WESTERN CIVILIZATION:
THE CONTINUING EXPERIMENT

DOLPHIN EDITION
VOLUME B 1300 TO 1815

THOMAS F.X. NOBLE
University of Notre Dame

BARRY S. STRAUSS
Cornell University

DUANE J. OSHEIM
University of Virginia

KRISTEN B. NEUSCHEL
Duke University

WILLIAM B. COHEN
Late of Indiana University

DAVID D. ROBERTS
University of Georgia

RACHEL G. FUCHS
Arizona State University

Houghton Mifflin Company
Boston   New York

WESTERN CIVILIZATION: THE CONTINUING EXPERIMENT
VOLUME I: TO 1715, DOLPHIN EDITION
by Thomas F.X. Noble, Barry S. Strauss, Duane J. Osheim, Kristen B. Neuschel, William B. Cohen, David D. Roberts, Rachel G. Fuchs
Copyright © 2006 by Houghton Mifflin Company. All rights reserved.

Publisher: Charles Hartford
Senior Sponsoring Editor: Nancy Blaine
Senior Development Editor: Julie Swasey
Senior Project Editor: Christina M. Horn
Editorial Assistant: Michelle O'Berg
Senior Art and Design Coordinator: Jill Haber
Senior Photo Editor: Jennifer Meyer Dare
Senior Composition Buyer: Sarah Ambrose
Manufacturing Coordinator: Chuck Dutton
Senior Marketing Manager: Sandra McGuire

Text credits: Page 76: Quote by Sappho from Ancient Greek Literature and Society, Second Edition, by Charles Rowan Beye. Copyright © 1987 by Cornell University Press. Reprinted by permission. Page 129: Poem from The Aeneid of Virgil, trans. Allen Mandelbaum. Copyright © 1971 by Allen Mandelbaum. Reprinted by permission of Bantam Books, a division of Bantam, Doubleday, Dell Publishing Group, Inc. Page 324: "Down there, around Ventadorn" from The Lyrics of the Troubador, Trouveres, translated by Frederick Goldin. Copyright © 1973 by Frederick Goldin. Used by permission of Doubleday, a division of Random House, Inc. Page 324: "Friend, if you had shown consideration" from lyrics by Castellozza, in The Women Troubadours by Meg Bodin (W. W. Norton, 1976). Copyright © 1976 by Magda Bogin. Reprinted by permission of Magda Bogin. Page 384: Poem by Michelangelo from The 1talian Renaissance Reader, edited and translated by Julia ConawayBondanella and Mark Musa. Copyright © 1987 by Julia Conaway Bondanella and Mark Musa. Used by permission of Dutton Signet, a division of Penguin Group (USA) Inc.

WESTERN CIVILIZATION: THE CONTINUING EXPERIMENT, DOLPHIN EDITION
by Thomas F.X. Noble, Barry S. Strauss, Duane J. Osheim, Kristen B. Neuschel, William B. Cohen, David D. Roberts, Rachel G. Fuchs
Copyright © 2006 by Houghton Mifflin Company. All rights reserved.

Publisher: Charles Hartford
Senior Sponsoring Editor: Nancy Blaine
Senior Development Editor: Julie Swasey
Senior Project Editor: Christina M. Horn
Editorial Assistant: Michelle O'Berg
Senior Art and Design Coordinator: Jill Haber
Senior Photo Editor: Jennifer Meyer Dare
Senior Composition Buyer: Sarah Ambrose
Manufacturing Coordinator: Chuck Dutton
Senior Marketing Manager: Sandra McGuire

Cover image: Street scene, Moscow, Russia, late 19th century (early-20th-century engraving). Photograph: Dagli OrtilBibliotheque des Arts Decoratifs, Paris/The Art Archive.

Text credits: Page 76: Quote by Sappho from Ancient Greek Literature and Society, Second Edition, by Charles Rowan Beye. Copyright @ 1987 by Cornell University Press. Reprinted by permission. Page 129: Poem from The Aeneid of Virgil, trans. Allen Mandelbaum. Copyright @ 1971 by Allen Mandelbaum. Reprinted by permission of Bantam Books, a division of Bantam, Doubleday, Dell Publishing Group, Inc. Page 324: "Down there, around Ventadorn" from The Lyrics of the Troubador, Trouveres, translated by Frederick Goldin. Copyright @ 1973 by Frederick Goldin. Used by permission of Doubleday, a division of Random House, Inc. Page 324: "Friend, if you had shown consideration" from lyrics by Castellozza, in The Women Troubadours by Meg Bodin (W. W. Norton, 1976). Copyright @ 1976 by Magda Bogin. Reprinted by permission of Magda Bogin. Page 384: Poem by Michelangelo from The Italian Renaissance Reader, edited and translated by Julia Conaway Bondanella and Mark Musa. Copyright @ 1987 by Julia Conaway Bondanella and Mark Musa. Used by permission of Dutton Signet, a division of Penguin Group (USA) Inc.

Custom Publishing Editor: Todd Corbin
Custom Publishing Production Manager: Tina Kozik
Project Coordinator: Andrea Wagner

Cover Design: Deborah Azerrad Savona

This book contains select works from existing Houghton Mifflin Company resources and was produced by Houghton Mifflin Custom Publishing for collegiate use. As such, those adopting and/or contributing to this work are responsible for editorial content, accuracy, continuity and completeness.

Printed in the United States of America.

ISBN: 0-618-66359-2
N-05134

1 2 3 4 5 6 7 8 9 – CCI – 07 06 05

Houghton Mifflin
Custom Publishing

222 Berkeley Street • Boston, MA 02116

Address all correspondence and order information to the above address.

Brief Contents

Contents

8
EARLY MEDIEVAL CIVILIZATIONS, 600–900
224

11

**CRISIS AND
RECOVERY IN
LATE MEDIEVAL
EUROPE,
1300–1500**

331

12

THE RENAISSANCE

369

15
EUROPE IN THE AGE OF RELIGIOUS WARS, 1560–1648
469

Preface

Chance discoveries reveal that fifteen centuries ago, boys in Ireland and in what is now Afghanistan were copying the biblical psalms with a view to memorizing them. Young Christians were learning these Latin and Greek translations of ancient Hebrew poems. This arresting development points to three big themes that inform this book and that contribute to an understanding of why we should study Western Civilization in the early twenty-first century.

First, what or where is the "West"? The West is sometimes understood geographically and sometimes culturally. For most people, the West means western Europe. And yet western Europe itself is the heir of the peoples and cultures of antiquity, including the Sumerians, Egyptians, Persians, Greeks, Romans, Jews, Christians, and Muslims. In fact, Europe is the heir of even earlier civilizations in Asia and Africa.

Let us turn back to the psalm-learning boys of Ireland and Afghanistan. Although Ireland is now considered European, it was not part of the classical world. In fact, the Romans placed the island "at the end of the world." Christian missionaries prepared Ireland's entry into Western Civilization, and it has been at the heart of the West for more than a millennium. Consider Saint Patrick, the exuberant beauty of Celtic art, the English entanglement with Ireland, the poetry of William Butler Yeats or Seamus Heaney, and the novels of James Joyce—all of these are part of our Western heritage. The question of Afghanistan is trickier. Persians touched this land, as did the soldiers of Alexander the Great. The Silk Road—that great artery of objects and ideas—passed through it. A few years ago, to the horror of the world, the Taliban, radical Muslims, destroyed two monumental Buddha statues at Bamiyan. The psalm-learning boys, their psalms, and their heirs had religious competitors. But those statues had unmistakably Greek features, and today Western troops police much of Afghanistan. It would be a fascinating thought exercise to ask whether Afghanistan is "East" or "West."

As a cultural phenomenon, "Western" implies many things: freedom and free, participatory political institutions; economic initiative and opportunity; monotheistic religious faiths (Judaism, Christianity, and Islam); rationalism and ordered thought in the social, political, and philosophical realms; an aesthetic sensibility that aspires to a universal sense of beauty. But the West has felt free to evoke tradition as its guiding light and also to innovate brilliantly; to accommodate slavery and freedom simultaneously; to esteem original thought and to persecute people who deviate from the norm. "Western" indeed has meant many things in various places at different times. This book constantly and explicitly attempts to situate its readers in place, time, and tradition.

Second, what exactly is civilization? No definition can win universal acceptance, but certain elements of a definition are widely accepted. Cities are crucial; with cities emerge complex social organizations that involve at least a minimal division of labor. Some people work in the fields, some in the home. Soldiers defend the city, and artisans provide its daily goods. Governing institutions have a wide measure of acceptance and have the ability to enforce their will. Complex cultures also develop religious ideas and authorities; a literature and law that may be oral or written; monumental architecture, especially fortifications, palaces, and temples; and arts such as music, painting, and sculpture.

Western Civilization has had an influence on almost every person alive today. The West deserves to be studied because its tale is compelling, but it demands to be studied because its story has been so central to the development of the world in which we live. Many of the world's dominant institutions are Western in their origin and in their contemporary manifestations—most notably parliamentary democracy. Commercial capitalism, a Western construct, is the world's dominant form of economic organization, and even its greatest rival, communism, is fundamentally Western: its theoreticians were Europeans who drew on utopian ideals, classical economics, Enlightenment doctrines, and the ideologies of the French Revolution. Western styles in architecture dominate the skyline of every major city in the world. Western popular culture, from movies and music to fast food, may be found everywhere. Communications technologies, from cell phones to e-mail, are as global in spread as they are Western in origin.

It must be said that some people, inside and outside the West, have grave reservations about the extent of Western influence in the modern world. Were those boys of fifteen centuries ago heirs and beneficiaries of a great tradition? Or were they dupes and victims of Western cultural aggression? Some critics challenge Western religious, philosophical, political, and economic ideas at their core. Others have no quarrel with Western ideas as such but regret that local cultures around the globe are vanishing before a relentless Western onslaught. Still others wonder why Western achievements in political stability and economic prosperity cannot be more widely shared. In other words, to say that the West is dominant is only to state the obvious, not to insist that such domination is inevitable or desirable. But the sheer, unassailable fact of that domination makes the careful study of the West essential for informed, responsible participation in the modern world. And such study can help us understand and appreciate an impressive cultural heritage.

Third, the subtitle of this book, "The Continuing Experiment," was chosen to signal our third theme, contingency or unpredictability. This subtitle conveys our resolve to avoid a deterministic approach. For students and teachers, an appreciation of continuity and change, or unity and diversity, can foster sympathetic participation in this often-bewildering world. We try to give individual actors, moments, and movements the sense of drama, possibility, and contingency that they actually possessed. We, with faultless hindsight, always know how things came out. Contemporaries often did not have a clue. We respect them. Much of the fascination, and the reward, of studying Western Civilization lies precisely in its richness, diversity, changeability, and unpredictability. No one in Israel in 500 B.C. or in Rome a millennium later could have predicted that Irish and Afghan boys would simultaneously cultivate a new and similar religious sensibility by reading Jewish poems in the Christianized versions of the classical languages. Who, a generation ago, could have predicted the collapse of the Soviet Union or the rise of Osama bin Laden? The experiment continues.

BASIC APPROACH

More than a decade ago the six authors of *Western Civilization: The Continuing Experiment* set out to create a textbook that would play a role in a course that will, as a total effort, inform students about essential developments within a tradition that has powerfully, though not always positively, affected everyone in the contemporary world. Although each of us found something to admire in all of the existing textbooks, none of us was fully happy with any of them. We were disappointed with books that claimed "balance," but actually stressed a single kind of history. We regretted that so many texts were uneven in their command of recent scholarship. Although we were convinced of both the inherent interest of Western Civilization and the importance of teaching the subject, we were disconcerted by the celebratory tone of some books, which portrayed the West as resting on its laurels instead of creatively facing its future.

We decided to produce a book that is balanced and coherent; that addresses the full range of subjects that a Western Civilization book needs to address; that provides the student reader with interesting, timely material; and that is up-to-date in terms of scholarship and approach—in short, a book that helps the instructor to teach and the student to learn. We have kept our common vision fresh through frequent meetings, correspondence, critical mutual readings, and expert editorial guidance. We have come together as one, and because each of us has focused on his or her own area of specialization, we believe that we have attained a rare blend of competence, confidence, and enthusiasm. Moreover, we have been able to profit from the experience of using the book, the advice and criticism of dozens of colleagues, and the reactions of thousands of students.

Western Civilization is a story. Therefore, we aimed at a strong chronological narrative line. Our experience as teachers tells us that students appreciate this clear but gentle orientation. Our experience tells us, too, that an approach that is broadly chronological will leave instructors plenty of room to adapt our narrative to their preferred organization, or to supplement our narrative with one of their own.

Although we maintain the familiar, large-scale divisions of a Western Civilization book, we also present some innovative adjustments in arrangement. For instance, Chapter 2 treats early Greece together with the whole eastern Mediterranean region in the period from about 1500 to 750 B.C. This approach both links kindred cultures and respects chronological flow better than customary treatments, which take western Asia to a certain point and then backtrack to deal with early Greece. We incorporate a single chapter on Late Antiquity, the tumultuous and fascinating period from about A.D. 300 to 600 that witnessed the transformation of the Roman Empire into three successors: Byzantine, Islamic, and European. One chapter studies those three successors, thereby permitting careful comparisons. But we also assign chapters to some of the greatest issues in Western Civilization, such as the Renaissance, the age of European exploration and conquest, the Scientific Revolution, and the industrial transformation. Our twentieth-century chapters reflect an understanding of the last century formed in its closing years rather than in its middle decades. What is new in our organization represents adjustments grounded in the best scholarship, and what is old represents time-tested approaches.

In fashioning our picture of the West, we took two unusual steps. First, our West is itself bigger than the one found in most textbooks. We treat the Celtic world, Scandinavia, and the Slavic world as integral parts of the story. We look often at the lands that border the West—Anatolia/Turkey, western Asia, North Africa, the Eurasian steppes—in order to show the to-and-fro of peoples, ideas, technologies, and products. Second, we continually situate the West in its global context. We must be clear: this is not a world history book. But just as we recognize that the West has influenced the rest of the world, we also carefully acknowledge how the rest of the world has influenced the West. We begin this story of mutual interaction with the Greeks and Romans, carry it through the European Middle Ages, focus on it in the age of European exploration and conquest, and analyze it closely in the modern world of industry, diplomacy, empire, immigration, and questions of citizenship and identity.

Another approach that runs like a ribbon throughout this textbook involves balance and integration. Teachers and students, just like the authors of this book, have their particular interests and emphases. In the large and diverse American academy, that is as it should be. But a textbook, if it is to be helpful and useful, should incorporate as many interests and emphases as possible. For a long time, some said, Western Civilization books devoted excessive coverage to high politics—"the public deeds of great men," as an ancient Greek writer defined the historian's subject. Others felt that high culture—all the Aristotles and Mozarts—were included to the exclusion of supposedly lesser figures and ordinary men and women. In the 1970s books began to emphasize social history. Some applauded this new emphasis even as they debated fiercely over what to include under this heading.

In this book, we attempt to capture the Western tradition in its full contours, to hear the voices of all those who have made durable contributions. But because we cannot say everything about everybody at every moment, we have had to make choices about how and where to array key topics within our narrative. Above all, we have tried to be integrative. For example, when we talk about government and politics, we present the institutional structures through which power was exercised, the people who possessed power as well as the people who did not, the ideological foundations for the use of power, and the material conditions that fostered or hindered the real or the would-be powerful. In other words, instead of treating old-fashioned "high politics" in abstract and descriptive ways, we take an approach that is organic and analytical: How did things work? Our approach to the history of women is another example. A glance at this book's table of contents and then at its index is revealing. The former reveals very few sections devoted explicitly and exclusively to women. The latter shows that women appear constantly in every section of this book. Is there a contradiction here? Not at all. Women and men have not been historical actors in isolation from one another. Yet gender is an important variable that has shaped individual and collective experience. Hence we seek to explain why certain political, economic, or social circumstances had differing impacts on men and women, and how such conditions led them to make different choices.

Similarly, when we talk of great ideas, we describe the antecedent ideas from which seemingly new ones were built up, and we ask about the consequences of those ideas. We explore the social positions of the authors of those ideas to see if this helps us to explain the ideas themselves or to gauge their influence. We try to understand how ideas in one field of human endeavor proved to be influential in other fields. For instance, gender is viewed as connected to and part of the larger fabric of ideas including power, culture, and piety.

We invite the reader to look at our narrative as if it were a mosaic. Taken as a whole, our narrative contains a coherent picture. Viewed more closely, it is made up of countless tiny bits that may have their individual interest but do not even hint at the larger picture of which they are parts. Finally, just as the viewer of a mosaic may find his or her eye drawn especially to one area, feature, color, or style, so too the reader of this book will find some parts more engaging or compelling than others. But it is only because there is, in this book as in a mosaic, a complete picture that the individual sections make sense, command our attention, excite our interest.

One word sums up our approach in this book: "balance." We tell a good story, but we pause often to reflect on that story, to analyze it. We devote substantial coverage to the typical areas of Greece, Rome, Italy, France, Great Britain, and so forth, but we say more about western Europe's frontiers than any other book. We do not try to disguise our Western Civilization book as a world history book, but we take great pains to locate the West within its global context. And we always assume that context means mutuality and reciprocity. We have high politics and big ideas alongside household management and popular culture. We think that part of the fascination of the past lies in its capacity to suggest understandings of the present and possibilities for the future.

Organization and Content Changes

As always, we have paid close attention to how our chapters "work." Accordingly, Chapter 5 includes revised material on Roman politics and the conflict of the orders, as well as material on the Roman household and the connection between family and government. Chapter 7 has reorganized material on the Catholic Church, and Chapter 9 has expanded coverage of the Crusades. The material on the Thirty Years' War in Chapter 15 has been fully reworked and now includes a section on the developments in eastern and central Europe. New material on the slave trade has been added to Chapter 18. In Chapter 23, a new discussion of women and charity has been added, focusing on Josephine Grey Butler, Annie Wood Besant, and others. Chapter 28 incorporates new scholarship on the role of Pope Pius XII during the Holocaust, as well as an expanded account of the Warsaw uprising. Finally, in light of the drastic changes in the world since this book was last revised, Chapter 30 has been thoroughly reworked to include coverage of the Iraq War, recent environmental issues, the expanding European Union, the changing demographics of Europe, and the issues of unilateralism and Western responsibility in an increasingly global community.

DISTINCTIVE FEATURES

Each chapter of the book begins with a vignette that is directly tied to an accompanying picture. These vignettes introduce the reader to one or more of the key aspects of the chapter. Then the reader encounters a thematic introduction that evokes interest while pointing clearly and in some detail to what follows.

This *Dolphin Edition* includes a boxed primary source feature in each chapter called "The Continuing Experiment." The feature reinforces one of the main themes of the text by including documents that show contingency, possibility, or uncertainty. Readers will encounter topics such as Egypt's startling religious experimentation, Archimedes' anticipation of the scientific method, Charlemagne's attempts to reform education, the complexities of Keynesian economics, and the varying outcomes of "women's liberation."

STUDENT WEBSITE

In addition to the main text, *Western Civilization, Dolphin Edition* shares *Western Civilizations,* the Fourth Edition's redesigned and expanded website. On the interactive site, students will find ACE self-assessment quizzes, annotated chapter outlines, and other supplemental material including web activities based on the "Continuing Experiment" features.

ACKNOWLEDGMENTS

The authors have benefited throughout the process of revision from the acute and helpful criticisms of numerous colleagues. We thank in particular: **James Burns, Clemson University;** Eleanor A. Congdon, Youngstown State University; **Eugene Cruz-Uribe,** Northern Arizona University; **Janusz Duzinkiewicz,** Purdue University North Central; **Ann R. Higginbotham,** Eastern Connecticut State University; **Vejas Gabriel Liulevicius,** University of Tennessee; **David A. Reid,** University of North Florida; and **Alice N. Walters,** University of Massachusetts, Lowell.

Each of us has also benefited from the close readings and careful criticisms of our coauthors, although we all assume responsibility for our own chapters. Barry Strauss has written Chapters 1–6; Thomas Noble, 7–10; Duane Osheim, 11–14; Kristen Neuschel, 15–19; William Cohen, 20–24; and David Roberts, 25–30.

The author team suffered the loss of a member, but Rachel Fuchs, a student of Bill Cohen, joined us to revise the chapters dealing with the nineteenth century. Our gratitude to Rachel is as immense as our pleasure at the quality of her work.

Thomas F. X. Noble

About the Authors

THOMAS F. X. NOBLE   After receiving his Ph.D. from Michigan State University, Thomas Noble taught at Albion College, Michigan State University, Texas Tech University, and the University of Virginia. In 1999 he received the University of Virginia's highest award for teaching excellence. In 2001 he became Robert M. Conway Director of the Medieval Institute at the University of Notre Dame. He is the author of *The Republic of St. Peter: The Birth of the Papal State, 680–825*; *Religion, Culture and Society in the Early Middle Ages*; *Soldiers of Christ: Saints and Saints' Lives from Late Antiquity and the Early Middle Ages*; and *Images and the Carolingians: Tradition, Order, and Worship*. Noble's articles and reviews have appeared in many leading journals, including the *American Historical Review*, *Byzantinische Zeitschrift*, *Catholic Historical Review*, *Revue d'histoire ecclésiastique*, *Speculum*, and *Studi medievali*. He has also contributed chapters to several books and articles to three encyclopedias. He was a member of the Institute for Advanced Study in 1994 and the Netherlands Institute for Advanced Study in 1999–2000. He has been awarded fellowships by the National Endowment for the Humanities (twice) and the American Philosophical Society.

BARRY STRAUSS   Professor of history and Classics at Cornell University, Barry Strauss holds a Ph.D. from Yale. He has been awarded fellowships by the National Endowment for the Humanities, the American School of Classical Studies at Athens, the MacDowell Colony for the Arts, the Korea Foundation, and the Killam Foundation of Canada. He is the recipient of the Clark Award for excellence in teaching from Cornell. He served as Director of Cornell's Peace Studies Program. His many publications include *Athens After the Peloponnesian War: Class, Faction, and Policy, 403–386 B.C.*; *Fathers and Sons in Athens: Ideology and Society in the Era of the Peloponnesian War*; *The Anatomy of Error: Ancient Military Disasters and Their Lessons for Modern Strategists* (with Josiah Ober); *Hegemonic Rivalry from Thucydides to the Nuclear Age* (co-edited with R. Ned Lebow); *War and Democracy: A Comparative Study of the Korean War and the Peloponnesian War* (co-edited with David R. McCann); *Rowing Against the Current: On Learning to Scull at Forty*; and *The Battle of Salamis, the Naval Encounter That Saved Greece—and Western Civilization*.

DUANE J. OSHEIM   A Fellow of the American Academy in Rome with a Ph.D. in history from the University of California, Davis, Duane Osheim is a professor of history at the University of Virginia. A specialist in late medieval and Renaissance social and institutional history, he is the author and editor of *A Tuscan Monastery and Its Social World*, *An Italian Lordship: The Bishopric of Lucca in the Late Middle Ages*, and *Beyond Florence: The Contours of Medieval and Early Modern Italy*.

KRISTEN B. NEUSCHEL After receiving her Ph.D. from Brown University, Kristen Neuschel taught at Denison University and Duke University, where she is currently associate professor of history. She is a specialist in early modern French history and is the author of *Word of Honor: Interpreting Noble Culture in Sixteenth-Century France* and articles on French social history and European women's history. She has received grants from the National Endowment for the Humanities and the American Council of Learned Societies. She has also received the Alumni Distinguished Undergraduate Teaching Award, which is awarded annually on the basis of student nominations for excellence in teaching at Duke. She is currently Director of Undergraduate Studies for the History Department.

WILLIAM B. COHEN After receiving his Ph.D. at Stanford University, William Cohen taught at Northwestern University and Indiana University, where he was professor of history. At Indiana, he served as chairman of the West European Studies and History Departments and was Director of Graduate Studies for the History Department. A previous president of the Society of French Historical Studies, Cohen received several academic fellowships, including a National Endowment for the Humanities and a Fulbright fellowship. He was the author of many works on French history and his research focused on the Algerian war and French memory.

DAVID D. ROBERTS After taking his Ph.D. in modern European history at the University of California, Berkeley, David Roberts taught at the Universities of Virginia and Rochester before becoming professor of history at the University of Georgia in 1988. At Rochester he chaired the Humanities Department of the Eastman School of Music, and he chaired the History Department at Georgia from 1993 to 1998. A recipient of Woodrow Wilson and Rockefeller Foundation fellowships, he is the author of *The Syndicalist Tradition and Italian Fascism; Benedetto Croce and the Uses of Historicism;* and *Nothing but History: Reconstruction and Extremity After Metaphysics,* as well as two books in Italian and numerous articles and reviews. He is currently the Albert Berry Saye Professor of History at Georgia.

WESTERN CIVILIZATION

The Ancestors of the West

(Egyptian Museum, Cairo)

They look at us with an up-to-date intensity, this nearly 5,000-year-old couple from early Egypt. Dressed in simple clothes, they each have movie star good looks, heightened by well-made wigs and expensive jewelry. Their bodies are shown in the regular way of Egyptian art: The man's body is largely bare, while the woman's is mostly covered; his skin is dark brown, hers is light yellow. They are depicted as partners but not as equals.

The writing identifies them as Rahotep and Nofret, husband and wife. We see them here in sculptures from their tomb of about 2600 B.C. The painted limestone statues, with inlaid eyes of quartz and rock crystal, show a powerful pair. Both were part of the royal court, and Rahotep was a general and high priest. The sculptures show us that early civilization was literate, technologically sophisticated, structured by rank and status, religious, and fascinated by the relationship between men and women.

The rich and complex world of Rahotep and Nofret rested on the most momentous inventions in human history. They began approximately 100,000 years ago, when the first modern humans evolved from humanlike ancestors. Human beings wrestled with an often-hostile environment, engaging in a continuing series of experiments, until beginning about 10,000 B.C. they learned how to plant crops and tame animals. The shift from a food-collecting to a food-producing economy dramatically increased the amount of human life that the earth could support. Between 3500 and 3000 B.C., human society became well organized in urban centers, supported by farmers in the surrounding territories, and able to keep written records: it had, in short, achieved civilization.

What we call Western civilization, however, was still more than two thousand years away. As a term, *Western civilization* is imprecise, inviting disagreement about its definition and about the lands, peoples, and cultures that it embraces at any given time. In this book we give Western civilization an evolving definition that permits comparison and reflection over time and space. In the strictest sense, Western civilization means the "West," and that, in turn, has traditionally meant the lands and peoples of western Europe.

Initially, however, the West embraced the Greek and Roman peoples, plus the foundational monotheistic religions of Judaism and Christianity. These first Westerners in turn borrowed many ideas and institutions from the earlier civilizations of western Asia and Egypt. (These civilizations are sometimes referred to as the Ancient Near East.) Indeed, civilization began in those lands and came only relatively late to Europe.

Western Asia and Egypt contributed greatly to the cultures of Greece and Rome and to the religious visions of the Jews and Christians. Yet those earlier civilizations are sufficiently different from the West and its society, politics, and religion that they are better considered as ancestors or forerunners of the West rather than as its founders. (For a longer discussion of the definition of Western civilization, see the Preface.)

So, after briefly surveying the origins of the human species, the historian of the West must begin with the emergence of civilizations after 3500 B.C. in two great river valleys: the valley of the Tigris and Euphrates in Mesopotamia (today, Iraq and Syria), and the valley of the Nile in Egypt. Impressive in their own right, Mesopotamia and Egypt influenced a wide range of other early civilizations in western Asia and northern Africa. Among them were the Hittites and the Syro-Palestinian city-states, whose own cultural contributions make them ancestors of the West as well. They are studied in this chapter. The Hebrews and the Greeks were also influenced by Mesopotamia and Egypt, but with the Hebrews and the Greeks, Western civilization begins, and so they are covered in Chapter 2.

ORIGINS, TO CA. 3000 B.C.

The earth is old; modern human beings are young; and civilization is a very recent innovation. Physical anthropologists, archaeologists, geneticists, and biochemists have made great strides in explaining human origins. Great disagreement still reigns nonetheless. Each decade seems to bring an exciting new discovery that calls for the reassessment of previous theories.

We can be more certain about the series of processes, beginning around 10,000 B.C., that led to the emergence of civilization by 3500 to 3000 B.C. The period studied in this chapter includes both prehistory—the term often used for time before the invention of writing—and recorded history. Writing appeared last among the complex of characteristics that marks the emergence of civilization. Over a period of several thousand years, many humans abandoned a mobile existence for a sedentary one. They learned to domesticate animals and to cultivate plants. They shifted from a food-collecting economy to a predominantly food-producing economy. They developed the first towns, from which, over several millennia, the first urban societies slowly evolved. The result—the first civilizations, found in western Asia and Egypt—laid the groundwork on which later would be built the founding civilizations of the West: Greece, Rome, and ancient Israel.

The First Human Beings　　Anatomically modern human beings, *Homo sapiens sapiens*—genus *Homo*, species *sapiens*, subspecies *sapiens*—first appeared about 100,000 years ago. The human family, or hominids, are much older, however. The hominids include many ancient and extinct species.

Both the first hominids and, much later, the first *Homo sapiens sapiens* were found in Africa, the continent that is the cradle of humanity. The first hominids appeared in Africa's tropics and subtropics over 4 million years ago. By 2.5 million years ago they had evolved into creatures who invented the first technology, simple stone tools. Prehistory is traditionally referred to as the Stone Age because stone was the primary medium from which hominids made tools. The hominids were migratory: not less than 1.6 million years ago and perhaps much earlier, they appeared in East Asia and the eastern edge of Europe. The next important stage in human evolution is *Homo erectus* ("upright person"), a hominid with a large brain who used more complex stone tools and may have acquired language. The appearance of *Homo erectus* is usually dated to 1.8 million years ago, but a recent discovery in China may date *Homo erectus* as early as 2.25 million years ago. Slowly, separate *Homo erectus* populations in different places gave way to the gradual emergence of various archaic forms of *Homo sapiens*.

But the most recent research suggests that all anatomically modern humans are descended from a single African ancestor. This conclusion is supported both by DNA evidence and by three recently discovered skulls in Ethiopia. These skulls are about 160,000 years old and represent the probable immediate ancestors of anatomically modern humans. About 89,000 years ago, the *Homo sapiens sapiens* from whom we are all descended was born in Africa. About 70,000 years ago, descendants of that man left Africa for the other continents. All humans today may be descended from only about two thousand individuals in Africa.

For many millennia humans struggled with the ebb and flow of glaciers. They lived during the Ice Age, as scholars refer to the period of fluctuating cycles of warm and cold, beginning about 730,000 years ago and ending only about 10,000 years ago. Early humans existed amid great contrasts in temperature, seasons, and landscapes, requiring considerable adaptation—but adapt they did.

Archaic humans first appeared in Europe about 800,000 years ago. Beginning about 400,000 years ago, Europe was home to the ancestors of the best-known archaic people, the Neandertals. Fully evolved by 130,000 years ago, Neandertal people lived in Europe and western Asia for the following 100,000 years, to about 30,000 years ago. Their strong and stocky physiques were perhaps an adaptation to the rugged climate of the Ice Age. The Neandertals were far from being the brutes they are usually imagined to be. They were, for example, among the first people to bury their dead, often with grave offerings—for example, flint, animal bones, or flowers—a practice that suggests they were sensitive enough to mourn their losses. Recent research shows both that Neandertals were clever enough to use tools to attack one another and caring enough to nurse their wounded back to health.

Neandertals, however, were not modern humans. Modern humans entered Europe about 40,000 years ago, having originated in Africa. Within 10,000 years Neandertals had disappeared—whether through war, disease, or an inability to compete with modern humans, we do not know. The first modern humans tended to be taller and less muscular than Neandertals and other archaic people. They also used their hands more precisely and walked more efficiently, and they lived longer. The modern human skull, with its high forehead and tucked-in face, is distinctive, but differences between the modern and archaic human brain are a matter of scholarly debate. What no one debates, however, is that, with the disappearance of Neandertals, modern humans put into effect a revolution in culture.

The Revolution in Human Culture, ca. 70,000–10,000 B.C.   Before the emergence of modern humans and perhaps before Neandertals, people had relatively little ability to change the natural environment. Modern humans changed that. They exploited natural resources largely by means of technology and organization. Thus they began the process of human manipulation of the environment that—sometimes brilliantly, sometimes disastrously—has remained a leading theme of the human experience ever since. The key to this change was a dramatic increase in the amount and complexity of information being communicated—what might be called the first information revolution. The twin symbols of the revolution are cave paintings and notations made on bone, signs that humans were thinking about their environment and their experiences.

It was long thought that these dramatic changes began in Europe about 40,000 B.C.* Recently, however, they have been traced to southern Africa, probably more than 70,000 years ago. The discovery there of carefully worked bone tools and stone spearheads pinpoints the dawn of modern human technology. Still, it is not in Africa but

---

*We follow the traditional practice in the West of expressing historical dates in relation to the birth of Jesus Christ (actually, to a now discredited calculation of his birth date, because in fact Jesus was not born in A.D. 1; see page 181). Dates before his birth are labeled B.C. (which stands for "before Christ"), and dates after his birth are labeled A.D. (*anno Domini*, Latin for "in the year of the Lord"). A widely used alternative refers to these dates as B.C.E. ("before the common era") and C.E. ("of the common era").

elsewhere that we can best trace the early evolution of the modern human mind. Europe from about 40,000 to about 10,000 B.C. provides reliable evidence of the way of life and the culture of early human hunter-gatherer societies, complex organizations that survived by a food-collecting economy of hunting, fishing, and gathering fruits and nuts. This period is sometimes called the Upper Paleolithic (Greek for "Old Stone") era. Then, around 10,000 B.C., western Asia offers evidence of a second revolution: the invention of a food-producing economy, consisting of the domestication of animals and the cultivation of crops. The period from about 10,000 to 3000 B.C. is some times called the Neolithic (Greek for "New Stone") era.

Archaeology tells us something about early people's way of life. So do analogies from contemporary anthropology, for even today a tiny number of people still exist in hunter-gatherer societies in isolated corners of the globe—for example, in the Kalahari Desert of Africa and in the Arctic. It is reasonable to speculate that early humans lived in small groups, numbering perhaps twenty-five to fifty persons, related by kinship or marriage. Early hunter-gatherers moved from place to place, following the seasonal migration of game, but by the eve of the invention of agriculture, some hunter-gatherers had settled down in villages. Hunting was largely a male preserve, while gathering nuts and berries fell into the female domain. Perhaps women brought their children with them as they worked or relied on kin or friends for child-care.

It was probably common for men and women to pair off, have children, and establish a family, much as marriage is a near-universal practice among humans today. Compared with other animals, humans produce extremely dependent infants requiring years of attention. In order to ensure the survival of the young to adulthood, men as well as women need to play a role in child rearing.

Early people found shelter by building huts or, frequently, by living in caves or rock shelters—hence our notion of the "caveman." Caves offered shelter, could be heated, and made a naturally good vantage point for observing prey and hostile humans. In the Upper Paleolithic era, about 30,000 years ago, caves were the site of the earliest representational art. The most spectacular Upper Paleolithic paintings discovered so far have been found in caves in southern France (for example, at Lascaux and at Chauvet Cave) and in Spain (at Altamira). European cave paintings of animals such as the bison, horse, reindeer, and woolly mammoth (a huge, extinct member of the elephant family with hairy skin and long, upward-curving tusks) attest to early human artistic skill. The presence of abstract shapes attests to an interest in symbols. The purpose of cave paintings is unknown, but perhaps they served as illustrations of myths or as attempts to control the environment through magic.

Other early representational art includes engravings on stone of animals, birds, and stylized human females, as well as female figurines carved from ivory or bone. Usually represented with exaggerated breasts or buttocks, the carvings are called Venus figurines, after Venus, the Roman goddess of love. They may represent an attempt to control fertility through magic.

Upper Paleolithic craftsmanship is as impressive as the art. The early human tool kit included the first utensils in such easily worked materials as antler and ivory. Stone tools became longer and the first polished bone tools appeared, as did the first stone and bone spear points and the first bows and arrows. The presence of bone needles and awls (pointed tools for punching holes) implies sewing, probably of animal skins.

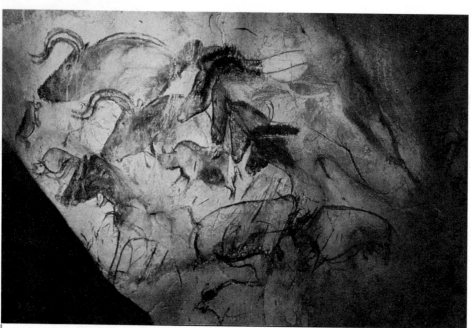

Chauvet Cave Art *This black-painted panel shows horses, rhinoceroses, and wild oxen. This painting and others in the cave, discovered in 1994 in southern France, are over 30,000 years old, making them perhaps the oldest known paintings in the world.* (Jean Cottes/Ministère de la Culture/Corbis Sygma)

The existence of Upper Paleolithic artists and skilled craftspeople demonstrates at least a limited specialization of skills and division of labor: society required organization, albeit on a limited scale. Hunting was a communal enterprise. Related families are likely to have joined together in clans, which in turn may have formed tribes. It is often thought that each of these groups was patriarchal (literally, "ruled by the father"); that is, the family was governed by the father, the tribe by a male headman or chief. To be sure, some later myths (for example, among the ancient Greeks) argue that women were the rulers of prehistoric society. Today some historians see the possibility of matriarchy (literally, "rule by the mother") in the Venus figurines. There is, however, no firm evidence of matriarchy. Male chiefs probably did exist, as in later periods, but some tribes may have had no chief at all, following the decision of the community rather than an individual leader.

The Coming of Agriculture, ca. 10,000–5000 B.C. The human discovery of agriculture was dramatic, meriting the name "Neolithic Revolution" that scholars sometimes give it. Yet if dramatic, the discovery spread slowly and unevenly. In most areas, hunting and fishing continued to be a major source of food, even though agriculture fed more people. Agriculture was first discovered sometime after 10,000 B.C. in western Asia, then discovered again independently in other parts of the world. By 5000 B.C. information about the new practices had spread so widely that farming could be found in many places around the world.

The story begins about 13,000 B.C., when humans began to specialize in the wild plants they collected and the animals they hunted. They had good reason to do so because hunter-gatherer society had become increasingly complex, and in some places permanent settlements had appeared. A settled existence probably produced more mouths to feed, stimulating the need for more food. The next step is not surprising: learning how to domesticate plants and animals.

People seem to have begun by domesticating dogs, which were useful in hunting. Then they learned to keep sheep, goats, and cattle. Next came farming. Humans learned first how to grow wheat and barley, then legumes (beans). With males occupied in hunting, it may well have been females who first unraveled the secrets of agriculture.

The earliest area of domestication is a zone of land stretching in a crescent shape west to east from what is today southern Jordan to southern Iran. Scholars call this region of dependable annual rainfall the Fertile Crescent. With domestication came small agricultural settlements, which were increasingly common after 7000 B.C. Thus was born the farming village, probably the place that most people have called home since the spread of agriculture around the world.

Scholars once thought of Neolithic villages as simple places devoted to subsistence agriculture, with no craft specialization, and as egalitarian societies lacking social hierarchies. In recent years, new evidence and a rethinking of older information have altered this picture considerably. The Neolithic village site of Çayönü Tepesi in eastern Anatolia, for example, provides evidence of metalworking (of copper) and specialization of labor (in beadmaking) from approximately 7000 to 6000 B.C. The site also contains the world's earliest known example of cloth, probably linen, woven around 7000 B.C. Other contemporaneous village sites reveal experiments in ironworking and craft specialization. Evidence points to long-distance trade between villages in pottery and in obsidian (a sharp volcanic glass used in tools). Artwork shows men wearing loincloths and headdresses, women wearing pants and halter tops, and both sexes wearing jewelry.

Consider the case of Jericho, in Palestine near the Dead Sea, perhaps the oldest settled community on earth. A small village around 9000 B.C., Jericho had by about 7000 B.C. become a town surrounded by massive walls 10 feet thick and 13 or more feet high. The walls, about 765 yards long, probably enclosed an area of about 10 acres. The most prominent feature of the walls was a great tower 33 feet in diameter and 28 feet high with an interior stairway. Inside the walls lived a densely packed population of about two thousand people.

An even larger Neolithic town was Çatal Hüyük in south-central Anatolia. Its population of six thousand people in 6000 B.C. made it by far the largest settlement of the era. It was probably a trading center and perhaps a religious shrine. Carbonization from fire has preserved a wealth of artifacts attesting to Çatal Hüyük's sophistication, including woven fabrics, obsidian mirrors, wooden vessels, and makeup applicators.

Agriculture made human populations richer and more numerous, but the resulting concentrations of population bred disease and probably increased the scale of war. More men than ever before were available to fight because agriculture proved to be so efficient a source of food that it freed people for specialized labor. Some became craftsmen, some artists, some priests, and some warriors.

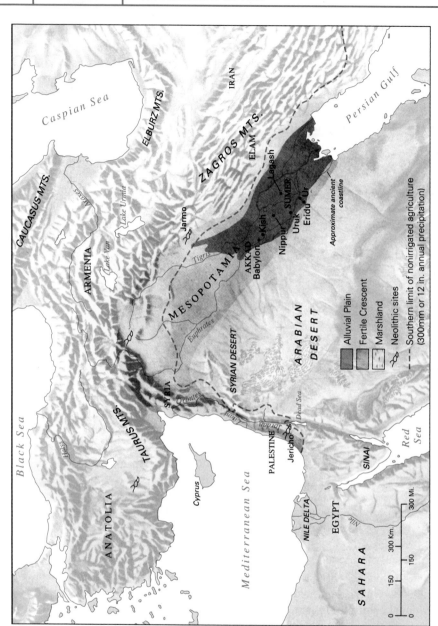

Western Asia The Neolithic Revolution began after 10,000 B.C. in the Fertile Crescent, an arc-shaped region of dependable annual rainfall. In this area between the Tigris and Euphrates Rivers known as Mesopotamia, the world's first urban civilization took root about 3500 to 3000 B.C.

This is not to say that war in Neolithic times was sophisticated. Indeed, the phenomenon perhaps consisted of group skirmishes and sporadic raids rather than systematic warfare. People added new weapons to the spear and the bow: the sling, the dagger, and the mace (a heavy war club). Spanish rock art shows a confrontation between two groups of archers, one following what seems to be a leader. The scene may be a ritual rather than a violent conflict, but we have physical cases of actual bloodshed. The earliest known evidence of organized warfare comes from a cemetery along the Nile River in the Sudan dating from 12,000 to 4500 B.C. The cemetery contains fifty-nine human skeletons, nearly half of whom died violently. Some were speared, some clubbed, and some killed by arrowheads. Some suffered multiple wounds. The victims include women and children.

Neolithic and Copper Age Europe, 7000–2500 B.C. Europe was one day to become the center of Western civilization, but the region lagged behind its neighbors at first. Innovations from the east reached Europe after 7000 B.C. and slowly transformed it. Europe was no empty vessel to be filled by eastern technologies, however: Europeans developed their own unique culture.

The term *Europe* refers to a vast peninsula of the Eurasian continent with several very distinct regions. Southern Europe is made up of a rugged and hilly Mediterranean coastal strip, linked to northern Africa and western Asia by the sea and by similarities in climate and landscape. High mountains are found in the Alps of south-central Europe, from which chains of lower mountains radiate toward the southwest and southeast. Northern Europe, by contrast, consists in large part of a forested plain, indented here and there by great rivers. In the southeast the plain, or steppe, becomes open and mostly treeless. The eastern boundaries of Europe are, in the north, the Ural Mountains and, in the south, the Caucasus Mountains. Georgia, Armenia, and Azerbaijan are all considered parts of Europe.

Before 7000 B.C. Europeans lived a traditional hunter-gatherer existence. Farming began in southeastern Europe around 7000 B.C., when migrants from western Asia introduced the settled way of life of the Neolithic village. That food-producing economy spread across Europe between about 6000 and 4500 B.C., borne alternately by colonization and by native adaptation of new technologies.

The farmers of Early Neolithic Europe (ca. 7000–ca. 4500 B.C.) were pioneers, living in hamlets or villages surrounded by larger hunter-gatherer populations. Not until 2500 B.C. did the majority of Europeans adopt a food-producing way of life. Between 4500 and 2500 B.C., a give-and-take between pioneers and natives led to the development of regional cultures. This era of European prehistory is known as the Late Neolithic Age, or the Copper Age, because copper came into use on the Continent during this time, as did gold. Both metals were used primarily as status symbols: the most dramatic example is a Bulgarian burial site dating from about 4000 B.C. in which a 45-year-old man is buried with 990 gold objects as well as copper and flint weapons.

Between about 4500 and about 3500 B.C., Copper Age Europeans developed their own cultures in relative isolation from the more advanced East. For example, European metallurgy probably developed independently. On Europe's northern and western edges people began to set up megaliths—stone tombs and monuments—often of huge blocks. Such monuments may illustrate an awareness of time created by the spread of agriculture, with its seasonal rhythms.

Between about 3500 and 2500 B.C., Copper Age Europe grew in sophistication. The urbanization of Mesopotamia (in modern-day Iraq) had an impact on southeastern Europe, which supplied raw materials for western Asia. Greece underwent the greatest transformation, to the extent that it developed its own urban civilization by about 2000 B.C. (see Chapter 2). Elsewhere, especially in the Balkans, technological innovations came into use, from the wheel, to complex metal-casting, to wine cups (evidence of a new taste). The recent discovery of a Copper Age corpse preserved in the ice of the Italian Alps opens a window into northern Italian society of about 3200 B.C.

In western Europe stone monuments are the most dramatic cultural achievements. On the Mediterranean island of Malta, for example, people built elaborate temple complexes constructed of massive limestone blocks. In Britain megalithic architecture reached its peak with Stonehenge, built in stages from about 2800 to 1500 B.C. This famous monument consists of a circle of stones oriented precisely on the rising sun of midsummer—a sign both of early Europeans' interest in the calendar and of their skill in technology.

Neolithic and Copper Age sculpture consists of many representations of females but few of males. Consider, for example, the ample, sculpted female figures found in Malta's temples. The enlarged buttocks and thighs of these statues might be symbols of fertility. Some scholars speculate that early Europeans worshiped goddesses, until warlike invaders after 2000 B.C., who brought male deities with them. The theory is, however, controversial.

The Emergence of Civilization, 3500–3000 B.C.
Civilization is derived from the Latin word *civitas*, meaning "commonwealth" or "city." The first civilizations, beginning in Mesopotamia and Egypt between 3500 and 3000 B.C., probably contained the first cities. What differentiated them from their predecessors, however, was not so much size (a city versus a town) as complexity. Civilization allowed human beings to think big. A large and specialized labor force, organized by a sufficiently strong government, made it possible to expand control over nature, pursue advances in technology, and trade and compete over ever widening areas. An elite class emerged that was able to pursue ever more ambitious projects in art and thought and to invent systems of writing. In short, the advent of civilization in the fourth millennium B.C. marked a major turning point. Thereafter, the human horizon expanded forever.

Civilization arose in Iraq, in the valley between the Tigris and Euphrates Rivers, a region that the Greeks named Mesopotamia (literally, "between the rivers"). At around the same time or shortly afterward, civilization also began in the valley of the Nile River in Egypt. Although these civilizations each developed largely independently, some borrowing between the two nonetheless took place.

Both Mesopotamia and Egypt are home to valleys containing alluvial land—that is, a relatively flat tract where fertile soil is deposited by a river. Otherwise, the two regions are quite different. Although the Nile Valley was easy to farm, much of the Tigris-Euphrates plain had to be tamed by would-be farmers. Every summer the Nile flooded in a relatively regular and predictable manner, bringing north to Egypt the waters of the monsoon rains of the Ethiopian highlands, where one of the river's sources—the Blue Nile—rises. The spring deluges of the Tigris and Euphrates were more sudden and less predictable. Moreover, the Nile's waters spread so broadly that it took less human effort than in Mesopotamia to irrigate most of the available farmland. In southern Mesopotamia, by contrast, most of the soil was alternately so dry or so marshy that agriculture would not have been possible without considerable irrigation and drainage—that is, the use of channels, dikes, or dams to control floodwaters and improve the fertility of the land. One Mesopotamian text describes a farmer as "the man of dike, ditch, and plow." Making matters worse, Mesopotamia was given to extreme heat and scorching winds. Some scholars argue that the very hostility of Mesopotamia's environment generated the cooperation and control that civilization requires.

It has long been thought that the first cities developed in southern Mesopotamia. A recent discovery, however, suggests that cities were found in northern Mesopotamia around the same time—that is, during the Uruk Period (3800–3200 B.C.). An excavation at Tell Hamoukar in northeastern Syria, near the Iraqi border, uncovered what appears to be a city from around 3500 B.C. The excavators found ovens and pottery, apparently used for large-scale food production, and they unearthed stamp seals and clay seal impressions, which may indicate a bureaucracy. A mud-brick fortification wall has tentatively been identified. In short, several signs point to a city.

If cities developed simultaneously in northern and southern Mesopotamia in the mid-fourth millennium B.C. they may share a common, earlier source: the Ubaid culture of mid-fifth-millennium B.C. Mesopotamia. Many questions arise, among them whether Ubaid cities existed as early as 4500 B.C., a thousand years earlier than cities were thought to have first appeared. We will have to wait for future excavation and study to answer such questions.

The first cities emerged through a slow, incremental process of action and reaction. Labor became more specialized, and agricultural production was maximized. When part of the population moves to a city, those who remain on the land must work harder or use better farming techniques or increase the amount of land under cultivation. In fourth- and third-millennium B.C. Mesopotamia, farmers did all three. Meanwhile, both the number and variety of settlements increased. Urban populations required the support of people in smaller units—towns, villages, and hamlets—clustered around a city.

Along with the growth of cities came the development of writing, about 3500 to 3100 B.C. in Mesopotamia. The development of writing from simple recordkeeping can be traced step by step. Before writing, Mesopotamian people used tiny clay or stone tokens to represent objects being counted or traded. By 3500 B.C., with 250 different types of tokens in play, the system had grown unwieldy enough for people to start using signs to indicate tokens. It was a short step to dispensing with the tokens and placing the signs on a clay tablet by making indentations in the clay with a reed stylus: writing. New words were soon added through pictographs (pictures that stand for particular objects). In time the pictographs evolved into ideograms—that is, abstract symbols that are no longer recognizable as specific objects and thus can be used to denote ideas as well as things.

In the centuries following its introduction, Mesopotamian writing became standardized. Scholars call the signs *cuneiform*, from the Latin for "wedge-shaped," a good description of what early writing looks like. In its first centuries, cuneiform was used almost entirely for economic records or commercial transactions. Then it was adapted to make brief records of offerings to the gods. By 2350 B.C. cuneiform had evolved into a mixed system of about six hundred signs, most of them phonetic (syllabic), with relatively few ideograms.

Experts used to think that writing began in Mesopotamia and spread to Egypt. Recent excavations, however, have found examples of early Egyptian writing securely dated to 3300 to 3200 B.C. In other words, Egyptian writing was independent: it was not derived from or related to cuneiform. Whether writing began in Egypt or Mesopotamia, therefore, is now an open question. What is clear, however, is that writing was invented to meet economic rather than creative needs. In Egypt the earliest writing includes records of the delivery of linen and oil as taxes to King Scorpion I. The writing consists of early *hieroglyphs* (literally, "sacred carvings"), a system of pictures and abstract signs that represent sounds or ideas, later to become more formal and standardized.

As we shall see, incising cuneiform on clay was much clumsier than writing with pen and ink on papyrus, as became possible in Egypt. Nonetheless, cuneiform was flexible enough to record the spoken language and to be used for poetry as well as for bookkeeping. Moreover, cuneiform became the standard script of various languages of western Asia for several thousand years. Clumsy it may have been, but cuneiform was writing, and writing is both a catalyst for change and the historian's best friend. Mesopotamia after 3000 B.C. was dynamic, sophisticated, and, best of all, intelligible to us.

MESOPOTAMIA, TO CA. 1600 B.C.

After 3000 B.C. the people of Mesopotamia flourished. They experimented in government, in cooperation and conflict among different ethnic groups, in law, and in the working out of class and gender relations. Keenly aware of human limitations and vanity, they sought divine justice, as their literary and religious texts show. Their engineering skill, mathematics, and astronomy set ancient science on an upward path. In later centuries, Western civilization would build on these foundations, and then take off in new directions.

Archaeologists sometimes refer to the third and second millennia in the eastern Mediterranean and western Asia as the Bronze Age. In this period people mastered the technology of making bronze, an alloy of copper and tin, and bronze frequently replaced stone as a primary material for everyday use.

The City-States of Sumer — Though their culture is long dead, the Sumerians live on. Whenever someone today counts the minutes, debates politics, or quotes the law, the Sumerians live, for these are all legacies of that ingenious society.

The dominant inhabitants of Mesopotamian civilization in its first flowering are named Sumerians. Present in southern Mesopotamia by 3200 B.C. and probably earlier, the Sumerians entered their great age in the third millennium B.C., when their city-states enjoyed a proud independence.

The formative era of Mesopotamian civilization is known as the Uruk Period (ca. 3800–3200 B.C.), after one of its major archaeological sites. During the Uruk Period the Sumerians invented the wheel and the plow, planted the first orchards—of dates, figs, or olives—and developed the first sophisticated metal-casting processes. They built some of the first cities, for example, Uruk. They expanded the size of territories and populations, the scale of war, the complexity of society, and the power of government. Finally, as if to cap a period of remarkable change, at the end of the Uruk Period the Sumerians invented cuneiform writing.

Mesopotamian cities flourished in this era. By the period that scholars have named the Early Dynastic Period (2800–2350 B.C.), named for the first royal dynasties (ruling families), a large Mesopotamian city had grown to the point where it might cover 1,000 acres surrounded by more than 5 miles of walls, within which lived about fifty thousand people. Such a city was part of a network of thirty such city-states with a common culture, commerce, and propensity to make war on one another. Hence the city-states of Mesopotamia may be called the first civilization.

It was a land of cooperation and conflict. The Sumerian cities had much in common: language, literature, arts and sciences, and religion. Yet the cities often quarreled. In some cases conflict erupted over the boundaries of adjacent farmlands. The scarcity of fresh water also led to disputes among cities over water rights.

Each city had its own small urbanized area and a larger agricultural hinterland irrigated by canals. Cities traded with one another and with the outside world. The primary political units of southern Mesopotamia for most of the third millennium B.C., Sumerian city-states were an incubator of civilization.

How were the Sumerian city-states governed? A Sumerian might have responded that they were governed by the gods, for the Sumerians believed that the gods had created, and thus owned, everything on earth. Historians study human government, but the lack of evidence makes it difficult to say much with assurance about Sumerian government before the Early Dynastic Period.

Certainly in early times Sumerian temples were wealthy and powerful. A simple structure around 5000 B.C., the temple had become by 4000 B.C. an elaborate, monumental work of architecture built on a raised platform. Each city had at least one temple, the house of its patron god and the common symbol of the community. There is no evidence, though, for the once-prominent theory that the early Sumerian cities were temple-states governed by priests.

By the beginning of the Early Dynastic Period, around 2800 B.C., political power in a Sumerian city rested largely in the hands of its Council of Elders, whose members were probably wealthy landowners. Some scholars argue that the council shared power with a popular assembly, creating, in effect, a bicameral legislature and perhaps even a primitive democracy. The evidence is ambiguous, however, leaving it highly debatable whether ordinary people took part in Sumerian government.

In Sumer, as elsewhere in western Asia and Egypt throughout ancient times, ordinary people often faced limits on their freedom. True, there seem to have been many free peasants. Yet these small "free" farmers often had to provide forced labor for the state as a kind of taxation—maintaining the vast Mesopotamian irrigation system, for example. There also seems to have been a large group of people who were only semi-free because they owned no land of their own but worked others' land. Finally, there were slaves—that is, people who could be bought and sold. Slaves were never very numerous in these societies because no large policing system existed yet to keep them from running away. Still, wealthy people usually had a few slaves to help in the household. Slaves were usually brought from abroad as war booty or merchandise, although some slaves were local people who had been sold into slavery to pay off a debt; often they were children (especially daughters) sold by their parents.

By about 2700 B.C. political power shifted. It was a time of chronic intercity warfare, and the times demanded a strong hand. The new ruler was not a Council of Elders but rather a "big man" (*lugal*) or, less often, a "governor" (*ensi*)—that is, a king or, occasionally, a queen. The monarch was first and foremost a warrior. He claimed to be the earthly representative of the gods, a position that gave him general responsibility for his subjects' welfare. Accordingly, kings sponsored irrigation works, raised fortification walls, restored temples, and built palaces.

The earliest Sumerian kings, dating from the period 2700 to 2600 B.C., are Enmebaragesi of the city of Kish; his son and successor, Agga; and Gilgamesh of Uruk, a hero of epic poetry whom many scholars consider a genuine historical personage. In the cities of Ur and Lagash, the king's wife was often a power in her own right. Kish was ruled by Ku-baba (r. ca. 2450 B.C.), the first reigning queen of recorded history.

Though warriors, Sumerian monarchs also recognized a responsibility for promoting justice. History's earliest known reformer of law and society was Uru-inim-gina, king of Lagash around 2400 B.C. Surviving documents describe Lagash as a society in which wealthy landowners encroached on the temples and oppressed the poor, and royal administrators mistreated ordinary people. The king's aims seem to have been both to correct abuses and to weaken independent sources of power threatening royal authority. Uru-inim-gina attempted to manage the bureaucracy, protect the property of humble people, and guard the temples. He also put into effect the first known wage and price controls. Uru-inim-gina's proclaimed intention was to promote impartial justice, a goal that he expressed in the formula "[the king] will protect the mother that is in distress, the mighty man shall not oppress the naked and the widow." If at the same time he also managed to increase his own power, then so much the better. As it turned out, Lagash was conquered only a few years after Uru-inim-gina's reign. His reforms nonetheless survived as the precedent for a long Mesopotamian tradition of royal lawgiving.

Conquest and Assimilation, ca. 2350–1900 B.C. Mesopotamian cities faced competition from the surrounding peoples of the desert and the mountains. Poor and tough, these people coveted Mesopotamia's wealth. Some conquerors came directly from the hinterland to the walls of the city they were attacking; others climbed to power from within the Sumerian city-states. Both groups were sufficiently impressed by Sumerian culture to adopt a great many Sumerian customs and ideas. The most successful warrior-king was Sargon (r. 2371–2316 B.C.), an unusual figure who rose from obscurity to a high position under the king of Kish before founding his own capital city, Agade. Even more important, Sargon was a native speaker not of Sumerian but of Akkadian.

The Akkadians were originally a seminomadic people who lived on the edge of the desert. Shepherds, they moved their flocks with the seasons. Their language, Akkadian, belongs to the Semitic group of languages, which also includes Arabic and Hebrew. Scholars formerly believed that the Akkadians came directly from the desert to conquer Sumer, but it is now known that they had begun settling in the northern cities of southern Mesopotamia by the end of the Uruk Period. This northern part of southern Mesopotamia was known as Akkad.

Akkadian Bronze *This stern-faced, life-size cast-bronze head, with its stylized ringleted beard and carefully arranged hair, shows Mesopotamian craftsmanship at its finest. Thought by some to be Sargon (r. 2371–2316* B.C.*) or Naram-sin (r. ca. 2250–2220* B.C.*), it was deliberately mutilated in ancient times.* (Claus Hansmann, München)

As commander of one of history's first professional armies, Sargon conquered all of Mesopotamia, and his power extended westward along the Euphrates and eastward into the Iranian Plateau. Rather than rule conquered peoples directly, the Akkadians generally were satisfied with loose control, as long as they could monopolize trade. They adopted Sumerian religion and wrote Akkadian in cuneiform.

Sargon's son inherited his throne. His dynasty boasted that it reigned over "the peoples of all lands" or "the four quarters of the earth." The Akkadian empire reached its greatest height in the reign of Sargon's grandson, Naram-sin (r. ca. 2250–2220 B.C.), but it did not survive the next reign. Sargon nonetheless proved to be one of western Asia's most influential figures. His dynasty's ideal of universal empire was one to which future conquerors would lay claim.

Sargon proved adept at using religion to legitimize his rule. A self-made monarch, he was sensitive to the charge of having stolen power. Indeed, he chose the throne name Sargon (Sharrum-ken in Akkadian) because it means "the king is legitimate." By claiming the status of the gods' representative on earth, Sargon strengthened his authority.

He once paraded a defeated enemy in a halter before the temple and priests of Enlil, the chief Sumerian god, confidently proclaiming that Enlil was on his side.

Assimilation was another lasting Akkadian legacy. Although Sargon made Akkadian the official language of administration, he made politic concessions to Sumerian sensibilities. For instance, his daughter Enkheduanna, whom he appointed high priestess at Ur and Uruk, wrote poetry in Sumerian, poetry powerful enough to be quoted often in later Sumerian texts. The first known woman poet, Enkheduanna described the union of Sumerians and Akkadians.

Around 2200 B.C. the Akkadian empire broke up into a series of smaller successor states. Then, after a century of rule by invaders from the Zagros Mountains on the eastern border of Mesopotamia, the Sumerians returned to power under the Third Dynasty of Ur (2112–2004 B.C.). Far from stripping away all Akkadian influence, the revived Sumerian rulers spoke of themselves as "kings of Sumer and Akkad." It was a title that would have a long and potent history: for the next fifteen hundred years, many of the great kings of western Asia would label themselves, among other honorifics, "king of Sumer and Akkad." By using this title, the Sumerian kings of Ur showed that they recognized the existence of a composite, common Mesopotamian society.

This society survived renewed political turmoil around 2000 B.C. A new kingdom under the rule of the Amorites, one of several raiding peoples, emerged around 1900 B.C. in southern Mesopotamia. The kingdom of the Amorites, Semitic-speakers, shared Mesopotamian culture and traditions. Babylon, northwest of Ur in the central part of Mesopotamia, became the Amorite capital. From Babylon, Amorite kings issued cuneiform decrees that, although written in a Semitic language, drew heavily on Sumerian material.

Hammurabi's Code

The most famous Amorite king, Hammurabi (r. 1792–1750 B.C.) ruled in Babylon about six hundred years after Sargon. Much of his forty-two-year reign was devoted to creating a Mesopotamian empire. A careful administrator who ushered in an era of prosperity and cultural flowering, Hammurabi is most famous for the text known as Hammurabi's Code. Although the work was less a "code" than a collection listing various crimes and their punishments—a kind of treatise on justice glorifying Hammurabi's qualities as a judge—we shall use the familiar name. Hammurabi's Code became both a legal and a literary classic, much copied in later times.

Hammurabi's Code offers a remarkable portrait of Mesopotamian society. The document contains nearly three hundred rulings in cases ranging from family to commercial law, from wage rates to murder. The administration of justice in Mesopotamia was entirely practical: we find no notion of abstract absolutes or universal principles, not even a word for "law."

Though occasionally less harsh than earlier law codes, which date as far back as around 2100 B.C., Hammurabi's Code was by no means lenient. Whereas earlier codes were satisfied with payment in silver as recompense for crime, Hammurabi's Code was the first to stipulate such ruthless penalties as mutilation, drowning, and impaling. It also introduced the law of retaliation for wounds: "If a man has destroyed the eye of a member of the aristocracy: they shall destroy his eye. If he has broken his limb: they shall break the (same) limb." Moreover, children could be punished for the crimes of their fathers.

Inscribed in forty-nine vertical columns on a stone stele about 7½ feet high and displayed in a prominent public place, Hammurabi's Code symbolized the notion that the law belonged to everyone. Although ordinary people could not read, it was possible for them to find a patron who could. Yet the societies of western Asia and Egypt were anything but egalitarian, and Hammurabi's society was no exception. Punishments there, as elsewhere, were class-based: crimes against a free person, for example, received harsher punishment than crimes against a slave or a semi-free person. Debt seems to have been a serious and widespread problem, frequently leading to debt slavery. Women could own and inherit property and testify in court. The overall direction of the code, however, was patriarchal: it enshrined the power of the male head of the family. For example, a son who struck his father had his hand cut off, while a woman who brought about the death of her husband "because of another man" was impaled on stakes.

Divine Masters   The Sumerians were polytheists—that is, they had many gods—and their gods (like the later gods of Greece) were anthropomorphic, or human in form. Indeed, Sumerian (and Greek) gods were thought to be much like human beings, by turns wise and foolish, except that they were immortal and superpowerful. Many Sumerian gods arose out of the forces of nature: An, the sky-god; Enki, the earth-god and freshwater-god; Enlil, the air-god; Nanna, the moon-god; and Utu (Semitic, Shamash), the sun-god. Other Sumerian gods embodied human passions or notions about the afterlife: Inanna (Semitic, Ishtar), goddess of love and war; and Ereshkigal, goddess of the underworld.

The Sumerians sometimes envisioned their gods holding an assembly, much like a boisterous Sumerian prototype. The Sumerians and Akkadians considered Enlil, city-god of Nippur, to be the chief god. The Babylonians replaced him with Marduk, city-god of Babylon.

Every Mesopotamian city had its main temple complex, the most striking feature of which was a *ziggurat,* or stepped tower. Constructed originally as simple raised terraces, ziggurats eventually became seven-stage structures. Unlike the pyramids of Egypt, ziggurats were not tombs but "stairways" connecting humans and the gods.

The keynote of Mesopotamian religion was a certain pessimism about the human condition. It is not surprising that the Mesopotamians, living in a difficult natural environment, regarded the gods with fear and awe. Although the gods communicated with humans, their language was mysterious. To understand the divine will, the Mesopotamians engaged in various kinds of divination: the interpretation of dreams, the examination of the entrails of slaughtered animals, and the study of the stars (which stimulated great advances in astronomy, as we will see). By building temples, offering prayers and animal sacrifices, and participating in public rituals and processions, Mesopotamians hoped to appease their gods and discern their wishes.

Most people expected nothing glorious in the afterlife, merely a shadowy existence. It was thought that with a person's last breath, his or her spirit embarked on a long journey to the Netherworld, a place under the earth. More than one Mesopotamian text describes the Netherworld as the "Land-of-no-return" and "the house wherein the dwellers are bereft of light, / Where dust is their fare and clay their food, / Where they see no light, residing in darkness."[1] The dead resided there permanently, though in some texts their spirits return to earth, often with hostile intent toward the living.

Archaeological evidence indicates a possible shift in such attitudes toward death, at least on the part of the Mesopotamian upper classes, by the late third millennium B.C. The kings and nobles of the Third Dynasty of Ur were buried with rich grave goods and with their servants, who were apparently the victims of human sacrifice following the master's death. Perhaps the rulers now expected to have the opportunity to use their wealth again in a comfortable immortality, possibly influenced by Egyptian ideas (see pages 24–25).

Arts and Sciences   The people of Mesopotamia were deeply inquisitive. They focused on the beginning and the end of things. "How did the world come into being?" and "What happens to us when we die?" are perhaps the two fundamental questions of their rich literature. Consider, for example, the Babylonian creation epic known from its first line as *Enuma Elish* ("When on high"). An epic poem is the story of heroic deeds, in this case the deeds of the gods of order, who triumphed over the forces of chaos. This poem also commemorates the political ascendancy of Babylon. The poem was recited annually during the New Year's festival by Babylonian priests. Another important Babylonian literary genre, known as wisdom literature, responded to life's vicissitudes with precepts that are sometimes simple, sometimes sophisticated. It proved eventually to influence the wisdom literature of the Hebrew Bible.

The best-known example of Mesopotamian literature is the *Epic of Gilgamesh*. Frequently translated and adapted by various western Asian peoples, *Gilgamesh* may be a Sumerian work dating to about 2500 B.C. Gilgamesh, king of Uruk, was probably a real historical personage, but the poem primarily concerns his fictionalized personal life, in particular his painful pilgrimage from arrogant youth to wise maturity. The main themes are friendship, loss, and the inevitability of death. Much of the poem discusses Gilgamesh's close relationship with Enkidu, who is first his rival, then his friend, and finally his educator. Enkidu's untimely death makes Gilgamesh aware of his own mortality. Distraught by his friend's passing, Gilgamesh goes on a vain quest for immortality. The *Epic of Gilgamesh* contains stories that presage the later biblical Eden and Flood narratives; there is little doubt but that those narratives found their way from Mesopotamia to the Hebrew Bible.

The Mesopotamians made advances in mathematics, astronomy, medicine, and engineering. The Sumerians had two systems of numbers: a decimal system (powers of ten) for administration and business and a sexagesimal system (powers of sixty) for weights and mathematical or astronomical calculations. Like the Babylonians, we still divide hours by sixty today. Furthermore, our modern system of numerical place-value notation—for example, the difference between 42 and 24—is derived, through Hindu-Arabic intermediaries, from the Babylonian system. The Babylonians were adept at arithmetic and could solve problems for which we would use algebra. A millennium before the Greek mathematician Pythagoras (who claimed to have studied the Mesopotamian tradition) proved the validity of the theorem that bears his name, they were familiar with the proposition that in a right triangle the square of the longest side is equal to the sum of the squares of the other two sides. In the first millennium B.C. the Babylonians developed a sophisticated mathematical astronomy (see page 39). As early as the seventeenth century B.C., they made systematic, if not always accurate, recordings of the movements of the planet Venus.

In medical matters they demonstrated considerable critical ability. Physicians made advances in the use of plant products for medicines and in very rudimentary surgery. The Babylonians had a simple pregnancy test of moderate accuracy, for example, and their surgeons were experienced at setting broken bones. When they became ill, however, most people in Mesopotamia set more store by magic and incantations than by surgery or herbal medicine.

Mesopotamian sculptors, particularly the Sumerians, were adept and sophisticated. They did not produce realistic representations of reality—that was not their purpose. Rather, they aimed at creating symbols of religious piety or political or military power. Sumerian statues tend to be stiff and solemn. The head and face are carved in detail, and the body is neglected, sometimes little more than a geometric form.

The most common type of Mesopotamian sculpture is relief sculpture, in which figures or forms are projected from a flat surface. Steles (upright stone slabs or pillars), plaques, and cylinder seals (small, carved stone or metal cylinders rolled over wet clay to make a stamp, indicating ownership) are all found.

EGYPT, TO CA. 1100 B.C.

From Babylon to the valley of the Nile River was about 750 miles by way of the caravan routes through Syria and Palestine—close enough to exchange goods and customs but far enough for a distinct Egyptian civilization to emerge. As in Sumer, civilization in Egypt arose in a river valley, but Egypt was much earlier than Mesopotamia in becoming a unified kingdom under one ruler. Moreover, ancient Egypt survived as a united and independent kingdom for over two thousand years (to be sure, with some periods of civil war and foreign rule). Egypt made great strides in a variety of areas of human achievement, from the arts to warfare. Western civilization borrowed much from Egypt, especially in technology and religion.

Geography as Destiny   Ancient Egypt is a product of the unique characteristics of the Nile River. Egypt was "the gift of the Nile," to use the well-known phrase of Herodotus, a Greek historian who visited Egypt in the fifth century B.C.

Yet most of present-day Egypt is desert. Only about 5 percent is habitable by humans, including a few oases, the Nile Delta, and the Nile Valley itself, which extends about 760 miles from Cairo to Egypt's modern southern border: Upper Egypt, a long and narrow valley never more than about 14 miles wide. North of Cairo, in Lower Egypt, the Nile branches out into the wide, low-lying delta before flowing into the Mediterranean Sea.

The fertility of the Nile River gave ancient Egypt a prosperous economy and optimistic culture. The river's annual floods, which took place during late summer and autumn, were generally benign. With less human effort than was required in Mesopotamia, the floodwaters could be used to irrigate most of the farmland in the Nile Valley. As a result, Egyptian agriculture was one of the wealthiest in the ancient world. Bread and beer were the national staples.

Egyptian culture celebrated the Nile's bounty. "Hail to Thee, O Nile, that gushest forth from the earth and comest to nourish Egypt!" So proclaims an ancient hymn that

Ancient Egypt and the Levant

The unique geography of the Nile Valley and its fertile soil left a stamp on ancient Egypt. Egypt enjoyed trade and cultural contact—and sometimes went to war—with nearby lands such as Nubia and the Levant.

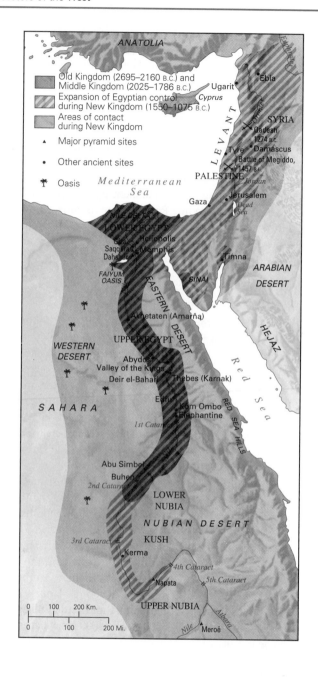

indicates the Egyptians' confidence in their natural environment. With its plentiful water and fertile land, Egypt suffered far less of the warfare that damaging floods and relative economic scarcity provoked in Mesopotamia.

Egyptian art and literature betray little of the despair over the unpredictability of the universe that developed in the harsher climatic conditions of Mesopotamia. The behavior of the Nile, furthermore, encouraged a static quality in Egyptian ideology.

Change seemed undesirable. Even death appeared to be a minor event compared with the eternal regularity of the Nile, which may help explain the prominence in Egyptian religion of belief in the afterlife. In addition, the static outlook helped promote the idea of an absolute, all-powerful, and all-providing king—namely, pharaoh.

Early Egypt developed a distinctive civilization, with no major invasion for nearly 1,500 years after the beginning of the historical period around 3100 B.C. Just how isolated was early Egypt, however, and just how distinctive was its civilization? Debate has arisen in recent years about the relationship of Egypt with western Asia, Europe, and the rest of Africa. Before World War II, most Egyptologists tended to think of Egypt more as part of the Near East (that is, of the culture of western Asia) than as part of Africa. Many imagined that ancient Egyptians looked much like modern Europeans: part of "the Great White Race."[2] More recently, with the liberation after World War II of Europe's former African colonies and with the awakening of a growing interest in Africa by African Americans, some people have argued that Egypt was primarily African in character and that the ancient Egyptians were black.

The truth lies in between these two positions. Much of Egypt's earliest culture is African, as evidenced by both artifacts, such as Neolithic artwork and pottery, and ideas, such as the notion that the ruler represents the ancestors and guarantees the fertility of the soil. Yet in its late Neolithic era (ca. 3400–3050 B.C.), Egypt imported new styles and techniques in art, architecture, ceramics, and metallurgy from western Asia. As for the population, it seems from the fourth millennium B.C., if not earlier, to have consisted of Africans mixed with immigrants from western Asia. The Egyptians considered themselves a distinct ethnic and racial group, unlike their neighbors in Africa or elsewhere. Egyptians were generally darker skinned than the ancient peoples of Europe or western Asia but often lighter skinned than the peoples of Africa south of the Sahara. They included a considerable variety of skin colors and body types. The Egyptians of the southerly Upper Nile were more likely to have the dark skin and facial features characteristic of sub-Saharan Africans.

Egypt was in continual contact with other regions of Africa, particularly the neighboring areas of ancient Libya and Nubia (roughly, modern Sudan). The people of Nubia, who were black Africans, borrowed from Egypt and were perhaps borrowed from in turn. Some scholars believe, for example, that the early Egyptian notion of monarchy originated in Nubia. In West Africa certain important institutions—including sacred royalty, the cult of the ram, and belief in the afterlife existence of a double of one's physical person—may be of Egyptian origin.

Divine Kingship   Agriculture and settled village life emerged in Egypt around 5000 B.C. By 4000 B.C. villages had grown into towns, each controlling a strip of territory. About a thousand years later, around 3100 B.C., the Nile Valley had become one unified kingdom of Egypt, with a capital city perhaps at Memphis. We do not know precisely how this process unfolded. Egyptians writing after 3000 B.C. assumed that the Nile Valley had originally been home to two kingdoms roughly corresponding to Upper and Lower Egypt. Then, around 3100 B.C., Menes, king of Upper Egypt, is said to have conquered Lower Egypt and united the two into a single realm.

We do not know how much (if any) of this tradition is true. We *do* know that between about 5000 and 3100 B.C., Egyptian communities up and down the Nile Valley succeeded in clearing marshes and expanding the amount of land under cultivation, which in turn could support a larger population. By 3200 B.C., monumental architecture, writing, and kingship appeared. For several centuries Egyptians consolidated their institutions. Although few specifics are known about this Archaic Period (3200–2695 B.C.), it clearly laid the groundwork for the next era. Around 2700 B.C., a remarkable, distinctive, and relatively well-documented period of creativity began, the Third (2695–2600 B.C.) and Fourth (2600–2500 B.C.) Dynasties (that is, ruling families) of the Old Kingdom.

The history of third- and second-millennium B.C. Egypt is usually divided into three distinct eras of great prosperity: the Old Kingdom (2695–2160 B.C.), the Middle Kingdom (2025–1786 B.C.), and the New Kingdom (1550–1075 B.C.). Between the kingdoms, central authority broke down in the Intermediate Periods. Broadly speaking, the Old Kingdom was an era of spectacular creativity and originality, symbolized by the building of the Great Pyramids; the Middle Kingdom, an era of introspection and literary production; and the New Kingdom, an era in which Egypt's traditional isolation gave way to international diplomacy and expansion.

The early Egyptian government was the first government in recorded history to govern a large territory. Indeed, a chart of Egypt's power structure would be strictly hierarchical, resembling a pyramid, with a broad base of laborers and artisans supporting a small commanding elite. The occupant of the highest point of power was considered so important that for centuries Egyptians referred to the office rather than to the person, calling it "the Great House"—in Egyptian, *per-aa*, or "pharaoh," as the ruler himself (or occasionally herself) was eventually called.

Egyptian kingship was sacred monarchy. In Mesopotamia, the king generally claimed to have been appointed by the gods. In Egypt pharaoh was deemed to *be* a god. He was referred to as the "good god" in his lifetime and the "great god" after death. Considered the physical child of the sun-god, Re, he was also equated with the sky-god Horus, and after dying he became Osiris, god of the underworld. Just as Egyptian myth recounted how the world was created when a god, sitting on a hill, made the waters recede, so pharaoh was thought to make the Nile rise and fall each year.

A wall of language and ceremony separated kings from ordinary human beings. Egyptians did not speak "to" the king but rather "in his presence." He was outfitted with a variety of crowns, headdresses, and scepters. Pharaoh's exalted status was apparent on the occasion of a "glorious appearance" before his subjects, especially at the Sed festival or jubilee, a ceremony designed to rejuvenate the king's divine powers.

The most dramatic symbol of the king's divinity, however, was not a festival but a building—or, rather, a series of buildings—the pyramids. The ancients built thirty-five major and many smaller pyramids, of which the best known are the Great Pyramids of Giza—three gigantic, perfectly symmetrical limestone tombs constructed during the Fourth Dynasty. Nearly five thousand years after its construction, the pyramid of King Khufu (r. 2589–2566 B.C., better known by his Greek name, Cheops) is still the largest all-stone building in human history. Near the Great Pyramids stands the Great Sphinx, a human-headed lion carved out of a huge rock outcropping, perhaps representing Khufu's son, King Khafre (r. 2558–2532 B.C.; Greek name, Chephren), for whom the second pyramid at Giza was built.

The pyramids were not just monuments to an ego but also temples where the king would continue to be worshiped and served in the afterlife. The structures served a po-

Great Pyramids of Giza   *Royal funerary monuments of three Egyptian kings of the twenty-sixth century B.C., the pyramids symbolize the power and ambition of the Old Kingdom. The pyramid of King Khufu (or Cheops, rearmost in the photo) is still the largest all-stone building in human history.* (Michael Holford)

litical purpose as well. When the Great Pyramids were constructed, the kingdom of Egypt was still young and fragile. By carrying out an astonishingly large project focused on his person, the king made a statement of his power—an eloquent, simple, and irrefutable statement. The sheer size of the Great Pyramids demonstrated the king's ability to organize a vast labor force. Indeed, it has plausibly been suggested that the encampment of workers at Giza represented the largest gathering of human beings to that date. Moreover, the pyramids and the rows of tombs surrounding them reinforced the hierarchical structure of Egyptian society, of which the king was the capstone. Only princes and select officials were given the privilege of erecting a tomb beside the royal pyramids, a privilege that Fourth Dynasty Egyptians viewed as a prerequisite to gaining access to eternal life. The principal royal wives were permitted to be buried in small pyramids of their own.

In theory, the king owned all the land, but in practice Egypt's economy was a mixture of private enterprise and centralized control. The king was thought to watch over Egypt carefully. In the Middle Kingdom, for example, he was represented as a good shepherd, appointed by the sun-god, Re, as one text says, "to keep alive the people and the folk, not sleeping by night as well as by day in seeking out every beneficial act, in looking for possibilities of usefulness." Even sleepless pharaohs needed help, however, and they delegated authority to a large group of officials. Indeed, Old Kingdom Egypt was one of the earliest great bureaucracies. The country was supervised by governors, mayors, military commanders, judges, treasurers, engineers, agricultural overseers, scribes, and others. The highest official was the vizier, a sort of prime minister who had more day-to-day power than pharaoh himself.

The essence of good government was what the Egyptians called *ma'at,* whose basic meaning is "order"—in government, society, or the universe. *Ma'at* can also mean "truth" or "justice." The god-king embodied what we would call law, but the administration of justice rested mainly on others' shoulders. Egypt had a well-functioning system of judges who heard lawsuits, and it probably also had a detailed law code, although few written laws survive.

Life and Afterlife

Later peoples, beginning with the Greeks, have assumed that the ordinary Egyptian chafed under royal power. It is true that Egyptians were burdened with a variety of taxes (paid in agricultural produce) and that free people, both men and women, had an obligation of forced labor service on public works, from irrigation projects to the pyramids. Sometimes this service caused resentment. We hear of worker discipline maintained by beatings, of desperate fugitives, of the pious hope that there would be no forced labor in the afterlife, and even, in one unusual case, of a workers' strike.

Both piety and practicality, however, dictated that most people make peace with their public burdens. Far from resenting the king's claim to divinity, ordinary people may have been reassured to be ruled by a god. Nor were the pyramid-builders slaves laboring under a tyrant, as Greek writers assumed. In fact, they might have given their labor gladly to raising the man-god's tomb, as an act of faith, just as people centuries later donated time and money to build medieval cathedrals. The workers reaped material compensations, too: ration supplements for ordinary laborers, steady employment for specialized craftsmen.

Egyptian life was suffused with religious practices, from daily rituals and seasonal festivals to ethical teachings and magic. Egyptian religion tended toward *syncretism*— that is, the blending of mutually opposed beliefs, principles, or practices. For example, Egyptian mythology taught variously that the sky was a cow, was held up by a god or by a post, or was a goddess stretched over the earth. No one was troubled by such inconsistencies, as a modern worshiper might be, because Egyptians believed that a fundamental unity underlay the varieties of nature. Another example of syncretism is the most important Egyptian god, Re, the sun, often called "universal lord." From time to time, Re was syncretized with other gods to create a powerful new god—for example, Re-Atum, a combination of Re and a creator-god.

But Egypt's religion had an abundance of greater and lesser deities, including human, animal, and composite gods. Various animals, from cats and dogs to crocodiles and serpents, were thought to represent the divine. Innumerable local deities and demons, as well as gods and goddesses of all of Egypt, peopled the spirit world. Important deities included Thoth, the moon-god and god of wisdom; Nut, goddess of the sky; Ptah, a creator-god; Osiris, who invented agriculture and became lord of the dead; Horus, son of Osiris, a sky-god imagined as a giant falcon; and Isis, wife of Osiris and mother of Horus, a mother-goddess. Temples were numerous and lavish.

Probably the most striking feature of Egyptian religion was its focus on the afterlife. Unlike the Mesopotamians, the Egyptians believed that death could be an extremely pleasant continuation of life on earth. Hence, they actively sought immortality. The wealthy placed great emphasis on building tombs, decorating them with paintings and inscriptions, and stocking them with cherished possessions for use in the world beyond. The most cherished possession of all, of course, was the body itself, and the Egyptians provided for its preservation through their mastery of the science of embalming—thus the Egyptian mummies. The Egyptians believed that a person's spirit could live on after death, but unlike later civilizations, they were not prepared to jettison the body altogether, believing instead that from time to time a person desired to return to the body after death. That belief made mummification necessary.

Reserved for the king and his officials in the Old Kingdom, the afterlife became, as it were, democratized by the Middle Kingdom. The Middle Kingdom and the First and Second Intermediate Periods were in many ways an inward-looking and reflective era, one in which materialism was de-emphasized and a sense of common humanity appears.

By the Middle Kingdom, even ordinary Egyptians believed they could enjoy immortality after death, as gods, as long as they could purchase for their graves funerary texts containing the relevant litanies. The texts emphasize ritual—incantations, magic spells, prayers—as the key to eternal life. Yet from time to time we find other texts, especially from the Middle Kingdom, that say that ritual is not enough; ethical behavior also is required. New Kingdom texts describe the details of a dead person's appearance before a divine court for judgment. Before forty-two judges of the underworld, the dead person declares his or her innocence of a variety of sins. A god then weighs the dead person's heart in the balance against a feather, the symbol of *ma'at*, or truth. The sinless are admitted into eternal life in the kingdom of the blessed. The guilty, their heavy hearts devoured by a beast, suffer a second, final death.

Such absolute judgments were not found in daily life. Consider relations between the sexes. Egyptian women did not enjoy equal status with men, but they had a considerably greater measure of equality than women in other ancient societies, particularly in legal matters. As in Mesopotamia, so in Egypt a woman could buy or sell, bequeath or inherit, sue or testify in court, but a married Egyptian woman, unlike her eastern sisters, could do so without a male guardian's approval. A married woman in Egypt retained the status of complete legal independence. She could even own property without her husband's involvement. But how often did women exercise such privileges? Relatively little evidence of female property owners survives from Egypt. Although Egyptian women could work outside the home in a variety of enterprises, they were rarely managers. Women worked in agriculture and trade, in the textile and perfume industries, in dining halls, and in entertainment, and women served as priestesses of various kinds. Yet in Egypt, as elsewhere, women were expected to make the home the focus of their activities. So although Egyptian women had more freedom outside the home than most ancient women, they exercised nothing like the freedom enjoyed by women in North America today.

Expansion, Reform, and Power Shifts, 1786–1075 B.C. The humane attitudes of the Middle Kingdom were swept away after about 1700 B.C., when Semitic-speaking immigrants from Palestine—the Hyksos, to employ the commonly used Greek term—conquered much of Egypt. In many ways gentle conquerors, the Hyksos worshiped Egyptian gods, built and restored Egyptian temples, and intermarried with natives. As foreigners, however, the Hyksos were unpopular. Eventually a war launched from Upper Egypt, which had retained a loose independence, drove the Hyksos out.

The first restored Egyptian ruler of the New Kingdom was Ahmose I (r. 1550–1525 B.C.). His proved to be a new Egypt indeed. The Hyksos had brought advanced military technology to Egypt, including the horse-drawn war chariot, new kinds of daggers and swords, and the composite bow. Made of laminated materials including wood, leather, and horn, the composite bow could hit a target at 600 yards. Having tasted foreign occupation, Egypt's new rulers determined to use such weapons in aggressive military campaigns abroad.

Warlike, expansionist, and marked by a daring attempt at religious reform, the New Kingdom's Eighteenth Dynasty (1540–1293 B.C.) has long held a special fascination for historians. One of the dynasty's memorable names is that of Queen Hatshepsut. Widow of Thutmose II (r. 1491–1479 B.C.), Hatshepsut first served as regent for her young stepson and then assumed the kingship herself (r. 1479–1457 B.C.). Other Egyptian queens had exercised royal power before, but Hatshepsut was the first to call herself king. Some statues show her wearing a false beard, and some of her inscriptions refer to Hatshepsut as "he," not "she." Although Hatshepsut dispatched Egyptian armies to fight, her reign is best known for peaceful activities: at home, public works and temple rebuilding; abroad, a commercial expedition over the Red Sea to the "Land of Punt" (perhaps modern Somalia, in eastern Africa).

After her death Hatshepsut was succeeded by her stepson, Thutmose III (r. 1479–1425 B.C.). Late in his reign, he tried to erase his stepmother's memory by having Hatshepsut's statues destroyed and her name expunged from records—an attempt, perhaps, to cut off a claim to the throne by her supporters. A warrior-pharaoh, Thutmose III led his dynasty's armed expansion in western Asia and northern Africa. Thutmose won his greatest victory during his first campaign, at the Battle of Megiddo in Palestine in 1457 B.C., where Egypt's triumph prevented the kingdom of Mitanni from expanding southward. Egypt now ruled an empire with territory in Nubia, Palestine, and Syria.

Empire brings power, and power often causes conflict. In imperial Egypt during the fourteenth century B.C., kings and priests struggled over authority. Consider the Amarna reform, named for a major archaeological site at the modern town of Tell el-Amarna.

The Amarna reform was carried out by Thutmose III's great-great-grandson, King Amenhotep IV (r. 1352–1336 B.C.). Earlier, the god Amun-Re had become the chief deity of the New Kingdom. As supporters of the ideology of imperialism, his temple priests had been so richly rewarded with land and wealth that their power now rivaled pharaoh's own. Amenhotep IV's dramatic response was to forbid the worship of Amun-Re and replace him with the god Aten, the solar disk. Changing his own name to Akhenaten ("pleasing to Aten"), the king ordered the erasure of Amun-Re's name from monuments throughout Egypt. As a further step, Akhenaten created a new capital city in central Egypt at an uninhabited site at the desert's edge: Akhetaten (modern Amarna). The new town had a distinctive culture. Akhenaten's wife, Nefertiti, figures prominently in Amarna art, and she too may have played an important role in the reform.

The reform shifted power away from the priests and toward the king, but we need not doubt the reformers' sincerity. Contemporary literature suggests intense religious conviction in Aten as a benevolent god and one who nurtured not only Egypt but all countries. Although the Aten cult focuses on one god, only Akhenaten and his family were permitted to worship Aten directly; the rest of the Egyptian population was expected to worship the god through pharaoh.

Bold as the reform was, sustaining so dramatic a break with tradition proved impossible. After Akhenaten's death his son-in-law and successor, Tutankhaten (r. 1336–1327 B.C.) restored good relations with the priests of Amun-Re, which he signaled by changing his name to Tutankhamun. The Amun-Re cult was revived, the Aten cult was abolished, and the city of Akhetaten was abandoned. After Tutankhamun's death the military exercised great influence over the remaining pharaohs of the Eighteenth Dynasty. Then, in 1291 B.C., a military officer founded a new dynasty as Ramesses I (r. 1291–1289 B.C.).

The Nineteenth (ca. 1291–1185 B.C.) and Twentieth (ca. 1185–1075 B.C.) Dynasties are known as the Ramesside Era, from the most common name of the pharaohs. Although the era witnessed great warrior-pharaohs and builder-pharaohs, over time the kings lost power to the priests of Amun. Abroad, Egypt remained a formidable power, but it faced armed invasions, some of which required major efforts to repel (see page 32). In any case, many foreigners settled peacefully in the rich farmland of the Nile Delta, giving Egypt a more cosmopolitan character. Both their presence and the building of a great new city in the delta by the Ramesside kings led to a power shift within Egypt. When the Twentieth Dynasty ended in 1075 B.C., the New Kingdom ended with it, and regional conflict between the Nile Delta and Upper Egypt broke out.

Arts and Sciences in the New Kingdom   The Egyptians were superb builders, architects, and engineers. In addition to pyramids and irrigation works, they constructed monumental royal tombs, palaces, forts, and temples, and they erected looming obelisks. At their best, Egyptian architects designed buildings in harmony with the unique landscape—one of the reasons for the structures' lasting appeal. Their most original and enduring work was done in stone. Stone temples, for example, culminated in the imposing pillared structures of the New Kingdom. That period also saw the construction of rock-cut temples, the most famous of which is Ramesses II's (r. 1279–1213 B.C.) project at Abu Simbel. In front of the temples sit four colossal statues of Ramesses, also carved out of rock. Obelisks were slender, tapering pillars carved of a single piece of stone. Inscribed with figures and hieroglyphs, and usually erected in pairs in front of a temple, obelisks were meant to glorify the sun-god.

Throughout history royal courts have excelled as patrons of the arts; the Egyptian court was one of the first and greatest. Egyptian craftsmen were master goldsmiths, glassmakers, and woodworkers. The major arts are well represented in tombs, which were decorated with rich, multicolored wall paintings, the first narrative depictions. Scenes of the gods, court ceremony, ordinary life, war, and recreation amid the crocodiles and hippopotamuses of the Nile Valley adorn subterranean walls. Like so much else in Egypt, painting had a religious purpose. Representations of living people were meant to perpetuate them in the afterlife.

Sculpture was another art form in which Egyptians excelled. Carved in stone, wood, or metal, Egyptian sculpture is a study in contrasts. The body posture is usually rigid and stiff, the musculature only sketchy; the face, in contrast, is often individualistic, the expression full of character and drawn from life. Statues represent kings and queens, gods and goddesses, husbands and wives, adults and children, officials, priests, scribes, animals. Mirroring broader cultural trends, statues of pharaohs underwent stylistic changes through the centuries. In the Old Kingdom, the royal expression was usually one of majesty and power, but in the Middle Kingdom, the king's face often appeared more human and weak. Statues of New Kingdom pharaohs often suggested imperial power, whereas Amarna sculptors emphasized introspective gazes and experimented with the grotesque. Eighteenth Dynasty sculpture often shows a striking interest in feminine beauty and grace.

Ancient Egyptian literature is notable for its variety. Religious subjects, historical and commemorative records, technical treatises in mathematics and medicine, and secular stories survive alongside business contracts and royal proclamations. A good example of Egyptian writing is the *Story of Sinuhe*, a Middle Kingdom prose tale. Sinuhe reveals both the charm of ancient Egyptian literature and its cultural chauvinism.

The vastness and variety of ancient Egyptian literature were made possible by the invention of a far more convenient medium for writing than the clunky clay tablets of Mesopotamia—papyrus. Egyptian writing is best known for hieroglyphs. Elaborate and formal, hieroglyphs were generally used after the Archaic Period only for monuments and ornamentation. Two simplified scripts served for everyday use.

The people who built the pyramids had to be skilled at arithmetic and geometry. Egyptians were able to approximate pi (the ratio of the circumference of a circle to its diameter) and to solve equations containing one or two unknowns. Mathematical astronomy never reached the heights in Egypt that it reached in Babylon (see page 39), but the Egyptian calendar was a remarkable achievement. Based on observation of the star Sirius, the Egyptian calendar, with its 365-day year, approximates the solar calendar. Corrected to 365¼ days, it survives to this day as the calendar of Europe, the Americas, and much of the rest of the world.

Egyptian medical doctors were admired in antiquity and in demand abroad. They knew how to set a dislocated shoulder and used a full battery of splints, sutures, adhesive plasters, elementary disinfectants (from tree leaves), and burn treatments (fatty substances). A brilliant treatise, the Edwin Smith Papyrus, demonstrates their sophistication and rationalism. Dating from around 1750 B.C., the document claims to be a copy of an original from 2700 B.C. (the veracity of that claim is uncertain). Possibly a manual for the treatment of battlefield wounds, it is an ancient prototype of modern triage, dividing diseases into three categories: treatable, possibly treatable, and untreatable. In addition to signs of careful observation is tantalizing evidence that Egyptian doctors undertook postmortem dissection in order to understand the human body better.

WIDENING HORIZONS: THE LEVANT AND ANATOLIA, 2500–1150 B.C.

Egypt and Mesopotamia tend to capture our attention, but other early, nearby civilizations are, if less important, also significant contributors to the West. Not only were they the cradle of Western languages and writing systems, but they took part in the first international system of states, a forerunner of later international relations between the West and its neighbors. Let us look in particular at the city-states of the Levant—the geographic region known today as Syria and Palestine or Israel—and at a kingdom in Anatolia, today's Turkey.

The City-States of Syria-Palestine, ca. 2500–1200 B.C. The discovery in 1974 of a huge cuneiform archive at Ebla (modern Tell Mardikh) in northern Syria revolutionized our knowledge of one such city-state in the mid-third millennium B.C. Another Levantine city-state, Ugarit (modern Ras Shamra), a cosmopolitan port, flourished in the second millennium B.C.

A prosperous city, Ebla was known for commerce and artisanry as well as scholarship. Its extensive cuneiform archives include the world's earliest known dictionaries. Sometime between 2500 and 2300 B.C., Ebla ruled a large kingdom, extending over much of Syria and possibly containing as many as 250,000 people, of whom perhaps 30,000 lived in the city. Ebla's government fostered trade by negotiating commercial treaties and arranging dynastic marriages. The treaty between Ebla and Ashur, a city about 435 miles to the east, is the earliest known agreement between two states. When diplomacy failed, Ebla resorted to war, with great success. Ebla's most notable conquest was Mari, a commercial competitor 300 miles downstream on the Euphrates.

Ebla was ruled by an oligarchy (a small, elite group) headed by fourteen regional governors who were probably also clan elders. The king, a sort of first among equals, was chosen by election rather than inheritance; his power was limited by the oligarchic council. Eblaites seem to have conceived of the state as a large family, the "children of Ebla." The queen and queen mother had significant government authority. The queen had her own properties, administered by officials who answered to her. If she was still alive, the queen mother, officially addressed as "the honored mother of the king," had considerable say in the succession.

Ebla fell to the Amorites around 2000 B.C. It remained a wealthy city, though much diminished in power. To find a much more vibrant city in Syria after 2000 B.C., we need only look at the coast and the city of Ugarit. Ugarit was a thriving Mediterranean port, especially around 1400 to 1200 B.C. Its cosmopolitanism made Ugarit distinctive among western Asian city-states. As a trading center, it linked ships coming from the eastern Mediterranean island of Cyprus or the Anatolian ports with land caravans heading to Babylonia. The native inhabitants of Ugarit spoke a Semitic language. Their culture and that of large numbers of people in southern Syria and Palestine is called Canaanite (from the Hebrew Bible, which calls Palestine "the land of Canaan"). The merchants of Ugarit, however, were often foreigners, and the bazaars echoed with a multitude of languages.

Ugarit played an important role in the spread of one of history's most important writing systems: the alphabet. Unlike the pictographic or syllabic systems of Mesopotamia, Egypt, and China, in an alphabet each sign stands for one and only one sound. In the 1300s B.C. scribes in Ugarit developed an alphabet. It was not the first alphabet, however. In Egypt, in the desert west of the Nile, limestone inscriptions have recently been found in a Semitic script with Egyptian influences. Dated to about 1900 to 1800 B.C., during the Middle Kingdom, the writing is now recognized as the earliest known example of an alphabet.

We do not know whether that alphabet was invented by Egyptians or by speakers of a Semitic language who were visiting Egypt. Nor do we know if that alphabet influenced Ugarit. What is clear is that Ugaritic scribes invented thirty cuneiform signs as an alphabet to write their Semitic language. Later adapted by the Phoenicians and, through them, the Greeks, the Ugaritic alphabet is the source of the Roman alphabet, used today by English and many other languages around the world.

The Hittites, 1650–1180 B.C.

Almost all the peoples of western Asia and Egypt whom we have discussed so far spoke a language belonging to the large Afro-Asiatic language family. But none of these languages survived antiquity in Europe. Instead, virtually every modern European language—as well as the dominant languages of Iran and India—are descendants of the long-lost proto–Indo-European language. These languages, from English and Russian to Iranian and Hindi, are said to belong to the Indo-European language family.

Indo-European–speakers probably originated between 4500 and 2500 B.C. in southern Russia, in the region of the Dnieper and Volga Rivers. A warlike, mobile people, they emigrated east and west. The first speakers of an Indo-European language to establish a civilization in western Asia were the Hittites, who came to Anatolia sometime before 1800 B.C. The Hittites were masters of the horse, which they harnessed to chariots and used in battle. They ruled Anatolia from their city of Hattusas (modern Boghazköy). Rich in minerals and farmland, Anatolia provided a solid foundation for power.

Hittite history is divided into several periods. After conquest and consolidation in the Old Kingdom (ca. 1650–1450 B.C.) came a period of retrenchment and loss of territory known as the Middle Kingdom (ca. 1450–1380 B.C.). During the New Kingdom (ca. 1380–1180 B.C.), the Hittites' power extended into Syria and northern Mesopotamia. Afterward came the Neo-Hittite era (ca. 1180–700 B.C.), when the Hittite kingdom had disintegrated into small successor states.

The Hittite Old Kingdom was a warrior society with a strong nobility and weak kings. Nobles supplied the king with troops and horses in return for land. The monarch was neither a god nor god's representative but only first among equals. The power of the nobility spelled trouble for central authority in the sixteenth century B.C., when conspiracy, feud, and assassination came close to destroying the Hittite kingdom. The powerful King Telepinu finally established himself and his family securely on the throne around 1500 B.C. In the Hittite New Kingdom the balance of power swung further in favor of the king, who was now addressed as "my Sun" during his lifetime and was deified after death.

Hittite queens and queen mothers had strong and independent positions, as at Ebla. Puduhepa, wife of King Hattusilis III (r. 1278–1250 B.C.), played a memorable role in state affairs. Puduhepa seems to have been the prime mover in making the Hurrian sun-goddess of Arinna (a shrine near Hattusas) the chief deity of the Hittite state. Hattusilis publicly declared that he would not have rebelled against the previous king had Puduhepa not first dreamed of divine support for the coup.

Hittite political thought stands out as sophisticated and original. Earlier peoples had kept lists and chronicles; Hittite annals are livelier and better argued. The royal annals of King Hattusilis III, for example, read in parts like a lawsuit, carefully pleading a justification of the king's actions. Hattusilis excused his usurpation of the throne by stating that the former king had unjustly stripped him of territory; furthermore, Hattusilis

Hittite God *This figurine in gold, standing only 1.5 inches high, represents Hittite art of the Old Kingdom (ca. 1650–1450 B.C.). The clothes, shoes, and conical hat are typical of Hittite depictions of gods.* (Louvre/R.M.N./Art Resource, NY)

rebelled openly. Hittite treaties with lesser states similarly argue their cases: each begins with an introduction providing historical background and justifying the relationship sworn to in the body of the text.

The First International System and Its Collapse, ca. 1500–1150 B.C. The Hittites and New Kingdom Egyptians exercised great military power, yet what is even more remarkable about these states and others is their ability to make and maintain peace. The years from about 1450 to about 1300 B.C. marked a period of peace among the great powers from Egypt to Anatolia and Mesopotamia—what historians call the first international system. The arts of peace are illustrated in surviving treaties and letters between monarchs, the most important of which comes from Amarna. The Amarna Archives (mid-fourteenth century), written in Akkadian cuneiform, illustrate formal communication among states. Rulers of great powers addressed each other as "brother," while Canaanite princes called pharaoh "my lord and my Sun-god" and assured him that they were "thy servant and the dirt on which thou dost tread." The texts reveal a system of gift exchange and commerce, politeness and formality, alliance and dynastic marriage, subjects and governors, rebels and garrisons. Two factors seem to have supported peace. First, shared values among kings created mutual respect and a willingness to compromise. Second, although no such concept as our balance of power existed then, a rough equality of power did prevail. Since no great power was likely to defeat the others, the parties avoided all-out war, preferring instead to compete by jockeying for allies among the small border states of Syria and Palestine.

But peace was not to last. By the late fourteenth century B.C., Egypt and the Hittites were back at war. At the Battle of Qadesh in northern Syria in 1274 B.C., twenty thousand Egyptian troops faced seventeen thousand Hittites. Predictably, neither of the two evenly matched powers managed to conquer the other. Instead, they used resources that would soon be dearly needed for defense.

Between about 1250 and 1150 B.C., the international system came to a crashing end. From Mesopotamia to Greece, from Anatolia to Egypt, one state after another collapsed during this time. Surviving evidence is fragmentary, but it suggests that both foreign and domestic problems led to the collapse. Raiders and invaders beset the eastern Mediterranean in this period. Called "Sea Peoples" by the Egyptians, they attacked

IMPORTANT EVENTS

ca. 4.4 million years ago Earliest hominids.

800,000 years ago First humans in Eruope.

ca. 100,000 years ago *Homo sapiens sapiens.*

40,000–10,000 B.C. Upper Paleolithic ear.

10,000–2,500 B.C. Neolithic era.

3,500–3,000 B.C. First civilizations.

3,500–3,100 B.C. First writing in Mesopotamia.

3,300–3,200 B.C. First writing in Egypt.

ca. 3,200 B.C. Unification of Nile Valley.

2,800–2,350 B.C. Early Dynastic Period.

2,695–2,160 B.C. Egyptian Old Kingdom.

2,500–2,350 B.C. Cuneiform texts from Ebla.

2,025–1,786 B.C. Egyptian Middle Kingdom.

1,650–1,180 B.C. Hittite Old, Middle, and New Kingdoms.

1,550–1,075 B.C. Egyptian New Kingdom.

1,450–1,300 B.C. First International System.

1,400–1,200 B.C. Height of prosperity at Ugarit.

1,250–1,150 B.C. Sea Peoples invade.

(All dates in this chapter are approximate.)

both on land and at sea. We do not know precisely who they were. In addition, some evidence of regional famine and climatic change indicates that natural causes may have led to disruption and rebellion.

Whatever the cause, what followed would prove to be a different world. Yet the end of the international system did not result in the disappearance of ancient cultures. Although new peoples appeared and old peoples changed, both continued to borrow from the cultures that had flowered before 1250 B.C.

NOTES

1. James B. Pritchard, ed., *Ancient Near Eastern Texts Relating to the Old Testament,* 3d ed., with Supplement (Princeton, N.J.: Princeton University Press, 1969), p. 107.
2. James H. Breasted, *The Conquest of Civilization* (New York: Harper & Bros., 1926), p. 112. Quoted in Brian Tierney, Donald Kagan, and L. Pearce Williams, eds., *Great Issues in Western Civilization from Ancient Egypt Through Louis XIV* (New York: McGraw-Hill, 1992), pp. 68–69.

SUGGESTED READING

Bertman, Stephen. *Handbook to Life in Ancient Mesopotamia.* 2003. A useful and informative introduction, offering thumbnail sketches, in encyclopedia form, of a wide variety of subjects from archaeology to ziggurats.

Bottéro, Jean, et al. *Everyday Life in Ancient Mesopotamia.* 2001. One of the most readable introductions to the subject.

Bryce, Trevor. *The Kingdom of the Hittites.* 1999. The best and most up-to-date introduction.

Cunliffe, Barry, ed. *The Oxford Illustrated Prehistory of Europe.* 1994. An introduction to European material culture from the Paleolithic era to the early medieval period, with chapters written by a dozen archaeologists. Especially valuable for its treatment of the early period and for its integration of Greco-Roman civilization and the wider continental context.

Johanson, D. C., and Edgar B. Johanson. *From Lucy to Language.* 1996. Excellent and relatively up-to-date introduction to human evolution, with outstanding photographs.

Murnane, William J. *The Penguin Guide to Ancient Egypt.* 1983. Both a well-illustrated travel guide and a scholarly, basic introduction.

Oates, Joan. *Babylon.* Rev. ed. 1986. A well-illustrated historical and archaeological introduction, from Sargon of Agade to the Greeks.

2

The Sword, the Book, and the Myths: Western Asia and Early Greece

The bull in brick relief shown here symbolizes power even today, twenty-six hundred years after it was molded and glazed. About 4 feet high, this bull was one of several dozen figures of bulls and dragons that decorated the massive Ishtar Gate, which led through the inner town wall of Babylon into the palace. The gate represents only a small part of a

34

magnificent reconstruction of the city by the Neo-Babylonian kings who ruled western Asia around 600 to 539 B.C.

Imagine the king's surprise had he known that under his nose an obscure prophet—we know him only as "Second Isaiah"—was preaching a bold message to his compatriots, a conquered people living in exile in Babylon. Isaiah reminded them that Yahweh, their god, was a god of justice and mercy—the one and only true god of the entire world—and that Yahweh had chosen the king of mountainous, backward Persia to conquer western Asia and redeem Yahweh's people. The Neo-Babylonian king might have laughed at the idea. Yet the Persians under Cyrus the Great conquered Babylon in 539 B.C. and proclaimed the freedom of Yahweh's people—the Jews—to return to Palestine and re-establish the Temple to their god in the city of Jerusalem. They did so, and around this time they wrote down their religious and historical traditions in large sections of what would become the Hebrew Bible, or Old Testament.

Also in the sixth century B.C., Pisistratus, the ambitious ruler of Athens, a tiny city-state a thousand miles northwest of Babylon, sponsored a literary project to preserve the religious and historical traditions of his people. The literary works whose texts were standardized under his patronage are the *Iliad* and *Odyssey*, the epic poems of Homer, who had composed them about two centuries before.

Both the Hebrew Bible and the Homeric poems are deeply religious in outlook, but there the similarities end. The Hebrew Bible is monotheistic and focuses on the individual's subordination to God. Homer is polytheistic and glorifies the hero, who, though doomed to fail, aspires to godlike achievement. For most scholars the Bible and Homer represent two poles of Western civilization: the sacred and the worldly, the reverent and the heroic, holy writ and poetic craftsmanship.

Israel and Greece are, along with Rome, the founders of the West. Israel's holy book, the Hebrew Bible, founded the Western religious tradition. Greece, which founded the Western tradition of philosophy and politics, had its first great literary flowering in the works of Homer, whose epic poems are based on Greek myths.

The Neo-Babylonians, along with the other great empires of the era, the Assyrians and Persians, are ancestors of the West. Conquerors, they came to power by the sword, but once in power they spread civilization, serving as conduits through which the achievements of Mesopotamia were transmitted. They built great empires whose institutions were eventually transformed into notions of mass citizenship under law and justice in a universal empire by the third founder of the West, Rome.

The first half of the first millennium B.C., therefore, left a divergent legacy to the West. On the one hand, new empires arose that were more systematically organized, farther-flung, and more diverse ethnically than those created before. On the other hand, prophets, philosophers, and poets looked in new and deeper ways into the human soul.

In this chapter we look at the deeply influential developments in empire, religion, and thought forged in the first half of the first millennium B.C. At the same time, we consider the peaceful expansion in this era, through trade and colonization, particularly under the Phoenicians. Finally, we examine the material innovation that has earned the period the title "Iron Age."

Assyrians, Neo-Babylonians, and Persians, ca. 1200–330 B.C.

Ancestors of the West, three great multi-ethnic empires emerged between the 800s and 500s B.C. Ruthless soldiers, brutal conquerors, and innovative administrators, the Assyrians established an empire in western Asia and Egypt during the ninth through seventh centuries B.C. They were followed in turn by a Neo-Babylonian empire in the late seventh and sixth centuries. However, neither of these was as successful or as durable as the empire of the Persians (ca. 550–330 B.C.). At its height the Persian Empire stretched from central Asia and northwest India in the east to Macedonia and Libya in the west. Persia's vast empire was loosely governed by a Persian ruling elite and its native helpers. Unlike the ironfisted Assyrians, the Persians were relatively tolerant and respectful of their subjects' customs. Many of Persia's kings were followers of Zoroastrianism, an ethical and forceful religion. A period of relative peace in most of Persia's domains from the 530s to the 330s B.C. fostered widespread economic prosperity.

Borrowing the administrative methods of the Assyrians and Medes and the long-established officialdom of Babylon, the Persians built a new and durable imperial government. Their official art stressed the unity of the peoples of the empire under Persian leadership. Persian rule represented the greatest success yet in implementing the notions of universal kingship that dated back to Sargon of Agade (r. 2371–2316 B.C.; see page 14). In turn, Persia transmitted the trappings of absolute kingship to later ambitious rulers, from Alexander the Great to the caesars of Rome and from the Byzantine emperors to the Muslim caliphs.

Assyrians and Neo-Babylonians The Assyrians, whose homeland was in what is today northern Iraq, spoke a Semitic language. For most of the second millennium B.C., they were a military and commercial power. Around 1200 B.C. the Assyrians' state collapsed during that era of international crisis (see page 32), but they held on to a small homeland of about 5,000 square miles, roughly the size of Connecticut. The toughened survivors emerged with an aggressive, expansionist ideology.

Assyria's greatest successes came in the eighth and seventh centuries. One by one, states large and small fell—Babylonia, Syria, the kingdom of Israel, Cilicia in southern Anatolia, even Egypt (though Assyrian rule there lasted only a generation). Assyria became the first state to rule the two great river valleys of the ancient Near East, the Nile and the Tigris-Euphrates.

The Assyrians were warriors. Ashur, their main deity, was a war-god. Theirs was an ideology of power, conquest, and control. The key to Assyria's success was its army—100,000 to 200,000 men strong—which made an unforgettable impression on observers and foes. The Israelite prophet Isaiah of Jerusalem ("First Isaiah") said of Assyrian soldiers: "[Their] arrows are sharpened, and all their bows bent, their horses' hoofs are like flint, their chariot wheels like the whirlwind. Their growling is like that of a lion" (Isaiah 5:28–29). He might have added that Assyrian spearmen, archers, and cavalrymen were equipped with weapons and armor of iron.

Thanks to new heating and cooling techniques, metal smiths in the ancient world produced an alloy of carbon and iron that was harder and more durable than bronze.

It was also easier to obtain since iron ore is widespread—unlike tin, an essential element of bronze. Iron tools and weapons were often stronger and cheaper than their bronze predecessors, which opened up new technical and military possibilities.

Adding to its might, Assyria was the first major state to employ regular cavalry units (rather than charioteers) as the main strike force. The Assyrians were also excellent engineers, adept at taking walled cities by siege.

In addition, the Assyrians displayed superb organizational skills. The central standing army was supplemented with draftees conscripted from around the empire. Provinces were kept small to prevent the emergence of separate power bases, and independent-minded nobles were regularly checked by the kings.

To control the restive subjects of their far-flung empire, the Assyrians met rebellion with ferocious reprisals. Disloyal cities were attacked and, if need be, destroyed. Sculptured reliefs and inscriptions were set up to show, often in gruesome detail, the fate awaiting Assyria's enemies. We see or read of cities burned to the ground; of men flayed alive, even though they had surrendered, and walls covered with their skin; and of piles of human skulls.

The Assyrians also engaged in mass deportations. They uprooted the people of a conquered country, resettled them far away—often in Assyria itself—and colonized their land with Assyrian loyalists. The so-called Ten Lost Tribes of Israel—the people of the northern Israelite kingdom (see page 49)—were conquered by Assyria in 722 B.C., and many of them were transported to Mesopotamia, where they disappeared from history. (Those who remained in Israel mixed with colonists, and the new group became known, and scorned, as Samaritans.)

Assyrian policy was the result of careful calculation. The political goal was to punish rebellion, the economic goal to create a varied labor force. For example, although it is estimated that the Assyrians deported several million people, they deported not whole populations but a carefully chosen cross section of professions. They also deported entire families together, to weaken deportees' emotional ties to their former homes.

Assyria's success also was due in part to the relative weakness of other powers. Egypt had been at the mercy of factions and invaders for much of the Third Intermediate Period (1075–656 B.C.). Around 950, for example, the kingship came into the hands of Libyan mercenaries. From the eighth century on, their rule was challenged in turn by invaders from the south, rulers of a new Nubian kingdom called Kush. Kushite pharaohs governed Egypt from around 719 until 656, when they withdrew back south. It was they who faced the Assyrian attacks in 671 and 667.

The conquest of Egypt marked imperial Assyria's greatest extent—and its overextension. A coalition army consisting of soldiers from a revived Babylonian kingdom and of Medes (who had formed a powerful state in Iran; see page 40) conquered Nineveh, the Assyrian capital, in 612 B.C. and defeated the remnants of the Assyrian army in battles in 609 and 605. Few of its subjects mourned the empire's passing.

The destruction of Assyria led to revival for Babylon, whose rulers attempted to recapture the glories of Hammurabi's day (see page 16). For a short period, until the Persian conquest in 539 B.C., the Neo-Babylonian dynasty (founded in 626 B.C.) and the Medes of Iran were the dominant military forces in western Asia. The Neo-Babylonian king Nebuchadrezzar II (Nebuchadnezzar in the Hebrew Bible; r. 605–562 B.C.) conquered the kingdom of Judah (in southern Palestine) in 598 and destroyed Jerusalem, its capital, in 586. He deported many thousands of Judeans to Babylon, an

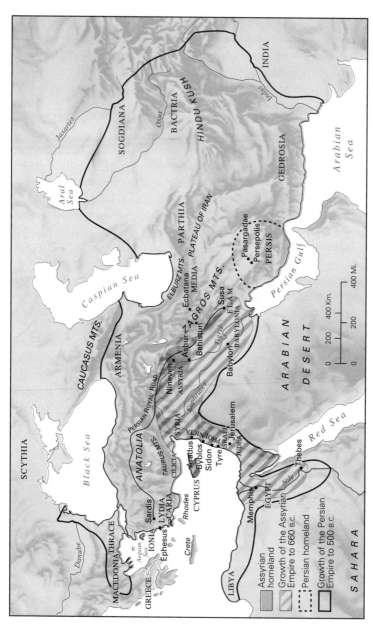

The Assyrian and Persian Empires

In the 660s B.C. the Assyrians ruled the largest empire the ancient world had seen, extending from the Tigris to the Nile. The Persian Empire was even greater. Around 500 B.C. it reached from its heartland in southwestern Iran westward to Macedonia and eastward to India.

event remembered by Christians and Jews as the Babylonian Captivity. Most of the rest of western Asia also fell to Nebuchadrezzar's troops. His most enduring achievement was rebuilding Babylon on a grand scale. In addition to the city's numerous temples, shrines, and altars, he created the so-called Hanging Gardens celebrated by later Greek writers. They describe the structure as a large terraced complex that Nebuchadrezzar built for his queen, although it may have been a plant-covered ziggurat.

The Neo-Babylonians and Assyrians both made great strides in astronomy. Their primary motive was not scientific but religious—that is, a belief in astrology (the study of the movements of heavenly bodies in the belief that they influence human affairs). Astrology led to advances in the scientific observation of the heavens. Assyrian priests had produced relatively accurate circular diagrams (astrolabes) that showed the positions of the major constellations, stars, and planets over the course of the year. By 600 B.C. Assyrian and Neo-Babylonian astronomers could predict solstices, equinoxes, and lunar eclipses.

Astronomy in Mesopotamia reached its heights in the centuries after 500 B.C. The zodiac, a diagram showing the movement of the sun and planets relative to the constellations, was invented in Persian-ruled Babylon in the fourth century B.C. In the third and second centuries B.C., when Babylonia was under Hellenistic Greek rule, native scientists made impressive advances in mathematical astronomy, composing tables that could be used to calculate movements of the moon and planets. More sophisticated mathematical astronomy would not be produced in the West until the Scientific Revolution of the sixteenth century A.D.

Another western Asian society during this period was created by trade, not war. In both the Hebrew Bible and Homer, the Phoenicians loom large as merchants and seamen, as "traders the world honored" (Isaiah 23:8). Phoenicians were Canaanites, speakers of a Semitic language and heirs to the civilization that had prospered in Ugarit around 1400 B.C. (see page 29). After the invasions of the Sea Peoples and others around 1200 B.C., the Canaanites' once-large territory was reduced to a narrow strip along the Mediterranean in the area of modern Lebanon and northern Israel. Between 1050 and 750 B.C., the inhabitants of the area flourished; historians call them, as did the ancient Greeks, "Phoenicians." Their purple-dyed textiles gave the Greeks their word for the color purple: *Phoenician.*

The Phoenicians were master shipbuilders and sailors. Around 600 B.C. their ships accomplished the first known circumnavigation of Africa. Around 450 B.C. they made the first known commercial sailing trip to the British Isles. Some scholars think they even reached Brazil. The most lasting Phoenician achievement at sea, however, was the planting of colonies in the Mediterranean, probably beginning in the ninth century B.C. Many of their colonies eventually became independent states. The greatest Phoenician colony was Carthage, founded by the city of Tyre around 750 B.C. It was the major port city of the western Mediterranean for much of the next thousand years.

Phoenician culture was open to outside influences. Phoenician religious art is full of Egyptian sphinxes, coffins that look like mummy cases, and women wearing wigs in the style of Egypt's New Kingdom. But Phoenician art also contains Near Eastern seals and figures out of Greek myths.

Phoenician traders introduced advanced material goods, slaves, and possibly law codes to the Greeks. It was probably from the Phoenicians, whose alphabet derived from Ugarit, that the Greeks adapted their alphabet.

Around 750 B.C. the Phoenician city-states lost their independence to the Assyrians, and in later years Neo-Babylonians, Persians, and other foreign conquerors followed. But Phoenician culture survived—at home, in the colonies, and among the many Mediterranean peoples influenced by it. The result, though unintended, was that Phoenician colonists exported the civilization of western Asia to the western Mediterranean.

Building the Persian Empire   A thousand miles east of Phoenicia, a great empire took root. Indo-European–speaking peoples, the Medes and Persians arrived in western Iran probably around 1500 B.C. but perhaps not until 900 B.C. The two peoples were closely related in language and customs. The Medes lived in the central Zagros Mountains. The Persians made their homeland farther south in Anshan (modern Fars). At first the Medes ruled the Persians, but in 550 B.C. the tables were turned when the Medes were suddenly conquered by the young Persian king Cyrus the Great (r. 559–530 B.C.).

It took Cyrus only twenty years to conquer most of western Asia and much of central Asia. Within five years of his death in 530 B.C., his son and successor, Cambyses (r. 530–525 B.C.), added Egypt and Libya. Cambyses' successor, Darius (r. 521–486 B.C.), corralled northwestern India and Thrace. The frontier regions, especially Egypt, were often in revolt, and the attempt of Darius and his successor, Xerxes (r. 486–465 B.C.), to extend Persian rule to Greece ended in failure (see pages 84–87). The Achaemenid Persian Empire (named after a legendary founder, Achaemenes) survived for two hundred years, until a Greco-Macedonian army under Alexander the Great, king of Macedon (r. 336–323 B.C.), destroyed it.

Let us consider several reasons for the success of Achaemenid Persia. The first was military prowess. Persia was ruled by a warrior aristocracy whose traditional values, according to the Greek historian Herodotus, were "riding, hunting, and telling the truth." The state was able to field a huge army of about 300,000 men, conscripted from the various subject peoples. Although the resultant hodgepodge of soldiers from across the empire did not always fight as a unit, a crack infantry group, the 10,000 Immortals, provided a solid core. The Persians excelled as bowmen and cavalrymen. Following the Assyrians, they made cavalry into the decisive strike force of the battlefield, assigning a more minor role to chariotry. Persia was even more innovative at sea, where it had its subjects build the first great navy. Although Persians served as marines and sometimes as commanders, the rowers and seamen were usually Phoenicians or Greeks.

The second reason for Persia's success was political. Unlike the Assyrians, the Persians considered generosity and tolerance to be more effective than terrorism and brutality. As Cyrus prepared to attack Babylon, he portrayed himself as the champion of the traditional Babylonian religion, and Babylon surrendered to him without a fight. Cyrus also emphasized his continuity with earlier Mesopotamian history by adopting the traditional title of "King of Sumer and Akkad." Nor did he hesitate to break with Assyrian and Neo-Babylonian population transfers, as witnessed in his edict permitting the Jewish exiles in Babylon to return to Judea.

The third reason for Persia's success was its skill at administration and organization. Darius played a crucial role in reorganizing the imperial administration and finances. Like the Assyrian Empire, the Persian domain was divided into provinces, called *satrapies*. Each of the twenty satrapies was a unit of administration and tax collection. For the first time, taxes could be paid with a stable, official coinage: the gold daric (named after Darius) and the silver shekel. Coins had been invented in the kingdom of Lydia in western Asia Minor in the seventh century B.C. Croesus (r. 560–547 B.C.), Lydia's king, was known for his wealth—hence the expression "rich as Croesus"—before Cyrus conquered him in 547 B.C.

The provincial governors, or *satraps,* were powerful, often quasi-independent figures. But the king tried to keep a firm hand on them. Each province had a royal secretary and was visited regularly by traveling inspectors called "the king's eyes." A network of good roads radiated from the capital cities of Susa and Persepolis. The most famous road, the so-called Royal Road, stretched 1,600 miles from western Iran to western Anatolia. Covering the whole distance took most travelers three months, but the king's relay messenger corps could make the trip in a week, thanks to a series of staging posts furnished with fresh horses.

Another unifying element was a society that was law-abiding and prosperous. Darius proclaimed in an inscription that he had fostered the rule of law: "These countries [of the empire] showed respect toward my law; as was said to them by me, thus it was done." Darius and other Persian kings helped create the conditions for compliance and security by taking an interest in the economy. For example, they opened to commercial traffic Persian roads and a canal connecting the Red Sea and the Nile.

Language, too, built unity. Not Persian, which relatively few people spoke, but Aramaic, the most widespread language of western Asia, became the empire's basic

Achaemenid Persian Silver *This silver rhyton (drinking vessel) is in the shape of a griffin, a mythological animal that is part lion and part eagle. Persian rulers commanded the talents of western Asia's best artists and craftsmen, silversmiths among them.* (Copyright © The British Museum)

language of commerce and administration. A Semitic language related to Hebrew, Aramaic was first used by the Aramaeans, a nomadic people who settled in northern Syria about 1100 B.C. and ruled an area extending into Mesopotamia before succumbing to Assyrian conquest about 725 B.C. The Aramaeans dominated the overland trade routes, which, combined with the simple and easily learned Aramaic alphabet, contributed to the spread of their language. Aramaic facilitated the development of literacy and recordkeeping. Aramaic would become the common language of western Asia for over a thousand years, until Arabic replaced it; Jesus Christ was to be its most famous native speaker.

The King of Kings   Despite its success, Persia's empire was fraught with several weaknesses. First, Cyrus had bequeathed a legacy as a charismatic war leader. Feeling the need to live up to his example, his successors sometimes undertook ambitious and expensive expeditions that failed, such as wars with the Scythians (a tough nomadic people in Ukraine) and the Greeks. Second, however mild Persian rule, however peaceful and prosperous, it was still rule by foreigners and it still involved taxation. Persian officials, military garrisons, and colonists were found—and were resented—in every corner of the empire. Native resentment, particularly in Egypt, and the independence of certain satraps led to intermittent provincial revolts.

The exaltation of the Persian king served as a counterweight to rebellious tendencies. From Darius on, the Persian monarch tried to overawe his officials with his majesty and might. The "King of Kings," as the monarch called himself, sat on a high, gold and blue throne, dressed in purple, decked out in gold jewelry, wearing fragrant oils and cosmetics, and attended by corps of slaves and eunuchs (castrated men employed in high positions). Although he was not considered a god, he had to be treated with reverence. Persians spoke of the king's *khvarna*, his "kingly glory," a mysterious aura of power. Anyone who came into the royal presence had to approach him with a bow to the ground, face-down.

Impressive as the court ceremonial was, Persian kings were not all-powerful. They were bound by the rule of law and by the considerable power of Persia's proud nobility, on whom they relied to fill the top administrative positions. Competing factions of ministers, wives, concubines, eunuchs, and sons often brought intrigue and discord to court, especially in the fourth century B.C., a time of frequent rebellion.

Royal authority was symbolized in the decoration of the great palaces at Susa and Persepolis, a project begun by Darius I and completed by his son and successor, Xerxes. The Susa palace, the larger of the two, reflected the universality of the empire in the variety of hands that built it Craftsmen from east and west took part in the construction. The Persepolis palace, too, displayed the heterogeneity of the empire in its architecture. The palace was placed on a terrace, as in Mesopotamia, but contained columned halls as in Egypt, with Assyrian-style column capitals or tops. In Persepolis, a frieze of sculpted relief panels lining a monumental stairway leading to the palace emphasized the king's vast power. The panels depict an endless procession of the peoples of the world paying homage to the King of Kings: from the nobility to the Immortals, to Median and Persian soldiers, to tribute-bearing subjects from the ends of the earth. The overall feeling of the scene is static, as if the Persian Empire would last forever.

Zoroastrianism   Like ancient Israel, Persia developed a highly ethical religion in the first millennium B.C. From obscure beginnings, Zoroastrianism became the religion of Persia that persisted until the Muslim conquest in the seventh century A.D. Although largely extinct in today's Iran, an Islamic country, Zoroastrianism still survives in small communities elsewhere, primarily in India. Some scholars argue that Zoroastrian beliefs eventually influenced Judaism and Christianity, as well as Roman paganism and Indian Buddhism.

It is easier to describe ancient Zoroastrianism in broad strokes than in detail, partly because the religion changed radically over the course of its ancient history, and partly because relatively little information survives before A.D. 300. This much is clear: The religion was founded by a great reformer and prophet named Zarathustra (Zoroaster in Greek). Zarathustra lived in eastern Iran. His teachings survive in the *Gathas* ("Songs"), a portion of the Zoroastrian holy book called the *Avesta*. Some scholars date Zarathustra as late as 550 B.C.; others prefer an earlier date, 750 or even 1000 B.C.

Zarathustra's society was dominated by warriors whose religion consisted of blood cults, violent gods, animal sacrifice, and ecstatic rituals in which hallucinogens were eaten. Zarathustra rejected such violent practices in favor of an inward-looking, intellectual, and ethical religion. He favored ceremonies involving fire, considered a symbol of purity. Zarathustra was not a strict monotheist like the Jews, but he did emphasize the power of one god over all people, the supremely good and wise creator of the universe, whom he called Ahura Mazda ("Wise Lord"). Unlike the Jews, Zarathustra considered the problem of evil to be the central question of religion. If god was one, good, and omnipotent, how could evil exist?

Zarathustra's answer might be called *ethical dualism* (dualism is the notion of a grand conflict between good and evil). Ahura Mazda had twin children: the Beneficent Spirit and the Hostile Spirit. Each spirit had made a free choice: one for the "truth" and the other for the "lie"—that is, one for good and the other for evil. Every human being faces a similar choice between good and evil. "Reflect with a clear mind—man by man for himself—upon the two choices of decision, being aware to declare yourselves to Him before the great retribution," says Zarathustra.[1] Indeed, humanity is caught in a great cosmic struggle in which individuals are free to make a momentous choice. Zarathustra distinguished between two states of being: the spiritual and the material. The more a person pursued spiritual purity, the greater was the person's ability to choose good rather than evil.

Zarathustra held a linear conception of history, similar to that in the Hebrew Bible. His religion is marked by a strong *eschatology* (interest in the end of the world) as well as *soteriology* (belief in a savior). He believed that one day, through an ordeal by fire, Ahura Mazda would judge all the people who had ever lived. Those who had chosen good would be rewarded, and those who had chosen evil would be punished. Then would follow a Last Judgment in which the dead would be transfigured and restored to a glorious bodily existence. There would be, Zarathustra promised, "long destruction for the deceitful but salvation for the truthful." The notion of a savior who would initiate the Last Judgment is an early Zoroastrian belief, if perhaps not a doctrine of Zarathustra himself.

In later centuries, Zarathustra's followers eased his uncompromising rejection of Iranian paganism. Under the leadership of priests, known as *magi* in western Iran, the religion changed considerably. Lesser deities beneath Ahura Mazda were added to the Zoroastrian pantheon, in part to suit the religion to the needs of the huge, multicultural Persian Empire.

It is tempting to attribute Cyrus's policy of toleration to the ethical teachings of Zarathustra, but it is uncertain whether Cyrus was Zoroastrian. We are on firmer ground with later Persian kings, particularly Darius I, who had an image of himself alongside Ahura Mazda carved on the face of an Iranian cliff. In an accompanying inscription Darius announces: "For this reason Ahura Mazda bore aid, and the other gods who . . . [exist], because I was not hostile, I was not a Lie-follower, I was not a doer of wrong—neither I nor my family. According to righteousness I conducted myself."[2]

ISRAEL, CA. 1500–400 B.C.

In the first millennium B.C. a small, often-conquered people turned imperialism on its head. Human achievement is meaningless, they argued; only the power of divinity matters. There is only one god, they said; all other gods are false. The one true god had revealed himself not to the awesome, imperialistic Assyrians but to the less powerful Hebrews—ancient Jews. They founded the Western tradition of religion. The God of ancient Israel eventually gave rise to the God of Christianity and of Islam as well as of modern Judaism.

The Hebrews, also known as Israelites, had existed as a people since about 1200 B.C. and perhaps for centuries earlier. They spoke a Semitic language.

The Hebrew Bible   As literature and as religious teaching, the Bible is one of the most important books in Western civilization. As a source of history, however, it presents difficulties. Much of the Hebrew Bible (called the Old Testament by Christians) is based on written sources that probably date back at least as far as the early Israelite monarchy of about 1000 B.C. Other parts of the Hebrew Bible are probably the product of an oral tradition, and the nature, antiquity, and reliability of that tradition are the subject of much scholarly debate.

Archaeological evidence from the area of ancient Israel, a small number of inscriptions (almost all after 800 B.C.), and some information in Greek and Roman writings provide an alternative source of information. Yet little of that alternative evidence sheds light on the period before about 1200 B.C., and it offers only partial insight into the later period. The historian needs both to pay attention to the Bible and to consider its nature.

The Hebrew Bible reached something close to its current form a century or two before the birth of Christ. It consists of three main sections: (1) the Torah (literally, "teaching"), also known as the Pentateuch, or five books of Moses (that is, the first five books of the Bible); (2) the Prophets, that is, the "historical" books of the early prophets (Joshua, Judges, Kings, and Chronicles) and the books of the later prophets (Isaiah, Jeremiah, Ezekiel, and the twelve "minor prophets"); and (3) the Writings, various books of poetry, proverbs, and wisdom literature.

The books of the Hebrew (and Christian) Bible are canonical: one by one, each was accepted by established authority as sacred. Two key dates stand out in the canonization of the Hebrew Bible: 622 B.C. and about 425 B.C. On the first date, Josiah, king of Judah (see page 49), assembled "the entire population, high and low" to swear to obey "the scroll of the covenant which had been discovered in the house of the Lord" (the scroll probably was Deuteronomy, now the fifth book of the Torah). On the second date, a similar assembly of the people, called by the religious leader Ezra, swore to accept the five books of the Torah that had by then been assembled. The introduction of the Torah made its worshipers into what they have been ever since: "a people of the Book," as the Muslims would put it many years later. The written tradition and literacy became central to the Hebrews.

The Hebrews are the first people we know of to have a single national history book. That book was written not as secular history but as sacred history. It is the story of the working out of God's pact, or covenant, with the Hebrews, his chosen people. All ancient peoples told stories of their semidivine foundation. Only the Hebrews imagined the nation created by an actual treaty between the people and their God.

The central fact of human existence in the Hebrew Bible is God's covenant with the Hebrews. Because of the covenant, history has meaning. History is the story of the success or failure of the Hebrew people in carrying out God's commandments. The emphatic focus is on the individual: on individual people taking actions that have not just moral but military and political consequences that unfold over time.

Many of the themes, narrative details, and styles of writing in the Hebrew Bible derive from earlier cultures. The biblical Flood story, for example, seems to have been modeled on a similar flood in the *Epic of Gilgamesh* (see page 18). Biblical poems in praise of God are often similar to Egyptian poems in praise of pagan gods, and biblical wisdom literature (that is, works containing proverbs and rules of conduct) often recalls Egyptian or Babylonian parallels. In spite of such borrowings, the Hebrew Bible is dramatically different from its predecessors because it subordinates everything to one central theme: God's plan for humanity and, in particular, for his chosen people—the Hebrews.

The Emergence of Hebrew Mono-theism, ca. 1500–600 B.C.	The earliest nonbiblical evidence of the Hebrews is an inscribed monument of the New Kingdom Egyptian pharaoh Merneptah (r. 1224–1214 B.C.). After a military expedition into Canaan (that is, roughly, Palestine), pharaoh declared triumphantly that "Israel is laid waste." Most scholars accept this

as evidence of an Israelite presence in Canaan, but the question is, how did they get there? The Bible says that the Israelites settled Palestine by conquering its earlier inhabitants. Most scholars now reject that account. Archaeological evidence suggests, rather, a more complex process. Perhaps the Israelites were a combination of three groups: armed conquerors, shepherds who gradually entered the country and later settled down to farming, and dispossessed and oppressed Canaanites who rebelled against their masters.

From such sources the Israelites may have emerged. The Bible, however, tells a different story of Israelite origins. Although much of it is credible, none of it is confirmed by nonbiblical sources. Still, the biblical story of Israelite origins has been so influential in later Western culture that we must examine it. If one follows the Bible, Hebrew history began sometime during the period 2000 to 1500 B.C. with the patriarchs, or founding fathers. Abraham, the first patriarch, migrated to Canaan from the city of

Haran in northern Mesopotamia. A seminomadic chieftain, Abraham settled on territory north and west of the Dead Sea, where he grazed his herds. Seminomadic clans in the region frequently made long migrations in antiquity, so the biblical account of Abraham and his descendants, Isaac and Jacob, is plausible.

The Bible, however, emphasizes the implausible: Abraham's extraordinary decision to give up Mesopotamian polytheism for belief in one god. This god commanded Abraham to leave Haran; indeed, he made a treaty, or covenant, with Abraham. In return for Abraham's faith, said the god, "As a possession for all time I shall give you and your descendants after you the land in which you are now aliens, the whole of Canaan, and I shall be their God" (Genesis 17:8). Abraham was not a strict monotheist: although he worshiped only one god, he did not deny the existence of other gods. (See, for a comparison, the discussion of Akhenaten on page 26.) Nevertheless, he took a giant step on the road to pure monotheism by coming to believe that only one god rules *all* peoples.

According to the Bible, the next important step took place several hundred years later. In a time of famine in Canaan, many of Abraham's descendants left for prosperous Egypt. At first they thrived there, but in time they were enslaved and forced to build cities in the Nile Delta. Eventually, Moses, a divinely appointed leader, released the Hebrews from bondage in Egypt and led them back toward Canaan and freedom.

The Exodus ("journey out," in Greek), as this movement has been called, is a rare example of a successful national liberation movement in antiquity. Among those who accept its historicity, a date in the thirteenth century B.C. is frequently assigned to the Exodus. According to the Bible, the Exodus marked the key moment of another covenant, this time between the god of Abraham and the entire Israelite people. At Mount Sinai, traditionally located on the rugged Sinai Peninsula between Egypt and Palestine, the Israelites are said to have first accepted as their one god a deity whose name is represented in Hebrew by the letters corresponding to YHWH. YHWH is traditionally rendered in English as "Jehovah," but "Yahweh" is more likely to be accurate. The Israelites accepted Yahweh's laws, summarized by the Ten Commandments. In return for obedience to Yahweh's commandments, they would be God's chosen people, his "special possession; . . . a kingdom of priests, . . . [his] holy nation."

The Ten Commandments are both more general and more personal than the laws of Hammurabi's Code. They are addressed to the individual, whom they commit to a universal standard. They emphasize prohibitions, saying more about what one should *not* do than about what one should do. The first three commandments establish Yahweh as the sole god of Israel, prohibit any sculpture or image of God, and forbid misuse of the divine name. The next two commandments are injunctions to observe the seventh day of the week (the Sabbath) as a day free of work and to honor one's parents. The sixth and seventh prohibit destructive or violent acts against neighbors, in particular adultery and killing. The final three commandments regulate community life by prohibiting stealing, testifying falsely, and coveting another man's wife or goods. In contrast to the starkness of the Ten Commandments, an enormous amount of detailed legal material is also found in the Hebrew Bible.

Many scholars doubt whether Hebrew monotheism emerged as early as the thirteenth century. In any case, the Bible makes clear that many ordinary Hebrews remained unconvinced. For centuries afterward, many Israelite worshipers deemed

The Covenant

The central event in the history of ancient Israel was the establishment, during the Exodus, of the covenant, or treaty, at Sinai between God and his chosen people. Before this time, ancient peoples had worshiped gods and tried to gain their favor, but with only a loose relationship. The covenant uniquely uses a treaty—something typically reserved for legal or political obligations—to bring God and man closer together and to make the relationship permanent. As this text of Moses demonstrates, the covenant required the Israelites to follow certain obligations in order to receive the protection and blessings of God.

Moses summoned all Israel and said to them: Israel, listen to the statutes and the laws which I proclaim to you this day. Learn them, and be careful to observe them. The Lord our God made a covenant with us at Horeb [Sinai]. . . .

It was not because you were more numerous than any other nation that the Lord cared for you and chose you, for you were the smallest of all nations; it was because the Lord loved you and stood by his oath to your forefathers, that he brought you out with his strong hand and redeemed you from the land of slavery, from the power of Pharaoh king of Egypt. Know then that the Lord your God is God, the faithful God; with those who love him and keep his commandments he keeps covenant and faith for a thousand generations, but those who defy him and show their hatred for him he repays with destruction: he will not be slow to requite any who so hate him.

You are to observe these commandments, statutes, and laws which I give to you this day, and keep them.

What then, Israel, does the Lord your God ask of you? Only this: to fear the Lord your God, to conform to all his ways, to love him, and to serve him with all your heart and soul. This you will do by observing the commandments of the Lord and his statutes which I give you this day for your good. To the Lord your God belong heaven itself, the highest heaven, the earth and everything in it; yet the Lord was attached to your forefathers by his love for them, and he chose their descendants after them. Out of all nations you were his chosen people, as you are this day. So now you must circumcise your hearts and not be stubborn any more, for the Lord your God is God of gods and Lord of lords, the great, mighty, and terrible God. He is no respecter of persons; he is not to be bribed; he secures justice for the fatherless and the widow, and he shows love towards the alien who lives among you, giving him food and clothing. You too must show love towards the alien, for you once lived as aliens in Egypt.

Source: Exodus 19:1, 3–6; 20:1-9, 12–17, in *The New English Bible with the Apocrypha.* © Oxford University Press and Cambridge University Press, 1989.

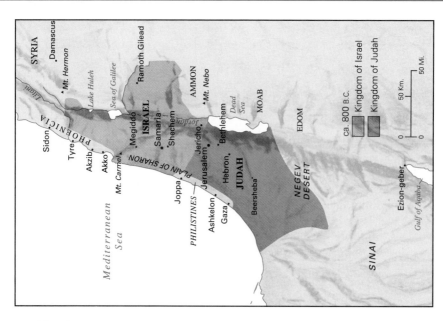

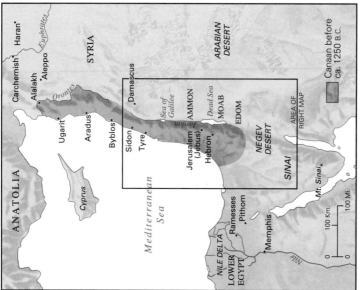

Ancient Israel The Israelites settled in the Canaanite hill country west of the Jordan River and the Dead Sea after 1200 B.C. (*left map*). Control of Israelite territory after 928 B.C. was shared between two monarchies (*right map*): the kingdoms of Israel (conquered by the Assyrians in 722 B.C.) and Judah (conquered by the Babylonians in 598 B.C.).

Yahweh their greatest god but not their only god. Unready for the radical innovation that monotheism represented, they carried out the rituals of various Canaanite deities, whom they worshiped on hilltop altars. Forging a national consensus for monotheism took centuries.

From the thirteenth to the late eleventh century B.C., the Hebrews were governed by a series of tribal leaders, referred to as "judges" in the Bible, but eventually the military threat posed by the Philistines persuaded the tribes to accept a centralized monarchy. The Philistines, one of the Sea Peoples, had captured the Palestinian coast in the twelfth and eleventh centuries and seriously endangered Israel. The first Israelite king, Saul (r. ca. 1020–1004 B.C.), had some success against them but eventually fell in battle along with his son, Jonathan. The next king, David (r. 1004–965 B.C.), a former mercenary captain for the Philistines, defeated them decisively.

David was Israel's greatest king. He extended the kingdom into parts of modern Jordan, Lebanon, and Syria and conquered the Canaanite city of Jerusalem, which he made Israel's capital. David's son and successor, Solomon (r. 965–928 B.C.), was also a great king, a centralizer who moved from a loose kingship toward a tightly organized monarchy. His most famous accomplishment was the construction of the magnificent Temple in Jerusalem. The Temple priesthood and sacrifices became the focus of the national cult of Yahweh. Previously, that focus had been a humble, movable wooden chest known as the Ark of the Covenant.

Solomon's reign represented the high-water mark of the power of the Israelite monarchy. Under his successors the monarchy was split into a large northern kingdom of Israel with a capital at Samaria and a smaller southern kingdom of Judah centered on Jerusalem. In 722 B.C., the Assyrians conquered the kingdom of Israel and deported its inhabitants. Judah survived, first as a state controlled by Assyria and then as an independent power.

The religious history of the period of the two kingdoms (928–722 B.C.) and the Judean survivor-state (722–587 B.C.) is marked by an intense drive toward monotheism. The kings of Judah in the seventh century B.C., especially Hezekiah (r. 715–686 B.C.) and Josiah (r. 640–609 B.C.), aggressively attacked the worship of all gods other than Yahweh and all centers of Yahweh worship other than the Temple in Jerusalem. The kings also began the process of canonizing the Hebrew Bible. Ambitious and independent, Hezekiah joined in a revolt against Assyria that was brutally suppressed in 701 B.C. and almost cost him his kingdom.

The Judean kings could not have succeeded without the help of the prophets, who were prominent from approximately 900 to 500 B.C. Seers uttering divinely inspired predictions were universal figures in ancient religion. No other culture of antiquity, however, has anything like the Hebrew prophets: charismatic, uncompromising, terrible figures who announced God's anger and ultimate forgiveness. The prophets remind us of the most radical spiritual teachings of Israel: absolute monotheism, an insistence on righteousness, contempt for materialism and worldly power, love of the powerless. They often supported the kings but did not shrink from confronting authority and insisting on uncompromising justice. Among them were Amos, a humble shepherd who preached the superiority of righteousness to ritual; Jeremiah, who prophesied the destruction of Jerusalem as punishment for the people's idolatry; and Isaiah, who predicted the coming of a savior who would inaugurate a new day of universal peace and justice.

A characteristic story of the prophets is the confrontation between Elijah, perhaps the most famous prophet, and Ahab, king of Israel (r. 871–852 B.C.). Ahab coveted the vineyard of one Naboth, but Naboth refused Ahab's offer to buy it. Spurred on by his wife, Jezebel, Ahab trumped up charges against Naboth, who was unjustly stoned to death. Ahab then confiscated the vineyard. God sent Elijah to declare to Ahab that, as punishment for committing murder, "dogs will lick [Ahab's] blood" and that of his family (1 Kings 21:19). In a remarkable scene, we witness not only Elijah's courage in confronting the king but also the king's surrender and repentance before Elijah's spiritual authority. Ahab (though not Jezebel) humbles himself and is spared, but his son and successor, King Ahaziah, who is equally wicked, is punished with a fatal injury. The Western tradition of civil disobedience owes much to the courage of the Hebrew prophets.

Exile and Return, 598–ca. 400 B.C. The prophets prepared the people of Judah for survival by correctly predicting ruin and exile and promising that divine providence would guarantee return. The tenacity of the Judeans in clinging to this message was remarkable. Indeed, it needed to be, for between 598 and 586 B.C. the Neo-Babylonians conquered Judah, destroying Jerusalem and the Temple. The cultural, political, and economic elite were deported to Babylon. Those who could, fled for Egypt. The dispirited remnant in Palestine shared their land with colonists from neighboring regions, with whom they intermarried and among whom their religion all but disappeared.

And that, given the usual fate of exiled and uprooted peoples in antiquity, should have been that. Yet not only did the Judeans in the Babylonian Captivity persevere in their religious loyalty; they actually returned to Palestine in large numbers.

The Neo-Babylonian rulers allowed Jewish deportees to continue to practice their religion. Jews* in Babylon were not slaves; rather they rented land on royal estates, and some became prosperous. Although some Babylonian Jews assimilated to local ways, many continued a Jewish religious life. Communal worship was observed in open places, perhaps with associated buildings. Some scholars argue that synagogues ("gatherings" in Greek), modest centers of prayer and study that have been the focus of Jewish worship ever since, first emerged in Babylon. It is also possible that the exiles put together the Torah in something like its current form. Elders led the community, while prophets continued to speak out: two examples are Ezekiel, who preached the restoration of the Temple, and the man known to us only as "Second Isaiah" (Isaiah 40–66). Second Isaiah emphasized the universal aspect of the god of Israel, who made empires rise and fall and would bring the exiles home from far-off Babylon.

The Temple in Jerusalem was rebuilt around 515 B.C., only seventy years after its destruction. This remarkable turn of events was possible partly because of the Persians, who conquered Babylon in 539 B.C. and proclaimed the freedom of the Jews to rebuild their Temple in Jerusalem. Still, Persian benevolence would not have been enough if the Judean elite had not kept the faith burning among the exiles.

Second Isaiah's message points to a second important development among the exiles of Judah. As striking as the return to Palestine was the survival of large numbers of

---

*Strictly speaking, the terms *Jew* and *Jewish* are anachronistic before the fifth century B.C.

Israelite Seal *This seal stone, which shows a roaring lion, was used by a man named Shema, an official of King Jeroboam of Israel. The stone was used to make an impression in hot wax, creating a seal on a document.* (Reuben and Edith Hecht Collection, University of Haifa, Israel/Erich Lessing/Art Resource, NY)

Judeans as an unassimilated people outside of Judah—in other words, as Jews. For the first time, membership in a community of worship was divorced from residence. Jewish communities flourished in Babylon, Persia, and Egypt, but the members often chose not to become Babylonians, Persians, or Egyptians. From the sixth century B.C. on, a majority of Jews were living outside Palestine, and the Jewish Diaspora ("dispersion") became a permanent fact of history.

The People of the Covenant A rough equality among the people of Israel, limited government, and the rule of law under God were all fundamental Israelite political notions. Eventually, they would become fundamental political ideals for many in the West, and they would be applied not only to Israelites but to all people.

According to Israelite belief, God made humans in his own image. Thus all individuals were equal in a fundamental sense; all were bound by God's law. A king who disobeyed this law was illegitimate. Indeed, Israel was ambivalent at best about the institution of kingship, which was tolerated as an evil made necessary only by the country's many armed enemies. God's covenant with the Hebrews was a religious contract with political consequences, rendering God the only true king of Israel. Far from being gods themselves or even God's representatives, Israel's kings were merely God's humble servants.

Israelite egalitarianism was restricted to men. Israelite women usually could not own or inherit property, as women could in Hammurabi's Babylon; or sue in court, as women could in pharaonic Egypt; or initiate a divorce, as women could in Classical Athens (see page 84). The powerful goddesses of other ancient cultures were absent in Israel. Women participated in the rituals of early Israelite religion and the original Temple (ca. 940–586 B.C.) but were segregated in a separate women's courtyard in the rebuilt Temple (ca. 515 B.C.–A.D. 79) and absent from Temple ritual. Indeed, the perspective of the Hebrew Bible is predominantly male. Consider just two examples. First, of the 1,426 names in the Hebrew Bible, 1,315 are male; only 111 women's names appear, about 9 percent of the total.[3] Second, only men and boys can bear the sign of the Lord's covenant with Israel—that is, circumcision.

Nevertheless, Israelite women enjoyed honor as mothers and partners in running the household. The Hebrew Bible states that woman (as exemplified by Eve, the first woman) was created as "a suitable partner" for man (Genesis 2:18, 20). Reproduction and hence motherhood assume great importance in the Hebrew Bible; the Lord enjoins humans to "be fruitful and multiply" (Genesis 1:28). The Bible also commands that children honor both their father and their mother: the two parents are equal in parental authority (Exodus 20:12).

The Hebrew Bible sometimes displays sympathy for and insights into the strategies that women used to counter the abuses of male power. Rebecca, for instance, thwarts her husband Isaac's plan to give his blessing to their son Esau. As the eldest, Esau was entitled to this honor, but Rebecca preferred her younger son Jacob, and she saw to it that he and not Esau obtained her husband's blessing.

Only about a half dozen women in the Hebrew Bible served as leaders of Israel, but that is more than in the literature of most other ancient cultures. Deborah (ca. 1125 B.C.), for example, a charismatic Israelite prophet, organizes an army that destroys the forces of a Canaanite commander. In a later book Esther, a Hebrew woman, becomes the wife of a Persian king whom the Bible calls Ahasuerus (probably Xerxes, r. 485–465 B.C.). Esther works ferociously at the Persian court to defeat a conspiracy to wipe out her people, and she saves them. The Book of Ruth (date uncertain) tells the story of a selfless and loyal woman, Ruth, who rescues her mother-in-law, Naomi, from ruin and poverty. The Bible celebrates Ruth as Naomi's "devoted daughter-in-law, who has proved better to you [Naomi] than seven sons."

Israelite culture prized women for their cunning, courage, and perseverance—qualities that allowed the people to survive. Military prowess was highly valued in men, but their inner qualities were appreciated as well. Schooled in defeat and exile, many Israelites came to the conclusion that "wisdom is better than weapons of war" (Ecclesiastes 9:18). Thus the Hebrew Bible stresses God's primary interest in goodness of soul: "The Lord does not see as man sees; men judge by appearances, but the Lord judges by the heart" (1 Samuel 16:7). The God of Israel prized righteousness above wealth, might, sacrifice, or ritual.

One might say that Israelite law reflected a similar tension between power and righteousness. On the one hand, just as the God of Israel was omnipotent and jealous, so the law of Israel was meant to be comprehensive and forceful. Capital punishment existed for murder, rape, incorrigible rebelliousness of a son against his parents, adultery by a married woman (both she and her lover were to be executed), a woman's loss of her virginity before marriage, and other offenses. Harsh punishment was mandated for Canaanite towns taken by siege: the entire population was to be killed so as not to corrupt Israel with their religious practices.

On the other hand, by taking intention into account, Israelite law echoed a note already present in Mesopotamia. The so-called Law of the Goring Ox, for instance, allowed a person to go unpunished for owning an ox that gores a person to death, unless the owner knew beforehand that the animal was dangerous. If the owner did know, however, the owner had to be put to death. Israelite law, moreover, demonstrated a belief in the sanctity of human life by prohibiting human sacrifice. An Israelite had to be ready in his or her heart (but *only* in his or her heart) to sacrifice his or her child to Yahweh, as Abraham was willing to sacrifice Isaac when Yahweh so commanded. After ascertaining Abraham's willingness to obey even to the point of sacrificing his son, Yahweh freed Isaac from the altar and supplied a ram as a substitute offering. Israelite monotheism thus rejected human sacrifice, as did the religions later derived from it.

EARLY GREECE, TO CA. 725 B.C.

The Greeks founded the Western tradition in politics and philosophy. The ancient Greek genius was at its height in the era of the Greek city-states (ca. 700–300 B.C.), but it is already visible in the *Iliad* and the *Odyssey*, the epic poems of Homer (ca. 725 B.C.). Both are products of the first millennium B.C. Civilization, however, flourished in Greece a thousand years earlier, and Homer's works have roots in this earlier era. Most of what we know of this earlier period, called "Aegean Greece" by scholars, is based on the discoveries of archaeologists. In particular, archaeology provides the evidence for the rise and fall of two monument-building, literate civilizations: the Minoans on the island of Crete and the Mycenaeans on the Greek mainland.

The Minoans and Early Greece, 3000–1375 B.C. Europe's first civilization appeared in Greece, on the Aegean island of Crete around 2000 B.C. From there, civilization spread to the Greek mainland.

Civilization came relatively late to Greece, but in comparison with Egypt and even western Asia, Greece is not a hospitable land. Mountainous, and watered by few rivers, it contains little cultivable farmland. Although pastureland and forest are more abundant, one-third of the country is entirely unproductive. Most of the farmland, moreover, is to be found in upland plains, which are divided by mountains, making it difficult to concentrate a large labor force to work the land efficiently. The south enjoys a mild Mediterranean climate but is quite dry. The north has a Balkan climate of hot summers and cold winters. The indented seacoast provides Greece with many harbors. Greece's geography influenced several recurring features of its history: contrasts between seafarers and mountaineers and between north and south, and the challenge of unifying so mountainous a terrain.

Agriculture preceded civilization in Greece. The first agricultural villages appeared shortly after 7000 B.C., bronze-making skills after 3000 B.C. After 3500 B.C. Greece became a supplier of raw materials for the new cities of western Asia. Both on the islands and the mainland, small towns appeared, sometimes fortified with stone walls, occasionally containing substantial stone and mud-brick structures. Between 3000 and 2400 B.C., people living on the Cycladic islands of the Aegean Sea produced exquisite marble sculptures and incised terra-cotta dishes.

Around 2000 B.C. civilization appeared on Crete. Its origins are hotly debated, but we know that it was literate because Cretan writing has survived. It consists of a syllabary, or system of simple syllables that form words, known as "Linear A." Although we know its language is not Greek, we do not know what it is. The island of Crete is located on the sea routes between the Greek mainland, Egypt, and Anatolia. The archaeological record contains many signs of trade and cultural contact between Cretans and nearby peoples, from one of whom, perhaps, the Minoans were descended. The evidence for Minoan civilization is concentrated in Crete's palaces—monumental structures that first appeared at various locations on the island around 2000 B.C. After destruction by earthquake, the palaces were rebuilt on an even grander scale, to flourish especially during the period from 1800 to 1550 B.C. Scholars call the palace-builders and their civilization "Minoan," after King Minos of later Greek myth. He was supposed to have ruled a great sea empire from his palace at Knossos. What the Minoans called themselves remains a mystery.

The Minoan palaces were not merely royal residences but centers of administration, religion, politics, and economics. Minoan palace bureaucrats supervised a large sector of the economy, just as their counterparts did in Ugarit, Egypt, the Hittite kingdom, and other ancient societies. The largest Cretan palace, as well as the first to be excavated, Knossos offers a striking example of Minoan civilization. The main building at Knossos covers 3 acres, the associated structures an additional 2 acres. The palace was built around a large central court, 180 feet long by 82 feet wide, probably used for public ceremonies. A mazelike structure surrounded the court. The palace had enormous staterooms, residence quarters, storage rooms, artisans' workshops, and bathrooms, in-

Palace of Knossos *A paved ramp and (partially restored) portico are part of an entranceway to the palace. The tapered columns and combination of stone and timber are characteristic features of Minoan architecture.* (Dmitrios Harissiadis/© Photographic Archive of The Benaki Museum)

terconnected by corridors, ramps, and stairways. Light wells admitted daylight, and brightly colored frescoes decorated the walls. Cretan architects were aware of palace architecture elsewhere in the eastern Mediterranean and may have borrowed from it, but precisely who influenced whom remains an open question.

The palaces make clear that the Minoans exploited Crete's considerable natural wealth in agriculture and timber. Archaeological and linguistic evidence indicates a widespread Minoan trading network from the Levant to Sicily. A Minoan settlement flourished on the Aegean island of Thera, 70 miles north of Crete. This settlement was destroyed in 1626 (or possibly 1628) B.C. by one of the most violent volcanic eruptions in history. So huge a catastrophe produced climate changes for several years, evident in the pattern of tree rings in ancient wood. That is why scholars can offer so specific a date for Thera's eruption.

From the lack of fortifications around Cretan palaces and the small amount of arms and armor found in burial sites, it appears that the Minoans lived in relative peace. Minoan frescoes show that women as well as men played important roles in cult and ritual. The women portrayed by Cretan artists are often beautiful, bejeweled, and elegant, the men often graceful and athletic. We see, for example, acrobats practicing the sport of bull jumping. Landscapes and animals are frequently illustrated. A statuette of a priestess holding a snake in either hand depicts Minoan interest in the relationship between humans and the natural world. In short, Minoan civilization gives an impression of peace, prosperity, and happiness. No wonder we sense a somewhat lost-Eden quality about the violent and relatively sudden destruction of Minoan civilization. All of the palaces except Knossos were destroyed around 1550 B.C.; Knossos fell around 1375 B.C.

No shortage of theories has surfaced about the cause of the destruction, but the archaeological evidence strongly supports the notion of an invasion. But by whom? To find the answer, let us look to the Greek mainland.

The Mycenaeans, to ca. 1200 B.C. A wave of destruction put an end to the Greek mainland's vigorous Copper Age (see page 9) around 2300 B.C. Centuries of relative poverty followed until, around 1700 B.C., signs of power and prosperity appear at a series of burial sites in central Greece and the Peloponnesus. The most dramatic are at Mycenae, where the royal burials contain a treasure house of objects in gold and other precious metals. Many of the other cities in Greece that would later become famous, such as Athens and Thebes, were also thriving cities in this period.

The inhabitants of Mycenae, unlike the earlier inhabitants of the Greek peninsula, were Greek-speakers. They and the wider civilization they represent are called Mycenaean. Just when and how the Mycenaeans got to Greece are tangled questions. Some scholars imagine migration, others invasion. Some believe the Mycenaeans' ancestors arrived as early as 2300 B.C., whereas others think it was not until 1700 B.C., more than half a millennium later.

The Mycenaeans adopted and adapted technology, ideas, and art from their advanced neighbors in Crete, Egypt, Anatolia, and Syria-Palestine. The Mycenaeans traded with these neighbors. They also fought with them, for Mycenaean society was dominated by warrior-kings, raiders who exchanged booty to show off their wealth.

Lion Gate at Mycenae *Carved about 1250 B.C. above the main gate of the citadel's massive walls, the lions—flanking a column, their front paws resting on altars—probably represent royal authority. Inside the walls is Grave Circle B, a royal burial site.* (Dmitrios Harissiadis/© Photographic Archive of The Benaki Museum)

Around 1550 B.C. the mainland warriors achieved their greatest feat: the conquest of Crete. They destroyed most of the palaces but spared Knossos, which did not fall until about 1375 B.C. (we do not know the cause of that destruction). The warlike Mycenaeans had conquered the sophisticated Minoans. In turn, the Mycenaeans learned from their subjects and adopted a Minoan-style palace economy.

Mycenaean civilization was at its height between about 1400 and 1200 B.C. Kings lived in palaces whose storerooms were crammed with treasures. They traveled through their kingdoms on a network of good roads and could muster rowers and ships. Mycenaean artists excelled at potterymaking and fresco painting, gold inlay work and ivory carving. Mycenaean builders constructed palaces, fortifications, bridges, huge vaulted tombs, and sophisticated drainage works.

Palace officials supervised considerable economic activity, often in minute detail, including agriculture, pasturage, and artisanry. Women and children as well as men were included in the labor force. Our knowledge of the palace economy comes primarily from thousands of clay tablets inscribed by palace scribes around 1200 B.C. They are written in a script scholars call "Linear B," mostly an early form of Greek consisting of a combination of syllabary and ideograms (a system of symbols that stand for words or ideas).

Mycenaean merchants replaced Minoans in trade in the central and eastern Mediterranean. From Sicily to the Levant, they exported wine and scented oils and imported metals, ivory, and perhaps slaves. Mycenaean warriors engaged in activities ranging from raids and skirmishes to formal battles.

In the thirteenth century B.C., at the height of Mycenaean power, some unknown threat prompted the Mycenaean kings to fortify the palaces at Mycenae and elsewhere with stone walls. By 1200 B.C. most of the fortified sites had been destroyed. Afterward, only a few people continued to live in the old towns. It appears likely that Mycenaean Greece suffered from a combination of internal weakness and foreign invasion similar to that experienced by most of the eastern Mediterranean around 1250 to 1150 B.C., the era of the Sea Peoples (see page 32).

Between Mycenae and the City-States, ca. 1100–725 B.C.   The era from the fall of Mycenae to the rise of the Greek city-states was long referred to as the Greek Dark Ages. But that gloomy term is used less often as archaeology increases our knowledge of the period from roughly 1100 to 800 B.C. The evidence does, however, suggest a considerable depopulation in Greece from the twelfth through the ninth century B.C. It seems that rich and poor alike were worse off than in Mycenaean times.

After the destruction of the palaces around 1200 B.C., Mycenaean culture continued to flicker before finally fading in the early eleventh century B.C. New peoples began to move into central and southern Greece around this time. They probably were the Dorians, speakers of a Greek dialect who came from northern Greece. Their material culture was rougher and ruder than that of Mycenae's descendants; it boasts few distinctions besides the iron slashing sword and the long bronze fastener. The Dorians drove out or dominated the Mycenaean Greeks, turning much of central and southern Greece, including Crete, into Dorian centers. Among major settlements, only Athens maintained its independence. The city served as an asylum for Mycenaean refugees, many of whom migrated eastward around 1000 B.C. to the Aegean coast of Anatolia, which was destined to become an important center of Greek culture.

Greece from roughly 1100 to 800 B.C. was largely a poor and illiterate society of small towns and low-level agriculture and trade. Nevertheless, it produced notable painted pottery and preserved an oral tradition of poetry handed down from the Mycenaean era. After 800 B.C. a huge change came over Greece.

First of all, peace contributed to a sharp population rise, and the economy shifted from herding to farming, a more efficient source of food. Greek commerce, too, expanded, thanks in part to the impact of Phoenician traders.

Under pressure from rising population, Greeks founded colonies around the Mediterranean and the Black Sea beginning around 750 B.C. Meanwhile, trade and colonization inspired change at home. Dramatic new experiments in politics, warfare, and culture were attempted. It was the dawn of the era of the Greek city-state. We look at these changes in detail in Chapter 3. Here we focus on a milestone in literary artistry that heralded a new age: the epic poetry of Homer.

Homer and History   Had ancient Greece produced a Bible, the *Iliad* and the *Odyssey* of Homer would have been its two Testaments. Only Hesiod, a poet who lived around 700 B.C., had as much influence on later generations, but his poems (*Theogony* and *Works and Days*), though composed in the epic tradition, were shorter than Homer's and arguably less dramatic. But Greece did not have a Bible. Homer and Hesiod were poets, not priests. (As far as we know, the Greek world never had a priestly class comparable to that of Egypt or western Asia.) Although their poems inspired, moved, and educated the Greeks—a large part of a Greek boy's education consisted of learning to recite Homer from memory—they were not divine writ.

Homer was not a historian either. He was a bard, a professional singer of heroic poetry—of songs praising the deeds of the great. Heroic poetry consciously glorifies and magnifies the actions of its subjects.

Yet both archaeology and the evidence of inscriptions suggest that the story of the Trojan War is based on a kernel of truth. Troy really existed: it was a big, wealthy city, strategically located near the entrance to the Hellespont (or Dardanelles), the straits that lead toward the Black Sea. The king of Troy was attached politically to the Hittite empire, and his city had strong trading relations with the Mycenaean Greeks. The people of Troy probably spoke Luvian, a language related to Hittite. Troy was destroyed violently, possibly by Mycenaean warriors. Previously, around 1225 B.C. seemed the likeliest date for the destruction, but recent excavation argues for about 1200–1180 B.C.

Most scholars today would date Homer to about 725 B.C. or later. Although Homer lived centuries after the end of Troy, he resided in an area whose culture had been affected by Troy and its neighbors. Homer lived in Ionia, a region of the central western coast of Anatolia, perhaps in the city of Smyrna. Homer was influenced by the earlier pre-Greek poets of Anatolia. A Luvian poem about Troy may have existed, and Homer could have drawn some of his material from it. In short, there might be more than a little history in Homer.

The author (or possibly authors) of the *Iliad* and the *Odyssey* worked in a continuous poetic tradition going back to the Mycenaean Age. Most scholars accept the theory that this tradition was oral, not written. Like oral poets elsewhere, Homer and his predecessors composed their poems as they sang them, making use of a stock of stories and formulaic expressions (such as the Greek equivalents of "swift-footed Achilles" and "grey-eyed goddess Athena"). In fact, Homer may have been illiterate.

Oral tradition gave Homer knowledge of a society that was long gone by his day. Although Homer's poems are studded with accurate details of Mycenaean palace life, the ideology of his characters generally reflects the beliefs of his own, post-Mycenaean society.

Both in Mycenaean times and in Homer's day, the Greeks were polytheists. The gods of Greece are similar in many ways to the gods of Sumer. They share the foibles and foolishness of humanity but are immortal and far more powerful than humans. The gods figure prominently in early Greek poetry, but they are less powerful than Yahweh, less immediate, and less interested in the inner life of men and women. Already emerging at the beginning of the Greek cultural tradition was the belief that became the hallmark of ancient Greece: that "man is the measure of all things," as the thinker Protagoras would declare in the fifth century B.C.

The Greek gods of the first millennium B.C. were worshiped in Mycenaean times— offerings to them are recorded on Linear B tablets. Because they were thought to live on

Mount Olympus, a 9,500-foot-high peak in northern Greece, the gods were called the Olympians. Hesiod's *Theogony* tells the story of the Olympians' birth and their triumph over an older generation of deities. The "household" of the Olympians—the early Greek pantheon was conceived of as a noble's household—included Zeus, a sky-god and the "father of gods and men," and his consort, Hera; Zeus's brother, Poseidon, god of the sea, earthquakes, and horses; Ares, god of war; and Aphrodite, goddess of love. Also in the "household" were Zeus's children: Athena, goddess of wisdom and cunning; Hephaestus, god of craftsmen; Hermes, god of travelers and thieves; Apollo, god of disease and healing; and Artemis, goddess of the hunt, of maidens, and of childbirth.

Flawed and sometimes unpredictable, the Greek gods often seem childish, but the natural world they symbolized seemed equally inconstant to the ancients. The gods embody the values of a warrior society that put a premium on *aretê*, or excellence, especially excellence in battle. The heroes in the *Iliad* and the *Odyssey* seek glory through military exploits. Homer's gods reward great warriors, but the gods insist on justice as well. Zeus punishes those who do evil—those who, for example, break oaths or give false judgments or violate the laws of hospitality. In the *Iliad,* the Trojan prince Paris sparks the Trojan War by abducting the beautiful Helen from her husband, the Greek king Menelaus, while he is a guest in Menelaus's household. In return, the Greeks attack Troy, a wealthy city in northwestern Anatolia. The gods destroy Troy as punishment for Paris's crime.

The *Iliad* and the *Odyssey* focus on the Trojan War and its aftermath. The *Iliad* is set in the tenth year of the conflict. The strain of fighting leads to a quarrel between Greek chieftains: Agamemnon, king of Mycenae and the leader of the expedition, and Achilles, the greatest Greek warrior. The most prominent Trojans, King Priam and his eldest son, Hector, are less petty but will suffer the greater ruin. The *Odyssey* tells the story of the struggle of the Greek hero Odysseus to return to Ithaca and to regain his kingship after a twenty-year absence, ten years in the war at Troy and ten years wandering homeward. It also focuses on the loyalty and ingenuity of Odysseus's wife, Penelope, who saves the household in her husband's absence, and the maturation of their son, Telemachus, who helps his father regain his kingdom.

Homer puts as much emphasis on brains as on brawn; Odysseus, for example, is not just strong but also smart and cunning. And Homer's gods are no brutes; they believe in justice, hospitality, and respect for parents. Finally, although the Homeric poems focus on the upper classes—and primarily on men—the poems have a strain of sympathy for ordinary people and for women. Indeed, they show sympathy for failure. Homer's heroes court death and often obtain it. Unlike the psalmist of the Hebrew Bible, a Homeric hero walks alone "through the valley of the shadow of death" (Psalm 23:4); he has no god to comfort or redeem him. He knows that the gods make human life hard and full of suffering. Human frailty, however, ennobles Homer's heroes.

Homer's princes are proud and jealous. In the *Iliad,* when Agamemnon is forced by divine command to return his "prize"—a girl captured in a raid—he demands in return the "prize" of Achilles, his greatest warrior—that is, Achilles' girl. Achilles' response is to sulk in his tent while the Trojans nearly defeat his fellow Greeks. In the *Odyssey,* a group of nobles lives off the absent Odysseus's estate, waiting to see which of them Odysseus's wife (and supposed widow) might marry. Odysseus's honor demands that he punish them by killing every last one. In both cases, Homer recognizes that the hero goes too far: Achilles' inaction leads to the death of his best friend, and ultimately to his own death; Odysseus's thirst for revenge leads to civil war.

World of the Heroes

Homer focuses on the elite. Homeric warriors and their women hold aristocratic values and tend to look down on ordinary people. But society in Homer's day was more level and egalitarian. Except for a small number of traders and craft specialists who lived in towns, most people in the Greece of 725 B.C. lived in villages and hamlets. Most farmed or herded pigs, goats, or sheep, and most were free. The people of each community were called the *demos*; the leading men, *basileis. Basileis* means "kings," but it is more accurate to understand them as chiefs. No great difference of wealth existed between the basileis and ordinary free farmers.

Although the basileis took the lead in both government and war, the demos played a crucial role. Homer spotlights contests between aristocratic champions, but his vivid battle scenes also include large companies of ordinary men fighting in mass combat in close formation. And if the basileis dominated Homeric government, the demos had at least a small say.[4]

The basic instruments of government that would exist for centuries in Greece appear in the *Iliad* and the *Odyssey:* generals, orators, judges, a council, and an assembly. When making decisions about war and peace, a council of elder basileis consults an assembly of the warriors. In this arrangement we see a fundamental principle of Greek government: the political community should be composed of the warriors.

Let us turn now to the ideology of Homer's basileis, which would greatly influence later generations in antiquity. In the epics, the chiefs make friendships and exchange goods across international boundaries. Greek and Trojan chiefs kill each other on the battlefield but rarely hate each other. Indeed, some are bound by hereditary ties of guest-friendship and so decline to fight each other.

The main activity of Homer's basileis is warfare. The *Iliad* consists largely of a series of battlefield contests. Since women did not take part in battle, they are not presented as men's equals. Yet Homer rarely criticizes women in general, as some ancient Greek writers would in later centuries. Homer's women are weaker than men, but they are neither timid nor helpless. Penelope, for example, personifies female resourcefulness: by refusing to marry until she has finished weaving a shroud for Odysseus's elderly father, and then by unraveling every night what she has woven during the day, she puts the noble suitors off for years. She is as concerned with honor as any Homeric man. By refusing to accept an offer of marriage while Odysseus might still be alive, Penelope does honor to her own good name and to her husband's.

Homeric women play important roles in encouraging men or in bolstering men's courage by playing the foils to their doubts and dreads. In the *Iliad,* Hector overcomes his own fears of battle by hearing his wife, Andromache, express *her* terror at the thought of his dying and leaving her a widow and their infant son an orphan. Moreover, by taking the burden of hearth and home on herself, Andromache allows Hector to define masculinity as making war.

Loyalty to the family played an important role in social relations. A person's obligations to kin included the duty to avenge crime or murder. Friendship, cemented by

IMPORTANT EVENTS

2000 B.C. First Minoan palaces on Crete

1800–1550 B.C. Height of Minoan civilization

1626 B.C. Eruption of Thera volcano

1550 B.C. Mycenaeans conquer Crete

1375 B.C. Palace at Knossos destroyed

1400–1200 B.C. Height of Mycenaean civilization

1250–1150 B.C. Sea Peoples invade Palestine

1200 B.C. Mycenaean palaces destroyed

ca. 1200–1000 B.C. Israelites settle Palestinian hill country

ca. 1050–750 B.C. Height of Phoenician city-states

1004–928 B.C. Reigns of David and Solomon

ca. 725 B.C. Homer

722 B.C. Assyrians conquer kingdom of Israel

612 B.C. Conquest of Nineveh ends Assyrian power

598 B.C. Neo-Babylonians conquer kingdom of Judah

559–530 B.C. Reign of Cyrus the Great

550–331 B.C. Achaemenid Persian Empire

539 B.C. Cyrus conquers Babylon; permits Jews to return to Palestine

ca. 425 B.C. Judean assembly accepts the Torah

an exchange of gifts, was another important social institution. Even humble peasants prided themselves on hospitality.

Such values served Homeric society well. Although they would survive in later centuries, they would be challenged after 700 B.C. by the increasing emphasis on public life as the Greek city-state evolved.

NOTES

1. S. Insler, *The Gāthās of Zarathustra: Acta Iranica*, 8 (Leiden: E. J. Brill, 1975), p. 33.

2. Roland G. Kent, *Old Persian: Grammar, Texts, Lexicon* (New Haven, Conn.: American Oriental Society, 1950), p. 132.

3. Carol L. Meyers, "Everyday Life: Women in the Period of the Hebrew Bible," in *The Women's Bible Commentary,* ed. Carol A. Newsom and Sharon H. Ringe (Louisville, Ky.: Westminster/ John Knox Press, 1992), p. 245.

4. Kurt A. Raaflaub, "Homer to Solon. The Rise of the *Polis:* The Written Sources," in *The Ancient Greek City-State: Symposium on the Occasion of the 250th Anniversary of the Royal Danish Academy of Science and Letters, July 1–4, 1992, Historisk-filosofiske Meddelelser* 67, The Royal Danish Academy of Sciences and Letters, ed. Mogens Herman Hansen (Copenhagen: Munksgaard, 1993), pp. 41–105.

SUGGESTED READING

Briant, Pierre. *From Cyrus to Alexander: The Persian Empire.* Translated by Peter T. Daniels. 2002. The fundamental introduction to the subject. Essential reading.

Dickinson, Oliver. *The Aegean Bronze Age.* 1994. Perhaps the best single introduction to a vast and fascinating subject.

Finley, M. I. *The World of Odysseus.* Rev. ed. 1978. A classic introduction to the Homeric poems; still good on society and ideology but out-of-date on historicity.

Markoe, Glenn. *Phoenicians.* 2000. An up-to-date introduction.

Oates, J. *Babylon.* Rev. ed. 1986. A well-illustrated survey, from the period of Sargon to the Hellenistic Greeks, with a section on Babylon's cultural legacy.

Saggs, H. W. F. *The Might That Was Assyria.* 1990. A readable introductory history celebrating the Assyrians' achievements.

Shanks, H., ed. *Ancient Israel: A Short History from Abraham to the Roman Destruction of the Temple.* 2d ed. 1999. Short, readable essays by scholars offering up-to-date introductions to the subject.

Wood, Michael. *In Search of the Trojan War.* 2d ed. 1998. A readable introduction to the new scholarship as of the mid-1990s.

The Age of the Polis in Greece, ca. 750–350 B.C.

3

(Photo: Julia M. Fair)

It is dawn. The light reveals a hillside in the city of Athens, a natural auditorium. Its rocky slopes, visible in the photograph here, would have been covered, beginning about 500 B.C., with wooden benches facing a platform cut into the rock. The six thousand men gathered there constitute a diverse group, ranging from farmers to philosophers, from dockyard workers to aristocrats. As they take their seats, these, the citizens of Athens, watch priests conducting prayers and offering a sacrifice. Then all eyes turn to the individual who mounts the platform—a herald. His booming voice asks the question that marks the start of business: "Who wishes to speak?" Someone rises to address the assembly. It is the first democracy in history—and the central laboratory in this great experiment in participation.

The assembly meeting recalls the defining features of what was, in its era, the characteristic political institution in much of Greece: the *polis* (plural, *poleis*). Usually translated as "city-state," the polis is better understood as "citizen-state." The polis was the product of communal activities—whether in the assembly, the military, or the theater—undertaken by its members: its citizens. Not every polis was a democracy, but every polis emphasized cooperative activities whose participants enjoyed at least a measure of equality. Every polis also sought a balance between the group and the individual, be that person the speaker, a military hero, or a freethinker.

Balance is a difficult state to achieve, however, and the equilibrium of the polis was frequently disturbed by tension and exclusion. Paradox marked the polis. Greek democracy failed to grant equal rights to women or immigrants, and it depended on slave labor. Relations among poleis were less often a matter of cooperation than of war. Although the Greeks created magnificent religious architecture, a portion of their intellectual elite came to the conclusion that the gods were of little importance in explaining the universe. Whereas one leading polis, Sparta, was a paragon of militarism, obedience, and austerity, scorning the life of the mind, another, Athens, prided itself on freedom and cultural attainments. Yet the Greeks made the most even of such tensions, exploring them in literary genres—tragedy, comedy, history, and philosophy—that focused on the polis as a central theme. Creative tensions also marked Greek achievements in sculpture, painting, and architecture.

The era of the polis proved to be a defining moment in Western history. Although the Greeks of this era borrowed much from neighboring cultures, they were remarkably original. In the mid-first millennium B.C., the monotheistic religious heritage of the West first emerged among the Jews. During that same era, the Greeks founded the Western tradition in a broad range of culture, including politics; philosophy; literary genres such as comedy, tragedy, and history; and the visual and plastic arts of painting, sculpture, and architecture.

SOCIETY AND POLITICS IN ARCHAIC GREECE, CA. 750–500 B.C.

Historians usually call the era in Greek history from roughly 750 to 500 B.C. the "Archaic period." In this context *archaic* refers to the style of sculpture in the two centuries before the "Classical period" (480–323 B.C.). Archaic Greece was a patchwork of hundreds of separate city-states, tribal leagues, and monarchies. Nevertheless, it displayed a distinctive style and outlook not only in art but also in politics, military arrangements, technology, economics, literature, and religion.

Although it was a period of paradox, the Archaic era laid the groundwork for much of lasting importance in Western civilization. Archaic Greece witnessed the simultane-

ous growth of individualism and a tight community spirit, the emergence of social co-
hesion despite a continual state of war, the coexistence of deep religious piety and the
West's first nontheistic philosophy. The Archaic period also saw the origin of characteristic Western types of governmental regimes—tyranny, oligarchy, and the first steps
toward democracy—and of fundamental Western notions of citizenship and the rule
of law.

Agriculture, Trade, Colonization, and Warfare	An observer of ninth-century B.C. Greece would hardly have predicted greatness of that poor, illiterate society of small settlements and low-level trade. Yet, as we saw in the discussion of Homer in Chapter 2, everything began to change in Greece

in the eighth century B.C. It was out of these changes that a new communal institution
emerged: the polis.

Change was a product of peace, which stimulated a sharp population rise. In response, the economy shifted from herding to farming, a more efficient source of food.
Seeking new agricultural land in the rocky Greek peninsula, farmers terraced hillsides
and drained marshes. The typical agricultural unit was the family farm. Most farms
were small and roughly equal in size, apparently a stimulus of social and political
equality in Greece.

Greek commerce, too, was expanding. Shortly before 800 B.C., Greeks from the island of Euboea, perhaps following the example of Phoenician merchants and seafarers
who had been casual traders in Greece for a century (see page 39), established a trading post in Syria at Al-Mina on the mouth of the Orontes River, at the terminus of the
chief caravan route from Mesopotamia. Shortly afterward, Euboeans established another trading post in the west, on an island in the Bay of Naples in Italy. In both east
and west, Greek merchants sought iron and luxury goods. What they offered in return
was probably silver, of which ancient Greece had rich deposits, and slaves.

From commerce it was but a short step to colonization in order to siphon off the
extra mouths created by population growth. In colonization as in trade, the Greeks
may have followed the example of the Phoenicians, who had begun establishing
colonies probably in the ninth century B.C. Between about 750 and 500 B.C., the Greeks
founded colonies throughout the Mediterranean and the Black Sea, planting nearly as
many cities as already existed in Greece. Colonization in Italy and Sicily began in
earnest around 750 B.C.; in the Chalcidice in the northeast Aegean perhaps a generation later; in the Sea of Marmara about 680 B.C.; in North Africa around 630 B.C.; and
in the Black Sea about 610 B.C. In the far west, Massalia (modern Marseilles) was established about 600 B.C. Southern Italy and Sicily, whose climate and landscape recalled the Aegean, were especially intense areas of Greek settlement, so much so that
the Romans later called the region *Magna Graecia* ("Great Greece"). In the long run,
Greek colonization proved to be of great importance for the spread of urban civilization westward, especially into Italy.

One important consequence of foreign contact was the introduction to Greece
of the alphabet, borrowed from the Phoenicians. The first datable examples of the
Greek alphabet were inscribed on pots in about 750 B.C. The alphabet spread rapidly
and widely in the next century. Literacy underlay the achievements in poetry, philosophy, and the law that Archaic Greece has left behind. However, so few people at

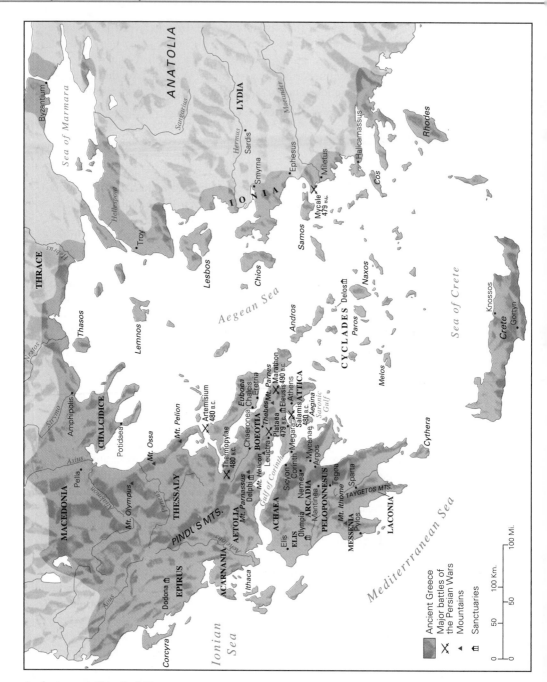

Archaic and Classical Greece

The region of the Aegean Sea was the heartland of Greek civilization around 750 to 350 B.C. The mountainous terrain, rugged coastline, and numerous islands encouraged political fragmentation.

the time could read and write well that ancient Greek culture remained primarily an oral culture.

Another consequence of foreign contact was the introduction of new military technology, which the increase in wealth allowed the Greeks to adopt. Social changes, furthermore, fostered new tactics on the battlefield. The result was the hoplite phalanx, a tightly ordered unit of heavily armed, pike-bearing infantrymen. The phalanx not only became the dominant military force in Archaic Greece, but, with relatively few changes in equipment and tactics, it remained supreme on land in Greece, western Asia, and other Mediterranean regions for centuries, until its defeat by a Roman army in 197 B.C.

The phalanx emerged through a process of evolution rather than in a revolutionary leap. Before 800 B.C., single combat among the *basileis* (elite) appears to have decided battles. Around 800 to 750 B.C. armies began to include more men, fighting in close formation. Around 700 B.C. came new armaments. The result was the phalanx. The heavily armed infantryman (hoplite) of the fighting unit (phalanx) wore bronze armor on his shins and chest and a bronze helmet slit with a narrow opening for eyes and mouth. He carried a heavy wooden shield in his left hand. His weapons were a pike—a heavy, wooden, iron-tipped thrusting spear at least 9 feet long—and a short, iron stabbing sword.

The men of the phalanx were arranged in close ranks, normally four to eight deep. Soldiers stood together in line, each man's shield overlapping his neighbor's. Hoplite combat involved set battles—head-to-head, army-against-army, all-or-nothing affairs— rather than individual skirmishes or guerrilla raids. Too unwieldy for Greece's mountains, the phalanx fought only in the plains. Battle usually consisted of an initial charge, followed by a grueling contest. The men in the front line pounded the enemy with their pikes, while the men in the rear pushed forward. Finally, one side would give way and run. The victors stayed and erected a trophy.

Greek hoplite warfare rested on deep societal roots. Only independent men of means could afford hoplite armor. Thanks to the spread of the family farm, such men were common in Greece by around 700 B.C. Hoplites were amateur soldiers. Most were full-time farmers outside the fighting season, which lasted only for the summer months. The notion of the farmer-soldier, independent and free, would have a lasting impact on Western political thought. So would the warrior values of what became a way of life in Greece.

Aretê, now translated as "excellence" or "virtue" but originally meaning "warrior prowess," was a central concept for the Greeks. In Homer a warrior fought mainly for personal and familial honor (see page 58). By around 650 B.C. aretê referred also to the community. According to the poet Tyrtaeus (ca. 650 B.C.), the ideal soldier not only fights bravely but "heartens his neighbor by his words." Should he die, his death brings glory not only to his father but also to his city and his countrymen. Although the battlefield remained the favored arena for displays of aretê, the assembly or the council house became increasingly acceptable as an alternative.

Greek women did not serve as soldiers, but they were expected to encourage their men to fight and die for the city. Women were praised for bearing and raising sons to serve as future soldiers.

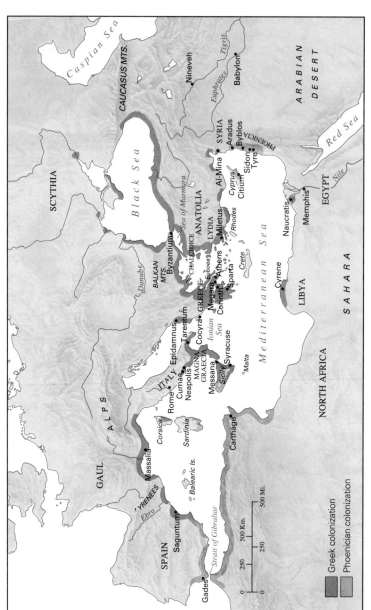

Phoenician and Greek Colonization

Both the Phoenicians (beginning perhaps after 900 B.C.) and the Greeks (beginning around 750 B.C.) established numerous colonies on the coasts of the Mediterranean and Black Seas.

Emergence of the Polis

Paradoxes abound in the origins of the polis. The polis was both a product of the changes of the eighth century B.C. and a stimulus for change. As an urban settlement, the polis existed as early as the ninth or even the tenth century B.C., but its intense communal spirit did not emerge until around 700 B.C. In agriculture, the most important single profession, the prevalence of the family farm created a kind of rough social equality, which was reflected in a cultural emphasis on equality. Yet the polis was marked by social inequality as some grew rich on the profits of trade.

Polis came to denote not just a city but the community as a whole, corresponding roughly to a country or nation. One crude gauge of the centrality of the polis is the number, not to mention the significance, of words the Greeks derived from it: among them, *polites* (citizen), *politeia* (constitution), *politeô* (to govern), *ta politika* (politics), and *politikos* (politician).

Most poleis were small, many less than 100 square miles in size. Athens was one of the largest. Its territory, known as Attica, covered 1,000 square miles (approximately the size of Rhode Island). At its height (ca. 430 B.C.) the population of Athens was about 400,000, but a typical polis contained only between 5,000 and 10,000 people. The philosopher Aristotle (384–322 B.C.) wrote that an ideal polis should be small enough that the citizens know one another personally.

The polis consisted of two parts: the urban area, which usually was tiny, and the surrounding countryside, where most people lived. From the earliest times, the urban public space included both a defensible hill (preferably with a water supply), called a "high city" (*acropolis*), and a "gathering place" (*agora*), used as a marketplace and meeting place. At least one temple usually served as a focal point. After around 500 B.C. stone buildings, including council houses, theaters, covered porticoes, gymnasia, and baths, became increasingly common.

What distinguished the early polis, however, was not its buildings but its spirit. As the poet Alcaeus (b. ca. 630 B.C.) puts it, "Not houses finely roofed or the stones of walls well-built, nay nor canals and dockyards, make the polis, but men able to use their opportunity."

The Greeks came to call the polis a "common thing" (*koinon*). It was a shared commonwealth. It belonged to its people, not to a few nobles or to a king or a god. As early as about 700 B.C., important public documents were inscribed in stone. Acts of state were attributed not to a personified polis but to the community—for example, not to Thera but to "the Thereans," not to Sybaris but to "the Sybarites." The emphasis is on the plurality.

The emphasis was on equality as well. The early polis developed an ethos of measure and moderation. The ideal citizen was thought to be neither rich nor poor but of moderate means. Women were generally not considered citizens and were excluded from taking part in politics. Yet women's behavior was considered important to the polis. Laws against extravagant jewelry or unrestrained mourning (mourning the dead was considered women's work), for example, were put into place in some poleis.

In theory, all citizens were supposed to be roughly similar, but this was not always true in practice, as the politics of the early polis makes clear.

Tyranny

Trade and colonization inspired change at home, for one thing, making increasing numbers of Greeks into seafarers.

This was a critical development, for as the historian Thucydides (ca. 455–397 B.C.) argues, a sea power tends to be more dynamic and innovative than a land power. Seafarers are likely to come into contact with new ideas and institutions. In antiquity, ships moved more quickly and cheaply than land transport; thus seafaring usually accelerated the rate of change.

One such change was Greece's growing wealth. To some extent, this wealth was general. The poet Hesiod (ca. 700 B.C.), for example, records the increasing size and prosperity of the class of free farmers. Some individuals, however, grew far wealthier than others. Yet many of these newly rich lacked the status of the *basileis,* the elite of landowning families who monopolized political power and honor. In order to claim a share, the newly rich seem to have made common cause with the independent farmers who staffed the hoplite phalanx. The result was tyranny.

Tyrant, a term borrowed from the East, possibly from Lydia (a wealthy kingdom in Anatolia), originally referred not to an arbitrary and oppressive ruler but rather to a champion of the people. Having overthrown a narrow and entrenched aristocracy, tyrants were popular at first. *Tyrant* did not become a pejorative word before roughly 550 B.C., when the people soured on the second and third generation of tyrants.

Greek tyranny began in Argos, a polis in the northeastern Peloponnesus, around 675 B.C. The first tyrant was an Argive named Pheidon. By 660 B.C. tyranny had spread to nearby Corinth. Over the course of the seventh and sixth centuries B.C., all the major Greek poleis except Sparta became tyrannies.

Sources of evidence for the first tyrannies are poor, and much about the tyrants is debated by scholars. Yet it does seem that in the seventh century B.C., wealthy men who had been denied political power rose on the shoulders of the hoplites and overthrew a narrow elite. They set up one-man rule, not in the name of the basileis, but on behalf of a much broader group: the prosperous farmers who fought in the phalanx.

Much of what the tyrants did, especially in the first generation, was popular and progressive. They stimulated the economy by founding colonies on trade routes, standardizing weights and measures, and encouraging the immigration of skilled craftsmen from other poleis. Corinth under the tyrant Cypselus (r. ca. 657–625 B.C.), for example, became the wealthiest city in Greece by exporting agricultural produce. Tyrants built temples and instituted festivals, providing both jobs and leisure-time activities.

When tyrants passed power on to their sons, however, the second generation tended to rule oppressively. Buoyed by the discontent of the demos, the basileis regrouped and tried to take back power. Thrasybulus of Miletus (ca. 600 B.C.), one second-generation tyrant, advised accordingly: to maintain power, a tyrant should "lop off the tallest ears of grain"—that is, execute or exile aristocrats in order to deny leaders to the opposition. But the tide of discontent was not to be stopped. Few tyrannies lasted beyond the third generation, when they were overthrown and replaced by oligarchy (literally, "rule by the few") or, less often, by democracy (literally, "power of the people"). By 500 B.C. tyranny had disappeared from most of Greece.

Sparta

Located in Laconia, a fertile valley in the south-central Peloponnesus, in the southern part of mainland Greece, Sparta seemed destined by geography for prosperity but not for glory. It was positioned not at a crossroads or beside a great harbor but rather by rugged mountains that might have left it isolated. Yet Sparta proved to be a powerful model of citizenship and constitutionalism, virtue and community, austerity and militarism.

The history of Sparta is not easy to write. Sparta was a closed military society, contemptuous of book learning, suspicious of foreigners, and secretive toward the outside world. Scholarship has lifted the veil a little, however. For example, Spartans believed that their unique system had been created at a stroke by the legendary lawgiver Lycurgus, who is supposed to have lived (according to the most common version) in the eighth century B.C. and whose charter for Sparta was a divine command. Nowadays, scholars argue for gradual innovations in Sparta rather than revolutionary change, for a process beginning around 650 B.C. and continuing for generations. And it is by no means clear that there ever was a Lycurgus. Let us consider the question of origins.

The foundations of Spartan society were laid around 650 B.C., when a three-part class system emerged. Helots, unfree laborers who worked the land for their masters, were at the lowest level. In the middle ranks were *perioikoi* (roughly, "neighbors"), who were free but under the thumb of the highest class. At the top stood Similars, who were the only full citizens. We do not know the number of helots, but we do know that they vastly outnumbered the other two classes.

Compared with individuals of the other classes, a Similar had a good life. If male and over age 30, he had the right to attend the assembly and to hold public office. Each male Similar, moreover, was given a basic allotment of land worked by helots, which freed him to fight. As the name implies, Similars were alike but not equal. Wealthy Similars owned more land than the basic allotment.

Although Sparta is remembered as a conservative society, the idea of a large group of men sharing power was radical in its day. When the system began around 650 B.C., Similars numbered about nine thousand. What gave them their clout and prestige? The Similars were probably hoplites, the backbone of Sparta's army.

In the mid-seventh century B.C., Sparta was even more dependent on its army than was the average polis; the reason is the helots. Most helots were Messenians, whose fertile territory had been conquered by Sparta in about 725 B.C. Although the Messenians were Greeks, they were forced to work for the conquerors. Sparta profited, but it now faced a security problem. The restive Messenian helots had to be policed, and a dramatic revolt sometime between 675 and 650 B.C. almost succeeded in expelling the Spartans. To keep Messenia, Sparta needed a crack army; to get that, it needed to train, support, and glorify its soldiers. The political and economic result was to make all Spartan hoplites into Similars.

Sparta was no democracy, however. The ancients classified the Spartan government as "mixed" because it distributed power among the Similars through a combination of monarchy, oligarchy (that is, rule by an elite few), and popular government. The assembly of Similars was the popular element in the regime, but its powers were limited. Real power was shared among those Similars who were kings, elders, and *ephors* (overseers), men generally belonging to a few wealthy families.

The elite did not lead lives of luxury, however, at least not after around 550 B.C., when austerity became the order of the day. Society was reordered to promote the discipline needed to keep control of the helots. For example, Spartans' diet was famous for its simplicity. The preferred food was a black broth of pork cooked in its own blood and spiced with salt and vinegar. To discourage consumption, Sparta issued no coins;

the official "currency" consisted of heavy and clumsy iron skewers. Since the outside world was considered corrupt, Sparta engaged in little trade and admitted few foreigners to its territory—and those who were admitted were subject to periodic expulsion.

Whereas other poleis offered little or no formal public education, Sparta schooled its sons from childhood to be soldiers—a system known as the *agoge* ("upbringing"). Limited to male Similars, the agoge created a life cycle unique in Greece. At birth babies were examined by public inspectors. Those who were considered deformed or unfit were "exposed"—that is, they were abandoned without food or shelter. The victims might die, but they might also be sold into slavery or even secretly adopted. (Other Greeks also practiced exposure of infants, but the choice was a family matter, not public policy.) Surviving children were raised at home up to the age of 7, at which point boys left the family to be boarded with a "herd" of their age mates. For the eleven years from age 7 to age 18, a boy went through rigorous training. On the theory that good soldiers should be strong and silent, boys learned only enough reading and writing for practical ends—for example, to transmit messages to and from military headquarters.

Many boys between the ages of 18 and 20 served in the *krypteia* (secret service), living secretly in the hills of Messenia, where they survived by hunting, foraging, and stealing. They spied on the ever rebellious Messenian helots, whom they could kill freely because every year Sparta declared war on helots. By age 20 all Similars had become hoplites, and they continued to serve in the army until age 60. Supported by helot labor, they devoted all their time to fighting and training the next generation.

Ironically, Sparta offered more opportunities outside the home to elite women than did other Greek states. For example, unlike most Greek girls, Spartan girls received a public education—limited, however, to physical training, which was thought to strengthen females for childbearing. Still, the sight of girls running, wrestling, and throwing the discus and javelin, which was common in Sparta, was unthinkable elsewhere in Greece. So was Sparta's unique recognition of the risks of maternity. Like Spartan men who died in battle, Spartan women who died in childbirth were allowed to have their names inscribed on their tombstones. All other Spartan burials were anonymous.

Spartan women were relatively more independent than women elsewhere in Greece. With the men consumed by military training or warfare, women ran the day-to-day operations of life, controlling the helot farmworkers and servants, and raising the girls and the very small boys. Women married around age 20, men around 30. Newlyweds were supposed to spend only enough time together to produce offspring. Often left on their own without a husband's interference, and having been schooled in assertiveness by youthful physical training outdoors, Spartan women also had the advantage of being able to inherit property, unlike Athenian women.

Beginning around 550 B.C., Sparta used its military might to build up a network of alliances (dubbed the "Peloponnesian League" by scholars) in the Peloponnesus and central Greece. It may seem paradoxical that a society that feared foreigners, as Sparta did, became the *hegemon* (literally, "leader") of an extensive alliance system, but Sparta's fear made its leadership slow and careful. Sparta intervened in the wider world only to prevent threats from arising on the horizon, and usually only after a great deal of debate and with the utmost caution.

By around 500 B.C. all of the Peloponnesian poleis except Argos had alliances with Sparta, and in central Greece Thebes came aboard shortly thereafter. Allies swore "to

Spartan Woman

This bronze statuette (4¾ inches tall) from Laconia (ca. 530 B.C.) shows a woman running. Unlike other Greek women, elite Spartan women underwent physical education. Although their personal freedom was limited, women in Sparta suffered fewer restrictions than their counterparts in democratic Athens. (National Archaelogical Museum, Athens/Archaeological Receipts Fund)

follow Sparta wherever it may lead and to have the same friends and enemies." Until its breakup in the aftermath of the Peloponnesian War (431–404 B.C.; see page 86), the Peloponnesian League was the dominant land power in Greece and, after the defeat of Persia in 480 B.C., in the entire eastern Mediterranean.

Sparta exemplified community spirit and respect for law. The people of Sparta, as the historian Herodotus (ca. 485–425 B.C.) quotes a Spartan king, "are free . . . , but not entirely free; for they have a master, and that master is Law, which they fear." Sparta was also an exemplar of equality—limited equality, to be sure, but equality extended to a wider group than ever before in Greece. The notion of the Similars, moreover, contains the germ of the idea of the citizen: a free member of the political community who, unlike a subject, has rights as well as duties. Few other poleis could match the stability and sense of civic duty fostered by Sparta. In the realms of equality and citizenship, however, Sparta was eventually outstripped by Athens. In the realm of liberty, Athens wrote a new chapter in Western history.

Early Athens   Around 650 B.C. the basileis of the Pedion, or Attic, Plain who proudly called themselves the Eupatrids ("well-fathered men"), ruled Athens. They served in one-year magistracies and afterward became life members of the Areopagus, a council of elders named for its meeting place on the "hill of Ares." By its prestige, this aristocratic council held the lion's share of power, both in politics and in justice, for it also served as a court. The demos (the people) met in an assembly. Probably from early times on, the assembly had, in theory, supreme lawmaking power as well as authority over war and peace, but voting was by shouting, and few people challenged Eupatrid wishes.

By 632 B.C. the aristocrats faced trouble in Athens as elsewhere because of corruption, economic change, and assertive hoplites. A failed attempt that year to establish a tyranny left the forces for change eager. In 621 B.C. a loose coalition opposed to Eupatrid rule forced a codification of the laws, which were then issued in writing. This Code of Draco, named for its main drafter, was infamous for its harsh provisions (hence the adjective *draconian*); it was written, a later commentator suggested, "not in ink but blood." Yet Draco's Code seems only to have whetted an appetite for change. A wealthy non-Eupatrid elite of hoplites was emerging, grown rich exporting olive oil. Some were merchants; most were prosperous farmers. They now wanted political power. As for ordinary Athenians, they typically worked small family farms. Over the years, bad harvests and soil exhaustion had sent many into debt. Those who had pledged their land as collateral became known as *hektemoroi* ("sixth-parters"), probably because they owed one-sixth of their crops to their creditors. Other farmers sank even further into debt and had only themselves or their children as collateral. Some ended up as slaves, sometimes sold abroad. Because both rich and poor Athenians had grievances against the Eupatrids, revolution was in the air.

Enter Solon (ca. 630–560 B.C.), who was appointed to the emergency position of sole *archon* (chief officer) for one year, probably 594 B.C. A Eupatrid who had become a merchant, Solon understood both the old and the new elite, and he was sympathetic to ordinary Athenians as well. As his surviving writings show, Solon was a moderate. He could have become tyrant, but he preferred to be a mediator; as such, he said, he "stood with a strong shield before both parties [the common people and the powerful] and allowed neither one to win an unfair victory."[1]

Solon's reforms were comprehensive, spanning both economics and politics. He helped ordinary people by the "shaking off of burdens," measures that abolished the institution of *hektemorage* and probably canceled some debts. He also abolished the practice of making loans on personal surety and set up a fund to redeem Athenians who had been sold into slavery abroad. By freeing the hektemoroi, Solon ensured Athens a large class of independent small farmers.

Solon's other economic reforms were aimed at encouraging Athenian trade. To foster the production of olive oil, a cash crop, he restricted all other agricultural exports. He changed Athenian weights, measures, and perhaps coins to conform to the most common Greek standard. The result was a commercial boom.

Solon made fundamental changes in Athenian government, too. He changed qualifications for office from birth to wealth, a boon to the non-Eupatrid elite. He established four census classes based on agricultural production. Most offices were reserved for men of property, but the poorest class, known as *thetes*, could participate in the assembly and courts. Solon probably established the Council of 400, which prepared the assembly's agenda. He is probably also responsible for regularizing council and assembly meetings and replacing the assembly's voice votes with the counting of hands.

Solon's moderation, respect for law, and liberation of the poor and downtrodden are milestones in Greek history. Yet Solon's reforms had an unexpected byproduct: the growth of slavery in Athens. Though booming, the Athenian economy lost its cheap labor when Solon freed debt slaves and hektemoroi. The solution was to buy slaves abroad and import them to Athens. At the time, the island city-state of Chios was the center of the slave trade in Greece. After Solon, Athens along with Chios developed one of history's first large-scale slave systems. Slaves worked in agriculture, crafts, trade, and elsewhere in the economy. Unlike helots, slaves could be bought and sold and were often uprooted, and the system was better policed than in earlier societies.

In the centuries after Solon, slavery grew widespread in Athens. Some slaves served in agriculture, some labored under miserable conditions in Athenian silver mines, and some were engaged in commerce or the military (where some rowers were slaves). Most, however, worked as domestics or in small workshops as, for example, metalworkers or furniture makers. The vast majority of slaves were non-Greek. Most were prisoners of war; some were victims of pirates or debtors from states where, unlike Athens, citizens might end up in debt slavery. Thrace (roughly, modern Bulgaria) and Anatolia were the main sources of slaves, but some slaves came from North Africa and other Mediterranean regions.

Living conditions for slaves were usually poor and those in the silver mines abysmal. Emancipation, however, was more common in Athens than in the American South before 1865. A few ex-slaves even rose to positions of wealth and power in Athens. A striking and unusual case is that of Pasion (d. 370 B.C.). Originally a slave employee of a banking firm, he bought his freedom and became the wealthiest Athenian banker of his day, as well as an Athenian citizen.

If free Athenians had any moral doubts about slavery, they went unrecorded. Yet there was much dissatisfaction with Solon's reforms, since his middle way satisfied neither Eupatrids nor champions of the free poor. After years of conflict, around 560 B.C. advocates of radical reform established a tyranny under Pisistratus (ca. 600–528 B.C.). He and his sons held power for forty of the next fifty years.

Supported by the thetes, the Pisistratids exiled many Eupatrids and confiscated and redistributed their land. Pisistratus kept the façade of Solon's reforms while ensuring that loyal supporters held all key offices.

A stable regime, the tyranny witnessed prosperity at home and the expansion of Athenian influence abroad. Yet Pisistratus's dynasty lasted only two generations. A steadfast opponent of tyrants, Sparta deposed his son, Hippias, in 510 B.C. Athens's elites by birth and wealth were ready to establish an oligarchy, but the way was open for an unexpected development: the emergence of popular government.

THE CULTURE OF ARCHAIC GREECE

While one trend in Archaic culture was communal solidarity, as reflected in the hoplite phalanx, another was the opposite: a growing elevation of individualism. Increased prosperity and mobility (social, geographic, and political) during the Archaic period encouraged the breakdown of old ties and left some people with a sense of their uniqueness. Archaic poetry and sculpture both demonstrate this new consciousness of the self.

Meanwhile, although most Archaic Greeks celebrated religion, a small group of thinkers expressed religious doubts. While monumental stone temples and international centers for divination were being erected to honor the pantheon of gods, Greek thinkers began to move away from divine and toward abstract and mechanistic explanations of the universe. Their defection marked the start of the Western philosophical tradition.

Revealing the Self: Lyric Poetry and Sculpture Between approximately 675 and 500 B.C., the dominant Greek literary form was lyric poetry. This genre consisted of short poems written in a variety of styles but sharing a willingness to experiment, sometimes by revealing private feelings, sometimes by commenting on contemporary politics (as in the poetry of Tyrtaeus). Epic poetry, by contrast, was longer, grander in theme and tone, and less personal.

Homer never speaks directly about himself, and Hesiod reveals only a few personal details. In contrast, Archilochus of Paros (ca. 700–650 B.C.), the earliest known of the lyric poets, flaunts the self. Born on the Cycladic island of Paros, Archilochus was the son, perhaps the illegitimate son, of a noble. He was a mercenary soldier (that is, he fought for pay for a foreign country) and a colonist before returning home and dying in a hoplite battle against a neighboring island. The varied subjects of Archilochus's poetry include love, travel, and war. Much of his poetry is satire, sometimes mocking and ironic, sometimes vicious and abusive. Archilochus takes a cynical and detached view of hoplite ideals, freely admitting that he once tossed away his shield to escape the battlefield: "And that shield, to hell with it! Tomorrow I'll get me another one no worse."[2]

Sappho of Lesbos (ca. 625 B.C.) is also famous as a private poet, one who composed unmatched descriptions of intimate feelings, among them love for other women. Sappho is one of the few women poets of antiquity whose work has survived—very little, unfortunately, but enough to show that she was educated, worldly, and versed in politics. Like a modern experimental poet, she uses language self-consciously. Sappho's sensuality comes through in a description of her feelings at seeing a woman whose company she desires talking with a man: her heart shakes, her tongue is stuck, her eyes cannot see, her skin is on fire. "I am greener than grass," Sappho writes, "I feel nearly as if I could die."[3]

Sappho discusses female sexuality, a subject that Greek elite culture, dominated by males, tended to ignore. We know little about the sexuality of Greek women or of non-elite males. Among the male elite, romantic love in Archaic and Classical Greece was homosexual love or, to be precise, *pederasty* ("boy love"). The ideal relationship was supposed to involve a man in his twenties and a boy in his teens. The male elite was, strictly speaking, bisexual. By age 30, a man was expected to marry and raise a family. Perhaps bisexuality prevailed among elite females as well; Sappho, for example, eventually married and had a child.

Another sign of Archaic Greece's interest in the personal is the growing attention paid to the depiction of the human body, both in painting (most of the surviving examples are painted pottery) and in sculpture. Archaic artists displayed increasing skill and sensitivity in depicting the human form. The rich marble deposits in Greek soil gave sculptors promising material; baked clay (terra cotta) and bronze were other common sculptural media.

Early Archaic marble sculpture (seventh century B.C.) was strongly influenced by the way Egyptian sculpture represented the human body. Like Egyptian statuary, early

Greek sculpture tended to be formal and frontal. But over the course of the seventh and sixth centuries B.C., Greek sculptors experimented with a greater variety of poses and with increasing realism in showing musculature and motion. This realism, however, was expressed within limits, for the favorite subject of Archaic sculptors was not ordinary people but idealized, beautiful youth. Typical sculptural forms were the naked young man (*kouros*) and clothed young woman (*kore*), which often served as grave markers or monuments. The goal was to show people not as they were but as they might be.

Religious Faith and Practice The Olympian gods who had been worshiped in the Mycenaean era survived in later ages, adapted to fit new political and social conditions. In the Archaic period, accordingly, the Olympian gods became gods of the polis.

Although the Olympians were revered throughout Greece, each polis had its patron deity: Apollo at Corinth, Hera at Argos and Samos, Athena at Athens and Sparta. Each polis also had its favorite heroes or demigods—for example, Theseus, the legendary founder of Athens, and Heracles (Hercules), a favorite of Dorian cities such as Sparta and Thebes. Devotees considered it important to build a "house"—that is, a temple—for the local patron god or at least for his or her statue. The first temples were built of wood; the earliest stone temple, a temple of Apollo at Corinth, was built around 550 B.C.

Temples were rectangular structures with long sides on the north and south, short sides on the east and west, a colonnade around all four sides, and a pitched roof. The columns were based loosely on those of Egyptian architecture. Greek temples faced east so sunlight would illuminate the interior, which consisted of two rooms: a small treasury, open to the west, and a larger main chamber, in which a statue of the deity stood. The interior decoration of the temple was simple. Outside, however, brownish red roof tiles, painted sculpture above the colonnade and in the pediments (the area between the gables and the front and rear doorways), and terra-cotta roof ornaments created a festive and lively effect. The bare white ruins seen today are misleading.

The emphasis on exterior rather than interior decoration in a Greek temple reflects the way the building was used. The main ceremony took place outside. A long altar stood in front of the temple and parallel to it. On feast days—and under the tyrants the number of such days was increased greatly, as a concession to the common people— temple priests would sacrifice animals (pigs, goats, lambs, and, less often, bulls) on the altar. Only the thighs would be burned for the gods. The rest of the meat would be boiled and distributed to worshipers.

As in other ancient cultures, so in Greece divination was an important element of religion. Divination was institutionalized in *oracles*, places where, it was believed, a god or hero might be consulted for advice. Of the various Greek oracles, that of Apollo at Delphi (in central Greece) became the most prestigious and respected. At Delphi, Apollo spoke through the Pythia, a priestess who went into a trance. The utterances of Apollo at Delphi were famous among the Greeks for being ambiguous. Because different people might interpret them in different ways, Apollo could always be absolved after the fact if things did not turn out as the listener expected.

The oracle of Delphi was regularly consulted by poleis wishing to establish colonies. The oracle gave advice about the choice of location and the appropriate patron god or goddess, and it helped settlers draft new law codes. Delphi was also active in the search for new constitutions in the old poleis of Greece. Tradition says that Sparta based its government on a pronouncement of the Delphic oracle.

Archaic thinkers pondered the theme of divine justice. In Archaic literature we see less of the petty squabbling among the gods than in Homer and more of Zeus's majesty and justice. Although the wicked might seem to prosper, Zeus eventually punishes them or their descendants. "It never escapes him all the way when a man has a sinful spirit; and always, in the end, his judgment is plain," says Solon.[4]

Archaic writers delighted in portraying human emotions, but they had no confidence about the human ability to master emotions. In Archaic literature, people are weak and insignificant; their fortune is uncertain and mutable. Further, the gods are jealous of human success. People who aim too high are guilty of *hubris*—arrogance with overtones of violence and transgression. Hubris inevitably brings *nemesis*, "punishment" or "allotment." The safest course is for a person to be pious and humble.

So Archaic religion taught a humbling, even pessimistic, lesson. Yet religious teachings were not always heeded. The pages of Archaic history are full of people who aimed high and sought success with seemingly little worry and no dire consequences. In Ionia (the territory of the Greek cities along the central western Anatolian coast), one group of Greek thinkers made a radical break with Archaic religion and invented speculative philosophy.

The Origins of Western Philosophy   Abstract, rationalistic, speculative thinking emerged in Greece during the sixth century B.C. The first developments took place in Miletus, an Ionian city. It is often said that the thinkers of Miletus (the Milesians) and their followers in other parts of Ionia invented philosophy. So they did, but we must be precise about what this means.

The Ionians were not the first to ask questions or tell stories about the nature and origins of the universe; virtually every ancient people did so. Nor did the Ionians invent science. They conducted no experiments. By 600 B.C., moreover, science—including mathematics, astronomy, medicine, and engineering—had been thriving for over two thousand years in Egypt and Mesopotamia, a heritage with which the Ionians were familiar and from which they borrowed.

The real importance of the Ionians is as pioneers of rationalism. They began the movement away from anthropomorphic or divine explanations and toward an abstract and mechanistic explanation of the universe. They themselves did not make a clear distinction between reason and revelation, but they made it possible for later Greek thinkers to do so. Later Greek philosophers were rarely (if ever) atheists, but they took for granted what the Ionians labored to establish: the primacy of human reason.

The Ionians saw themselves as students of nature—*physis* (from which the word *physics* is derived). Although they also commented on morality and politics, their interest in natural phenomena is what makes the Ionians significant. In their own day, the Ionians were called "wise men" (*sophoi*); to a later generation, they were "lovers of wisdom," *philosophoi* (from which *philosopher* comes).

Thales, the first Milesian thinker, made a name for himself by successfully predicting a solar eclipse in 585 B.C. He is credited with founding Greek geometry and astronomy. Little survives of his writings or those of the other Milesians, but it is clear that he created the first general and systematic theory about the nature of the universe. According to Thales, the primary substance, the element from which all of nature was created, was water. He emphasized the mobility of water and its ability to nourish life.

A reply was not long in coming. Around 550 B.C. Anaximander of Miletus wrote the first known book of prose in Greek, expounding his own philosophy of nature. He attacked Thales for oversimplifying and for failing to do justice to the dynamism of nature. Anaximander accepted Thales' monist assumption—that all matter originated from one primary substance—but he called the substance "the unlimited" or "the undefined" rather than water. A third Milesian, Anaximenes, replied that the primary substance might be unlimited but it was not undefined. It was air, whose properties of condensation and rarefaction symbolized the dynamic and changing nature of things.

Humble as these theories might seem today, they represent a dramatic development: an open and critical debate among thinkers, each of whom was proposing an abstract and rational model of the universe. Many scholars have speculated about the origins of this development. Why Miletus? Why the sixth century B.C.? There are no sure answers, although certain influences have been suggested. Among them are Miletus's contacts on the trade routes with sophisticated Babylon, the proximity of Ionia to non-Greek peoples and the resulting Milesian appreciation of variety and complexity, and the search for law and order in contemporary Greek political life and its extension to the philosophical plane.

In its second generation early Greek philosophy moved to other Ionian cities and then migrated westward across the Mediterranean. Heracleitus of Ephesus (ca. 500 B.C.) proposed fire as the primary substance. Although fire was ever changing, it had an underlying coherence. According to Heracleitus, this paradox nicely symbolized the nature of the universe. He summed up the importance of change by the aphorisms "All things flow" and "You cannot step into the same river twice." The universe witnessed a constant struggle of opposites, yet an essential unity and order prevailed. To describe this order, Heracleitus used the term *logos*. This key concept of Greek philosophy is difficult to translate; among other definitions, *logos* can mean "word," "thought," "reason," "story," or "calculation."

Heracleitus's contemporary, Pythagoras of Samos, was both a rationalist and a religious thinker. On the one hand, Pythagoras was a mathematician who discovered the numerical ratios determining the major intervals of the musical scale—that is, the range of sound between high and low. It is less certain if, as tradition has it, he discovered the so-called Pythagorean theorem—that in a right triangle the hypotenuse squared is equal to the sum of the squares of the other two sides.

On the other hand, Pythagoras believed that the purity of mathematics would improve the human soul. Just as he had imposed numerical order on the musical scale, so could philosophers understand the entire universe through number and proportion. The resulting knowledge was no mere academic exercise but a way of life. Pythagoras devoted himself to "observation" or "contemplation"—to *theoria* (from which *theory* comes).

In Croton in Magna Graecia (southern Italy), Pythagoras founded a religious community. Its members observed strict secrecy, but it appears that they abstained from meat because they believed in the kinship of all living things. They also believed in the reincarnation of the human soul, though not necessarily into a human body. Pythagoras is said to have stopped a man from beating a dog because he recognized from the barking that the dog was the reincarnation of a friend who had died.

The early Greek philosopher whose work is most fully preserved is Parmenides of Elea in Magna Graecia. Parmenides (b. ca. 515 B.C.) completely distrusted the senses. He believed that reality was a world of pure being: eternal, unchanging, and indivisible, comparable to a sphere. To Parmenides, change was a mere illusion. Parmenides, therefore, is the first Western philosopher to propose a radical difference between the world of the senses and reality. This fundamental strain of Western thought would be taken up by Plato and his followers and then passed to Christianity.

To sum up, in philosophy as in so many other endeavors, the Archaic Greeks were great borrowers and even greater innovators who left a profound mark on later ages. By the late sixth century B.C., Archaic Greece was poised on the brink of a revolution that would give birth to the Classical period of Greek civilization.

CLASSICAL GREECE

The word *democracy* comes from the Greek word *demokratia*, coined in Athens early in the fifth century B.C. *Demokratia* literally means "the power (*kratos*) of the people (*demos*)." A modern democracy is characterized by mass citizenship, elections, and representative government. Athenian demokratia, in contrast, was a direct democracy in which elections mattered less than direct participation, citizenship was narrowly restricted, women were excluded from politics, resident aliens could almost never become citizens, and citizens owned slaves and ruled an empire. Modern democracies may cover a huge territory, but Athens encompassed only 1,000 square miles. Modern democracies tend to emphasize individual rights. Athens, in contrast, often placed the community first. In spite of these differences, Athenian demokratia established principles that are enshrined in democracy today: freedom, equality, citizenship without property qualifications, the right of most citizens to hold public office, and the rule of law.

The young democracy's greatest achievement was to spearhead Greece's victory over the Persian invaders in 480 B.C. After that victory, Athens became Greece's leading sea power. Yet Sparta remained the superior land power, and the two poleis were soon locked in a cycle of competition and war. The result nearly destroyed Athenian democracy. Even more serious, it undermined Greece's very independence.

The Development of Demokratia, 508–322 B.C. Tyranny often gave way to oligarchy—to government by wealthy men, both Eupatrids and non-Eupatrids. In Athens after Pisistratid rule, however, conditions were ripe for revolution. Solon had left a society of independent small farmers, while the Pisistratids had strengthened the ranks of immigrants and weakened the Eupatrids. Elite leaders nonetheless tried to establish an Athenian oligarchy. We may imagine strong popular opposition.

Ironically, a Eupatrid, a member of the Alcmeonid clan by the name of Cleisthenes (d. ca. 500 B.C.), led the revolution. Originally Cleisthenes aimed to head the oligarchy, but his rivals shut him out of power. He turned then to the demos, whose leader he became. The watchwords of the day were *equality* and *mixing* (that is, mixing people from different regions of Attica in order to break down local, aristocratic power bases).

Greek Trireme *Olympias is a hypothetical reconstruction of an Athenian war galley of about 400 b.c. Rowed by 170 oarsmen arranged on three decks, the trireme fought by ramming an enemy ship with the bronze ram attached to its bow.* (Courtesy of the Trireme Trust)

Frightened by the assertive populace, the oligarchs called for Spartan military assistance, but to no avail: Cleisthenes rallied the people to victory. The Athenian triumph proved, in Herodotus's opinion, "that equality is an excellent thing, not in one way only but in many. For while they were under a tyranny, [Athenians] were no better at fighting than any of their neighbors, but once they were rid of tyrants they became by far the best."[5]

Cleisthenes extinguished Eupatrid power once and for all by attacking its local bases of support. For example, he abolished the four traditional tribes and apportioned the people among ten new tribes. Immigrants and their descendants, who had been excluded from the old tribes, now joined natives in the new tribes. The tribes formed the basis of a new Council of 500 to replace Solon's Council of 400. The council was divided into ten tribal units, each serving as a kind of executive committee for one of the ten months of the civic year.

The centerpiece of the government was the assembly, some of whose members, emboldened by the new spirit of equality, now spoke up for the first time. The new Council of 500, like its predecessor, prepared the assembly's agenda, but assemblymen felt free to amend it. Only the Areopagus council remained a privileged preserve.

The last and most unusual part of the Cleisthenic system was ostracism, a sort of annual *un*popularity contest that received its name from the pieces of broken pottery (*ostraka*) on which the names of victims were chiseled. The "winner" was forced into ten years of exile, although his property would not be confiscated. Ostracism was meant to protect the regime by defusing factionalism and discouraging tyrants. Judging by Athens's consequent political stability, it worked.

In 508 b.c. the poorest Athenians had relatively little power in Cleisthenic government. But a change in conditions by the 450s made Athens even more democratic.

During that period the oldest principle of Greek politics came to the fore: Whoever fights for the state governs it. To counter the Persian threat against Greece in the 480s (see page 85), Athens built a great navy. The standard ship was a trireme, an oared warship rowed by 170 men on three decks. The core of the rowers consisted of Athenian thetes. Just as hoplites supported new regimes in Greece after 700 B.C., so rowers supported new regimes in Greece after 500 B.C.

A second revolution occurred around 461 B.C., when Ephialtes (d. ca. 460 B.C.) and his young associate Pericles (ca. 495–429 B.C.) targeted the last bulwark of privilege, the Areopagus. They stripped away the council's long-standing supervisory powers over the regime and redistributed those powers to the Council of 500 and the people's court. The decade of the 450s B.C. saw another innovation: payment for public service, specifically for jurors, who received a half-drachma (perhaps half a day's wages) for a day of jury duty. Eventually other public servants also received pay. Conservatives complained bitterly because they perceived, rightly, that state pay made political activity by poor people possible. State pay was, an Athenian said, "the glue of demokratia."

Demokratia became closely connected with Pericles, who inherited the constituency of Ephialtes after his assassination around 460 B.C. For much of the next thirty years, Pericles dominated Athenian politics. An aristocrat who respected the common people, an excellent orator who benefited from an education in philosophy, an honest and tireless worker, and a general who led in peace as well as war, Pericles was a political giant. Under his leadership, demokratia became firmly entrenched as the government and way of life in Athens.

Athenian democracy survived, with occasional oligarchic intrusions, for 150 years after Pericles' death. During those years it became more institutionalized and cautious, but it also became more thoroughly egalitarian.

How Demokratia Worked   Unlike most modern democracies, Athenian demokratia was direct and participatory. Pericles once claimed that in Athens "people pay attention both to their own household and to politics. Even those occupied with other activities are no less knowledgeable about politics."[6] This is part boast, but only part. Large numbers of ordinary citizens attended the assembly from time to time and held public office or served on the Council of 500 for a year or two.

The instruments of government are easily sketched. The central institution was the assembly. Open to all male citizens over age 20, assembly meetings were held in the open air, on a hillside seating several thousand on benches (see the photograph on page 63). In the fourth century B.C. the assembly gathered a minimum of forty times per year, about once every ten days.

The assembly heard the great debates of the day. It made decisions about war and peace, alliance and friendship; it conferred honors and issued condemnations; it passed decrees relating to current issues and set up commissions to revise fundamental laws. In the assembly top orators addressed the people, but everyone, however humble, was theoretically entitled to speak.

The judicial branch consisted of courts, which, with a few exceptions, were open to all citizens, no matter how poor. Aristotle or a member of his school comments that "when the people have the right to vote in the courts, they control the constitution." Juries were large, commonly consisting of several hundred men chosen by lottery; small juries, it was felt, were easily bribed. After a preliminary hearing, cases were decided in a single day.

The executive consisted of the Council of 500 and some seven hundred public officials (also, under Athens's empire in the fifth century B.C., several hundred others living abroad). All male citizens over age 30 were eligible to serve. Most public officials were chosen by lottery, which put rich and poor, talented and untalented, on an equal footing. To guard against installing incompetents or criminals, all officials had to undergo a scrutiny by the council before taking office and an audit after the term. Most magistracies, moreover, were boards, usually of ten men, so even if a bad man managed to pass this scrutiny, he would be counterbalanced by his colleagues. Only generals and treasurers were chosen by election.

Athens had a relatively weak executive and no chief executive such as a president or prime minister. Generals and orators led assembly debates and sometimes exercised great influence, but ordinary people set the agenda and made the decisions by taking votes at each assembly meeting. On the local level, every deme (county) had an annually chosen executive and a deme assembly of all citizens.

So novel and populist a system of government has not been without critics, either in antiquity or today. Some have charged that the Athenian people were uneducated, emotional, and easily swayed by oratorical tricks. Others say that demokratia degenerated into mob rule after the death of Pericles. Still others complain about the lack of a system of formal public education, which denied many citizens equality of opportunity.

Another serious charge against Athenian demokratia is that it was democracy for a small elite only. Adult male citizens never accounted for more than one-tenth of the population, approximately 40,000 out of a total population—men, women and children, resident aliens, and slaves—of about 400,000. To become a citizen, a boy at age 18 had to prove that he was the legitimate son of a citizen father and a citizen maternal grandfather. Girls were never officially registered as citizens. Although the term *citizeness* existed, Athenian citizen women were usually referred to as "city women." As for resident aliens, whether male or female, they rarely attained citizenship.

In the fifth and fourth centuries B.C., Athens had a large population of foreigners. Some were transient. Others were officially registered resident aliens, or *metics*. Metics came by the thousands from all over the Greek world and beyond. Some, like Aristotle (a native of a Greek colony in Macedonia), were attracted by the city's schools of philosophy, but most came because of its unparalleled economic opportunities. Metics could not own land in Athens, and they had to pay extra taxes and serve in the Athenian military. Nevertheless, they prospered in Athenian commerce and crafts.

Athenian women were excluded from politics and played only a modest role in commerce as small retailers. In legal matters women were almost always required to be represented by a male guardian. Demokratia also promoted an ideal of the male as master of his household. Women were expected to be obedient and remain indoors.

Practice, however, was another matter. As Aristotle asks rhetorically, "How is it possible to prevent the wives of the poor from going out?" *Poor* is a synonym for *ordinary* in ancient Greek. Ordinary women could not stay at home because they had to run errands, draw water, and sometimes even help make ends meet. Ordinary houses, moreover, were small and cramped, and in the Mediterranean heat women could not stay inside all the time.

We occasionally get glimpses, sometimes more, of Athenian women resisting or working behind the scenes to correct male mistakes. An inheritance case reveals a woman go-between interceding among her quarreling male relations. Greek comedy shows women mocking male pretensions and establishing sisterly friendships. A woman who brought a large dowry into a marriage could use it and the threat of divorce to influence her husband (the dowry had to be returned to the woman's father or guardian if there was a divorce). In short, Athenian women had some access to the world outside the household and some influence within the household. There existed, nonetheless, a real disparity in power between men and women.

Athenian demokratia lacked many features of modern democracy, including a notion of universal human rights, the possibility for immigrants to become citizens, gender equality, the abolition of slavery, and public education. To its small citizen body, however, Athenian demokratia offered extraordinary freedom, equality, and responsibility, as well as a degree of participation in public life seldom equaled. Demokratia was a model of what democracy could be but not of who could take part.

The Persian Wars, 499–479 B.C.   In 500 B.C. Sparta, hegemon of the Peloponnesian League, was the most prominent power of the Greek mainland. Across the Aegean Sea in Anatolia, the Greek city-states had been under Persian rule for two generations, since Cyrus the Great's conquest in the 540s B.C. In 499 B.C., however, events began to unfold that not only would revolutionize that balance of power but also would throw the entire eastern Mediterranean into two hundred years of turmoil.

Led by Miletus, the Ionian Greek city-states rose in revolt against Persia in 499 B.C. Athens sent troops to help, but despite initial successes, Athens reconsidered the alliance and withdrew its forces. The Ionian coalition broke down thereafter and was crushed by Persia. Miletus was besieged and destroyed, but otherwise Persia was relatively lenient in Ionia.

Upstart Athens, however, could not go unpunished. In 490 B.C. Darius I sent a large naval expedition to Athens. About 25,000 infantrymen and 1,200 cavalrymen (with horses) landed at Marathon, some 24 miles from the city of Athens. Athens sent 10,000 men (including 1,000 allies) to defend Marathon, and a great battle ensued.

Persian overconfidence and the superiority of the Greek phalanx over Persia's loosely organized infantrymen won Athens a smashing victory. Persia suffered 6,400 casualties, Athens only 192. (The story, unconfirmed, that a messenger ran from the battlefield to the city of Athens with the news, "Rejoice, we conquer!" is the inspiration for the modern marathon race, a slightly longer distance of about 26 miles.) After the battle, Athens experienced a burst of confidence that propelled it to power and glory.

Meanwhile, Persia sought a rematch. After Darius's death in 486, his son and successor, Xerxes, amassed a huge force of about a thousand ships and several hundred thousand soldiers and rowers, vastly outnumbering potential Greek opposition. Athens, under the leadership of Themistocles (ca. 525–460 B.C.), prepared by building a fleet of two hundred ships. Athens joined Sparta and twenty-nine other Peloponnesian poleis in the Hellenic League of defense, with Sparta in overall command. Most poleis either stayed neutral or, like Thebes and Argos, collaborated with Persia. The Greeks had over three hundred ships and about fifty thousand infantrymen.

Amazon Queen *This red-figure Athenian cup (ca. 440 B.C.) shows the Greek warrior Achilles about to slay the Amazon queen Penthesilea during the Trojan War, in which she fought on Troy's side. She was a symbol of feminine courage and beauty.* (Staatliche Antikensammlungen und Glyptothek, Munich)

Persia invaded Greece in 480 B.C. and won the opening moves. At the narrow pass of Thermopylae in central Greece, the Persians outflanked and crushed a small Spartan army, who died fighting to the last man, including their king, Leonidas. This sacrifice added to the Spartan reputation for courage but left the road south open. Abandoned by its defenders, Athens was sacked.

The tide then turned. The Greeks lured the Persian fleet into the narrow straits between Athens and Salamis. The Persians could not use their numerical superiority in this confined space, and the Greeks had the home advantage. The result was a crushing Persian defeat under the eyes of Xerxes himself, who watched the battle from a throne on a hillside near the shore.

Because their sea links to the Levant had been cut, Xerxes and the remainder of the Persian fleet left for home. Soon afterward the united Greek army under Spartan leadership defeated Persian forces on land at Plataea (just north of Attica) in 479 B.C. At about the same time, the Greek fleet defeated a reorganized Persian fleet off the Anatolian coast near Mycale. The victorious Greeks sailed the coast and liberated the Ionians. Not only did Persia fail to conquer the Greek mainland, but it also lost its eastern Aegean empire.

Greeks did not remember the invader fondly. After 480 they thought of Persians not merely as enemies but as barbarians—that is, cultural inferiors. At the same time, Greeks became more conscious of their own common culture.

Struggles to Dominate Greece, 478–362 B.C.

The Greek unity forged by the struggle against Persia was fragile and short-lived. What followed was a constant struggle in diplomacy and war among city-states, usually arranged in leagues under hegemons.

Following the Greek victory over Persia, Athens expanded its power as hegemon of a new security organization. Founded on the island of Delos in the Aegean Sea, the so-called Delian League aimed both at protecting Greek lands and at plundering Persian territory. The number of allies grew from about 150 in 477 B.C. to about 250 in 431 B.C. at the height of the league.

Because they feared entanglement outside the Peloponnesus, most Spartans preferred to leave the Aegean to Athens. Some Spartans nonetheless watched with unease and jealousy as Athenian power boomed.

Afraid of the new titan, the major allied states rebelled, one by one, beginning with Thasos in 465 B.C., but Athens crushed each rebellion. Sometimes after surrender, rebels were executed and their wives and children sold into slavery. Allied complaints began to stir Sparta. A conflict between Greece's greatest land power, Sparta, and Greece's greatest sea power, Athens, started to look all but inevitable.

The Peloponnesian War, as this conflict is known today, came in 431 B.C. and lasted intermittently until 404 B.C. The war proved bloody and bitter. Battles between huge fleets, economic warfare, protracted sieges, epidemic disease, and ideological struggle produced a devastating war. It was clear that the Greeks could not maintain their unity against Persia; indeed, they appeared to be destroying themselves.

In this era both democratic Athens and oligarchic Sparta sought to promote their respective ideologies. Some unfortunate states became ideological battlegrounds, often at great cost of life. In Corcyra (modern Corfu), for example, bloody civil war marked a series of coups and countercoups in the 420s B.C.

Given Spartan supremacy on land and Athenian mastery of the sea, it is not surprising that the Peloponnesian War remained undecided for a decade and a half. The balance of power shifted only after an Athenian blunder, an expedition to conquer Sicily (415–413 B.C.) that became a quagmire and then a disaster, leading to total defeat and thousands of Athenian casualties. In the aftermath most of the Athenian empire rose in revolt. Persia re-emerged and intervened on Sparta's side—in return for Sparta's restoration of Ionia to Persia, an ironic counterpoint to Sparta's role in driving Persia from Greece in 479. Athens, nevertheless, was sufficiently wealthy and plucky to hold out until 404 B.C.

Sparta won the Peloponnesian War, but establishing a new Greek order proved beyond its grasp. Spartans were soldiers, not diplomats; infantrymen, not sailors; and commanders, not public speakers. They made poor leaders. Sparta took over Athens's former empire and quickly had a falling-out with its allies, Persia, Corinth, and the Boeotian city-states, especially Thebes.

In addition, Sparta suffered a vast decline in the number of citizens. The original nine thousand Similars of the seventh century B.C. had dropped to only about fifteen hundred in 371 B.C. The main problem seems to have been greed. Rich Spartans preferred to get richer by concentrating wealth in fewer hands rather than open the elite to new blood. Thousands of men could no longer afford to live as elite soldiers.

The result was military disaster. In 371 B.C. the Boeotian army crushed the Spartans at the Battle of Leuctra, killing a thousand men (including four hundred Similars) and a Spartan king. In the next few years Boeotia invaded the Peloponnesus, freed the Messenian helots, and restored Messenia to independence, after some 350 years of bondage. It was a fatal blow to Spartan power, but Boeotia, too, was exhausted and its main leaders, Epaminondas (d. 362 B.C.) and Pelopidas (403–364 B.C.), were dead. None of the Greek city-states had been able to maintain hegemony.

Nothing better demonstrates the fatal excess of individualism in Classical Greece and the absence of cooperative virtues than the wars of the city-states in the fourth century B.C. They accomplished nothing but leaving a weakened Greece prey to outsiders.

THE PUBLIC CULTURE OF CLASSICAL GREECE

The word *classical* means "to set a standard." The culture of Greece between 480 and 322 B.C. proved so influential in the later West that it may justly be called classical. Classical Greek culture was public culture. Poets were not inward-looking or alienated figures. Rather, to quote the Athenian playwright Aristophanes (ca. 455–385 B.C.), they were "the teachers of men," who commented on contemporary public debate. (As the quotation might also suggest, men, especially citizens, dominated public life.) Dramas were performed in a state theater at state religious festivals. The philosopher Socrates (469–399 B.C.) discussed philosophy in marketplaces and gymnasia. It was not private individuals but the public that was the major patron of sculpture and architecture.

Public life, accordingly, is the central theme of Classical Greek art and literature. In tragedy, for example, regardless of the particular hero or plot, the same character always looms in the background: the polis. The Classical historians Herodotus, Xenophon, and especially Thucydides focus on public affairs rather than private life. Classical philosophy ranged from biology to metaphysics, but politics was undoubtedly its central focus.

Religion and Art   A hallmark of Classical culture is the tension between the religious heritage of the Archaic period and the worldly spirit of the Classical age. The Classical period was a time of prosperity, political debate, and military conflict. "Wonders are many on earth, and none more wondrous than man," said the Athenian tragedian Sophocles (ca. 495–406 B.C.). Yet Sophocles was a deeply religious man who also believed that people were doomed to disaster unless they obeyed the laws of the gods. Sophocles mirrored a widespread debate, for he knew his countrymen well. He was not only a popular playwright but also a general, state treasurer, priest, and friend of Pericles.

Classical religion was less sure of itself than its Archaic predecessor. A few people even questioned the very existence of the gods, although most Greeks wanted religion to be adapted to the new age, not discarded altogether. Thus Athenian religion was tailored to the needs of a democratic and imperial city. In the 440s B.C., under Pericles' leadership, Athens embarked on a vast, ambitious, and expensive temple-building project, using Delian League funds and serving as a large public employment program. Temples were built in and around the city, most notably on the Athenian Acropolis.

To adapt religion to a new age, new cults also were introduced. The most popular was the worship of Asclipius, god of healing. Traditionally a minor figure and considered a son of Apollo, Asclipius became enormously popular in his own right beginning in the late fifth century B.C., perhaps in response to the high mortality of the Peloponnesian War. Outside Athens, large shrines to Asclipius at Epidauros (in the Peloponnesus)

The Parthenon *The temple of Athena Parthenos ("the Maiden") on the Athenian Acropolis, the Parthenon was dedicated in 438 B.C. One of the largest and most complex Greek temples, it was built of fine marble. The partially restored ruins symbolize the wealth, power, and greatness of Classical Greece.* (William Katz/Photo Researchers)

and Cos (an island off the Anatolian coast) became pilgrimage centers in the fourth century B.C. for ailing people in search of a cure.

Women played a major role in Classical Athenian religion. They were priestesses in more than forty major cults. They participated each year in many festivals, including several reserved only for women. One such festival, the Thesmophoria, a celebration of fertility held each autumn, featured a three-day encampment of women on a hillside in the city, right beside the Athenian assembly amphitheater. Women also attended public funeral orations in honor of soldiers who had died in battle. They probably attended plays as well.

Pericles was very much influenced by a woman, Aspasia. She belonged to the small group of noncitizen women called *hetairai,* or courtesans (that is, prostitutes patronized by men of wealth and status). An educated woman from Miletus, Aspasia was for many years Pericles' mistress and bore him a son. Aspasia and Pericles gathered around them a glittering circle of thinkers and artists. Some say that Aspasia even influenced Pericles' political decisions.

In art, Classical sculptors completed the process begun by their Archaic forebears of mastering the accurate representation of the human body. In anatomical precision, Classical Greek sculpture was the most technically proficient sculpture the world had seen. Like Archaic sculpture, it was not, however, an attempt to portray humans "warts and all" but rather an idealization of the human form.

The Sophists and Socrates

Success in democratic politics required a knowledge of oratory. This demand was met in the late fifth century B.C. by the arrival in Athens of itinerant professional teachers of *rhetoric,* the art of speaking. They were known as Sophists (from a word meaning "instruct" or "make wise"). Sicilian Greeks invented rhetoric around 465 B.C. by drawing up the rules of argument. For a fee—rarely small and sometimes astronomical—Sophists taught young Athenians the art of speaking. Their curriculum consisted not only of rhetoric but also of the rudiments of linguistics, ethics, psychology, history, and anthropology—in other words, any aspect of "human nature" that might help an aspiring politician. Within a few years most ambitious young Athenians of prosperous families were studying with Sophists.

At their best, Sophists sharpened young minds. Athenian tragedians, historians, and philosophers all benefited from sophistic teaching. Protagoras (b. ca. 485 B.C.), perhaps the best-known Sophist, summed up the spirit of the age in his famous dictum "Man is the measure of all things"—an appropriate credo for the interest in all things human that is apparent in Classical literature and art. There is, however, a more troubling side to the Sophists. As teachers of rhetoric, they taught respect for success, not for truth. Thus they acquired a reputation as word-twisters who taught men how to make "the weaker argument defeat the stronger."

Much to the distress of conservatives, Sophists drew a distinction between *nomos,* a word that means "law" or "convention," and *physis,* which means "nature." The distinction had revolutionary potential. In general, Sophists had little respect for the established order, or nomos. They considered it mere convention. A great man trained by a Sophist might rise above convention to realize the limitless potential of his nature, or physis. If he used his skill to overturn democracy and establish a tyranny, so much the worse for democracy. Indeed, the Sophists trained both unscrupulous democratic politicians and many of the oligarchs who launched coups d'état against Athenian democracy at the end of the fifth century B.C. As a result, *sophist* became a term of abuse in Athens and remains so to this day.

Classical Greek advances in rhetoric, therefore, were as problematic as they were brilliant. The Sophists had a wide-ranging effect on many different branches of thought. Consider, for example, the work of the philosopher Democritus (b. ca. 460 B.C.), a native of the northern Greek polis of Abdera but a visitor to Athens. Democritus was not a Sophist, but he shared the common Sophistic notion that the reality of nature was far more radical than conventionally thought. He concluded that all things consisted of tiny, indivisible particles, which could be arranged and rearranged in an infinite variety of configurations. He called these particles *atoma,* "the uncuttable" (from which the word *atom* is derived).

The physicians of the Aegean island of Cos are known as Hippocratics, from Hippocrates (b. ca. 460 B.C.), the first great thinker of their school. If they were not directly influenced by the Sophists, they shared similar habits of thought. Like the Sophists, the Hippocratics were religious skeptics. They considered disease to be strictly a natural phenomenon in which the gods played no part. Hippocratic medicine was noteworthy for its methodology, which emphasized observation and prognosis (the reasoned prediction of future developments). The Hippocratics were the most rigorously naturalistic physicians to date, although no more successful in healing illness than earlier practitioners.

In the fifth century B.C. not all thinkers welcomed the conclusions of the Sophists. Perhaps their most notable critic, and the greatest of all fifth-century B.C. philosophers, was Socrates (469–399 B.C.). Unlike the Sophists, he charged no fees, had no formal students, and did not claim to teach any positive body of knowledge. His main virtue, he believed, was his awareness of his ignorance. Unlike the Sophists, most of whom were metics, Socrates was an Athenian citizen.

Socrates, however, resembled the Sophists in his intense interest in political theory. Like any good Athenian citizen, Socrates served in the military—as a hoplite during the Peloponnesian War. He had his doubts about democracy, which he criticized for inefficiency and for giving an equal voice to the uneducated. He preferred rule by a wise elite. Nonetheless, Socrates was too loyal an Athenian to advocate revolution.

Yet Socrates made many enemies because of his role as a self-styled "gadfly." He stung the pride of Athens's leaders by demonstrating their ignorance. Mistakenly considered a Sophist by the public because of his unconventional opinions, Socrates was tried, convicted, and executed in 399 B.C. by an Athenian court for alleged atheism and "corrupting the young." The Athenian public soon had second thoughts, and the trial of Socrates is usually considered one of history's great miscarriages of justice, as well as one of Athenian democracy's greatest blunders.

Socrates was trained in the Ionian natural philosophy tradition. He went beyond it, as the Roman thinker Cicero later said, by bringing philosophy "down from the heavens into the streets"; he changed the emphasis from the natural world to human ethics. Like most Greeks, Socrates believed that the purpose of life was the pursuit of aretê. Unlike his contemporaries, however, he did not consider aretê to be primarily excellence in battle or in public life but rather excellence in philosophy. One became good by studying the truth, which is part of what Socrates meant by his saying "Virtue (aretê) is knowledge." He also meant that no one who truly understood goodness would ever choose to do evil.

Teach people well, Socrates says, and they will behave morally. Socrates has gone down in history as an inspiring teacher despite his protestations of not teaching anything. His emphasis was not on research or writing, and in fact he refused to write anything down. He believed that truth can be found only in persons, not through books—that philosophy requires a thoughtful verbal exchange. His favorite technique was to ask people difficult questions. Pedagogy that relies on inquiry is still called the "Socratic method."

Plato and Aristotle   Because Socrates never wrote anything down, we are dependent on others for our knowledge of him. Fortunately for us, he inspired students who committed his words and ideas to paper. Socrates' most distinguished student, and our most important source for his thought, was Plato (427–348 B.C.), who in turn was the teacher of Aristotle (384–322 B.C.). Together, these three men laid the foundations of the Western philosophical tradition. They were thinkers for the ages, but each was also a man of his times.

Socrates grew up in confident Periclean days. Plato came of age during the Peloponnesian War, a period culminating in the execution of Socrates. Shocked and disillusioned, Plato turned his back on public life, although he was an Athenian citizen. Instead of discussing philosophy in public, Plato founded a private school in an Athenian suburb, the Academy. Plato held a low opinion of democracy, and when he did intervene in politics, it was not in Athens but in far-off Syracuse (in Sicily). Syracuse was governed by a tyranny, and Plato hoped to educate the tyrant's heir in philosophy—a vain hope, as it turned out.

In an attempt to recapture the stimulating give-and-take of a conversation with Socrates, Plato did not write straightforward philosophical treatises but instead dialogues or speeches. All of Plato's dialogues have more than one speaker, and in most the main speaker is named "Socrates." Sometimes this figure is the historical Socrates, sometimes merely a mouthpiece for ideas Plato wished to explore.

A voluminous writer, Plato is not easily summarized. The word that best characterizes his legacy, though, is *idealism,* of which Plato is one of Western philosophy's greatest exponents. Like Parmenides, Plato believed that the senses are misleading. Truth exists but is attained only by training the mind to overcome commonsense evidence. The model for Plato's philosophical method is geometry. Just as geometry deals not with this or that triangle or rectangle but with ideal forms—with a pure triangle, a pure rectangle—so the philosopher could learn to recognize purity. A philosopher would not be misled by, for example, comparing aretê in Athens, Sparta, and Persia; a philosopher would understand the meaning of pure, ideal aretê. No relativist, Plato believed in absolute good and evil.

Philosophy is not for everyone, according to Plato. Only a few people have the necessary intelligence and discipline. In the *Republic,* a dialogue that is perhaps his best-known work, Plato demonstrates the nature of his idealism and its political consequences. He envisioned a society whose elite would study philosophy and attain enlightenment. They would understand the vanity of political ambition but would nonetheless accept the responsibility of governing the masses. Plato never makes clear precisely why they should assume this burden. It is possible he was enough of a traditionalist, in spite of himself, to consider a citizen's responsibility to the polis to be obvious. In any case, Plato's ideal state was one in which philosophers would rule as kings, benevolently and unselfishly.

Plato explored the details of such a state in the *Republic* and in other dialogues, particularly the *Laws.* It is not clear how wedded he was to specific details; indeed, some of them may have been meant merely to shock or to satirize. An overall picture emerges, however. The ideal state would be like a small polis: self-sufficient and closed to outside corrupt influences like Sparta, but committed to the pursuit of things intellectual like Athens. Society would be sharply divided into three classes—philosophers, soldiers, and farmers—with admission to each class based on merit rather than heredity. Poetry and drama would be strictly censored. Plato advocated public education and toyed with more radical notions: not only gender equality but also the abolition of the family and private property, institutions that he felt led to disunity and dissension.

Plato's ideas have always been controversial but almost never ignored. Even in his own day, most people considered Plato far too radical. The writings of his great student Aristotle were more to contemporary tastes. Originally from Macedonia, Aristotle spent most of his life in Athens, first as a student at the Academy, then as the founder of his own school, the Lyceum. Like Plato, Aristotle wrote dialogues, but none has survived. His main extant works are treatises, largely compilations by students of his lecture notes. One of the most wide-ranging intellectuals, Aristotle had a voracious appetite for knowledge and for writing. His treatises embrace politics, ethics, poetry, botany, physics, metaphysics, astronomy, rhetoric, zoology, logic, and psychology.

Though influenced by Plato's idealism, Aristotle was a far more practical, down-to-earth thinker. His father had been a doctor, which may account for Aristotle's interest in applied science and in biology and the biological method. Unlike Plato, Aristotle placed great emphasis on observation and fieldwork and on classification and systemization.

Aristotle agreed with Plato about the existence of absolute standards of good and evil, but he emphasized the relevance of such standards to everyday life. Unlike Plato, Aristotle considered the senses important guides. Change, he believed, was not an illusion but rather an important phenomenon. Aristotle's view of change was teleological—that is, he emphasized the goal (*telos* in Greek) of change. According to Aristotle, every organism changes and grows toward a particular end and is an integral and harmonious part of a larger whole. The entire cosmos is teleological, and each and every one of its parts has a purpose. Behind the cosmos was a principle that Aristotle called "the unmoved mover," the supreme cause of existence.

Aristotle defined an object's aretê as the fulfillment of its inherent function in the cosmos. The aretê of a horse, for example, was to be strong, fast, and obedient; the aretê of a rose was to look beautiful and smell sweet. As for the aretê of a human being, Aristotle agreed with Plato: only the philosopher achieved true aretê. As a pragmatist, however, Aristotle did not imagine philosophers becoming kings. Even so, he did not advocate democracy, which he considered mob rule. Instead, he advocated a government of wealthy gentlemen who had been trained by philosophers—not the best regime imaginable but, in Aristotle's opinion, the best one possible.

Aristotle believed that men had stronger capacities to make judgments than women and so should rule over them. He condemned states like Sparta that accorded power to women. Hence Aristotle would be cited in later centuries to justify male dominance. Ironically, however, Aristotle was more enlightened on gender issues than most of his contemporaries. For example, he believed that since women played a crucial role in the family, they should receive education in morality.

Aristotle may be the single most influential thinker in Western history. His scientific writings not only were the most influential philosophical classics of Greek civilization, and of Roman civilization as well, but they remained so during the Middle Ages in the Arabic and Latin worlds. It took nearly two thousand years for serious rivals to challenge Aristotle's intellectual supremacy.

Athenian Drama

Perhaps the greatest art form that emerged in the polis was drama. Modern comedy and tragedy find distant ancestors in the productions of Athens's theater of Dionysus, named for the god of unrestraint, liberation, and wine. Comedy and tragedy began in religious festivals honoring Dionysus (also known as Bacchus) but quickly became an independent forum for comment on public life. Ancient drama was poetry, not prose. Because it highlighted the relation of the individual to the community, drama proved to be the most suitable poetic medium for the ideology of the polis.

According to ancient tradition, tragedy was first presented at the Dionysian festival in Athens by Thespis in the 530s B.C. (hence the word *thespian* for "actor"). The first surviving tragedy dates from the 470s B.C., the first surviving comedy from the 420s B.C. A play in the fifth century B.C. consisted of a chorus (a group of performers work-

Theater at Delphi *Open to the air, an ancient Greek theater contained tiers of stone benches above a circular area where the action took place, behind which backdrops could be erected. The audience often had a view of stirring scenery that, at Delphi, included the temple of Apollo and the valley below.* (Vanni/Art Resource, NY)

ing in unison) and three individual actors, who played all the various individual speaking parts. Plays were performed in an open-air theater on the south hillside of the Acropolis. Enormously popular, drama spread all over Greece, and eventually most poleis had a theater.

Classical Athenian tragedy was performed at the annual Dionysia in March. Each playwright would submit a trilogy of plays on a central theme, plus a raucous farce to break the tension afterward. Comedies, which were independent plays rather than trilogies, were performed both at the Dionysia and at a separate festival held in winter. Wealthy producers competed to outfit the most lavish and impressive productions. Judges would award prizes for the best plays—a typical reflection of Greek competitiveness.

Tragedy is not easy to define, except generally: a serious play with an unhappy ending. Perhaps a short tag from the playwright Aeschylus can be said to sum up tragedy: *pathos mathei,* "suffering teaches." The essence of tragedy is what has been called the tragic sense of life: the nobility in the spectacle of a great man or woman failing but learning from failure. In *Oedipus the Tyrant* (ca. 428 B.C.) by Sophocles, for example, the hero unknowingly kills his father and unknowingly marries his mother. Oedipus cannot escape the consequences of his deeds, but he can react to his fate with dignity and heroism; he can try to understand it. Oedipus loses his power as tyrant and goes into exile, but he retains a degree of honor. He carries out his own punishment by blinding himself. As Aristotle observed, tragedy derives its emotional power from the fear and pity that it evokes and from the purification of the senses (*katharsis*) that it leaves in its aftermath.

The great period of Attic tragedy began and ended in the fifth century B.C. Aeschylus (525–456 B.C.), Sophocles (ca. 495–406 B.C.), and Euripides (ca. 485–406 B.C.) were and are considered the three giant playwrights. Although other tragedians wrote plays, only the works of these three men (or, rather, a small fraction of their works) have survived. Aeschylus was perhaps the most pious of the three. His plays—notably the trilogy of the *Oresteia* (the *Agamemnon,* the *Libation Bearers,* and the *Eumenides*), the only surviving tragic trilogy, dating from 458 B.C.—take as their central question the justice of Zeus. The subject is the myth of the House of Atreus—in particular, the murder of King Agamemnon by his much-wronged wife, Clytemnestra, and her murder in turn by their son, Orestes, avenging his father. Aeschylus casts this primitive saga into an epic of the discovery of justice. In fulfillment of the will of Zeus, Athena puts an end to vengeance killings and institutes the supposed first court of law: the court of the Areopagus in Athens.

Sophocles, too, was interested in divine justice. His tragedies focus on the relationship between the individual and the community. Heroic individuals have a spark of the divine in them, but their towering virtues are threats to ordinary people. In *Antigone* (ca. 442 B.C.), for example, the heroine refuses to compromise with injustice. Her late brother had committed treason, for which his corpse is denied burial—the standard Greek punishment. Antigone, however, insists on following a higher law, Zeus's law, which demands that all bodies be buried. Turmoil, disorder, and death ensue, but Antigone stays true to principle.

Of the three tragedians, Euripides is the least traditional and the most influenced by the Sophists. His plays reflect the disillusionment of the Peloponnesian War era. Euripides was more impressed by divine power than by divine justice. The central gods of Aeschylean drama are Zeus the father and Apollo the lawgiver, while Sophocles focuses on semidivine heroes, but Euripides' major deities are Dionysus and Aphrodite, goddess of erotic passion. In the *Bacchae* (406 B.C.), for example, an arrogant young king named Pentheus is punished for refusing to recognize the power of Dionysus (Bacchus). When he goes to the hills to spy on drunken women, called "Bacchae," who are worshiping the god, he ends up as their prisoner. Driven to frenzy by Dionysus, the women do not recognize the king. Indeed, Pentheus's own mother, one of the Bacchae, mistakes him for an animal and kills him.

The changes in tragedy from Aeschylus to Euripides reflect the changes in Athens as first imperial arrogance and then the Peloponnesian War took their moral toll. Aeschylus's confidence in the goodness of the community gives way first to a focus on the individual struggling to be good and then to a fundamental doubt about the possibility of goodness. The civic order, celebrated so confidently at the end of the *Oresteia* (458 B.C.), looks less certain in Sophocles' *Oedipus* (ca. 428 B.C.) and by the time of Euripides' *Bacchae* (406 B.C.) seems terrifyingly weak.

Comedy, too, was invented in Athens in the Classical period. Like tragedy, comedy offers a moral commentary on contemporary Athenian life. Unlike tragedy, which is usually set in the past and takes its characters from mythology, Athenian comedy (the so-called Old Comedy) is set in the present and pokes fun at politicians and public figures. Whereas tragedy is generally serious and sad, comedy is light, biting, and humorous.

The greatest writer of comedy in the fifth century B.C. was Aristophanes (ca. 455–385 B.C.). His extant plays are lively, ribald, even scatological, and full of allusions to contemporary politics. Aristophanes loved to show the "little guy" getting the better of the powerful and women deflating the pretensions of men. In *Lysistrata* (411 B.C.), his best-known play, he imagines the women of Greece stopping the Peloponnesian War by going on a sex strike, which forces the men to make peace.

Historical Thought and Writing Like drama, history flourished in the exciting intellectual atmosphere of classical Athens. Indeed, its two greatest historians, Herodotus (ca. 485–425 B.C.) and Thucydides (ca. 455–397 B.C.), are among the founders of history-writing in the West. This judgment is not meant to discount the contributions of, for example, the Hittites or Hebrews, or the chronicles, inventories, and genealogies of early Greece. Herodotus and Thucydides, however, are more rationalistic than their predecessors, and their subject matter is war, politics, peoples, and customs—what we think of as the stuff of history-writing today. Indeed, the word *history* comes from a word used by Herodotus, *historiai,* meaning "inquiries" or "research."

The works of Herodotus (*The Histories*) and Thucydides (*The Peloponnesian War*) have unifying themes. The thread through *The Histories* is the cyclical rise and fall of empires. Herodotus sees the Persian Wars as merely one episode in a vast historical drama. Again and again, hardy, disciplined peoples conquered their neighbors, grew wealthy, were corrupted by a life of luxury, and were eventually conquered in turn. Success made people arrogant, driving them to commit injustices, which were eventually punished by Zeus. The breadth of Herodotus's vision is noteworthy. A native of Halicarnassus (a polis on the southwestern coast of Anatolia), Herodotus traveled widely, eventually settling in Athens. He wrote not only about Greeks but also about Persians, Egyptians, and a host of other peoples in Europe, Asia, and Africa.

Only a child at the time of the Persian Wars, Herodotus gathered information by interviewing older people in various countries as well as by checking what limited written public records existed. Herodotus also wrote about previous centuries and places he had not visited, but with uneven accuracy. He could rarely resist a good story, and alongside solid research are tall tales, unconfirmed accounts, and myths.

Thucydides, by contrast, prided himself on accuracy. He confined himself mainly to writing about an event that he had lived through and participated in: the Peloponnesian War. A failed Athenian general, Thucydides spent most of the Peloponnesian War in exile, carefully observing, taking notes, and writing.

Like Herodotus, Thucydides was influenced by the grandeur of Classical tragedy. He also shows the signs of the Sophist movement, especially in the finely crafted speeches he includes in his writing. Thucydides' great theme is the disastrous effect of war on the human soul. His case study, the Peloponnesian War, proved that war is a harsh teacher: it strips away the veneer of civilization and reveals the savagery of human nature. In Thucydides' opinion, Periclean Athens was a high point in the history of civilization. The strain of prolonged war, however, destroyed Athens's moral fiber as well as its empire.

IMPORTANT EVENTS

ca. 750 B.C. Greek colonization of Magna Graecia begins

ca. 725 B.C. Sparta conquers Messenia

ca. 675 B.C. Pheidon becomes tyrant of Argos

ca. 625 B.C. Sappho active as poet

594 B.C. Solon is archon in Athens

ca. 560 B.C. Pisistratus becomes tyrant of Athens

508 B.C. Cleisthenes begins reforms in Athens

499 B.C. Ionians revolt against Persia

490 B.C. Battle of Marathon

480–479 B.C. Persia invades Greece

477 B.C. Delian League founded

460–429 B.C. Pericles at peak of power

458 B.C. Aeschylus's Oresteia first performed in Athens

431–404 B.C. Peloponnesian War

399 B.C. Trial of Socrates

395–386 B.C. Corinthian War

371 B.C. Battle of Leuctra

NOTES

1. Excerpt from a poem by Solon, quoted in Aristotle, *Constitution of Athens,* trans. Barry S. Strauss.
2. Charles Rowan Beye, *Ancient Greek Literature and Society,* 2d ed. (Ithaca, N.Y.: Cornell University Press, 1987), p. 78.
3. Ibid., p. 79.
4. Adapted from Richmond Lattimore, trans., *Greek Lyrics,* 2d ed. (Chicago: University of Chicago Press, 1960), p. 19.
5. Herodotus, *The Histories,* trans. Barry S. Strauss.
6. Thucydides, *The Peloponnesian War,* trans. Barry S. Strauss.

SUGGESTED READING

Biers, W. *The Archaeology of Ancient Greece: An Introduction.* 2d. ed. 1996. A clear presentation of the achievements and variety of archaeological excavation in Greece.

Boardman, John. *The Greeks Overseas: Their Early Colonies and Trade.* 4th ed. 1999. The standard introduction; authoritative, vivid, updated, and beautifully illustrated.

Cartledge, Paul. *The Spartans: The World of the Warrior-Heroes of Ancient Greece.* 2003. A lively and reliable introduction by a great expert on ancient Sparta.

Connolly, Peter, and Hazel Dodge. *The Ancient City: Life in Classical Athens and Rome.* 1998. Connolly's gorgeous illustrations and outstanding reconstructions distinguish this introduction to daily life in the two cities.

Hanson, Victor Davis. *The Wars of the Ancient Greeks*. 1999. A good introduction, especially to land warfare, by a leading military historian.

Martin, Thomas. *Ancient Greece from Prehistoric to Hellenistic Times*. 2000. A readable and scholarly introduction emphasizing politics and war.

Pomeroy, Sarah B. *Goddesses, Whores, Wives, and Slaves: Women in Classical Antiquity*. 1975. An overview of women in politics and society in Greece, the Hellenistic world, and Rome; still the best introduction to the subject.

Pomeroy, Sarah B., Stanley M. Burstein, Walter Donlan, and Jennifer Tolbert Roberts. *Ancient Greece: A Political, Social, and Cultural History*. 1999. A balanced introduction from the prehistoric to Hellenistic periods, with special emphasis on Classical Greece.

Strauss, Barry S. *Salamis: The Greatest Naval Battle of the Ancient World*. 2004. Opens a window onto Greece and Persia while telling a gripping story.

4

Alexander the Great and the Spread of Greek Civilization, ca. 350–30 B.C.

The young men in the pebble mosaic shown here wield ax and sword against the stag whom they are hunting. The artist, named Gnosis, was a master at rendering perspective and drama. Clearly, no expense was spared on the work, dated around 325 B.C. Both the vigor of the scene and the quality of the craftsmanship symbolize the spirit of a young man who was born in Pella, the Macedonian capital where the mosaic was displayed: that man was Alexander the Great. Alexander was a fearless warrior and one of the most brilliant generals in the history of the world. In just twelve years he conquered all the territory between Greece and India, as well as Egypt.

Alexander created new realities of power as king of Macedon (r. 336–323 B.C.). A northeastern Greek kingdom that had previously been only a fringe power, Macedon rose meteorically under Alexander's father, Philip II (r. 359–336 B.C.), to become the leading military power in Greece. Philip was a brilliant and ambitious general, but Alexander outstripped him.

Alexander laid the foundations of a new Greek world: the world of the Hellenistic period (323–30 B.C.), in which Hellenic, or Greek, language and civilization spread and were transformed. This era was distinct in many ways from the preceding Hellenic period (ca. 750–323 B.C.). In Hellenistic times, Macedonians and Greeks replaced Persians as the ruling people of Egypt and western Asia. Large numbers of Greek-speaking colonists moved south and east. Governed by Macedonian dynasties, Egypt and the Levant became integral parts of the Greek world and remained so until the Arab conquest in the seventh century A.D. Greek-speaking kingdoms thrived briefly as far east as modern Afghanistan and Pakistan. At times the new ruling elite was open to natives who learned Greek and adopted Greek ways, but more often natives were excluded and exploited.

Conquest put huge amounts of wealth into Greek hands. Alexander and his successors built great new cities: Antioch in Syria, Pergamum in Anatolia, Seleucia in Mesopotamia, and, greatest of all, Alexandria in Egypt. Trade increased and expanded southward and eastward. In political life, individual cities continued to be important, but federal leagues (that is, unions of city-states) and monarchies ruled most of the Greek-speaking world.

Material and political expansion led to unanticipated cultural changes, which may be summarized as a turn inward. Frequently finding themselves among strange peoples, the Greeks sought comfort in new philosophies, religions, and modes of literary and artistic expression. Many of these new cultural forms emphasized people's emotions and intentions, not simply their actions. Science, meanwhile, flourished under royal patronage, as did the emerging discipline of literary criticism. The prestige of royal women tended to promote improvements in the overall status of Greek women.

Hellenistic Greeks boasted of having created one world—a common, or ecumenical (from the Greek *oikoumene*, "inhabited") region. In truth, that world was complex. Native cultures flourished, while Greeks adapted and Hellenized a number of Egyptian and Asian deities.

Hellenistic Greek contact with one native culture in particular—Judaism—proved to have a lasting impact on the West. Under the impact of the Greeks, Judaism became more self-conscious and placed a greater emphasis on salvation, martyrdom, and individual study and prayer. Some Jews resisted Greek culture, others adopted it, and still others resolved to convert Greeks to Judaism. Reshaped by its contacts with the Greeks, Hellenistic Judaism was poised to transform Western religion.

PHILIP AND ALEXANDER

The Hellenistic world was founded by two conquerors: Philip II of Macedon (382–336 B.C.) and his son, Alexander III, known as Alexander the Great (356–323 B.C.). After a century of indecisive warfare among the Greek city-states, Philip swept south and conquered them in twenty years. In even less time Alexander conquered Egypt and all of western Asia as far east as modern India. The legacy of these impressive conquests was to spread Greek civilization and to change it, both of which consequences were revolutionary developments.

The Rise of Macedon

Macedon was a border state, long weaker than its more advanced neighbors but capable of learning from them and ultimately of conquering them. Though rich in resources and manpower, Macedon lacked the relatively efficient organization of the polis. It included both tribal groups and scattered cities. Several dialects of Greek were spoken, some unintelligible to southern Greeks, who considered Macedonians "barbarians" (from the Greek *barbaros,* meaning "a person who does not speak Greek"). Ordinary Macedonians lived rough, sturdy lives, while the king and the royal court inhabited a sophisticated capital city, Pella, where they sponsored visits by leading Greek artists and writers. Philip confounded Greek stereotypes of Macedonian barbarism by turning out to be a brilliant soldier and statesman—a man of vast ambition, appetite, and energy. A hard drinker, vain, and a man with numerous wives and lovers, he was also an excellent orator and general. Philip's goals were to make himself dominant in Macedon and then, after neutralizing opposition in Greece, to conquer the Persian Empire, or at least its holdings in Anatolia. He accomplished all but the last.

The instrument of Philip's success was his army, a well-trained, professional, year-round force. Macedon, with its plains and horses, was cavalry country, and Philip raised cavalry to a new level of importance. In battle, the Macedonian phalanx would first hold the enemy phalanx until the cavalry could find a weak spot and break the enemy line. Then the phalanx would attack and finish the job. Macedonian hoplites carried extra-long pikes to keep the enemy at a distance. Philip also mastered the technology of siegecraft, raising it to a level unseen since Assyrian days (see page 36).

Philip used his army effectively. After capturing the lucrative gold mine of Mount Pangaeum in Thrace (the region east of Macedon), he turned to the Greek city-states nearby. Olynthus, the most important, fell in 348 B.C. Led by the Athenian Demosthenes (ca. 385–322 B.C.), the main Greek city-states prepared to make a stand. Demosthenes was a superb orator, but his attempts to forge a unified force came too late. By 338 B.C., when an Atheno-Theban army met the Macedonians, Philip had already won over much of the Greek world through diplomacy, bribes, and threats. His complete military victory at Chaeronea in Boeotia was followed up with a lenient settlement in which all the Greeks except Sparta acknowledged Philip's hegemony. The Greeks would rebel against Macedon more than once but always in vain, until they fell under the even greater power of Rome. The polis would no longer decide the fate of the eastern Mediterranean.

In 336 B.C. Philip was murdered by a disgruntled courtier, and the invasion of the Persian Empire fell to his 20-year-old son, Alexander, the new king.

Alexander the Conqueror

Alexander III of Macedon (r. 336–323 B.C.) is as famous in art as in literature, in romance as in history, in Iran and India as in Europe and America. Yet the evidence for the historical

Alexander is almost as problematic as that for the historical Socrates or Jesus. After Alexander's untimely death at age 32, contemporaries wrote histories and memoirs, but none has survived. Several good historical accounts, based on earlier texts, are extant, but none was written less than three hundred years after Alexander's day. Alexander, moreover, was not only a legend in his own time but also a master propagandist. Many of the incidents of his life took place in remote regions or among a few individuals, and they tended to grow with the telling.

Still, Alexander's virtues are clear. He was charismatic, handsome, intelligent, and well educated; as a teenager he had Aristotle himself as a private tutor. Alexander was ruthless as well as cultured. He began his reign with a massacre of his male relatives, but he brought a team of Greek scientists along with him on his expedition through the Persian Empire. Although he destroyed peoples and places, Alexander founded twenty cities. One of those cities was born in 331 B.C., at the site of a fishing village in the northwestern part of Egypt's delta. Alexander and his advisers planned a great trading center to replace Tyre, whose inhabitants had been killed or enslaved by the Macedonians who had stormed the town in 332 B.C. The new city, called Alexandria, later grew into the largest city in the Mediterranean.

For all his varied interests, Alexander was first and foremost a warrior. Battlefield commander of the Macedonian cavalry at age 18, he devoted most of the rest of his life to warfare. As a leader of men, Alexander was popular and inspiring, and he shared risks with his troops. He knew the value of propaganda and took pains to depict his

Alexander Mosaic *This detail of a Roman-era mosaic from Pompeii shows Alexander the Great in battle, probably at Issus. Shining in his battle armor, Alexander is bareheaded, with a wide-eyed, intense gaze betokening his power. The larger scene includes the Persian king Darius, fleeing in his chariot.* (Scala/Art Resource, NY)

expedition to the Greek city-states as a war of revenge for Persia's invasion of Greece in 480 B.C. instead of what it actually was: the onslaught of Macedonian imperialism. He loved the colorful gesture. He began his expedition to conquer Persia in 334 B.C. by sacrificing animals to the gods at Troy, a site evoking Homer's heroes.

On the eve of invasion, Persia vastly outnumbered Macedon on both land and sea. Darius III of Persia was rich; Alexander's treasury was virtually empty. The Macedonian expeditionary force was short on supplies. The peoples in Persia's multi-ethnic empire were restive, but so too were Alexander's Greek allies, the mainstay of his fleet. One of Darius's advisers proposed a naval campaign to raise a revolt in Greece and force the Macedonians home. How, then, did Alexander propose to conquer Persia?

The answer was the Macedonian army. Although Alexander invaded Anatolia with only about thirty-five thousand men, they were the fastest-marching, most experienced, and most skilled army in the eastern Mediterranean. If Persia would fight the Macedonians in a set battle, Alexander might be confident of victory—and it appeared that Persia would indeed fight. Persian elite ideology impelled the army to face the enemy head-on. Darius, moreover, was a new monarch and a usurper, and so under pressure to prove himself in the field. As expected, Macedon crushed the enemy. The war was de-

Conquests of Philip and Alexander

Between 359 and 323 B.C., the armies of Macedon conquered first the Greek city-states and then the Persian Empire. Macedonian power extended from Greece and Egypt eastward to modern India.

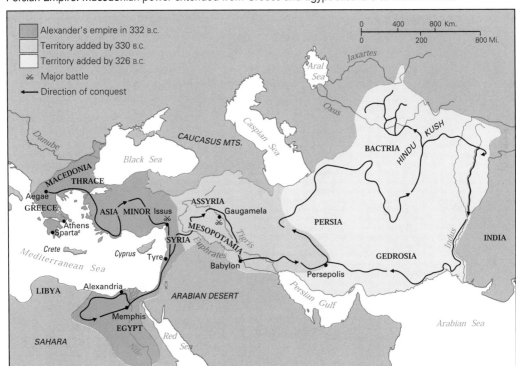

cided in three great battles: at the Granicus River in Anatolia (334 B.C.), at Issus in Syria (333 B.C.), and at Gaugamela in Mesopotamia (331 B.C.). Darius fled into Iran and was deposed, assassinated, and replaced by a man whom Alexander captured and executed. By 328 B.C. Alexander's claim to be king of Persia was sealed with blood and iron.

Having conquered the Persian heartland, Alexander turned eastward. The last seven years of his career are marked by three themes. First is the continuing and, in Alexander's mind, apparently open-ended military campaign. He pushed his army not only into the eastern parts of the Persian Empire but beyond, into modern Pakistan, which had not been controlled by Persia since the early fifth century B.C. The Macedonians won a major victory there in 326 B.C. near the Hydaspes River (modern Jhelum River) over the army of King Porus, a force employing as many as two hundred elephants. Alexander's infantry suffered considerable casualties before inflicting enough wounds on the elephants to make them uncontrollable. Alexander prepared to continue eastward, perhaps as far as the Bay of Bengal, but his exhausted and homesick men had other plans. They mutinied beside the Hyphasis River (modern Beas River, near the modern Indo-Pakistani border) and forced Alexander finally to turn back. He reached Persia in late 325 B.C.

The second theme of Alexander's later career is his increasing despotism. After conquering Persia, Alexander turned on the Macedonian nobility, among whom he feared potential rivals, for Macedonian nobles had a tradition of rebelling against strong kings. The years after 330 B.C. were marked by conspiracy trials, purges, and assassinations. The most spectacular took place in 328 in Maracanda (modern Samarkand, located in Uzbekistan), where, after a drunken quarrel, Alexander murdered Cleitus, one of his senior commanders.

Another sign of Alexander's growing despotism was his demand for the trappings of Persian kingship. After conquering Persia, for example, he made independent-minded Greeks and Macedonians bow down before him. He required that the Greek city-states deify him. "If Alexander wishes to be a god, let him be," was the concise reply of the Spartans, but Alexander had set a precedent for both Hellenistic monarchs and Roman emperors.

The third theme of Alexander's later career is his novel policy of fusion. After returning from the Indian subcontinent, Alexander began training an army of thirty thousand Iranians and dismissed a large number of Macedonian troops. He forced his main commanders to marry Iranian women, just as he himself did. In 324 B.C. Alexander staged a grand banquet in Mesopotamia for nine thousand, at which he prayed for "concord and a partnership in rule between Greeks and Persians." Such actions were a sharp break with the traditional Greek belief in their national superiority. Aristotle, for example, had referred to the peoples of western Asia as fit only to be slaves. Alexander's policy probably owed less to idealism than to a desire for a new power base independent of the Macedonian nobility.

Alexander died in Babylon in June 323 B.C., a month before he turned 33, probably of malarial fever, although some contemporaries suspected poison and some historians have suggested drunkenness. Alexander did not designate a successor. His wife, pregnant at his death, would give birth to a son and heir, but he was shunted aside by the Macedonian generals, who began a long and bloody round of wars over the spoils of empire. It took approximately fifty years of fighting, from 322 to 275 B.C., to make clear

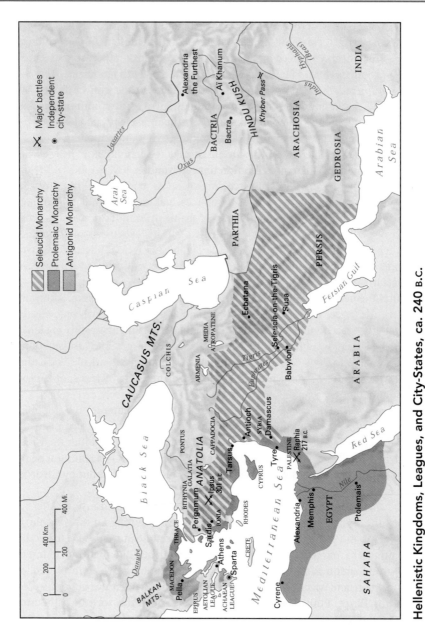

Hellenistic Kingdoms, Leagues, and City-States, ca. 240 B.C.

After Alexander's death, his empire lost its political unity. Great new cities and kingdoms arose in the lands he had conquered.

that three large kingdoms—Macedon (under the Antigonid dynasty), Ptolemaic Egypt, and the Seleucid realm—would inherit most of Alexander's empire. The rest was divided among small kingdoms, federal leagues, and independent city-states.

In the long run, Alexander's life was far more influential than his death. His conquests did nothing less than lay the foundations of the Hellenistic world. It is ironic to measure in such impersonal terms the achievements of one who, more than most people in history, exemplifies individual success. Whether it was exalting a savior or debunking a hero, much of Hellenistic culture centered on the myth of heroism that Alexander had engendered. Historians who insist that the individual is insignificant will rarely have a more challenging refutation than Alexander.

THE HELLENISTIC KINGDOMS, 323–30 B.C.

Variety, flexibility, and the creation of a new elite to transmit Greek culture compose the Hellenistic political legacy. Hellenistic political units ranged from multi-ethnic kingdoms to small, ethnically homogeneous city-states. The Greek peninsula saw both a monarchy with republican pretensions and experiments in federalism and social revolution. In Asia and Egypt, a new ruling elite emerged consisting both of Greeks and Macedonians and of natives. Although the first group tended to dominate high office, natives were by no means excluded. The immigrants wanted land, wealth, or adventure. Their paths were smoothed by a new ideology that identified being Greek less with loyalty to an individual city than with participation in a common Greek civilization.

Although the Hellenistic world became relatively peaceful after 275 B.C., conflict among the kingdoms continued. Generally waged at a low level of intensity, with bribes and diplomacy as weapons, the conflict nonetheless sometimes broke out into major battles. A number of small states emerged in Anatolia, notably Pergamum, whose wealthy rulers were patrons of literature and art, and Galatia, carved out by Celtic invaders from Europe.

Colonialism, Greek Style Many Greeks and Macedonians emigrated from home during the fourth and third centuries B.C., but we do not know how many. The few available statistics indicate a significant migration but not a mass exodus. By the second century B.C. the colonizing impulse had diminished in Greece and Macedon, but a large number of Jews left war-torn Palestine, particularly for Egypt. Ptolemaic Egypt and the Seleucid realm were also the most common destinations for Greek and Macedonian migrants.

Greek migrants could take advantage of a new definition of being Greek that had begun to emerge even before Alexander's conquests. Disappointed by the narrow and self-destructive localism of the Greek city-states, Isocrates (428–338 B.C.), an Athenian teacher of rhetoric, sought a wider horizon. Isocrates redefined the meaning of Greek identity. He promoted the idea that Greece was not a collection of city-states but a civilization. "The people we call Hellenes"—that is, Greeks—he wrote, "are those who have the same culture as us, not the same blood."[1]

The ideal of Greek culture made it easier for the migrants to maintain a Greek identity. For that matter, it was now possible for foreigners to become Greek by learning the

Clay Flask in Form of Black Boy *This vase was made in the shape of a squatting figure in the late third century B.C. The subject shows the Hellenistic world's interest in black Africa, while the posture reveals the artist's search for an unusual pose.* (Martin von Wagner Museum der Universität Würzburg. Photo: K. Oehrlein)

Greek language and literature. The number of Hellenized foreigners was relatively small, yet their very existence marked a break from the Classical polis, where even a resident genius such as Aristotle could not obtain Athenian citizenship because he was not of Athenian descent.

The Greek language also served as a common denominator, along with Aramaic, both of which became the languages of trade in the eastern Mediterranean. To get a sense of the importance of Isocrates' redefinition of Hellenism, consider that one of the most famous Greek-speakers of all antiquity was Paul, the Christian apostle who was born a Jew in Tarsus, a city in southern Anatolia.

Immigrants sought to realize dreams of prosperity or adventure. Although agriculture was the main economic pursuit, trade, industry, finance, administration, and military service also offered opportunities. The large Ptolemaic bureaucracy needed administrators and tax collectors.

In the Ptolemaic and Seleucid realms, administration was a joint effort of both immigrants and natives. The Macedonian conquerors might have preferred to rely on Macedonians and Greeks, but their territories never attracted enough immigrants from "home" to make that possible. Besides, the new rulers needed both the goodwill and the local knowledge of the people whom they had conquered. Thus the upper echelons of government were dominated by Greek and Macedonian immigrants and their descendants, but native elites held government positions as well. Especially after about 200 B.C., some natives served the new rulers as administrators or soldiers, usually in low- or mid-level positions but sometimes in high office. Others worked in the traditional native administrative structures that survived largely intact in the new kingdoms—for example, as judges or village headmen or priests.

Consider, for example, soldiers. To create a permanent, hereditary military group living in the countryside, Ptolemy I settled his soldiers on land allotments. Native Egyptians were excluded from the army at first but served as policemen. By the second century B.C., however, the dynasty turned to native Egyptians as a new source of soldiers. In return for military service, natives now received land, tax breaks, and the right to call themselves Hellenes. Their Hellenism sometimes merely scratched the surface, but other times it went deeper.

An Egyptian named Plenis, a villager in middle Egypt in the late second century B.C., is a good example of this cultural cross-fertilization. Plenis was a tenant farmer on a royal estate and a priest in a local Egyptian cult. His horizon was not narrow, however. Like his father before him, Plenis served as a soldier in the Ptolemaic army. Plenis, moreover, could write Greek as well as Egyptian, and he even used a Greek name: Dionysius, son of Kephalas.

Temples, which often administered large estates, represented important sources of native power. Priests shaped local opinion and were in a position, therefore, both to enjoy considerable independence and to demand royal patronage. Both Ptolemies and Seleucids complied: from Babylon to Edfu, money poured into temple-building and renovation.

The Seleucids addressed the security needs of their far-flung realms by establishing over seventy colonies extending to central Asia. Some colonies were civilian, but most were military, composed of retired or reserve soldiers, mostly Greeks or Macedonians, but also including Jews and other non-Greek peoples. Colonists received land allotments. Greek-style public buildings were erected, and some cities were laid out according to a rectilinear grid reminiscent of the Classical polis. The gymnasium attained a great practical and symbolic importance as both the center of Greek culture and the preparatory school for entry into the elite. The Hellenistic gymnasium offered education in literature, philosophy, and oratory as well as athletics.

Some Seleucid colonies developed into flourishing cities. For example, Greek cities dominated the Syrian coastline and much of Anatolia until the coming of Islam in the seventh century A.D. Greek urbanization should not create the false impression, however, that the Seleucids were motivated by some civilizing mission. They were not. They established colonies to increase their power.

| Economic Expansion | Immigration and colonization were not the only sources of new economic opportunities. At the beginning of the Hellenistic era, Alexander turned the huge gold and silver reserves |

of Persia into coinage and released it onto the market virtually all at once. Although Alexander's action stimulated a rapid inflation lasting about seventy-five years, it also had the positive effect of greatly stimulating commerce. In particular, the economy of Hellenistic Egypt became highly monetarized, even on the village level. Barter continued to exist in Egypt, but the widespread presence of money served to increase the production and circulation of goods, helping to render Egypt an economic powerhouse. Another stimulus to trade was the creation of thriving new Hellenistic cities, especially Alexandria with its great harbors, canals, marketplaces, and infrastructure of banks, inns, courts, and shipbuilding facilities.

During Hellenistic times, trade and commerce tended to shift from Greece proper to Anatolia and Egypt. The island of Rhodes, located off the southwest tip of Anatolia, grew into a major trading center, especially for grain. This development was the result of excellent harbors; a location on the merchant routes between Asia, Africa, and southeastern Europe; and a superb fleet. The Rhodian aristocracy grew rich off taxes and duties, wisely reinvesting a portion of the profits in naval infrastructure (such as arsenals and dockyards) and in campaigns against pirates. Egypt, too, had many products to trade. Grain was the most important, but textiles, glass, papyrus (from which a kind of paper was produced), and luxury goods were also significant. Egyptian goods were sold throughout the Mediterranean. A network of canals connecting Alexandria to the Nile and the Red Sea beyond also made possible active trading with Sudan, Arabia, and India.

The Seleucid kingdoms controlled rich trade routes to Arabia, India, and central Asia. Commerce was facilitated by good roads, safe sea travel between the Persian Gulf and India, and a unified royal coinage. The Seleucids traded agricultural goods and manufactured products such as textiles, glassware, and metalwork for spices from India and Arabia. In the first century B.C. they even had trade contacts with China, whose silk garments reached the Mediterranean. The kingdom of Pergamum, which stretched inland from Anatolia's northwest coast, exported the agricultural products of the rich hinterland it controlled, as well as the local gray-blue building stone and, as an alternative to Egyptian papyrus, parchment.

Slavery was an important part of the Hellenistic social and economic scene. Although war and piracy were the main sources of enslavement, some people were born into slavery. In Sicily and southern Italy, slaves worked huge plantations, but eastern Mediterranean slaves were commonly found in the household or in administration, and in cities rather than in the countryside. Many unfree laborers worked on farms in Egypt and western Asia. Following the pre-Greek traditions of those regions, they were generally tenant farmers tied to kings or potentates rather than outright slaves.

On some plantations conditions for slaves were harsh enough to lead to mass uprisings. It was not unusual, however, for domestic or administrative slaves to buy their freedom, sometimes using savings they were allowed to keep, sometimes borrowing money from the master or from friends. Greeks enslaved fellow Greeks, but often, it seems, with guilty consciences; they frequently made special efforts to help Greek slaves win their freedom. Even in bondage, therefore, Greeks had special privileges.

Macedon and Greece

Macedon was the last of the three great Hellenistic kingdoms to emerge from civil war after Alexander's death. Not until 276 B.C. was Antigonus Gonatas, grandson of Alexander's general Antigonus the One-Eyed, established firmly on the throne. His Antigonid dynasty lasted about a century, when the conquering Romans made Macedon first a republic and then a Roman province.

True to the traditions of Macedon, the Antigonids projected an image of simplicity and toughness. Like Philip II and Alexander the Great, Antigonus immersed himself in the culture of the Greek city-states, partly because he admired it, partly because it brought him prestige. As a young man, Antigonus had studied the new school of Stoic philosophy in Athens (see page 122). As king, he devoted himself to the Stoic dictates of duty, describing his office as "noble servitude" and his diadem as a mere "rag." Antigonus shared the traditional Macedonian ambition to dominate the Greek city-states, but he faced rival powers. Besides Ptolemaic Egypt, there was the kingdom of Epirus in northwestern Greece and two new federal leagues in the south, the Aetolians (north of the Corinthian Gulf) and the Achaeans.

The federal leagues were more tightly organized than Classical Greek military leagues (such as the Peloponnesian League) and larger than the Boeotian League, a fourth-century B.C. federal alliance that had covered a relatively small territory. The new leagues permitted some participation by ordinary men but were dominated by the wealthy; they were not democracies.

Yet the leagues interest us as models of federalism that would one day influence the founders of the United States. The Aetolians, for example, practiced proportional representation by population in a federal council for constituent cities. The Achaeans successfully balanced local and federal authorities. Constituent cities kept their own constitutions while recognizing federal jurisdiction. The federal government consisted of a governing general (both president and commander-in-chief) and ten subordinate magistrates, an executive council, and a general assembly.

Athens, less successful than Sparta in maintaining independence, repeatedly experienced Macedonian rule. Through a combination of war and diplomacy, however, Athens won periods of freedom from the late fourth to the mid-second century B.C., when Rome held sway over Greece. Athens remained a vibrant democracy until the late third century B.C., when the oligarchic upper classes finally won the upper hand for good.

Extremes of wealth and poverty, problems of debt, and class conflict challenged Hellenistic Greece. The decline of democracy enabled the wealthy to contribute less to the public good in taxes and to amass private fortunes. The result was sometimes class conflict, but the elite usually made just enough concessions to avoid full-scale revolution.

Sparta was an exception. In the late third century B.C. a social revolution was launched from above by Agis and Cleomenes, two Spartan kings working together. After defeat in the fourth century B.C., Sparta had become impoverished (see page 86). The reformers now offered debt relief, redistribution of land, and restoration of Classical Spartan austerity and equality. Popular in Sparta, the revolution threatened to spread elsewhere. Peloponnesian oligarchs called in Macedonian forces, which crushed Sparta in 222 B.C. and ended the revolution.

Ptolemaic Egypt   The wealthiest, most sophisticated, and longest-lasting Hellenistic kingdom was Ptolemaic Egypt. One of Alexander's great generals, Ptolemy (d. 283 B.C.), became governor of Egypt in 323 B.C. and proclaimed himself king in 304 B.C. His dynasty lasted until Rome annexed Egypt in 30 B.C., after the suicide of the last of the line, Queen Cleopatra (see page 120). By contrast, Macedon was absorbed by Rome a century earlier, in 146 B.C.; Pergamum was annexed in 133 B.C.; and the Seleucid kingdom succumbed to Rome in 64 B.C.

Unlike the Antigonids, the Ptolemies did not pursue the simple virtues but rather gloried in wealth and grandeur. Ptolemy I showed the way to his successors when he had Alexander's funeral procession hijacked on its way to Macedonia and established a tomb and then a cult in the capital city, Alexandria—a Greek hero-shrine in the land of the pyramids. Ptolemy I made arrangements to have himself proclaimed "savior-god" after his death; his successors, less reticent, took divine honors while still alive.

The most important Ptolemaic borrowing, however, was the pharaonic tradition of royal intervention in the economy, which the Ptolemies combined with Greek customs of literacy and the use of money rather than barter. The result was a highly complex and profitable economy. Putting to use the science of the Museum, the great institute in Alexandria (see page 114), the Ptolemies sponsored irrigation and land reclamation projects, the introduction of new crops (for example, new varieties of wheat), and the greatly expanded cultivation of old ones (such as grapes for wine).

Most of the people of Egypt made their living in agriculture, either as independent small farmers or as tenants on large estates. Government enriched itself through taxes, rents, demands for compulsory labor, state monopolies (on such diverse items as oils, textiles, and beer), and various internal tolls and customs duties. The result was boom times under strong kings and queens in the third century B.C. Egypt became the most prosperous part of the Hellenistic world, and Alexandria became the wealthiest, most populous city in the Mediterranean, as well as its literary capital. In the second century B.C., however, continued economic prosperity was derailed by decline. Weak kings, bureaucratic corruption, inflation of the currency, and the end of Greek immigration created conditions for revolt.

Since pharaonic times, tendencies toward regional independence had bedeviled Egypt's government. The Ptolemaic period was no exception. Regional unrest stirred in the 240s B.C. and then mushroomed after the Battle of Raphia in 217 B.C., a struggle in Gaza between the Ptolemies and Seleucids for control of Palestine. The Ptolemies won, but only by enrolling thousands of Egyptians in the Macedonian phalanx, responding to a shortage of Greek mercenaries. Emboldened by their new military power, people in Upper Egypt soon broke into armed revolt against the government in far-off Alexandria. Rival kings appeared in the south, and unrest continued for about a century.

To advance their cause, the rebels inflamed anti-Greek sentiment. High taxes and regional rivalries, however, probably carried more weight than nationalism in the minds of most people. Although friction between immigrants and natives sparked from time to time, most Egyptians accepted the Ptolemies as pharaohs as long as they brought peace and prosperity.

Nor did the Ptolemies allow national sentiment to stand in the way of reasserting their power. In 196 B.C., for example, Ptolemy V Epiphanes celebrated his coronation in full pharaonic ceremonial in Memphis. Egyptian priests commemorated the occasion in a decree written in Egypt's traditional language of kingship in a trilingual inscription (Greek, hieroglyphic, and demotic—ordinary—Egyptian). This inscription, discovered by French soldiers in 1798 and dubbed the Rosetta stone (named for the place where it was found), led to the modern European deciphering of hieroglyphics.

Despite the frictions, evidence points to native-settler cooperation, especially in the countryside, where intermarriage and bilingualism became common. Many an ordinary Greek became fully assimilated to Egyptian ways, and even wealthy, sophisticated, urban Greeks adopted a smattering of Egyptian customs. The Egyptian calendar, Egyptian names, and mummification were all in use. By 98 B.C. assimilation was evident in the cultural hybrid of a group of 18- and 19-year-old male youths who received traditional Greek military and literary training but prayed to Egypt's crocodile-god.

Seleucids and Attalids

The kingdom founded by Alexander's general Seleucus (ca. 358–281 B.C.) experienced shifting borders and inhabitants. The Seleucid kingdom began when Seleucus took Babylon in 312 B.C. and ended in 64 B.C. when Syria became a Roman province. Many territorial changes occurred in between. The first three kings ruled a domain stretching from the Aegean to Bactria (modern Afghanistan), but by the early second century B.C. most of the Iranian Plateau and lands eastward had been lost. At its height, in the third century B.C., the Seleucid kingdom had three nerve centers: Ionia (in western Anatolia), with a capital at Sardis; Syria, with a capital at Antioch; and Babylonia, whose capital was Seleucia-on-the-Tigris (near modern Baghdad).

Unlike the compact Nile Valley, with its relatively homogeneous population, the far-flung and multi-ethnic Seleucid lands presented an enormous administrative challenge. To govern such a conglomerate, the kings took over the Persian system of satraps (provincial governors), taxes, and royal roads and post (see page 41), to which they

Laocoön *This famous statue group of the second or first century B.C. shows the Trojan priest Laocoön and his sons being strangled by snakes sent by the gods. The scene's emphasis on extreme emotion is typical of Hellenistic art.* (Scala/Art Resource, NY)

added an excellent army trained according to Macedonian traditions, a common coinage, and a Hellenistic ruler cult. The chief Seleucid innovation was the establishment of colonies. Greek and Macedonian soldiers and administrators dominated, but natives also filled bureaucratic slots.

The greatest Seleucid city was Antioch, which became one of the wealthiest and most luxurious of all eastern Mediterranean cities; only Ptolemaic Alexandria outstripped it. The intellectual and artistic capital of Greek Asia in Hellenistic times, however, was not Antioch but Pergamum, in northwestern Anatolia.

The rulers of Pergamum, the Attalid dynasty of kings, carved out a small kingdom that became independent of the Seleucids in 263 B.C. and fell into Roman hands in 133 B.C. The Attalids made Pergamum into a showplace of Greek civilization, a would-be second Athens. As in Athens, public building was focused on a steep acropolis. The upper city of Pergamum was laid out on hillside terraces rising to a palace and fortified citadel. One of the terraces housed the famous Pergamum Altar, a huge monument to an Attalid victory over the Celts, who first invaded Anatolia in 278 B.C. and whose advance the Attalids checked. They could not, however, stop the Celts from settling in central Anatolia, where they created their kingdom of Galatia.

Pergamum was famous for its sculptors and for a library second only to Alexandria's. Pergamene writers focused on scholarship, to the exclusion of poetry, perhaps as a result of the influence of Stoic philosophers, who disapproved of poetry's emotionalism.

The Greco-Indian Interaction

The Seleucids' hold on Alexander's vast eastern domains turned out to be temporary. A new Persian dynasty, the Parthians, achieved independence in the mid-third century B.C. and over the next century carved out an empire extending westward into Mesopotamia. But to the east, Bactria remained Greek, if not Seleucid. From the mid-third century B.C. an independent Greek Bactria prospered.

Vivid evidence of Greek colonization in Bactria comes from the site of Aï Khanum (its ancient name is unknown) in northern Afghanistan. This prosperous and populous city contained many reminders of Greece, among them a gymnasium, theater, and library. A pillar in the gymnasium was inscribed in the mid-third century B.C. with 140 moral maxims from Delphi in Greece, over 3,000 miles away.

In the second century B.C. Bactrian kings extended their rule into the Indus River valley and the Punjab, a region with a modest Greek presence since the fifth century B.C., when the Persians settled Greek mercenaries there. Virtually no literary evidence survives, but monuments and, particularly, coins demonstrate Greco-Indian cultural interaction. For example, some coins from the second century B.C. show bilingual inscriptions in Greek and Indian languages. Their designs include a variety of Indian religious motifs, such as the lotus plant, symbol of Lakshmi, goddess of wealth and good fortune. Indians admired Hellenistic astronomy; one text goes so far as to say that Greek scientists should be "reverenced like gods."

The Hellenistic world seems to have intrigued King Asoka (r. ca. 270–230 B.C.), who ruled almost the entire subcontinent, the largest empire in India to date. Asoka is best remembered as a religious reformer. A convert to Buddhism, he played a major role in its spread, which proceeded under the slogan of *dhamma*—that is, "morality" or "righteousness." One of his inscriptions records "victory" by dhamma, "where reigns the

Greek king named Antiochus, and beyond the realm of Antiochus in the lands of the four kings named Ptolemy, Antigonus, Magas, and Alexander," which is generally thought to refer to embassies to the Hellenistic kingdoms.[2]

The envoys apparently found few converts, for it is difficult to find any trace of Buddhism in Hellenistic Greek culture, at least outside the Greco-Indian kingdoms. There one of the most powerful Greek rulers, Menander Soter Dikaios (r. ca. 155–130 B.C.), may have converted to Buddhism in the mid-second century B.C. But certain aspects of Indian religion—especially India's powerful currents of asceticism, mysticism, and monasticism—interested Greek intellectuals around the Mediterranean in Hellenistic and Roman times. Observers on Alexander's expedition, Hellenistic envoys, merchants, and philosophers in search of Eastern wisdom all served as conduits between East and West. One of the most influential was Megasthenes, a Seleucid ambassador to the court of Asoka's grandfather, who published his *Indika*, a description of India, around 300 B.C.

Yet the degree to which this interest influenced Greek and Roman culture is debatable. Although ancient writers mention Greek or Roman philosophers who were attracted by Indian culture, modern scholars tend to be cautious. The ancients had a weakness for tall tales and stories of exotic inspiration. Consider, for example, the following reports. Pyrrho of Elis, founder of the Hellenistic philosophical school of skepticism (see page 123), supposedly based his notion of the imperturbable sage on one Calanos, an Indian whom Pyrrho saw step calmly on a funeral pyre when Pyrrho was part of Alexander's expedition. Around A.D. 40 Apollonius of Tyana, a pagan religious thinker, is supposed to have traveled to India to study with its sages. Two centuries later the great Neo-Platonic philosopher Plotinus (A.D. 235–270) is reported to have traveled with the Roman emperor Gordian's army eastward, hoping in vain to reach India. Some scholars see Indian influence in Plotinus's mysticism and pantheism, but others dismiss these various reports.

Central Asian nomads overran Bactria in the late second century B.C. The Hellenistic kingdoms of India and Pakistan, however, survived until about the time of Christ, and some Greek communities lasted until the fifth century A.D. The Gandharan sculptors who flourished in a formerly Greek-ruled region in about A.D. 200 used Greek artistic techniques to depict Buddhist subjects, which might suggest the impact of Indian culture on the remaining Greek population.

THE ALEXANDRIAN MOMENT

By the first century B.C. Alexandria was a city of half a million or more inhabitants. It was one of the largest, wealthiest, and most important cities in the world. The bulk of the people were Egyptian, but Greeks and Jews made up large minorities, and no one would have been surprised, in this cosmopolitan center, to see an Indian or a Celt, an Italian or a Persian.

The capital of Egypt, Alexandria was also perhaps the most important place where Greek culture was spread and transformed in the Hellenistic era. At the same time, it was a mix of ethnic cooperation and conflict. Underwater archaeologists, for example, looking for submerged parts of the city in Alexandria harbor, have found Egyptian sphinxes and obelisks as well as Greek statues. Written sources portray a picture of social change in the elite, an increase in leisure time, a growth in educational opportunities for both sexes, royal patronage of culture, and the value of even a limited knowledge of Greek literature as the ticket to advancement.

The Anti-Epic Temperament

In 294 B.C. King Ptolemy I invited the deposed tyrant of Athens, Demetrius of Phalerum, to found an institution of culture in Alexandria. A writer himself, Ptolemy was no less sincere because the new foundation would bring him prestige and keep his engineers up to date on new technology for warfare and agriculture. Demetrius had studied with Aristotle's successor at the Lyceum, Theophrastus (ca. 370–288 B.C.), a practical man interested in compiling and cataloging knowledge.

The new institution was called the Museum (literally, "House of the Muses," or the home of the female deities who inspired creativity). The Museum was a residence, study, and lecture hall for scholars, scientists, and poets. One of its key components was the Library, in its day the largest collection of Greek writing in the world. In the third century B.C.—at the height of the Ptolemaic kingdom—the Library contained 700,000 papyrus rolls, the equivalent of roughly 50,000 modern books. Its nearest competitor, at Pergamum, contained less than a third as many rolls.

The Library reflects the growth of the Hellenistic reading and writing public. As independence vanished, city-states converted their military training programs for 18- and 19-year-old men into educational programs in literature and philosophy. The names of over a thousand writers of the Hellenistic era survive, and after 300 B.C. anthologies, abridgments, and school texts multiplied.

Though modeled on Athens's Lyceum, the Museum represented a break from the public culture of the Classical period. The denizens of the Museum were an elite, dependent on royal patronage and self-consciously Greek and not Egyptian. At the Museum, culture was an object of study, not a part of civic life, as it had been in Classical Athens. A clever remark of Timon, a philosopher from the Peloponnesus who lived in the third century B.C., rings true: "In Egypt, land of diverse tribes, graze many pedants, fatted fowls that quarrel without end in the hen coop of the Muses."

Before we examine Alexandrian literature further, it is worth noting how greatly Hellenistic Athenian literature diverged from Classical culture. The greatest Hellenistic Athenian writer, a man famous throughout the ancient world, was Menander (ca. 342–292 B.C.). He was the master of a style of comedy called "New Comedy," as distinguished from the "Old Comedy" of Aristophanes, which had flourished a century earlier (see page 95). Where Old Comedy was raucous and ribald, New Comedy was restrained; where Old Comedy focused on public matters such as war and politics, New Comedy was domestic and private. New Comedy was typical of the turn away from public life in Hellenistic times.

Menander wrote over seventy plays, but only one complete work has survived, *Dyskolos* (*The Grouch*). There are also large excerpts from several other comedies as well as Roman imitations. Witty and fluent, Menander favored stock plots and stock characters: the boastful soldier, the clever slave, the dashing but inept young man, the sweet maiden, and the old miser. Within those limitations, Menander created realistic and idiosyncratic characters. As a Hellenistic critic asked rhetorically: "O Menander and Life, which of you imitated the other?"

Street Musicians *The lively scene of a mixed group of young and old, male and female, recalls the jaunty mimes popular with the Hellenistic public. A mosaic from about 100 B.C., the artwork comes from a private villa in the Greco-Italian city of Pompeii.* (Museo Nazionale, Naples)

Like Menander, Alexandrian writers spurned public themes, but in Alexandria the characteristic literary figure was not the playwright but the critic. He was a professional man of letters, and he aimed at establishing a literary canon and standardizing the texts of the canonical authors. Adopted by the Romans, Alexandrian critical standards have influenced the West to this day.

Of the three greatest Alexandrian writers, two—Callimachus (305–240 B.C.) and Apollonius of Rhodes (b. ca. 295 B.C.)—worked at the Library; the third, Theocritus (ca. 300–260 B.C.), probably lived on a stipend from the Ptolemies. Popular for centuries, Callimachus was probably the most influential, the complete Hellenistic poet. A native of Cyrene who came to Alexandria as a schoolteacher, Callimachus found a position in the Library. There he composed a virtually universal history of all recorded Greek (and much non-Greek) knowledge.

A prolific writer, Callimachus generally preferred short to long poems: "Big book, big evil" was his maxim. Earlier Greek poets were usually austere and public-minded; Callimachus preferred the private, the light, and the exotic. "Don't expect from me a big-sounding poem," he writes. "Zeus thunders, not I."[3] Callimachus was expert at the pithy statement in verse—the epigram.

Another major Alexandrian writer was Callimachus's student Apollonius of Rhodes. Tradition claims that Apollonius retired to Rhodes after his epic poem *Argonautica* (*Voyage of the Argo*) was poorly received. The subject is the legend of Jason and the heroes who travel on the ship *Argo* to Colchis, at the far end of the Black Sea, in pursuit of the Golden Fleece (the skin of a winged ram). With the help of the Colchian princess Medea, who falls in love with Jason, the heroes succeed and return home safely after numerous adventures.

The most striking thing about Apollonius is his doubt about the very possibility of heroism. Apollonius's Jason is no hero of old. Whereas Homer describes Odysseus as "never at a loss," Apollonius describes Jason as "helpless." Men move the action in the *Iliad* and the *Odyssey;* Jason depends on a woman, Medea, for his success. Indeed, much of the *Argonautica* focuses on Medea and in particular on her love for Jason. With the exception of the works of Sappho, previous Greek poetry generally either ignored female eroticism or presented it in a hostile light. Apollonius's work illustrates both the improved status of women in Hellenistic ideology and the great interest of the age in the life of the emotions. All in all, the *Argonautica* is less a traditional epic than an anti-epic.

Like Callimachus, Theocritus, a native of Syracuse, wrote short, polished poetry. He composed thirty-one subtle and refined poems, conventionally known as idylls. The best known of the poems focus on country life. They are the first known pastoral poems; indeed, Theocritus probably invented the genre. Theocritus's pastorals explore nature, but always self-consciously, always with the city in mind. His peasants and shepherds are marvelously cultured, more like townspeople on an excursion than true rustics. Through his Roman admirers, Theocritus's love of nature has exerted a powerful hold on the Western literary imagination.

Outside the Museum, Alexandria had a lively popular culture, much of it Egyptian or influenced by Egyptian models. A glimpse of this culture is offered in the seven surviving mimes, or farces, of an obscure writer named Herondas or Herodas. Though written in literary Greek, they discuss commonplace subjects—shopping for shoes, tourism, lawsuits, and beatings at school—and titillating themes such as adultery and prostitution. Lively, bawdy, funny, and filled with the grit of everyday life in the third century B.C., they are a reminder of just how specialized the culture of the Museum was.

Advances in Science and Medicine

The Ptolemies not only reaped practical benefits in military and agricultural technology from their Museum, but they also became the patrons of a flourishing period in the history of pure scientific inquiry. They unwittingly promoted a split between philosophy and science that has characterized much of Western culture since. Antigonid patronage of ethical and political philosophy helped keep Athens preeminent in those fields. In contrast, the study of science tended to shift to Alexandria. The rulers of Pergamum and, far to the west, Syracuse, a flourishing Hellenistic city in Sicily, were great patrons of science as well. Wealth, improved communications and literacy, continued warfare, and cross-fertilization between Greek and non-Greek traditions, especially Greek and Babylonian astronomy, were all catalysts of Hellenistic science.

Some of the best-known figures of Hellenistic science were mathematicians. In his *Elements,* the Alexandrian Euclid (active ca. 300 B.C.) produced a systematic exposition of geometry that was hugely influential in both Western and Islamic civilizations. A Sicilian Greek, Archimedes of Syracuse (287–212 B.C.), did original work on the geometry of spheres and cylinders, calculated the approximate value of pi (the ratio of a circle's circumference to its diameter), and made important discoveries in astronomy, engineering, optics, and other fields. Archimedes was as great an inventor as he was a theoretician. One of the most important of his innovations was the water snail, also known as Archimedes' screw—a device to raise water for irrigation. Invented by Archimedes during a stay in Egypt, the screw made it possible to irrigate previously barren land, as did the ox-driven water wheel, another Ptolemaic invention.

Advances in mathematics promoted advances in astronomy. Aristarchus of Samos (active ca. 275 B.C.) is known for his heliocentric hypothesis, which confounded tradition by having the earth revolve around the sun, instead of the sun around the earth. He was right, but Hellenistic astronomy lacked the data to prove his theory, so its rejection was not unreasonable at the time. Eratosthenes of Cyrene (active ca. 225 B.C.) was saddled with the frustrating nickname of "Beta" (the second letter of the Greek alphabet) because he was considered second best in every branch of study. This "second best" nonetheless calculated through simple geometry an extraordinarily accurate measurement of the earth's circumference.

Hellenistic medicine thrived in Alexandria. Both Greece and Egypt had long-established medical traditions. Egyptian drugs, and possibly Egyptian doctors' knowledge of the eye as well as their emphasis on measurement, helped stimulate Alexandrian medical progress, as no doubt did the mere fact of cross-fertilization. The key to medical advance, however, was the dissection of human cadavers in Alexandria, a first in the history of science. In Greece, as in many ancient societies, religious tradition demanded that dead bodies not be mutilated. But in the frontier atmosphere of early Alexandria, this traditional taboo lost much of its force. Although Egyptians did not practice dissection, they did practice embalming, which may have helped Alexandrian Greeks overcome the prohibition against cutting open the human body. Ever supportive of research, the Ptolemies provided corpses to Greek scientists for dissection. Indeed, they had condemned criminals sent from prison for live dissection by scientists. The practice, only a short-lived experiment in the early third century B.C., outraged many writers in antiquity, just as today it would be considered an atrocity.

The leading scientific beneficiary was Herophilus of Chalcedon (ca. 320–250 B.C.), a practicing physician in Alexandria. Among his achievements was the recognition (against Aristotle) that the brain is the center of the nervous system, a careful dissection of the eye, the discovery of the ovaries, and the description of the duodenum, which he named (*duodenum* is a Latin translation of a Greek word meaning "twelve fingers," describing the organ's length). In addition, Herophilus developed a detailed theory of the diagnostic value of measuring pulse rates.

Hellenistic technology has long fascinated and frustrated scholars. The great engineers invented both numerous engines of war and various "wonderworks" to amuse the royal court. Among the latter were mechanical puppets and steam-run toys. Given these advances, why did the Greeks achieve neither a scientific revolution, along the lines of the one begun in the early modern era by thinkers such as Copernicus and Galileo, nor an industrial transformation, such as was ushered in by the steam engine around A.D. 1800? Historians are not entirely sure but can venture a guess. Greek machine-making technology was not as sophisticated as that of eighteenth-century Europe. The prevalence of slavery in antiquity, moreover, discouraged the invention of laborsaving machines; steam was used only for playthings and gadgets. A related point

Archimedes' Experiment

Archimedes of Syracuse (ca. 287–212 B.C.) was the greatest mathematician of Greek antiquity and a notable inventor. In this crude but brilliant experiment, Archimedes proved that when an object is submerged in a fluid, it feels a buoyant force equal to the weight of the fluid that it has displaced. The anecdote is an intriguing reminder that although the ancient world did not have a Scientific Revolution like that of the early modern era, ancient scientists could conduct experiments.

[King Hiero of Syracuse asks Archimedes to test a gold crown, which, Hiero suspects, has been watered down with silver.]

The latter [Archimedes], while the case was still on his mind, happened to go to the bath, and on getting into a tub observed that the more his body sank into it the more water ran out over the tub. As this pointed out the way to explain the case in question, without a moment's delay, and transported with joy, he jumped out of the tub and rushed home naked, crying with a loud voice that he had found what he was seeking; for as he ran he shouted repeatedly in Greek, "Eureka, Eureka!" [you-REE-kuh] ("I have found it! I have found it!").

Taking this as the beginning of his discovery, it is said that he made two masses of the same weight as the crown, one of gold and the other of silver. After making them, he filled a large vessel with water to the very brim, and dropped the mass of silver into it. As much water ran out as was equal in bulk to that of the silver sunk in the vessel. Then, taking out the mass, he poured back the lost quantity of water, using a pint measure, until it was level with the brim as it had been before. Thus he found the weight of silver corresponding to a definite quantity of water.

After this experiment, he likewise dropped the mass of gold into the full vessel and, on taking it out and measuring as before, found that not so much water was lost, but a smaller quantity: namely, as much less as a mass of gold lacks in bulk compared to a mass of silver of the same weight. Finally, filling the vessel again and dropping the crown itself into the same quantity of water, he found that more water ran over for the crown than for the mass of gold of the same weight. Hence, reasoning from the fact that more water was lost in the case of the crown than in that of the mass, he detected the mixing of silver with the gold, and made the theft of the contractor perfectly clear.

Source: Vitruvius, *The Ten Books of Architecture*, trans. Morris Hicky Morgan (Cambridge, Mass.: Harvard University Press, 1914), p. 254.

is the elitist bias of Greek intellectual life. After Archimedes' death, for example, it was claimed that although he had written copiously on theoretical matters, he never bothered to write about his mechanical inventions because he considered them "ignoble and vulgar."

Perhaps the most important point is the Greek attitude toward nature. Whereas Jews and Christians learned from the Bible that human beings have dominion over nature, thereby making possible the conclusion that it is appropriate to conquer nature, the Greeks thought in more restricted terms. They believed that nature set limits, that a virtuous person tried to follow nature, not subdue it. Thus Greek engineers were not inclined to make the revolutionary changes that their modern counterparts have promoted.

Men and Women in Art and Society

Like Hellenistic literature, Hellenistic art attests to changing male attitudes toward women and toward gender issues. The portrait of Jason and Medea in Apollonius's *Argonautica* makes fun of masculine pretensions and celebrates the triumph of female intelligence. It also presents a sympathetic portrait of a woman's romantic desire for a man, as does Theocritus's work. In the Classical period, depictions of romantic love were generally restricted to male homoeroticism. Accordingly, statues of naked males were common, but women were almost always depicted clothed. Hellenistic sculpture, by contrast, affords many erotic examples of the female nude.

There are indications that the Hellenistic Greek male of the elite was much more willing than his Classical predecessor to see lovemaking as a matter of mutuality and respect. Classical vase-painting often depicts heterosexual lovemaking with a lusty and explicit mood. In contrast, in Hellenistic vase-painting the emphasis is more often on tenderness and domesticity. Hellenistic men wrote with sensitivity about satisfying a woman's needs and desires. The vogue for representations of Hermaphrodite, the mythical creature who was half-female and half-male, may suggest a belief that the feminine was as important a part of human nature as the masculine.

Many a Hellenistic artist or writer seems to be as interested in emotion as in action and to focus on the inner as much as on the outer life. Hellenistic art often depicts women, children, and domestic scenes. Representations of warriors are as likely to focus on their unrestrained emotions as on their soldierly self-control.

Hellenistic women enjoyed small improvements in political and legal status and considerable improvements in economic and ideological status. A number of reasons explain these advances. First, Greek women, particularly in the elite, benefited from the spread of monarchy. For one thing, queens and princesses in royal courts had power and prestige that had been denied women in city-states. For another, under monarchy the notion of the loyal and prosperous subject replaced that of the independent citizen-warrior. Citizens in the Classical polis had been encouraged to be aggressive and exaggeratedly masculine to the point of hostility toward women. Subjects in Hellenistic monarchies were meant to cultivate the more passive and reflective virtues of legalism, obedience, and economic enterprise. Because Greek men associated these virtues with women, their respect for female qualities tended to increase. Also, in the new cities, as in many a frontier society, women were permitted to inherit and use property more often than in old Greece.

It was an era of powerful queens: Olympias, Alexander the Great's mother, played kingmaker after her son's death. Arsinoe II Philadelphus was co-ruler of Egypt with her husband (who was also her brother) for five years at the height of Ptolemaic prosperity around 275 B.C. The most famous Hellenistic woman, Cleopatra VII, was queen of Egypt from 51 to 30 B.C. Although she was the lover of two of the most powerful men in the world, the Romans Julius Caesar and Mark Antony, Cleopatra was no exotic plaything. Rather, she was a brilliant and ambitious strategist who nearly succeeded in winning a world empire for her family.

Writers in the new Hellenistic cities often described freedom of movement for women. Theocritus and Herondas, for example, show women visiting a temple or a show. Nor did Hellenistic men, even in Athens, obey Pericles' injunction not to speak

Aphrodite of Cnidos This 7½-foot-tall marble statue is a Roman copy of an original by Praxiteles (ca. 350–330 B.C.). Perhaps the most famous of Hellenistic female nudes, the statue was housed in a special shrine where it could be viewed in the round to accommodate all the interest it generated. (Vatican Museums)

of women, even good women. In Hellenistic Athens, aristocratic fathers put up inscriptions in honor of their daughters who had participated in the cult of Athena. Although women generally continued to need a male guardian to represent them in public, in some situations, at least in Egypt (where the evidence is most plentiful), a woman could represent herself. A woman could petition the government on her own behalf. Widows and mothers of illegitimate children could give their daughters in marriage or apprentice their sons. A few cities granted women citizenship and even permitted them to hold public office.

Some Hellenistic cities admitted women to the gymnasium, previously a male preserve. Heretofore only Sparta had promoted physical education for women, but by the first century A.D. women were even competing in the great Pan-Hellenic games. Gymnasia were also centers of education in music and reading. One consequence of growing literacy was the re-emergence of women poets and the first appearance of women philosophers in the West. Before dying at age 19, Erinna, who lived on the Aegean island of Telos during the late fourth century B.C., wrote the *Distaff*, a poem in memory of her childhood friend Baucis. This three-hundred-line poem, famous in antiquity, describes the shared experiences of girlhood. Hipparchia of Maroneia (b. ca. 350 B.C.), like her husband, Crates of Thebes, studied Cynic philosophy. The Cynics, like another philosophical school, the Epicureans, supported a measure of equality between women and men. Hipparchia and Crates led an itinerant life as popular teachers and the Hellenistic equivalent of counselors or psychologists.

Much of the explanation for the relative freedom of elite women lies in the new economic power of this group. The new cities generally imposed fewer restrictions on women's economic roles than had Classical poleis such as Athens. In many cities women could sell land, borrow money, and decide whether their husbands could make loans or contracts on the strength of their dowries. Free women could manumit slaves as well.

The role reversals of male and female in Hellenistic art and literature are indicators of genuine social change. Hellenistic women never attained the equality that sometimes exists between men and women today, but they did enjoy genuine though limited improvements in status. Men and women played new roles in a changed, complex world. The new Hellenistic philosophies and religions attempted to address that complexity.

THE TURN INWARD: NEW PHILOSOPHIES, NEW FAITHS

The events of the Hellenistic era—emigration, a trend from independent city-states to monarchies and federal leagues, new extremes of wealth and poverty, and contact with foreign peoples and customs—all generated uncertainty. In response, Greek culture was spread and transformed. As literacy expanded, more Greeks than ever before could participate in cultural debate. New philosophies and religions arose to meet new spiritual concerns, generating ideas that would be influential for centuries.

The meeting of Jews and Greeks proved to be just as significant. Challenged by Greek conquest, Greek colonization, and their own migration to Greek lands, Jews alternately embraced Hellenism and engaged in resistance, both cultural and armed. In the process, first Judaism and then Hellenism were changed forever.

Cynics, Stoics, Epicureans, and Skeptics

Although the polis lost its military and political pre-eminence in the fourth century B.C., philosophy continued to thrive. It was, however, much changed. With the city-state losing significance as a focus of loyalty, and with the Greek-reading public growing in size and geographic extent, Hellenistic philosophy paid less and less attention to politics. Moreover, as we have seen, Hellenistic science tended to become a separate discipline from philosophy. What was left as the primary subject of philosophy was ethics, the discovery of the best way to live. The essence of the good life, most philosophers agreed, was finding peace of mind, or freedom from troubles. Hellenistic philosophers won wide followings; indeed, for many people, primarily in the elite, philosophy became a way of life, even a religion.

Several competing philosophical schools emerged. The first to attract attention was Cynicism. Never a widespread philosophy, Cynicism is nonetheless important as a precursor of the two most popular doctrines, Stoicism and Epicureanism. Finally, Skepticism rejected the main philosophies as mere dogmatism and proposed instead a commonsense attitude toward ethics.

The first Cynic was Diogenes of Sinope (ca. 400–325 B.C.). An exile in Athens, Diogenes developed a philosophy that rejected all conventions. People find happiness, he decided, by satisfying their natural needs with simplicity. Accordingly, Diogenes chose a life of poverty. A beggar in rags, he delighted in shocking conventional morality. Famous for wit and shamelessness, he was nicknamed "Dog" (*kuon*) because the Greeks considered dogs to be shameless animals; his followers were called "Doglike" (*kunikoi*, whence the name *Cynic*).

Although he founded no school, Diogenes cast a wide shadow. Among those whom he indirectly influenced was Zeno (335–263 B.C.), who began one of the most important philosophical systems of antiquity: Stoicism. Zeno came to Athens in 313 B.C. from Citium in Cyprus, a multi-ethnic city; he was possibly of Phoenician origin. Influenced by both Cynicism and Socratic philosophy, Zeno developed his own doctrines, which he taught in the *Stoa Poikile* ("Painted Porch," whence the name *Stoic*), a public building.

Like Plato and Aristotle, Zeno sought an absolute standard of good on which to base philosophical decisions. He found it in the divine reason (*logos*), which he considered the organizing principle of the universe and the guide to human behavior. The best life was a life in pursuit of wisdom—that is, a life of philosophy. Only that rare and forbidding figure, the Sage, could truly attain wisdom; ordinary people could merely progress toward it. What was required was study and the attempt to be free from all passion.

Stoicism may seem harsh. It is not surprising that *stoical* has come to describe austere indifference to pain. In some ways, however, Stoicism was comforting. First, freedom from passion was meant to bring peace of mind and happiness. Second, unlike Plato, the Stoics were empiricists—that is, they trusted the evidence of the senses, an attitude that they thought would inspire confidence and security. Third, the common share in divine logos entailed a common human brotherhood—led, to be sure, by a Greek-speaking elite. Fourth, because brothers have a duty to one another, the Stoics argued that a good person should play an active role in public life.

Like Hellenistic poets or portraitists, the Stoics emphasized the inner life. They believed that intentions matter. This Stoic belief was an important departure from Greek tradition, which tended to emphasize the outcome of an action, not its motivation.

Stoicism also departed from traditional Greek localism, embracing a more cosmopolitan outlook. "This world is a great city, [and] has one constitution and one law," wrote Philo of Alexandria (30 B.C.–A.D. 45), a Stoic and a Jew. Many Stoics believed in a natural law or law of nations—that is, that overarching and common principles governed international relations.

With its emphasis on duty and order, Stoicism became popular with Greek ruling elites, both Macedonian kings and their opponents in city-states and leagues. Stoicism would enjoy even greater success with the Romans, who found its strictures congenial to their own stern morality and who used its concept of a universal state to justify their empire. A great deal of Stoicism was later embraced by early Christian writers.

Epicurus (341–270 B.C.), an Athenian citizen, founded his philosophical school at around the same time as Zeno founded Stoicism. There were other similarities: both schools were empiricist and materialist (that is, they tended to trust the evidence of the senses), both sought peace of mind, and both inspired widespread followings. Epicurus, however, taught not in a public place but in a private garden. Whereas the Stoics encouraged political participation, the Epicureans counseled withdrawal from the rough-and-tumble of public life. "Calm" and "Live in hiding" are famous Epicurean maxims.

Epicurus's materialism is based on the atomic theory of Democritus (see page 89). It envisions a thoroughly mechanistic universe in which the gods exist but play no active role in events. Individuals need fear neither fickle deities nor an unhappy afterlife because the soul is merely a combination of atoms that ceases to exist after death. What might be the purpose of life in such an unheroic universe? The answer was the avoidance of pain and the pursuit of pleasure. The latter component of Epicureanism was called hedonism (from *hedone,* Greek for "pleasure"), but not, as the word has come to mean today, indulgence in food, drink, or sex. Instead, Epicureans meant intellectual pleasure. Friendship and fraternity were Epicurean ideals—the private analogs, as it were, of Stoic brotherhood.

The Epicureans raised eyebrows and sometimes ire, occasionally suffering persecution by the state. They were accused of atheism and sensuality; to this day, *epicurean* connotes a fondness for luxury and pleasure. Classical Greek philosophy defined virtue as the highest good. The Epicurean emphasis on pleasure, even spiritual pleasure, seemed perverse to some. Yet Epicureanism was simple, sure of itself, and practical, and it offered both friendship and a sense of community. It became a popular philosophy, especially among the wealthy.

Skepticism was founded by Pyrrho of Elis (ca. 360–270 B.C.), a Greek who traveled with Alexander to India. Like Stoics and Epicureans, Skeptics sought peace of mind. They rejected those thinkers' conclusions, however, on the grounds that they were dogmatic—that is, based not on positive proof but merely on opinion (*doxa*). Considering the senses unreliable, Skeptics rejected the commonsense approach of Stoics and Epicureans. They preferred to suspend judgment on the great philosophical questions (hence our term *skepticism* for a doubting state of mind). Whoever was able to do so could accept the customs of the community, avoid politics, and thereby obtain peace of mind.

The Mystery Religions

The name "mystery religion" comes from the Greek word for "secret." A mystery religion initiated worshipers into secret teachings. Long a feature of Greek religion, the mystery religions—there were several different ones—grew very popular in Hellenistic times. Their rise is a sign of the decline of the traditional Greek religion of the Olympian gods.

The old Greek gods came under attack on every front in the Hellenistic era. First, the newly divinized kings stole the spotlight. Second, Hellenistic philosophers, like their Archaic and Classical predecessors, criticized the Olympians as primitive, unsophisticated, and immoral. A third attack came from science and scholarship. Around 300 B.C. Euhemerus of Messene wrote in his *Sacred Scripture* that Zeus, Ouranos, and Kronos were not divine beings but merely great kings of the past who were rewarded with deification, much as a Hellenistic monarch might be. Debunking the Olympians became a popular literary pastime.

The Olympians retained their temples, but the rituals seemed hollow and antiquarian. What was to replace them? Of the several new religious movements that marked the age, three stand out: the divinization of kings, the cult of Tyche (Fortune), and the mystery religions.

Under the Ptolemies and Seleucids, the ruler-worship that Alexander had demanded became standard procedure. Many subjects no doubt considered the divinity of their king or queen merely a patriotic formality. Others treated the divinized monarch as something like a patron saint who could intercede in heaven. The old Greek city-states, especially the democracies, bristled at ruler-worship. "To transfer to men the honor due to the gods," the Athenian playwright Philippides (active ca. 300 B.C.) wrote, "is to dissolve the democracy."

He might have said much the same about the Hellenistic cult of Tyche (Fortune or Luck), often worshiped as a goddess, sometimes as the protector of a particular city. The most famous example was the Tyche of Antioch, personified as a statue of a woman wearing the battlements of the city on her head as a kind of crown—a very popular statue, to judge by the many copies found around the Hellenistic world.

The mystery religions offered relief similar to that of the philosophical schools: ethical guidance, comfort, release from worries, reassurance about death, and a sense of unity. Consider the cult of Demeter at Eleusis, a town just outside the city of Athens. Demeter was the goddess of fertility. Her daughter, Persephone, supposedly spent half the year in the underworld, among the dead, but came back to earth each spring. As told to initiates, the myth symbolized the promise of a blessed afterlife. The precise details of the ritual remain unknown to this day. What is clear is that they included fasting, ritual bathing in the sea, a procession, and a torch-lit ceremony in the great hall at Eleusis.

Various new mystery religions from outside Greece became more popular, particularly the Hellenized Egyptian cults of Serapis and of Isis. Created under Ptolemy I, Serapis was meant to combine Osiris, the Egyptian god of the afterlife, with Apis, the god of the Nile flood. Serapis also suggested Pluto, the Greek god of the underworld. Hence it is an early example of the common Hellenistic practice of religious syncretism, or fusion. Despite its roots, Serapis-worship had little appeal to native Egyptians, but the god became popular in the Greek world as the patron of healing and sailing.

Another traditional Egyptian deity, Osiris's wife, Isis, also became a popular Greek and, later, Roman goddess. Called the Goddess of Ten Thousand Names, Isis was said to symbolize all the female deities of antiquity. Hers was a cult of the afterlife and of the suffering but tender and loving mother; she was particularly popular among women. Thus, under Ptolemaic sponsorship, ancient Egyptian cults were recast and spread throughout the Greek-speaking world, circulating such notions as the suffering mother, the Last Judgment, and blessed eternal life after death. Early Christianity was much influenced by such Greco-Egyptian religious notions, but it was more directly the product of debate and ferment within Hellenistic Judaism.

Hellenistic Judaism Few consequences of Alexander's conquests had so lasting an impact as the mixing of Greeks and Jews. Even before Alexander took Judea from the Persians in 332 B.C., the two peoples were in occasional contact, but in the Hellenistic era, their fates became intertwined. The Greeks governed Judea and then lost it to a Jewish independence movement. Meanwhile, millions of Jews settled in Egypt, Syria, Anatolia, and Greece.

Changed by its contact with Greek culture, Hellenistic Judaism placed a greater emphasis on salvation, martyrdom, and individual study and prayer. Jewish responses to Greek culture varied: they ranged from admiration to resistance to outreach—that is, the desire to convert Greeks to Judaism. In its creative ferment, Hellenistic Judaism proved to have a long-lasting impact on the West.

Hellenistic Judea was governed first by the Ptolemies until 200 B.C., then by the Seleucids, until the establishment of an independent Jewish state in 142 B.C., which came under Roman suzerainty in 63 B.C. The Greeks were not absentee rulers. Rather, they established a large number of Greek colonies in and around Judea, especially under the Seleucids. Many Jews, especially wealthy ones, adopted some degree of Greek culture. Not all of these so-called Hellenizers abandoned Judaism. Indeed, some reshaped Jewish traditions to appeal to a Greek audience. Yet some Hellenizers abandoned Jewish customs altogether for the Greek gymnasium, theater, and political institutions. With the help of the Seleucid king Antiochus IV Epiphanes (r. 175–163 B.C.), Jewish Hellenizers in 175 B.C. had Jerusalem proclaimed a Greek polis, renamed Antioch, like many a Seleucid city; they even built a gymnasium at the foot of the Temple Mount. In 167 B.C. they went further by outlawing Sabbath observance, prohibiting circumcision, and rededicating the Temple to Olympian Zeus.

The traditionalists, however, resisted. Aided by the political ineptitude of their opponents, who raised taxes, they rallied the Jewish masses into opposition. Soon a guerrilla revolt began in the countryside, led by the Hasmonean family, also known as the Maccabees, whose successes are celebrated today by Jews during the religious holiday of Hanukkah. The guerrilla movement developed into a disciplined armed uprising, which forced the Seleucids to tolerate an independent state under the Hasmonean dynasty. Religiously conservative at home, the state was expansionist abroad, conquering nearby territories such as the Galilee and forcing their inhabitants to convert to Judaism.

During the struggle over Hellenism, new elements of lasting significance became part of Judaism. First, the Jews developed a literature of spiritual resistance to the foreigner. This literature was apocalyptic—that is, it claimed to reveal dramatic, heretofore secret truths. Drawing on both biblical and Mesopotamian traditions, Jewish apocalyptic writing predicted a future cataclysm, when a royal redeemer would evict the foreigner and establish a new kingdom of Israel. The redeemer was often identified with another notion that first became popular in this era: the Messiah (literally, "anointed one"), someone anointed with oil signifying his election as king, a descendant of King David, who would save Israel. Another new aspect of Hellenistic Judaism was martyrdom, the notion of the holy sacrifice of one's life for a religious cause. There was also a growing belief in a final Judgment Day and resurrection, when God would raise the meritorious dead to live again on earth in their own bodies.

Hellenistic Judaism was far from monolithic. Various sects each proposed its own version of Judaism. Among these sects were the Sadducees ("righteous ones"), a wealthy establishment group for whom the rituals of the Temple in Jerusalem were the heart of Judaism. Their opponents, the Pharisees ("those who separated themselves"), insisted on the validity of the oral tradition of interpretation alongside the written law of the Hebrew Bible and the Temple rituals. The Pharisees proposed a kind of democratization of Judaism, emphasizing study and prayer in small groups. A third group was the Essenes, generally identified with the Qumran community in the Judean desert (see page 181). As for the Hellenizers, although some were merely status seekers, others sincerely wished to combine Jewish ethical monotheism with the cosmopolitan spirit of Hellenistic civilization. They wanted, in short, to bring Jewish teachings to non-Jews, or Gentiles ("the nations").

Most Jews of the Hellenistic era lived outside Judea. The Diaspora had spread into (among other places) Syria, Anatolia, the Greek mainland, and Egypt, where a strong

IMPORTANT EVENTS

359–336 B.C. Reign of Philip II of Macedon

ca. 342–292 B.C. Life of playwright Menander

338 B.C. Greece falls to Philip at Battle of Chaeronea

336–323 B.C. Reign of Alexander the Great

331 B.C. Battle of Gaugamela completes Persian defeat

322–275 B.C. Wars of the Successors

313 B.C. Zeno founds Stoic philosophy in Athens

312 B.C. Seleucus I conquers Babylon

304 B.C. Ptolemy I king of Egypt

294 B.C. Museum founded in Alexandria

276 B.C. Antigonus Gonatas king of Macedon

263 B.C. Kingdom of Pergamum founded

ca. 246 B.C. Parthia revolts from Seleucids

ca. 245 B.C. Bactria gains independence

244–222 B.C. Reforms of Agis and Cleomenes in Sparta

ca. 225 B.C. Eratosthenes of Cyrene calculates earth's circumference

217 B.C. Battle of Raphia brings Palestine under Ptolemies

167–142 B.C. Maccabean revolt in Judea

146 B.C. Antigonid Macedonia becomes a Roman province

64 B.C. Seleucid Syria becomes a Roman province

30 B.C. Ptolemaic Egypt becomes a Roman province

Jewish presence during the Persian period grew even stronger, particularly in Alexandria. Jews served the Ptolemies as soldiers, generals, bureaucrats, and tax collectors. They also prospered in private enterprise. Jewish success, as well as their maintenance of a separate culture, led to hostility among ordinary Greeks and Egyptians. Such attitudes spawned the first anti-Semitic literature as well as sporadic violence that at times broke into riots and persecution. Yet there was also considerable admiration among Greek intellectuals for what they saw as Jewish virtue and antiquity.

Greek was the common tongue of Diaspora Jews. Between around 300 and 100 B.C. in Alexandria the Hebrew Bible was translated into Greek. Known as the Septuagint, or Seventy, from the number of translators who, legend has it, labored on the project, this text made the Bible accessible to a Jewish community increasingly unable to understand Hebrew or Aramaic. In later centuries the Septuagint became the Old Testament of Greek-speaking Christians.

Foreign conversions and immigration into the Diaspora began to change the meaning of the word *Jew*. The word came to mean less "inhabitant of Judea" than "practitioner of Judaism." In short, *Jew* came to denote as much a religion as a nation.

NOTES

1. Isocrates, "Panegyricus," trans. H. I. Marrou, in *A History of Education in Antiquity,* trans. George Lamb (New York: Mentor Books/New American Library, 1956), p. 130.
2. Romila Thapar, *Aśoka and the Decline of the Mauryas* (Oxford: Oxford University Press, 1961), p. 256.
3. Quoted in Charles Rowan Beye, *Ancient Greek Literature and Society,* 2d ed. (Ithaca, N.Y.: Cornell University Press, 1987), p. 265.

SUGGESTED READING

Bosworth, A. B. *The Legacy of Alexander: Politics, Warfare, and Propaganda Under the Successors.* 2001. A study of the emergence of the Hellenistic kingdoms in the thirty years after Alexander's death.

Bowman, Alan K. *Egypt After the Pharaohs.* 1986. An excellent and highly readable introduction to the social history of the Ptolemaic and later periods.

Cohen, Shaye. *From the Maccabees to the Mishnah.* 1987. An excellent introduction by a distinguished scholar of Second Temple Judaism.

Grant, Michael. *From Alexander to Cleopatra: The Hellenistic World.* 1982. A lively and readable introduction; at its best on cultural history.

Green, P. *Alexander to Actium: An Essay in the Historical Evolution of the Hellenistic Age.* 1989. A collection of elegant essays synthesizing scholarship on a wide variety of topics in political, cultural, and social history.

Long, A. A. *Hellenistic Philosophy: Stoics, Epicureans, Sceptics.* 2d ed. 1986. A concise critical analysis of the main ideas and methods of thought of the major Hellenistic philosophers.

Shipley, Graham. *The Greek World After Alexander, 323–30 B.C.* 2000. A thorough, sophisticated, and learned introduction to the Hellenistic era; well versed in and prudent about recent scholarly controversies.

Wood, Michael. *In the Footsteps of Alexander the Great.* 1997. An engaging story that retraces Alexander's path today while it narrates his history; magnificent color photos of seldom-seen sites.

5

Rome, from Republic to Empire, ca. 509–31 B.C.

(Michael Yamshita/ Woodfin Camp & Associates)

Here is the Roman Forum. We are standing in the heart of the ancient city, under the arch of the emperor Septimius Severus, looking south toward two columns that once held statues of great citizens. Beyond them are the Sacred Way, Rome's oldest street, and the three elegant columns of the Temple of Castor and Pollux. In the background, beyond a market and vaulted warehouse, is the Palatine Hill. The photograph takes us from an arch celebrating military triumph to ruins evoking citizenship and piety, to a reminder of the everyday needs of the masses of Rome, and finally to a historic hill. On this hill shepherds founded the city of Rome, and on this hill, centuries later, emperors lived. We see, in short, the civic center of the city destined to give the Western world many of its fundamental ideas about government and empire. It is arguably the single most important public space in the history of the world.

The ancient Romans were a practical people. Virgil (70–19 B.C.), for example, the greatest Roman poet (see pages 167–168), celebrates not his countrymen's artistry or cultivation but rather their pragmatic accomplishments:

> For other peoples will, I do not doubt,
> still cast their bronze to breathe with softer features,
> or draw out of the marble living lines,
> plead causes better, trace the ways of heaven
> with wands and tell the rising constellations;
> but yours will be the rulership of nations,
> remember, Romans, these will be your arts:
> to teach the ways of peace to those you conquer,
> to spare defeated peoples, tame the proud.[1]

The Romans turned an Italian city-state into one of the largest empires in history, including all the countries of the Mediterranean as well as large parts of western Asia and of northern and central Europe. By holding this empire for centuries and by promoting prosperity in every corner, Rome planted in what would become Britain, France, Germany, and Spain (among other places) the seeds of the advanced civilizations of the Mediterranean.

Rome is no less important for its influence on the Western civic tradition. Much of the modern vocabulary of politics, from *president* to *inauguration* to *forum,* can be traced back to Rome. After an early period of monarchy, Rome was for centuries a republic (Latin, *res publica,* literally "public thing") before becoming essentially a monarchy again under the Caesars. The Roman Republic mixed popular power with government controlled by wealthy landowners. The government was divided into three branches, which created a system of checks and balances that tended toward consensus. The result was efficiency and, for centuries, stability.

Roman politicians sought to control ordinary citizens but in some ways were more flexible than Greek democrats. Unlike Greece, Rome extended its citizenship to a large population, first throughout Italy and then across its entire empire. The modern nation-state with its mass citizenship owes much to Rome. Indeed, although Rome was not democratic, modern democracy—that is, popular government with a large population, whose officials are elected by the people—has roots in the Roman Republic as well as in the Greek city-state.

Fueled by fear, ambition, and greed, Roman expansion generated its own momentum. Rome's arrogance matched its success: in consolidating power over huge territories, the Romans committed atrocities, enslaved whole peoples, and destroyed cities with little provocation. Ironically, military success slowly undermined both Rome's political stability at home and the socioeconomic basis of its army. Meanwhile, the Romans showed great open-mindedness in borrowing from other societies, in particular from the Greeks, to whom the Republic owed great cultural debts. Also fascinating is the shrewdness and generosity with which the Romans shared their citizenship with the elites whom they had conquered, thereby winning their loyalty and strengthening Rome's grip on their territories.

Historians conventionally divide the Republic into three periods: Early (509–287 B.C.), Middle (287–133 B.C.), and Late (133–31 B.C.). This chapter begins with the origins of the city of Rome in the early first millennium B.C. and then traces the Republic from its foundation to its imperial conquests to its collapse under their weight. Success spoiled Rome. The unintended consequences of conquest on Rome's society, politics, and culture led to a revolution that, in the century beginning in 133 B.C., saw the Republic's downfall.

BEFORE THE REPUBLIC, 753–509 B.C.

The ancient Romans believed that their city was founded on April 21, 753 B.C., by Romulus, a descendant of refugees from the Trojan War. Although the name "Romulus" supplies a convenient etymology for "Rome," little stock can be placed in this story. Nevertheless, archaeology shows that Rome was already an important settlement by the eighth century B.C. A simple village of farmers and shepherds—a collection of huts— was established then on the Palatine Hill, one of the seven hills on which Rome would cluster and the place where tradition puts the settlement of 753. But the first settlers on the hills of Rome came even earlier, around 1000 B.C., as pottery and graves show.

Archaeological evidence raises some basic questions: What were Rome's origins, and how did it grow? Are seeds of Roman greatness visible in its early history? By examining the data of archaeology and of those elements in ancient historiography that seem to be based on accurate tradition, we can answer these questions, at least in outline.

Archaic Rome and Its Neighbors   Italy is a long peninsula, shaped roughly like a boot, extending about 750 miles from the Alps into the Mediterranean. In the far north, the high Alps provide a barrier to the rest of Europe. To the east, the Adriatic Sea separates Italy from modern Slovenia and Croatia; to the west, the Tyrrhenian Sea faces the large islands of Sardinia and Corsica (and the smaller but iron-rich island of Elba) and, beyond, the coasts of France and Spain. Off the "toe" of the Italian boot, and separated from the mainland by a narrow, 3-mile strait of water, is the large island of Sicily, rich farm country in ancient times. Sicily is only 90 miles from North Africa. In short, Italy is centrally located in the Mediterranean. It was both a target for conquerors and a springboard for conquest.

Italy contained some of the ancient Mediterranean's most fertile and metal-rich land. From the watershed of the Po and Adige Rivers in the north, the agriculturally

Early Italy and Region of City of Rome

Early Italy comprised a variety of terrain and peoples. Rome is located in the central Italian region of Latium. The Alps separate Italy from northern Europe. The Apennine mountain range runs almost the entire length of the Italian peninsula. Much of the rest of Italy is fertile plain.

Latium

0   15 Km.
0   15 Mi.

Lake Sabatinus
Tiber
Ar
Veii
Tibur
AEQUI
Anio
Gabii
Rome
Praeneste
Tusculum
HERNICI
Anagnia
Ostia
Lake Albanus
Mt. Albanus
Trerus
Lavinium
Lake Nemorensis
Cora
Tyrrhenian Sea
Ardea
Norba
Satricum
V O L S C I
Privernum
Antium

Roman territory, ca. 500 B.C.

ALPS

Ligurian Sea

LIGURES

VENETI
Adige
Po
Mantua
Spina
ETRUSCANS
Felsina (Bologna)
Ravenna
Faesulae
Arno
Adriatic Sea
ILLYRIA
Volaterrae
UMBRI
Arretium
PICENTES
ETRURIA
Perusia
Populonia
Clusium
Vetulonia
Volsinii
Elba
ETRUSCANS
LIGURES
Vulci
SABINES
APENNINES
Alalia
Tarquinii
Veii
Corsica
Caere
Rome
SAMNITES
LATIUM
APULI
LATINS
Capua
CAMPANIA
Cumae
Neapolis (Naples)
MESSAPII
Puteoli
Herculaneum
OSCI
Pithecusae
Pompeii
Tarentum
Bay of Naples
LUCANI
Sardinia
Gulf of Tarentum
Tharros
Tyrrhenian Sea
Sybaris
SARDI
BRUTTII
Carales
Croton

Mediterranean Sea

Messana
Panormus
SICANI
SICULI
Utica
Cape Bon
Sicily
Carthage
MAGNA GRAECIA
Acragas (Agrigentum)
Syracuse

NORTH AFRICA

Malta

0   50   100 Km.
0   50   100 Mi.

Etruscans of Etruria
Expansion of Etruscans
Greeks
Carthaginians
OSCI Other peoples

rich plains of Etruria (modern Tuscany), Latium (the region of Rome), and Campania (the region of Naples) unfold southward down Italy's west coast. Although the Apennine mountain range runs north-south along most of the Italian peninsula, they are low compared with the Alps and contain many passes, permitting the movement of armies.

A sensational recent archaeological discovery opens a window into second-millennium B.C. Italy. Poggiomarino is a prehistoric village consisting of houses that were built on oak pilings and separated by canals. The village, located on a river near Naples, was inhabited from around the 1500s B.C. to around 700 B.C. A masterpiece of prehistoric engineering, the village covered at least 7 acres and was a center of bronze production.

In the first millennium B.C., Italy was a hodgepodge of peoples and languages. They included the Etruscans in the north, Greek colonists in southern Italy and in Sicily, and such mountain peoples as the Sabines and the Samnites. The Samnites spoke Oscan, an Indo-European language, as did the Campanians, who lived around Naples, and the Lucanians, who lived in south-central Italy. Both the Samnites and the Lucanians were warlike peoples who conquered their neighbors before finally being conquered by Rome.

Latium was home to a number of small Latin-speaking towns, one of them Rome. In the fifth century B.C. another important people arrived on the Italian scene: Celts (called Gauls by the Romans), large numbers of whom crossed the Alps and settled in northern Italy after roughly 500 B.C. Most of these various peoples spoke Indo-European languages, of which Latin, the language of the Romans (as well as other peoples of Latium), was one.

Rome's location in Italy was central and protected. Rome is located in Latium, which is about halfway down the Italian peninsula. Located 15 miles inland on the Tiber, the largest river on Italy's west coast, Rome had access to the sea. A midstream island makes Rome the first crossing place upstream from the Tiber's mouth, offering the Romans freedom of movement north and south. Yet strategically, Rome was protected. It was far enough from the sea to be safe from raiders and pirates. And its seven hills offered a natural defense—from nature as well as humans, because the Tiber often flooded its banks.

In the seventh century B.C. Archaic Rome (as the pre-Republican period is called) began to change from a large village into a city. In this era Rome saw its first stone houses, its first public building, and its first forum or civic center. In the sixth century B.C. streets, walls, drains, temples, and a racetrack followed. What caused the transformation? Perhaps the key factor was contact with Magna Graecia, the Greek colonies to the south. Established in the eighth and seventh centuries B.C., the colonies transported westward the sophisticated urban civilization of the eastern Mediterranean.

More controversial is the impact on early Rome of its neighbors to the north, the Etruscans. The twelve Etruscan city-states were organized in a loose confederation centered in Etruria. They grew rich from the mining of iron, copper, and silver, from piracy, from trade, and from a network of influential Etruscan emigrants throughout central Italy, probably including Rome's last three kings (traditionally dated 616–509 B.C.).

The Etruscans were brilliant, wealthy, and warlike. We know less about them than we would like, from their language, which is only partly understood, to their origins, which probably lay in Italy but possibly in Anatolia. Etruscan power extended to many places in central, northern, and even southern Italy. Many scholars argue that the

Etruscan Tomb Painting   *This wall painting from Tarquinia shows a married aristocratic couple at a banquet. The style of the figures is derived from Greek art, but the depiction of husband and wife dining on the same couch is characteristically Etruscan.*   (National Museum, Tarquinia/Scala/Art Resource, NY)

Etruscans conquered pre-Republican Rome, but the evidence does not support that theory. Rather, an Etruscan nobleman, Lucius Tarquinius Priscus, migrated to Rome and was eventually elected king. Under him and his son (or perhaps grandson), Lucius Tarquinius Superbus, who was Rome's last king, Etruscan culture left an impact on Rome. For example, the Tarquins sponsored several building projects in Rome, including the great Temple of Jupiter on the Capitoline Hill in the center of Rome. But scholars disagree as to whether the Etruscan impact on Roman culture was superficial or deep.

At least we can be sure that the Etruscans were great artists and architects and very religious. They believed that it was possible to learn the will of the gods by interpreting the sight and sound of lightning and thunder and by carefully examining the internal organs, especially the liver, of sacrificial animals. Etruscan elite women had high status compared with their Greek or Roman counterparts. Etruscan women kept their own names, and Etruscan children bore the names of both parents. In addition, Etruscan elite women were permitted to attend athletic contests in spite of the presence of naked male athletes.

The Roman Monarchy   Tradition says that Rome was ruled by seven kings before the foundation of the Republic. Although the number of kings may be a later invention, their existence is undoubted. In addition to traces of the monarchy in Republican institutions, there is archaeological proof: a form of the Latin word *rex* ("king"), for example, has been found inscribed on a Roman monument from the early sixth century B.C. The king's power, called *imperium* (from *imperare,* "to command"), was very great, embracing religious, military, and judicial affairs.

The king was advised by a council of elders, called the "fathers" (*patres* in Latin) or the "senate" (*senatus,* from *senex,* "old man"). In theory, the senate was primarily an advisory body, but in practice it was very powerful. Senators were the heads of the most important families in Rome, so the king rejected their advice at his peril. Romans spoke of the senate's *auctoritas,* a quasi-religious prestige.

Most senators were patricians, as early Rome's hereditary aristocracy was known. The rest of the people, the bulk of Roman society, were called plebeians. Plebeians were free; most were ordinary people, though some were wealthy. Patricians monopolized the senate and priesthoods, and they did not intermarry with plebeians.

The whole people, probably both patricians and plebeians, met in an assembly organized in thirty local units, or *curiae,* hence the name *curiate assembly.* Although the assembly's numbers were large, its powers were limited. Before becoming law, resolutions of the assembly required approval by the senate.

Early Rome was a class-based society, but it was open to foreigners. Among others, Etruscans, Sabines, and Latins—as the inhabitants of other Latin-speaking towns are called—came to settle in Rome. The Tarquins, whose family is traditionally said to have provided two kings of Rome, including the last, may have originally come from Corinth. Unlike Athenians, who tried to hide the presence of immigrants in their country by a myth of indigenous origins, Romans openly discussed their mixed roots. Foreigners at first had low status, but they gained equality around 550 B.C., for pragmatic purposes. Rome needed soldiers to fight its wars; in order to expand the body of loyal infantrymen, the immigrants were granted citizenship—a reform traditionally associated with King Servius Tullius (578–535 B.C.).

Servius probably introduced to Rome the hoplite phalanx (see page 67), with immigrants included in its ranks. The changes in the army contributed to the process that, within several generations of Servius's reform, took Rome from monarchy to republic.

GOVERNMENT AND SOCIETY IN THE EARLY AND MIDDLE REPUBLICS, CA. 509–133 B.C.

Tradition says that the Roman Republic was established in 509 B.C., when the kings were overthrown. Nowadays, scholars envision a long process rather than a single, dramatic upheaval. In either case, the new Republic was destined to have a unique influence on Western political institutions, so it is worth a close look.

The Republic differed from the monarchy in two basic ways. First, the Republic stood for liberty, which for the Romans meant both freedom from the arbitrary power of a king and freedom to participate in public affairs. Second, the Republic was a commonwealth, in Latin, *res publica,* literally "public thing," as opposed to *res privata,* "private thing," as the Romans characterized monarchy. As a kingdom Rome belonged to the royal family, but as a republic it belonged to the Roman people. In theory, the Roman people were sovereign—that is, the people ruled the state.

But which people? This is a key question because the Romans did *not* embrace another principle that might seem to follow from liberty: equality. Rather, they believed in order, balance, and competition, all of which are central themes of Roman Republican history. Roman society and culture, moreover, were conservative. Once the young Republic had its new values in place, it tried to maintain those values over the centuries with little change. Nor did the Republic give up entirely on the old values of the monarchy. Rather, it continued some of those values.

What Kind of Republic?	We know relatively little about the Early Republic (509–287 B.C.) but enough to know that it witnessed centuries of social and political conflict. The Middle Republic (287–133 B.C.)

was a shorter and better-documented period of relative consensus at home and massive expansion abroad. Social and political conflict broke out again with a vengeance in the Late Republic (133–31 B.C.), ultimately rendering the Republic a deathblow.

The best and most even-handed ancient analyst of Roman politics is the historian Polybius (ca. 200–118 B.C.). A Greek and former hostage who lived in Rome, Polybius observed his adopted city with an outsider's careful eye. Polybius argued that in the Middle Republic of his day, Rome was a "mixed constitution," balancing the power of the masses with the authority of the elite. The result was a strong and stable state.

Polybius divides Roman political institutions into three branches: executive, deliberative, and legislative. The American founders adopted a similar division, but they combined the legislative and deliberative functions and added a judicial branch. In Rome the executive branch also administered justice. Rome's executive branch was made up of magistrates—that is, public officials; the deliberative branch consisted of the Roman senate; and the legislative branch was composed of four different assemblies of the people.

Polybius argued that the assemblies were democratic, the senate oligarchic, and the magistrates a royal element. Not all historians agree. Polybius's critics say that he was misled by the democratic façade of Rome's assemblies. In the last analysis, they maintain, oligarchs controlled the state. They monopolized high office, rigged elections, dominated proceedings in the senate, set the course of cultural life, and controlled religion in a society that knew no separation of church and state.

Although these criticisms contain some truth, they overstate the case. Rome experienced real political competition and a real need to court the voters; all laws were debated, often fiercely, in public meetings; candidates for office ran ambitious campaigns, which suggests that the results were not rigged; the people's representatives could veto any action taken by public officials; and freed slaves became citizens, which was rarely true in a democratic Greek state such as Athens. Of course, the wealthy elite had considerable power, but that power was limited, which means that, as Polybius writes, the Roman political system was balanced and competitive.

In short, Rome was a mixed constitution. It was not always a stable society, however. Let us survey Rome's political institutions and then examine the conflicts of the Early Republic and the compromises that resolved them in the middle era. We will turn to the revolution that destroyed the Late Republic at the end of this chapter.

Political Institutions	Executive power lay in the hands of Rome's powerful magistrates. They were elected and not chosen by lottery, as in

Greek democracy. Election required campaigning, which in turn took money and connections. Magistracies were time-consuming jobs but offered no salary, unlike in Greek democracy. Thus only a wealthy few could afford to hold public office in Rome.

Eager for strong magistrates but afraid that power corrupts, Romans imposed the principles of *collegiality* and *annuality* on their officials. Every magistrate had one or more colleagues and held office for only one year. The chief magistrates were eventually called consuls, of which there were two. Each consul had the power to veto the other's actions. Like the former king, each consul had *imperium,* the power to issue commands and order punishments, including execution.

From about 500 B.C. to about 300 B.C., other public offices were created to help the consuls as administration grew more complex. In addition, the Romans elected two censors, older men chosen once every few years for eighteen-month terms. At first their job was to supervise the census, the military register of citizens that recorded each man's property class. Later the censors became, as it were, supervisors of public morals, since they could punish "bad" citizens.

The Republic's government adapted flexibly to trying circumstances. In times of emergency, for example, the Republic turned power over to a single magistrate. The dictator, as he was called, made binding decisions, but he held office for only six months.

The Roman senate guided and advised the magistrates. During most of the Republic, the senate consisted of three hundred men, all former magistrates and each of whom served for life. Senators possessed great authority. They supervised public expenditures and were for all practical purposes in charge of foreign policy.

Only the assemblies of the people could make laws. There were four assemblies: the curiate assembly, the centuriate assembly, the council of the plebs, and the tribal assembly. Roman assemblies combined democratic and nondemocratic features. On the one hand, all decisions were made by majority vote, and only after speeches or campaigning. Assembly meetings were often preceded by public meetings, typically in the forum, which featured lively debate. Women, free noncitizens, and even slaves could attend. On the other hand, voting took place by groups, and those groups were unrepresentative. Furthermore, in contrast to Greece, assembly participants stood rather than sat down and received no salary for attendance.

Although the curiate assembly of the monarchy survived, in the Republic it had a largely ceremonial role. The centuriate assembly held real power: it elected magistrates, voted on laws and treaties, accepted declarations of war and peace, and acted as a court in cases of treason, homicide, and appeals of the magistrates' decisions. But this assembly was dominated by wealthy men, especially the equestrians, or cavalrymen. The poorest men, known as *proletarii* ("breeders"), often did not have even the chance to vote.

The two other assemblies were the council of the plebs and the tribal assembly. The tribal assembly eventually replaced the plebs and, in fact, became Rome's main legislative body in the third century B.C., outstripping the centuriate assembly in making laws. To understand the evolution and workings of the tribal assembly, we turn now to the class conflicts in Rome during the fifth through third centuries B.C.

Conflict of the Orders

Social and political conflict severely tested the Roman state between 494 and 287 B.C. In the end, a more stable state was hammered out, led by a wider elite and offering a measure of popular power. As Rome reached a domestic political consensus, it presented a stronger military front to its enemies. By 300 B.C. Rome was ready to grow from local power to dominance in Italy and then the Mediterranean.

Tradition gives Rome only 136 patrician families in 509 B.C., but they dominated the Early Republic. The plebs, in contrast, comprised masses of peasants and a tiny number of men who, though wealthy, were not patricians. There were plebeian artisans, traders, and shopkeepers, but they made up only a small part of the population. The various plebeian groups each wanted to break patrician power. Wealthy plebeians wanted access to high office, from which they had been largely excluded. Ordinary plebeians demanded relief from debt, redistribution of land, and codification and publication of the law. For a century and a half, the two groups of plebeians made common cause, writing an important chapter in the history of political resistance.

Debt and hunger loomed large in the Early Republic. If a free man could not repay a loan, he had to work off what he owed, often for the rest of his life. Plebeians wanted this harsh system abolished. The average farm was too small to feed a family, so most peasants depended on public land for farming and grazing. Time and again throughout Republican history, however, public land was taken by the wealthy, who denied access to the poor. The only plebeian hope was to change the system.

The story of the plebs in the fifth century B.C. is one of solidarity. They organized themselves as a kind of state within the state, complete with their own assembly (the council of the plebs) and officials (the tribunes of the plebs). The decisions of the council of the plebs, called *plebiscita* (from which *plebiscite* comes), were binding only on the plebs; they did not receive the full force of law for over two hundred years. Yet the plebs did not retreat. On several occasions during the Early Republic, they resorted to secession: the plebs as a whole left the city, often for the Aventine Hill, where they stayed until their grievances were addressed.

The ten tribunes, elected annually by the plebs, were the people's champions. A tribune's house stood open to any plebeian who needed him, and he could not leave the city limits. Inside the city of Rome, a tribune also had the right to veto any act of the magistrates, assembly, or senate that harmed plebeians. In return, the plebs swore to treat the tribunes as sacrosanct and to lynch anyone who harmed them.

But the patricians struck back. They controlled important priesthoods and had many supporters in the military. Furthermore, the new tribal assembly, created around the same time as the council of the plebs, used a system of representation that heavily favored landowners such as patricians. The tribal assembly elected lower magistrates and, like the centuriate assembly, voted on laws and acted as a court of appeals.

Still, the plebeians pressed onward and forced concessions from the patricians, until finally the patricians retreated. They decided to neutralize the poor by meeting the main demands of the plebeian elite. The outcome was a new nobility that combined patricians and plebeians. The patricians had decided to compromise to keep most of their privileges. The personnel changed, but the elite maintained power in Rome.

The specific events in the patrician-plebeian conflict follow two lines of development: concessions to wealthy plebeians and concessions to poor ones. A key moment came in 449 B.C. with publication of the law code known as the "Twelve Tables," eventually, if not at first, on twelve bronze tablets in the Forum. By modern standards, the code was tough and primitive, but its very existence was a plebeian victory because published law was accessible and dependable. Unfortunately, the complex legal procedure remained a secret of the priests for another 150 years, which meant that no poor man could go to court without the help of a rich patron.

Continued plebeian pressure slowly yielded other gains through the fourth century B.C. Around 445 B.C. the patricians accepted patrician-plebeian intermarriage, but it took nearly another eighty years, until 367 B.C., until they agreed to plebeian consuls. That same year saw a debt-relief law, and further debt relief came in 326 B.C.

Finally, in 287 B.C., the patrician and plebeian orders were formally merged, and a law called the "lex Hortensia" made decisions of the council of the plebs and the tribal assembly binding on the whole community, including patricians. Rome's new, combined patrician-plebeian elite was based on wealth, not heredity. Most Romans were non-elite, but at least they had won something: debt relief, access to the published laws, increased power for their assembly, and, most important, protection from arbitrary power.

The problems of poverty continued, but during these same Early Republican years, the poor began to find another form of relief in the new land that Rome acquired through conquest.

The Roman Household

Roman government was once thought to be nothing more than the maneuvering of a few powerful families. Today a more balanced picture of Rome's constitution prevails. Yet there remains no doubt that elite Roman families wielded great power.

The Latin word *familia* is broader in meaning than the English word *family*. Better translated as "household," it connotes slaves, animals, and property, as well as the mem-

Shrine of a Wealthy Household *This painting from Pompeii shows the spirit of the paterfamilias in a toga, which is wrapped around his head in keeping the Roman procedures of sacrifice. He is flanked by the spirits of departed ancestors. A snake symbolizes fertility.* (Alinari/Art Resource, NY)

bers of a nuclear family and their ancestors or descendants. The familia was the basic unit of Roman society and a model of political authority. In theory, though not always in practice, the Roman household was an authoritarian institution governed by a male; thus the familia is an example of patriarchy.

The legal head of the familia was the *paterfamilias*—the oldest living male, usually the father. According to Roman law, the paterfamilias had supreme power within the household. Although he was supposed to call a council of senior male relatives to consult on major decisions, he was not required to follow their advice. He had the right to sell family members into slavery and the rarely used power to kill an errant wife or child. A son, no matter how old, was always legally subject to the authority of a living paterfamilias.

Roman respect for the paterfamilias stemmed from Roman esteem for ancestors, who were more important than in Greek culture. All patricians and some plebeians belonged to a *gens* (plural, *gentes*), a kinship group that traced its ancestry back to a purported common ancestor. All Roman males had a personal and a family name, and patricians and elite plebeians also had a third (middle) name, indicating their gens—for example, Gaius Julius Caesar, whose personal name "Gaius" was followed by the gens name "Julius" and the familia name "Caesar."

In theory, the paterfamilias was the focus of power in the household, but practice was more complex. The sources are full of fathers who showed affection, love, and even indulgence toward their children. Moreover, Roman women usually married in their late teens and men in their late twenties. Given the low life expectancies, it was common for a man of 25 to have already buried his father. Many, perhaps even most, adult males were independent of a paterfamilias.

Unlike men, Roman women never became legally independent, even on the death of a paterfamilias. Instead of receiving a personal name, a daughter was called by the name of her father's gens. For example, Gaius Julius Caesar's daughter was called Julia; if Caesar had had a second daughter, she would have been Julia Secunda ("Julia the Second"). Although fathers were expected to support all male children, they had to support only the first of their daughters. In other words, they were free to "expose" additional daughters—that is, leave them in the open to die or, as was perhaps more likely, to be adopted or raised as a slave. A father also arranged a daughter's marriage and provided her with a dowry. In theory, again, the customs suggest a most severe relationship, but the evidence shows considerable father-daughter affection, including married daughters who sought advice or aid from their fathers.

Most women in early Rome married *cum manu* (literally, "with hand")—that is, they were "handed over" to their husbands, who became their new paterfamilias. Even so, Roman wives and mothers had more prestige and freedom than their counterparts in Classical Greece. Legends of early Rome mention some who were peacemakers, negotiators, or catalysts of quarrels among men. Roman women regularly shared meals and social activities with their parents and were expected to take an interest in their husbands' political lives.

Patrons and Clients   *Patron* (derived from *pater*, "father") means "defender" or "protector." *Client* means "dependent." Just as the Roman family was hierarchical, so Roman society consisted of pyramidal patron-client networks. Most patrons were in turn clients of someone more powerful; only a very few men stood at the top of the pyramid. To the Romans, justice meant not that patron and client treated each other as equals but rather that they showed each other respect and fulfilled mutual obligations.

Various paths led to the status of client. A peasant in need of help on his farm might ask a wealthy neighbor to become his patron. A manumitted slave became the client of his former owner. A conquered foe became the client of the victorious general. The status of client or patron was hereditary.

Patron and client might help each other in various ways. A patron might provide a client with food or with property for a dowry. He might settle disputes or provide legal assistance. In return, a client owed his patron respect and service. He escorted his patron in public on important occasions—possession of a large clientele signified prestige and power. If his patron sought political office, the client voted for him and urged others to do so.

Cloaked in an elaborate language of goodwill, the patron-client relationship was considered a matter of *fides* ("good faith" or "trustworthiness"). Romans spoke not of a client submitting to a patron's power but rather of a client "commending himself" to the patron's fides. A patron spoke not of his clients but of his "friends," especially if they were men of standing or substance.

A patron was supposed to put his clients before his kin by marriage; only blood or adoptive relations were to take precedence. According to the Twelve Tables, a patron who defrauded his client was accursed and subject to death with impunity.

Patronage played an important role in Roman domestic politics. A wealthy patron expected his humble clients to vote as he wished, but he abused them at his peril. If a man's clients grew discontented, they might find a new patron. Patronage was more straightforward in foreign affairs. Experience as patrons schooled Roman leaders in treating the peoples they conquered as clients, often as personal clients. Moreover, the Roman state sometimes took foreign countries into its collective fides—much as a patron did a client—thus allowing Rome to extend its influence without the constraints of a formal alliance.

| Religion and World-View | If we knew nothing about early Roman religion, we could deduce much about it from the familia and patronage. We could expect to find an emphasis on powerful fathers and binding |

agreements, and both are indeed present. The task of a Roman priest, whether an official of the state or an individual paterfamilias, was to establish what the Romans called the "peace of the gods." Roman cults aimed at obtaining the gods' agreement to human requests, at "binding" the gods—the Latin term for which is *religio*.

The earliest Roman religion was animistic—that is, it centered on the spirits that, the Romans believed, haunted the household and the fields and forests and determined the weather. The Lares, or spirits of departed ancestors, guarded the house, and the Penates watched over stored grain. The spirit of the hearth was Vesta, of the door Janus, of the rain and sun Jupiter (later identified with the Greek sky-god and the father-god Zeus), and of the crops and vegetation Mars (later identified with the Greek war-god Ares). The Romans believed that these spirits needed to be appeased—hence the contractual nature of their prayers and offerings. Over the years, as a result of Greek influence, anthropomorphism (that is, the worship of humanlike gods and goddesses) replaced Roman animism.

Roman state religion grew out of house religion. Vesta, the hearth-goddess, became goddess of the civic hearth; Janus, the door-god, became god of the city's gates; Jupiter became the general overseer of the gods; and Mars became the god of war. When trade and conquest brought the Romans into contact with foreign religions, the Romans tended to absorb them. The senate screened and sometimes rejected new gods, but by and large Roman polytheism was tolerant and inclusive.

The Republic sponsored numerous priestly committees, or colleges, to secure the peace of the gods. Originally restricted to patricians, most of the highest priesthoods were opened to plebeians by law in 300 B.C. Although some priesthoods were full-time jobs, most left the officeholder free to pursue a parallel career as a magistrate or a senator. The two most important priestly colleges were the augurs, who were in charge of foretelling the future from omens and other signs, and the pontiffs, who exercised a general supervision of Roman religion. The chief pontiff, the *pontifex maximus,* was the head of the state clergy. He was chosen by election. The pontiffs alone controlled the interpretation of the law until the fourth century B.C. The Romans allowed priests to interpret the law on the theory that an offense against humans was also an offense against the gods.

The system provided for only two colleges of priestesses: those of Ceres, goddess of fertility and death, and those of the Vestal Virgins. The six Vestals tended the civic hearth and made sure that its fire never went out. They served, as it were, as wives of the whole community, as guardians of the civil household. The Vestals were the only Roman women not under the authority of a paterfamilias. Chosen between the ages of 6 and 10 by the pontifex maximus, they had to remain virgins for thirty years or face death.

Roman ideology promoted simple and austere farmers' virtues—discipline, hard work, frugality, temperance, and the avoidance of public displays of affection even between spouses. Such virtues underlined the difference between the Republic and the kings, with their luxury and sophistication. At the same time, these virtues papered over class distinctions between rich and poor and so promoted stability.

Other Roman ideals included the supreme virtue of the household, *pietas*—devotion and loyalty to the familia, the gods, and the state. Household duties and gender obligations were defined clearly. Women were to be modest, upright, and practical. Men were to project *gravitas* ("weight" or "seriousness"), never lightness or levity. A serious man would display self-control and constancy, the ability to persevere against difficult odds. The masculine ideal was *virtus* (literally, "manliness"), which indicated excellence in war and government.

Roman men who attained virtus considered themselves entitled to the reward of *dignitas,* meaning not only public esteem but the tangible possession of a dignified position and official rank—in short, public office. The ultimate test of virtus, however, was in battle. Rome's wars supplied ample occasion to display it.

FROM ITALIAN CITY-STATE TO WORLD EMPIRE, CA. 509–133 B.C.

At the beginning of the Republic (ca. 509 B.C.), Roman territory comprised about 500 square miles. By 338 B.C. Rome controlled the 2,000 square miles of Latium and was moving north into Etruria and south into Samnite country. Three-quarters of a century later, in 265 B.C., Rome controlled all of the Italian peninsula south of an imaginary line from Pisae (modern Pisa) to Ariminum (modern Rimini), an area of about 50,000 square miles. By 146 B.C. Roman provinces included Sicily, Cisalpine Gaul (northern-most Italy), Sardinia, Corsica, and Spain (divided into two provinces). Once-great Carthage was the Roman province of Africa (roughly, modern Tunisia), and once-mighty Macedon was the province of Macedonia, whose governor was also effectively in charge of Greece. The Seleucid kingdom was free but fatally weakened. Rome was the supreme power between Gibraltar and the Levant. It was the greatest empire of the ancient West. How and why had Rome, from its humble beginnings as a local power, reached this breathtaking height?

Republican Expansion: The Conquest of Italy, ca. 509–265 B.C.
Romans maintain that they conquered an empire without ever committing an act of aggression. When war was declared, a special college of priests informed the gods that Rome was merely retaliating for foreign injury. True, the Romans were frequently attacked by others, but often only after provocative behavior by Rome had left its rivals little choice.

Rome's early conquests reveal many of its lasting motives for expansion. No doubt lust for conquest played a part, as did fear and hatred of outsiders, but self-control and shrewdness were stronger Roman characteristics. Greed, particularly land-hunger, was a perennial theme. Sometimes a domestic political motive was at work, for foreign adventure was a convenient way of deflecting plebeian energies. Perhaps the most significant factors, however, were the personal ambitions of a warrior elite and the presence of conflict in early Italy.

Victory in battle promised both prestige and booty and the political success that might follow. Military achievement brought unique acclaim. For example, certain victorious generals were allowed to celebrate a triumph; no such ceremony rewarded the feats of peacemakers or distinguished judges or other public benefactors. The triumphant general rode a chariot through the city to the Temple of Jupiter on the Capitoline Hill. He was accompanied by his troops, by the spoils of victory including famous captives, and by the magistrates and senators.

The harsh reality of Italian politics also ruled against pacifism. Without the willingness to fight, Rome could never have maintained its freedom. Yet what began as a pragmatic response to present dangers hardened into a habit of meeting even remote threats with force. In the fourth century B.C., having gained control of Latium, Rome considered the Samnites of central and southern Italy to be a potential threat. In the third century B.C., once Rome controlled Italy, it felt threatened by Carthage. After Carthage, the threat of Macedon was squelched, and after Macedon, Seleucid Syria, and so on.

Though flexible and far-reaching, Roman diplomacy sometimes ended up in war. Rome made formal alliances with some states, granting protection in return for

Roman Italy, ca. 265 B.C.

Rome controlled a patchwork of conquered territory, colonies, and allied states in Italy, held together by a network of treaties and of roads. The city of Rome (*inset*) was built on seven hills beside the Tiber River.

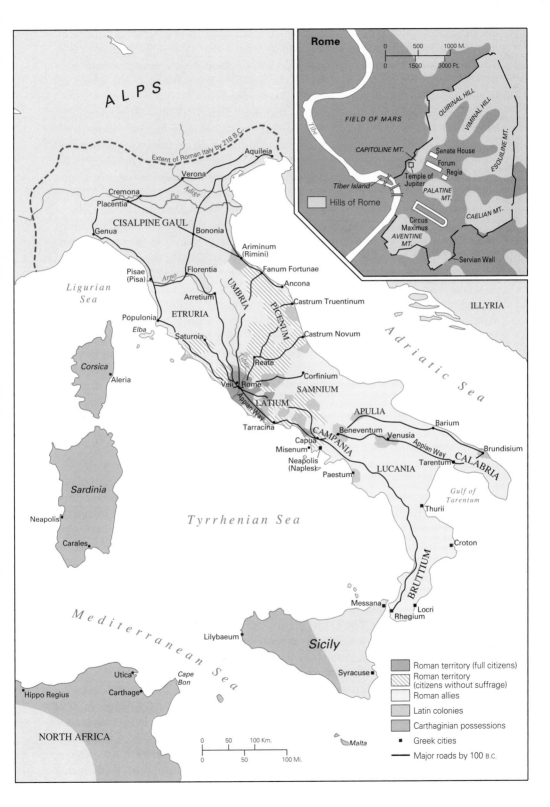

ALPS

Extent of Roman Italy by 218 B.C.

Aquileia

Verona

Cremona
Placentia

Adige
Po

CISALPINE GAUL

Genua

Bononia

Pisae
(Pisa)

Arno

Florentia

Ariminum
(Rimini)

Fanum Fortunae

Ancona

Ligurian
Sea

Arretium

UMBRIA

Castrum Truentinum

PICENUM

Populonia

ETRURIA

Elba

Saturnia

Castrum Novum

Corsica

Reate

Aleria

Veii Rome

Corfinium

SAMNIUM

LATIUM

Appian Way

Tarracina

CAMPANIA

APULIA

Beneventum

Barium

Venusia

Appian Way

Capua

Misenum

Brundisium

Neapolis
(Naples)

Paestum

Tarentum

CALABRIA

LUCANIA

Gulf of
Tarentum

Sardinia

Thurii

Neapolis

Tyrrhenian Sea

Carales

Croton

BRUTTIUM

Messana

Locri

Rhegium

Mediterranean Sea

Sicily

Lilybaeum

Syracuse

Utica

Cape
Bon

Carthage

Hippo Regius

Malta

NORTH AFRICA

ILLYRIA

Adriatic Sea

Rome

| 0 | 500 | 1000 M. |
| 0 | 1500 | 3000 Ft. |

FIELD OF MARS

QUIRINAL HILL

VIMINAL HILL

Tiber

CAPITOLINE MT.

Senate House

Forum

Regia

ESQUILINE MT.

Temple of
Jupiter

Tiber Island

PALATINE
MT.

CAELIAN MT.

Hills of Rome

Circus
Maximus

AVENTINE
MT.

Servian Wall

0   50   100 Km.

0   50   100 Mi.

Roman territory (full citizens)

Roman territory
(citizens without suffrage)

Roman allies

Latin colonies

Carthaginian possessions

■ Greek cities

— Major roads by 100 B.C.

obedience and troops or ships when needed by Rome. Short of a formal commitment, however, Rome might accept a state "into its fides"—that is, treat the state as a client. The result was only a moral, and not a legal, commitment, which sometimes sufficed to frighten any would-be aggressor from harassing Rome's new friend. If not, Rome had to go into battle to prove its trustworthiness as a patron.

Military success requires tenacity, discipline, and flexibility—all qualities that Rome cultivated. Roman organizational ability and love of order made the Roman military camp a much more regular and systematic place than anything seen since Assyrian days. Beginning in the fourth century B.C., Rome began to reward its soldiers with regular pay; this and the distribution of conquered land improved morale. Two other points are even more significant: the willingness to utilize foreign military technology and the combination of generosity and firmness with which Rome treated its allies.

Borrowed from the Greeks in the sixth century B.C., the hoplite phalanx suited Rome on the relatively level ground of Latium but fared poorly in the rugged Apennines against the Samnites. Following a major defeat in 321 B.C., the Romans adopted with great success the Samnites' equipment and tactics.

Unlike the phalanx, which overpowered the enemy by fighting as one thickly massed unit, a Roman legion was flexible and adaptable. Legions were drawn up into three lines, thirty maniples ("handfuls"), and sixty centuries (literally "hundreds," although the number of men per century varied); each century was commanded by a centurion. A legion marched in a checkerboard pattern, leaving gaps in the lines. In battle each line closed its gaps as it attacked in turn. Unlike hoplites, who engaged the enemy at short range, legionnaires first threw their javelins at long range. Then, having broken the enemy's order, they charged and fought with sword and shield. The semi-independence of the maniples, each with its own commander and banner, created a more maneuverable army than that of the phalanx and one better suited for mountain fighting. When Rome's legions beat the Macedonian phalanx decisively in 197 B.C., military history entered a new era.

Rome was the leading power among the Latins, whom it led in an alliance known as the Latin League. Rome was first among equals, but the citizens of even the humblest Latin state had reciprocal rights of intermarriage and commerce with Romans and the right to become a citizen of another state by migrating there. Under Roman leadership the Latin League successfully defended Latium's borders against a series of enemies during the fourth and fifth centuries B.C. But eventually Rome had to confront a bitter two-year-long Latin revolt (340–338 B.C.).

The year 338 B.C. marked a turning point. Defeated peoples in the ancient world were often executed, deported, or enslaved. Victorious against the Latins, Rome, by contrast, pursued generosity. The Latin League was dissolved. Some of its member states were annexed, and their inhabitants became Roman citizens; others retained independence and alliance with Rome though no longer with one another. The non-Latin allies of the former rebels were also annexed by Rome, but they received the unique halfway status of "citizenship without suffrage." They shared the burdens of Roman citizenship but also all the rights except the vote; they also retained the right of local self-government. The settlement of 338 B.C. broke new ground by making it possible for Rome and its former allies and enemies to live together on the basis of relative equality.

The settlement also set a precedent for future Roman expansion. As Rome conquered Italy, a number of privileged Italian cities (called *municipia*) received the status

The Appian Way *Named for the censor Appius Claudius Caecus, who proposed its construction, Rome's first great road was built in 312 B.C. during the Samnite Wars. It originally ran 132 miles from Rome to Capua and was extended an additional 234 miles, probably by 244 B.C., to Brundisium, on Italy's southern Adriatic coast.* (F. H. C. Birch/Sonia Halliday Photographs)

of citizenship without suffrage. Others remained independent but were tied to Rome by perpetual alliance. Romans often annexed a portion of the land of these states.

If municipia were the carrots of Roman imperialism, the stick was a network of military roads and colonies crisscrossing Italy, allowing Rome to keep an eye on potential rebels. Roman roads allowed the swift movement of troops and linked the growing network of colonies. Colonies were established in strategically vital areas. The inhabitants, Roman and Latin, owed military service to Rome.

In later years, Italians would complain about treatment by Rome, but compared with inhabitants of Roman provinces outside Italy, they had a privileged status. Romans too would complain about allied demands for equality, but Rome received from its allies a huge pool of military manpower. The allies staffed the Roman armies that conquered the Samnites, Etruscans, and Gauls, all of whom came into the Roman orbit by the early third century B.C. Manpower abundance won Rome's war (280–276 B.C.) against the Greek general Pyrrhus of Epirus (319–272 B.C.), an adventurer who intervened in southern Italy. Although Pyrrhus won battle after battle, he was unable to match Roman willingness to sustain thousands of casualties time and again. Pyrrhus's seeming victories, therefore, turned out to be defeats, which sent him home to Greece disappointed and left us with the expression "Pyrrhic victory."

As for Rome, by 265 B.C. it emerged as the ruler of all of Italy south of the Pisae-Ariminum line. One might say that Rome unified Italy, although Italy was less a unity than a patchwork of Roman territory and colonies and of diverse cities, states, and peoples each allied to Rome by separate treaties.

Rome Versus Carthage: The Punic Wars, 264–146 B.C. The conquest of Italy made Rome one of two great powers in the central Mediterranean. The other was Carthage. Founded around 750 B.C. by Phoenicians from Tyre, Carthage controlled an empire in North Africa, Sicily, Corsica, Sardinia, Malta, the Balearic Islands, and southern Spain. (The adjective *Phoenician* is *Punicus* in Latin, hence the term *Punic* for *Carthaginian*.) Like Rome, Carthage was guided by a wealthy elite, but it was mercantile in character rather than agrarian. Rome was a land power, Carthage a sea power. Rome had virtually no navy. Carthage commanded a great war fleet, and its merchant ships dominated the western Mediterranean and played a major role in the east.

Carthage was an economic powerhouse. The Carthaginians exploited the mineral-rich mines of Spain. They were the first Mediterranean people to organize large-scale plantations of slaves for the production of single crops. Even though the Romans zealously wiped out most of Carthaginian elite culture, they did make sure to preserve one Carthaginian classic: a multivolume work on agriculture by Mago. Translated from Punic into Latin by order of the senate, Mago's treatise had an enormous impact on Roman landowners, who, with the importation of massive numbers of slaves, adopted the plantation system in Italy (see page 150).

Carthage boasted brilliant generals, especially in the Barca family, whose most famous member was Hannibal (247–183 B.C.). Carthage might have been a handicapper's favorite at the outbreak of its long wars with Rome in 264 B.C., yet the end result was disaster for Carthage. A combination of Carthaginian weaknesses and Roman strengths accounts for the outcome.

Carthaginian Craftsmanship *These pendants of male heads are made of colored glass and come from Carthage. The Phoenicians and their colonists excelled in glasswork as a medium for the production of luxury goods.* (Erich Lessing/Art Resource, NY)

Unlike Rome, Carthage did not have a citizen army. The commanders were Carthaginian, but most of the soldiers were mercenaries and of questionable loyalty. Unlike Rome, which treated its Italian allies well, Carthage showed contempt for its troops, who repaid the favor by revolting whenever they had the chance. Carthage fielded large armies but not as large as Rome's.

At the start of the Punic Wars, Rome had no navy or commanders to match the Barca family, but it proved adaptable, tenacious, and ruthless. To win the First Punic War (264–241 B.C.), for example, Rome not only built a navy but outlasted the enemy in a long and bloody conflict. After initially granting a mild peace treaty, Rome took advantage of later Carthaginian weakness to seize Sardinia and Corsica and to demand an additional indemnity.

Forced to give in to Rome's demands, Carthage decided to build a new and bigger empire in Spain, beginning in 237 B.C., under Barca family leadership. Hannibal's father, the general Hamilcar Barca (d. 229 B.C.), had gone undefeated in the First Punic War and is said to have raised his son to seek a rematch. With Spain's rich deposits of silver and copper in its hands, Carthage once again posed a credible threat to Rome. In the mid-220s B.C., an ever watchful Rome challenged Carthaginian power in Spain through a Roman client there. The new Carthaginian commander, 27-year-old Hannibal Barca, was not to be cowed, however, and the Second Punic War ensued (218–201 B.C.).

Carthage was willing to risk war because Hannibal promised a quick, cheap, and easy victory. Because Carthage no longer had a fleet, the Romans felt secure in Italy; Hannibal surprised them by marching overland to Italy, making a dangerous passage across the Alps. A tactical genius, Hannibal reckoned that with his superior generalship, he could defeat the Romans in battle and cause them enormous casualties, and he was right. Hannibal's forces dominated the battlefield. Among his victories was the Battle of Cannae in Apulia (southeastern Italy), where, in 216 B.C., Carthage gave Rome the bloodiest defeat in its history, killing perhaps thirty thousand Romans.

But huge casualties alone could not bring Rome to its knees. Nor did all of Rome's allies revolt, as Hannibal had hoped. Most stood by Rome, which had treated them relatively well in the past and which now threatened rebels with reprisals. After Cannae, Rome's leadership followed a cautious strategy of harassment, delay, refusal to fight, and attrition. Hannibal was stymied by an enemy who lost battles but refused to surrender. In addition, Hannibal did not have the power to take the city of Rome.

In the meantime, Rome had bought valuable time to regroup. A new military star emerged: Publius Cornelius Scipio (236–183 B.C.), a Roman who finally understood Hannibal's tactics and matched them. First Scipio conquered Carthage's Spanish dominions, and then he forced Hannibal back to North Africa for a final battle in 202 B.C. near Zama (in modern Tunisia). Scipio won the battle and gained the surname Africanus ("the African"). As for Hannibal, he played a prominent role in Carthaginian politics for about a decade, until Rome forced him into exile in Syria. In about 183 B.C., after taking part in the Seleucids' unsuccessful war against Rome, he committed suicide rather than face extradition to Rome.

The peace settlement of 201 B.C. stripped Carthage of its empire. Yet soon its economy rebounded, reviving old Roman fears of Carthage's political ambitions. In the Third Punic War (149–146 B.C.), Rome mounted a three-year siege under the leadership of Scipio Aemilianus (185–129 B.C.), finally destroying the city of Carthage in 146 B.C. Approximately a century later, Carthage was resurrected as a Roman colony and

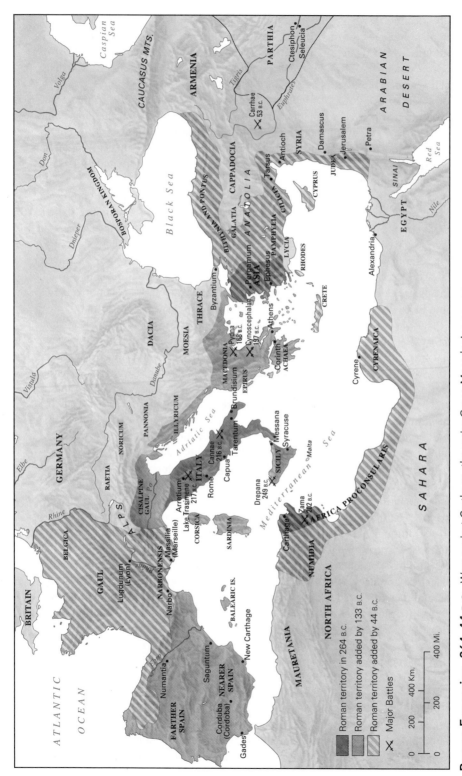

Roman Expansion, 264–44 B.C. Wars against Carthage, the major Greco-Macedonian powers, Gauls, Germans, North Africans, and other peoples brought Rome an empire on three continents.

became one of the empire's greatest cities. In the meantime, it was left desolate, its people killed or enslaved.

Rome emerged from the Punic Wars as the greatest power in the Mediterranean. It had acquired new provinces in Sicily, Sardinia, Corsica, Spain, and North Africa (where Carthage's former territory was annexed as the province of Africa). The road to further conquest seemed to lead in all directions.

Victories in the Hellenistic East, ca. 200–133 B.C.   Most countries would have savored peace after an ordeal such as the Punic Wars, but Rome immediately leaped into a long conflict in Greece and Anatolia. Its aims were to weaken the power of Macedon, which it feared might threaten Rome one day, especially since the Macedonian king Philip V (r. 221–179 B.C.) had made an alliance with Hannibal after Cannae. Rome won a relatively quick and easy victory when in 197 B.C. the legions crushed the Macedonian phalanx at Cynoscephalae in central Greece.

Rome had hoped to impose a patron-client relationship on Greece and Macedon, thereby avoiding having to sustain a permanent military presence, but that hope failed. The independent-minded Greeks chafed at Roman domination. Several years of miscommunication and intrigue followed, only to lead to renewed wars. First the Seleucids, under the ambitious king Antiochus III (r. 223–187 B.C.), challenged Rome for hegemony on the Greek peninsula. It was in this war that Hannibal took a small, doomed part. Roman forces made short work of the enemy. Driven out not only from Greece but from Anatolia as well, the Seleucids in effect recognized Roman supremacy in the Mediterranean (188 B.C.).

Then came another two rounds of war that pitted Rome against Macedon and various Greek states (171–167 and 150–146 B.C.). Victorious in both wars, Rome deprived the Greeks and Macedonians of their independence. Wherever democracy had survived in Greece, it was replaced with oligarchy. In 146 B.C. Rome destroyed Corinth, one of Greece's wealthiest cities, as a warning against further rebellion. Greece then suffered Roman neglect and taxation for nearly two hundred years.

By annexing Carthage, Macedon, and Greece in the mid-second century B.C., Rome created a dynamic for expansion around the entire Mediterranean. Before the century was over, southern Gaul was annexed, and Rome had gained a foothold in Asia. The kingdom of Pergamum (northwestern Anatolia) had supported Rome throughout Rome's wars in the east. When Attalus III of Pergamum died without an heir in 133 B.C., he surrendered his kingdom to the Roman people, who made it into a province of Asia.

Two great Hellenistic states remained independent: the Seleucid kingdom, that is, Syria, and Ptolemaic Egypt. Roman ambassadors and generals frequently interfered in their affairs, however, and no one was surprised when, in the first century B.C., they too were annexed by Rome.

The Socioeconomic Consequences of Expansion   Expansion led to enormous and unintended changes in Rome's society, economy, and culture. Already wealthy, the Roman elite now came into fabulous riches. Huge profits awaited the generals, patrons, diplomats, magistrates, tax collectors, and businessmen who followed Rome's armies. In Italy most profits were in the form of land; in the provinces wealth was found not only in land but also in slaves, booty, and graft. One of the worst grafters, Gaius Verres, governor of Sicily from 73 to 71 B.C., was prosecuted by Cicero (see pages 158–159), then beginning his oratorical career, for allegedly extorting tens of thousands of pounds of silver from his province. But even Cicero skimmed off several thousand pounds of silver as governor of the province of Cilicia (southern Anatolia) from 51 to 50 B.C.

The first Roman coinage, traditionally dated to 289 B.C., facilitated commercial transactions. Previously, the Romans had made do with barter, uncoined bronze, and cast bronze bars, but now they imitated the workmanship and style of Greek coins. Equally prominent in the homes of wealthy Romans were Greek metalwork, jewelry, art objects, and other luxury goods. Conservatives bemoaned the decline of traditional Roman austerity, but they fought a hopeless rear-guard action.

Ordinary Romans needed no reminder of the virtues of austerity, for they did not share in the elite's profit from Roman expansion. Indeed, a century of intensive warfare—from the outbreak of the Punic Wars in 264 B.C. to the destruction of Carthage and Corinth in 146 B.C.—strained the lot of the Roman people to the breaking point. Hannibal's invasion left much of the farmland of southern Italy devastated and Italian manpower considerably reduced. Yet most people might have rebounded from these problems within a generation or two, if they had not faced other serious troubles.

Conscription had become the norm. The average term of military service between ages 17 and 46 was six years; the maximum term was twenty years. Because experienced legionnaires were at a premium, commanders were loath to release them from service. But the longer a man was away in the army, the harder it was for his wife and children to keep the family farm running. With help from a patron, they might be able to make do, though most patrons in fact added to the problem through the introduction to Italy of large-scale agricultural entrepreneurship. Those who sought wealth monopolized Italian farmland, imported huge numbers of slaves, and brought ruin on the free peasantry of Italy.

The last two centuries B.C. witnessed the transformation of Roman rural society from one of independent farmers to one in which slave labor played a major role. By the end of the first century B.C., Italy's slave population was estimated at two million to three million, about a third of the peninsula's total. Prisoners of war and conquered civilians provided a ready supply of slaves. Most worked in agriculture or mining, and their treatment was often abominable; the fewer house slaves were usually better off.

Wealthy Romans wanted to invest in large landed estates, or *latifundia,* worked by slaves. These estates were either mixed farms (most often devoted to cultivating vines, olives, and grain) or ranches (establishments where animals were raised for meat, milk, and wool). One devotee of the latter was the prominent conservative Marcus Porcius Cato (234–149 B.C.), known as Cato the Censor. Cato argued that there were only three ways to get rich: "pasturage, pasturage, and pasturage." All a would-be entrepreneur needed was land, which Rome had conquered a huge amount of in Italy. Called public land, Rome's new territory belonged to the Roman people, but an individual was legally entitled to claim about 320 acres as his own. Many entrepreneurs flouted the law, however, and grabbed much more than their fair share of public land. In addition, they often forced families of absent soldiers off private land, either by debt foreclosure or by outright violence. Sometimes families would leave the land for the city, but usually they stayed as tenants.

Before about 170 B.C., poor Romans were sometimes able to find land in colonies. By 170 B.C., however, Rome had established all the colonies in Italy that its security demanded, so this avenue of escape from poverty was closed. A displaced farmer who wanted to compete in the labor market would have found it difficult to underbid cheap slave labor. In any case, Roman ideology frowned on wage labor by citizens. Nor was it practical for a poor farmer to sue a wealthy patron who seized his land, because a plaintiff himself had to bring the accused into court.

The situation of the Italian peasantry was becoming increasingly miserable by the mid-second century B.C. As one modern scholar has put it, "In conquering what they were pleased to call the world, the Romans ruined a great part of the Italian people."[2]

The Impact of Greece on Rome and Its Empire

Rome learned much from its new encounters with foreign peoples—and from none more than the Greeks. Wealthy Romans cultivated interests in Greek art, literature, rhetoric, and speculative thought; poor and rich alike enjoyed Greek drama. Before the mid-third century B.C. Roman literature was virtually nonexistent. An oral tradition of songs, ballads, and funeral oratory kept alive the deeds of the famous, for writing was generally restricted to commercial and government records and inscriptions. In short, the Romans conquered Italy without writing about it.

Contact with the Greek cities brought changes. Large numbers of Roman soldiers in Magna Graecia (southern Italy and Sicily) were introduced to comedy, tragedy, mimes, and sophisticated song lyrics, and many developed a permanent taste for them. It is no accident that the first production of a drama at Rome took place in 240 B.C., the year after the end of the First Punic War. Afterward, the annual production of such dramas became standard procedure.

No one could accuse the Romans of rushing headlong into a new age, however. The authorities continued to have their doubts about theater, which seemed excessively emotional and probably corrupt. They did not allow the building of a permanent theater in Rome until 55 B.C., insisting that the wealthiest city in the Mediterranean make do with makeshift wooden structures. Nor did the Roman elite readily become playwrights or poets. The first gentleman poet in Rome, Lucilius (180–102 B.C.), did not arrive until the second century B.C., and he was a Latin, not a Roman. His predecessors, the founders of Latin literature, were all of low social status; little of their work survives.

The two great early Latin playwrights are Titus Maccius Plautus (ca. 254–184 B.C.) and Publius Terentius Afer, today known as Terence (ca. 195–159 B.C.). Both of them wrote comedies on the model of the great Greek comic playwright Menander (see page 114). Plautus was an Umbrian and a poor man who learned his Latin in Rome; Terence was a North African slave, educated and freed in Rome. Twenty-one plays by Plautus and six by Terence survive. Plautus's plays are generally earthy slapstick farces. They are invariably set in Greece, not Rome, in part out of escapism (many were written during the Second Punic War), in part out of the censorial demands of the Roman authorities. They nonetheless reveal much about Roman society. Terence's plays are more subtle than Plautus's, indicating the growing sophistication of Roman theatergoers.

Latin prose developed more slowly than did poetry and drama. The first histories by Romans, composed after the Second Punic War, were written in Greek, for Latin lacked the vocabulary or the audience for history. Cato the Censor was the first historian of Rome to write in Latin. His *Origines*, of which we have only remnants, recounted Roman history from the origin of the city to about 150 B.C. The earliest surviving Latin prose work is Cato's *On Agriculture.*

In the traditional education of a Roman aristocrat, parents and close family friends played the primary role. Although this practice continued, wealthy Romans in the second century B.C. began acquiring Greek slaves to educate their sons in the Greek language and Greek literature. Soon Greek freedmen began setting up schools offering the same subjects. Before long, similar Latin grammar schools also opened.

One of the forms of Greek literature that appealed most to the practical-minded Romans was rhetoric. Roman orators studied Greek models, and many would say that they eventually outdid the Greeks. Cato was the first Roman to publish his speeches, and he also wrote a book on rhetoric. Both gave impetus to the spread of sophisticated rhetoric in Rome.

Scipio Aemilianus, conqueror of Carthage in 146 B.C., had a distinguished political and military career. He was also patron of a group of prominent statesmen and soldiers who shared his love of Hellenism. Among the writers whom they supported were the playwright Terence, the poet Lucilius, the historian Polybius, and the Stoic philosopher Panaetius (ca. 185–109 B.C.). The Stoic emphases on duty, wisdom, and world brotherhood appealed both to Rome's traditional ideology and to its more recent acquisition of empire. Yet not all Romans shared Scipio's admiration of Greek culture; Cato, for example, was famously ambivalent.

Cornelia, Scipio Aemilianus's mother-in-law, was an educated lover of Hellenism who wrote letters that existed several hundred years later as examples of elegant Latin prose. Her villa in the resort of Misenum on the Bay of Naples was well known for the distinguished guests whom she received there. When her husband, an outstanding statesman and general, died, Cornelia chose to remain a widow. One of the men who tried to change her mind was no less a figure than the king of Egypt. The widow spent her time managing her own estate and supervising the education of her two sons, the future tribunes Tiberius and Gaius Gracchus.

Although Cornelia's privileges were extraordinary, she is nonetheless a reminder of the opportunities that imperial expansion offered to wealthy Roman women. Marriage practices are one example of change. Few women were married *cum manu* anymore—that is, handed over by their fathers to their husbands. A woman's father or nearest male relative, not her husband, was most likely to be her paterfamilias, which meant that a husband's control over his wife's dowry was limited. The result was more freedom, at least for wealthy women.

Cornelia is also a reminder of the fundamental conservatism of Roman society. Although we know the years of birth and death of numerous elite Roman males of the second century B.C., we do not know Cornelia's. Nor did her literary interests entail any neglect of home and family. Cornelia bore twelve children, though only three of them lived to adulthood (such was the reality of infant mortality even for the wealthiest Romans).

THE REVOLUTION FROM THE GRACCHI TO THE CAESARS, 133–31 B.C.

A citizen of the Roman Republic in the mid-second century B.C. might have looked forward to a long and happy future for his country, unaware that the Republic—after 350 years of expansion—was about to begin a century of domestic and foreign unrest that would bring down the whole system. Why and how did the Republic collapse? More than a century of warfare weighed heavily on the ordinary people of Italy—the Romans and allied peasants whose farms were ruined while they were off fighting. The Roman elite was bitterly divided over what to do about the problems of the peasants. One group wanted to redistribute land on behalf of the poor; another group had no sympathy for them.

By the Late Republic the city of Rome was crowded and populous: scholars estimate the number of inhabitants to have reached one million by the end of the first century B.C. The government had to take charge of the grain supply. But elite politicians exploited the issue for partisan purposes. Once before, during the struggle between the patrician and plebeian orders in the Early Republic, the elite had been similarly divided and had resolved its differences through compromise (see pages 137–138). The Late Republic, however, was an age of individualism, sophistication, and cynicism. Ambitious nobles were no longer willing to subordinate themselves to the community. Thwarted from above, it was not long before competing armies of land-hungry peasants were marching across Italy.

The Gracchi   Many Romans fretted over the military dimension of the agrarian crisis. In modern societies, draftees are often the poorest people. In Rome, military service was a prestigious activity, so a property qualification was imposed and the poor were not drafted. As fewer and fewer potential soldiers could afford to own property, however, during the second century it became necessary to reduce the property qualification several times. By 150 B.C. a conscript had to own property worth only 400 denarii—roughly a small house, a garden, and some personal belongings. If the peasantry continued its decline, Rome would either have to drop the property qualification for the military altogether or stop fielding armies. Clearly, something had to be done.

Into the breach stepped Tiberius Sempronius Gracchus (d. 133 B.C.), one of the ten tribunes for the year 133 B.C. The son of Cornelia and a distinguished general and ambassador (whose name Tiberius shared), Tiberius belonged to the eminent Gracchi family. He seemed an excellent spokesperson for a group of prominent senators who backed land reform. He proved, however, to be arrogant and overly ambitious. In pursuit of his goals, he deposed one of his fellow tribunes, Octavius, an opponent of reform, and thereby shocked and angered conservatives.

Tiberius's proposed law restored the roughly 320-acre limit to the amount of public land a person could own (plus an exception for a man with two sons, who was allowed to hold about 667 acres). A commission was to be set up to repossess excess land and redistribute it to the poor, in small lots that were to be inalienable—that is, the wealthy could not buy them back. The former landowners would be reimbursed for improvements they had made, such as buildings or plantings.

The proposal was moderate, but wealthy landowners repudiated it outright. Many senators suspected that Tiberius wanted to set himself up as a kind of superpatron, buoyed by peasant supporters. The senate was in fact more disturbed by Tiberius's methods than by the substance of his proposed law because those methods threatened the senate's power. In addition to deposing Octavius, Tiberius, when the bill became law, intervened in the senate's bailiwicks of foreign affairs and finances by earmarking tax receipts from the new province of Asia to finance land purchases. Finally, Tiberius broke with custom by running for a second consecutive term as tribune. While the tribal assembly prepared to vote on the new tribunes, some senators led a mob to the Forum and had Tiberius and three hundred of his followers clubbed to death.

This shocking event marked the first time in the Republic that a political debate was settled by bloodshed in Rome itself. The ancient sources agree that it was the beginning of a century of revolution. Tiberius's killers had not merely committed murder, but had attacked the traditional inviolability of the tribunes. Yet over the next century public violence grew as a weapon of politics in the Republic. The land commission went ahead with its work, even without Tiberius. His younger brother, Gaius (d. 121 B.C.), ready to continue Tiberius's work, became tribune himself in 123 B.C. Gaius expanded Tiberius's coalition, adding to it supporters from the equestrian order and the urban populace, mainly composed of slaves and freedmen. He gave the plebs cheap grain at subsidized prices. The equestrians were wealthy, landed gentry, similar to senators in most respects except for their failure to have reached the senate; they yearned for political power. A small but important group of equestrians was engaged in commerce and tax collection in the provinces. The senate regulated their activities through the so-called extortion courts, which tried corruption cases. Gaius staffed those courts with equestrians. Alluding to the new equestrian power, Gaius remarked, "I have left a sword in the ribs of the senate."

Gaius's ultimate aims are unclear, but one thing is certain: he posed a dangerous threat to the senate's power. He sponsored an extension of his brother's agrarian law, new colonies, public works, and relief for poor soldiers. Eventually Gaius ran aground on a plan to include the Italian allies as beneficiaries of agrarian reform—a farsighted notion but one unpopular with the Roman people, who were jealous of their privileges. Gaius was denied a third term as tribune in 121 B.C. (he had won a second the previous year). Soon his supporters engaged in violent scuffling with their opponents. The senate responded to his action by passing a declaration of public emergency, empowering the magistrates to use any means necessary to protect the state.

One of the consuls had Gaius and 250 of his followers killed. Another 3,000 Gracchans were executed soon thereafter. Within a few years the Gracchan land commission was abolished. It is estimated that approximately 75,000 citizens had been given land. The law, however, was amended to permit the resale of redistributed land, and with the wealthy poised to buy land back, the settlers' future was uncertain. The senatorial oligarchy was back in control.

Or so it seemed. In fact, Roman politics had become an unstable brew. In time, it became clear that the Gracchi had divided the political community into two loose groupings. On one side were the *optimates* ("the best people"; singular, *optimas*), conservatives who asserted the rule of the senate against popular tribunes and the maintenance of the estates of the wealthy in spite of the agrarian crisis. On the other side were the *populares* ("men of the people"; singular, *popularis*), who challenged the rule of the senate in the name of relief of the poor. The populares were not democrats. Like the optimates, they were Roman nobles who believed in hierarchy, but they advocated the redistribution of wealth and power as a way of restoring stability and strengthening the military.

Marius and Sulla   By 100 B.C. Rome's agrarian crisis had become a full-scale military crisis, too. Roman armies under senatorial commanders fared poorly, both in Numidia (modern Algeria) and in southern Gaul against Germanic invaders. The situation was saved by an outsider to established privilege, an equestrian named Gaius Marius (157–86 B.C.), the first member of his family to be elected consul, for 107 B.C. This "new man" proved to be a military reformer and a popularis. Marius made several moves to streamline and strengthen the Roman army: Camp followers were reduced in number, and individual soldiers were made to carry their own equipment. To meet the Germans, who attacked in overwhelming waves, maniples—the tactical subunits of a legion—were reorganized and combined into larger units called cohorts, rendering the army firmer and more cohesive. Most important, Marius abandoned altogether the property qualification for the military. As a result, Roman soldiers were no longer peasants doing part-time military service but rather landless men making a profession of the military.

Politically they became a force to be reckoned with. As an indispensable general, Marius demanded and won six elections to the consulship, unconstitutional though that was. Furthermore, after winning the wars in North Africa and Gaul, Marius championed his soldiers. In 100 B.C. he asked that land be distributed to them. The senate refused, but its victory was temporary. The poor recognized that only military leaders such as Marius desired to meet their need for land. As a result, ordinary Romans, who were all now eligible for the army, transferred their loyalty from the senate to their commander.

The Republic was weak, and it became weaker still as a result of two new wars. First, its Italian allies rose against Rome in a bloody and bitter struggle from 91 to 89 B.C. known as the "Social War"—that is, war with the *socii* ("allies"). The allies fought hard, and Rome, in order to prevail, had to concede to them what they had demanded at the outset: full Roman citizenship. The war wrought devastation in the countryside, further destabilizing the Republic. The other conflict of this period pitted Rome against Mithridates (120–63 B.C.), a rebellious king in northern Anatolia. Mithridates conquered Roman territory in western Anatolia and slaughtered the numerous Italian businessmen and tax collectors there. Once again a military man rose to save the day for Rome: Marius's rival and former lieutenant, Lucius Cornelius Sulla Felix (ca. 138–78 B.C.), consul for the year 88 B.C., patrician and optimas.

Yet Marius was jealous, and his troops and Sulla's fought over the issue of the command against Mithridates. Sulla's forces won the first round by marching on Rome, but after they departed for the east, Marius's men retook the city and settled scores. Victorious over Mithridates, Sulla returned to Italy in 83 B.C. and engaged in all-out civil war. Sulla defeated Marius's men in battle (minus Marius himself, who had died in 86), then sealed his victory with proscription. He had posted the names of his political opponents, as many as two thousand men. Their land was confiscated, their sons disenfranchised, and they were executed. Sulla settled his veterans, about eighty thousand men, on land in Italy from which he had expelled entire communities that had opposed him.

Having assumed the long-dormant office of dictator—but without a time limit on his tenure—Sulla attempted to restore the senatorial rule of pre-Gracchan days. To this end, he greatly weakened the tribunate and strengthened the senate, whose size he doubled, from about three hundred to about six hundred members.

The most long-lasting of Sulla's measures was his reform of the courts. He abolished trials before popular assemblies and equestrian-staffed courts. Criminal cases were now heard before one of seven standing courts, whose juries were composed of senators. Although later Roman criminal law evolved considerably, it was founded on Sulla's actions. Generally only wealthy people had access to the standing courts; alleged crimes involving ordinary people were heard before lesser magistrates.

Sulla retired in 79 B.C. and died a year later. His hope of restoring law and order under the senate died with him. Within ten years the old powers of the tribunes had been restored. Discontent smoldered among the men whose land Sulla had confiscated. Equally serious, many senators, aspiring to what Sulla had done and not to what he had said, pursued personal power, not the collective interests of the senate.

Pompey and Caesar

New would-be Mariuses or Sullas now arose. The dominant leader of the seventies and sixties B.C. was the optimas Pompey the Great (106–48 B.C.), a brilliant general and a supporter of Sulla. Young Pompey went from command to command: he put down an agrarian rebellion in Italy and a rebellion in Spain, cleared the Mediterranean of pirates, defeated Mithridates again, and added rich conquests to the empire in Anatolia, Syria, Phoenicia, and Palestine. In the fifties B.C. the tide began turning in favor of Gaius Julius Caesar (100–44 B.C.), an even more gifted general and politician—indeed, perhaps one of history's greatest. A popularis, Caesar had family connections to Marius and his supporters. Caesar's career depended on his dazzling oratory, his boldness, and his sheer talent at war and politics. Caesar conquered Gaul, gained a foothold in Britain, and laid the foundations of Roman rule in Egypt.

While the elite of the Late Republic struggled to maintain order and secure power, ordinary people struggled for survival itself. Violence had become a way of life in rural Italy. Many once-prosperous farmers, dispossessed peasants, and runaway slaves ended up as robbers or bandits. It was also an era of slave revolts, the most serious of which lasted from 73 to 71 B.C. under the leadership of Spartacus, a Thracian slave who had been a gladiator. An able commander, Spartacus beat nine separate Roman armies in two years before finally suffering defeat. At the same time, Rome also faced major wars in Spain and Anatolia.

Roman women were sometimes pawns, sometimes partners in the political careers of Pompey and Caesar. In 80 B.C., for example, Pompey divorced his first wife to advance his career by marrying Aemilia, Sulla's stepdaughter. Aemilia was not only married at the time but pregnant by her first husband. Soon after her divorce and remarriage, she died in childbirth. Caesar took many mistresses, among whom was the queen of Egypt, Cleopatra. Caesar had a penchant for certain Egyptian institutions, such as the Egyptian calendar, and he toyed with becoming a monarch himself, an inclination that Cleopatra perhaps encouraged. Another of Caesar's mistresses was Servilia, stepsister of Marcus Porcius Cato (Cato the Younger, 95–46 B.C.), great-grandson of the famous censor (see page 150). She was also the mother of Brutus, the man who would eventually help murder Caesar.

Pompey was an optimas, Caesar a popularis, but the two of them agreed that they, not the senate or the assemblies, should dominate Rome. Each man's ambition was more important to him than any political principles. In 60 B.C. they entered into a pact with a third ambitious noble, Marcus Licinius Crassus (d. 53 B.C.). Known today as the "First Triumvirate," this coalition amounted to a conspiracy to run the state. Their individual ambitions rebuffed by the senate, each man had an agenda that could be achieved by pooling resources in the triumvirate: for Pompey, ratification of his acts in the east and land for his veterans; for Caesar, who became consul for 59 B.C., a long period of command in Gaul and a free hand in his behavior there; for Crassus, a rebate for the tax collectors of Roman Asia, whom he championed, and eventually a command in Syria to make war on Parthia (the new Persian Empire).

Having achieved its goal, the triumvirate did not long survive, but its very existence shows how little the Republic now meant. Crassus died in an inglorious defeat at Carrhae in Syria in 53 B.C., tarnished further by the Parthians' successful capture of Roman legionary standards. Frightened by Caesar's stunning victories in Gaul, Pompey returned to the senatorial fold, now led by Cato the Younger. Cato and his supporters stood for the traditional rule of the senatorial oligarchy. In 49 B.C. they ordered Caesar to give up his command in Gaul, but instead Caesar marched on Italy with his army. Italy's northern boundary was marked by a tiny stream called the Rubicon; when Caesar defiantly crossed it, he declared, "The die is cast." Indeed it was, for civil war. Caesar swept to victory against the senate's army, led by Pompey, at Pharsalus in Greece in 48 B.C. Pompey fled but was assassinated. The complete destruction of the senate's forces took until 45 B.C.

The years of civil war took Caesar from Spain to Anatolia. During the fighting he showed the qualities that made him great: he was fast, tough, smart, adaptable, and a risk-taker. He was a diplomat, too, offering mercy to any of his enemies who joined him. A talented writer, Caesar published two books about his military campaigns—*On the Gallic War* and *On the Civil War*—the latter appearing after his death. These works glorified Caesar's conquests and defended his decision to wage civil war.

Back in Rome, Caesar sponsored a huge number of reforms. His political goal was to elevate Italians and others at the expense of old Roman families. To achieve this, Caesar conferred Roman citizenship liberally, on all of Cisalpine Gaul (northernmost Italy) as well as on certain provincial towns. He enlarged the senate from six hundred to nine hundred, adding his supporters, including some Gauls, to the membership. Caesar sponsored social and economic reforms, too, including reducing debt and founding the first colonies outside Italy, where veterans and poor citizens were settled. He undertook a grand public building program in the city of Rome. Caesar's most long-lasting act was to introduce the calendar of 365¼ days, on January 1, 45 B.C. Derived from the calendar of Egypt, it is known as the Julian calendar.

Caesar did not hide his contempt for Republican constitutional formalities. By accepting a dictatorship for life he offended the old guard; by flirting with the title of king he infuriated them. With one eye toward avenging Crassus and another toward equaling the achievements of Alexander the Great, Caesar made preparations for a war against Parthia, but in vain. His career ended abruptly on March 15, 44 B.C. (the Ides of March by the Roman calendar), when sixty senators stabbed him to death. The assassination took place in the portico attached to the Theater of Pompey, in front of a statue of Pompey himself, where the senate was meeting that day. It had been eighty-nine years since the murder of Tiberius Gracchus.

The assassins called themselves Liberators, believing that they were freeing themselves from tyranny just as the founders of the Republic had done centuries before. Indeed, one of the chief conspirators, Marcus Junius Brutus (ca. 85–42 B.C.), claimed descent from Lucius Junius Brutus, traditional leader of the revolt against the Tarquins that was thought to have established the Republic. Like his co-conspirator Gaius Longinus Cassius (d. 42 B.C.), Brutus had been a magistrate, military officer, and provincial administrator.

The assassination of Caesar threw Rome back into turmoil. Civil war followed for the next thirteen years, first between the Liberators and Caesar's partisans and then between the two leading Caesarians. The final struggle pitted Mark Antony (Marcus Antonius, ca. 83–30 B.C.), Caesar's chief lieutenant and the man who inherited his love affair with Cleopatra, against Octavian (Gaius Julius Caesar Octavianus, 63 B.C.–A.D. 14), Caesar's grandnephew and adopted son and heir to Caesar's name and his huge fortune. At first it looked as if Antony had the upper hand because Octavian was young and inexperienced, was not a general, and was cursed with poor health. Octavian was, however, a man of unusual cunning and prudence. His forces defeated Antony and Cleopatra at the naval battle of Actium (off northwestern Greece) in 31 B.C.; their suicides followed shortly. The Roman world held its breath to see how Octavian would govern it.

| The World of Cicero | Marcus Tullius Cicero (106–43 B.C.) is one of the best-known figures of all antiquity. Like Marius, he was a wealthy equestrian from the central Italian town of Arpinum who, as consul |

(in 63 B.C.), became a "new man." Cicero was an optimas and defender of the senate, though ready for compromise with the equestrians, from whose ranks he himself had arisen. He made his name by successfully leading the opposition to Lucius Sergius Catilina, a down-and-out patrician who organized a debtors' revolt in Etruria; the army smashed the rebellion.

Cicero was intelligent, ambitious, and talented. As a young man he studied philosophy and oratory in Greece. As a result, he produced elevated and serious writings. Never as original as Plato or Aristotle, Cicero nonetheless was crucial in making the Latin language a vessel for the heritage of Greek thought. A prolific writer, Cicero produced over a hundred orations, of which about sixty survive; several treatises on oratory; philosophical writings on politics, ethics, epistemology (the study of the nature of knowledge), and theology; poetry, of which little survives; and numerous letters. After his death in 43 B.C., his immense correspondence was published, with little censored. The letters and speeches provide a vivid, detailed, and sometimes damning picture of politics.

Politics in the Late Republic was loud and boisterous. The elite prided itself on free speech and open debate. In senate deliberations, court cases, and public meetings in the Forum that preceded assembly votes, oratory—sometimes great oratory—was common. Few orators in history, though, have matched Cicero's ability to lead and mislead an audience by playing on its feelings. He knew every rhetorical trick and precisely when each was appropriate.

Because of increased freedom and greater educational opportunities, during the Late Republic it was possible for elite women as well as men to study oratory. Private tutors were common among the aristocracy, and girls often received lessons alongside their brothers. Girls sometimes also profited from a father's expertise. A particularly dramatic case is that of Hortensia, daughter of Quintus Hortensius Hortalus (114–50 B.C.), a famous orator and rival of Cicero. An excellent speaker herself, Hortensia defied tradition by arguing successfully in the Roman Forum in 42 B.C. against a proposed war tax on wealthy women.

Cicero pilloried one elite woman who enjoyed considerable freedom: Clodia (b. ca. 95 B.C.). Sister of the notorious populist gang leader Clodius and wife of optimas politician Metellus Celer (d. 59 B.C.), Clodia moved in Rome's highest circles. Cicero accused her of poisoning her husband (the charge was unprovable). She is better remembered from the poems of Catullus (ca. 85–54 B.C.), where she is called Lesbia. In passionate and psychologically complex verse, Catullus describes the ups and downs of their affair, which Clodia eventually ended.

Ordinary people lacked the education and freedom to express themselves in the manner of a Catullus or Hortensia, but a less civilized means of expression was open to them: the political gang. Brawls and violence between the rival groups of Clodius, a supporter of Caesar, and Milo, a supporter of the senate, became increasingly common in the fifties B.C. As dictator, Caesar abolished the gangs.

Cicero's works provide evidence of a crucial development in the practice of Roman law. Often unheralded, what Cicero's contemporaries did was invent the notion of the legal expert, a person devoted to explaining and interpreting the law. Roman law needed interpretation because it was complex and intricate. Much of it was the work not of legislators but of magistrates, who issued annual statements setting forth how their courts would work. The result was unsystematic and sometimes contradictory and cried out for someone to make sense of it. Enter the jurisconsults, legal interpreters who emerged in the third and second centuries B.C. At first they had no special standing, but in the first century B.C. they became true jurists; their interpretations began to be considered authoritative. No earlier Mediterranean society had a professional class of legal experts, but no earlier society had faced issues as complicated and turbulent, or had grown to three million citizens, as the Roman Republic did in the mid-first century B.C. The Western tradition of legal science has its roots in Rome.

Rome's political system, unlike its legal system, did not adapt flexibly to changing circumstances. The disenfranchised of the Late Republic had reasonable goals: land for those who had fought for their country and admission to the senate of a wider group. Yet the old elite resisted both. Cicero's solution was to build on Sulla's reforms by uniting the senatorial and equestrian orders and by widening the Roman ruling class to include the elite of all Italy. The expanded ruling class could close ranks and establish *otium cum dignitate*, "peace with respect for rank." Cicero's proposed new order was distinctly hierarchical.

In the turbulent times of the Late Republic, the Roman elite often turned to the Hellenistic philosophers. The poet Lucretius (ca. 94–55 B.C.) describes the Epicurean ideal of withdrawal into the contemplative life in a long didactic epic called *On the Nature of Things*. Most elite Romans, however, including Cicero, preferred the activist philosophy of Stoicism (see pages 122–123). Cicero put forth a generous view of human brotherhood. He argued that all people share a spark of divinity and are protected by natural law. Consequently, all persons have value and importance and should treat others generously. Such ideas would be influential in the new Roman Empire when, under the leadership of Augustus, fair treatment of provincials was a major theme. For Cicero, however, these ideas existed more as theory than as practice.

Cicero did not hide his lack of sympathy for his fellow citizens who were poor. In one speech he castigated "artisans and shopkeepers and all that kind of scum"; in a letter he complained about "the wretched half-starved populace, which attends mass meetings and sucks the blood of the treasury." Cicero also made his disdain for democracy clear: "The greatest number," he said, "should not have the greatest power."

Elitist as Cicero's views were, they were by no means extremist. Cassius, Brutus, and the other Liberators had little interest in even Cicero's limited compromises. Their stubbornness proved to be their downfall, for dispossessed peasants and ambitious equestrians transferred their loyalties to Julius Caesar and, later, to Augustus. One of Caesar's supporters, Sallust (86–ca. 34 B.C.), wrote biting and bitter works of history that indicted the greed and corruption of the optimates, whom he blamed for the decline of the Republic. In any case, peace was not restored, for the generation of Liberators was wiped out in renewed civil war, and a new generation emerged, weary for peace.

IMPORTANT EVENTS

753–509 B.C. Monarchy (traditional dates)

509–287 B.C. Early Republic

449 B.C. Law of the Twelve Tables

338 B.C. Latin League dissolved; Roman citizenship extended

289 B.C. First Roman coinage (traditional date)

287–133 B.C. Middle Republic

264–146 B.C. Punic Wars

240 B.C. First play produced at Rome

197 B.C. Rome defeats Macedonian phalanx

146 B.C. Rome destroys Carthage and Corinth

133–31 B.C. Late Republic

133–121 B.C. The Gracchi

107–78 B.C. Marius and Sulla

73–71 B.C. Spartacus's revolt

66–62 B.C. Pompey's eastern campaigns

63 B.C. Consulship of Cicero

58–51 B.C. Caesar conquers Gaul

44 B.C. Caesar assassinated

31 B.C. Antony defeated at Actium; Octavian in power

NOTES

1. *The Aeneid of Virgil,* trans. Allen Mandelbaum (Berkeley: University of California Press, 1971), pp. 160–161.
2. P. A. Brunt, *Social Conflicts in the Roman Republic* (New York: Norton, 1971), p. 17.

SUGGESTED READING

Barker, H'., and T. Rasmussen. *The Etruscans.* 1997. Excellent historical introduction and guidebook, written with gusto.

Beard, Mary, and Michael Crawford. *Rome in the Late Republic: Problems and Interpretations.* 2d ed. 1999. An unusual and innovative approach to the subject, emphasizing sociocultural and institutional analysis more than narrative.

Brunt, P. A. *Social Conflicts in the Roman Republic.* 1971. A fine, non-Marxist view of the importance of class conflict throughout Republican history.

Cornell, T. J. *The Beginnings of Rome: Italy and Rome from the Bronze Age to the Punic Wars (c. 1000–264 B.C.).* 1995. A readable and ambitious survey combining archaeological and literary evidence, often in support of iconoclastic conclusions.

Cornell, T. J., and J. Matthews. *Atlas of the Roman World.* 1982. A readable introduction to Roman history written by two scholars; the maps and photos are beautiful.

Crawford, Michael. *The Roman Republic.* 2d ed. 1993. The best short introduction; sophisticated, lively, and concise.

Dixon, Suzanne. *The Roman Family.* 1992. A good historical study in complexity; strongly aware of the difference between the myth and reality of the Roman family and nicely written.

Goldsworthy, Adrian. *Roman Warfare.* 2000. A concise and expert introduction.

Talbert, Richard A. *Barrington Atlas of the Greek and Roman World.* 2000. The most thorough, detailed, and scholarly atlas of this subject ever attempted.

Ward, A. M., F. M. Heichelheim, and C. A. Yeo. *A History of the Roman People.* 3d ed. 1998. The best introductory textbook; scholarly and readable.

6 Imperial Rome, 31 B.C.—A.D. 284

(Scala/Art Resource, NY)

The imperial family of Rome walks in stately procession to a sacrifice: Livia, wife of Augustus, first of the emperors; his daughter, Julia; Julia's husband, Agrippa; and various cousins and in-laws and their children. They are formally dressed in togas and gowns, heads wreathed. The men and women gaze seriously; the boys and girls have impish looks, betraying thoughts of mischief as they hold their parents' hands. They are all carved in stone, one of several sculptured reliefs decorating the walls of a public monument in Rome. Dedicated on Livia's birthday in 9 B.C., the monument shown here illustrates the propaganda themes of the new regime, among them the happy family as symbol of peace after generations of civil war. The senate, which had commissioned the monument, called it the *Ara Pacis Augustae,* or "Altar of Augustan Peace."

Having made peace was no idle boast on Augustus's part. Not only did he end the Roman revolution, but he began a period of two hundred years of prosperity and stability in the Roman Empire. Augustus took advantage of Rome's war-weariness to create a new government out of the ruins of the Republic. Like the builders of the Early Republic's constitution, Augustus displayed the Roman genius for compromise. He had superb political instincts. Although he retained the final say, he shared a degree of power with the senate. He made financial sacrifices to feed the urban poor and distribute farms to landless peasants. He ended Rome's seemingly limitless expansion and stabilized the borders of the empire. He began to raise the provinces to a status of equality with Italy.

The *pax Romana* ("Roman peace"), at its height between A.D. 96 and 180, was an era of enlightened emperors, thriving cities, intellectual vitality, and artistic and architectural achievement in an empire of 50 million to 100 million people. Yet it was also an era of slavery. More positively, the Roman peace was a period of heightened spirituality. In the peaceful and diverse empire, ideas traveled from people to people, and the religious beliefs of an obscure sect from western Asia began to spread around the Mediterranean and into northern Europe. The new religion was Christianity.

After 180 Rome slowly passed into a grim period marked in turn by bad emperors, civil war, inflation, plague, invasion, and defeat. After reaching a nadir around 235 to 253, Rome's fortunes began to improve under a series of reforming emperors who would forge a stronger and vastly different empire.

Augustus and the Principate, 31 B.C.–A.D. 68

In 31 B.C. Gaius Julius Caesar Octavianus (63 B.C.–A.D. 14), or Octavian, as Augustus was then known, stood at the top of the Roman world. His forces had defeated those of Mark Antony and Cleopatra at the Battle of Actium in northwestern Greece, whereupon his two chief enemies committed suicide. Few could have predicted the vision and statesmanship that Octavian now displayed. He spent the next forty-five years healing the wounds of a century of revolution. He did nothing less than lay the foundations of the prosperous two centuries enjoyed by the empire under the Roman peace.

The Political Settlement   Octavian was both an astute politician and a lucky one. He was lucky in the length and violence of the civil wars. After Actium, most of his enemies were dead, so establishing the oneman rule that he claimed was necessary to restore stability was relatively easy. He was also lucky to live to be nearly 80—he had plenty of time to consolidate his rule. He was

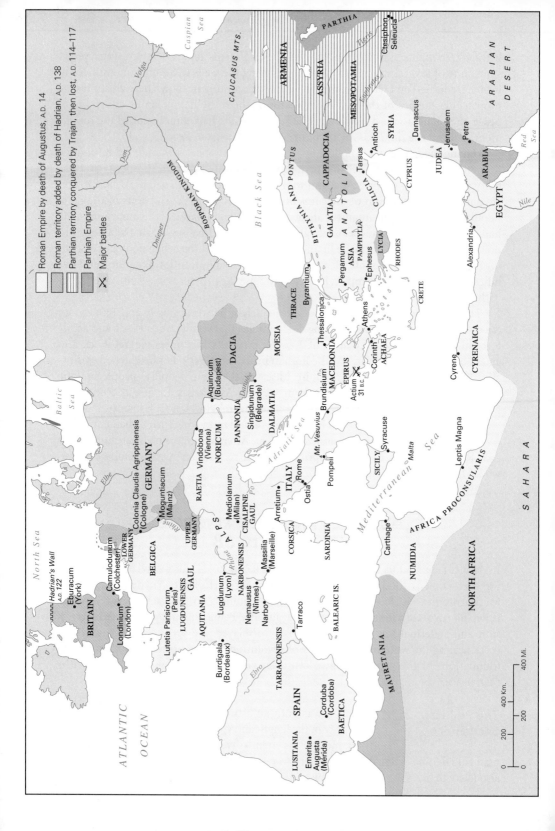

Roman Empire by death of Augustus, A.D. 14

Roman territory added by death of Hadrian, A.D. 138

Parthian territory conquered by Trajan, then lost, A.D. 114–117

Parthian Empire

X Major battles

North Sea

ATLANTIC
OCEAN

Baltic Sea

Hadrian's Wall A.D. 122
BRITAIN
Eburacum (York)
Camulodunum (Colchester)
Londinium (London)

Elbe

LOWER GERMANY
Colonia Claudia Agrippinensis (Cologne)
GERMANY
Moguntiacum (Mainz)
UPPER GERMANY
Rhine

BELGICA
Lutetia Parisiorum (Paris)
GAUL
LUGDUNENSIS
Lugdunum (Lyon)
AQUITANIA
Burdigala (Bordeaux)
NARBONENSIS
Nemausus (Nimes)
Narbo
Massilia (Marseille)
Rhône

RAETIA
Vindobona (Vienna)
NORICUM
Mediolanum (Milan)
CISALPINE GAUL
ALPS
Po

PANNONIA
Aquincum (Budapest)
Danube
Singidunum (Belgrade)
DALMATIA

DACIA
MOESIA

Volga

Don

Dnieper

Caspian Sea

BOSPORAN KINGDOM

CAUCASUS MTS.

Black Sea

ARMENIA
PARTHIA
ASSYRIA
MESOPOTAMIA
Tigris
Euphrates
Ctesiphon
Seleucia

THRACE
Byzantium
BITHYNIA AND PONTUS
CAPPADOCIA
GALATIA
ANATOLIA
Pergamum
ASIA
Ephesus
LYCIA
PAMPHYLIA
RHODES

CILICIA
Tarsus
SYRIA
Antioch
Damascus
Jerusalem
JUDEA
Petra
ARABIA

ARABIAN DESERT

Red Sea

MACEDONIA
Thessalonica
EPIRUS
Actium 31 B.C. X
ACHAEA
Athens
Corinth
CRETE

ITALY
Rome
Ostia
Arretium
CORSICA
SARDINIA
Mt. Vesuvius
Pompeii
Brundisium
Adriatic Sea

SPAIN
LUSITANIA
Emerita Augusta (Mérida)
TARRACONENSIS
Tarraco
Ebro
BAETICA
Corduba (Cordoba)
BALEARIC IS.

Mediterranean Sea
SICILY
Syracuse
Malta

MAURETANIA
NORTH AFRICA
NUMIDIA
Carthage
AFRICA PROCONSULARIS
Leptis Magna

CYRENAICA
Cyrene

EGYPT
Nile
Alexandria

SAHARA

0   200   400 Mi.
0   200   400 Km.

a cagey man and a sharp judge of others. Octavian learned the lesson of Caesar's greatest mistake. He understood that the Roman elite, however weakened, was still strong enough to oppose a ruler who flaunted monarchical power. To avoid a second Ides of March, therefore, Octavian was infinitely diplomatic.

Rather than call himself dictator, Octavian took the title of *princeps* ("first citizen"), an old title of respect in the senate. From *princeps* comes *Principate*, a term often used to describe the constitutional monarchy of the "Early Empire," the name that historians have given to the period from 31 B.C. to A.D. 192. Four years after Actium, in 27 B.C., the senate granted Octavian the honorific title *augustus,* symbolizing the augmentation, or increase, of his authority. He was also known as *Caesar* and *divi filius* ("son of a god"), which tied him to Julius Caesar. Another name, *imperator* ("commander" and, later, "emperor"), recalled the military might that Augustus (as we shall henceforth call him) could call on if needed.

In 27 B.C. Augustus proclaimed "the transfer of the state to the free disposal of the senate and the people"—that is, the restoration of the Republic. Remembering similar claims by Sulla and Julius Caesar, few Romans were likely to believe this, and few would have wanted the Republic restored in any case. They no doubt appreciated their ruler's tact, however.

Two strokes of genius marked the new regime. First, Augustus held power without monopolizing public offices. He held the civil authority of the tribunate without being a tribune and the military authority of provincial generals without holding a specific command. Generalships remained open to ambitious Romans as long as they accepted Augustus's power. Second, the new government divided the provinces between Augustus and the senate. To check any new would-be Caesar, Augustus kept for himself the frontier provinces, with the main concentration of armies, as well as grain-rich Egypt (which had been annexed as a Roman province after Actium). The local commanders were loyal equestrians who owed their success to Augustus. Most of the other provinces continued to be ruled as before by senators serving as governors.

Augustus wanted advice without dissent. He used the senate, or rather a committee of senators and magistrates, as a sounding board; the group evolved into a permanent advisory body. Ordinary senate meetings, however, what with informers and secret agents, lost their old freedom of speech. The popular assemblies fared even worse, as their powers were limited and eventually transferred to the senate. Nor would unruly crowds be tolerated. Augustus established the city of Rome's first police force and also stationed there his own personal guard. Called the praetorians, or Praetorian Guard, the name used for a Roman general's bodyguard, the guard would play a crucial role in future imperial politics.

More important for the public good, Augustus established the first civil service, consisting of a series of prefectures—or departments—supervising, for example, the city watch, the grain supply, the water supply, the building of roads and bridges, tax collection, and the provisioning of the armies. Equestrians and freedmen were prominent

The Roman World in the Early Empire

Many modern cities are built on the sites of Roman foundations, evidence of the immense extent of the Roman Empire at its height.

in these prefectures and in provincial government, so they enthusiastically supported the Principate.

Although one may speak loosely of "imperial bureaucracy," neither Augustus nor his successors ever established a tight administrative grip on their far-flung empire. As in all ancient empires, Roman government tended to be decentralized and limited. In an age in which few public officials received a salary, bribes were winked at.

The Economic and Social Settlement The old Roman ruling class made its peace with Augustus, but some never forgave him for ending their ancient privileges. The conservative historian Tacitus (ca. A.D. 55–117) looked back wistfully to the Late Republic as a golden era of freedom, eloquence, and "the old sound morality." Even Tacitus, however, was forced to admit that most people in the Roman world welcomed and admired the Principate. The reason is simple: Augustus and his successors brought peace and prosperity after a century of disasters under the Late Republic.

The Augustan period enjoyed affluence, especially in Italy; the other provinces caught up with Italy by the second century A.D. Agriculture flourished with the end of civil war. Italian industries became leaders in exports. Italian glass bowls and window-panes, iron arms and tools, fancy silver eating utensils and candlesticks, and bronze statues and pots circulated from Britain to central Asia.

The perennial problem of the Late Republic had been land-hunger, which drove peasants into the arms of ambitious generals. Augustus kept his troops happy by compensating 300,000 loyal veterans with land, money, or both, often in new overseas colonies. At first he paid out these rewards from his own private sources; after A.D. 6, he made the rich pay via new taxes. The result kept the peace, but many nonsoldiers in Italy remained poor, as of course did the huge number of slaves.

As for the renegade commanders who had bedeviled the Late Republic, Augustus cut their potential power base by reducing the size of the army, gradually cutting the number of legions from over sixty to twenty-eight. The total size of the army, including light infantry and cavalry, was about 300,000. This reduction lightened Rome's tax burden but left Augustus with little room to expand the empire. In A.D. 9 Rome lost three legions to a native revolt against Rome's plan to extend its rule in Germany as far east as the Elbe River. Short of manpower, Augustus had to accept the Rhine River as Rome's new German frontier.

Imperial defense remained a major issue. Strong Roman armies were a necessity along the hostile European frontier. On the friendlier border in western Asia and northern Africa, Augustus and his immediate successors set up client kingdoms, such as Judea and Armenia, to protect Roman territory. As for Parthia, Augustus compromised. He won no new territory but did achieve the symbolic victory of a return of the legionary standards lost by Crassus at Carrhae in 53 B.C.

Back in Rome the urban poor, many of them freedmen, enjoyed a more efficient system of free grain distribution under Augustus and a large increase in games and public entertainment—the imperial policy of "bread and circuses" designed to content the masses. Augustus also set up a major public works program, which provided jobs for the poor. He prided himself on having found Rome "a city of brick" and having left it "a city of marble."

To promote his ideology of renewal, Augustus sponsored social legislation embodying the old Republican virtues. He passed a series of laws encouraging marriage and childbearing and discouraging promiscuity and adultery. Such legislation was so flagrantly disobeyed that in 2 B.C. Augustus felt compelled to make an example of his own daughter, Julia (39 B.C.–A.D. 14), his only child, whose adulteries were the talk of Rome. As punishment she was banished to a barren islet.

Augustus's era marks the beginning of the classical period of Roman jurisprudence, during which the professionalism that had begun to mark Roman law in the Late Republic became a permanent fact. It was probably Augustus who established the practice, followed by later emperors, of granting a few distinguished jurists the exclusive right to issue legal opinions "on behalf of the princeps." He ensured, therefore, that experts guided the administration of justice. The first law school was opened in Rome under Augustus. Roman jurists, many of them provincials, adapted Roman law to the practices of the provinces. Although various provincial legal systems remained in use, the international system of Roman law was also used widely in the provinces.

In religion, too, Augustus was a legislator and reformer. He restored once-neglected cults and temples in order to appear as Rome's savior. He would probably have approved when, after his death, he was deified, just as Julius Caesar had been. Even while he was still alive, Augustus was worshiped in the provinces as a god—in both the East, where the cult of Roma and Augustus grew in popularity, and the West, where centers of emperor-worship were established at the sites of Lyon and Cologne. The imperial cult, an important part of state propaganda until the empire became Christian in the fourth century A.D., was well underway.

Deification, whether formal or informal, was a heady brew, but Augustus deserved it more than most. He not only ended the Late Republican era of civil wars but established the Roman Empire on a completely new footing. Republican freedom was gone, but the emperor and bureaucrats brought stability. The peace of the Augustan Principate would last, with few interruptions, for two hundred years. Few people in history have created order so successfully.

The Culture of the Augustan Age   Like *Periclean,* the adjective *Augustan* has come to signify an era of literary and artistic flowering. In both periods strong elements of classicism shaped the arts—that is, an attempt to project fundamental, heroic, and idealized values, the values that the self-confident rulers of each epoch wished to promote. Both prose and poetry flourished in Augustus's empire. The emperor and his close adviser Maecenas (d. 8 B.C.) were patrons of a number of important poets, chief among them Virgil (70–19 B.C.) and Horace (65–8 B.C.). The historian Livy (59 B.C.–A.D. 17), who wrote his history of Rome from the founding of the city to 9 B.C. under Augustus, also elicited the princeps's interest in his work. All three men contributed in their writings to the Augustan renewal and rededication of Rome.

In many ways Virgil speaks for his contemporaries. In the *Eclogues*—poems that, following an Alexandrian model (see page 114), have rustic settings—Virgil describes the miseries of the civil wars and the blessings of peace under Augustus. "A god created this peace for us; for he will always be a god to me," one character says. In the Fourth Eclogue, Virgil speaks of the birth of a child to usher in a restored Golden Age. At the

Mosaic of the Doves
This exquisite mosaic shows a number of doves drinking from or positioned around a gilded bronze basin on a marble pedestal. Derived from a Hellenistic work from Pergamum, this mosaic comes from a wealthy house in Pompeii. (Scala/Art Resource, NY)

Council of Nicaea in A.D. 325 (see page 199) and later, this poem was given a Christian interpretation. In the *Georgics,* Virgil describes the glories of Italian agriculture, which, thanks to Augustus, could be practiced peacefully again.

Virgil's masterpiece is an epic poem, the *Aeneid,* "the story of Aeneas," the legendary Trojan founder of Rome, or at least of the Latin town from which Rome's founders eventually came. Legend also makes Aeneas the ancestor of Augustus. Thus the *Aeneid* indirectly celebrates Augustus, often considered Rome's second founder. The poem explores the pain and burden as well as the glory of empire.

If Virgil's work has the grandeur of marble, Horace's poems—*Odes, Epodes, Satires, Epistles,* and *Ars Poetica (Art of Poetry)*—are more like finely cut gems. They tend to be polished, complex, and detached. Like Virgil, Horace explores the themes of war and peace and praises Augustus. "With Caesar [Augustus] holding the lands, I shall fear neither turmoil nor violent death," declares one of the *Odes.* Both Horace and Virgil successfully adapted Greek models and, in the process, created something new. Few writers have had a greater influence on the later Western literary tradition.

Only 35 of the original 142 books of Livy's ambitious history have survived. Livy is both a master storyteller and a superb ironist. His anecdotes of Roman history are vivid and told in a grand rhetorical style. Livy is our major source for the Roman monarchy and Early Republic, although his account of early Rome is long on myth and short on fact. Nevertheless, Livy is not merely an entertaining stylist but a profound thinker on the meaning of history. He embroiders the facts and engages in frank, subjective judgments intended to inspire both patriotism and reflection on the ironies of history.

Another patron of writers in Augustus's circle was Messalla, himself an orator as well as a statesman. Love poetry was his special interest. Among the poets Messalla supported were Ovid, best known for works on love and mythology; Tibullus, an elegist; and his ward, Sulpicia. Although little survives of Sulpicia's work, more of her work exists than of any other Roman woman. She describes her passion for one Cerinthus: "a worthy man . . . at last a love . . . of such a kind that my shame, Gossip, would be greater if I kept it covered than if I laid it bare."[1]

Augustus and his entourage were also great patrons of the arts and of architecture, which they considered propaganda tools. They sponsored many major building projects throughout the empire, especially in Rome, which gained temples, a new Forum of Augustus, the Theater of Marcellus, the Baths of Agrippa, the Pantheon, and the Mausoleum of Augustus.

The Julio-Claudians   Augustus and his successors presented the imperial household to the world as the ideal family, the very model of social order. Behind the walls of the palace, however, dwelt a troubled reality. Augustus had only one child, Julia, from his first marriage, which ended in divorce. In 38 B.C. Augustus took as his second wife Livia (58 B.C.–A.D. 29), who divorced her husband to marry Augustus even though she was pregnant with their second son. She did not bear Augustus children. Seeking a male successor, Augustus used Julia as a pawn in a game of dynastic marriage, divorce, and remarriage, but to no avail. Julia's first two husbands both predeceased her, as did two sons, each of whom Augustus had adopted. (In Rome it was common for a man without a birth son to adopt a son.) In the end, Augustus was forced to choose as successor, and adopt, a man he disliked, Tiberius (42 B.C.–A.D. 37), Livia's elder son.

Livia was among the most powerful women in Roman history. One of Augustus's main advisers, she developed a reputation for intrigue, aimed, so gossip had it, at securing the succession for Tiberius. Livia's enemies accused her of poisoning many people, including Julia's husbands and sons; her own grandson, Germanicus (a brilliant general whose popularity threatened Tiberius's); and even Augustus himself, who died in bed after a short illness in A.D. 14.

From A.D. 14 to 68, Rome was ruled by other emperors from Augustus's family. The dynasty, known as the Julio-Claudians, consisted of Augustus's stepson Tiberius, great-grandson Caligula, grandnephew Claudius, and great-great-grandson Nero. For many elite Romans, this era was one of decadence, scandal, and oppression of the old nobility. Ordinary people, however, generally enjoyed the benefits of stable, effective, and peaceful government.

The reign of Tiberius (r. 14–37) was later remembered by the elite for its treason trials and murders. The senate complained as it steadily lost power to the princeps. The Roman masses grumbled because Tiberius cut back on games and building projects. But despite his shortcomings, Tiberius was a skilled and prudent administrator. He wisely drew back from war on the borders, reduced taxes and spending, and promoted honesty among provincial governors.

His successor, his nephew Gaius (r. 37–41), nicknamed Caligula ("Baby Boots," after the boots he had worn as a little boy in his father's army camp), humiliated the senate. It was bad enough that he tried to have himself declared a living god. On top of that, he appointed his favorite horse not only high priest of a new cult in his honor but also a member of the senate. Caligula raised taxes and accused people of treason in order to confiscate property. He wanted to have his statue erected in the Temple at Jerusalem, and he would have done so, but he was assassinated first, the victim of a high-level conspiracy. After his death the senate debated restoring the Republic, but it was not to be.

Caligula's uncle, Claudius, was named emperor by the Praetorian Guard, which forced the senate to support him. Physically handicapped, Claudius (r. 41–54) was often the butt of jokes, but he was a man of substance: a historian, politician, and priest and someone fully versed in the cunning ways of his family. An activist emperor, he expanded the imperial offices with their powerful freedmen; oversaw the construction of an artificial harbor at Rome's silt-clogged port of Ostia; and conquered Britain, where Roman arms had not intervened since Julius Caesar's forays in 55 to 54 B.C.

Claudius's death may have been the result of poisoning by his wife, who was also his niece, Agrippina the Younger (15–59); in any case, her son by a previous marriage, Nero, became emperor (r. 54–68). Nero's scandalous behavior rivaled Caligula's, and his treason trials outdid Tiberius's. After a great fire destroyed half of Rome in 64, Nero mounted a big rebuilding program and was accused of having started the fire just so that he could become famous as a builder. He found a scapegoat for the fire in the members of a small religious sect, the Christians, whom he persecuted. Ordinary Romans supported Nero because he gave them good government. He was unpopular with the senators and, more serious, with the army, because he failed to pay all his troops promptly. Confronted with a major revolt in 68, Nero committed suicide.

The next year, 69, witnessed Rome's first civil war in about a century. Three men claimed the imperial purple after Nero. A fourth, Vespasian (Titus Flavius Vespasianus, r. 69–79), commander of the army quelling a revolt in the province of Judea, was able to make his claim stick. Peace was restored, but not the rule of Augustus's family. Vespasian founded a new dynasty, the Flavians (r. 69–96), which was followed in turn by the Nervo-Trajanic (r. 96–138) and Antonine (r. 138–192) dynasties. The ultimate tribute to Augustus may be that his regime was stable enough to survive the extinction of his family.

THE ROMAN PEACE AND ITS COLLAPSE, A.D. 69–284

Much about Rome in the second century A.D. appears attractive today. Within the multi-ethnic empire, opportunities for inhabitants to become part of the elite were increasing. The central government was on its way to granting Roman citizenship to nearly every free person in the empire, a process completed in the year 212. The emperors emphasized sharing prosperity and spreading it through the provinces. Italy was no longer the tyrant of the Mediterranean, but merely first among equals. To be sure, rebellions were crushed, but few people rebelled. This period, known as the *pax Romana,* or "Roman peace," seems particularly golden in contrast with what followed: the disastrous and disordered third century A.D., in which the empire came close to collapse but survived because of a radical and rigid transformation.

The Flavians and the "Good Emperors"	The Flavian dynasty of Vespasian (r. 69–79) and his sons Titus (r. 79–81) and Domitian (r. 81–96) provided good government, and their successors built on their achievements. Unlike

the Julio-Claudians, Vespasian hailed not from the old Roman nobility but from an Italian propertied family. A man of rough-and-ready character, Vespasian is supposed to have replied when Titus complained that a new latrine tax was beneath the dignity of the Roman government, "Son, money has no smell." Unlike his father and brother, Domitian reverted to frequent treason trials and persecution of the aristocracy, which earned him assassination in 96, although the empire as a whole enjoyed peace and sound administration under his reign.

The so-called Five Good Emperors are Nerva (r. 96–98), Trajan (r. 98–117), Hadrian (r. 117–138), and the first two Antonines, Antoninus Pius (r. 138–161) and Marcus Aurelius (r. 161–180). They are in several ways examples of the principle of merit. Trajan, a Roman citizen born in Spain, was Rome's first emperor from outside Italy. Hadrian and Marcus Aurelius also came from Spain, and Antoninus Pius from Gaul. Each of the Five Good Emperors except Marcus Aurelius adopted the most competent person, rather than the closest blood relative, as his son and successor, thus elevating duty over sentiment. Marcus Aurelius, a deeply committed Stoic, gave full vent to his sense of duty in his *Meditations*, which he wrote in Greek while living in a tent on the Danube frontier, where he fought long and hard against German raids. Antoninus was surnamed "Pius" (Dutiful) because he was devoted to his country, the gods, and his adoptive father, Hadrian.

The Five Good Emperors made humaneness and generosity the themes of their reigns. Trajan, for example, founded a program of financial aid for the poor children of Italy. They also went to great lengths to care for the provinces. These emperors not only commonly received petitions from cities, associations, and individuals in far-off provinces but answered them. Yet humaneness does not mean softness. Hadrian, for instance, ordered a revolt in Judea (132–135) suppressed with great brutality.

Like the Julio-Claudians, the Five Good Emperors advertised their wives to the world as exemplars of traditional modesty, self-effacement, and domesticity. In fact, they were often worldly, educated, and influential. Trajan's wife, Plotina, for example (d. 121 or 123), acted as patron of the Epicurean school at Athens, whose philosophy she claimed to follow. She advised her husband on provincial administration as well as dynastic matchmaking. Hadrian's wife, Sabina, traveled in her husband's entourage to Egypt (130), where her aristocratic Greek friend, Julia Balbilla, commemorated the trip by writing Greek poetry, which she had inscribed alongside other tourists' writings on the leg of one of two statues of Amenhotep III at Thebes, referred to in classical times as the "colossi of Memnon."

A darker side of the second-century empire was the problem of border defense. Augustus and the Julio-Claudians had established client kingdoms where possible, to avoid the expense and political dangers of raising armies. The emperors of the day tended to be more aggressive on the borders than their predecessors. They moved from client kingdoms to a new border policy of stationary frontier defense. Expensive fortification systems of walls, watchtowers, and trenches were built along the perimeter of the empire's border and manned with guards. A prominent example is Hadrian's Wall, which separated Roman Britain from the enemy tribes to the north. Stretching 80 miles, the wall required fifteen thousand defense troops.

The most ambitious frontier policy was that of Trajan, who crossed the Danube to carve out the new province of Dacia (modern Romania) and who used an excuse to invade Parthian Mesopotamia. He won battles as far away as the Persian Gulf, but he lost the war. As soon as his army left, Mesopotamia rose in revolt, followed by Germany. Trajan's reign marked the empire's greatest geographic extent, but Trajan had overextended Rome's resources. When he died, his successor, Hadrian, had to abandon Trajan's province of Mesopotamia.

Prosperity and Romanization in the Provinces Compared with a modern economy, the Roman economy was underdeveloped. Most people worked in agriculture, employed primitive technology, and lived at a subsistence level. Even so, the Roman Empire experienced modest economic growth during the first two centuries A.D. The chief beneficiaries were the wealthy few, but ordinary people shared in the economic expansion as well. In addition to stability and peace, several other factors encouraged economic development. The western provinces witnessed the opening of new lands to agriculture, where improved techniques were applied. The growth of cities increased agricultural demand. Changes in Roman law aided commerce by making it easier to employ middlemen in business transactions. Travel and communications were relatively easy and inexpensive.

Trade boomed, as a recent archaeological discovery in the Italian city of Pisa recalls. Nineteen Hellenistic and Roman ships were found at the site of the ancient harbor beginning in 1999. Several are merchant ships, both coastal freighters and small harbor craft. One of the ships was filled with amphoras (storage jars), still stacked in neat rows

Double Portrait, Pompeii *This wall painting from a house joined to a bakery depicts a married couple, possibly the wealthy baker P. Paquius Proculus and his wife. The portraiture is realistic. The couple carry symbols of education: she holds wax tablets and a stylus (pen), while he grasps a sealed scroll.* (Scala/Art Resource, NY)

and filled with wine and sand. Both of those goods come from the region of the Bay of Naples, whose sand was used for concrete that could set underwater. The finds, which seem to date from the mid-second century A.D., offer a vivid picture of trade up and down the west coast of Italy. When the cargo was unloaded at Pisa, the ships probably picked up the local grain and marble, which was shipped in turn to Rome.

Rome was an economic magnet, but so, to a lesser extent, were all cities, and the second century A.D. was a great age of city life. New cities were founded far from the Mediterranean. They began as veterans' colonies, market towns, and even army camps, and some grew into cities of permanent importance in European history: Cologne (Colonia Claudia Agrippinensis), Paris (Lutetia Parisiorum), Lyon (Lugdunum), London (Londinium), Mérida (Emerita Augusta), Vienna (Vindobona), and Budapest (Aquincum).

Whether old or new, cities attracted large elite populations. The Principate was not a domain of country gentry but one in which ambitious people wanted to live in great cities, in emulation of the greatest city of the empire, Rome, which was by Augustus's day a city of perhaps a million people. In cities men competed for positions as magistrates, in imitation of the two consuls, or for seats on the local town council, often called a *curia*, like the senate in Rome. Town councilors were called *decurions* and known collectively as the *curial order*. Decurions played one-upmanship in sponsoring public buildings in the Roman style—one man endowing a new forum, another a triumphal arch, a third a library, a fourth an amphitheater, and so on. From Ephesus in Anatolia to Colchester in Britain, from Mainz in Germany to Leptis Magna in Libya, a Roman could find familiar government institutions, architecture, and street plans. At Zeugma on the Euphrates River, for example, a city of seventy thousand people, aristocrats on Rome's eastern frontier lived in Italian-style villas decorated with classical frescoes and mosaics and adorned with bronze statues of the Greco-Roman gods.

Unlike men, women did not usually hold magistracies, but wealthy women of the empire could and did lavish money on public benefactions. Women endowed temples and synagogues, amphitheaters and monumental gateways, games and ceremonies. They were rewarded with wreaths, front-row seats, statues, priesthoods, and inscriptions honoring them as "most distinguished lady," "patron," and even "father of the city," to cite an extraordinary case from Roman Egypt.

The buildings were visible examples of Romanization, although the Romans did not use the term. If they had, it would have had a limited meaning because the emperors neither would nor could impose a lockstep cultural uniformity on their subjects. The empire was too big and ancient technology too primitive for that. The total population of the empire consisted of between 50 million and 100 million people, most of whom lived in the countryside. The small and largely urbanized Roman administration had little direct contact with most people. So, for example, only a minority of the inhabitants of the empire spoke Latin; in the East, Greek was the more common language of administration. Millions of people spoke neither Greek nor Latin. Celtic, Germanic, Punic, Berber, Coptic, Aramaic, and Syriac were other common languages in Roman domains. In short, the empire lacked the unity of a modern nation-state.

What, then, besides buildings and language might Romanization entail? One index has already been suggested: the participation of provincials in the central government, even as emperor. By around A.D. 200, for example, about 15 percent of the known

Roman equestrians and senators came from North Africa. By this time the senate was no longer dominated by Italians but was representative of the empire as a whole.

Participation in government implies another index of Romanization—the extension of Roman citizenship outside Italy to magistrates, decurions, or even whole cities. Citizens took Roman names reflecting the emperor or promagistrate who had enfranchised them. Thus the provinces were full of Julii, Claudii, and Flavii, among others.

The spread of Roman customs is another measure of Romanization. For example, the gladiatorial shows that Romans loved became popular from Antioch to England. These combats advertised both Roman culture and Roman brutality.

By the same token, native customs might be adopted by Romans. Consider the case of Egypt, where, in the late 1990s, archaeologists discovered a vast Roman-era cemetery about 230 miles southwest of Cairo, in the Bahriya Oasis, Roman Egypt's wine country. The population was Romanized here. Yet the cemetery, with its dozens of gilded mummies from the first and second centuries A.D., shows the persistence of the mummification processes of the pharaohs.

Another ambiguous symbol of Romanization is found in A.D. 212. In a law known as the *Constitutio Antoniana,* the emperor Caracalla (r. 211–217) rendered nearly all of the free inhabitants of the empire Roman citizens. On the one hand, the law is a historical landmark. Near-universal Roman citizenship was a kind of halfway point between ancient empire and modern mass democracy. On the other hand, the *Constitutio Antoniana* was something of a gimmick. It was probably less an instrument of unification than of taxation, for citizens had a heavier tax burden than noncitizens.

The Roman army, by contrast, did promote Romanization. In antiquity as today, military service offered education and social mobility. Only citizens could join the legions; non-Romans served as auxiliaries. They received Roman citizenship after completing their regular term of service, twenty-five years, and with good reason: a Syrian or Gallic peasant, for example, who served in the Roman military would experience a way of life with old and deep roots in central Italy.

Non-Italians had, and took, the opportunity to rise high in the army or government. This was all to Rome's credit. Yet as Italians became a minority in the Roman army, and as ever larger numbers of frontier peoples were recruited, it became conceivable that someday the army might abandon its loyalty to Rome.

Roman Law on Class and Marriage Roman law is one of the ancient world's most influential and enduring legacies. Logical, practical, orderly, and—within the limits of a society of slaves and masters—relatively fair, Roman law has influenced the legal systems of most Western countries and many non-Western countries. The law governing Roman citizens was called *ius civile,* or "civil law." Originally this term covered a very broad range of legal matters, but in the empire its meaning was narrowed to private matters. Criminal law became a separate category.

The law helped Rome administer its empire. Roman law was not universal, and noncitizens continued to use their own laws for local matters, but the governors used Roman law to run their provinces, so local elites had to become familiar with it. Like so many Roman customs, the law was both hierarchical and flexible. Let us consider two areas in which the law affected daily life: class and marriage.

The law reflected Roman society's ingrained social inequality. Traditional special classes such as senators and equestrians survived, to be joined by the new distinction between citizens and noncitizens. Another important division cut across the citizen-alien distinction, that between *honestiores* (in general, the curial order) and *humiliores* (everyone else). Privileges previously inherent in citizenship, such as exemption from flogging by officials, now tended to be based on this new distinction, enshrined in private and criminal law.

The most basic legal distinction was that between free and slave—and the empire contained millions of slaves. A third category, ex-slaves or freedmen, also became increasingly important. Freedmen technically owed service to their former masters, who became their patrons, and most freedmen were humble. A few, however, grew rich in commerce or wielded enough power in imperial administration to lord it over even Roman aristocrats. The result was strong elite hostility toward freedmen, which is often reflected in Roman literature. Witness the stereotype of the vulgar freedman, embodied in Trimalchio in the *Satyricon*, a novel by Petronius (first century A.D.). Trimalchio had more estates than he could remember and so much money that his wife counted it by the bushel-load.

As regards marriage, Roman family law was strict and severe in principle. In practice, however, it often proved pragmatic and even humane. Consider three cases: elite marriages, slave marriages, and soldiers' marriages.

As in the Late Republic, so in the Early Empire most Roman women married without legally becoming members of their husbands' families—or their children's. This gave women a degree of freedom from their husbands, but it left elite women, who owned property, with a problem: technically that property was controlled by their fathers or brothers. Yet society recognized a woman's wish to leave her property to her children, and imperial law increasingly made it possible for her to do so—although the conservative Romans waited until the sixth century A.D. before abolishing completely the rights of greedy uncles. Another case is a mother's right to have a say in her children's choice of marriage partner. This maternal prerogative became accepted social practice even though Roman law gave women no such right.

Roman slaves married and had children, but they had to do so in the face of both legal and practical obstacles. Roman law gave slaves no right to marry, and it made slave children the property of the owner of the slave mother. Owners could and did break up slave families by sale. Even if a slave was freed, the law expressed far more concern with the continuing obligations of freedmen to their former masters than with the rights of slave families. Yet during the Early Empire cracks appeared in the wall of law that allowed slave families to slip through.

For example, although the law insisted that a slave be age 30 before being freed, it made an exception for an owner who wished to free a female slave younger than 30 in order to marry her. To take another example, the law conceded that slave children owed devotion and loyalty (*pietas*) to their slave parents.

Career soldiers from at least the time of Augustus on could not marry, probably on the grounds of military discipline. Yet many soldiers cohabited anyhow, often with noncitizen women in the areas where they served, and frequently children were the result. Not until the reign of Septimius Severus (r. 193–211) were soldiers permitted to marry formally, and then only after twenty-five years of service. Yet not only had commanders permitted cohabitation for two centuries, but the law also made concessions now and then. For example, the Flavians gave soldiers a degree of freedom to make wills, which could allow them to leave property to illegitimate children. Various emperors gave groups of soldiers the privilege, on discharge, to legalize a marriage with a noncitizen, which ordinary Romans were not permitted to do.[2]

The Culture of the Roman Peace

In Latin poetry the century or so after the death of Augustus is often referred to as the "Silver Age," a term sometimes applied to prose as well. The implication is that this period, though productive, fell short of the golden Augustan era. It might be fairer to say that the self-confidence of the Augustan writers did not last. As the permanence of monarchy became clear, many in the elite looked back to the Republic with nostalgia and bitterness. Silver Age writing often takes refuge in satire or rhetorical flourish. Writing under Trajan, for example, the historian Tacitus poured scorn on the Julio-Claudians and Flavians. Other Silver Age writers indulged in flattery and obsequiousness toward the emperor.

The Silver Age was an era of interest in antiquities and in compiling handbooks and encyclopedias; it was also an era of self-consciousness and literary criticism. In the first two centuries A.D., Roman writers came from an ever greater diversity of backgrounds and wrote for an ever wider audience, as prosperity and educational opportunities increased. Consider Lucian (ca. A.D. 115–185), an essayist and satirist. A native of Syria who probably spoke Aramaic before learning Greek, he served as an administrator in Roman Egypt.

Many writers of the era pursued public careers, which offered access to patronage. Tacitus, for instance, rose as high as proconsul of the province of Asia. Prominent literary families emerged, such as that of Pliny the Elder (A.D. 23–79), an encyclopedic author on natural science, geography, history, and art; and his nephew, Pliny the Younger (ca. A.D. 62–ca. 113), an orator and letter writer. The most notable literary family is that of Seneca the Elder (ca. 55 B.C.–A.D. 40), a historian and scholar of rhetoric; his son, Seneca the Younger (ca. 4 B.C.–A.D. 65); and Seneca the Younger's nephew, the epic poet Lucan (A.D. 39–65).

Born in Cordoba, Spain, the younger Seneca moved at an early age to Rome, where he became a successful lawyer and wealthy investor. He was banished in A.D. 41 for alleged adultery with a sister of Caligula. Recalled in 49, he became tutor to the young Nero. When Nero became emperor in 54, Seneca became one of his chief advisers and helped bring good government to the empire. Seneca eventually fell out of favor, however, and was forced first into retirement and then, in A.D. 65, into suicide. He had been the major literary figure of his age, a jack-of-all-trades: playwright, essayist, pamphleteer, student of science, and noted Stoic philosopher.

A literary career was safer under the Five Good Emperors. Consider Tacitus and his contemporary, the poet Juvenal (ca. A.D. 55–130). Juvenal's *Satires* are bitter and brilliant poems offering social commentary. He laments the past, when poverty and war had supposedly kept Romans chaste and virtuous. Amid "the woes of long peace," luxury and foreign ways had corrupted Rome, in his opinion. Critics often blame society's troubles on marginal groups. Juvenal, for example, launches harsh attacks on women and foreigners. Tacitus, too, is sometimes scornful of women.

Yet if he is biased on matters of gender, Tacitus is far from ethnocentric. Few historians have expressed graver doubts about the value of their country's alleged success. For example, Tacitus highlighted the simple virtues of the Germanic tribes, so different from the sophisticated decadence of contemporary Rome. Nostalgia for the Republic pervades his two greatest works, *The Histories,* which covers the civil wars of A.D. 69, and *The Annals* (only parts of which survive), chronicling the emperors from Tiberius through Nero. A masterpiece of irony and pithiness, Tacitus's style makes an unforgettable impression on the reader.

Plutarch (ca. A.D. 50–120), whose *Parallel Lives of Noble Greeks and Romans* later captured the imagination of Shakespeare, is probably the best-known pagan Greek writer of the first two centuries A.D. Like Livy, Plutarch emphasizes the moral and political lessons of history. A careful scholar, Plutarch found his true calling in rhetorical craftsmanship—polished speeches and carefully chosen anecdotes. As in Rome, rhetoric was the basis of much of Greek literary culture in this period.

Another star of Greek culture at this time was the physician Galen of Pergamum (A.D. 129–?199). In his many writings, Galen was to medicine what Aristotle had been to philosophy: a brilliant systematizer and an original thinker. He excelled in anatomy and physiology and proved that the arteries as well as the veins carry blood. He was destined to have a dominant influence on European medicine in the Middle Ages.

The Crisis of the Third Century, A.D. 235–284	Leaving the relative calm of the second century A.D. behind, the third-century Roman Empire descended into an ever widening spiral of crisis. Barbarian invasions, domestic economic

woes, plague, assassinations, brigandage, urban decline—the list of Rome's problems is dramatic. The empire went "from a kingdom of gold to one of iron and rust," as Dio Cassius put it, summing up Roman history after the death of Marcus Aurelius in 180, when the seeds of crisis were sown.

Stability first began to slip away during the reign of the last of the Antonines, Marcus Aurelius's birth son, Commodus (r. 180–192), a man with Nero's taste for decadence and penchant for terrorizing the senatorial elite. His predictable assassination led to civil war, after which Septimius Severus, commander of the Danube armies, emerged as the unchallenged emperor (r. 193–211). He founded the Severan dynasty, which survived until 235.

Severan reformers attempted to re-establish the empire on a firmer footing, but they only brought the day of crisis nearer. The main theme of Septimius's reign was the transfer of power—from the senate to the army and from Italy to the provinces. To extend the Roman frontier in North Africa and western Asia, Septimius expanded the army and improved the pay and conditions of service. These measures might have been necessary, but Septimius went too far by indulging in war with Parthia (197–199)—unnecessary war, because the crumbling Parthian kingdom was too weak to threaten Rome. What the war did accomplish, however, was to inspire the enemy's rejuvenation under a new Eastern dynasty, the Sassanids.

The Sassanid Persians spearheaded increased pressure on Rome's frontiers. The Sassanids overran Rome's eastern provinces and captured the emperor Valerian himself in 260. The caravan city of Palmyra (in Syria) took advantage of Rome's weakness to establish independence; its most famous leader was the queen Zenobia. Meanwhile, two Germanic tribes, the Franks and the Goths, hammered the empire from the northwest and northeast.

Fending off invasions at opposite fronts stretched Rome to the breaking point. To pay for defense, the emperors devalued the currency, but the result was massive

Hadrian's Wall   *Built in A.D. 122–126, this extensive structure protected Roman England from raids by the tribes of Scotland. It represents the strategy of stationary frontier de-fense.*   (Roy Rainford/Robert Harding Picture Library)

inflation. As if this were not bad enough, a plague broke out in Egypt at midcentury and raged through the empire for fifteen years, compounding Rome's military man-power problems.

Assassinations and civil wars shook the stability of the government. Between 235—when the last Severan emperor, Severus Alexander, was murdered—and 284, twenty men were emperor, however briefly in some cases. Civilians suffered in the resulting disorder.

Yet the empire rebounded, which is a tribute to Roman resilience as well as a sign of the disunity and lack of staying power among the empire's enemies. Recovery began during the reign of Gallienus (r. 253–268), who ended the Frankish threat and nearly polished off the Goths. By 275 Aurelian (r. 270–275) had defeated the Goths and re-conquered the eastern provinces, including Palmyra. Gallienus excluded senators from high military commands and replaced them with professionals. Moreover, he began a new, more modest policy of border defense. The Romans now conceded much of the frontier to the enemy and shifted to a defensive mode: fortified cities near the frontier served as bases from which to prevent deeper enemy penetration into Roman territory. They also concentrated mobile armies at strategic points in the rear, moving them where needed.

Gallienus's reforms pointed the way to imperial reorganization, but they remained to be completed by the two great reforming emperors at the end of the third century and the beginning of the fourth: Diocletian (r. 284–305) and Constantine (r. 306–337), subjects of the next chapter. When their work was done, the new Roman Empire of Late Antiquity might have been barely recognizable to a citizen of the Principate.

EARLY CHRISTIANITY

Increasing contact between Rome and its western provinces served to plant Roman cities, Roman law, and the Latin language (or its derivatives) in western Europe. As Rome in turn owed much to other Mediterranean peoples, it may be said that the Roman Empire was a vessel that transported ancient Mediterranean civilization to northern and western Europe. No feature of that civilization was to have a greater historical impact than the religion born in Tiberius's reign: Christianity.

Christianity began in the provincial backwater of Palestine among the Jews, whose language, Aramaic, was understood by few in Rome. It immediately spread to speakers of the two main languages of the empire, Greek and Latin, and the new movement addressed the common spiritual needs of the Roman world. By the reign of Diocletian, Christians had grown from Jesus's twelve original followers to perhaps millions, despite government persecution. In the fourth century A.D., Christianity unexpectedly became the official religion of the entire Roman Empire, replacing polytheism—one of the most momentous changes in Mediterranean history. We turn to that change in the next chapter; here we consider the career of Jesus and the early spread of the Christian Gospel (literally, "Good Tidings"). But first, to set the stage, we look at other religions of the Roman Empire.

Mystery Religions   The Romans were polytheists. They did not try to impose a single, unified religion on the empire. Instead, Romans were usually willing to admit new gods to their pantheon, as long as their worshipers took part in the patriotic emperor cult. Roman conservatism, moreover, engendered respect for other peoples' traditional faiths. Although Roman authorities had tried occasionally to expel these faiths from the city itself, the spread of new religions during the first three centuries A.D. proved irresistible. Besides Christianity and Judaism, the most important religions were Greek mystery cults, the cults of Isis and Mithras, and Manichaeism. These religions displayed a tendency toward syncretism, often borrowing rites, doctrines, and symbols from one another.

Greek mystery cults included the cults of Dionysus, the god of wine, and of Demeter, the goddess of grain, who was worshiped at annual ceremonies at Eleusis, a town outside Athens. The "mystery" consisted of secret rites revealed only to initiates. In the case of Demeter, the rites apparently had something to do with the promise of eternal life.

The cult of Isis derived from the ancient Egyptians' worship of Isis (see page 24), her brother and husband, Osiris, and their son, Horus. Like the cult of Demeter, its central theme was eternal life, through the promise of resurrection achieved by moral behavior in this life. Isis, the "Goddess of Ten Thousand Names," was portrayed as a loving mother, and elements of Isis were later syncretized in the cult of the Virgin Mary. Her followers were known to march in colorful, and at times terrifying, parades through Roman streets, flagellating themselves as a sign of penitence.

Although men joined in the worship of Isis, the cult appealed particularly to women. The goddess's popularity crossed class lines; devotees ranged from slaves to one Julia Felix, whose estate at Pompeii included a garden shrine to Isis and Egyptian statuettes. By contrast, the worship of Mithras was dominated by men, and especially by soldiers. Mithras, a heroic Persian god of light and truth, also promised eternal life.

His worshipers believed that Mithras had captured and killed a sacred bull whose blood and body were the source of life. Accordingly, Mithraism focused on bull sacrifice carried out in a vaulted, cavelike temple called a *Mithraeum*. Initiates were baptized with bull blood and participated in various other rituals, among them a sacramental meal. Their moral code advised imitating the life of their hero.

Manichaeism also originated in Persia, but later, in the third century A.D. Its founder, the Persian priest Mani, was martyred by conservative religious authorities. Manichaeism attempted to be the true synthesis of the religious beliefs of the period, recognizing not only Jesus but also Zoroaster and Buddha as prophets. The main tenet of Manichaeism was philosophical dualism, which emphasized the universal struggle between good (Light) and evil (Darkness). According to believers, the world had been corrupted by Darkness, but eventually the Light would return. In the meantime, good Manichaeans were to attempt to lead pure lives. Manichaeism was a powerful religious force for two centuries, and its believers were spread as far as India. The great theologian Augustine even flirted with it before becoming a Christian.

A new philosophy that developed in the same intellectual world as these Roman religions was Neo-Platonism, which was founded by Plotinus (A.D. 209–270). Using the works of Plato as a starting point, Plotinus developed a philosophy in which the individual could first seek inner unity and then achieve oneness with the supreme unity of what Plotinus called the One or the Good. By this he meant an intangible and impersonal force that is the source of all values. Like the mystery cults, Plotinus's philosophy was difficult to understand, but it promised a kind of salvation. Neo-Platonism was destined to have a great influence on Western thought.

Jesus of Nazareth   Christianity begins with Jesus. For all its historical importance, Jesus's life is poorly documented. The main source of information about it is the New Testament books of Matthew, Mark, Luke, and John. Jesus left no writings of his own. Early Christians, however, wrote a great deal. Between the second and fourth centuries A.D., Christians settled on a holy book consisting of both the Hebrew Bible, called the "Old Testament" by Christians, and a collection of writings about Jesus and his followers, called the "New Testament." The account of the Gospel according to Mark, probably the earliest Gospel, was most likely written about forty years after Jesus's crucifixion; several of the letters written by Paul of Tarsus (see page 184) date from the 40s A.D.; and the earliest non-Christian sources are later in date and are scanty. In 2002 some archaeologists thought that they had found new documentation of Jesus in the form of an ancient burial box supposed to have held the bones of Jesus's brother, James. But the box has been judged a fake by most experts.

No personality has generated as much discussion among Western scholars as has Jesus. Many would distinguish the Jesus of theology, the object of faith, from the Jesus of history, the figure who really lived in first-century Palestine. Recent work argues that the historical Jesus must be understood within the Judaism of his day. He was a product of the popular culture of the Palestinian countryside, a culture that was peasant and oral. Much of what the Gospels have to say about Jesus, some argue, must be rejected as later invention. These are controversial points, but many scholars would agree with one thing: we must be careful to avoid anachronism. By A.D. 200 two new religions had emerged, orthodox Christianity and rabbinic Judaism. The proponents of both religions claimed to be the rightful heirs of the biblical covenant. They engendered new perspectives that have colored the way Christians and Jews envisage the past before 200. The following account of Jesus seeks a middle ground among today's schools of interpretation.

Jesus was born a Jew. A speaker of Aramaic, he may also have known at least some Greek, widely spoken by both Jews and non-Jews in the several Hellenized cities of Palestine. To his followers, Jesus was Christ—"the anointed one" (from the Greek *Christos*), the man anointed with oil and thus marked as the king of Israel. They considered him the Messiah (from the Hebrew for "anointed one"), foretold in the Hebrew Bible, who would redeem the children of Israel and initiate the kingdom of heaven. The dynamism and popularity of his teachings led to a clash with Jewish and Roman authorities in Jerusalem, the capital city of Judea, and to his crucifixion. His mission began, however, in a corner of the Jewish world, in the northern region of Galilee, where he lived in the town of Nazareth.

Jesus was probably born not long before the death in 4 B.C. of Herod, the Roman-installed client-king of Judea. (The date of A.D. 1 for Jesus's birth, a mistaken calculation of Late Antiquity, does not accord with the data of the New Testament.) At around age 30, Jesus was baptized by the mysterious preacher John the Baptist. Soon afterward Herod Antipas, the Romans' client-king of Galilee, ordered the execution of John. John had preached that God's kingdom was about to arrive—a time of universal perfection and an end of misery. In preparation, sinful humankind needed to repent. Just how much influence John had on Jesus is a matter of debate, as is the question of John's relationship to the religious community of the Essenes. Debate may be appropriate, for Judaism in the first century A.D. was in a state of creative disagreement. This era endorsed no one normative Judaism but rather a variety of Judaisms.

The Essenes lived apart from society in pursuit of a new covenant with God. The community at Qumran in the Judean desert, whose history is documented in the Dead Sea Scrolls, ancient texts discovered in 1947, was probably Essene. The tenets of Qumran included frugality, sharing, participating in a sacred communal meal, and avoiding oath-taking. Adherents anticipated the coming of the Messiah and an end of days in which God would punish the wicked. Although Essene doctrine has much in common with early Christianity, early Christians did not withdraw from the world as the Essenes did but instead faced it.

There are both similarities and differences between Jesus's teaching and contemporary doctrines of Palestinian Judaism. The most popular group among Palestinian Jews, the Pharisees, focused on the spiritual needs of ordinary folk (see page 126). The Pharisees believed that law was central to Judaism but argued that it could be interpreted flexibly, in light of the oral tradition that had grown up alongside the written text of the Hebrew Bible. The Pharisees emphasized charity toward the poor and spoke in parables—vivid allegories that made their teaching accessible.

Jesus argued similarly. Like the Pharisees, he strongly criticized the pillar of the Jewish establishment, the Sadducees, the priests and wealthy men who saw the Temple at Jerusalem and its rites as the heart of Judaism. Also like the Pharisees, Jesus rejected the growing movement of the Zealots, advocates of revolt against Roman rule, although there were Zealots among his followers. Yet Jesus was neither a Pharisee nor an Essene. His teaching went further than the Pharisees' in rejecting the need to follow the

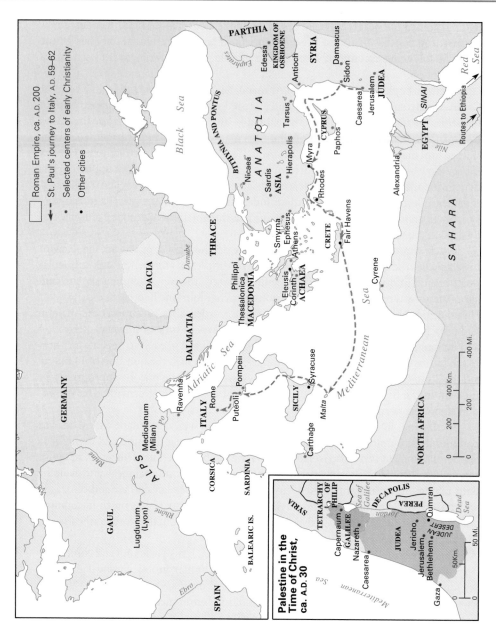

Map legend:
- Roman Empire, ca. A.D. 200
- St. Paul's journey to Italy, A.D. 59–62
- Selected centers of early Christianity
- Other cities

Palestine in the Time of Christ, ca. A.D. 30

The Expansion of Christianity to A.D. 200

After its origin in Palestine, early Christianity found its main centers in the Greek-speaking cities of the Roman East. Missionaries such as Paul also brought the new faith to the Latin-speaking West, as well as to Ethiopia and Mesopotamia.

letter of biblical law. Inward purity became the key principle, as reflected in Jesus's statement to his disciples (that is, his close followers): "Whoever does not accept the kingdom of God like a child will never enter it" (Mark 10:15). Only an adult could become expert in biblical law, but it is probably easier for a child than for an adult to attain spiritual innocence.

Jesus argued that the kingdom of God, which John the Baptist had said was coming soon, was actually already beginning to arrive. Moreover, Jesus said that he himself, acting through the direct order of God, could forgive sins. He emphasized the notion of God as a loving and forgiving father. He often spoke in parables and announced himself through miracles, particularly faith healing. He welcomed marginalized groups, including prostitutes and lepers.

Jesus's teaching is typified in the Sermon on the Mount, addressed to his many followers in Galilee. He praised the poor and the humble and scorned the pursuit of wealth instead of righteousness. He called for generosity and forgiveness, recalling the traditional Jewish golden rule—to treat others as one would like to be treated. He said that prayer, fasting, and acts of charity should be conducted in private, not in public, in order to emphasize purity of motive. He called on his followers to endure persecution in order to spread his teachings: "You are light for all the world," he told them.

Jesus spoke with conviction and persuasiveness—with "authority," as his followers said. In Galilee they greeted him as king. For some this was a purely spiritual designation; others planned an overthrow of Roman rule, although Jesus rejected that course of action. In any case, his teachings won him hostility from some Pharisees, who considered his claim to be able to forgive sins blasphemous, and from Sadducees stung by his criticisms. Neither group accepted Jesus as the Messiah. It should be emphasized, nevertheless, that most of Jesus's followers were Jewish.

Jesus challenged central authority by going to Jerusalem and teaching and healing in the Temple under the eyes of the priests whom he criticized. Nor did he confine his opposition to words: he drove merchants and moneychangers away from the Temple precincts by overturning their tables and perhaps even threatening them with a whip. Jesus attracted large crowds of followers, at least some of whom were armed. Sadducee authorities feared trouble, and so did the overlords of Judea, the Romans. The governor, Pilate (Pontius Pilatus), had already endured vehement Jewish objections to the display in Jerusalem of an imperial medallion and of an inscription that seems to have asserted Augustus's divinity. Pilate had no need of further uproar. Temple police and Roman soldiers were called on to arrest Jesus quietly.

Jesus's subsequent trial and execution have always been controversial. The New Testament emphasizes the role of the Jewish leadership and the Jerusalem mob in Jesus's death. Written after the First Jewish Revolt (A.D. 66–70), however, the Gospels may reflect anti-Jewish sentiment in the empire. Crucifixion, the method used to execute Jesus, was a Roman penalty (the traditional Jewish method was stoning), and Jesus was executed by Romans, not Jews. Jesus probably appeared in informal and hurried proceedings before both the Jewish Council and Pilate. He suffered slow death by crucifixion on Golgotha (Calvary) Hill, just outside the city. It was a spring Friday, on the eve of the Passover festival, around A.D. 30.

Paul of Tarsus

According to the Gospel writers, Jesus died on a Friday and rose from the dead on Sunday, an event commemorated by

The Good Shepherd
This ceiling painting comes from a Christian catacomb in Rome dating before A.D. 284. The pastoral image, common in the early church, recalls Christ's ministry. It symbolizes both his beneficence and his sacrifice, as well as his closeness to ordinary people. (Scala/Art Resource, NY)

Christians at Easter. He is said to have then spent forty days on earth, cheering and commissioning his disciples in Galilee and working miracles, before finally ascending to heaven. Heartened, the disciples returned to Jerusalem and spread Jesus's teachings. They preached in synagogues, private households, and even the Temple, and to Greek-speaking as well as Palestinian Jews. Their movement spread in the thirties and forties A.D. throughout Palestine and into Syria. In Jerusalem Christians were known as Nazarenes—that is, followers of Jesus of Nazareth; it was at Antioch that they were first called "men of Christ" (*christianoi*).

The leaders of the movement were known as apostles, from the Greek *apostolos*, "one who is sent" and who enjoys the authority of the sender. The apostles believed that Jesus had sent them and given them authority. The apostles included Jesus's twelve original followers, or disciples. The most prominent disciple was Peter, a Galilean fisherman whom Jesus endowed with particular authority. After the crucifixion, Peter became a miracle-worker and leading apostle. According to a reliable tradition, he went to Rome, whose church he headed and where he died as a martyr in A.D. 64.

It was not clear at first that Christians would form a new religion separate from Judaism. Although the Sadducees and Jewish civil officials were hostile, Christians found much support among the Pharisees. Some Christians, however, contemplated a radical break; among them no one was more important than Paul of Tarsus (d. A.D. 67?).

Only Jesus himself played a greater role than Paul in the foundation of Christianity. A remarkable figure, Paul embodied three different and interlocking worlds. Born with the name of Saul, he was a Jew of the Diaspora from the southern Anatolian city of Tarsus. A learned Pharisee, Paul was a native speaker of Aramaic and knew Hebrew and Greek. His father was one of the few Jews to attain Roman citizenship, a privilege that

Paul inherited. Paul's heritage speaks volumes about the variety of the Roman peace, and his religious odyssey speaks volumes more.

At first Paul joined in the persecution of the Christians, whom he considered blasphemous. Around A.D. 36, however, he claimed to see a blinding light on the road to Damascus, a vision of Jesus that convinced him to change from persecutor to believer. It was a complete turnaround, a *conversio* ("conversion"), to use the Latin word that would grow so important in years to come. Saul changed his name to Paul and became a Christian.

He also changed what being a Christian meant. The key to Paul's faith was not so much Jesus's life, although that was a model for Christian ethics, as it was Jesus's death and resurrection. Jesus's fate, Paul wrote, offered all humanity the hope of resurrection, redemption, and salvation. Paul retained his belief in Jewish morality and ethics but not in the rules of Jewish law. Following the law, no matter how carefully, would not lead to salvation; only faith in Jesus as Messiah would.

Such doctrines bespoke a break with Judaism, as did Paul's attitudes toward converts. Hellenistic Judaism had long reached out to Gentiles. Some became Jews. Others, scattered throughout the cities of the Roman Empire, were known as "God-fearers"—that is, they accepted the moral teachings of Judaism but refrained from following strict dietary laws, circumcision, and other Jewish rituals. Seneca the Younger, writing in the sixties, complains about the spread of Judaism: "The customs of this accursed race have gained such influence that they are now received throughout the world."[3]

The Jerusalem church baptized converts and considered them Jews, but Paul considered them not Jews but converts in Christ. For Pauline Christians, circumcision, dietary laws, and strict observance of the Sabbath were irrelevant. From the late forties to the early sixties A.D., Paul tirelessly undertook missionary journeys through the cities of the Roman East and to Rome itself. He aimed to convert Gentiles, and so he did, but many of his followers were Hellenized Jews and "God-fearers." Paul started Christianity on the road to complete separation from Judaism. Events over the next century widened the division. First, while Pauline churches prospered, departing ever more from Jewish customs, the Jerusalem church was decimated. Jewish authorities persecuted its leaders, and after Rome's suppression of the First Jewish Revolt and destruction of the Jerusalem Temple in A.D. 70, the rank and file of Palestinian Jews rallied to the Pharisees. Second, Jews and Christians competing for converts emphasized their respective differences. Third, although many Jews made their peace with Rome in A.D. 70, enough Jewish-Roman hostility remained to lead to uprisings in the Diaspora in 115 and to the Second Jewish Revolt in 132 to 135. Both were suppressed mercilessly by Rome, and Judaism became ever more stigmatized among Gentiles.

Bereft of the Temple at Jerusalem, Judaism nonetheless continued to prosper as a religion. Indeed, Jewish missionary activities continued, although they did not keep pace with the number of converts gained by Christianity. More striking is the emergence of the rabbis (the religious leaders of the Pharisees) as the mentors of Judaism. Popular among Jews, the rabbis also attracted the Romans because most rabbis opposed revolt. After both A.D. 70 and 135, the Romans made the rabbis responsible for Jewish self-government in Palestine. The rabbis left their mark on history, however, not in administration but in an intellectual movement. Continuing in the tradition of the Pharisees, the rabbis amplified the oral law—that is, they wrote interpretations of the Hebrew Bible that clarified the practice of Judaism. They developed the notion of the "dual Torah," elevating the oral law to equal authority with the written law of the Hebrew Bible. The notion legitimized the rabbis' enterprise, which made it possible for Judaism to evolve flexibly. The basic text of rabbinic Judaism is the Mishnah (ca. A.D. 200), a study of Jewish law. In rabbinic Judaism lies the basis of the medieval and modern forms of the Jewish religion.[4]

Expansion, Divergence, and Persecution

Although Jesus's mission was mainly in the countryside, early Christianity quickly became primarily an urban movement. Through missionary activity and word of mouth, the religion slowly spread. It was concentrated in the Greek-speaking East, but by the second century A.D. Christian communities dotted North Africa and Gaul and, beyond Roman boundaries, appeared in Parthian Iraq and in Ethiopia.

By around A.D. 200, an orthodox (Greek for "right-thinking") Christianity had emerged. Rooted in Judaism, it was nonetheless a distinct and separate religion that found most of its supporters among Gentiles. A simple "rule of faith," emphasizing the belief in one God and the mission of his son, Jesus, as savior, united Christians from one end of the empire to the other. Christianity attracted both rich and poor, male and female; its primary appeal was to ordinary, moderately prosperous city folk. Believers could take comfort from the prospect of salvation in the next world and in a caring community in the here and now. Christians emphasized charity and help for the needy, qualities all too often absent in Greco-Roman society. A Christian writer justly described a pagan's amazed comment on Christian behavior: "Look how they love each other." Most early Christians expected Christ's return—and the inauguration of the heavenly kingdom—to be imminent.

Early churches were simple and relatively informal congregations that gathered for regular meetings. The liturgy, or service, consisted of readings from the Scriptures (the Old and New Testaments), teaching, praying, and singing hymns. Baptism was used to initiate converts. The Lord's Supper, a communal meal in memory of Jesus, was a major ritual. The most important parts of the meal were the breaking and distribution of bread at the beginning and the passing of a cup of wine at the end; these recalled the body and blood of Christ. As organizational structures emerged (see pages 200, 201), churches in different cities were in frequent contact with one another, discussing common concerns and coordinating doctrine and practice.

Just as Jewish women were not rabbis, so early Christian women did not hold the priesthood. Jewish women, however, did hold office in the synagogue, and Christian women likewise served as deaconesses. Both endowed buildings and institutions. For example, consider the Italian Jewish woman Caelia Paterna, an officeholder honored by her congregation as "mother of the synagogue of the people of Brescia." Or the two Christian deaconesses, both slaves, whom Pliny the Younger tortured during his governorship of the Anatolian province of Bithynia (ca. A.D. 110) in an attempt to extract information about the worrisome new cult. Deaconesses played an active part in church charities and counseling and now and then preached sermons.

As Christianity spread, its troubles with the authorities deepened. For one thing, Christians met in small groups, a kind of assembly that conservative Romans had long suspected as a potential source of sedition. More troubling, however, was Christians' refusal to make sacrifices to the emperor. The Romans expected all subjects to make

Caesar and Christ

The Romans valued law and order. They considered Christianity a threat to both because Christians refused to worship the emperor as a god. Yet the Romans wanted to avoid a full-scale persecution of Christianity because that, too, would disrupt public order. So they tried a policy of limited tolerance, as shown in this exchange of letters in about A.D. 110 between the governor of Roman Bithynia (northwest Anatolia), Pliny the Younger, and the emperor Trajan. Ultimately the policy failed.

To the Emperior Trajan

It is a rule, Sir, which I inviolably observe, to refer myself to you in all my doubts; for who is more capable of guiding my uncertainty or informing my ignorance? Having never been present at any trials of the Christians, I am unacquainted with the method and limits to be observed either in examining or punishing them. Whether any difference is to be made on account of age, or no distinction allowed between the youngest and the adult; whether repentance admits to a pardon, or if a man has been once a Christian it avails him nothing to recant; whether the mere profession of Christianity, albeit without crimes, or only the crimes associated therewith are punishable in all these points I am greatly doubtful.

In the meanwhile, the method I have observed towards those who have been denounced to me as Christians is this: I interrogated them whether they were Christians; if they confessed it I repeated the question twice again, adding the threat of capital punishment; if they still persevered, I ordered them to be executed. For whatever the nature of their creed might be, I could at least feel no doubt that contumacy and inflexible obstinacy deserved chastisement. There were others also possessed with the same infatuation, but being citizens of Rome, I directed them to be carried thither.

. . . Those who denied they were, or had ever been, Christians, who repeated after me an invocation to the Gods, and offered adoration, with wine and frankincense, to your image, which I had ordered to be brought for that purpose, together with those of the Gods, and who finally cursed Christ, none of which acts, it is said, those who are really Christians can be forced into performing, these I thought it proper to discharge.

Trajan to Pliny

The method you have pursued, my dear Pliny, in sifting the cases of those denounced to you as Christians is extremely proper. It is not possible to lay down any general rule which can be applied as the fixed standard in all cases of this nature. No search should be made for these people; when they are denounced and found guilty they must be punished; with the restriction, however, that when the party denies himself to be a Christian, and shall give proof that he is not (that is, by adoring our gods) he shall be pardoned on the ground of repentance, even though he may have formerly incurred suspicion. Accusations without the accuser's name signed must not be admitted in evidence against anyone, as it is introducing a very dangerous precedent, and by no means agreeable to the spirit of the age.

Source: Pliny the Younger, *Letters,* trans. William Melmoth, rev. W. M. L. Hutchinson, Loeb Classical Library (Cambridge, Mass.: Harvard University Press, 1915), pp. 401–403, 407, slightly modified.

IMPORTANT EVENTS

31 B.C. Octavian defeats Antony and Cleopatra at Actium

27 B.C. Augustus establishes Principate

27 B.C.–A.D. 68 Julio-Claudian dynasty

19 B.C. Death of Virgil

ca. A.D. 27–30 Ministry of Jesus

ca. 67 Death of Paul of Tarsus

69–96 Flavian dynasty

70 Temple in Jerusalem destroyed

79 Eruption of Vesuvius

96–180 The "Five Good Emperors"

ca. 117 Death of Tacitus

193–235 Severan dynasty

ca. 200 Mishnah and New Testament each completed

212 Almost all free inhabitants of empire awarded Roman citizenship

235–284 Period of military anarchy

such sacrifices as a sign of patriotism. The only exception was the Jews, who were permitted to forgo the imperial cult because their ancestral religion prohibited them from worshiping idols. The Christians, however, were a new group, and the Romans distrusted novelty.

As a result, the emperors considered Christianity at best a nuisance and at worst a threat. Christians were tested from time to time by being asked to sacrifice to the emperor; those who failed to do so might be executed, sometimes in the arena. More often, however, the Romans tacitly tolerated Christians as long as they kept their religion private. Christians could not proselytize in public places, put up inscriptions or monuments, or build churches. Christianity thus spread under severe restrictions, but spread it did, particularly in the cities of the East. The willingness of martyrs to die for the faith made a strong impression on potential converts. Although the number of Christians in the empire is not known, it is clear that by the late third century they were a significant and growing minority.

NOTES

1. Mary R. Lefkowitz and Maureen B. Fant, trans., *Women's Life in Greece & Rome: A Source Book in Translation,* 2d ed. (Baltimore: Johns Hopkins University Press, 1992), p. 9.

2. This discussion of marriage and laws owes much to Susanne Dixon, *The Roman Family* (Baltimore: Johns Hopkins University Press, 1992), pp. 36–60.

3. Seneca, *De Superstitione,* trans. Menachem Stern, in *Greek and Latin Authors on Jews and Judaism,* vol. 1 (Jerusalem: Israel Academy of Sciences and Humanities, 1976), p. 431.

4. On these points, see Lawrence H. Schiffman, *From Text to Tradition: A History of Second Temple and Rabbinic Judaism* (Hoboken, N.J.: Ktav Publishing House, 1991), pp. 1–16.

SUGGESTED READING

Adkins, Leslie, and Roy A. Adkins. *Handbook to Life in Ancient Rome.* 1998. An excellent reference book, arranged thematically, by two archaeologists.

Earl, D. C. *The Age of Augustus.* 1968. A beautifully illustrated introduction to government, society, and religion.

Fantham, Elaine, Helene Peet Foley, Natalie Boymel Kampen, Sarah B. Pomeroy, and H. A. Shapiro. *Women in the Classical World: Image and Text.* 1994. Chapters 10–13 provide an excellent introduction to the social and cultural history of women in the Roman Empire.

Köhne, Eckart, and Cornelia Ewigleben. *Gladiators and Caesars: The Power of Spectacle in Ancient Rome.* 2000. Originally written as an exhibition catalog, this well-illustrated collection of essays serves as a very good introduction to the subject.

Pagels, Elaine. *Beyond Belief: The Secret Gospel of Thomas.* 2003. Elegant and readable study of competing arguments and faiths within early Christianity.

Ramage, Nancy H., and Andrew Ramage. *Roman Art.* 3d ed. 2000. An excellent introductory text; especially good on the Roman Empire.

Wells, Colin. *The Roman Empire.* 2d ed. 1995. A sweeping, lively, and thoughtful overview of the subject from 44 B.C. to A.D. 235.

7

The World of
Late Antiquity,
284–ca. 600

"Solomon, I have outdone you!" Tradition holds that the emperor Justinian (r. 527–565) uttered these words when he saw for the first time the magnificent Church of Hagia Sophia ("Holy Wisdom"), which he erected in Constantinople. Justinian's reign, words, and building provide an excellent entry into the late antique period. Justinian looked back to the biblical king Solomon in speaking of his church. The church itself is composed of two intersecting rectangular basilicas surmounted by a dome. Justinian's religious, military, and administrative policies were consistent with those of his predecessors for two centuries, and his legal reforms grew out of centuries of tradition. In many ways Justinian, perhaps Late Antiquity's greatest ruler, was a traditional Roman. But his church was unlike any building the Roman world had ever seen. Justinian's massive law code was more comprehensive and systematic than any of its predecessors. His military aspirations were audacious, as were his administrative plans. Justinian's reign points out the dynamic tensions of the late antique period: continuity and change, tradition and innovation, past and future.

Two centuries before Justinian the reigns of Diocletian (284–305) and Constantine (306–337) inaugurated a period that scholars now label "Late Antiquity." For many years educated people, often taking their lead from the elegant and influential *Decline and Fall of the Roman Empire* by the British historian Edward Gibbon (1737–1794), believed that, beset by insurmountable problems, the Roman Empire "fell" in the fifth century. With that fall, such a view insisted, the glories of classical civilization gave way to the gloom of the "Dark Ages." Today, on the contrary, specialists in the period from roughly 300 to 600 see vigor and achievement. They emphasize continuity and coherence over calamity and collapse. No one denies that the Roman world of 600 was different from the Roman world of 300. But recent scholarship stresses how the Romans themselves created a stable framework for change. No catastrophic time, place, or event marked the "fall of Rome."

From the time of its founding, the Roman Empire had suffered from various structural problems. In particular, the Roman world was vast geographically and diverse in its human and material resources. Changes were inevitable in such a world. This chapter identifies the most important changes that took place while the Roman Empire was evolving into its medieval European, Byzantine, and Muslim successors.

REBUILDING THE ROMAN EMPIRE, 284–395

The third-century Roman Empire had lurched from crisis to crisis. Decisive action was needed if Rome was to survive. The chronic civil wars had to be brought to an end. The army needed to be reformed and expanded to meet new threats on the frontiers. And the economy had to be stabilized to bring in the revenue the government needed for administrative and military reforms. Rome was fortunate in raising up two rulers, Diocletian and Constantine, with more than fifty years of rule between them, who understood the empire's problems and legislated energetically to address them. Although these rulers thought of themselves as traditional Romans, they actually initiated a far-reaching transformation of the Roman Empire.

The Reforms of Dio-cletian (r. 284–305) The son of a poor Dalmatian farmer, Diocletian rose through the ranks of the army until he attained a key position in the emperor's elite guards. When the emperor was murdered, the soldiers elevated Diocletian to the imperial office.

In about 293 Diocletian devised a regime that historians call the "tetrarchy," or rule by four. He intended to address both the political instability of the Roman regime and

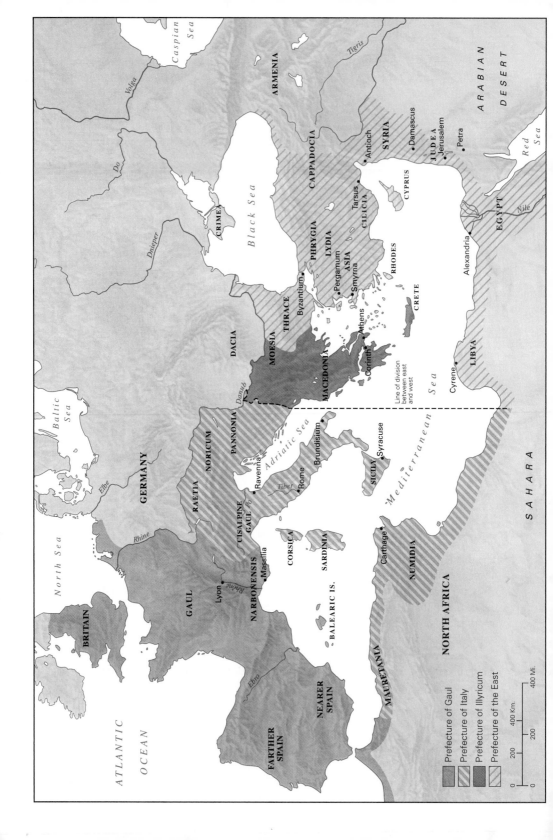

the awesome size and complexity of the empire. First Diocletian decided to divide the empire into eastern and western halves and then selected an imperial colleague for himself. Ruling from Nicomedia and retaining the position of senior emperor, he took charge of the wealthy and militarily threatened eastern half of the empire. Diocletian and his colleague each selected a subordinate official who would eventually succeed to the imperial office. The advantage of the tetrarchy was that it yielded four men of imperial rank who could lead armies and make decisions in political and administrative matters. Diocletian hoped that the tetrarchy would provide orderly succession to the imperial office and promote experienced, respected men.

Historians call the regime instituted by Augustus in 31 B.C. the "Principate" because the emperor pretended to be the "first citizen" and heir of the Republican magistrates, even though his real power depended on control of the army. By contrast, Diocletian abandoned all pretense of being a magistrate. Scholars call his regime the "Dominate," from the Latin *Dominus,* meaning "lord and master." Diocletian adopted Eastern, especially Persian, habits, such as wearing a gilded cloak and a jeweled diadem, sprinkling gold dust in his hair, sitting on an elevated throne, rarely appearing in public, and requiring those who approached to prostrate themselves before him. Diocletian succeeded in enhancing the prestige of the imperial office but did so at the price of making the emperor more remote from his subjects.

Given its size and problems, the Roman Empire was dramatically *under*governed. The empire had some fifty provinces, which varied greatly in size, population, wealth, strategic importance, and degree of Romanization, but the imperial administration was made up largely of aristocratic amateurs and numbered only a few hundred men when Diocletian ascended the throne. Rome had traditionally asked for relatively little from its empire—primarily taxes, military recruits, and loyalty. Local authorities generally did the tax collecting and military recruiting, with little interference from imperial agents.

Diocletian increased the number of officials and doubled the number of provinces by dividing old, large provinces into smaller ones. He then organized groups of provinces into thirteen dioceses and joined the dioceses into four prefectures. Diocletian subordinated each prefecture to a tetrarch and equipped each prefecture with a force of military, legal, financial, and secretarial officials headed by a praetorian prefect. By 350 the number of officers from the provincial to the prefectorial level had risen from a few hundred to thirty-five or forty thousand. Diocletian wished to fill the bureaucracy with trained administrators instead of with wealthy senators and equestrians, who viewed government service as a means of enriching themselves and advancing the interests of their families.

Diocletian also attended to Rome's military problems. His major initiative was an attempt to double the size of the army from about 300,000 to 600,000 men, although the final total ended up being only around 450,000. Diocletian also built new forts

Diocletian's Division of the Roman Empire, 286

Diocletian divided the empire into eastern and western halves; each half was divided into two prefectures. Thus four regions, rulers, and bureaucratic administrations replaced the ineffective rule of one man.

Tetrarchy *Ideal and reality are both evident in this sculpture of the tetrarchy. The rulers, depicted equal in size, embrace one another but also bare their weapons—to one another and to the world.* (Scala/Art Resource, NY)

along the frontiers and improved the roads that supplied frontier defenders. He began the systematic incorporation of barbarians into the army, a step that led to a blurring of the distinction between Romans and barbarians. Military service had long been attractive to people in the empire because it provided Roman citizenship as well as a secure income. After 212 almost every free man in the empire enjoyed automatic citizenship. As a result, mainly noncitizen barbarians living along the frontiers, whose only hope of citizenship was military service, found the army attractive. For a while the army tended to Romanize the barbarians, but as the proportion of barbarian soldiers and officers grew, the culture and ethos of the army began to change.

Diocletian's reforms were expensive and required a predictable income. Thus Diocletian attempted to regularize the tax system in the empire. The government conducted a census to identify all taxpayers and assessed the productive value of land. To address the mounting inflation of the third century, Diocletian issued in 302 the Edict of Maximum Prices, which froze the costs of goods. Since senators successfully defended their long-standing exemptions from taxes and the taxation of business ventures remained low, virtually the whole cost of the Roman system continued to fall on agriculture, in particular on small farmers. Diocletian's reform of the tax structure brought in more revenue, but it also caused hardships. A rising tax burden threatened those who were most vulnerable. And with more officials handling vastly greater sums of money, corruption ran rampant. Most people never saw the emperor, but they saw too much of his tax-gouging local minions.

The rationale behind Diocletian's reforms is easy to understand; their results were less easy to anticipate. The actions were costly in three unintended respects: moral, social, and economic. The emperors had always been military dictators, but Diocletian removed all pretense that they served at the behest of the Roman people. His frankness may have enhanced the aura of the imperial office, but it also loosened the ties between the ruler and his subjects. By reducing the official duties of the senatorial order, Diocletian alienated an influential group of about two thousand leading citizens. The enlarged imperial administration necessarily impinged on the autonomy of cities and their local leaders, for three centuries the key components of the imperial system. Finally, the expanded administration and army cost dearly in real cash. That cash had to be extracted from an empire that was in serious economic distress.

The Reforms of Constantine (r. 306–337)

Diocletian's careful plans for the imperial succession collapsed almost immediately after his voluntary retirement in 305. When Diocletian's Western colleague (Constantius I) died in 306, his troops reverted to the hereditary principle and declared his son, Constantine, emperor. From 306 to 313 as many as six men claimed to be emperor somewhere in the empire. From 313 to 324 Constantine shared rule with one man, and from 324 to 337 he ruled alone over a reunited empire, although he made his sons subordinates in various parts of the empire. This compromise between the hereditary and tetrarchal systems persisted for the next two centuries.

Constantine had entered the imperial court as a young man in 293, when his father was made co-emperor, and he later served with his father in Britain and Gaul. He knew the system well and maintained the administrative structure that Diocletian had introduced. Constantine continued the eastward shift of power by creating a second imperial capital in the East. In 324 he selected an old Greek city, Byzantium, and renamed it after himself, "Constantine's polis" or Constantinople (modern Istanbul). Byzantium's location, more than its size, wealth, or fame, recommended it. The city straddled military roads between the eastern and western halves of the empire, overlooked crucial trade lanes to and from the Black Sea region, and was well sited to respond to threats along both the Balkan and the eastern frontiers.

In financial affairs, too, Constantine's work echoed his predecessor's. He issued a new gold *solidus,* the principal money of account in the Roman Empire. This coin promoted monetary stability in the Mediterranean world for nearly a thousand years. Unfortunately, both a stable currency and Diocletian's price controls braked but could not stop the headlong rush of inflation.

In military affairs, Constantine believed that Rome's frontiers stretched too far to be held securely by garrisons, so he expanded the use of mobile field armies. These armies, recruited largely (as under Diocletian) from barbarians living along or beyond the frontiers, were stationed well inside the borderlands so that they could be mobilized and moved quickly to any threatened point. They were given their own command structures, under officers whom the Romans called "Masters of the Soldiers." The praetorian prefects were deprived of their military responsibilities and became exclusively civilian officials. The separation of civilian and military command made sense administratively and politically because it meant that no individual could combine the command of an army with the authority of a government post.

Whereas Diocletian will always be remembered for launching the last persecution of Christianity (303–305), Constantine legalized the new faith. Each man's motivation has evoked scholarly controversy. Diocletian was a Roman of conventional piety, who seems to have been convinced that the presence of Christian soldiers in his army offended the ancestral gods and denied victory to the Roman troops. Constantine's mother, Helena, was a devout Christian, and there were Christians in his father's court circle. In 312, while marching toward Rome to fight one of his rivals, Constantine believed that he saw in the sky a cross accompanied by the words "In this sign you shall conquer." Persuaded, Constantine put a chi-rho (from the first two letters of *Christos*, "Christ" in Greek) monogram on his soldiers' uniforms. He defeated his foe at the Milvian Bridge near Rome, and, certain that Christ had assured his victory, he and his Eastern colleague issued the Edict of Milan in 313, granting Christianity full legal status in the empire.

Diocletian's persecution had been harsh and systematic. He ordered churches to be closed and the Scriptures seized, arrested members of the clergy, and required all citizens to make a public act of sacrifice in a temple. Constantine did far more than merely stop the persecution or legalize Christianity. He granted the church tax immunities, exempted the clergy from military and civic obligations, and provided money to replace books and buildings that had been destroyed in the persecution. He and his mother sponsored the construction of impressive churches, such as Saint Peter's in Rome and the Church of the Holy Sepulcher over the traditional site of Christ's tomb in Jerusalem.

Scholars have long debated the strategic and political wisdom of Constantine's arrangements. Moving experienced troops away from the frontiers may have invited rather than deterred attacks. Recruiting barbarians into the field armies and leaving frontier defenses to barbarian auxiliaries may have created divided loyalties and conflicts of interest. Most Roman provincials had not lived near soldiers. Now the soldiers and the veterans of the field armies became daily companions. One certain result of the reforms of Diocletian and Constantine was the militarization of Roman society—the transformation of the Roman Empire into a vast armed camp. The financial resources of that empire were now largely devoted to maintaining an expensive military establishment that was socially diverse and potentially politically volatile. Christians were still a minority of the population in Constantine's lifetime, so his legalization and patronage of the new faith may have been visionary but certainly offended the elites of his day.

Diocletian and Constantine responded with imagination to the third-century crisis. They created a new kind of rulership and a new type of imperial regime. Constantine erected a statue of himself in Rome that was more than 30 feet high; its head alone was about 8 feet tall. This statue is an indicator of the late antique imperial ideology. Constantine's size in stone serves to emphasize a distance that the viewer cannot articulate but cannot help feeling. The huge statue does not so much depict Constantine as proclaim emperorship. The majesty of Constantine and his long, productive reign, in conjunction with Diocletian's success and longevity, stands in stark contrast to the troubles of the third century. But we may ask, as contemporaries did, whether order was purchased at too high a price in terms of personal freedom.

The Fourth-Century Empire: A Fragile Stability   Diocletian and Constantine considered themselves to be Roman traditionalists, but their wide-ranging reforms had actually introduced deep changes in the Roman system. When

Constantine died in 337, the Roman Empire was more peaceful and stable than it had been throughout the crisis-ridden third century. But Rome's rulers were now more despotic; Rome's government was bigger, more intrusive, and more expensive; and Rome's military was larger and increasingly barbarian in composition. The open question in 337 was whether Rome would revert to the chaos of the third century or continue along the path marked out by the reforms of Diocletian and Constantine.

Succession to the imperial office remained a troubling issue despite the introduction of the tetrarchy. Constantine had employed a combination of the tetrarchal and dynastic systems. He had three subordinates, all of them his sons. They did not base their activities in the four prefectures, and they succeeded him jointly when he died. Constantine's sons had no heirs of their own, and when the last of them died in 361, the army turned to Julian (331–363), Constantine's nephew. Julian was a great leader and a man who looked out for his troops. Nevertheless, people were trying to find a legitimate heir to Constantine, not merely a general who would reward the army.

Julian ruled for only two years before he was killed fighting in Mesopotamia. Because Julian had no heirs, the army controlled the succession. The choice fell on Valentinian (r. 364–375) and his brother, Valens (r. 364–378). Valentinian ruled in the west, his brother in the east. Valentinian established a dynasty that ruled the Roman world for ninety-one years (364–455). In 378, when Valens was killed in battle, Valentinian's sons sent their brother-in-law, Theodosius I (r. 379–395), who had risen through the military ranks in Spain, to the east to restore order.

Until his own death in 395 Theodosius was the most powerful man in the Roman world and, after his last brother-in-law died in 392, sole ruler. He enjoyed the confidence of the people and the army—the former because he was exceptionally competent and honest and the latter because he was an old military man and a superb general. He divided the empire between his two sons without dynastic or military challenge. His branch of the family lived on until the deaths of Theodosius II in the East in 450 and Valentinian III in the West in 455. Later rulers of the dynasty sometimes ruled alone, sometimes with chosen colleagues or subordinates. Dynastic and tetrarchal systems were thus blended effectively.

Following the reforms of Diocletian and Constantine, the army was supposed to protect the empire, not play a role in Roman politics. Events proved otherwise. In the 340s the Romans faced a renewed threat in the east from Persia, where an ambitious king sought to revive the glories of his ancestors. The Romans did not take this Persian threat lightly, for they knew that in the Persians they faced an old and formidable foe. In the west, Rome faced one serious challenge from the Visigoths (discussed later in this chapter). These military provocations inevitably enhanced the role of the army in public life and elevated military concerns over civilian ones. The presence of new threats contributed to the army's prominence in selecting emperors.

The fourth century did not witness the kind of intensive and sustained administrative reforms that characterized the reigns of Diocletian and Constantine. But emperors did introduce many modest measures, some of which had outcomes very different from those intended by their implementers. One example may stand for many.

During the reign of Valentinian I, a soldier raised to the imperial office by the army, the emperor wanted to make military careers more attractive and soldiers' lives more comfortable. To achieve these ends, Valentinian proposed providing soldiers with plots of land and seed grain. He aimed to supplement soldiers' pay, to tie them more securely to a particular region, and to make them more loyal to him. This creative idea complemented earlier military reforms.

Nonetheless, Valentinian's program angered the senators, who were still rich and influential. They agitated against the reform because, they said, the emperor was spending too much time worrying about the army, and he was depriving them of lands they desired. The senators also complained that the new program was expensive, and they were absolutely right. To pay for land and seed, Valentinian had to raise taxes.

Higher taxes were especially unpopular in the cities, where the burden of collecting them fell on the *decurions,* the main local officials who composed the town councils. From the time of Valentinian in the late fourth century, evidence points to a steady decline in loyalty to Rome among these provincial urban elites. Part of Rome's success under the Principate had been directly tied to the regime's ability to win over local elites all over the empire. Now a military reform whose rationale was clear and defensible actually provoked suspicion and disloyalty among senators and decurions.

When Theodosius died in 395, the Roman world still seemed reasonably secure. The families of Constantine and Valentinian had produced effective rulers. Scattered threats clouded the frontiers, but for the moment conditions appeared stable. Programs of institutional and economic reform continued apace, generally along the lines marked out by Diocletian and Constantine.

In the late fourth century, the empire may have numbered 50 million to 60 million inhabitants. Of these, not more than 5 million to 10 million lived in towns. Because Roman government was based on towns, the actual capacity of the Roman administration to keep track of, tax, coerce, and Romanize the population as a whole was limited. Nevertheless, as the Roman Empire became an increasingly militarized state, its towns were being dominated by central authorities as never before, and its rural population was being pressed hard by tax policies necessitated by larger civil and military structures. The reforms of Diocletian and Constantine continued to provide the framework within which these changes took place.

THE CATHOLIC CHURCH AND THE ROMAN EMPIRE, 313–604

While Rome's rulers were trying to stabilize the state during the fourth century, the empire was experiencing a dynamic process of religious change. The formerly small and persecuted communities of Christians were achieving majority status in the Roman world. The Christianization of the empire's population, first in towns and then in the countryside, and the emergence of the Catholic Church as a hierarchical, institutional structure were two of the greatest transformations of the ancient world. Many Christians, now able to practice their faith in public, discovered that they had sharp disagreements with one another on fundamental points of doctrine. Attempts to resolve those controversies entangled the church with the Roman authorities and strengthened the bishops of Rome. Moreover, numerous Christians—monks and nuns—sought a life of perfection away from the bustle of the world.

Emperors, Bishops, and Heretics   Constantine discovered that his support of the church drew him into heated disputes over doctrine and heresy. *Heresy* comes from a Greek word meaning "to choose." Heretics are persons who choose teachings or practices that religious or state authorities deem wrong. The two greatest and most difficult heresies of Late Antiquity involved the central doctrines of Christianity: the deity of Jesus Christ himself and the relationship between his divine and human natures.

Christian belief holds that there is one God who exists as three distinct but equal persons: Father, Son, and Holy Spirit. But around 320 a priest of Alexandria, Arius (ca. 250–336), began teaching that Jesus was the "first born of all creation." Christians had long been stung by the charge that their monotheism was a sham, that they really worshiped three gods. Arianism, as the faith of Arius and his followers is called, preserved monotheism by making Jesus slightly subordinate to the Father. Arianism won many adherents.

Constantine was scandalized by disagreements over Christian teachings and distressed by riotous quarrels among competing Christian factions. He dealt with religious controversies by summoning individual theologians to guide him and by assembling church councils to debate controversies and reach solutions. In 325 at Nicaea, near Constantinople, the emperor convened a council of more than three hundred bishops, the largest council by far that had met up to that date. This was the first of many "ecumenical"—or all-world—councils in church history. The Council of Nicaea condemned Arius and his teachings. The bishops issued a creed, or statement of beliefs, which maintained that Christ was "one in being with the Father," co-equal and co-eternal.

Religious unity remained elusive, however. The Council of Nicaea's attempt to eliminate Arianism was unsuccessful in the short term. Constantius II (r. 337–361), Constantine's son and successor in the eastern half of the empire, was an avowed Arian, as were some later emperors. For more than forty years, Rome's rulers occasionally embraced a faith that had been declared heretical. It was during this time that the Visigothic priest Ulfilas entered the empire, was converted to Arian Christianity, and returned to spread this faith among his people. Arian Christianity spread widely among the barbarian peoples living along the empire's frontiers. By the time those people began to enter the empire in significant numbers (see pages 206–207), catholic Christianity had triumphed over Arianism, leaving the barbarians as heretics.

One emperor—Constantine's nephew Julian, called "the Apostate" by his Christian opponents—made a last-ditch attempt to restore paganism during his short reign (361–363). He did not resort to persecution but forbade Christians to hold most government or military positions or to teach in any school. Although Christianity had been legalized only in 313, by the 360s it was too well entrenched to be barred from the public sphere, and Julian's pagan revival died with him.

In the fifth century Monophysitism—literally "one-nature-ism"—emerged as a result of bitter quarrels between Christian thinkers in Alexandria and Antioch. Theologians were struggling to find a way to talk about the divine and human natures in Christ. Some emphasized one nature, some the other. Logically either proponent could have been called a Monophysite, but true Monophysites stressed the divine over the human nature of Christ. In 451 the Eastern emperor Marcian called a new council at Chalcedon to deal with the issue of Monophysitism. Like his predecessors, the emperor sought unity, and he was willing to let the theologians define the doctrines. At Chalcedon the theologians condemned the Monophysites and pronounced that Jesus Christ was true God and true man—that he had two authentic natures.

The Institutional Development of the Catholic Church, ca. 300–600

The earliest Christian communities were urban and had three kinds of officials, whose customary titles in English are *bishop, priest,* and *deacon.* Deacons were clearly subordinate to the other two. They were responsible for charitable works and for arranging meetings. Bishops and priests presided at celebrations—most prominently the Eucharist (or Holy Communion, as it came to be called)—preached, and taught. Distinctions between bishops and priests developed over time. Depending on their relative size, towns would have many independent Christian groups, each headed by a priest. By about 200, as a sign of unity and authority, the eldest priest came to be called "overseer," the literal meaning of *bishop.* As more people converted, as the church acquired property, and as doctrinal quarrels began to cause divisions among the faithful, bishops began to be influential local officials. By the late fourth century, the bishops in the major cities of the empire were called *metropolitan bishops,* or sometimes *archbishops,* and they had responsibility for territories often called *dioceses.* In essence, the church was adapting to its own purposes the administrative geography of the Roman Empire.

From its earliest days the Christian community had espoused the doctrine of *apostolic succession.* In other words, just as Jesus had charged his apostles with continuing his earthly ministry, that ministry was passed on to succeeding generations of Christian bishops and priests through the ceremony of ordination. When one or more bishops laid their hands on the head of a new priest or bishop, they were continuing an unbroken line of clerics that reached back through the apostles to Jesus himself. The bishops of Rome coupled this general notion of apostolic succession with a particular emphasis on the original primacy of Peter, in tradition the leader of the apostles and the first bishop of Rome. The theory of "Petrine Primacy" was based on Matthew's Gospel (16:16–18), where Jesus founded his church on Peter, "the Rock," and conferred upon him the keys to the kingdom of heaven. The theory held that just as Peter had been the leader of the apostles, so the successors to Peter, the bishops of Rome, continued to be the leaders of the church as a whole. By the late fourth century the bishop of Rome was usually addressed as *papa,* or "pope" in English. The steadily growing importance of bishops everywhere was a marked feature of the age, and the growing authority of the bishop of Rome within the church is the most striking organizational process of the fourth and fifth centuries.

Christians in the Roman world frequently disagreed on matters of jurisdiction and theology. Attempts to resolve these controversies strengthened the ecumenical council as a regular organ of church government, increased the power of the papacy, and drew emperors more deeply into the public life of the church. In a series of laws issued between 378 and 381, Theodosius virtually outlawed the pagan cults, thereby making Christianity and Judaism the only legal religions, and required all Christians to believe as the bishop of Rome did, in the hope of imposing religious unity on battling groups of Christians. Unity under Roman leadership was essential, Theodosius said, because Peter had transmitted the unblemished faith directly to Rome and Peter's successors had preserved it there. The bishops of Rome took an ambivalent view of Theodosius's actions. On the one hand, they were glad to have the emperor's support. On the other hand, they did not wish for their authority or teaching to rest on imperial decrees. Theodosius's decree reflects the growing power of the bishop of Rome and demonstrates the degree to which the state and the church were becoming intertwined. The decree itself failed to achieve the unity Theodosius desired. Accordingly, in 381 he summoned another ecumenical council in Constantinople. This council again condemned Arianism, which thereafter declined in significance within the empire, although it remained vigorous among the barbarian peoples living along Rome's frontiers.

Ever since Nicaea, councils, with active participation by the emperors, had settled major disagreements in the church. Pope Leo I (r. 440–461) began to assert papal prerogatives. He had sent representatives to the Council of Chalcedon bearing his doctrinal formulation. Leo insisted that as the bishop of Rome, he had full authority to make decisions in doctrinal controversies. The emperor Marcian skillfully steered Leo's "Tome" to acceptance by the council, but to appease many Eastern bishops, who felt that too much authority was being claimed by the pope, the emperor also encouraged the council to assert that the bishop of Constantinople (or patriarch, as he was often called) was second in eminence and power to the bishop of Rome. Leo, the greatest exponent of "Petrine Primacy" though not its originator, objected strenuously to the Council of Chalcedon's procedures. He disliked the prominent role of the emperor, complained that Eastern bishops had no right to challenge his doctrinal authority, and particularly opposed the elevation of Constantinople's status. Indeed, Leo said, Rome's position derived from its Petrine succession and not from imperial or conciliar decrees.

A generation later Pope Gelasius I (r. 492–496) sent a sharply worded letter to the emperor Anastasius (r. 491–518), who had intervened in a quarrel between the Catholics and the still-numerous Monophysites. Gelasius protested the emperor's intervention. He told the emperor that the world was governed by the "power" of kings and by the "authority" of priests. Ordinarily, the pope said, the jurisdictions of kings and priests are distinct. In a controversy between them, however, priestly authority must have precedence, because priests are concerned with the salvation of immortal souls, whereas kings rule only mortal bodies. Gelasius was telling the emperor to stay out of theology, but he was implying much more. His opposition of the words *power*—meaning mere police power, the application of brute force—and *authority*—legitimacy, superior right—was of great importance. Gelasius elevated the church, with the pope at its head, above the whole secular regime, with the emperor at its head. Despite his lofty claims, Gelasius had no means of coercing emperors. Moreover, many clergy in the eastern Mediterranean refused to accept the idea that the pope had supreme authority in either doctrine or church government.

The pontificate of Pope Gregory I "the Great" (r. 590–604) exemplifies the position of the papacy as Late Antiquity drew to a close. Gregory was the scion of an old senatorial family. He had risen through several important positions in the Roman administration but then decided to abandon public life, sell off his family's property, and pursue a life of spiritual retreat. Soon, however, the Roman people elected him pope. His reputation for holiness was important to his election, but so too were his impeccable social credentials and wide political connections. Rome was threatened by the Lombards (a barbarian group that had entered Italy in the 560s), the local economy was in a shambles, and relations with the imperial government had been strained. Gregory did not wish to be elected pope, but given his conventional Roman sense of duty and obligation, he had little choice but to accept the office. Immediately he undertook dangerous diplomatic measures to ward off the Lombard threat. He also tried hard to

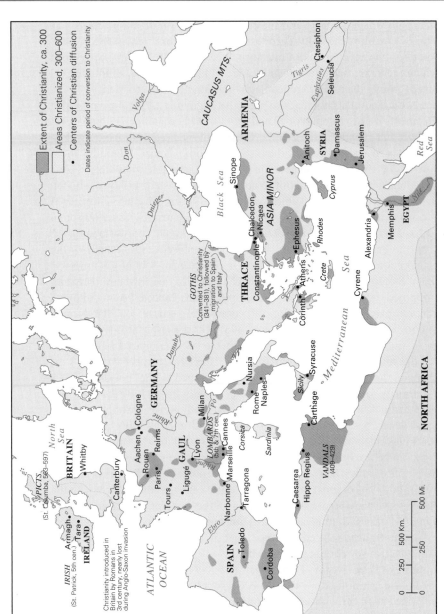

The Spread of Christianity to A.D. 600

From its beginnings in Palestine, Christianity, while still illegal, spread mainly in heavily urbanized regions. After Constantine legalized Christianity, the faith spread into every corner of the Roman world.

improve relations with the emperor. And he put the local economy on reasonably sound footing. He reorganized the vast patrimonies of the church to place their products and revenues at the disposal of the Romans. In the absence of effective imperial administration in and around Rome, Gregory also began to attend to urban services and amenities, such as streets, aqueducts, and baths.

By 600, then, the bishop of Rome—the pope—viewed himself as the head of a universal, or catholic, church. Many members of the clergy disputed that view. Some simply disagreed with specific papal teachings. Others claimed that Jesus had given his authority equally to all the apostles and not uniquely to Peter and thus to Peter's successors. Emperors, too, rejected papal overreaching. After all, they had always claimed for themselves authority in all aspects of their subjects' lives, religious affairs included. By 600, however, there were no longer emperors in the West, and the Eastern rulers had few means of controlling the bishops of Rome. For their part, the bishops of Rome were gradually focusing their efforts on the western regions of the old Roman world.

The rise of the pope in the church as a whole was paralleled by the rise of bishops throughout the empire. By the last years of the fourth century, various ranking members of the social elite were everywhere entering the clergy and rising to its highest offices. This capture of the elite was the final, decisive factor in the triumph of Christianity.

The clergy was an outlet for the talents and ambitions of the elite. For some time senators had been excluded from military offices and reduced in civilian influence, and decurions were growing dissatisfied with public service. The *episcopal* office (that is, the office of bishop) was desirable to prominent men for many reasons. It was prestigious. Bishops wore distinctive clothing when officiating and were addressed by special titles—traditional Roman marks of respect. They had opportunities to control patronage in the way that prominent Romans always had done. They could intervene on behalf of individuals at the imperial court. They controlled vast wealth, as the generosity of pious Christians put more resources at their disposal. Communities elected their own bishops, and by the middle of the fifth century the dominant person in most towns was the bishop, not a civilian official. The bishops, however, were the same persons, from the same families, who had once dominated local society through civic service. The overall effect of these social changes was dramatic in the long run, but it happened very gradually.

The change from a secular to an ecclesiastical elite in Roman cities even led to alterations of the topography of the cities themselves. The elite usually financed local building projects, such as temples, basilicas, forums, and amphitheaters. Such benefactions declined sharply during the third century because of the uncertainty of the times. The fourth century at first saw little building on private initiative, but then came the construction of Christian cathedrals (a bishop's church, from *cathedra,* the chair or seat of the bishop's authority), episcopal residences, baptisteries, and local parish churches. Such buildings as a rule were not placed in the old city centers, which had associations with the pagan past. Instead, they were placed on the edges of populated districts. In the future these Christian centers served as poles around which ancient towns were reconfigured. The Roman elites built to show pride in their cities and to promote themselves. This did not change in Late Antiquity, but this time the elites were bishops or rich Christians, and the buildings were religious.

The Rise of Christian Monasticism For some men and women the call of the Gospel was radical. They yearned to escape the world and everything that might come between them and God. To do so, many of them embraced a new way of life—monasticism. Christian monks and nuns developed a theology and an institution that were among the most creative and long-lived achievements of Late Antiquity.

The practice of rigorous self-denial (*askesis*) was common to several religious and philosophical sects in antiquity—for example, the Pythagoreans and the Stoics—and was well known among the Jews in the time of Christ, as the Essenes show (see page 181). Ascetics believed that if they could conquer the desires of the body, they could commune with the supernatural beings who were greater and purer than humans encumbered by lust for food, drink, knowledge, sex, and adventure. Sometimes ascetic practices were adopted by tightly knit groups, sometimes by heroic solitaries.

The founder of Christian monasticism was a young Egyptian layman, named Anthony (d. 356). At age 19 Anthony gave away all his possessions and took up in the Egyptian desert a life of prayer and renunciation. His spiritual quest became famous, and many disciples flocked to him. Finally he decided to organize these seekers into a very loose community. His followers remained in solitude except for worship and meals. Anthony's form of monasticism is called *eremitic,* from the Greek *heremos,* or "desert," hence the word *hermit.*

Pachomius (290–346) created a more communal form of monastic life. A former Roman soldier, he was baptized a Christian in 313 and retired to the Egyptian desert, where he studied with a hermit. Eventually Pachomius founded a community of ascetics, which before long had grown to thousands of members. Perhaps because of his military background, or because his religious instincts favored order and unity, Pachomius wrote the first Rule, or code for daily living, for a monastic community. He organized most aspects of his community by designing a common life based on routines of private prayer, group worship, and work. By the time of his death, Pachomius led nine male and two female communities. Pachomius's pattern of monasticism is called *cenobitic,* from the Greek for "common life." People living this common life were called *monks,* and the place where they lived was called a *monastery.* The head of the community was designated the *abbot,* a word meaning "father." In later times the term *abbess,* meaning "mother," was coined for the woman who led a female community, and a community of nuns came to be called a *convent.*

Monasticism spread from Egypt by means of texts such as the *Life of Anthony* (a late antique "bestseller"), collections of the wise sayings of famous desert abbots, and books written by persons who went to Egypt seeking a more perfect life—among whom were several prominent women. One attraction of monasticism among the devout was that it seemed to be a purer form of Christian life, uncorrupted by the wealth, power, and controversy of the hierarchical church. Many pious women embraced monasticism at least partly because they could not be ordained priests. Positions in monasteries, including that of abbess, provided responsible roles for talented women. Monasticism gave women a chance to choose a kind of family life different from the one available in households dominated by fathers and husbands.

Eremitic monasticism was prominent in Palestine and Syria and eventually throughout the Greek-speaking world. Eastern monasticism produced a great legislator in Basil

(330–379), whose Rule was the most influential in the Orthodox Church (see page 219). Generally these monks assembled only for weekly worship and otherwise ate, prayed, and worked alone.

Eremitic monasticism arrived in the West in the person of Martin of Tours (336–397). Like Pachomius, Martin was a pagan Roman soldier who, after his military service, embraced both Christianity and asceticism. Even though he was elected bishop of Tours, Martin kept to his rigid life of denial. Martin's form of monasticism influenced many in the western regions of the Roman world but set especially deep roots in Ireland. There the whole organization of the church was based on monasteries. At Kildare the abbess Brigid (d. 523) had more authority than the local bishop.

In the West cenobitic monasticism became the dominant pattern. Benedict of Nursia (480–545) abandoned his legal studies and a potential government career to pursue a life of solitary prayer in a mountain cave east of Rome. Benedict's piety attracted a crowd of followers, and in about 520 he established a monastery at Monte Cassino, 80 miles south of Rome. The Rule he drafted for his new community is marked by shrewd insights into the human personality. It emphasizes the bond of mutual love among the monks and obedience to the abbot. The Rule assigns the abbot wide powers but exhorts him to exercise them gently. The Rule allows monks a reasonable diet and decent, though modest, clothing. Although providing for discipline and punishment, the Rule prefers loving correction. In later centuries Benedict's Rule dominated monastic life.

Eremitic or cenobitic, East or West, monasticism was a conscious alternative and an explicit challenge to the civic world of classical antiquity. Monks and nuns did not seek to give their lives meaning by serving the state or urban communities. They went into remote places to serve God and one another. They sought not to acquire but to abandon. Spiritual wisdom was more important to them than secular learning, and they yearned for acknowledgment of their holiness, not recognition of their social status. Still, monasticism was sometimes controversial. Whereas many people admired and emulated these holy men and women, others disputed their claims to elite spiritual status.

At the dawn of Late Antiquity the church was persecuted and struggling. By the end of the period the church was rich and powerful, its leaders were prominent and prestigious, and in the monasteries, at least, its spiritual fervor was deep. This change was gradual but fundamental.

THE RISE OF GERMANIC KINGDOMS IN THE WEST, CA. 370–530

The years from the 370s to the 530s were decisive in the history of the Roman Empire in the West. When this period opened, the dynasty of Valentinian was firmly in control. When it closed, the western provinces of the empire had become a number of Germanic kingdoms, most of which maintained some formal relationship with the eastern Roman Empire. Roman encounters with the barbarians took many different forms, ranging from violent conflict to peaceful accommodation. The key point to understand is that although the barbarians supplanted Roman rule in the West, they did so slowly and often with Roman permission and assistance.

Frankish Woman's Necklace
This sixth-century "choker" necklace consists of brightly colored beads of glass, amber, amethyst, and rock crystal. The Franks were accomplished glassmakers, and this necklace provides some insight into women's taste. (Staatliche Museen zu Berlin, Museum für Vor- und Frühgeschichte/Bildarchiv Preussischer Kulturbesitz/Art Resource, NY. Photo: Klaus Goken)

Invasions and Migrations

Few images of the ancient world are more fixed in the popular imagination than the overrunning of the Roman Empire by hordes of barbarians who ushered in a dark age. The Romans inherited the word *barbarian* from the Greeks, who had divided the world between those who spoke Greek and those who did not. Barbarians were literally babblers, foreigners who spoke an unknown language. After the Romans granted citizenship to virtually everyone in the empire in 212, they adopted a Greek-style differentiation between Romans and barbarians. Technically the latter were merely foreigners, but in practice Romans thought barbarians inferior to themselves.

Individual groups of barbarians did invade the empire in various places at different times, but there was never a single, coordinated barbarian invasion of the Roman world that had well-formulated objectives. The Romans and barbarians did not face one another as declared enemies. Indeed, peaceful encounters outnumbered violent confrontations in the history of Romano-barbarian relations. The Romans had long traded with the barbarian peoples, carried out complicated diplomacy with them, and recruited them into their armies. Barbarian veterans were settled in most provinces of the empire.

If we cannot label one grand movement as "the barbarian invasions," we must also avoid the idea that the barbarians were naturally nomadic and migratory. Holding this view would tempt us to see the entry of the barbarians into the empire as one stage in a long process of human movement. Archaeological evidence collected to date makes it clear that the barbarians were settled agriculturists. They lived in villages, farmed the surrounding country, and raised livestock. If barbarians moved from one place to another, their movement must be explained with reference to specific developments and cannot be attributed to migratory habits.

Who were the barbarians? Linguists classify them as belonging to the Germanic branches of the Indo-European family of languages. The Germanic peoples can be differentiated from the Celts and Slavs with whom they shared much of central and eastern Europe, but apart from some minor linguistic variations, it is difficult to distinguish one Germanic group from another. What are we to make of the profusion of names offered to us by our sources: Franks, Saxons, Vandals, Visigoths, Ostrogoths, Lombards, Burgundians? The Romans referred to the Germanic peoples as tribes, but that does not mean that they were actually groups of related people. Every Germanic "tribe" was a confederation, and these confederations formed, dissolved, and re-formed many times. For example, the Visigoths who crossed the Danube in 376 included Visigoths proper and more than a half dozen other peoples. The confederations were formed either by powerful leaders who coerced less powerful people to join them or by groups of villages that banded together to protect themselves from aggressive neighbors. As a tribe was forming, its constituent peoples would intermarry and adopt the language, law, and lifestyle of the dominant group.

Incorporating the Barbarians   The transformation of the western Roman Empire began as a result of an unexpected set of events involving the Huns, nomadic warriors from the central Asian steppes. After plundering the frontiers of Persia and China for centuries, they turned west in search of booty and tribute. In 374 or 375 they fell on the Ostrogoths, who lived near the Black Sea, and frightened the Visigoths, who requested permission to cross the Danube and enter the empire.

Recent years had been difficult for the empire. Julian had fallen in battle with the Persians in 363, and dynastic quarrels were disturbing the West. The Romans thus delayed responding to the Visigoth request. Fearful of the Huns, the Visigoths crossed the Danube on their own and then asked if they might settle in the Balkans. Reluctantly, Valens (r. 364–378) agreed but postponed permanent arrangements. While the central government considered how to deal with the Visigoths, local authorities sold them food at exorbitant prices and even traded dog meat for Gothic children, who were then enslaved. When the Visigoths revolted, Valens foolishly marched north to meet them with a small force. The Visigoths defeated his army and killed him at Adrianople in 378.

The history of the Visigoths thus presents an instructive example of Romano-Germanic relations. They had served as auxiliary troops entrusted with defending a stretch of the Danube frontier for a long time when they requested permission to enter the empire in 376. They did not cross the border as part of a massive invasion but because they were sorely threatened. In 382 Theodosius, whom we have met several times already, marched east to pacify the situation. He agreed to grant the Visigoths what they had been demanding: land to settle on and a Roman military title—that is, official status—for their king. A spokesman for Theodosius explained the emperor's motives: "Which is better: To fill Thrace with corpses or with farmers? To fill it with graves or with people? To travel through wilderness or cultivated land? To count those who have perished or those who are ploughing?" For decades barbarians had been settling inside the Roman frontiers, and they had served loyally in the army. Beginning in the fourth century, most high military officers in the Roman world were barbarians. The only peculiarity about the Visigoths' situation was that never before had the Romans admitted a whole people.

For about thirty years the Visigoths struggled to improve the terms of their settlements in the Balkans. Alaric, the Visigothic king after 395, grew tired of unfulfilled promises and forced matters by attacking Italy. In 410 the Visigoths sacked Rome. The taking of the city for the first time in eight hundred years shocked the entire Roman world and has loomed large for centuries in people's ideas about the "fall" of the Roman Empire. Actually it was a ploy by Alaric to improve the terms of his already official status. Alaric died in 410, and his brother led the Visigoths north into southern Gaul. For good measure the new Visigothic king captured the Western emperor's sister, Galla Placidia, and forced her to marry him. However objectionable this act must seem, the Visigoths viewed it as a further demonstration of their loyalty to Rome and their determination to effect a satisfactory new treaty.

In 418 the Roman government gave in. A treaty permitted the Visigoths to settle in southern Gaul, with Toulouse as their base of operations. They were assigned the task of protecting the area from marauding bands of brigands. In return for their service, the Visigoths were given land allotments and a portion of Roman tax receipts as pay.

The Visigoths' treaty with Rome made theirs the first Germanic kingdom on Roman soil. From 418 to 451 the Visigoths' king, Theodoric I, served Rome loyally and earned the respect of the Gallo-Roman aristocrats among whom he ruled. Between 466 and 484 the Visigothic kingdom in Gaul reached its high point and continued to receive official recognition from Roman rulers. Southern Gaul, one of Rome's oldest provinces, gradually passed from the hands of the Roman bureaucracy and the local nobility into the control of the Visigoths. Nevertheless, from Constantine's first treaty with the Visigoths through the continuing recognition by the Romans of Visigothic kings, it was Roman policy more than Visigothic policy that determined the accommodation of this first Germanic kingdom within the framework of the western Roman Empire.

While they were dealing with the Visigoths, the Roman authorities realized that the Huns, who had settled in the Danube basin after driving the Visigoths into the empire, were a serious menace. They raided the Balkans, preyed on trade routes that crossed the region, and demanded tribute from the Eastern emperor. In 434 the fearsome warrior Attila murdered his brother and became sole ruler of the Huns. In return for a huge imperial subsidy, he agreed to cease raiding the Balkans. At the same time, a Roman general in Gaul concluded an alliance with the Huns in an attempt to use them to check the expansion of the Burgundians, an allied people who lived in the central Rhineland.

Together Attila and the Romans routed the Burgundians, but Attila realized the weakness of the Roman position in the West. He attacked Gaul in 451 and was stopped only by a combined effort of Romans, Visigoths, Burgundians, and Franks. Attila turned to Italy in 452, even approaching Rome, where Pope Leo I, not the emperor, convinced or bribed him to withdraw. Attila died in 454, and before another year was out, the short-lived Hunnic kingdom, largely Attila's personal creation, had vanished.

More Kingdoms: The End of Direct Roman Rule in the West

To meet threats in Gaul and elsewhere, the Romans had begun pulling troops out of Britain in the fourth century and abandoned the island to its own defense in 410. Thereafter, raiding parties from Scotland and Ireland, as well as seaborne attackers—called "Saxons" by contemporaries because some of them came from Saxony in northern Germany—ravaged Britain. The British continually appealed to the military authorities in Gaul for aid, but to no avail. Between 450 and

600 much of southern and eastern Britain was taken over by diverse peoples whom we call the "Anglo-Saxons." The newcomers jostled for position with the Celtic Britons, who were increasingly confined to the north and west of the island. Amid these struggles was born the legend of King Arthur, a Briton who defended his people and led them to victory. Gradually several small kingdoms emerged. Although Britain retained contacts with Gaul, the island had virtually no Roman political or institutional inheritance.

Valentinian III (r. 425–455) was born in 419 and became emperor of the West as a 6-year-old. Even when he came of age, his court was weakened by factional strife, and his regime was dominated by military men. After Valentinian, the western empire saw a succession of nonentities, the last of whom was deposed by Odoacer, a Germanic general, in 476. Ruling in Italy, Odoacer simply sent the imperial regalia to Constantinople and declared that the West no longer needed an emperor. This is all that happened in 476, the traditional date for the "fall" of the Roman Empire.

After the vast coalition defeated the Huns in Gaul in 451, the remaining Roman authorities in the Paris region discovered that the Visigoths were expanding north of the Loire River into central Gaul. To check this advance, the Roman commander in Paris forged an alliance with the Franks. The Franks, long Roman allies, had been expanding their settlements from the mouth of the Rhine southward across modern Holland and Belgium since the third century.

The fortunes of the Frankish kingdom, indeed of all of Gaul, rested with Clovis. He became king of one group of Franks in 481 and spent the years until his death in 511 subjecting all the other bands of Franks to his rule. He gained the allegiance of the Frankish people by leading them to constant military victories that brought territorial gains, plunder, and tribute. The greatest of Clovis's successes came in 507, when he defeated the Visigoths and drove them over the Pyrenees into Spain.

Clovis was popular, not only with the Franks but also with the Gallo-Roman population, for three reasons. First, Clovis and the Romans had common enemies: Germanic peoples still living beyond the Rhine and pirates who raided the coast of Gaul. Second, whereas most of the Germanic peoples were Arian Christians, the majority of the Franks passed directly from paganism to Catholicism. Thus Clovis and the Gallo-Romans had a shared faith that permitted Clovis to portray his war against the Visigoths as a kind of crusade against heresy. Third, Clovis eagerly sought from Constantinople formal recognition and titles, appeared publicly in the dress of a Roman official, and practiced such imperial rituals as distributing gold coins while riding through crowds. The Frankish kingdom under Clovis's family—called "Merovingian," from the name of one of his semilegendary ancestors—became the most successful of all the Germanic realms.

Several early Germanic kingdoms were short-lived. The Burgundian kingdom, which had once prompted the Romans to ally with the Huns, was swallowed up by the Franks in the 530s. The Vandals, who crossed the Rhine in 406 and headed for Spain, crossed to North Africa in 429. They were ardent Arians, who persecuted the Catholic population. They refused imperial offers of a treaty on terms similar to those accepted by other Germanic peoples. And they constantly plundered the islands of the western Mediterranean and the Italian coast, even sacking Rome in 455. Roman forces from Constantinople eliminated the Vandals in 534.

The Ostrogoths, allies who had been living in Pannonia since the 370s as subjects of the Huns, began to pose a threat to the eastern empire after Attila's death. In 493 the

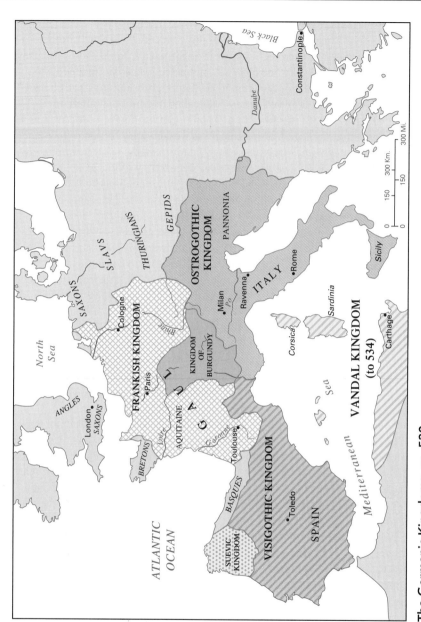

The Germanic Kingdoms, ca. 530

By 530 the western provinces of the Roman Empire had evolved into Germanic kingdoms. Just as Roman provincial boundaries had changed numerous times, the existence and extent of Germanic kingdoms were also impermanent.

emperor decided to send them to Italy to remove Odoacer, who had earned the displeasure of the Roman administration by laying hands on the sentimentally significant land of Italy—and doing so on his own initiative instead of the emperor's directive. The government at Constantinople was familiar with the Ostrogoths' king, Theodoric, because he had been a hostage there for several years. The emperor also wished to remove the Ostrogoths from the Danube basin. Sending Theodoric to Italy seemed like a way to solve two problems simultaneously.

Theodoric ousted Odoacer quickly enough and set up his capital in Ravenna, the swamp-surrounded and virtually impregnable city that had sheltered the imperial administration for much of the fifth century. Through the force of his personality, and by a series of marriage alliances, Theodoric became the dominant ruler in western Europe. In Italy he promoted peace, stability, and good government. Still, Theodoric had two strikes against him. First, he and his people were Arians. Second, although the population of Italy was accustomed to having an imperial court dominated by barbarians

Amalasuntha, Daughter of Theodoric   *This ivory plaque (ca. 530) depicts Amalasuntha in the way that Roman consuls and emperors had long been depicted on their assumption of office. Since the late fifth century empresses had been depicted this way, too. Amalasuntha projects an image of legitimacy. Compare her appearance with that of Theodora on page 215.*   (Kunsthistorisches Museum, Vienna)

and to having Germanic military men in Gaul as the real powers in the state, they had never been directly ruled by a barbarian, and some of them could not accept Theodoric. By the 520s Theodoric grew increasingly suspicious and dictatorial.

When Theodoric died, his daughter Amalasuntha (498–535) served as regent for her son Athalaric from 526 to 534 and then briefly served as queen. A contemporary said that she was beautiful and well educated. Clearly she favored the Romans in Italy and promoted cultural fusion. For this she evoked the keen hatred of the staunch Goths, who deposed and then murdered her. Her death was Justinian's pretext to launch the Gothic Wars (535–554), which put an end to the Ostrogothic kingdom.

By the 530s the western Roman Empire had vanished, the conclusion of a process initiated by the entry of the Visigoths into the Balkans in 376. Of all the peoples who had contested for a share of Rome's legacy, only the Franks in Gaul, the Visigoths in Spain, and the Anglo-Saxons in Britain had created durable political entities. Most of two prefectures with their several dozen provinces had turned into a small number of kingdoms.

Why did the Roman government perish in the West? Beginning with Diocletian, Rome's best rulers were resident in and concerned mainly about the East. The Visigoths and other peoples were settled in their own kingdoms on Roman soil instead of being enrolled in and dispersed among Roman army units. Also during Diocletian's rule, the army was increasingly Germanized, and Germanic military men gained high offices in the state. Those leaders often dominated imperial courts and negotiated the series of treaties that submitted former provinces to barbarian peoples. Provincial elites had long been accustomed to having prominent Germans in their midst. The new situation was not unusual to them. Churchmen readily embraced the Catholic Franks and tolerated Arians, such as the Visigoths, when they promoted peace and good government without abusing the Catholic population.

Old and New in the West The Germanic kingdoms had a great deal in common with one another and very much resembled the late Roman Empire, which had been their common tutor. Each realm was led by a king who usually appeared in two distinct guises. To his people, the king was the military leader. The essential bond of unity among each Germanic people was loyalty to the leader, who repaid his followers in booty, tribute, land, legal protection, and military security. To the Romans, the king appeared as an ally and magistrate. Almost all Germanic kings bore Roman titles such as *consul* or *patrician,* and in these officially conferred titles resided the authority necessary to govern Roman populations. The kings also succeeded to a long line of Germanic Masters of the Soldiers, the title of the highest military officers in a prefecture. Each monarchy was led by a dynasty—for example, the Merovingians among the Franks—that was pre-eminent in wealth and possessed a sacral aura not unlike that of the Roman emperors.

The most common local officials were counts, a combined civilian-military position that made its first appearance in the fifth century. Initially a direct representative of the emperor, a count had financial, judicial, and military responsibilities. Local notables, usually great landowners, initially resented counts but gradually aspired to the office. Kings were careful to promote important locals, both Romans and their own people, to the office of count.

Local administration remained based in cities and towns. Taxes continued to be paid to royal governments throughout the sixth century. Provincial populations did not find this policy odd or unjust. Their taxes had always gone primarily to pay for the Roman military establishment, and the monarchies were the heirs of that establishment. Latin persisted as the language of administration. Until the end of Late Antiquity, notaries continued to draw up wills, records of land transactions, and legal documents of all kinds. Law codes issued by the Germanic kingdoms were largely adaptations of Roman provincial law. In other words, the legal conditions under which most people lived stayed pretty much the same. In sum, people's daily lives changed surprisingly little as a result of the replacement of Roman provinces by Germanic kingdoms.

THE ROMAN EMPIRE IN THE EAST, 395–565

The creation of the tetrarchy at the end of the third century had separated the eastern and western halves of the Roman Empire administratively. In theory, there was only one empire, ruled by one senior emperor, but in practice the Eastern and Western courts followed different policies in many areas, notably in their relations with the Germanic peoples. Fundamental cultural differences also distinguished East from West. The East was more populous, more heavily urbanized, and more prosperous. The eastern Mediterranean was Greek in culture and livelier intellectually than the West. From Diocletian in the third century to Justinian in the sixth, the eastern Roman Empire evolved slowly along the path marked out by its first great reformers. Moreover, the eastern empire survived as the western empire was being parceled out into kingdoms.

Constantinople and Its Rulers

Constantius II (r. 337–361), Constantine's son and his successor in the East, began making Constantinople a truly imperial city. He gave "New Rome" its own senate and urban magistrates, placing the city on an equal constitutional footing with Rome. Constantinople did not have an ancient aristocracy, so Constantius had to create a senatorial order. This he did by recruiting some Romans and promoting prominent and cultivated persons from cities in the eastern half of the empire, thereby forging bonds between the capital and its hinterland. Constantius and his successors also built palaces, public buildings, and churches to give the city a truly imperial character.

With the exception of the founder, the ablest members of the dynasty of Valentinian ruled in the East. The greatest of these was Theodosius II (r. 408–450), who enjoyed the longest imperial reign in Roman history. Through skillful diplomacy and the occasional application of force, he managed to keep the eastern empire free of serious Germanic incursions and the Persians at bay in Mesopotamia. To protect his capital on the landward side, he built massive walls, whose ruins are impressive even today. He promoted learning in the city and both added and beautified important buildings. Theodosius and his family made the new capital a real intellectual center.

Born in 401, Theodosius ascended the throne as a child. Throughout his life the two greatest influences on him were his sister, Pulcheria (399–453), and his wife, Athenais-Eudoxia (ca. 400–460). Theodosius's moderate religious policy owed much to his wife, while his deep personal piety seems attributable to his sister. Pulcheria achieved the appointment and dismissal of imperial officers, guided foreign policy, and patronized scholars and churchmen. Only rarely do surviving sources permit us to observe the activities of imperial women. The cases of Pulcheria and Eudoxia hint at how much we do not know.

Theodosius's greatest achievement was his law code of 438. The most comprehensive collection of Roman law yet produced, this code brought together all Roman laws issued since Constantine and arranged them in systematic fashion. The principal Germanic kingdoms were established just after the Theodosian code was issued. From this text, and from the Roman institutional structures that employed it, the barbarians were taught the rule of law and regulations for the conduct of daily affairs.

The Emperor Justinian (r. 527–565) After Theodosius II died in 450, the eastern empire endured seventy-seven years of rule by military men who lacked the culture, vision, or administrative capacity of their predecessors. But they preserved the empire and kept its government functioning. It was from these rough soldiers that Justinian emerged to become the greatest ruler of Late Antiquity, one of the greatest of all Rome's emperors.

Justinian was born in an Illyrian village (Croatia, today), entered the army, and secured high office under his illiterate uncle Justin, who had likewise risen from the peasantry to the imperial office (r. 518–527). Despite growing up in rural military camps, Justinian showed a wide range of interests and abilities. He surrounded himself with remarkable people and gave them considerable latitude. In 525 he flouted convention by marrying the actress Theodora (ca. 497–548). A woman of intelligence, imagination, and great courage, Theodora was one of Justinian's key advisers. Contemporaries believed that she guided the emperor's religious policy. She certainly spent lavishly on charitable activities, not least on homes for former prostitutes. Justinian also identified and promoted such previously obscure figures as the gifted general Belisarius, the administrative genius John the Cappadocian, and the greatest legal mind of the age, Tribonian. He entrusted two mathematicians, Anthemius of Tralles and Isidore of Miletus, with the task of designing the Church of Hagia Sophia, which remains his principal monument.

Almost immediately on assuming the throne, Justinian put John the Cappadocian to work reforming an administration that had been little altered in two centuries despite vast changes in the scope of the empire. John worked particularly to secure tighter control of provincial administrators, to ensure a steady flow of tax revenue, and to eliminate official corruption. Tribonian and a commission were assigned the task of producing the first comprehensive collection of Roman law since that of Theodosius II in 438. Between 529 and 533 Justinian's code was issued in three parts. The *Code* was a systematically organized collection of all imperial legislation. The *Digest* was a collection of the writings of the classical Roman jurists, the legal philosophers of the Early Empire. The *Institutes* was a textbook for law students. Justinian's code is the most influential legal collection in human history. It summarizes a thousand years of legal work, remained valid in the eastern empire until 1453, and has subsequently influenced almost every legal system in the modern world.

Not long after undertaking his legal and administrative reforms, Justinian launched an ambitious attempt to reunite the empire by reconquering its lost western provinces.

Theodora   *This magnificent sixth-century mosaic from Ravenna depicts the empress Theodora in all her power and majesty.*   (Scala/Art Resource, NY)

Belisarius retook Africa from the Vandals and Italy from the Ostrogoths. Justinian also landed an army in Spain in an unsuccessful attempt to wrest Iberia from the Visigoths.

Justinian's ability to sustain major campaigns in the West was limited by the need to ward off constant threats in the East. The empire faced new enemies—Bulgars and Slavs—in the Balkans and a resurgent old foe—the Persians—in Mesopotamia. Costly treaties and humiliating subsidies bought a string of cease-fires but no definitive settlements in these areas. The emperor's campaigns were so expensive that his administrative reforms wound up looking like contrivances to make more money for the emperor to waste. In 532 violent mobs coursed through the streets of Constantinople demanding the dismissal of John the Cappadocian and other imperial agents. Justinian almost fled, but Theodora persuaded him to put down the riot. In 542 the Mediterranean world was visited by the most devastating plague in centuries, one more blow to the empire.

Justinian's religious policy also met with sharp opposition. A genuinely pious man, Justinian legislated frequently on behalf of the church and, along with Theodora, practiced generous charitable benefactions. Still, by both personal conviction and a sense of official duty, Justinian desired religious unity. Justinian was mildly Monophysite, and his wife was enthusiastically so. Justinian tried again and again to find a compromise that would bring all parties together. His church council of 553 assembled amid high hopes, but his proposed doctrinal compromises alienated the clergy in Syria, Egypt, and Rome.

To create a monument equal to his lofty vision of the empire, Justinian sought out Anthemius and Isidore. He charged the two great mathematicians to design a church that would represent the place where heaven and earth touched. Regular meetings in this place of the emperor, the patriarch, and the people gave repeated symbolic confirmation of the proper ordering of the state. There is no evidence that Justinian dictated the form of his church—the Church of Hagia Sophia—but the fact that he did not turn to any of the city's regular builders suggests that he was not looking for a traditional basilica.

Hagia Sophia was the largest Christian church until the construction of Saint Peter's in Rome (1503–1614). The building begins with a square just over 100 feet on a side, 70 feet above which are four great arches. Two of the arches are solid and form the nave walls of the church; the other two give way to semicircular continuations of the nave. Above the main square is a dome that seems to float on the blaze of light that pours through its windows. The inside is a riot of color, achieved by marble fittings in almost every imaginable hue and by the mysterious play of light and shadow. The effect of the whole is disorienting. The space in most basilicas is ordered, controlled, elegant. The space in Hagia Sophia is horizontal and vertical, straight and curved, square and round. The inside is by turns dark and light, purple and green, red and blue. It is indeed as if one has entered a realm that is anchored to this world but gives access to another.

It is appropriate that in assessing his church, Justinian should have looked backward to Solomon, the Hebrew king who built Jerusalem's Temple. In almost all respects Justinian was a traditional, backward-looking ruler. His concern for the administrative minutiae of his empire would have made perfect sense to Diocletian. His combination of military and diplomatic initiatives would have been appreciated by Theodosius I, whose namesake, Theodosius II, would have admired Justinian's legal code. In his religious policies, especially his quest for unity, Justinian drew from a deep well of imperial precedent. Even in his attempt to restore direct rule in Rome's former western provinces, Justinian showed himself a traditionalist.

SOCIETY AND CULTURE IN LATE ANTIQUITY

During these centuries of the ascendancy of the eastern Roman Empire, and the splintering of the western, the daily lives of men and women of every social class changed relatively little in terms of power relationships and economic opportunities. Nevertheless, provincial elites, members of the clergy, and barbarians gained unprecedented influence. Ordinary farmers, the overwhelming majority of the population, experienced changes in their legal status but not in their material well-being. Secular intellectual life lost most of its vitality, but a vibrant Christian culture flourished in the writings of the Church Fathers. Christianity added yet another element to the diversity that always characterized the Roman world.

Social Hierarchies and Realities Roman society had long been hierarchical, and from Republican times Rome had been governed by a hereditary class. Although the members of this class affected a style of life that set them apart, they were never a closed caste. First, they did not reproduce themselves very effectively. About two-thirds of the Roman aristocracy was replaced every century—a typical pattern in premodern societies. This turnover created significant opportunities for social mobility. Second, just as the empire had been born in a social transformation that brought the Italian aristocracy into the Roman governing class, so Late Antiquity was characterized by a transformation that brought provincial elites and barbarians into the framework of power. Paradoxically, social change was always masked as social continuity, because when new men reached the top, they tried to embrace the culture and values of those whom they had replaced.

Three ideals guided the lives of elite men: *otium, amicitia,* and *officium. Otium,* "leisure," meant that the only life worth living was one of withdrawal in which the finer things in life—literature especially—could be cultivated. *Amicitia,* "friendship," implied several things. It could mean the kinds of literary contacts that the thousands of surviving letters from Late Antiquity reveal. Friendship also could mean patronage. The doorstep of every noble household was crowded every morning with hangers-on who awaited their patron's small offerings and any commands as to how they might do his will. *Officium,* "duty," was the sense of civic obligation that Roman rulers communicated to the provincial upper classes.

Aristocrats governed in both public and private ways, which are almost impossible to differentiate. Though gradually excluded from key military and administrative posts, nobles did not lose their influence. They used their wealth to win or reward followers, bribe officials, and buy verdicts. In towns decurions controlled local market privileges, building trades, police forces, fire brigades, and charitable associations. Their public and private means of persuasion and intimidation were immense. In the West, in the growing absence of an imperial administration, Roman public power did not so much "decline and fall" as find itself privatized and localized. Patronage and clientage in Roman society had a benevolent dimension, but they also revealed the raw realities of power.

In Roman society power was everything, and those who lacked power were considered "poor," regardless of their financial status. On this reckoning, much of the urban population was poor because they lacked access to the official means of coercion and security that the notables enjoyed. Merchants, artisans, teachers, and others were always vulnerable because their social, political, or economic positions could change at a moment's notice. They lacked the influence to protect themselves.

Most citizens of the late antique world can be classed as farmers, but this categorization is misleading because it lumps together the greatest landowners and the poorest peasants. Late Antiquity saw a trend in the countryside that continued into the Middle Ages: freedom and slavery declined simultaneously. Many small, independent farmers, probably people who had long been the clients of local grandees, handed over their possessions—*commended* them is the technical term—and received back the use of them in return for annual rents in money or in kind. They became *coloni,* "tenants." Their patrons promised to protect them from lawsuits and from severe economic hardship. More and more, these coloni were bound to their places of residence and forced to perform services or pay fees that marked their status as less than fully free. At the same time, many landlords who could no longer afford to house, feed, and equip slaves gave them their freedom and elevated them to the status of coloni. Probably the day-to-day lives of the great mass of the rural population and their position at the bottom of the social hierarchy changed very little.

Women's lives are not as well known to us as men's. "Nature produced women for this very purpose," says a Roman legal text, "that they might bear children and this is their greatest desire." Ancient philosophy held that women were intellectually inferior to men, science said they were physically weaker, and law maintained that they were naturally dependent. In the Roman world women could not enter professions, and they had limited rights in legal matters. Christianity offered women opposing models. There was Eve, the eternal temptress through whom sin had fallen on humanity, and then there was Mary, the virginal mother of God. The Bible also presented readers with powerful, active women, such as Deborah and Ruth, and loyal, steadfast ones, such as Jesus's female disciples. Amid this varied popular and learned opinion, we can still detect some possibilities for independent and influential activity on the part of women.

Girls usually did not choose their marriage partners. Betrothals could take place as early as age 7 and lawful marriages at 12. Most marriages took place when the girl was around 16; husbands were several years older. A daughter could reject her father's choice only if the intended man was unworthy in status and behavior. Women could inherit property from their fathers and retained some control over their marital dowries. Divorce was possible but only in restricted cases. A divorced woman who had lost the financial security provided by her husband and father was at a distinct disadvantage legally and economically unless she had great wealth.

Christianity brought some interesting changes in marriage practices. Since the new faith prized virginity and celibacy, women now had the option of declining marriage. The church at Antioch supported three thousand virgins and widows. Christian writers tried to attract women to the celibate life by emphasizing that housework was drudgery. Christianity required both men and women to be faithful in marriage, whereas Roman custom had permitted men, but not women, to have lovers, prostitutes, and concubines. Christianity increased the number of days when men and women had to abstain from sex. Ancient cultures often prohibited sexual intercourse during menstruation and pregnancy, but Christianity added Sundays and many feast days as forbidden times. Further, Christianity disapproved of divorce, which may have accorded women greater financial and social security, although at the cost of staying with abusive or unloved husbands.

Traditionally women were not permitted to teach in the ancient world, although we do hear of women teachers such as Hypatia of Alexandria (355–415), renowned for her knowledge of philosophy and mathematics. Some Christian women, such as Melania, were formidably learned. Until at least the sixth century the Christian church had deaconesses who had important responsibilities in the instruction of women and girls. Medical knowledge was often the preserve of women, particularly in areas such as childbirth, sexual problems, and "female complaints."

Christianity also affected daily life. Churchmen were concerned that women not be seen as sex objects. They told women to clothe their flesh, veil their hair, and use jewelry and cosmetics in moderation. Pious women no longer used public baths and latrines. Male or female, Christians thought and lived in distinctive new ways. All Christians were sinners, and so all were equal in God's eyes and equally in need of God's grace. Neither birth, wealth, nor status was supposed to matter in this democracy of sin. Theological equality did not, however, translate into social equality.

The church also introduced some new status distinctions. Holiness became a badge of honor, and holy men and women became Late Antiquity's greatest celebrities. After their death they were venerated as saints. Sanctuaries were dedicated to them, and people made pilgrimages to their tombs to pray and seek healing from physical and spiritual ailments. Miracle stories became popular. Thus in some ways Christianity produced a society the likes of which the ancient world had never known, a society in which the living and the dead jockeyed for a place in a hierarchy that was at once earthly and celestial. But in other ways Christianity reoriented traditional Roman patron-client relations so that client sinners in this world were linked to sanctified patrons in heaven.

The Quest for a Catholic Tradition   By the middle of the fifth century the Nicene Creed, first spelled out in 325, had taken definitive shape; it is still recited regularly in many Christian churches. With the Council of Nicaea we see the first clear evidence that people were striving for a *catholic* form of Christianity. This Greek word means "universal." Strictly speaking, catholic Christianity would be the one form professed by all believers. A fifth-century writer said that the catholic faith was the one believed "everywhere, all the time, by everyone." It is no accident that the Catholic Church grew up in a Roman world steeped in ideas of universality. The most deeply held tenet of Roman ideology was that Rome's mission was to civilize the world and bend it to Roman ways.

One intriguing development in Late Antiquity is the emergence of several Christian communities claiming fidelity to a universal, or catholic, tradition. The Latin Christian church in the West clung tightly to the doctrinal formulations of Nicaea and Chalcedon and took its bearings from Latin church writers. In the eastern Mediterranean writers tended to use the word *Orthodox,* which means "right believing" but also carries clear implications of catholicism, or "universality." The Orthodox Church centered primarily on the emperors and patriarchs, used Greek, and followed Greek Christian writers. The Coptic Church in Egypt was Monophysite, followed the teachings of the patriarchs of Alexandria, and used the Coptic language. The Jacobite Church, a mildly Monophysite, Syriac-speaking group, was originally strong in Syria, from which it spread to Mesopotamia and beyond. Each of these churches produced a literature, an art, and a way of life that marked its members as a distinct community. These traditions did not reflect the emergence of something new in Late Antiquity so much as a Christian reinterpretation of very old cultures and ideals. Each of these traditions exists today.

Christianity drew much from the pagan and Jewish environments within which it grew, but its fundamental inspiration was the collection of writings called in modern times the Bible. In antiquity this material was called *ta hagia biblia* or *sacra biblia,* meaning "the holy books." It was understood to be a collection of sacred writings, and the individual items in that collection had different meanings. From the second century, Christian writers began trying to define a canon, a definitive list of genuine Old and New Testament scriptures. It was widely recognized that without an official, standardized set of Christian writings, there could be no uniformity of Christian belief. This process of determining authentic Scripture was not completed until the middle of the fifth century.

While the search was underway for an authoritative list of books, it was also necessary to try to get uniform versions of the books that were being pronounced canonical. The Greek East used the Greek version of the Old Testament and the Greek New Testament. But that version was unsuitable in the West, where Latin was the principal

Sarcophagus of Junius Bassus *Junius Bassus, prefect of Rome, died in 359 and was laid to rest in this splendid sarcophagus (from the Greek "body eater"). Three points are important: First, as members of the Roman elite became Christian, they could afford to employ the finest craftsmen. Second, as Christianity became legal, it could search for artistic expression. Third, these Old and New Testament scenes proclaim Christ's divinity but, in an age of intense theological quarrels, glide over his humanity.* (Hirmer Verlag München)

tongue. Late in the fourth century Pope Damasus commissioned Jerome (331–420), a man who had renounced his wealth for a life of monasticism and scholarship, to prepare a Latin version based on a new translation of the Hebrew Scriptures and Greek New Testament. Jerome's version was called the "Vulgate Bible" because it was the Bible for the "people" (*vulgus*) who knew Latin.

The development of a scriptural canon paralleled the elaboration of a creedal statement that would set down precisely what Christians believed. As we have seen, the Councils of Nicaea and Constantinople defined the nature of the Trinity, and Chalcedon formulated the relationship between the human and divine natures of Christ. There were also debates about the nature of the priesthood, the structure and authority of the church, and the problem of human free will. Practical questions came up, too. How could Christians fulfill the moral demands of their faith while living in a world whose values were often at odds with church teachings?

Answers to these kinds of questions were provided by a group of Greek and Latin writers who are called the "Church Fathers" and whose era is called "patristic" (from *patres*, the Latin word for "fathers"). In versatility and sheer output they have few rivals at any time. Their intellectual breadth was matched by their elegant style and trenchant reasoning.

Many Christian writers addressed the problems of moral living in the world. In his treatise *On Duties*, Ambrose of Milan (339–397) attempted to Christianize the public ethos that Cicero had spelled out many years before in his book of the same name. Cicero talked of citizens' obligations to one another and to the law and the need for those in power to be above reproach in the conduct of their personal lives. Ambrose reinterpreted these obligations as duties that Christians owed to one another because of their common worship of God.

Pope Gregory I wrote *The Pastoral Rule* to reformulate Cicero's and Ambrose's ideas in ways that made them relevant to society's Christian leaders, the clergy. John Chrysostom (347–407), a patriarch of Constantinople and one of the most popular and gifted preachers of Late Antiquity (his name means "golden tongued"), bitterly castigated the immorality of the imperial court and aristocracy: by setting a bad example, they endangered the souls of their subjects.

Boethius (480–524) illustrates contemporary themes well. Descended from one of Rome's oldest families, he held high offices but eventually earned the enmity of Theodoric the Ostrogoth, who imprisoned and executed him. He was a prolific writer, whose Latin translations of Greek philosophical texts bequeathed those writings to the Middle Ages. In his most famous book, *The Consolation of Philosophy,* written while he was in prison, Boethius describes how the soul could rise through philosophy to a knowledge of God. Once again we see the classical and the Christian blended in a new synthesis.

Saint Augustine and the Christian Tradition

The most influential Christian thinker after Saint Paul was Augustine of Hippo (354–430). Augustine was born in North Africa to a pagan father and a Christian mother. His family was of modest means, but at great sacrifice they arranged for him to receive the best education available. He embarked on a career as a professor of rhetoric. Once he had established himself, he moved on to Rome and then to Milan, which in the fourth century was the unofficial Western capital. Augustine fell under the spell of Ambrose and embraced the Christianity that his mother, Monica, had been urging on him throughout his life. Later Augustine chronicled his quest for truth and spiritual fulfillment in his *Confessions,* a classic of Western literature. In 395 Augustine became a bishop and until his death served the North African community at Hippo, and the wider Christian world, with a torrent of writings.

Not a systematic thinker, Augustine never set out to provide a comprehensive exposition of the whole of Christian doctrine. Instead, he responded to problems as they arose. Crucial among these were the relationship between God and humans, the nature of the church, and the overall plan of God's creation.

In the early fifth century some people believed that they could achieve salvation by the unaided operation of their own will. Augustine responded that although God did indeed endow humankind with free will, Adam and Eve had abused their will to rebel against God. Ever since that first act of rebellion, a taint, called by theologians "original sin," predisposed all humans to continual rebellion, or sin, against God. Only divine grace can overcome sin, and only by calling on God can people receive grace. Here was a decisive break with the classical idea of humanity as good in itself and capable of self-improvement, perhaps even perfection, in this world. According to Augustine, all people are sinners, in need of God's redemption.

Some North African heretics taught that sacraments celebrated by unworthy priests are invalid. Augustine believed that the validity of the church's sacraments—those ritual celebrations that are considered to be channels for the communication of grace, of God's special aid and comfort to the faithful—does not depend on the personal merit of the minister. A priest or a bishop acts in God's place and through divine grace.

Therefore, faith in God is paramount. The church is thus a community of acknowledged sinners led by the clergy in a quest for eternal salvation. To Augustine, God alone is perfect. Clergy, rulers, and churches are all human institutions, all more or less good in particular circumstances.

To many adherents of the traditional Roman religion, the sack of Rome by the Visigoths in 410 was repayment for Rome's abandonment of its traditional gods. To refute them, Augustine wrote the most brilliant and difficult of all his works, *The City of God*. This book is a theology of history. Augustine sees time not as cyclical—the traditional classical view—but as linear. Since the creation of the world, a plan has been in operation—God's plan—and that plan will govern all human activity until the end of time. History is the struggle between those who call on divine grace, who are redeemed, who are citizens of the City of God, and those who keep to the ways of the world, who persist in sin, who live in the earthly city. One may observe the unfolding of the divine plan by seeing how much of the earthly city has been redeemed at any given time.

Even though the Roman Empire was officially Christian, Augustine refused to identify his City of God with it. Nor would he say that the church and the City of God were identical. What he did say was that the sack of Rome was a great irrelevance because many kingdoms and empires had come and gone and would continue to do so, but only the kingdom of God was eternal and, in the long run, important. To a Roman people whose most cherished belief held that the world would last exactly as long as Rome's dominion, Augustine's dismissal of Rome's destiny sounded the death knell of the classical world-view.

Augustine also addressed the problem of education. He regarded salvation as the goal of life but realized that people have to carry on with their ordinary occupations. He also knew that almost the entire educational establishment was pagan in design and content. Education was confined mainly to the elite, who sought schooling partly to orient themselves within their cultural tradition and partly to gain employment, often in the imperial or urban service. This education had three mainstays. Latin or Greek grammar—rarely both—was the first. Augustine, for instance, knew little Greek, and by the sixth century few people in the East knew Latin. The second mainstay of education was rhetoric, once the art of public speaking but now, increasingly, literary criticism. The third was dialectic, or the art of right reasoning. In Late Antiquity public schools were fast disappearing as the need for them slipped away. But the church still needed educated persons, so it provided schools in cathedrals and monasteries.

In a treatise entitled *On Christian Doctrine*, Augustine expressed some ideas about education that proved influential for a millennium. He argued that everything a person needs to know to achieve salvation is contained in the Bible. But the Bible, written in learned language, is full of difficult images and allusions. How is an ordinary person to learn what he or she needs to know in order to master this great book of life? Only by getting some schooling, and that education would inevitably be in the classical languages and literatures. To express his attitude toward that schooling, Augustine used the image of "spoiling the Egyptians," borrowed from the account of the Hebrews' Exodus from Egypt, when they took with them whatever they could use. Augustine's attitude toward classical learning was that it was useful only to the extent that it equipped individuals to read the Bible, to understand it, and to seek salvation. Classical culture had no intrinsic merit. It might give pleasure, but it was equally likely to be a distraction or a temptation to immorality.

The Italian writer Cassiodorus (ca. 485–580) gave this Augustinian interpretation of the classical heritage its definitive statement in his treatise *On Divine and Human Readings.* After the fall of the Ostrogothic kingdom, whose king Theodoric he had served loyally, Cassiodorus retired and set up a school of Christian studies. His treatise served as a kind of annotated bibliography and curriculum of the major writings on school subjects, such as grammar, rhetoric, and dialectic, and on biblical commentary. For centuries, schools organized on Augustine's and Cassiodorus's model did an estimable job of preparing the clergy to carry out their functions.

SUGGESTED READING

Bowersock, G. W., P. Brown, and O. Grabar, eds. *Late Antiquity: A Guide to the Post-Classical World.* 1999. Though basically an encyclopedia, this masterful volume contains long entries on all the major topics and up-to-date essays on big themes.

Brown, Peter. *The World of Late Antiquity.* 1971. A sprightly and beautifully illustrated interpretation of cultural crosscurrents by the most gifted interpreter of Late Antiquity.

Clark, Gillian. *Women in Late Antiquity: Pagan and Christian Lifestyles.* 1993. A first-ever attempt to capture the lives of late antique women in all respects.

Liebeschuetz, J. H. W. G. *The Decline and Fall of the Roman City.* 2001. A remarkable assessment of all aspects of urban change from the fourth to the seventh century.

Markus, Robert. *The End of Ancient Christianity.* 1990. This stimulating and beautifully written book explores the changing meanings of sacred and secular in the period from 400 to 600.

IMPORTANT EVENTS

284–337 Reforms of Diocletian and Constantine

300–400 Origins and spread of Christian monasticism

325–553 First five ecumenical councils of the Christian church

325–360 Foundation and development of Constantinople

350s–ca. 600 Age of the Church Fathers

370s–530s Beginnings of the Germanic kingdoms inside the Roman Empire

379–395 Reign of Theodosius I, last emperor of a united empire

408–450 Reign of Theodosius II; consolidation of eastern Roman empire

410 Visigoths sack Rome

412–418 Visigoths settle in Gaul

430 Vandals begin conquest of North Africa

440–604 Development of the Roman papacy

450–600 Anglo-Saxons settle in Britain

476 Last Roman emperor in the West deposed

481–511 Clovis founds Frankish kingdom

493 Beginning of Ostrogothic kingdom in Italy

527–565 Reign of Justinian I

8

Early Medieval Civilizations, 600–900

(Christopher Rennie/
Robert Harding Picture
Library)

The Great Mosque of Cordoba, erected by Abd ar-Rahman I in 786–787, at first glance appears much like a late antique building: elegant columns, arches arranged in arcades, rectangular space. But this is a *mosque,* an Islamic house of worship, and it was built in Spain, one of Rome's oldest provinces. We saw in Chapter 7 that Spain had fallen to the

Visigoths in the sixth century and that Justinian had been unable to reconquer the region. Between 711 and 716 an army of Arabs and North African tribesmen overwhelmed Spain and inaugurated seven centuries of Islamic rule on the Iberian Peninsula. A time traveler transported to the Mediterranean world of 600 would almost certainly have predicted only two heirs to Rome: the eastern empire and the kingdoms of the barbarian West. It is extremely unlikely that our intrepid wanderer would have foreseen one of the most dramatic developments in the history of Western civilization: the rise of the Arabs and their Islamic faith.

In this chapter three areas and histories engage our attention: the Islamic East, the Byzantine Empire, and the Latin West. For each, the seventh century was an era of dramatic change, the eighth century a period of reform and consolidation, and the ninth century a time of upheaval. A new imperial tradition developed in all three areas. Muslims, Orthodox Christians, and Catholics all believed themselves to be chosen by God, and their rulers defined themselves as God's earthly agents. In all three realms the interaction of local traditions and the Roman past produced new forms of central government that would prove influential for centuries. Commercial ties began to transform the Mediterranean world into a community of peoples who needed to balance mutual interests with bitter rivalries.

The Great Mosque serves as a remarkable reminder of how much changed—and how much remained the same—in the early Middle Ages. Arches and arcades graced classical architecture for more than a millennium. But Cordoba's arches are horseshoe shaped, a minor innovation. The arches incorporate alternating bands of red and cream-colored stone. These shapes and colors may be local traditions, an imitation of the Roman aqueduct at Mérida, Byzantine imports, or Syrian characteristics. The building is basilican in shape. In a basilica the space is oriented to the area where officials presided—to an altar when the basilica is a church. In a mosque the space is oriented to the *qibla* wall—the wall facing Mecca, the birthplace of Muhammad and Islam. The elements of the Great Mosque were old, but the overall effect was new.

The period from 600 to 900 is commonly called the "early Middle Ages." What does this term mean? In the seventeenth century a Dutch scholar wrote of the *Medii Aevi,* the "Middle Times" that lay between antiquity and the dawning modern world. The name stuck. As a label for the post-Roman world, "Middle Ages" (whose adjectival form is "medieval") has become traditional. The fact that we no longer talk of an abrupt and catastrophic "fall" of the Roman Empire means that we no longer use the word *medieval* in negative ways.

THE ISLAMIC EAST

Ancient writers took little notice of the Arabs, who inhabited much of the area from the Arabian peninsula to the Euphrates River. Around 600 the prophet Muhammad (570–632) appeared among them preaching a faith old in its basic elements but new in its formulation. With unprecedented spiritual and military fervor, converts to that new faith conquered territories from Spain to the frontiers of China. Slowly, they built an imperial system with a coherent government and ideology. At the same time, cultural elites began forging a new civilization out of the ethnic, religious, and historical diversity of that vast realm.

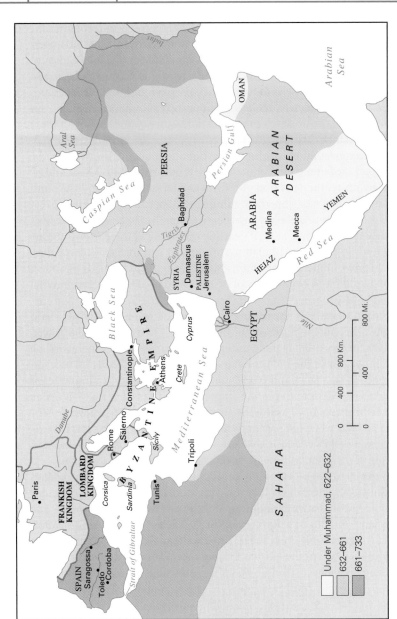

Arab Conquests to 733

This map vividly illustrates the spectacular gains by the Arabs in the time of Muhammad, under the first caliphs, and under the Umayyads. Later slow, steady gains in Africa, central Asia, and India expanded the empire even farther. Muslim conquest did not at first mean widespread conversion to Islam; Egypt, for example, was not majority Muslim before the tenth century.

Under Muhammad, 622–632
632–661
661–733

Arabia Before Muhammad

The Arab world in the early seventh century was large and turbulent. Long dominated by the Roman and Persian Empires, the region had no stable, large-scale political entities. People belonged to close-knit clans, or extended families, that in varying associations formed tribes. In theory, tribes were groups of people tracing descent from a known ancestor; in reality—and in this, Arab and Germanic peoples were alike—tribes were complex groups of relatives, allies, and political or economic clients.

As complex as its political situation was the region's ethnic and religious composition. The Roman world was overwhelmingly Christian, although there were many kinds of Christians. The Persian realm was officially Zoroastrian, but it had Jewish, Christian, Manichaean, and Buddhist minorities. The Arabs themselves were generally pagans, but Arabia had Jewish and Christian minorities.

The Arab East was also economically intricate and fragile. Bedouins (Arabs who were nomadic pastoralists) provided for their own needs from their herds of sheep and goats, from small-scale trading in towns, and from regular raids on one another and on caravans. Some farmers worked the land, but in many areas soils were too poor and rain was too infrequent to support agriculture. Cities supported traders who carried luxury goods, such as spices, incense, and perfumes, from the Indian Ocean region and southern Arabia along caravan routes to the cities of the eastern Mediterranean. These traders formed the economic and political elite of Arabia, and they led the tribes. Mecca, dominated by the powerful tribe of the Quraysh, was the foremost city of Arabia, but competition among cities and tribes was fierce.

A solution to the competition among tribes and towns for control of trade routes was the institution of *harams*, or sanctuaries—places where contending parties could settle disputes peacefully. Mecca was one of the chief harams in Arabia, and its founding was attributed to the Israelite patriarch Abraham and one of his sons, Ishmael. The focus of the sanctuary was the black stone shrine known as the Kaaba, founded by Abraham, according to Arab tradition. For centuries people from all over Arabia had made pilgrimages to Mecca, to the Kaaba, supposedly following Abraham's example.

The Prophet and His Faith

Muhammad was born in 570 to a respectable though not wealthy or powerful clan of the Quraysh tribe. His father died before he was born, his mother shortly afterward, leaving Muhammad under the care of his grandparents and an uncle. Like many young Meccans, he entered the caravan trade. By the time he was 20, Muhammad had such a reputation for competence and moral uprightness that he became financial adviser to a wealthy Quraysh widow, Khadija (555–619). Though older than Muhammad, she became his wife in 595, and they had a loving marriage until her death.

From his youth Muhammad was a man of spiritual insight. In 610 he received the first of many revelations that commanded him to teach all people a new faith that called for an unquestioned belief in one god, Allah, and a deep commitment to social justice for believers. Muhammad began teaching in Mecca, but he converted few people outside his own circle; his wife was his first convert. Some Meccans were envious of Muhammad. Others feared that his new faith and new god might call into question the legitimacy of the shrines in Mecca and jeopardize the traditional pilgrimages to the Kaaba and the trade that accompanied them. By 619 Muhammad's well-connected wife and uncle were dead, and his position was precarious.

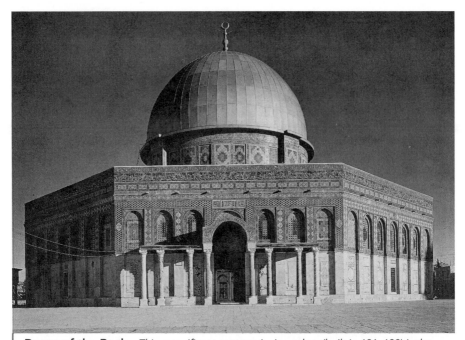

Dome of the Rock *This magnificent mosque in Jerusalem (built in 691–692) is the third-holiest shrine of Islam—after the Kaaba in Mecca and the Prophet's mosque in Medina. Muslims believe that Muhammad ascended to heaven from this spot.* (Michael Holford)

At this juncture citizens from Medina, a smaller trading community wracked by dissension among pagan Arabs, Jews, and followers of Muhammad, asked Muhammad to establish a haram there. In the summer of 622 small groups of Muhammad's disciples made their way to Medina, and in September Muhammad joined them. His journey from Mecca to Medina, the *hijra*, marks the beginning of a new era, symbolized to this day in the Arab world by a calendar that dates "In the year of the Hijra."

Although Muhammad was fully in control in Medina, Mecca remained the focus of his attention. In addition to his sentimental attachment to Mecca, its political and economic importance were critical to his emerging desire to convert all of Arabia. His followers began attacking Meccan caravans and battled with the Meccans several times in the 620s. In 630 Muhammad and many of his followers returned to Mecca in triumph. Muhammad left the Quraysh in control, and he retained the Kaaba as a focus of piety. After making local arrangements, he returned to Medina and set about winning over the bedouins of the Arabian desert. By the time Muhammad died in 632, he had converted most of Arabia.

To what exactly had Muhammad and his followers converted? At the most basic level, people were asked to surrender completely to Allah, the one true God—that is, they were asked to make *al-Islam*, "the surrender." Those who surrendered became *Muslims* and joined the *umma muslima*, a completely new kind of community in which membership depended only on belief in Allah and acceptance of Muhammad as Allah's prophet. No longer were one's duties confined to a particular clan, tribe, or town. All members of the umma were understood to have personal and communal responsibility for all other members. Because of the experience of the hijra, Islam was a religion of exile, of separation from the ordinary world, and of reliance on God.

The basic teachings of Islam are traditionally described as "Five Pillars": (1) the profession of faith, "There is no God but Allah and Muhammad is His Prophet"; (2) individual prayer five times daily, plus group prayer at noon on Friday in a *mosque*, a Muslim house of prayer; (3) the sunup-to-sundown fast for one month per year; (4) the donation of generous alms to the poor; and (5) a pilgrimage to Mecca at least once in a person's lifetime. These pillars are still the central requirements of Islam.

In the early decades the pillars sustained a faith that stressed strict monotheism and practices that affirmed Islam and built up a sense of community. At certain times of the day all Muslims everywhere bowed in prayer, with their heads facing toward Mecca. Everyone paid alms, creating thereby a feeling of solidarity among all members of the umma. Mecca itself and the experience of pilgrimage were central to all Muslims. Originally there was no elaborate theology, intricate doctrinal mysteries, creed, or clergy. Men called *imams* led the Friday prayers in the mosque and usually offered sermons that applied Muslim teaching to the issues of the day, but Islam involved no ordained priesthood as in Judaism or Christianity and no hierarchy as in the Christian churches.

Muhammad communicated God's teaching to his followers, always insisting that he was transmitting a direct, verbal revelation and not offering his own interpretations. That revelation came in the form of "recitations" that make up the *Quran*, the Scriptures of Islam. Not long after Muhammad's death his closest followers arranged the recitations into 114 *Suras,* or chapters. The Quran contains legal and wisdom literature like the Hebrew Scriptures and moral teaching like the Christian New Testament. It also prescribes regulations for diet and for personal conduct. For example, the Quran forbids alcohol and gambling, censures luxury and ostentation, and imposes strict sexual restraints on both men and women.

Initially the Quran was interpreted rather freely within the umma, doubtless because there was no clergy to impose a uniform interpretation. After the Prophet's death, some people felt the need for an authoritative teaching—as early Christians had felt the need for a canon of Christian scripture and teaching—and their efforts resulted in the collections called the *sunna,* which means roughly "good practice"—that is, the words and customs of Muhammad himself. Crucial in the development of the sunna were the *hadith,* the "sayings" of the Prophet, the comments he sometimes made about how God's revelation was to be understood and applied. Extant compilations of the sunna date from the ninth century, and scholars are not sure what portion of them derives authentically from the age of the Prophet.

The Arab Conquests   Muhammad's death brought a crisis. Who or what was to succeed him? In 632 the Meccan elite chose Abu Bakr as *caliph,* or "successor to the Prophet." Abu Bakr was elderly, an early convert to Islam, and a former secretary to Muhammad. He and his three successors down to 661 (Umar, Uthman, and Ali) were all Meccans, relatives of the Prophet by marriage, and early converts. Islamic tradition calls them the "Rightly Guided Caliphs."

Abu Bakr left his successor, Umar, a united Arabia, no small feat in that fractious world. Umar began the lightning conquests by the Arabs of much of the Roman and

Persian Empires. He initiated the policy of granting choice positions in the expanding caliphate, the Arab empire, to old converts and of ranking them according to precedence in conversion. As the old elite divided up the new provinces of the caliphate, some of them became *emirs* (governors), and others became lower administrators. Arab administrators then collected from all conquered people personal taxes and land taxes. Converts to Islam paid only land taxes. Arab settlers paid no taxes and received salaries from the taxes paid by others.

Umar was murdered by a slave in 644, leaving his successor, Uthman, a huge empire to administer. A great centralizer, Uthman chose emirs, regulated the finances of the provinces, and authorized the preparation of the definitive text of the Quran. In attempting to preserve the advantages of the old Meccan elite, Uthman alienated many people, particularly in Egypt, Syria, and Iraq, who had benefited from conquest and who guarded jealously their newfound local wealth and power. Uthman was murdered in 656 and replaced by Ali, Muhammad's son-in-law, whose goal was to create a truly Islamic government by emphasizing the religious side of the caliph's office as the leader of the umma. Ali was in turn killed by a disillusioned follower in 661. Years later some Muslims looked back to Ali as the true model for the caliph. These Muslims formed the *Shi'a,* the "Party of Ali."

When Ali was killed, the caliphate passed to Mu'awiya, a Meccan who was the governor of Syria and commander of the finest army in the Arab world. That army ensured Mu'awiya's position. From 661 to 750 the Umayyads, as Mu'awiya's family is called, built many of the caliphate's institutions.

The Umayyads instituted greater centralization. This involved the introduction of a unified coinage, the Arabization of the administration (granting all key positions to Arabs), and taking tight control of provincial government and taxation. The Umayyads moved the capital of the caliphate to Damascus in their own power base of Syria, more centrally located than the old towns of Mecca and Medina and closer to the militarily active zones in eastern Iran and along the Byzantine frontier in Syria. In addition, the Umayyads presided over the final territorial expansion of the caliphate. To the west, the caliph's forces took North Africa and Spain and conducted raids deep into Gaul. In the east, though stymied by unsuccessful sieges against Constantinople, campaigns moved the frontier against the Byzantine Empire into the mountains of southern Anatolia and, farther east, established nominal authority as far as the Indus River valley.

Rome's empire expanded for 350 years, but the caliphate reached its zenith in scarcely 100. How can we account for the astonishingly rapid creation of such a vast empire? External factors were important. Byzantium and Persia had financially and militarily weakened themselves in a series of wars that ended just as the caliphate of Umar commenced. Moreover, the Byzantine and Persian states were exceedingly diverse, and the Arab armies dismantled them piecemeal. Both old empires, but especially the Byzantine, had deep religious divisions. Coptic Egypt and Jacobite Syria, for example, willingly yielded to the Arabs, who demanded taxes and submission but otherwise left them alone. The Byzantines and Persians tended to depend on static frontier garrisons and large armies that could not be quickly mobilized and moved long distances. The Arabs rarely risked great pitched battles. They preferred a gradually expanding military frontier gained by numerous lightning strikes.

Internal factors were more significant, however. For centuries, raiding and plundering had been a way of life in Arabia, but because Islam forbade Muslims from raiding other Muslims, a new outlet for traditional violence was needed. The Prophet himself had believed firmly in the need to expand the faith, and his successors shared that belief. Muslim ideology divided the world into the "House of Islam" and the "House of War." In the House of Islam the justice of Allah reigned supreme. In the House of War *jihad,* or holy war, was the rule. Christians and Jews, as fellow "Peoples of the Book"—sharers in a scriptural tradition reaching back to Abraham—were spared the choice of conversion or death, but "infidels" were expected to submit and convert. The Arab conquests were carefully planned and directed to channel violence out of Arabia, to populate much of western Asia with loyal Muslims, and to reward members of the umma.

The Abbasid Revolution

Despite their military and administrative successes, the Umayyads were not popular. Many people resented their bureaucratic centralization. Such resentment was acute in areas heavily populated by recent converts, who had always disliked the old Arabian elites, and in frontier provinces, where Arab immigrants along with local converts desired autonomy. The secular nature of Umayyad rule also offended those pious Muslims who expected a high standard of personal morality from their rulers. The opposition came to a head in a series of rebellions that culminated in the naming of a rival caliph, Abu'l Abbas, in 749. In 750 he defeated his Umayyad opponent.

The Abbasids reigned until the thirteenth century. Initially, especially in the caliphate of Harun al-Rashid (r. 786–809), they brought the Islamic world its first golden age. Harun's reign was marked by political stability, economic prosperity, and cultural achievements. Abbasid successes are attributable to political acumen and ideological restructuring.

With their frontier origins, the Abbasids were sympathetic to the caliphate's provincial populations. Thus they created a more international regime. Non-Arabs and recent converts felt toward Islam, the Prophet, and the Prophet's family a loyalty that they would not grant to the old Arabian potentates who had led and initially benefited from the Arab conquests. The Abbasid polity was based on the idea of the fundamental equality of all believers, old or new, Arab or not.

Members of the Abbasid family received some key government posts, as did Iranians and other non-Arabs. Most important, however, local persons got more choice positions than Meccan or Syrian aristocrats. The capital of the caliphate was moved from Syria to Iraq, but to avoid favoring any existing group or region, the Abbasids built a new city, Baghdad, which they called "the navel of the universe." By addressing regional and ethnic sensitivities in an effective way, they were able to maintain, even extend, the centralized state of the Umayyad period.

The daily business of governing was usually in the hands of the *wazir,* who headed the administration, advised the caliph, and often exercised a powerful formative influence on the caliph's children and heirs. The first caliphs chose administrators from loyal Arabs and from experienced Christian subjects. Under the Umayyads the regime was Arabized. Then under Harun al-Rashid the government became international, professional, and hereditary. The chief agency of government was the treasury, which had separate branches dealing with Muslim alms, land and poll taxes paid by subjects, and land taxes paid by converts. Alone among early medieval governments, the caliphate could draw up annual budgets. Alongside the treasury in exerting power was a prestigious group of palace servants. They did not hold major offices, but their informal influence on the caliph and his family was great. The army was another prominent body within the state.

The central government had several links to the provinces. In addition to controlling the army and provincial governorships, the caliph employed a network of regular envoys and spies. The court, especially under the Abbasids, drew able young men from all over into the service of the caliph and created hopes among provincial elites that they, too, might be chosen. In every district and city there were judges, or *qadi*, to oversee the application of Islamic law. Qadi were under the authority of the caliph.

The death of Harun in 809 sparked a century of problems. Intense family rivalries touched both the succession to the caliphate and the possession of key provincial positions. The bureaucracy became an increasingly influential pressure group, and the palace servants began to foment intrigues. The army became more and more a professional body comprising non-Arabs, especially Turks, hired from the frontiers and beyond because Arabs, enjoying their salaries, declined to serve. The parallel with the Germanization of the late Roman army is striking. The army, the bureaucracy, and the courtiers all had different and conflicting interests and did not hesitate to press their own advantages. Religious divisions persisted, even intensified. Many felt that the Abbasids had not gone far enough in erecting a truly Islamic regime, but some felt that the caliphs had gone too far in claiming both the political and religious authority of the Prophet. Whole regions took advantage of Abbasid leniency in granting local autonomy and began to fall away. After the early tenth century the Abbasid caliphs had little effective power.

The Emergence of Islamic Culture   Two currents are apparent in the culture of the Islamic East: One is the elaboration of religious thought; the other is the assimilation of multiple cultural heritages. Both were influenced by the spread of Islam that mixed Greek, North African, Iranian, Turkish, and even Hindu elements into a culture already rich with Arab, Christian, and Jewish ingredients.

Muslims assembled for prayer in mosques, the often beautiful buildings usually modeled on the original mosque in Medina. The worshipers—with men and women in separate areas—arrayed themselves in parallel rows and were led in prayer by an imam. In time the imams started offering interpretations of the Quran, and collections of these interpretations began to circulate. Similarly, Muslim judges began to issue opinions on how the Quran and sunna might be applied to the daily lives of believers. Teachers in mosque schools also were influential. Together these authority figures, collectively the *ulama,* developed a body of religious thought. Lacking elaborate theology and creeds, Islamic religious thought pertains to practice and allegiance more than ideas. The point is less to *know* Islam than to *live* it.

The late ninth and early tenth centuries saw the emergence of a religious split in the Islamic world that persists to this day. The opposing groups are Shi'ite and Sunni Muslims. Shi'ites believe that caliphs should be chosen only according to strict standards of moral and spiritual worthiness. Further, they insist that the only way to ensure such worthiness is to choose caliphs from the line of Ali, the fifth caliph, husband of

Muhammad's daughter Fatima and, in 661, a victim of assassination. Moreover, they believe that the whole ulama should measure up to Shi'ite standards. Sunni Muslims, always the vast majority, proclaim that only they adhere to the sunna, the "good practice" of Muhammad himself. Sunnis accept the legitimacy of the whole line of Umayyad and Abbasid caliphs and the teachings of the ulama.

In 832 an Abbasid caliph endowed the "House of Wisdom," an academy for scholars in Baghdad (compare Charlemagne's palace school; see pages 249, 251), and from this point on Muslim scholars had the leisure and wherewithal to begin tackling the corpus of Greek thought, especially the scientific writers. The earliest Arab scholars sought mainly to master the learning of the past. Greek, Persian, and Indian works were collected and translated, manuscripts were copied, and libraries were built. Muslims showed little interest in the *literary* heritage of antiquity, the ancient legacy that was so important and controversial to Christian scholars.

So we may ask: Was the Islamic caliphate part of the West or not? Was it brother, or cousin, to the emerging Byzantine and Latin worlds? From the vantage point of 900, the answer we might give to those questions—"largely Western"—differs from the answer we might give today—"largely Eastern." In later chapters we will see how the Islamic world became less Western and more Eastern.

THE BYZANTINE EMPIRE

The century after Justinian's death in 565 was difficult for the eastern Roman Empire. Attacks by Persians, Bulgars, and Muslims; riots and rebellions; plagues and famines; and some weak rulers put the empire in a perilous position. Two fundamental changes transformed the eastern Roman Empire into a new civilization that we call "Byzantine," from "Byzantium," the ancient Greek name for the capital city, Constantinople. In external affairs the empire experienced a sharp geographic contraction until it stabilized into the shape it would hold into the thirteenth century. In internal affairs the empire changed both its basic administrative structures and its cultural orientation.

External Changes   In 600 the empire still laid claim, along the southern and eastern shores of the Mediterranean, to most of the lands that Rome had ruled for centuries. But in the East the empire had been suffering recurrent losses to Persia. In 610 Heraclius, a gifted ruler, ascended the throne. Between 622 and 629 Heraclius campaigned brilliantly and recovered almost everything that had been lost. But he faced a cruel irony. When the Arab expansion began under Umar, Heraclius's empire was militarily and financially exhausted. As the seventh century wore on, Arabs captured Syria, Palestine, and Mesopotamia and began a centuries-long push into Anatolia. Eventually they even threatened the capital, Constantinople.

In the Balkans Heraclius and his successors fought constant battles, with mixed results. They checked the advance of the Slavic peoples, who had been expanding southward for some years. The Slavic advance was partly generated by social and political forces among the Slavs themselves and partly a result of pressure from the Avars and Bulgars. These peoples, who were related to the Huns, had begun penetrating into the Danube basin in the late sixth century. The empire tried hard, with varying success, to check their forward march.

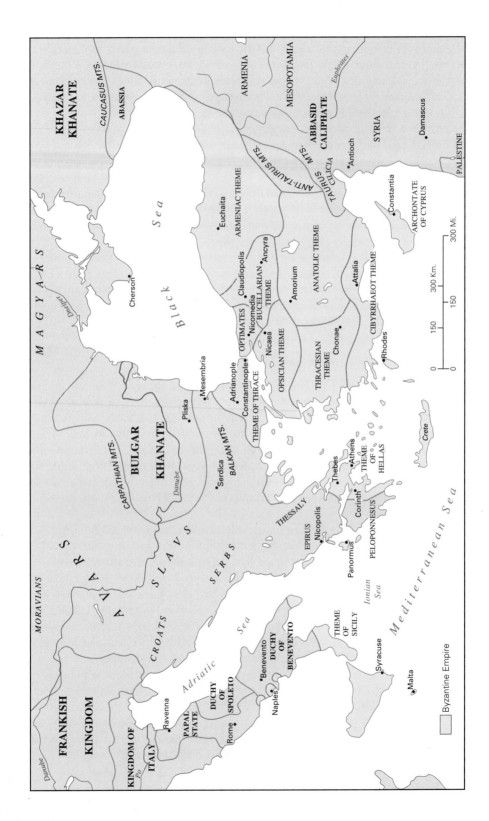

Where the West was concerned, Heraclius and his successors were powerless to stop the Arab advance in North Africa and Spain. In Italy imperial control was confined to a few outposts around Rome, Ravenna, and Sicily. Generally Italy was too far away and strategically insignificant to attract much attention from the imperial government.

By around 700 the empire was assuming the basic geographic shape it would hold for centuries. In contrast to the vast lands once ruled by Rome, the empire was now confined to the eastern Balkans and western Anatolia. Then in 717 Leo III "the Isaurian" (Leo was actually Syrian, but later legends made him a resident of Isauria in Anatolia), became emperor in a moment of acute crisis. Arab armies had seized much of Anatolia and had laid siege to Constantinople. The city would surely have fallen had it not been for the "Greek fire" that made it impossible for the attacking navy to operate beneath the seaward walls. Leo repulsed the attack and then ruled successfully until 741. He was followed by his able and charismatic son, Constantine V (r. 741–775). Constantine held the line in Anatolia and enjoyed decades of military success along the Balkan frontier.

In Italy alone Isaurian policy was unsuccessful. When Justinian reconquered Italy from the Ostrogoths (see page 214), his armies devastated the region and left it poor and weak. Into the gap stepped the Lombards, who gradually built a kingdom in the north of Italy—Lombardy still bears their name—and set up a series of duchies in the center and south of Italy. The Byzantines prudently dedicated their resources to holding their Balkan and Anatolian frontiers, but this strategy left their subjects in Italy clamoring for aid. Eventually the popes put themselves at the head of a movement in Italy that turned to the Franks for protection. In 755 and 756 the Frankish king marched to Italy, defeated the Lombards, and donated the territories he seized from them to the pope. On the one hand, this inaugurated the "Papal States," the ever changing set of lands in Italy whose current remnant is Vatican City. On the other hand, this military encounter put an end to effective Byzantine control in Italy, except for the areas around Naples and Sicily. In 827 Muslims seized Sicily, and in the ensuing decades they subjected southern Italy to continuous raids and occasional conquests.

Constantine V's promising son, Leo IV (r. 775–780), survived him only briefly. He left a 6-year-old heir, Constantine VI, and a remarkable widow, Irene (ca. 752–803), as regent for her son. Irene was a skilled politician, but under her the army grew restive because she preferred to make treaties, sometimes on unfavorable terms, than to send troops into the field. She did not trust the military's loyalty. Moreover, Irene had to contend with a foolish son who spent his time trysting with ladies of the court rather than attending to his official duties. In 797 Irene had him blinded, ironically in the very palace chamber where she had given birth to him. This was not a barbaric act in the Byzantine way of thinking. By mutilating Constantine VI, she merely rendered him unfit to rule: Roman ideology held that only a physically perfect person could reign; the

The Byzantine Empire in the Eighth and Ninth Centuries

After suffering tremendous territorial losses to the barbarians and Arabs, the Byzantine Empire transformed its military, institutional, and cultural structures to create a regime that lasted until it was conquered by Crusaders in 1204. This map shows the *themes*, Byzantium's major institutional innovation.

Coin of Empress Irene *This gold* nomisma *of the Empress Irene was struck between 797 and 802. The text reads "Irene, Empress." Note the craftsmanship of the Byzantine moneyers.* (Copyright © The British Museum)

alternative would have been to murder him. In any case, Irene's credibility sank to nothing, and in 802 she was deposed by a wily old soldier, Nicephorus (r. 802–811).

Whether in some ideal situation Nicephorus might have been successful is impossible to say. His problems came from two fearsome foes. In Anatolia he faced the redoubtable and aggressive Harun al-Rashid, and in the Balkans he contended with the clever Bulgarian Khan Krum (r. ca. 803–814). Nicephorus got a break when Harun died in 809, but he fell in battle with Krum, who gruesomely made a drinking cup out of his skull. The Isaurian reputation for invincibility died on that battlefield.

For two generations Byzantium suffered through short reigns, usurpations, political unrest, and military reverses. In 867 a rough soldier, Basil I (r. 867–886), seized the throne and, like Heraclius and Leo III before him, reversed the fortunes of the state. He established a new dynasty, the "Macedonian," and for the first time in years won important military victories. Faced as they were by worthy foes in both Anatolia and the Balkans, the Byzantines, the heirs of the Romans, might have vanished from history. But capable leaders emerged just often enough, especially in the eighth century, to preserve a state that, even in a vastly reduced shape, carried the Roman legacy into the future.

Internal Changes Even as its territory was shrinking, Byzantium undertook military and administrative reforms, revised its laws, and refocused its culture, particularly its religious practices. In the early Middle Ages a distinctive "Byzantium" emerged in place of Rome.

Leo and Constantine, the Isaurians, are reminiscent of Diocletian and Constantine, or of Justinian. They energetically brought to completion military reforms that had been pursued intermittently since the late sixth century. These reforms amounted to a major administrative change. For centuries Rome had recruited, trained, and paid professional troops out of tax revenues; they even used tax revenues to settle barbarian soldiers in their midst. Leo and Constantine put the finishing touches on a new "theme" system.

Men from frontier regions were now recruited and settled on farms in military districts called *themes*. All themes, whether land-based army ones or sea-based naval ones, were under the command of a leader who was simultaneously the civil and military chief of his theme. The farmer-soldiers did not pay taxes on their farms but discharged their obligation to the state by personal service. Some standing troops were retained, mainly around the capital, but henceforth the thematic armies formed the backbone of the Roman system.

The new system was less of a drain on the state treasury than the old one. Lower tax revenues were needed, and, correspondingly, so were fewer bureaucrats to collect the money. The empire was smaller than in the past and needed a different kind of army: smaller squadrons concentrated near the threatened frontier regions in Anatolia and the Balkans rather than large armies that were expensive to maintain and cumbersome to transport over long distances.

The Isaurians undertook other reforms, too. Leo issued the *Ecloga*, the first major revision and updating of Roman law since Justinian's. Issuing a law code was a matter of pride and a clear representation of power and authority. But the *Ecloga* was "a selection of laws," an abridgment whose purpose was to provide a simplified code adapted to the empire's new circumstances.

Leo and Constantine also instituted far-reaching reforms in imperial administration, which had changed little in centuries. Roman bureaucracy had consisted of a few large departments headed by officials with immense responsibilities and power. The revised Byzantine system was characterized by a profusion of departments under officers who had little real power or sway. The emperor neutralized the bureaucrats by drawing them from all social classes, paying them well, and giving them pompous titles and lots of public recognition, all the while dividing their responsibilities, curbing their influence, and making them dependent on himself. The Byzantine government was never a breeding ground for factional squabbles as in the caliphate.

Byzantine culture came to be increasingly defined by the church. The massive Arab conquests that stripped Byzantium of so much territory also removed the ancient patriarchates of Alexandria, Jerusalem, and Antioch from effective contact with Constantinople. Often in the past the empire had been disturbed by severe theological quarrels generated by the differing views held in the several patriarchates. These disputes had been disruptive, but they had also prompted a great deal of learned religious writing. Now, deprived of this stimulus, Byzantium turned inward.

Inside the smaller Byzantine Empire, monasticism gradually assumed a more prominent place in religious life. So many members of elite families sought to become monks that the Isaurians actually tried to limit entry into the religious life. Byzantine monks tended to be deeply learned, intensely critical of the patriarchs of Constantinople— whom they regarded as worldly and political—and opposed to imperial interference in the church. In Theodore of Studion (759–826) Byzantine monasticism found its greatest reformer and legislator since Basil, four centuries earlier (see page 204).

In 726 Emperor Leo III embarked on a bold new religious policy: iconoclasm. For centuries a beautiful and inspiring religious art had been emerging that troubled the emperor. Leo, a man of simple but fervent piety, believed that the presence of religious images, called "icons," in churches and public places was offensive to God. Moreover, Leo was convinced that the military disasters suffered by the empire in recent years were attributable to divine displeasure at the violation of Moses's prohibition of "graven images." Accordingly, he and his son banned religious images. They and some of their more enthusiastic followers even destroyed a few of them. Hence they were called "iconoclasts," which means "image breakers." Iconoclasm was officially proclaimed by a church council in 754, repudiated by another council in 787, proclaimed again in 815, and then definitively rejected in 843.

Although it might seem like an odd and local dispute, iconoclasm had several important consequences in its own time and reveals important aspects of emerging Byzantium to the modern observer. Iconoclasm was categorically rejected as heretical by the popes. This difference drove a sharp wedge between Eastern and Western Catholics. The debates over iconoclasm finally sharpened Byzantine thinking on the role and function of art in religious life. To this day the icon plays a more prominent role in religious devotion in the East than in the West. Moreover, the battle over iconoclasm evoked some of the most sophisticated Greek religious writing since Late Antiquity. Writers such as John of Damascus (675–749) and Theodore of Studion wrote learned treatises in defense of religious art that drew on Greek patristic writing (see page 220) and on ancient Greek philosophy in ways that sharply differentiated Byzantine and Western religious thought.

As the Byzantines turned more and more deeply into their own traditions, they exposed other differences between themselves and the West. Some of these were important, such as the dispute over the so-called *filioque*. In the East people taught and believed that the Holy Spirit proceeded "from the Father." In the West people said that the Holy Spirit proceeded "from the Father *and from the Son*" (*filioque* in Latin). Greek monks shaved the front of their heads, whereas Western monks shaved a circlet on the top. The Greek church used leavened (with yeast) bread in worship, whereas the Western church used unleavened bread. Taken together these differences amounted to a sharpening of the divide between Christian groups whom we may now label "Orthodox" and "Roman Catholic." Neither group wished to see a division in the Christian world, but physical separation and independent cultural evolution were producing two different traditions based, paradoxically, on a single late antique Christianity.

With its new geographic shape and its Orthodox faith, Byzantium was at once something old and something new. In official Byzantine ideology, the Roman Empire had always been one and inseparable. It is interesting to ask how familiar Augustus Caesar would have found the empire of Constantine V. With its indebtedness to classical and Christian traditions, there can be no question that Byzantium was a part of the West. But in its comparatively modest size, its constantly threatened frontiers, and its Orthodox traditions, Byzantium was going to have a somewhat different future than the portions of the West situated inside Rome's former western provinces. It is worth noting, too, that as was the case in the Muslim world, the seventh and ninth centuries were acutely tumultuous in Byzantium, whereas the eighth was marked by consolidation and achievement.

CATHOLIC KINGDOMS IN THE WEST

In the Latin West the seventh century also was marked by challenges, the eighth century by innovation and accomplishment, and the ninth century by new threats and in some areas near collapse. The social and political heritages of both the Germanic and the Roman past interacted with Christianity and the church to produce the third early medieval civilization: Catholic Europe. Crucial to these developments were the evangelization of the countryside, the growth of an ecclesiastical hierarchy, the shift of papal interests away from the Mediterranean world toward western Europe, and the evolving relationship between royal governments and the Catholic Church.

The Struggles of Visigothic Spain	After their defeat at Clovis's hand in 507, the Visigoths were never able to re-establish dynastic continuity. As a result, Spain witnessed rebellions and usurpations more frequently than

any other area in the West. In addition to internal struggles, Spain faced external threats from the Franks, the Ostrogoths in Italy, the Byzantines, and finally the Muslims.

The accomplishments of the Visigothic king Leovigild (r. 568–586) seem remarkable given the state of Spain on his accession. He nearly unified the country, and he established a capital (Toledo) and a seat of government—which the Visigoths had been lacking since they lost Toulouse in 507. Leovigild was a good general and a charismatic leader who understood the value of enhancing the royal office. He wore royal vestments, sat on a throne, and issued coins with his own image and name. Leovigild's greatest problem was the Arianism of the Visigothic minority in the midst of the Catholic population. An Arian himself, he tried hard to convert Catholics to Arianism but failed. In 589, under King Reccared (r. 586–601), the Visigoths officially embraced Roman Catholicism.

The conversion of the Visigoths permitted close cooperation between the church and the monarchy and placed the resources of the church at the disposal of the king as he attempted to unite and govern the country. The career of Archbishop Isidore of Seville (560–636) is a prime indicator of those resources. He came from an old Hispano-Roman family, received a fine education, and wrote histories, biblical commentaries, and a learned encyclopedia. By the mid-seventh century, economic prosperity, a high degree of assimilation between Goths and Hispano-Romans, and a brilliant culture marked the high point of Visigothic Spain. The succession problem, however, was never overcome, and a stable central government was beyond reach.

In 711 Muslims from North Africa invaded Spain. Within five years Berbers (native North Africans and recent converts to Islam who were led by Arabs) completed the conquest of much of the Iberian Peninsula, except for the northwest. In 716 the caliph at Damascus introduced an emir who ruled from Cordoba. The emirate of Cordoba struggled to make good its authority over all of Spain but failed to do so. Christians in the rugged mountains of the northwest—the region called Asturias—could not be dislodged, and the Muslims' part of Spain—known as al-Andalus—was plagued by the same divisions as the Islamic East: Arab factions against other Arab factions, Arabs against non-Arab Muslims, and Muslims against non-Muslims. Secure in mountainous Asturias, Christian kings built a capital at Oviedo and, in the ninth century, launched attacks against al-Andalus. For six hundred years this conflict between Christians and Muslims was the chief dynamic of Spanish history.

Italy and the Papal States	In 600 the Italian political scene was crowded. Several Germanic groups, several Byzantine outposts, and the popes were all contending for power. By the late eighth century the Franks

dominated northern Italy, the popes had created a state in the center, and the Byzantines clung to Naples and Sicily, much of which they lost to Muslims in the ninth century.

As we have seen, the Lombards conquered most of the Italian peninsula after the Gothic Wars. Neither numerous nor united, the Lombards were also Arians. Although the Lombard kings converted to Catholicism by 680, formed a strong government, and issued the most sophisticated Germanic law code, they always faced a dilemma. The kings had not systematically organized the conquest of Italy. From their capital at Pavia they dominated the Po Valley, but other Lombards settled elsewhere and created independent duchies. Kings were weakened because they did not control the duchies and because between Lombardy and the duchies lay Rome and Ravenna, which were nominally Byzantine.

The strongest Lombard king of the eighth century, Aistulf (r. 749–757), decided to risk the consequences of attacking Ravenna and Rome. He conquered the former but caused the pope to turn to Pippin III, the king of the Franks, for aid and protection. Pippin came to Italy, defeated Aistulf, and forced him to give to the pope all the lands he had taken from Rome and Ravenna. A few years later Aistulf's successor reopened hostilities in central Italy. In 774 Charlemagne, Pippin's son and successor, defeated the Lombards, deposed their king, and took the Lombard crown for himself.

The Franks guaranteed to the popes undisputed possession of a substantial territory in central Italy. This first Papal State was the culmination of three processes. First, as Roman imperial power declined in Late Antiquity, bishops often became the effective leaders of their towns. This position brought them power and prestige but also burdens. The popes found themselves responsible for Rome's food and water supply, the upkeep of its public buildings, and local charitable services. To pay for these functions, the popes began to organize the efficient bureaucratic administration of the patrimonies, the lands of the Roman church.

Second, the popes took the lead in protecting many people in central Italy, whether they lived on the patrimonies or not, thus preserving their purses from Byzantine taxes and their souls from heresy. This effort, too, forged bonds between the popes and the Italians.

Third, eighth-century Rome spawned a justification for papal temporal rule. According to the *Donation of Constantine,* a document written in Rome (probably in the 760s), when Constantine departed Rome for the East in the 320s, he allegedly gave to the pope the authority to rule Rome and the whole West. In reality, no pope ever made such grandiose claims, and no concrete claims were ever based on the *Donation.* But the existence of the document signals a crucial progression from protection to direct rule. From the beginning, however, the Papal States were vulnerable and required a protector.

The Fate of the British Isles

Britain was less thoroughly Romanized, more quickly abandoned by the Romans, and more deeply influenced by Germanic peoples than any other locality in the West. Around 600 the small Anglo-Saxon kingdoms created in the sixth century took the first steps toward converting to Christianity, transforming Britain into England, and joining England inseparably to the European world. And another history was unfolding in the British Isles, that of the Celtic peoples in the north and west of Britain itself and in Ireland.

Lindisfarne Gospels: Opening Page of the Gospel According to Matthew   *In the last years of the seventh century in the north of England, scribes and painters produced this exquisite book, which combines the artistic styles of the Mediterranean and Celtic worlds.*
(British Library)

The Celts—Britain's inhabitants before the Romans invaded in the first century—were related to peoples who lived in a broad band from Anatolia to Ireland and Spain. The Anglo-Saxons confined the British Celts to the western regions of Cornwall and Wales and to the northern area of Scotland. Ireland, seemingly beyond reach, had almost no Roman or Anglo-Saxon imprint.

The period between 600 and 900 saw only the faint beginnings of consolidation in the Celtic realms, where the development of the Catholic Church preceded large-scale political organization. Each Celtic region produced an elaborate mythology connected with heroic missionaries who supposedly brought the Christian faith in Late Antiquity. The best-known stories swirl around Ireland's Saint Patrick (390?–461?). The son of a Roman official in the north of Britain, Patrick was captured by pirates, enslaved in Ireland, freed, and eventually made a priest; he then returned to Ireland as a missionary. From his base at Armagh, Ireland's first bishopric, Patrick and his successors spread Christianity, and a vigorous monasticism, throughout the island. Historical, too, is the Irish aristocrat Columba (521–597), who, after his family lost a great battle, migrated in 563 to the isle of Iona off the coast of Scotland. From his monastery on Iona, Columba and his successors began the evangelization of the native Picts in Scotland.

Among the most successful Anglo-Saxon kingdoms were Wessex, Northumbria, and Mercia. Each had a reasonably large population and territory and opportunities for expansion. Wessex, for example, spread south and west into Devon, Cornwall, and Wales; Northumbria, which stretched along the North Sea coast, spread west to the Irish Sea and north into lowland Scotland. These kingdoms had ambitious rulers whose wars provided booty, land, and glory for old followers and new recruits. English kings quickly adopted symbolic aspects of rule to legitimize their authority and enhance their prestige. Archaeologists have found fine scepters and coins bearing early kings' names. The kings of Northumbria presided in a magnificent wooden hall, and their movements were preceded and announced by banners.

Relations with the church were important also. Two issues proved crucial: the conversion to Christianity and the development of an ecclesiastical hierarchy. In 597 Pope Gregory I sent a small band of missionaries under a Roman monk named Augustine (d. 604) to King Aethelbert of Kent, whose Christian wife, Bertha, had prepared the ground for the newcomers. From their base of operations at Canterbury in southeastern England, Augustine and his successors had limited success spreading Christianity, but a new field of influence was opened to them when Aethelbert's daughter married a king of Northumbria and took missionaries to her new home. Monks from Iona, as noted, were already introducing Christianity into central and lowland Scotland. When later Northumbrian kings turned to Iona for missionaries and bishops, Roman and Celtic Christianity came face-to-face in Northumbria.

The Christianity brought from Ireland did not differ in fundamental ways from the Roman Christianity imported at Canterbury. Indeed, the Irish were Roman Catholics. But Ireland had been isolated from the centers of Christian life since Late Antiquity, and its church had developed a number of distinctive local customs. For example, the two traditions used different calendars and thus celebrated Easter—the commemoration of the resurrection of Jesus Christ and the central celebration of the Christian year—on different days. In 664 a Northumbrian king called a church council at the monastery of Whitby, whose abbess was the former royal princess Hilda (614–680), a champion of Celtic customs. At Whitby, Roman and Irish representatives debated their positions. The king, choosing the universal over the particular, decided for Rome.

In 668 the pope sent to England a new archbishop of Canterbury, Theodore (r. 668–690). He was a Syrian monk who had traveled widely in the East, lived for a time in Rome, gained great experience in church administration, and acquired a reputation for both learning and discretion. The church in England was in an administrative shambles. Working tirelessly, Theodore built up a typical Roman ecclesiastical structure, introduced authoritative Roman canon law for the church, and promoted Christian education. Theodore laid the foundations for a unified English church that contributed to the eventual political unification of England.

Ecclesiastical peace led to the flourishing of monastic life. Monasteries played two important roles in this period. First, they led the way in bringing Christianity to ordinary people. Despite early gains among kings and nobles, Christianity had barely begun to penetrate the countryside. Second, monks maintained international connections, ranging from Ireland to Rome, that attached England to the major intellectual currents of the day and enabled the English to make their own contributions.

After Theodore's school at Canterbury, the most important early center of learning was in Northumbria. There English, Irish, Frankish, and Roman currents flowed together in the monasteries of Lindisfarne, Wearmouth, and Jarrow and in the cathedral school of York. British schools produced some of the most beautiful illuminated manuscripts—books whose texts are adorned with gorgeous paintings—of the early Middle Ages.

The greatest product of this intellectual tradition was Bede (673–735). When he was 7, his parents placed him in the monastery at Wearmouth. He soon transferred to neighboring Jarrow and spent the rest of his life there. Bede was a teacher of genius, an erudite scholar, and a superb Latin stylist. His *Ecclesiastical History of the English People,* the most important source for English history from the fifth century to the eighth, did much to identify the Anglo-Saxons as a single English people. His biblical commentaries remained influential all over Europe for centuries. His studies of temporal reckoning popularized the use of A.D. dating, which replaced a bewildering array of local systems.

The career of King Offa of Mercia (r. 757–796) shows the trends in early Britain. His ancestors were pagans, but he was a patron of the church, convener of councils, and recipient of papal envoys. He dominated all of Britain and was the first to call himself "King of the English." He issued a law code, reformed Mercia's institutions, and signed England's first international trade agreement—with Charlemagne.

After Offa's death, Viking raiders (see page 253) destroyed whatever unity had been achieved. For two generations local rulers struggled just to survive, and in 865 a Viking army launched a conquest of the whole country. In 871 Alfred the Great (r. 871–899) ascended the throne of Wessex, won a series of military victories, rallied the English, and began the slow reconquest of northern and eastern England from the Vikings. Alfred promoted intellectual recovery, church reform, and political stability. After half a century of chaos, Alfred revived the centralizing and unifying work of his eighth-century predecessors and laid the foundations for the English state of the tenth and eleventh centuries.

Britain's integration into the wider world is revealed by a seventh-century ship burial unearthed near Sutton Hoo (in East Anglia) in 1939. The ship, either a grave for or a memorial to an unknown king, had been hauled up onto the land, filled with treasures, and buried. The array of goods found at Sutton Hoo is astonishing. The hull contained Byzantine silver, represented by spoons and a large dish; Frankish gold, in the form of dozens of coins, jewelry, and personal adornments from many places; and pots, beakers, and other domestic items of varied provenance. The artistic decorations on these items demonstrate influences ranging from the Mediterranean to the Rhineland, Scandinavia, and Ireland.

THE CAROLINGIAN EMPIRE

Clovis and the Franks created the most effective of the early Germanic kingdoms. During the seventh century that kingdom, too, experienced difficulties but did not disappear. Just as Roman aristocrats had borne the ancient heritage into the Middle Ages, so now a Frankish family, called "Carolingian" from the name of its greatest member, Charlemagne, assembled the talent and resources of the Frankish realm in a new way. Charlemagne reformed his government and church, patronized learning, and resurrected the western empire. Early medieval civilization reached its culmination in the work of Charlemagne and his dynasty.

The Rise of the Carolingian Family, 600–768

When Clovis died in 511, he divided his realm among his sons, and thereafter several kingdoms coexisted. The Merovingian royal families feuded constantly, sought to expand at one another's expense, and drew local aristocracies into their battles. Trade and intellectual life declined, and some regions that had been conquered in the sixth century slipped away.

Nevertheless, the *idea* of a single kingdom of the Franks persisted. Kings and aristocrats in the small kingdoms competed for leadership of the realm as a whole. The flourishing culture of late antique Gaul was largely gone, but a creative Christian monastic culture was growing up in all parts of the Frankish kingdom. Monks began accomplishing the difficult task of converting the countryside to Christianity. The seventh century, in other words, was a time when the late antique regime was slowly changing into the medieval regime.

Central to this development was the rise to prominence of the Carolingians. The family appeared in history just after 600 and thereafter monopolized the office of mayor of the palace (sort of a prime minister) to the king in Austrasia (the easternmost kingdom). The Carolingians were the boldest and wealthiest family in Austrasia, perhaps in the Frankish world. Within two generations they unified the Frankish realm and increased their own power.

The Carolingians used several methods to accomplish their ends. They formed alliances with powerful noble families in many regions. They waged war against the enemies of the Franks to restore the territorial integrity of the kingdom. Charles Martel (d. 741), Charlemagne's grandfather, led the Frankish forces that put an end to Arab raiding in Gaul, defeating a large force near Poitiers in 733. With booty from their wars, tribute from conquered peoples, spoils taken from recalcitrant opponents, and even lands seized from the church, the Carolingians attracted and rewarded more and more followers until no one was a match for them. The Carolingians also allied themselves very early with leading churchmen, both episcopal and monastic. They aided missionaries in the work of converting central Germany, thereby expanding Frankish influence in that area.

For years the Carolingians were content with the office of mayor of the palace. Then in 749 Pippin III (son of Charles Martel) decided to send envoys to the pope to ask whether it was right that the person who had all the power in the land of the Franks was not the king. The pope responded that this situation ran counter to the divine plan. Accordingly, in 751 the last Merovingian king was deposed, and Pippin was elected in his place (r. 751–768). Pippin had prepared his usurpation very carefully with his Frankish supporters, but he appealed to the pope to make it appear that he had become king with divine approval and not by crude seizure. Hard-pressed by the Lombards in Italy, the pope probably gave Pippin the answer he wanted primarily to enlist him as an ally. Three years later the pope visited the Frankish kingdom, where he crowned and anointed Pippin and his sons, including Charlemagne. (The practice of anointing the head of a ruler with holy oil, which renders the recipient sacred, dates back to the kings of Israel. The head and hands of Catholic bishops also were anointed. The anointing of rulers and churchmen persisted throughout the Middle Ages and into the modern world.) The pope also forbade the Franks ever to choose a king from a family other than the Carolingians and received from their new favorites a promise of aid in Italy.

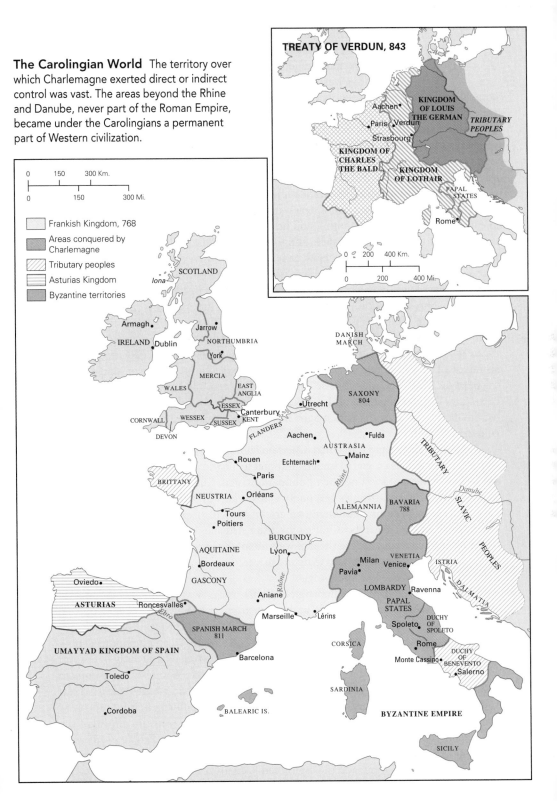

The Carolingian World The territory over which Charlemagne exerted direct or indirect control was vast. The areas beyond the Rhine and Danube, never part of the Roman Empire, became under the Carolingians a permanent part of Western civilization.

TREATY OF VERDUN, 843

KINGDOM OF LOUIS THE GERMAN

TRIBUTARY PEOPLES

Aachen
Paris Verdun
Strasbourg

KINGDOM OF CHARLES THE BALD

KINGDOM OF LOTHAIR

PAPAL STATES

Rome

0   200   400 Km.
0   200   400 Mi.

0   150   300 Km.
0   150   300 Mi.

Frankish Kingdom, 768
Areas conquered by Charlemagne
Tributary peoples
Asturias Kingdom
Byzantine territories

SCOTLAND
Iona

Armagh
IRELAND Dublin
Jarrow
NORTHUMBRIA
York
WALES MERCIA
EAST ANGLIA
CORNWALL WESSEX ESSEX
Canterbury
KENT
DEVON SUSSEX

DANISH MARCH

Utrecht

SAXONY 804

FLANDERS
Aachen
Fulda
AUSTRASIA
Mainz
Rouen Echternach
BRITTANY
Paris
NEUSTRIA Orléans
Rhine
Tours
Poitiers
ALEMANNIA
BAVARIA 788

TRIBUTARY

Danube

SLAVIC

BURGUNDY
Lyon
AQUITAINE
Bordeaux
GASCONY
Aniane
Rhône
Marseille Lérins

VENETIA
Milan Venice
Pavia
LOMBARDY Ravenna

PEOPLES

ISTRIA

DALMATIA

Oviedo
ASTURIAS Roncesvalles
Ebro
SPANISH MARCH 811

UMAYYAD KINGDOM OF SPAIN
Barcelona
Toledo
Cordoba

BALEARIC IS.

CORSICA

SARDINIA

PAPAL STATES
Spoleto DUCHY OF SPOLETO
Rome
Monte Cassino DUCHY OF BENEVENTO
Salerno

BYZANTINE EMPIRE

SICILY

The Empire of Charlemagne, 768–814

Charlemagne (Carolus Magnus, "Charles the Great" in Latin) was a huge man, and his stature has grown in European history and legend. Like all great leaders, Charlemagne (r. 768–814) was complex. He spoke and read Frankish, Latin, and some Greek but never learned to write. He promoted Christian morality but perpetrated unspeakable brutalities on his enemies and enjoyed several concubines. Many battles were fought in his name, but he rarely accompanied his armies and fought no campaigns that are remembered for strategic brilliance. Determination and organization were the hallmarks of his forty-six-year reign.

It took until the mid-780s for Charlemagne to assess and understand his world. His first major achievement was the articulation of a new ruling ideology in the Latin West. In capitularies—royal executive orders—of 789, Charlemagne required all males to swear an oath of allegiance to him, and he compared himself to a biblical king in his responsibility to admonish, to teach, and to set an example for his people. He referred to the people of his realm as a "New Israel," a new chosen people. Interestingly, this chosen people was not exclusively Frankish. No distinctions were to be made among Franks or Bavarians or Saxons. Everyone was to be equal in allegiance to the king and in membership in a sort of Augustinian City of God.

Einhard (ca. 770–840), Charlemagne's friend and biographer, reports that Augustine's *City of God* (see page 222) was the king's favorite book. The king understood it to mean that two opposing domains contended for power on earth: a City of God consisting of all right-thinking Christians—the "New Israel"—and a City of Man consisting of pagans, heretics, and infidels. This idea is similar to the Islamic umma (see pages 228–229). To Charlemagne and his advisers, it was obvious that as God was the sole legitimate ruler in heaven, Charlemagne was the sole legitimate and divinely appointed ruler on earth.

Modern readers may think that Charlemagne had crossed a boundary between church and state. It is crucial to understand that to Charlemagne, as to his Muslim and Byzantine contemporaries, no such boundary existed. Church (or religion) and state were complementary attributes of a polity whose end was personal salvation, not military security or personal fulfillment. Charlemagne's ideological legacy was twofold. On the one hand, it created possibilities for bitter struggles later in the Middle Ages between secular rulers and ecclesiastical powers about the leadership of Christian society. On the other hand, it made it hard to define the state and its essential purposes in other than religious terms.

The most disputed event in the reign of Charlemagne was his imperial coronation in Rome on Christmas in 800. It is important to separate how this event happened from what it meant to the participants. In April 799 some disgruntled papal bureaucrats and their supporters attacked Pope Leo III (r. 795–816) in an attempt to depose him. Leo was saved by an ally of Charlemagne and then traveled all the way to Saxony, where the king was camped with his army. Charlemagne agreed to restore the pope to Rome and, as his ally and protector, to investigate those who had attacked him. No real offenses could be proved against the pope, who appeared publicly in Rome to swear that he had done nothing wrong. Everything was handled to avoid any hint that the pope had been put on trial. When Charlemagne went to Saint Peter's Basilica on Christmas Day, he prayed before the main altar. As he rose from prayer, Pope Leo placed a crown on his head, and the assembled Romans acclaimed him as emperor.

Debate over this coronation arises from a remark of Einhard, who said that if Charlemagne had known what was going to happen, he would not have gone to church that day, even though it was Christmas. Einhard's point was not that Charlemagne did not wish to be emperor. For at least fifteen years, prominent people at the Carolingian court had been addressing Charlemagne in imperial terms in letters, treatises, and poems. Moreover, some were saying that because of Irene's usurpation (see page 235), the imperial throne was vacant—implying that a woman could not truly rule. What Einhard did mean was that Charlemagne saw himself as a Frankish and Christian emperor, not as a *Roman* emperor. The imperial office dignified his position as leader of the Frankish "Israel." Charlemagne did not wish to be beholden to the pope or to the Romans.

Charlemagne's policies did not change after his coronation. He continued his program of legal and ecclesiastical reform and put the finishing touches on some military and diplomatic campaigns. In 806 he divided his empire among his three legitimate sons. Two of them died, so in 813 he made Louis his sole heir and successor. Charlemagne outlived most of the friends and companions of his youth and middle age. He outlived four wives and many of his children. Old and alone, ill and lame, he died in early 814.

Charlemagne's legacy was great. He brought together the lands that would become France, Germany, the Low Countries, and northern Italy and endowed them with a common ideology, government, and culture. He provided a model that Europeans would look back to for centuries as a kind of golden age. His vast supra-regional and supra-ethnic entity, gradually called "Christendom," drew deeply on the universalizing ideals of its Roman, Christian, and Jewish antecedents but was, nevertheless, original. With its Roman, Germanic, and Christian foundations, the Carolingian Empire represented the final stage in the evolution of the Roman Empire in the West.

Carolingian Government

Charlemagne accomplished much through the sheer force of his personality and his boundless energy. But he also reformed and created institutional structures. These helped him to carry out his tasks, guaranteed a measure of permanence to his reforms, and created government patterns that lasted in many parts of Europe until the twelfth century.

The king (or emperor—the offices differed little in practical importance) was the heart of the system. In theory, the king ruled by God's grace and did not have to answer for his conduct to any person. In reality, the king necessarily sought consensus through a variety of means. The king controlled vast lands, which gave him great wealth of his own and also the means to reward loyal followers. By controlling appointments to key positions, the king required men to come to him for power, wealth, and prestige.

The Eastern contemporaries of the Carolingians relied on large numbers of carefully trained, paid civil servants. In contrast, the Carolingians employed a limited number of men who were tied to them by bonds of familial and personal allegiance. The Carolingian court included several ceremonial officers and a domestic staff, all desirable positions. For example, the constable, an officer in charge of transporting the royal entourage, was usually a great aristocrat; the real work of the office was carried out by underlings. The treasurer was the keeper of the king's bedchamber, where the royal treasure chest was kept. Several chaplains, whose primary duty was to see to the spiritual needs of the court, kept official records. The queen controlled the domestic staff and the stewards who managed the royal estates.

Local government was mainly entrusted to counts. About six hundred counts, and several times that number of minor officials, managed the empire. As in Merovingian times, the counts were administrative, judicial, and military officials. Most came from prominent families, and the office increased the wealth and importance of its holders. Counts had to promulgate and enforce royal orders and preside in regular sessions of local courts. They got one-third of the fines, so the zealous pursuit of justice was in their interest.

The royal court and the localities were linked in several ways. Under Charlemagne and his successors it became usual for all major officers, whether secular (counts and their subordinates) or ecclesiastical (bishops and abbots), to be *vassals* of the king. Vassals solemnly pledged loyalty and service to the king. Vassalage drew on both Roman and Germanic customs. Patron-client ties had always been socially and politically important among the Romans, and the allegiance of warriors to a chief was a key Germanic bond. But by connecting personal loyalty with public office, Charlemagne created something essentially new. Only a few thousand men, a tiny fraction of the total population, were vassals at any time. They constituted the political and social elite.

Another connection between the king and his local agents was the assembly that met in various places once or twice a year. In theory, all free men could attend these gatherings, which sometimes had separate secular and ecclesiastical sessions, to advise the king on matters of great importance, such as war and peace or legal reforms. In practice, only the vassals had the means or the interest to ensure their presence. Most of the great Carolingian reforms were formulated in these assemblies by cooperation between the king and his most important subjects. The assemblies served to defuse dissension, but the king also brought his power to bear locally by traveling widely. The monarchy possessed estates all over the heartlands of the kingdom, and the royal entourage often moved from one place to another. Monasteries and cathedrals provided hospitality to the king. As the royal party traveled about the realm, they were able to check on local conditions and to compel local officials to comply with royal wishes.

In 788 Charlemagne began to build a palace at Aachen, and in the last twenty years of his life he usually resided there. The later Carolingian rulers all tended to have fixed

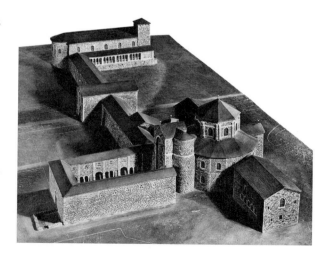

Model of Charlemagne's Palace at Aachen *In the foreground is the octagonal chapel and throne room of Charlemagne's palace at Aachen. It is joined by galleries to the residential quarters in the background. Construction was begun in 788. The models for these buildings were found in Rome, Trier, and Ravenna.* (Römisch-Germanisches Zentralmuseum)

residences, as did the Byzantines and the Abbasids. In adopting fixed residences and elaborate court rituals, the Carolingians may have been returning to Roman precedents or copying their contemporaries to appear as sophisticated as they. Elegant courts and intricate rituals project an aura of grandeur that enhances people's respect for their rulers. It is no accident that a key innovation of Charlemagne's reign coincided with his permanent residence in Aachen. In the late 780s he began to send out pairs of roving inspectors, or *missi dominici*, envoys of the lord king. Their function was to see that royal orders were being observed, that counts were dispensing justice honestly, and that persons of power were not oppressing the powerless.

The Carolingian Renaissance   Charlemagne's reforms culminated in a revival of learning that scholars have named the "Carolingian Renaissance" (*renaissance* is French for "rebirth"). Charlemagne's fundamental ideas are revealed by the constant use in contemporary sources of words such as *rebirth, renewal, reform,* and *restoration.* Charlemagne, his advisers, and his successors looked back for inspiration to Christian and papal Rome, to Saint Peter and Constantine, and to the Church Fathers. To them the rebirth of Western society as a "New Israel" was equivalent to the theological rebirth of an individual in baptism. The Carolingians were the driving force behind intellectual growth in their era, and in all areas they subordinated learning to their ideological program.

To accomplish his objectives, Charlemagne required every cathedral and monastery to establish a school. To set up and run those schools, he summoned to his court many of the most able and influential intellectual figures of the day, among them Franks, such as his biographer Einhard, grammar teachers from Italy, and Visigothic theologians from the Spanish border. His most famous recruit was the Anglo-Saxon Alcuin (735–804), the most learned man of his day and the heir of Bede and of the brilliant culture of Northumbria.

Much of the work of Alcuin and his associates was devoted to producing textbooks and to teaching elementary knowledge. Charlemagne was convinced that people needed to be taught the basic truths of Christianity if he were to accomplish his task of leading them to salvation. A massive effort was thus undertaken to copy manuscripts of the Bible and the writings of the Latin Church Fathers. These books, the essential resources for the whole program, needed to be disseminated as widely as possible. The process of copying was facilitated by a new script, Caroline minuscule.

It is significant that Charlemagne could attract Alcuin from York, the most renowned school in the West, to head his palace school, just then forming. Alcuin recognized that Charlemagne could place more resources at his disposal than anyone else and had the will to do so. Alcuin also saw the long-term benefits that would come from his work. Alcuin's pupils spread out in the next generation to create a network of schools that went right on multiplying across the ninth century. That is a powerful legacy. And Alcuin did more than just teach. He wrote learned works and poetry and was for twenty years Charlemagne's most trusted adviser.

With his plan, personnel, and schools in place, Charlemagne took many concrete steps. He secured from Rome a copy of the authoritative canon law of the church. In 789, after some years of study by his court scholars, this law was issued for his whole kingdom. In about 786 Charlemagne got from the pope a *sacramentary,* a service book

Charlemagne's Efforts at Educational Reform

Charlemagne equated the rebirth of Western society with spiritual renewal, so he addressed his major reforms to the church and its leaders. In about 789 Charlemagne sent letters like this one to every bishop and ordered them to transmit the letters to the churches and monasteries in their territories, for it was in those institutions that schools were to be found. Christianity is a faith of books, and of the Bible above all. Charlemagne was trying to reform the church and Christian practices, and to achieve his goals he saw a need to attend to a basic program of education. Proper schooling, he believed, would produce proper behavior.

Be it known to your devotion, which is most pleasing to God, that we, together with our faithful men, have considered it to be useful that the bishoprics and monasteries entrusted by the favor of Christ to our control . . . ought to be zealous in the cultivation of learning and in teaching those who by the gift of God are able to learn, according to the capacity of each individual. Thus just as the observance of the rule [that is, the guidelines observed in a monastery] imparts grace and order to their conduct, so also zeal in teaching and learning may do the same for their sentences, so that those who desire to please God by living rightly should not neglect to please him also by speaking correctly. For although conduct may be better than knowledge, nevertheless knowledge precedes conduct. In the past few years letters were often sent to us from several monasteries in which it was stated that the brethren who dwelt there offered on our behalf sacred and pious prayers. We have noticed in most of these letters both correct thoughts and uncouth expressions, because what pious devotion dictated faithfully to the mind, the tongue, uneducated on account of the neglect of study, was not able to express without error. So we began to fear that perhaps, as the skill in writing was less, so also the wisdom for understanding the Holy Scriptures might be much less than it ought to be. For we all know well that, although errors of speech are dangerous, far more dangerous are errors in understanding. Therefore, we exhort you not only to avoid neglecting the study of literature, but also with most humble mind, pleasing to God, to study earnestly so that you may be able more easily and correctly to penetrate the mysteries of the divine Scriptures. Since, moreover, images, tropes, and similar figures are to be found in the sacred pages, no one doubts that each one will in reading them understand the spiritual sense more quickly if previously he shall have been fully instructed in letters. Such men are to be chosen for this work who have both the will and ability to learn and the desire to instruct others. For we desire you to be devout in mind, learned in discourse, chaste in conduct, and eloquent in speech.

Source: Adapted from Dana C. Munro, *Translations and Reprints from the Original Sources of European History,* vol. 6 (Philadelphia, 1899), pp. 12–16.

for worship in cathedral churches, and, again after a period of examination, this was imposed throughout the kingdom. Charlemagne sought an authoritative copy of the *Rule of St. Benedict,* and after study and commentary, this Rule was imposed on all monasteries in the kingdom.

Secular reforms mirrored religious ones. Orders regularized the management of all royal estates. Charlemagne attempted to update local law codes and to make them as uniform as possible. Not since Rome had governments possessed either the interest in or the means to promote such centralization. It is striking that in the eighth century the caliphate, the Byzantine Empire, and the Carolingian Empire were engaged in similar centralizing activities.

Versatility was a hallmark of Carolingian learning. Various scholars excelled at poetry, history, and biography. Biblical studies and theology attracted a lot of attention. One figure who personifies the Carolingian Renaissance is the Visigoth Theodulf (ca. 760–821). He came to court in about 790 and served thereafter as a missus, royal adviser, abbot of several monasteries, and bishop of Orléans. He issued important legislation for his diocese. He was the foremost Old Testament expert of his day and the only one who knew Hebrew. He wrote the official Frankish response to Byzantine iconoclasm. He also composed theological treatises, many letters, and dozens of poems. At Germigny he designed a church that is a masterpiece of early Carolingian architecture.

Carolingian art is a crowning glory of the age. The manuscripts decorated under Charlemagne's patronage and then, for three generations, under the patronage of his descendants and of prominent churchmen show versatility, respect but not awe for the past, and innovation. Several distinct currents inspired and informed Carolingian art. Most prominent were the animal and geometric decorative motifs of Irish and Anglo-Saxon art; the elegance, formality, and sense of composition of classical art; basic elements of style from Byzantine painting; actual scenes from papal Rome; and the mysteries of Christian theology. Every element was borrowed, but the finished product was new.

Architecture shows the same trends. Charlemagne's palace complex at Aachen has parallels in imperial Constantinople, papal Rome, and Ostrogothic Ravenna. Workers and building materials were fetched from all over the empire. From 768 to 855, 27 cathedrals were built along with 417 monasteries and 100 royal residences. For basic buildings the Carolingians adapted the basilica. The classical basilica was a horizontal building, but the Carolingians, by altering the western end and façade (the "westworks"), added the dimension of verticality. In Romanesque and Gothic architecture this innovation would have a long career (see pages 326–328).

The Fragmentation of Charlemagne's Empire, 814–887 The Carolingian Empire did not outlive the ninth century. Rome's empire lasted much longer, as did Byzantium's and Islam's. All of these realms were fatally weakened by similar problems, but those problems arose more quickly and acutely in the Carolingian world than elsewhere. By the end of the ninth century small political entities had replaced the unified Carolingian Empire.

Size and ethnic complexity contributed to the disintegration of the empire. The empire included many small regions—Saxony, Bavaria, Brittany, and Lombardy, for example—that had their own resident elites, linguistic traditions, and distinctive cultures, which had existed before the Carolingians came on the scene and persist to this day. The Merovingian and Carolingian periods were basically a unifying intrusion into a history characterized by regional diversity. The Carolingians made heroic efforts to build a common culture and to forge bonds of unity, but the obstacles were insuperable.

Another key issue in the breakup of the Carolingian Empire was political and dynastic. The Carolingians regularly tried to create subkingdoms for all their legitimate sons while preserving the imperial title for one of them. This was a creative attempt to concede limited autonomy to particular regions by means of local kingships—for instance, in Bavaria, Italy, and Aquitaine—while preserving the "Augustinian" unity of the empire as a whole. Unfortunately, younger sons rarely yielded to their older brothers, and the bonds of loyalty among cousins, nephews, and grandchildren grew weak. Frequent divisions of the empire, or of segments of it, placed local nobilities in the difficult position of changing their allegiance frequently and of jeopardizing their offices and landholdings.

In the Treaty of Verdun in 843 the three grandsons of Charlemagne—Charles the Bald, Louis the German, and Lothair—divided the empire into three realms: the West Frankish, the East Frankish, and the Middle Kingdoms. After fierce battles among the brothers, each appointed forty members to a study commission that traversed the empire to identify royal properties, fortifications, monasteries, and cathedrals so that an equitable division of these valuable resources could be made. Each brother needed adequate resources to solidify his rule and to attract or hold followers. The lines drawn on the map at Verdun did not last even for a generation.

Slowly large West Frankish and East Frankish Kingdoms emerged, swallowing the Middle Kingdom, and created a framework for the future France and Germany. But they had to compete with many smaller entities. Some of these—in Italy, the Rhineland, and southern France—were old and distinctive regions that recaptured their former independence. Others were essentially new creations, born in the absence of firm Carolingian control. Newcomers also appeared on the scene, most prominently Scandinavian and Slavic principalities.

Before the ninth century, Scandinavia had known only small-scale political units under local chieftains and their trusted followers. Economic and political pressure from the Carolingians gradually began to push both Denmark and Norway in the direction of greater political consolidation. A single Danish monarchy has a continuous history from the late ninth century, and Norway's monarchy dates from the early tenth.

To the east of the Carolingian Empire lay a vast swath of Slavic lands. The Carolingians fought, allied, and traded with these peoples for decades. Charlemagne destroyed the Avar khanate in the Danube basin in campaigns between 788 and 804. By the middle of the ninth century the princes of Great Moravia dominated the region and played a complicated diplomatic game between the East Frankish rulers and the Byzantine emperors. To the east of the Moravians, the Bulgarians profited from the Avar and then the Carolingian collapse to expand their kingdom. For two centuries the Bulgarians dominated the northern Balkans and threatened Byzantium.

The most durable consequence of this political restructuring along the eastern frontier of the Frankish world was religious. In 863, on an invitation from Moravia and in hopes of countering the Franks, the Byzantine emperor sent the missionaries Cyril (826–869) and Methodius (805–884) into eastern Europe. The emperor hoped to erect an Orthodox union of his own realm, the southern Slavs, and the newly converted Bulgarians. Likewise he was seeking a diplomatic bulwark between the Bulgarians in the East and the Franks in the West. Unfortunately for Byzantium, Cyril and Methodius agreed with the pope to introduce Roman Catholic Christianity in return for the pope's permission to use the Slavonic language in worship. Cyril and Methodius were formidable linguists who created a religious literature in "Church Slavonic" that went far toward creating a new cultural realm in central Europe.

Finally a new wave of attacks and invasions contributed decisively to the fragmentation of the Carolingian Empire. In the middle decades of the ninth century, Muslims, Vikings, and Magyars wreaked havoc on the Franks.

Based in North Africa and the islands of the western Mediterranean, Muslims attacked Italy and southern France. The Byzantines lost Sicily to raiders from North Africa in 827 and found themselves seriously challenged in southern Italy. In the 840s Muslims raided the city of Rome. These same brigands preyed on trade in the western Mediterranean and even set up camps in the Alps to rob traders passing back and forth over the mountains.

"From the fury of the Northmen, O Lord, deliver us," was a plaintive cry heard often in ninth-century Europe. Those Northmen were Vikings, mainly Danes and Norwegians, seeking booty, glory, and political opportunity. Most Viking bands were formed by leaders who had lost out in the dawning institutional consolidation of the

Oseberg Ship   *Discovered in 1880, the Oseberg ship was buried in Norway in (probably) the tenth century. The ship may have belonged to a king and contained the remains of Queen Asa. It is 70 feet long and 16 feet wide. Its crew would have been thirty to forty men.*   (© Museum of Cultural History—University of Oslo, Norway)

northern world. Some were opportunists who sought to profit from the weakness of Carolingian, Anglo-Saxon, and Irish rule. In the mid-ninth century, Vikings began settling and initiated their own state-building activities in Ireland, England, northwestern France ("Normandy"—the region of the Northmen), and Rus (early "Russia").

Magyars, relatives of the Huns and Avars who had preceded them into eastern Europe, were accomplished horsemen whose lightning raids, beginning in 889, hit Italy, Germany, and even France. East Frankish Carolingians tried to use the Magyars as mercenaries against the troublesome Moravians. In the end, the Magyars destroyed the incipient Moravian state and raided with impunity.

All of these attacks were unpredictable and caused local regions to fall back on their own resources rather than look to the central government. Commerce was disrupted everywhere. Schools, based in ecclesiastical institutions, suffered severe decline. The raids represented a thousand pinpricks, not a single deadly sword stroke. Yet their collective effect amounted to despair and disruption on a massive scale.

Even though the Carolingian Empire itself disintegrated, the idea of Europe as "Christendom," as a single political-cultural entity, persisted. The Latin Christian culture promoted by Carolingian schools and rulers set the tone for intellectual life until the twelfth century. Likewise, Carolingian governing structures were inherited and adapted by all of the successor states that emerged in the ninth and tenth centuries. In these respects the Carolingian experience paralleled the Roman, and the Islamic and Byzantine, too. A potent, centralizing regime disappeared but left a profound imprint on its heirs. For hundreds of years Western civilization would be played out inside the lands that had been Charlemagne's empire and between those lands and their Byzantine and Muslim neighbors.

EARLY MEDIEVAL ECONOMIES AND SOCIETIES

The economic and social history of the early Middle Ages provides additional evidence of the similarities among the three early medieval civilizations, while also revealing differences. Overall the world remained rural, society was hierarchical, and women were excluded from public power. Although broad political frameworks changed, the lives of most people changed rather little.

Trade and Commerce
In the simplest terms, trade is a mechanism for exchanging goods from one person or group to another. There are many such exchange mechanisms. The Roman government, for example, moved large amounts of goods from the center of the empire to the frontiers to supply its armies. Roman, Byzantine, and Islamic governments raised taxes in one place, bought goods in another, and then consumed their purchases someplace else. Tribute and plunder were also effective exchange mechanisms, as were diplomatic gifts: a caliph, for example, sent Charlemagne an elephant.

The most common exchanges were intensely local, but several major trading networks operated during the early Middle Ages. In the East, Mesopotamia was linked by rivers to the Persian Gulf, East Africa, and southern Asia; by land and sea to Byzantium; and by land and rivers to the Black Sea region, Slavic Europe, and the Baltic. Byzantines traded mainly by sea. The whole Mediterranean was open to them, and from the Black Sea they received the products of the Danube basin. The Muslim world was fundamentally a land empire that had relatively poor roads and primitive wheeled vehicles, so transport considerations were crucial: a caravan of some five hundred camels could move only one-fourth to one-half the cargo of a normal Byzantine ship.

The West had many trade routes. The Rhône-Saône river system carried goods, as did the land routes through the Alpine passes. The North and Baltic Seas were the hubs of a network that linked the British Isles, the whole of the Frankish north (by means of its rivers), the Rhineland, Slavic Europe, Byzantium, and the Muslim world. The Danube was also a major highway. The major trade networks intersected at many points. Despite religious and ideological differences, Rome's three heirs regularly traded with one another. Recent research has documented hundreds of east-west and north-south contacts across the early medieval period.

Food and other bulk goods never traveled very far because the cost was prohibitive. Most towns were supplied with foodstuffs by their immediate hinterlands, so the goods that traveled long distances were portable and valuable. Cotton and raw silk were transported to the Mediterranean, where they were made into cloth in, respectively, Egypt and Byzantium. Paper and pottery were transported around the caliphate. Asian spices and perfumes were avidly sought everywhere. The Byzantines traded in silk cloth, fine ivories, delicate products of the gold- and silversmiths' art, slaves, and naval stores. Byzantium, with its large fleet, usually controlled the Black and Mediterranean Seas. Reduced in prosperity, the empire could no longer dictate trade terms to subject peoples and competed badly with the Muslims. Trade in the West was partly in high-value luxury goods but mainly in ordinary items such as plain pottery, raw wool, wool cloth, millstones, weapons, and slaves.

Town and Countryside

To think of the ancient world is to think of cities, but to think of the medieval world is to envision forests and fields. Actually 80 to 90 percent of people in antiquity lived in rural settings, and in the early Middle Ages the percentage was not much higher. What changed was the place occupied by towns in the totality of human life. Fewer government functions were based in towns, cultural life was less bound to the urban environment, and trade in luxuries, which depended on towns, declined.

Towns in the West lost Roman governmental significance but often survived as focal points of royal or, more often, ecclesiastical administration. A cathedral church required a large corps of administrators. Western towns were everywhere attracting *burgs,* new settlements of merchants, just outside their centers. Because Vikings frequently raided these burgs, their existence was precarious. Few Western towns were impressive in size or population. Rome may have numbered a million people in the time of Augustus, but only about thirty thousand lived there in 800. Paris had perhaps twenty thousand inhabitants at that time. These were the largest cities by far in Catholic Europe.

In the Byzantine East, apart from Constantinople, the empire had a more rural aspect after the Muslims took control of the heavily urbanized regions of Syria, Egypt, and parts of Anatolia in the seventh century. The weakening of the caliphate in the second half of the ninth century was a spur to renewed urban growth in the Byzantine Empire. In provincial cities population growth and urban reconstruction depended heavily on military conditions: cities threatened by Arabs or Bulgarians declined.

The Arabs were great city-builders. Baghdad—four times larger in area than Constantinople, with a million residents to the latter's 400,000—was created from scratch. The most magnificent city in the West was Cordoba, the capital of Muslim Spain. Its population may have reached 400,000, and its Great Mosque, begun in 786, held 5,500 worshipers, more than any Latin church except Saint Peter's. The city had 900 baths, 1,600 mosques (Rome had about 200 churches), 60,000 mansions, and perhaps 100,000 shops. Its libraries held thousands of books, while the largest Carolingian book collections numbered a few hundred.

Agriculture nevertheless remained the most important element in the economy and in the daily lives of most people in all three realms. Farming meant primarily the production of cereal grains, which provided diet staples such as bread, porridge, and beer. Regions tended to specialize in the crops that grew most abundantly in local circumstances. For example, olives and grapes were common in the Mediterranean area, whereas cereals predominated around the Black Sea and in central Gaul. Animal husbandry was always a major part of the rural regime. English sheep provided wool and meat. In Frankish and Byzantine regions pigs, which were cheap to raise, supplied meat, but for religious reasons pork was almost absent in the Muslim East—Islam adopted the Jewish prohibition against it.

A key development in the Frankish West was the appearance of a bipartite estate, sometimes called a "manor." On a bipartite estate, one part of the land was set aside as a reserve (or *demesne*), and the rest was divided into tenancies. The reserve, consuming from one-quarter to one-half of the total territory of the estate, was exploited directly for the benefit of the landlord. The tenancies were generally worked by the peasants for their own support. The bipartite estate provided the aristocrats with a livelihood while freeing them for military and government service.

Estates were run in different ways. A landlord might hire laborers to farm his reserve, paying them with money exacted as fees from his tenants. Or he might require the tenants to work a certain number of days per week or weeks per year in his fields. The produce of the estate might be gathered into barns and consumed locally or hauled to local markets. The reserve might be a separate part of the estate, a proportion of common fields, or a percentage of the harvest. The tenants might have individual farms or work in common fields. Although the manor is one of the most familiar aspects of European life throughout the Middle Ages, large estates with dependent tenants also were evolving in the Byzantine and Islamic worlds.

Social Patterns   Most of the surviving medieval records were written by elite members of society and reveal little about the middle and lower orders of society. Nevertheless, certain similarities are evident in the social structures of all levels in all three societies. The elites tended to be large landholders, to control dependent populations, and to have access to government offices. There were regional differences, too. Scholars ranked higher in Byzantium and the caliphate than in the West; churchmen, especially bishops, were powerful in Christian societies but had no counterparts in Muslim ones. Literature, surely reflecting social realities, portrays the cultivated Muslim gentleman in the Abbasid period. This social type, marked by learning, good manners, and a taste for finery, does not appear in Byzantium or in the West until the twelfth century.

The middling classes show some disparities among the regions. Merchants, for example, often rose through the social ranks to become great aristocrats in Muslim society. Islamic society often evinced great mobility because of its restless, expanding nature and because Islamic ideology rejected distinctions in the umma. In Byzantium traditional Roman prejudices against merchants and moneymaking activities persisted. Thus rich merchants whose wealth gave them private influence frequently lacked public power and recognition. In the West merchants were neither numerous nor powerful in the Carolingian period. In some towns, moreover, commerce was in the hands of Jews, always outsiders in a militantly Christian society.

Merchants were not the only people occupying the middle rungs of the social ladder. All three societies, in fact, possessed both central elites and provincial elites. Service at the Carolingian, Byzantine, or Abbasid court counted for more than service in a provincial outpost. It was one thing to be abbot of a great monastery and quite a different thing to preside over a poor, tiny house. The thematic generals in Byzantium were lofty personages; their subordinates held inferior positions. The vassals of a Carolingian king formed a real aristocracy, but vassals' vassals were of decidedly lower rank.

Degrees of freedom and local economic and political conditions shaped the lives of peasants. In all three societies some farmers were personally free and owed no cash or labor services to anyone but the central government. In areas such as Abbasid Iraq ordinary free farmers led a comfortable life. In the Frankish world most peasants existed outside the dawning manorial system. They were free, and if they lived in areas of good land and political security, such as the Paris basin, their lives most likely were congenial. Byzantine peasants, though free, often lived in areas of military danger, and in some parts of the Balkans they eked out a living from poor soils. Highly taxed and perpetually endangered, they may have viewed their freedom as small compensation for their economic and personal insecurity. All peasants were alike in their subjection to political forces over which they had no control.

At the bottom of the social scale everywhere were slaves. Christianity did not object to slavery in general but forbade the enslavement of Christians. Islam likewise prohibited Muslims from enslaving other Muslims. Slaves, therefore, tended to be most common in pagan societies—Scandinavia, for example—or in frontier regions where neighboring pagans could be captured and sold. There were more slaves in the Muslim world than in Byzantium, which had, in turn, more than the West.

Women were bound to the same social hierarchies as men. Predictably enough, women had few formal, public roles to play. Their influence, however great, tended to function in the private sphere, rarely revealed to us by sources that stem from the public realm of powerful men. Aristocratic women had opportunities and power that were denied ordinary women. Irene ruled at Byzantium as empress. Frankish and Anglo-Saxon queens were formidable figures in their realms. Carolingian queens managed the landed patrimony of the dynasty—dozens of huge estates with tens of thousands of dependents. The combination of a lack of evidence and the rigorous exclusion of women from public life in the Islamic world means that virtually no Muslim women emerge as distinct personalities in the early Middle Ages.

The conversion of England to Christianity was fostered by women. Most convents had aristocratic abbesses who presided over complex enterprises and often schools. In the Frankish world aristocratic women secured some learning, and one, Dhuoda, wrote in 841 a manual of advice for her son that conveys biblical and patristic teachings as well as practical wisdom. The Frankish convent at Chelles was a renowned center for the copying of manuscripts. Some Anglo-Saxon nuns owned ships and invested in commercial activities to support their convents. Almost all aspects of the cloth industry were in women's hands.

One example of the problems in the evidence concerning women relates to church roles. Women could not hold priestly office, and although deaconesses served at Hagia Sophia in the sixth century, they disappeared soon after and had long before vanished in the West. Religious power could come from personal sanctity as well as holding office. One study of some 2,200 saints from the early Middle Ages finds only about 300 females. It was hard for women to gain recognition as saints. And if a woman became a saint, her holiness was inevitably described either as "manly"—an extreme ascetic was praised for having the strength and courage of a man—or as beautiful, virginal, and domestic—in other words, with female stereotypes.

The domestic sphere is another difficult realm to enter. The Quran permitted a man to have up to four wives if he could care for them and would treat them equitably.

IMPORTANT EVENTS

570–632 Life of Muhammad

597 Pope Gregory I sends missionaries to England

610–641 Reign of Heraclius in Byzantium

622 Hijra

632–733 Muslim conquests

661–750 Umayyad caliphate

664 Council of Whitby

711–716 Muslim conquest of Spain

717–802 Isaurian dynasty at Byzantium

726–787, 815–842 Byzantine iconoclasm

750 Founding of Abbasid caliphate

751 Lombard conquest of Ravenna

755–774 Frankish conquest of Lombards

755–756 Foundation of Papal States

757–796 Reign of Offa of Mercia

768–814 Reign of Charlemagne

780s–860s Carolingian Renaissance

786–809 Reign of Harun al-Rashid

800 Imperial coronation of Charlemagne

843 Treaty of Verdun creates three Frankish kingdoms

867–886 Reign of Basil I

A Muslim woman, however, was given her dowry outright, and multiple marriages may have meant that relatively more Muslim women could gain a measure of security. In Byzantium and the West, families rarely arranged marriages for more than one or two daughters. Others remained single or entered convents. Women at all social levels tended to pass from the tutelage of their fathers to that of their husbands. In antiquity a suitor usually paid a fee, or "bride price," to his prospective wife's father and then endowed his wife with a "morning gift," money or possessions of her own. Gradually this practice changed to a system whereby a bride's father paid a dowry to her future husband. Thus a wife who was cast aside could be left impoverished, for in most places the law did not permit her to inherit land if she had brothers. Females were such valuable property in the marriage market that rape was an offense not against a girl but against her father. A man could divorce, even kill, his wife for adultery, witchcraft, or grave robbing and then marry again. A woman could usually gain a divorce only for adultery, and she could not remarry. For the vast majority of women, daily life was hedged about with legal limitations and personal indignities.

SUGGESTED READING

Becher, Matthias. *Charlemagne.* 2003. Brief yet detailed, up-to-date, and readable; by a distinguished German historian.

Berkey, Jonathan P. *The Formation of Islam: Religion and Society in the Near East, 600–1800.* 2003. Compact yet comprehensive and readable; equipped with fine "Suggestions for Further Reading," this book is now the place to start on the Islamic world.

Bitel, Lisa M. *Women in Early Medieval Europe, 400–1100.* 2002. Entertaining and informative, this is the first comprehensive treatment of early medieval women.

Brown, Peter. *The Rise of Western Christendom.* 2d ed. 2003. A verbal feast, now fully documented, this book presents a stimulating assessment of the place of Christianity in the rise of Western culture.

Denny, Frederick M. *An Introduction to Islam.* 2d ed. 1994. By far the most accessible, readable account of the Islamic faith; the book covers all periods but is helpful for the early centuries.

McCormick, Michael. *Origins of the European Economy: Communications and Commerce AD 300–900.* 2001. A stupendous achievement, this richly detailed book is *the* starting point for an understanding of the early medieval commercial economy.

Whittow, Mark. *The Making of Orthodox Byzantium, 600–1025.* 1996. Lively, readable, controversial, and engaging, this book challenges standard views.

9

The Expansion of Europe in the High Middle Ages, 900–1300

(Michael Holford)

The picture here represents one small section of the Bayeux Tapestry, a narrative account—in words and illustrations—of the conquest of England in 1066 by Duke William of Normandy. This scene is an apt introduction to the central theme of this chapter: expansion.

This section of the 230-foot-long tapestry depicts William setting sail for England. William had already gained greater authority in the duchy of Normandy than any duke before him. Now he was about to press his claim to the throne of England. He gathered soldiers from all over western France and boldly crossed the English Channel. Leaving nothing to chance, he transported horses, too, as you can see in the picture.

One group of Normans conquered England, while another seized control of southern Italy. Still other Normans played a decisive role in the period's most prominent manifestation of expansion: the Crusades. Meanwhile, certain Scandinavians settled Iceland and Greenland to the west, while others founded the first state on Russian soil. Spanish Christians pushed back the Muslims in Iberia. From the Baltic to the Balkans, Slavic rulers founded new states and pressed hard against their neighbors. German rulers crossed the Alps into Italy, French kings reached the Pyrenees, and English monarchs pushed into Wales, Scotland, and Ireland. Seldom has Europe's political geography expanded so dramatically as during the High Middle Ages.

Between 900 and 1300 Europe's population began one of its longest periods of sustained growth. People brought more land under cultivation, introduced new crops, and made agriculture more efficient. Villages, towns, and cities grew in number and size. Trade expanded in every material and in every direction.

Europe witnessed the re-emergence of centralizing monarchies in France, England, and Spain. Some new realms, such as Denmark and Hungary, built strong central governments. And an explosion of new states occurred along the frontiers of the old Carolingian Empire.

The "West" began taking on a more *western European* character. The Crusades complicated relations between Christian Europeans and Muslims, and both the Crusades and increasing religious differences alienated western Europe from Byzantium, and Roman Catholics from Orthodox believers. The center of Western civilization became more and more anchored to northwestern Europe. And that same western Europe was expanding to influence lands in Scandinavia and the Slavic world that had played no role at all in the West's classical, Mediterranean phase. The High Middle Ages repeatedly posed the question: Where is the West?

ECONOMIC EXPANSION

The economic expansion of Europe is manifest in many kinds of evidence that are more often qualitative than quantitative. Medieval people did not keep the kinds of records of births, deaths, population, or business activity that modern states routinely accumulate. Literary anecdotes can be revealing, of course, but they are no substitute for hard data. After about 1000 every available indicator points to a growing population and an expanding scale and sophistication of economic activity.

The Growing Population The population of Europe began rising slowly in the Carolingian period and may have doubled between 1000 and 1200. Scattered bits of evidence suggest that the total population of western Europe grew from around 30 million in 1000 to 55 million or 60 million in 1200. In the thirteenth century population growth gradually slowed.

In a few regions where family size can be estimated, fertile marriages were producing on the average 3.5 children in the tenth century and from 6 to 7 in the twelfth.

People were also living longer than their forebears. Studies of aristocrats, high clergy, and soldiers show that a surprising 40 percent of them were over 40 years old. Male life expectancy was surely longer than female because of the dangers of childbirth, always the great killer of women in the premodern world. The general trend is clear: more babies being born, more infants living into adulthood, more adults living longer.

Everywhere in Europe new land was brought into cultivation. More than half of the French documents relating to land in the twelfth century mention *assarting*, the bringing of previously untilled land under the plow. Thousands of acres of forest were felled. Marshes were reclaimed from the sea. Some 380,000 acres were drained along the western coast of France and probably twice that amount in both Flanders and England. This activity is inexplicable without assuming a growing number of mouths to feed.

Agriculture benefited from a warmer and drier climate through this whole period. Not a single vegetable blight was recorded. Food was more abundant and more nutritious. Animals were increasingly reared for their meat, and higher meat consumption meant more protein in the diet. Beans and other legumes, also rich in protein, were more widely cultivated. Fine grains such as wheat replaced poorer cereals—ryes and spelts—in many areas. People of every class and region were almost certainly eating better and living longer and healthier lives.

Technological Gains

The eleventh century was a decisive period in the spread of new technologies in Europe. Innovations occurred in agriculture, transportation, mining, and manufacturing. Agricultural changes came first as a rising population created an increased demand for food that could be met only by new practices. By the late twelfth century an acre of farmland in a fertile region was probably yielding a crop three to four times larger than in the Carolingian era. Given the combination of more land under cultivation and more yield per acre, the overall gains in the food supply were enormous.

The increases can be accounted for in several ways. Horses were more frequently used as draft animals. They were more expensive to acquire than oxen but no more costly to feed, and they did, in a day, a third or half again as much work. For much less "fuel" horses could haul loads farther and faster than oxen. Thus fewer people could, with horses, cultivate more land than their predecessors managed with oxen. In addition, they could cultivate the land more frequently and increase yields because more seed would fall on more finely plowed soil. The dissemination of the horse collar made possible the expanded use of horses—older forms of harnesses suitable for the low-slung, broad-shouldered ox would have choked a horse.

Plows, too, were improved. The light wooden scratch plow used by the Romans was satisfactory for the thin soils of the Mediterranean region but barely disturbed the heavy soils of northern Europe. The invention of a heavy wheeled plow with an iron coulter (or plowshare) and a moldboard was a real breakthrough. The iron plowshare cut deep furrows, and then the moldboard turned and aerated the soil. This heavy plow allowed farmers to exploit good soils more fully without exhausting the ground too rapidly. This plow seems to have been introduced into Carolingian Europe from the Slavic world, but it was not widely adopted before the eleventh century.

Wider adoption of nitrogen-fixing crops, such as peas and some kinds of beans, retarded soil exhaustion and also put more protein in the diet. Leaving land fallow was another means of avoiding soil exhaustion. In the early Middle Ages this meant setting aside about half of the arable land every year (the two-field system) or working the land intensively for a few years and then moving on. By the twelfth century three-field schemes of crop rotation were common.

Under the three-field system, two-thirds of the arable land saw nearly constant use. The amount of an estate under cultivation rose from 50 to 67 percent. Crop rotation brought other benefits as well. Horses ate oats, but (except in a few places such as Scotland) medieval people generally did not. If farmers wished to use horses, they had to dedicate some of their land to growing oats. A three-field rotation allowed some flexibility. Finally the alternation of winter crops (wheat and rye), spring crops (oats, barley, and legumes), and fallow ensured against a single season of unusually harsh weather.

Surplus produce was intended mainly for the growing towns. To supply that market, improvements in transportation were necessary. Kings often passed laws to secure the safety of highways, and popes three times (in 1097, 1132, and 1179) threatened highwaymen—robbers who preyed on travelers—with excommunication. Landlords required their dependents to maintain roads and bridges. Many stone bridges were constructed in France between 1130 and 1170 because wooden bridges were so vulnerable to fire. Indeed, fire destroyed the bridge at Angers (in western France) five times between 1032 and 1167.

Transport improved not only because of safer roads but also thanks to better vehicles. Documents and pictures in manuscripts agree that the old two-wheeled cart, drawn by oxen, began giving way to the sturdy four-wheeled, horse-drawn wagon. Because greater quantities of foodstuffs could be moved farther and faster, urban communities

Twelfth-Century Timbered House, Rouen, France
The house at the center of this picture was destroyed in World War II after holding its place for nearly eight hundred years. It shows one of the many uses of timber, and its narrow street gives an authentic feel of a medieval town. (Roger-Viollet/ Getty Images)

could be supplied from larger areas. This was a crucial factor in enabling cities to grow and in providing urban residents with a predictable and diverse range of foods.

Evidence from several parts of Europe points to the years after 925 as the beginning of real growth in the mining industry. Notable improvements occurred in both the quarrying of stone and the extraction of metals. Mines were not deep because people lacked the means to keep the shafts and galleries free of water. Still, the exploitation of surface and near-surface veins of ore—principally iron but also tin and silver—intensified, to supply the increased demand for plowshares, tools, weapons, construction fittings, and coins. Stone quarrying, the most common form of mining in the Middle Ages, benefited directly from more efficient stone saws and indirectly from improvements in transport. Better techniques in stonecutting, construction, and conveyance help to explain, for example, the increase in the number of England's stone religious buildings from sixty to nearly five hundred in the century after 1050.

Forms of Enterprise	Agricultural specialization became common. People began to cultivate intensively those crops that were best suited to local conditions. The area around Toulouse, for example, concen-

trated on herbs from which blue and yellow dyes were made. The central regions of France focused on cereal grains, while the Bordeaux and Burgundy regions emphasized the grapes that produced wine. Northern Germany specialized in cattle raising; northern England favored sheep.

Agricultural specialization helps to explain the growth in trade everywhere. For certain commodities local trade continued to flourish. Italian wines and olive oil, for example, were not produced for far-off markets; they tended to move from countryside to town within a region. The same was true of French or English grains. However, French wines were much prized throughout Europe, especially in England, and certain products, such as English wool and Flemish cloth, were carried far and wide. Salt fish from the Baltic found its way all over the continent. Lumber was routinely traded across the Mediterranean to the wood-poor Muslim world. Spain was a source of warhorses. Southern Europe supplied the northern demand for spices, oranges, raisins, figs, almonds, and other exotic foodstuffs. Caen, in Normandy, sent shiploads of its beautifully colored and textured stone to England for the construction of churches and monasteries. Rising population, higher productivity, and greater prosperity added up to a larger volume of goods moving farther and more frequently.

The lumber industry reveals many facets of medieval economic activity. Before the twelfth century wood was the main building material, and even later it yielded to stone mainly for the church and aristocracy. But wood could be used for more than construction. For example, the Venetian shipyards needed about twenty oaks, twenty towering pines, and fifty or so beeches to make a ship. In the early twelfth century the Venetians were making about ten vessels a year, twice the number they had been building two centuries earlier. Whether for ships or for homes, the demand for wood grew steadily.

Wood exemplifies the expansion and interconnectedness of the medieval economy and society. Forests were essential to daily life, providing the wood for houses, fences, and fuel in villages and towns. Animals, especially pigs, were grazed at the edges of the forest to permit as much land as possible to be dedicated to food crops. Wild animals were hunted in the forest. For aristocrats hunting was as much for sport as for food. For poorer rural people, however, wild game made up a significant part of the regular diet.

The forest was also a plentiful source of fruits, nuts, and honey. Thus the decision to cut down a stand of trees was a serious one.

The Roles of Cities and Towns All over Europe towns grew impressively in size and importance. Such growth also occurred in cities in Flanders, such as Bruges and Ghent, and in Paris, London, and other cities that were becoming national capitals. Ghent expanded its city walls five times between 1160 and 1300, a sure sign of growth even in the absence of population figures. Similar forces were operating in the countryside. In 1100 about 11 fortified villages surrounded Florence, but by 1200 the city was ringed by 205 such villages.

For the first time since late antiquity, cities were becoming centers for many activities. Governments, which required larger staffs of trained personnel, settled in towns. The towns of Italy and Flanders, though not national capitals, ruled over extensive hinterlands. Schools and eventually universities (see pages 319–320) were urban institutions. Mercantile, industrial, and legal organizations were located in towns. Ecclesiastical organization was always urban based. Towns began to compete with royal and aristocratic courts as literary centers, and cathedrals, the great buildings of the age, were exclusively urban.

One distinctive urban phenomenon was the rise of guilds. In 1200, for example, Paris had one guild of merchants and four or five craft or trade associations. By 1270 the city had 101 craft or trade guilds, and by 1292 the number had risen to 130.

The guilds had many functions. Their main purpose was economic: to regulate standards of production, to fix prices, and to control membership in their respective trades. But as towns grew larger and more impersonal, these associations of people engaged in similar occupations fostered a sense of belonging, a feeling of community. Members tended to live in the same areas and to worship together in a parish church. Growing wealth in general, coupled with fierce local pride, produced building competitions whose results are still visible in the huge neighborhood churches that survive in most European towns. The guilds indulged in elaborate festivals and celebrations, which sometimes turned into drunken debauches despite being held to honor saints. The guilds were also mutual assurance societies. That is, they assisted colleagues who fell on hard times, saw to the funeral expenses of members, and provided for widows and orphans.

The guilds had a damaging impact on women. As more economic activity came under the umbrella of the guild structures, women were more systematically excluded from guild membership. Usually women could become guild members only as wives or widows. They could not open economic enterprises of their own, although they were workers in many trades. Despite a growing, diversifying economy, women were increasingly denied opportunities, although later centuries would find women establishing their own guilds.

Commercial Growth and Innovation Towns were focal points in commercial networks. The basic trade routes and networks had existed since Carolingian times, but a novelty of the twelfth century was the emergence of the Champagne fairs as a meeting point for the commerce of north and south. Since the early Middle Ages, a few locations hosted permanent fairs, and many places sponsored occasional fairs. By the middle of the twelfth century, however, the spices, silks, and dyes of the Mediterranean, the wool of England, the furs and linens of Germany, and the leather products of Spain began to be sold in a series of six fairs held in the Champagne region of France from spring to autumn.

At any time of year, travel was difficult and costly. Few dared to venture across the Alps in the winter, and the northern seas, especially the passage around Denmark, were treacherous in cold weather. Even in the relatively calm Mediterranean, the Venetians refused to send out their trading fleet between November and March. Overland trade was impeded by snow, rain, mud, and highwaymen. Governments tried to restrain robbers, but no one could change the weather.

Seaborne trade expanded. The stern rudder, better sails, the compass (in use by 1180), and better navigational charts facilitated sea travel, as did the growing use of larger ships. An Italian fleet sailed to Flanders in 1277, and within a few years the old overland trade routes, and with them the Champagne fairs, began a decline that was not reversed until the invention of the railroad in the nineteenth century.

Changing Economic Attitudes   As medieval society generated more wealth and populations concentrated in cities, people who were relatively well-off became more conscious of those who were less fortunate. Moralists began to argue that the poor were a special gift of God to the rich, who could redeem their own souls by generous charitable benefactions. Most towns established schemes of poor relief. But the numbers of poor people grew so rapidly, particularly in large towns, that helping seemed hopeless, and some gave up trying. Hospitals, for example, began to refuse abandoned babies for fear that they would be deluged with them.

Efforts to alleviate the condition of the poor constituted one ethical concern of medieval thinkers, but two issues attracted even more attention. First, theologians and lawyers alike discussed the "just price," the price at which goods should be bought and sold. Christian teaching had long held that it was immoral to hoard food during a famine or knowingly to sell a damaged item. But what was the correct price in ordinary circumstances? A theological view, often dismissed as unrealistic, held that items could be sold for only the cost of the materials in them and the labor absolutely necessary to produce them. A commercial view, often dismissed as immoral, insisted that a fair price was whatever the market would bear, regardless of costs or consequences. A working consensus held that a just price was one arrived at by bargaining between free and knowledgeable parties.

The other ethical issue concerned usury, the lending of money at interest. Christian writers were always hostile to commercial enterprise, and they had plenty of biblical warrant for their view. Psalm 15 warned that no one can be blameless "who lends his money at usury." Luke's Gospel admonished Christians to "give without expecting to be repaid in full." Luke actually forbade the profit that makes most commercial enterprises possible. In the twelfth century churchmen began to be much more assiduous in their condemnations of usury, a practice that had been winked at for centuries.

Prohibitions against usury in twelfth-century Europe (a society in full economic expansion) produced some remarkably inventive ways to get around the prohibitions. One person might agree to sell another person an item at a certain price and then buy it back on a fixed date at a higher price. Exchange rates between currencies could be manipulated to mask usurious transactions. Gradually thinkers began to defend usury on the grounds that a person who lent money incurred a risk and deserved to be compensated for that risk.

Investment demands credit, and credit requires some payback for the lender. Even in the face of deep hostility, credit mechanisms spread in thirteenth-century Europe. They were held up to minute scrutiny by theologians and popular preachers and were found to be evidence of man's sinfulness, acquisitiveness, greed. But all these practices persisted, fueled by the expansion of the European economy, and began putting individual profit alongside community interest at the heart of social and economic thought.

THE HEIRS OF THE CAROLINGIAN EMPIRE: GERMANY, ITALY, AND FRANCE

The scope of political and institutional life expanded everywhere between 900 and 1300. In 900 the Carolingian Empire was collapsing. By 1300 France had emerged as a large, stable kingdom, and Italy had turned into several reasonably coherent regional entities. One might have predicted these post-Carolingian outcomes from the pre-Carolingian experience of these two areas. The most surprising political development within the old Carolingian lands, indeed within Europe as a whole, was Germany's rise to a premier position in the tenth century and then its long, slow decline. The states that evolved out of the Carolingian Empire faced common challenges: the achievement of territorial integrity; the growing responsibility of the central government; complicated political relations among kings, aristocrats, and churchmen; and the elaboration of new ideas about the state and its responsibilities.

Germany and the Empire, 911–1272 From the ninth century to the present, no state in Europe has been less stable territorially and politically than Germany and the German Empire. Time after time the Germans confronted new possibilities and challenges. An investigation of three questions in particular will help us comprehend German history after the Carolingians. First, what role did dynastic instability play in German history? Second, what rules governed political development in the German lands? Third, how did the German rulers regulate relations with the leaders of the church?

When the Treaty of Verdun (see page 252) assigned an East Frankish kingdom to Louis the German in 843, it created something essentially new. Frankish rulers had long claimed authority over some of the lands that eventually became Germany, but before 843 no unified kingdom had ever existed in the territories east of the Rhine River. The Carolingians tried hard to impose common institutions on the diverse regions running from Saxony in the north to Bavaria in the south, but they faced immense difficulties in doing so. The lands had no tradition of common or unified rule. There was no single "German" people; Saxons thought of themselves as Saxon, for example, not as German. Roman culture had barely penetrated into German lands, and Christian culture was recent and fragile. "Germany" had—has—no natural frontiers. Germany was, finally, the most thoroughly rural area of the Carolingian world.

After the last East Frankish Carolingian died in 911, the dukes, or leaders, of Germany's major regions chose one of their number as king. In 919 they did so again, their

Germany and Its Duchies, ca. 1000–1200

The chief political dynamic in Germany was a contest for power between the kings and the dukes. The duchies emerged in the ninth and tenth centuries and outlived one dynasty of kings after another.

choice this time falling on Duke Henry of Saxony. Henry and his successors, each of whom was named Otto, ruled capably until 1024, when Henry II died without an heir. This time the German dukes turned to a distantly related family, the Salians. The Salian family died out in the middle of the twelfth century and was replaced by the Staufer, who ruled until 1250. Then, after twenty-two years without a recognized ruler, the Germans elected a member of the Habsburg family. This record of frequent dynastic change might be contrasted with the situation in France (see pages 275–279), where one family reigned from 987 to 1328. Our task now is to see how this dynastic instability affected the course of German history.

Who were these dukes, and why were they so influential? German romantic tradition regarded them as the heroic leaders of distinct ethnic communities, the so-called Tribal Duchies. In fact, the dukes were the descendants of local rulers introduced by the Carolingians. They were wealthy and powerful; they contested with kings for control of the bishops and abbots in their duchies; and sometimes they managed to make vassals out of the lower ranks of the aristocracy in their territories, effectively denying kings connections with these people. In sum, the dukes were extremely jealous of their independence.

At the beginning of Saxon (Ottonian) rule, Germany comprised five duchies: Saxony, Franconia, Lorraine, Swabia, and Bavaria. When the Ottonians came to power, they concentrated on using both force and strategic alliances to attempt to control one or more of these duchies. Hoping to win new territories and distract troublesome aristocrats, the Ottonians began Germany's centuries-long drive to the east, into Slavic Europe. In 955 Otto I gained power and prestige when he led a combined German force to victory against the Magyars at Lechfeld.

The Ottonians also tried to control the church, especially bishops and abbots, to gain the allegiance of powerful and articulate allies. In 962 Otto I, who had begun expanding into Italy in 952, was crowned emperor in Rome by the pope. Why did he seek to revive the Carolingian imperial office? The imperial title conferred two benefits on the German kings: it gave them immense prestige and power that owed nothing to the dukes, and it raised the possibility of securing huge material resources in Italy, where, as emperors, they did not have to share power the way they did in Germany. The marriage of Otto II to a Byzantine princess was a sign of Germany's growing stature. Their son, Otto III, sponsored a brilliant court, patronizing writers and painters. When he died in 1002, Germany was the pre-eminent land in Europe.

The eleventh century and early twelfth century brought dramatic changes to Germany. The Salians, distant relatives of the Ottonians, mounted the throne in 1024, opening opportunities for political disruption. When the second Salian ruler, Henry III, died in 1056, he left behind a 6-year-old heir and a decade of civil war. Military expansion virtually ceased, and powerful aristocrats struggled with one another and with their kings. Chief among these aristocrats were the dukes, who had chafed under Ottonian and Salian efforts to control them.

When Henry IV came of age in 1066, he faced opposition on all sides, controlled no duchies, was not yet emperor, and had lost much of his father's control of the church. When he tried to make church appointments in the traditional way, he encountered the fierce opposition of the newly reformed papacy in the person of Pope Gregory VII (r. 1073–1085). Gregory was brilliant, proud, and inflexible—and determined to bend

Henry IV, Duchess Matilda of Tuscany, and Abbot Hugh of Cluny *The embattled Henry IV here implores Matilda, a tremendously wealthy landowner and ally of Pope Gregory VII, to intercede with the pope. The powerful abbot of Cluny looks over the scene protectively. Written documents do not portray women's power as vividly as this image does.* (Vatican Library, Rome)

Henry to his will. Their battles inaugurated the so-called investiture controversy, which lingered on until 1122, when both of the original foes were long dead.

What was the investiture controversy, how had it come about, and what impact did it have on Germany? In the middle of the eleventh century a group of ardent church reformers appeared in Rome. Committed to improving the moral and intellectual caliber of the clergy all over Europe, they targeted the chief impediment to reform: the control of church appointments by laymen—or "lay investiture," as they called it. This brought the reformers into direct conflict with the Salians, who, like Charlemagne and the Ottonians before them, believed that they reigned supreme in the "City of God." These German rulers stood, in their own view, nearest to God in a great hierarchy; the clergy occupied the rungs beneath them in human society. Thus the king was God's specially chosen agent on earth, and the higher clergy were the king's natural helpers in governing the realm. To the reformers, the proper organization of society was just the opposite: the clergy, with the pope at its head, stood nearest to God, with secular monarchs subordinate to the church.

When these reformers challenged royal supremacy on ideological grounds, the particular quarrel over the appointment of churchmen mushroomed into a general struggle for leadership in Christian society. In Germany the struggle between Henry IV and Gregory VII became a pretext for ducal and aristocratic opposition to the king. Even though the kings could not control the dukes, they had sometimes wrest the naming of bishops from them. Meanwhile, Henry expended time and resources in Italy trying in vain to control Rome and the pope.

The Concordat of Worms, concluded in 1122 between Henry V (r. 1106–1125) and Pope Calixtus II (r. 1119–1124), brought the investiture controversy to an end. The decree stipulated that episcopal (bishopric) elections should be free and conducted according to church law. Only after a man had been duly elected bishop could a king, or emperor, invest him with the symbols and offices of secular authority. The Concordat was a blow to the German political system as it had existed for centuries. When Otto III died in 1002, Germany was powerful and confident. When Henry V died in 1125, Germany was weak, disunited, and searching for new bases of authority.

With the accession of Frederick Barbarossa ("Red Beard") in 1152, a new family, the Staufer, consolidated its hold on the German throne. Frederick, whose base was in Swabia, patiently worked to get the other dukes to recognize his overlordship, even though he was powerless to demand payments or services from them. His plan was slowly to build up the idea that the king was the highest lord in the land (a plan that his French and English contemporaries used effectively). In 1158 Frederick summoned representatives of the major northern and central Italian cities to demand full recognition of his regalian, or ruler's, rights. These included military service; control of roads, ports, and waterways; administration of tolls, mints, fines, vacant fiefs, and confiscated properties; appointment of magistrates; construction of palaces; and control of mines, fisheries, and saltworks. No German king had ever possessed these kinds of rights before. Frederick's attempts to control northern Italy resulted in the creation of the Lombard League, a union of Italian cities that inflicted a humiliating defeat on German forces at Legnano in 1176.

Frederick also struggled for more than twenty years to get the popes to recognize his claim to the imperial office, which he viewed as a source of prestige and as a legitimation of his right to rule Italy. When he spoke of his "Holy Roman Empire," he meant that his power came, on the one hand, from God himself and, on the other hand, from the Romans via Charlemagne. Theory did not match reality, however, and the papacy was able to thwart virtually all his political initiatives. The handsome, energetic, and athletic Frederick accomplished much, and he might have done more had he not drowned in Anatolia in 1190 while on his way to the Third Crusade.

Frederick's successor, Henry VI (r. 1190–1197), ruled for only a short time and left behind an infant son, Frederick II (r. 1212–1250). Frederick II had been born in Sicily. His mother, Constance, had no standing in Germany and little influence in Italy. Accordingly, she placed her son under the tutelage of Pope Innocent III. By the time Frederick came of age, he so despaired of governing Germany that he conceded the "Statute in Favor of the Princes," which lodged royal power in ducal hands in return for a vague acknowledgment of his overlordship. Frederick concentrated his own efforts in Italy, where he sought to institute a sophisticated regime based on Byzantine and Norman (see page 275) models. Although he made good progress, he faced constant opposition from the popes, who were unwilling to trade a German ruler with interests in Italy for an essentially Italian ruler with interests in Germany. When Frederick II died in 1250, effective central authority in both Germany and Italy collapsed. After twenty-two years of weak or contested rule, the German dukes turned to Rudolf of Habsburg whose descendants remained influential in German politics until the early twentieth century.

Neither the Habsburgs nor any subsequent German emperors restored the position held by the Ottonians.

An understanding of Germany's fate requires that we return to the questions with which we began this discussion. One wonders: Might a long-lived dynasty have made a difference? Germany was not without great rulers: Otto I, Otto III, Frederick Barbarossa, and even Frederick II were the equals of any contemporary ruler. But repeated changes of ruling family in the context of a fragile political regime provided repeated opportunities for fragmentation. The German monarchy had a very limited territorial base and, compared with these kings' Carolingian predecessors and their French and English contemporaries, they possessed unimpressive government institutions. The kings themselves were dukes, and as such their areas of truly effective control were usually limited to one duchy. The Saxons were based in the north, the Salians in the center, and the Staufer in the south. Thus continuity of rule was constantly threatened by huge dynastic, institutional, and geographical challenges.

Was the Italian venture a mistake? Germany's involvement with Italy and the imperial title has occasioned no end of controversy. To some, royal involvement in Italy signals a failure to deal imaginatively with Germany itself. To others, the quest for prestige, power, and money in Italy was actually a creative solution to the monarchy's relative impotence in Germany. There was, of course, always a danger that Italy itself would become the prime object of the German ruler's attention, as actually happened under Frederick II. In the end the struggle for control of Italy brought Germany's rulers two unforeseen consequences. First, since the imperial title had to be obtained in Rome from the pope, the papacy was handed an unprecedented opportunity to meddle in German politics. That opportunity evolved from an initial request for protection, through periodic demands for political concessions, to a claim that the pope actually had the right to decide whether a particular individual was morally fit to be crowned emperor. Second, leading Italian cities were not content to be ruled by the Germans. The dramatic German defeat at Legnano is representative of the ongoing challenges and provocations to German authority.

With its promise, undoubted achievements, and yet ultimate failure, Germany is the political mystery of medieval Europe. In turning now to other regions of Europe, we will continue to explore the roles dynasty, geography, institutions, and ideology played there.

The Varying Fortunes of Italy

The history of Italy has always been played out in three regions: north, central, and south. The Carolingians and the Germans after them laid a heavy hand on northern Italy. In the center of the peninsula the Papal States was the key player. Outsiders always dominated the south, but their identities changed often.

As we have seen, German attempts to impose their authority on northern Italy met with limited success. One key obstacle to German rule was the communal movement, the most dynamic element on the Italian scene. Two conditions help to explain the rise of communes. The first relates to economic expansion. In the early eleventh century Italian towns began to rid the Mediterranean of Muslim pirates. By 1100 Italian merchants could trade anywhere in the Mediterranean world with confidence.

The second contributing factor relates to political developments in Italian towns. The Carolingians governed towns through resident counts, and German emperors tried to maintain this system. The powers of the counts tended to be weak, however, so the Germans also relied on bishops, who were, in Italy as in Germany, key props to the system of imperial rule. But bishops and counts were not alone in holding urban power. Since the late tenth century both bishops and counts had been granting fiefs to local men in order to strengthen their own authority and to procure defenses for the towns. Gradually these men, whose lands made them wealthy in the expanding economy, moved into the towns and, in turn, gave fiefs to other men in the countryside. These lords were wealthy and jealous of their power.

Communes were sworn associations of the local nobility—these landed lords—and their vassals. Commune members swore to uphold one another's rights and called themselves the *popolo*, or "people," although the people as a whole had nothing to do with the early communes. A commune accorded a high degree of participation to its members in choosing leaders and in coming together in an assembly that voted on matters of common concern. The leaders of the early communes were usually called *consuls*—a deliberate attempt to evoke the Roman past. Usually elected for a single year, the consuls varied in number from four to twenty in different cities. The consuls proposed matters to an assembly for ratification. By the 1140s every significant city in northern and central Italy had a commune.

The communes did not necessarily originate as attempts to make cities independent. Frequently, however, as communal governments became more established and confident, that is what they did. One by one, cities either refused to recognize papal or imperial overlordship or else renegotiated the terms under which they would acknowledge the rule of their historic masters. The working out of this ongoing relationship was a major development in the history of the Italian cities in the twelfth century.

Although each Italian commune constituted an entity unto itself, a fairly coherent evolution is evident. By the late twelfth century the consular communes were still governed by oligarchies of men whose wealth and power came from land, trade, and industry. Guild interests, however, gained in prominence at the expense of the landed groups among whom the communal movement had arisen, and ordinary workers began to clamor for participation. The communes were becoming increasingly volatile and violent.

One solution to this potential crisis was the introduction of the *podestà*, a sort of city manager chosen by the local oligarchy. The podestà often came from the outside, served for a set period (usually six months or a year), and underwent a careful scrutiny at the conclusion of his term. He was expected to be competent not only at ordinary administration but also at military leadership, so that he could police the city as well as defend it. He brought with him a group of seasoned officials as subordinates. Normally he could not be a property owner in the town, marry into local society, or dine privately with any citizen. By the middle of the thirteenth century some podestàs were becoming virtual professional administrators. One man, for example, was elected sixteen times in nine cities over a period of thirty-four years, four times in Bologna alone.

The Italian commune was a radical political experiment. Everywhere else in medieval Europe power was thought to radiate downward—from God, the clergy, the emperor, the king. In a commune power radiated upward from the popolo to its leaders. For several centuries the Italian city was arguably the most creative institution in the Western world. When Frederick Barbarossa tried to introduce tight imperial control, the future of northern and central Italy hung in the balance. But his defeat at the hands of the Lombard League at Legnano in 1176 left the Italian cities free to continue their distinctive political evolution.

Although some communes emerged in central Italy—even, briefly, in Rome in the 1150s—the key power in this region was the papacy, and the main political entity was the Papal States. In the political turmoil of the tenth and eleventh centuries, the papacy lost a great deal of territory. Throughout the twelfth and thirteenth centuries, therefore, a basic objective of papal policy was to recover lost lands and rights. This quest to restore the territorial basis for papal power and income helps explain why the popes so resolutely opposed German imperial influence in Italy.

The most striking development pertaining to the papacy is the expansion of its institutions. Gradually there emerged what historians have long called the "Papal Monarchy." This term is meant to characterize a church whose power was increasingly centralized in the hands of the popes. In Rome the pope presided over the *curia,* the papal court. The College of Cardinals, potentially fifty-three in number, formed a kind of senate for the church. They elected the popes (by majority after 1059 and by a two-thirds majority after 1179), served as key advisers, headed the growing financial and judicial branches of the papal government, and often served as legates. Legates were papal envoys, some of whom were sent to particular people or places provisionally, to communicate a message or to conduct an investigation, and some of whom were more like resident ambassadors who represented the pope on a continuing basis. Lateran Councils met often and gathered the clergy from all over Europe to legislate for the church as a whole. The hierarchical structure of the church became more visible as ecclesiastical business tended to accumulate in Rome.

High medieval popes also reserved to themselves certain jurisdictional and coercive prerogatives. Only popes could officially canonize a saint, a powerful reservation of rights against local communities. Popes could excommunicate persons—that is, exclude them from the sacraments of the church and the community of Christians. This was a form of social death in that excommunicated persons could not eat, converse, or socialize with others. Popes could lay a territory under interdict. This decree forbade all religious services except baptisms and burials and was designed to bring maximum pressure to bear on a particular individual. Finally, popes could invoke the inquisition. Despite horror stories about the inquisition, this was a judicial mechanism fully rooted in Roman law and widely used in the medieval West. Basically, an inquisition involved churchmen taking sworn testimony in an attempt to discover heresy.

Who were the popes? What were they like? Most of them had been cardinals with years, if not decades, of experience in the government of the church. Many of the twelfth- and thirteenth-century popes were lawyers, which may explain, in part, their dedication to institutional and legal reforms. Not a single pope from this period has been canonized as a saint. One Englishman was elected; the rest were Roman, Italian, or French. Most were noblemen.

Institutions were important, but personalities mattered, too. Innocent III (r. 1198–1216), for example, was the most powerful man ever to hold the papal office. He came from a minor Italian noble family, received early training in theology and law, and entered the papal administration while in his twenties. His entire life was dedicated to promoting the legal prerogatives of the papacy and the moral improvement of Christian society. As a young man Innocent wrote *On the Contempt of the World,* in which he expressed his hope for a life of peace and contemplation. As an older man he hurled legal thunderbolts at the greatest public figures of the day.

From the ninth century on, the region south of Rome was contested among Byzantines, North African Muslims, and local potentates. In 1026 Norman pilgrims bound for the Holy Land landed in southern Italy, where local people invited them to enlist in the fight against the Muslims. By the 1040s the original Normans had been joined by many more who were seeking land and adventure. Initially opposed to the Normans, the papacy later allied with their leader as a counterweight against the Germans.

From his capital at Palermo, Roger II, also known as "Roger the Great" (r. 1130–1154), ruled a complex state that blended Byzantine, Lombard, and Norman structures. In Italy, as in England (see page 279), the Normans showed a genius for adaptation. Perched advantageously at the juncture of the Latin, Greek, and Arab worlds, the Norman court was more advanced in finance and bureaucratic administration than any of its European contemporaries. No one forgot for a moment, however, that the Normans were primarily great warriors. A chronicler said of the Normans, "They delight in arms and horses."

When the male Norman line died out, its heiress, Constance, married Henry VI of Germany (Barbarossa's son) and gave birth to Frederick II. For two generations the papacy struggled to break German control of southern Italy. Once the popes had defeated Frederick II, they decided to look for more pliant allies in the south. They invited a succession of French and Spanish princes to assume the Crown, thus touching off long-standing rivalries in the area. A profusion of outsiders always dominated southern Italy.

Capetian France, 987–1314

When the Treaty of Verdun created the West Frankish Kingdom in 843, no one knew what the future of France might be. Referring to France's tremendous diversity, the twentieth-century French leader Charles de Gaulle once quipped, "It is impossible to govern a country with 325 kinds of cheese." During the late ninth century and much of the tenth, the area suffered cruelly from constant waves of Viking attacks and from repeated failures of the Carolingian family to produce adult heirs to the throne. Chroniclers often quoted the lament of King Solomon: "Woe to thee, O land, whose king is a child." At the end of the tenth century, however, the Carolingians were replaced by the Capetians, the family of Hugh Capet (r. 987–996). The Capetians ruled France for more than three hundred years—an impressive achievement in light of the repeated failure of German dynasties. The first key issue we must pursue pertains to the power and prestige of the monarchy. Then, bearing in mind de Gaulle's joke, we explore how a large but very complex group of territories was assembled into a kingdom. Finally we look at the nature of government in medieval France and the principles on which that government rested.

From the very beginning the Capetian kings of France sought to preserve the royal office, increase its prestige, and consolidate its political base. Hugh Capet inaugurated the tradition of crowning his son as his successor during his own lifetime. This meant that when the old king died, a new king was already in place and the nobility could not easily meddle in the succession. Robert II (r. 996–1031) displayed the "royal touch," a ceremony in which the king was believed to be able to cure people of scrofula (a common respiratory ailment) by touching them. No French nobleman, no matter how powerful, ever laid claim to such miraculous powers. Louis VII (r. 1137–1180) began to make elegant tours of the country to put himself, his office, and his sparkling entourage on display.

The Capetians were heirs of the dukes of Paris. This meant that initially they controlled no more than Paris and its immediate region. They contested for control of this region with a number of ambitious and aggressive families. Louis VI (r. 1108–1137) systematically ground down all his local opponents and made his area, the Ile de France, one of the best-governed regions in all of France. Capetian kings also capitalized on their control of the old, rich, prestigious, and centrally located city of Paris. The kings promoted the shrine of Saint Denis, the legendary first bishop of Paris, as a kind of "national" shrine for France. The kings also controlled about two dozen bishoprics and some fifty monasteries in northern France. This power base gave the kings unrivaled opportunities to extend their influence and, in turn, to build up a cadre of loyal and articulate supporters. Although French kings provoked a few battles with the papacy, France experienced no investiture controversy.

For more than a century Hugh Capet and his successors steadily turned the French monarchy into a prestigious office on solid, if local and limited, political foundations. During the reigns of Louis VI and Louis VII the two great dynamics of high medieval French history come into view: First, the territory ruled by France's kings expanded enormously. Second, the kings finally overwhelmed the territorial princes after a centuries-long struggle.

France's territorial expansion was tightly connected to military success. The background to French military success is complicated. In the late eleventh and early twelfth centuries one family of French magnates, the counts of Anjou, acquired control over a good deal of western France by marriage, diplomacy, and intimidation. Then Geoffrey of Anjou married the heiress of the duchy of Normandy, whose father, William the Conqueror, we will meet later. A bit later Geoffrey's son and heir married Duchess Eleanor of Aquitaine, the recently divorced wife of Louis VII of France. In 1154 Henry of Anjou, as a result of incredibly complicated political and matrimonial alliances, became King Henry II of England, but he still retained control of about 60 percent of France.

For several generations the kings of France hammered away at this Angevin Empire. Henry of Anjou's four sons were viciously jealous of one another, and the French kings exploited their rivalries to weaken Angevin authority in western and southwestern France. When one of Henry's sons, King John of England, absconded with the fiancée of a vassal of King Philip II (r. 1180–1223), the king of France, Philip summoned John to court to answer for his conduct. John's refusal to appear led to war in 1202. By1204 Philip had won a resounding victory and control over a substantial portion of western France. The English and French kings came to blows over their competing claims to French territory several more times in the thirteenth century. Each time the French won, including a major victory over an allied English and German army at Bouvines in 1214.

Southeastern France was gained by wars of a different kind. In the last decades of the twelfth century several cities in the southeast became hotbeds of the Albigensian heresy—an important religious movement (see pages 309–310). Some Catholic locals and many churchmen urged the kings to undertake military action against the heretics. The French kings were prudent and bided their time until they had the resources to deal with

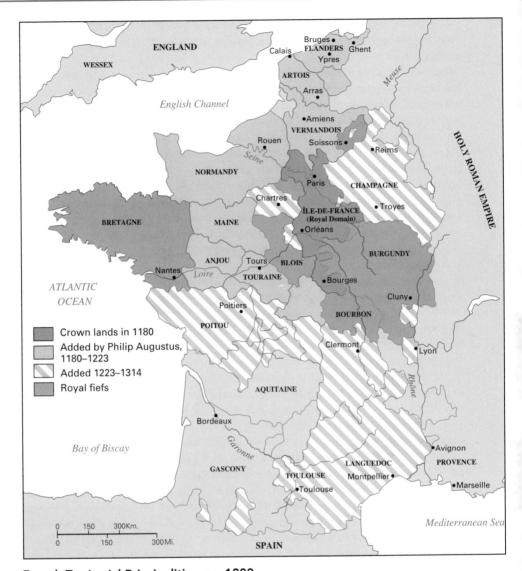

French Territorial Principalities, ca. 1200

As the Carolingian West Frankish Kingdom broke down and feudal bonds proliferated, many territories arose under counts and dukes. Their struggles to impose control locally and to fight off royal supervision animated French history.

this turbulent region. Under Louis VIII (r. 1223–1226) and Louis IX (r. 1226–1270) the French monarchy finally extended its authority to France's Mediterranean coast.

The chief political dynamic in France was the contest for power between the kings and the territorial princes. At stake was the monarchy's ability to introduce effective rule into the lands won in all those battles. Who were the territorial princes? They were locally powerful magnates, rather like the German dukes, most of whose ancestors had been officials appointed by the Carolingians. But whereas Germany comprised five major duchies, France had a dozen or more territorial principalities. In the tumultuous circumstances of the tenth and eleventh centuries some individuals and families had been remarkably successful in building castles, reducing the local population to subjection, and gathering into their own hands the powers that the Carolingian kings had once exercised in their localities.

Ironically, the territorial princes also faced localized rivalries for power and influence. Countless individuals built castles, brutally subjected local peasants, and became lords. Sometimes these individuals were the vassals of the territorial princes—say, the dukes of Normandy or the counts of Anjou—and sometimes they had vassals of their own. In the Carolingian world the number of vassals was small, their fidelity reasonably solid, and their services reliable. By 1100 the number of vassals was immense, their fidelity was constantly shifting, and they tended to provide only local military service. Scholars call this shift from effective Carolingian government to myriad local lordships a "feudal revolution."

For the kings of France to re-create central government, they had to overcome the disruptive tendencies of this revolution and then consolidate institutions. Under Louis VI and Louis VII some of the most powerful men in the realm visited court and swore allegiance to the Crown. Under Philip II and Louis IX the Capetians gradually turned this ceremonial obedience into effective subjection, just as Frederick Barbarossa had tried but failed to do in Germany.

In the twelfth and thirteenth centuries the Capetians followed a few basic policies to increase their ability to govern. They circumvented the local lords as much as possible. When they won military victories, the kings did not dole out the seized lands to lords as new fiefs but instead kept them in their own hands, or in the hands of family members as *appanages*. What is more, the kings introduced into these lands local officials, called bailiffs or provosts, who were of modest social background, had no personal ties to their assigned regions, often had some schooling in law, and were intensely loyal to the kings. By the time of Louis IX, officials called *enqueteurs* were sent around the country to inspect the work of bailiffs and provosts. Such roles had been unheard-of since the Carolingian *missi dominici* (see page 249). Louis also began to issue *ordonnances*, what we might call executive orders, that were binding on all the land under the king's control. These precepts are reminiscent of Carolingian capitularies (see page 246).

If in 1000 France was a land of innumerable tiny lordships, then by 1300 it was the best-governed kingdom in Europe. Indicative of France's position is the outcome of two battles between King Philip IV (r. 1285–1314) and Pope Boniface VIII (r. 1294–1303). First Philip attempted to tax the French clergy, and then he sought to bring a bishop before his court. Boniface angrily objected to Philip's intervention in ecclesiastical affairs. But things had changed drastically since the fateful confrontation between Henry IV and Gregory VII. Boniface had to back down.

The Welsh humorist Walter Map (1140–1209) provides this assessment of France in his day:

> The emperor of Byzantium and the king of Sicily may boast about their gold and silken cloth, but they have no men who can do more than talk, men incapable of war.

The Roman emperor or, as they say, the emperor of the Germans, has men apt in arms and warlike horses, but no gold, silk or any other wealth. . . . The king of England lacks nothing and possesses everything, men, horses, gold, silk, jewels, fruits and wild beasts. And we in France have nothing except bread, wine and joy.[1]

Walter comically underestimates the resources of the French. In 1300 theirs was the largest, richest, and best-governed kingdom in Europe. French culture and language were increasingly dominant. In Louis IX the Capetian family actually produced a saint of the Catholic Church—Saint Louis. Considering France's situation in 900, and compared with Germany's in 1300, these were impressive achievements.

THE BRITISH ISLES

In the British Isles expansion had three dimensions: the tremendous growth of the English government, England's relentless push into the Celtic world, and the emergence of states in the Celtic world. England, about the size of Alabama, is smaller than France or Germany and more homogeneous in population, culture, and language than either of them, or than Italy. Building effective governance in England was, therefore, a somewhat easier task than it was elsewhere. Nevertheless, England faced some acute dynastic, military, and political crises. Moreover, England shared an island with two Celtic neighbors, Wales and Scotland, whose inhabitants were close kin to the people of England's neighboring island, Ireland. For better or worse, the fates of the English and Celtic inhabitants of the British Isles are inseparable.

Viking and Norman Invasions in England   Alfred (r. 871–899; see page 243) heroically rallied the English against the Vikings, and his descendants ruled England for more than a century. They gradually rolled back the frontier of the "Danelaw," the areas of eastern and northern England controlled by Viking settlers (mainly Danes, hence the name). Alfred and his successors built strong central institutions. All free men in the realm owed allegiance to the king and could in principle be called to the militia, or *fyrd*. The great men of the realm attended meetings of the royal council, or *witan*, which was partly a court of law and partly a deliberative, consultative body. The king could issue writs—executive orders rather like Carolingian capitularies. The Danegeld—literally "money for the Danes"—was originally collected solely in times of danger and then slowly transformed into a regular tax. All of England was divided into shires, and each shire had a royally appointed officer the *shire-reeve* (or sheriff).

Late in the tenth century English leadership failed in the face of a severe threat from a new generation of Vikings. The powerful king of Denmark, Swein Forkbeard, conquered England in 1014, but survived his conquest by only two years. His son Cnut then ruled from 1016 to 1035, at which point power passed to Cnut's sons.

Cnut did not match the stereotype of the wild and woolly barbarian. He was simultaneously king of Denmark and England, and for a time of Norway, too. He wed his daughter to Emperor Henry III and himself to Emma, the widow of the last English king. He was cultured, Christian, and an acquaintance of the pope.

When Cnut's sons died in 1042 without heirs, the English nobles called over from Normandy Edward, called "the Confessor," the son of the last English king. Edward,

Northern and Eastern Europe, ca. 1200

Apart from Germany, the core states of Europe emerged inside the former Roman frontiers or right alongside them. After 900 an arc of new states emerged, from the Celtic realms and Iceland in the west, to Scandinavia in the north, to the western, southern, and eastern Slavs in eastern Europe.

who was unusually pious, had taken a vow of chastity. Because he was not going to have an heir, claimants to the English throne began jockeying for position. Edward seems to have promised his throne to William, the duke of Normandy. Most of the English nobles preferred Harold of Wessex, one of their number. In Norway Harald Sigurdson (who became known as Hardrada, or "Hard-Ruler") prepared to make a claim as Cnut's rightful heir.

When Edward died, the English elected Harold, and immediately he learned that Hardrada had invaded. He marched to meet the Norse challenger and won an impressive victory at Stamford Bridge, only to learn that William had meanwhile landed in the south. Foolishly Harold rushed south to meet William, without resting or reinforcing his troops. At Hastings William defeated Harold, and England was his for the taking.

Amid these frequent changes in rulers one thing remained constant: the smooth functioning of the Anglo-Saxon state. It is no surprise that neither Cnut nor William, known as "the Conqueror" (r. 1066–1089), desired to dismantle or replace the old English institutions. But William had won England by conquest, and he did introduce some changes. He turned most of the estates in England into fiefs and distributed them among some 180 of his most loyal followers. Each of these vassals held his fief in return for a fixed quota of soldiers for the royal army. To raise the approximately five thousand soldiers required by William, each of his vassals had to create vassals of his own. The technical name for this process of vassals creating vassals is *subinfeudation*. In 1087 William exacted the Salisbury Oath, which established the principle of liege homage, according to which the king was the final lord of all vassals. To avoid creating compact territorial principalities on the French model, William scattered his vassals' holdings around the kingdom. Finally, to learn as much as he could about his new kingdom, and about the fiefs he had assigned to his followers, William conducted a massive survey of England that resulted in 1086 in the *Domesday Book,* named for the Day of Judgment, against which there was no appeal. No comparable survey of any state was accomplished until the American census of 1790.

The Development of English Law and Government William was succeeded by two of his sons in turn, William II (r. 1089–1100) and Henry I (r. 1100–1135). Henry's only son drowned in a shipwreck, and the English nobles would accept neither his daughter Matilda as their queen nor her husband Geoffrey of Anjou as their king. Owing to William's conquest and settlement, most of the English elite were in fact Normans, and the Normans and Angevins were old foes. Consequently, the English turned in 1135 to a French prince, Stephen of Blois, who was a grandson of William the Conqueror through a daughter. Stephen I died childless in 1154 and bequeathed his kingdom to Henry of Anjou, the son of Geoffrey and Matilda, who ruled as Henry II (r. 1154–1189).

Henry was as much a French prince as an English king. From his father, mother, and wife (Eleanor of Aquitaine; see page 276), he had inherited a large part of France and was much preoccupied with his continental realm. He constantly battled his four sons for control of these vast French holdings. Two of these sons eventually became king. Richard I, also known as "Richard the Lionhearted" (r. 1189–1199), was a dashing prince who spent only ten months in England, preferring to pass his time on crusade or campaigning in France. John (r. 1199–1216) was defeated by France's Philip II, inducing contemporaries to mock him as "John Lackland" and "John Softsword."

On the surface it looks as though dynastic turmoil and military adventures make up the central themes of England's history. But just as Viking and Norman rulers built on the solid foundations of the Anglo-Saxon state, so the Anglo-Normans and Angevins retained and expanded those very foundations. They refined the financial machinery of the English government, the Exchequer, named for the checkerboard table on which the accounts were reckoned. They vastly improved the judicial institutions. Henry I began to send itinerant justices around the realm. He brought the royal court, with its swift, fair, and competent justice, within the reach of most people, and he made royal justice more attractive than the justice available in local lords' courts. Henry II expanded the work of the courts and created an extensive system of writs. These documents, available to almost anyone, had the effect of transferring cases into the royal courts. This expansion of the work of the royal courts led to the emergence of a common law in England—a law common to all people, courts, and cases.

Henry II used the sworn inquest to learn about his realm. He conducted an inquest of knights' service to find out what service vassals owed to which people. He conducted an inquest of sheriffs to learn how the sheriffs were performing their jobs and replaced those found shirking their responsibilities. This action is the context for the Robin Hood stories about the cruel sheriff of Nottingham and the kind king who looks out

Swift and Certain Justice *This picture from about 1130 depicts some of the forty-four thieves hung by Sheriff Ralph Basset in 1124. As a common law spread throughout England, criminals were more likely to be caught and punished.* (The Pierpont Morgan Library, New York/ Art Resource, NY)

for the people. Finally the Anglo-Norman and Angevin kings employed in their government "men raised from the dust," as one aristocratic contemporary contemptuously called them. These were men from the middling ranks of society, perhaps with some training in law, who were loyal to the king and advanced his interests against the aristocrats, who were intensely jealous of their own rights and privileges.

England's relations with the church fell somewhere between Germany's and France's in both intensity and outcome. Anglo-Saxon kings generally enjoyed cordial relations with the church on a traditional Carolingian model. William the Conqueror controlled the church with an iron hand but introduced reforms and reformers who were acceptable to Rome. Perhaps Gregory VII left William alone because he did not wish to fight on too many fronts simultaneously. Archbishop Anselm of Canterbury and Henry I had a quarrel that lasted several years, but they finally mended their differences in a settlement that anticipated the terms of the Concordat of Worms. Henry II was always anxious to extend the influence of his courts. In 1164 he decided that "criminous clerks," or members of the clergy who had committed a crime, should be judged in royal courts. The archbishop of Canterbury, Thomas Becket (ca. 1118–1170), protested that clerics could be tried only in church courts. Although the two sides came to a reconciliation, a band of overly zealous knights murdered Becket, believing that they were doing the king's bidding. In fact, the crime so outraged the church and the public that Henry had to back down on criminous clerks and give up some authority to Rome. Despite these religious quarrels, however, England experienced no investiture controversy.

John's conflict with the church resulted in far more dramatic changes for England. The loss of Normandy had been costly in terms of prestige and resources. In difficult circumstances John got into a row with Pope Innocent III because he refused to admit to England the pope's candidate for archbishop of Canterbury. John had already had minor scrapes with ecclesiastical officials because of his exploitation of the church's revenues. Eventually he submitted because Innocent had laid England under interdict and John needed the pope's support for his planned war against Philip II of France. True to his nickname "Softsword," John lost at Bouvines (see page 276) and thus ended his quarrel with Rome.

With John's inglorious defeat and shameful capitulation, the barons of England had had enough. These barons (a general name for the upper ranks of English society) were increasingly upset that an expanding royal government limited their influence. In 1215 a large group of disgruntled barons forced King John to sign the Magna Carta, or "Great Charter" (so called because it was written on an unusually large sheet of parchment). This document required the king to respect the rights of feudal lords, not abuse his judicial powers, and consult his "natural" advisers—that is, the barons.

John tried to wiggle out of the Magna Carta, but he died in 1216, leaving only a minor heir, and the barons exacted many concessions from the regency government. When Henry III came of age in 1234, he struggled to win a limited application of the Magna Carta. The barons, on the contrary, wanted a voice in devising royal policy, especially military policy, in light of recent defeats. They also wished to have some say in naming the king's closest advisers and in controlling the work of the king's agents, especially judges. This tension between king and barons led to several meetings of the royal court, often called *parliaments,* a French word meaning, roughly, "talking together." (The genuine ancestors of England's historic Parliament met in 1265 and 1295.) Initially these meetings had no fixed rights or procedures, no set group of attendees, and no defined role. The kings viewed them as clever political devices to win support for royal policies. The barons viewed them as opportunities to play a real role in a government that had been marginalizing them. In retrospect we can see that the English were groping to find a way to build consultation into their system.

The reign of Edward I (1272–1307) sums up the achievements of England's rulers in the High Middle Ages. Like his predecessors, Edward instituted sworn inquests to ascertain his rights and resources. He issued numerous statutes, laws that bear comparison with Louis IX's *ordonnances* (see page 278)—which earned him the nickname "the English Justinian." He worked skillfully with the newly emerging Parliament. And like other English rulers before him, Edward balanced political and military accomplishments, bravely fighting for years on the Welsh and Scottish frontiers.

The Celtic Realms When the Romans appeared on the scene, Celtic peoples could be found in virtually every region from Ireland to Anatolia. Most Celts were absorbed by more numerous and powerful Germanic and Slavic peoples. It was in the British Isles that the most durable and distinctive Celtic regions evolved into Ireland, Wales, and Scotland. Two essential dynamics characterized each of these regions. First, tiny political entities gradually turned into larger kingdoms. Second, relations between England and the Celtic realms were everywhere decisive in the historical development of the latter.

In each of the Celtic realms the movement toward greater unity was opened by the efforts of powerful, ambitious leaders to subjugate numerous well-entrenched local potentates, many of whom had expanded their power during the period of Viking invasions. In Ireland Brian Boru (r. 976–1014) became the first ruler to exercise real authority over most of the island. In Wales Rhodri the Great (d. 898) and Howell the Good (d. 950) were the first rulers to gain at least nominal authority over the whole of the land. Although disunity is a continuous theme of Scottish history, the centuries after the reign of Kenneth MacAlpin (843–858) reveal the slow creation of a national tradition.

The course of development in the Celtic lands was disrupted by the English in the eleventh and especially the twelfth centuries. The Norman Conquest of England brought adventurers to the frontiers of Wales and Scotland. Sometimes these continental knights advanced with the support of William the Conqueror and his sons, but more often they looked to wild frontier regions for opportunities to escape tight control. In Wales some Normans allied with various local princes who resented the growing power of the Welsh kings. Prince Grufydd ap Cynan (d. 1137) then turned to King Henry I in 1114 and promised allegiance if Henry would aid him in his quest to establish his authority throughout Wales. From that time forward, the actual power of Welsh rulers varied greatly, and English kings usually claimed some authority over the region. Scottish kings managed to enlist a good many Norman knights into their service, but this recruitment effort angered the English kings and clouded the lines of allegiance in Northumbria, where many of those knights had been sent in the first place. Civil disturbances in Ireland induced King Rory O'Connor (r. 1156–1186) to turn to King Henry II of England for mercenaries to help him establish his power. But by 1171

Henry had invaded Ireland himself and inaugurated the complicated English involvement that persists to this day.

Edward I of England intervened repeatedly in the Celtic world. In 1277 he invaded Wales with the intention of totally subduing the Welsh. He built immense castles, whose ruins are still impressive today. Edward also made his son the Prince of Wales—still the title of the heir to the British throne. Between 1100 and 1260 England and Scotland went to war four times, and Edward resolved to put an end to this struggle by annexing Scotland. The Scots, however, rallied to the standard of Robert Bruce (r. 1306–1329), a dashing knight who was, ironically, of Norman extraction. Robert managed to free Scotland for centuries.

THE GROWTH OF NEW STATES

The proliferation of new states constitutes one of the most remarkable examples of expansion in high medieval Europe. In Spain Christian rulers waged a steady war of reconquest against the Islamic caliphate of Cordoba that led to the emergence of the kingdoms of Portugal, Castile, and Aragon. In Scandinavia mighty leaders built durable kingdoms in Denmark, Norway, and Sweden. Local rulers created a band of new Slavic states running from the Baltic to the Balkans, from Poland to Bulgaria. To the east of those Slavic realms, around the city of Kiev, the Scandinavian Rus founded the first state on Russian soil. Between 900 and 1300 the geographic range of Europe's political entities more than doubled.

Reconquista and Kingdom Building in Spain Historians perceive two driving forces in the rich and colorful history of medieval Spain. One is the bloody experience of several centuries of war along an expanding frontier. The other is the constant interplay within the Iberian Peninsula of three vibrant cultures: Christian, Jewish, and Muslim. We describe the first of these forces in this chapter and the second in the next.

The emirate of Cordoba (see page 239) began breaking up after 1002, and the weakness of the tiny successor realms afforded an unprecedented opportunity to the Christians living in the north of the peninsula. King Sancho I (r. 1000–1035) of Navarre launched an offensive against the Muslims. This war, carried on intermittently until the fifteenth century, came to be called the *Reconquista*, the "Reconquest."

Before Sancho died, he divided his realm among his sons; thus the kingdoms of Aragon and Castile arose alongside Navarre. Alfonso I (r. 1065–1109) of Castile really advanced the Reconquista. In 1085 his forces captured the Muslim stronghold and old Visigothic capital of Toledo, an important moral and strategic victory. Alfonso's military successes owed much to the dashing warrior Rodrigo Díaz de Vivar, known as "El Cid" ("the Lord," from the Arabic *sayyid*). Rodrigo, a gifted but slightly unscrupulous mercenary, fought for both Muslims and Christians. The Reconquista was moving on three fronts. In the east the emerging kingdom of Aragon-Catalonia advanced along the Mediterranean coast. In the center León-Castile pressed hard against al-Andalus. In the west the nascent kingdom of Portugal became a factor in Iberian politics. Rodrigo's successes, and the reconquest of Toledo, led the retreating Muslims to summon aid in the 1150s from militant North African Muslims. The Christian advance temporarily stopped.

In the early thirteenth century Pope Innocent III stirred up crusading zeal and lent encouragement to clerics and nobles in Spain who wished to reopen hostilities against the Muslims. In 1212 a combined Castilian-Aragonese army won a decisive victory at Las Navas de Tolosa, south of Toledo. The victory of Las Navas de Tolosa was a great turning point in Spanish history. The outcome of the Reconquista, which did not conclude until the fifteenth century, was never again in doubt.

Twelfth-century Spanish kings, especially in Castile, imposed hereditary rule and exacted oaths of allegiance from their free subjects. The kings tried to force powerful nobles to become their vassals. They were more successful on the military frontier than back in their homelands because in the war zones nobles could be assigned new fiefs carved out of recent conquests. Kings profited from the Reconquista to enhance their status and power.

In the thirteenth century Spain produced kings of genius, especially James I of Aragon (r. 1213–1276) and Ferdinand III (r. 1217–1252) and Alfonso X (r. 1252–1284) of Castile. These rulers were pious men, genuinely inspired by the ideal of the Crusades (discussed later in this chapter) and zealous in the promotion of the church. They also were hardheaded rulers. James turned Aragon-Catalonia into the greatest naval power of the western Mediterranean and a formidable economic power. Ferdinand and Alfonso derived great prestige from their successful wars. Those wars provided a flow of booty and a supply of lands to reward the Castilian nobles who spent their energy on the frontier rather than on attacking the king. These kings built strong central governments. Increasingly they used professional officers in key government posts and dispatched roving officials from the court to check on local rulers. Alfonso issued a major law book for the whole of Castile. These laws were based on Roman law and emphasized royal power. The Cortes, a representative assembly made up primarily of urban notables, began forging an alliance between the king and the towns. Iberia was not united in the thirteenth century, but it had evolved into four coherent blocks: a small and impotent Muslim region in Valencia and Granada, and three vibrant kingdoms centered on Portugal, Castile, and Aragon.

Scandinavia   Europe's expanding map saw new states in Scandinavia, the
                               Roman name for the lands that became Denmark, Norway,
and Sweden. Although the faint beginnings of political consolidation in Denmark can be traced to the Carolingian period, actual development of the states of Scandinavia dates from the tenth and eleventh centuries. Overseas expansion played one key role in northern political development. Another was the slow achievement of political unity by kings who had to overcome powerful local interests.

The sea, not the land, is the great fact of Scandinavian history. Norway has more than 1,000 miles of coastline, and no point in Denmark is more than 35 miles from the sea. Scandinavia did not offer opportunities for large, land-based kingdoms or empires, but the sea provided Scandinavians with a wide scope for activities.

More than any other people of the north, the Vikings capitalized on the sea as a highway. Vikings were raiders, of course, but also settlers. Much of northeastern England, the Danelaw, was settled by Northmen. In 911 the Norwegian Rollo and his followers settled what became Normandy in northern France. Between 870 and 930 many Norwegians and some Danes settled Iceland and a little later established bases in Greenland. In 862 a Swedish force, accustomed to raiding and trading along the rivers of what would become Russia, established a base at Novgorod. Raiders, traders, and settlers, the Scandinavians fostered the expansion of Europe.

Because the sea made exit from Scandinavia so easy, and because the whole region had absolutely no tradition of unified government, kings had a hard time establishing their power. Essentially kings were war leaders with loyal bands of followers. Territorial states were thus built up as powerful leaders persuaded or forced more and more men to join them. Denmark's was the first of the northern monarchies to emerge in the early tenth century. Norway's monarchy arose a little later in the tenth century, but for much of the eleventh century Norway was under Danish control. As the Danes fell more and more under German influence in the eleventh century, Norway managed to break free. Sweden's monarchy was the last to emerge in the northern world; it was not fully stable until the twelfth century, but by 1300 it had become the most powerful.

Christianity came rather late to Scandinavia, with the first missionaries entering the region in the ninth century and widespread conversion ensuing in the eleventh. Norway's King Olaf (r. 1016–1028), affectionately remembered as Saint Olaf, was the first northern king who actively promoted Christianization. Scandinavian kings viewed the church as a useful adjunct to their power. They cooperated in creating bishoprics on the assumption that members of the high clergy would be educated, talented allies in the process of building central governments. Ironically, the church was a stabilizing force in Scandinavia during the very years when the investiture controversy wreaked havoc in Germany.

The Slavic World   In eastern Europe, between the Elbe and Dnieper Rivers, lived numerous peoples customarily called Slavs. Their languages were once much alike but differentiated over time. Partly because of language differences and partly because of the areas in which these people settled, scholars divide them into western, southern, and eastern Slavs. These peoples were never conquered by the Romans, assimilated few influences from the classical world, and received Christianity later than western Europe. Still, as states began emerging in eastern Europe, they exhibited many of the same problems that older and more westerly states had encountered: shifting frontiers, clashes between ambitious rulers and powerful nobles, and outside military and cultural influences.

The first western Slavic state was Great Moravia, created in the 830s by capable dukes while the Carolingian Empire was experiencing civil wars. As we saw earlier (see pages 252–253), the Moravian leaders invited the missionaries Cyril and Methodius to their realm, thereby beginning the establishment of Christianity in eastern Europe. Moravia's early promise was cut short in 906 by the Magyars. Also in the late ninth century the Přemysl dynasty forged a kingdom in Bohemia that lasted through the Middle Ages, although for long periods it was under German domination.

The greatest of the western Slavic states was Poland. In the 960s and 970s Duke Mieszko (d. 992) unified a substantial territory and received Christianity from Rome. The first action created the Polish state, and the second anchored Poland firmly within the orbit of the Latin West. Mieszko's descendants, the Piast dynasty of kings, ruled until Boleslav III divided the kingdom among his three sons in 1138. For more than two centuries Polish development was retarded as weak rulers contested for power with local magnates, who themselves were successfully subordinating both peasants and men of middling status.

The creation of a Hungarian state played a decisive role in dividing the western and southern Slavs. The Magyars were disruptive raiders from the 880s until their defeat by Otto I in 955. After that disaster the Magyars concentrated on building a state within the Danube basin, the home base from which they had launched their raids. The Magyars, who were related to the Huns and Avars, blended with the local Slavs. King (later Saint) Stephen (r. 997–1038), who received Christianity from Rome, was the real founder of Hungary. Like Poland, Hungary was attached to the Latin West. Stephen's family, the Arpads, ruled in Hungary for centuries. They built ruling centers at Buda and Esztergom, created an impressive territorial organization, and promoted the growth of the church. They also expanded in almost every direction.

The southern Slavs built a band of states that extended across the Balkans. The first, reaching back to the seventh century, was Bulgaria. The Bulgars were a Turkic people who first led and then merged into the local Slavic population. The first Bulgarian state lasted until the early eleventh century, when the Byzantines, who had suffered many defeats at Bulgarian hands, destroyed it. By the late twelfth century, when Byzantium itself had weakened, a new Bulgarian state emerged, but its rulers never had the firm control that their predecessors had wielded. Under Khan Boris (r. 852–879) Bulgaria made the momentous decision to accept Orthodox Christianity from Constantinople instead of Roman Catholicism, despite the pope's best efforts.

To the west of Bulgaria lay Serbia, a region dominated until the fourteenth century by Bulgaria and Byzantium. Perhaps because of constant outside threats, Serbia made little progress toward internal unity. The region accepted Orthodox Christianity. To the west of Serbia lay Croatia, a land formed when two originally independent areas, Dalmatia on the Adriatic coast and Croatia itself, were joined together in the early tenth century. Through much of the tenth and eleventh centuries, Croatia managed to preserve itself and evade the clutches of Hungary, Byzantium, and Venice. By 1107, however, Croatia was incorporated by Hungary as a more or less autonomous region. Croatia, owing to Italian and Hungarian influence, became Roman Catholic.

The creation of the major eastern Slavic state is shrouded in mystery and legend. It seems that in 862 a Swedish Viking named Rurik and his followers, called Varangians, established or seized a trading camp at Novgorod. A few years later Oleg (r. 879–912) took over Kiev and made it his base of operations. Thus was founded Kievan Rus, a state that, like Hungary and Bulgaria, began with an outside, elite leadership over a local Slavic majority. Kievan Rus lasted until the Mongols destroyed it in 1240.

Kiev was ruled by grand dukes who pursued four basic policies. They created a vast trading network that linked Germany, Scandinavia, Byzantium, and the caliphate. They shared power with regional nobles who built up several important towns of their own. They received Orthodox Christianity from Constantinople in 988. And, finally, they struggled to defend Kiev, indeed Rus territory as a whole, from wave after wave of invaders from the eastern steppes.

Eventually Kievan Rus was destroyed by the Mongols. These were a loose coalition of pastoral nomads from Mongolia (lands lying east of the Caspian Sea and north of China) and Turkic soldiers. The charismatic leader Jenghiz Khan (1154–1227) turned the Mongols into an invincible fighting force. He and his successors built an empire stretching from China to eastern Europe. In 1221 the Mongols began their attacks on Rus, and in 1240 Kiev fell.

Jenghiz Khan's empire was divided into several khanates on his death, with Rus dominated by the Golden Horde, so called because of the splendid golden tent from which they ruled. The Mongols accorded subject people considerable autonomy, but they demanded heavy taxes and occasionally carried out brutal raids to remind everyone who was in control. Through their domination of trade, the Mongols weakened the urbanization and commerce built up by Kievan Rus. Throughout the West, people were alarmed by the Mongol onslaught.

When Charlemagne was crowned emperor in 800, only Bulgaria existed as a state in the vast lands of eastern Europe. But the overriding trends of the era inexorably swept into that region. Three centuries later those lands were home to several small states and also to some impressively large and successful ones. The Slavic world was thoroughly pagan in 800 and largely Christian by 1200. State building and Christianization in eastern Europe represent two significant examples of European expansion in the High Middle Ages.

THE CRUSADES, 1095–1291

In 1096 an army of Christian knights who called themselves pilgrims left Europe to liberate the Holy Land from the Muslim "infidel." (This was the first of many crusades, so called because the warriors were *crucesignati*, "signed by the cross.") By the late eleventh century Europe was a fortress that had marshaled its resources for an attack on the world around it. Europe's expanding population, economic dynamism, political consolidation, and buoyant optimism made possible not only the First Crusade but also many more over two centuries.

The Background: East and West   With the accession in 867 of the Macedonian dynasty in the person of Basil I, the Byzantine Empire experienced a period of vigorous, successful rule that lasted until 1025. Although the Macedonians fostered striking cultural achievements, carried out significant administrative reforms, and established the kind of tight control of the church that had been so elusive in the iconoclastic era (see pages 237–238), they were primarily great soldiers. Along the Balkan frontier the Macedonian rulers kept both the Bulgarians and Kievan Rus at bay while also neutralizing many smaller Slavic principalities. Basil II (r. 976–1025), called "the Bulgar Slayer," wore down Bulgaria in a series of relentless campaigns. In the West the Macedonians maintained an effective diplomacy with Venice that permitted lucrative commercial opportunities in the Adriatic. In the East the Macedonian rulers profited from the gradual dissolution of the Abbasid caliphate by expanding their frontier in Anatolia.

By contrast, throughout the ninth and tenth centuries the ability of the caliphs in Baghdad to control their vast empire declined precipitously. Egypt and North Africa escaped Baghdad's control almost completely, and religious strife between Sunni and Shi'ite Muslims further destabilized the Islamic state.

After Basil II's death in 1025, Byzantium suffered a long period of short reigns and abrupt changes in policy. Great aristocratic families in Anatolia slipped from imperial control. In the capital factional squabbling swirled around the imperial court, and in

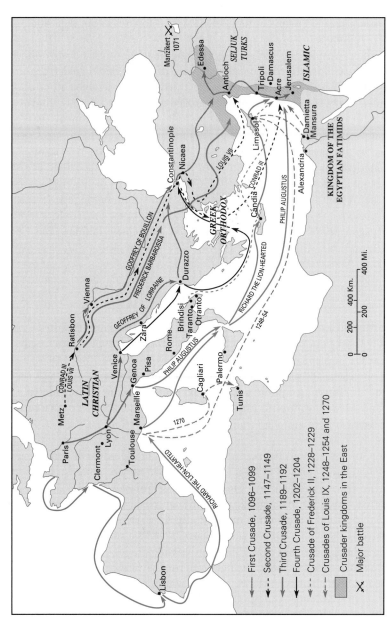

The Crusades, 1096–1270

The long-standing Western interest in the Holy Land is vividly illustrated by the Crusades. Note the numerous routes taken, lands traversed, destinations attained, and points of cultural encounter.

First Crusade, 1096–1099
Second Crusade, 1147–1149
Third Crusade, 1189–1192
Fourth Crusade, 1202–1204
Crusade of Frederick II, 1228–1229
Crusades of Louis IX, 1248–1254 and 1270
Crusader kingdoms in the East
Major battle

the person of Patriarch Michael Cerularius (r. 1043–1058) the church sought to break out from two centuries of domination. When in 1054 Cerularius and Pope Leo IX (r. 1049–1054) quarreled so bitterly over ecclesiastical customs that they excommunicated each other, the traditionally cooperative papal-Byzantine religious diplomacy gave way to a deep schism between the Catholic and Orthodox Churches that still exists. Religious tensions were complicated when the staunchly anti-Byzantine Normans began creating their kingdom in southern Italy.

It was in these divisive circumstances that the Seljuk Turks appeared on the eastern frontier of Anatolia. Bands of Turks, peoples from central Asia, had been serving the caliphs as mercenaries since the ninth century. With new leaders at their head, and with both the caliphate and the empire distracted, the Turks broke into Anatolia with a vengeance. In 1071 at Manzikert a skirmish between Byzantine and Turkish soldiers turned into a rout in which Byzantium lost an army, an emperor, and the Macedonian reputation for military prowess.

Ever since the emergence of the Turkish threat in the early eleventh century, the Byzantines had been seeking mercenary help. The imperial defeat at Manzikert made their search more urgent and led to appeals to the West. Some troops were rounded up but not enough, so in 1095 Emperor Alexius Comnenus (r. 1081–1118) sent envoys to ask Pope Urban II (r. 1088–1099) to support a plea for mercenary help against the Turks.

To most people in western Europe, the Turkish threat to Byzantium mattered little. What *did* alarm Westerners was Turkish attacks on pilgrims to Jerusalem. The popes saw in the plight of the Byzantines and of Western pilgrims some opportunities to manifest their leadership of the church. The papacy also wanted very much to heal the Roman-Orthodox rift. The popes, therefore, placed a high value on aiding the Byzantines.

Moreover, a crusade was perfectly consonant with the ethos of the knights of western Europe. Knights were born and trained to fight. The literature of the age glorified war and warriors. But churchmen had for some years been advancing an ideal of Christian knighthood that stressed fighting God's enemies. In the late tenth century there arose, first in France and then in many other places, peace movements called the "Peace of God" or the "Truce of God." These movements sought to prevent war in certain seasons, such as around Christmas and Easter, and on certain days of the week, chiefly Sunday. Peace movements also attempted to outlaw fighting near churches, protect noncombatants, and soften the treatment of enemies and captives. Together the movements induced knights to fight non-Christians outside Europe. Along with religious zeal, a quest for fame and fortune motivated many young men whose political prospects at home were limited.

The "Pilgrimage" to Jerusalem

Pope Urban II received Alexius's envoys in 1095 and then left Italy for France. He was actually a fugitive because Henry IV controlled Rome. In November at Clermont, Urban delivered a rousing speech to a vast Christian assembly. He ignored the Eastern emperor's appeal for aid and instead promised salvation to soldiers who would enlist in a great struggle to free the Holy Land. The crowd acclaimed his words with a shout of "God wills it!"

By 1096 four large armies, which eventually swelled to perhaps a hundred thousand men—mostly French knights, with a smattering of troops from other parts of Europe— assembled under the leadership of the pope's legate. The forces were to rendezvous at

Constantinople, where they seem to have expected a cordial imperial welcome and all necessary assistance. Alexius, however, took a rather different view, for several reasons. First, a ragtag band of ordinary people preceding the Crusaders had torn through the Balkans like a plague of locusts. Second, the crusading armies themselves sorely taxed the imperial authorities, who spent a lot of time and money arranging their passage from the frontier of Hungary to the gates of Constantinople. Finally, Alexius wanted mercenaries to fend off Turks in Anatolia, not armed pilgrims intent on liberating Palestine.

After receiving nominal promises of loyalty and the return or donation of any lands captured, Alexius moved the Crusaders into Anatolia. Almost immediately the Latin army defeated a Turkish force, thus earning a valuable, though short-lived, reputation for invincibility. The troops then entered Syria and laid siege to Antioch, which did not fall until 1098. At this point rivalries among the Crusaders came into the open. One force went to the frontier of Armenia and carved out a principality. One of the ubiquitous Normans kept Antioch for himself. The main army pressed on to Jerusalem and, after a short but fierce siege, conquered it in July 1099. A Muslim historian describes the scene:

> In the Masjid [Mosque] al-Aqsa the Franks slaughtered more than 70,000 people, among them a large number of Imams and Muslim scholars, devout and ascetic men who had left their homelands to live lives of pious seclusion in the Holy Place. The Franks stripped the Dome of the Rock [the Mosque of Umar, near the al-Aqsa mosque, pictured on page 243] of more than forty silver candelabra, each of them weighing 3,600 drams [almost 40 pounds], and a great silver lamp weighing forty-four Syrian pounds, as well as a hundred and fifty smaller candelabra and more than twenty gold ones, and a great deal more booty.[2]

Godfrey of Bouillon, leader of the troops that had "liberated" Jerusalem, was named "Advocate of the Holy Sepulcher" and became ruler of the Christians in the East. He lived only a short time, however, and was replaced by his brother, Baldwin, as king of Jerusalem in 1100.

Judged on its own terms, the First Crusade was a success. The Holy Land was retaken from the infidel, and the pilgrim routes were passable once more. Entirely uncertain, however, were the prospects of the crusader states, the future course of Western relations with Byzantium, and the reaction of the Islamic world once it recovered from its initial shock.

The Later Crusades

Crusading was intended to protect the Holy Land and keep open the pilgrim routes to Jerusalem. The creation of the small crusader states in the hostile environment of Syria and Palestine made continued crusading almost inevitable. In 1144 the tiny crusader state at Edessa on the Armenian frontier fell to a Muslim army. Although the news saddened Europeans, it took immense efforts by the papacy and other religious leaders to launch another crusade. Finally Conrad III of Germany and Louis VII of France agreed to lead it, but because neither would willingly submit to the other's authority, the Second Crusade accomplished little. Its one achievement was an accident. In 1147 an army of English, French, and Flemish soldiers who were proceeding to the Holy Land by sea put in

Saladin Routs the Franks   *This vivid image of Saladin defeating the Franks—that is, the Crusaders—at the Battle of Hattin (1187) comes from a thirteenth-century history by Matthew Paris. In this battle the Franks lost an army and their relic of the true cross and shortly afterward lost control of Jerusalem. These shocking defeats precipitated the Third Crusade.*   (Courtesy, Master and Fellows of Corpus Christi College Library, Cambridge)

on the Iberian coast and captured Lisbon. This opened a new front in the Reconquista and laid the foundations for the later kingdom of Portugal.

The papacy called for the Third Crusade when Saladin (1138–1193), a powerful local leader typical of the disintegrating Abbasid caliphate, recaptured Jerusalem in 1187. It is a measure of the force of the crusading ideal that the greatest crowned heads of the day—Frederick Barbarossa, Philip II, and Richard the Lionhearted—answered the call. It must be said, however, that only Frederick did so enthusiastically. Frederick died en route in 1190, while Philip returned home in 1191 and Richard in 1192. Because neither Richard nor Philip would stay in Palestine to fight Saladin, this crusade merely won access to Jerusalem for pilgrims.

Disappointed with the results of the Third Crusade, Innocent III began calling for another crusade immediately on his election in 1198. Popular preachers summoned an army, once again largely French, and the pope and the Fourth Crusade's military leaders engaged the Venetians to construct a fleet of war and transport ships. In less than eighteen months they produced 50 galleys and 450 transports, a tribute to the awesome capabilities of the Venetian shipyards.

Ships, however, were expensive, and the Venetians drove hard bargains. When too few Crusaders and too little money appeared, the Venetians suggested that the Crusaders could discharge some of their debt by recapturing from the Hungarians the formerly Venetian port of Zara on the Dalmatian coast. This idea outraged the pope, but he could do little about it. Then into the camp of the Crusaders came a pretender to the Byzantine throne, who promised that if the Crusaders would help him to claim his patrimony, he would contribute to the cost of the Crusade. The Venetians urged the indebted Crusaders to accept this offer, and, to the horror of Innocent III, the Fourth Crusade turned to Constantinople.

Once in Constantinople the Crusaders learned that their new ally had few friends in the Byzantine capital, but the venture hardly collapsed. The Venetians saw an opportunity to expand business opportunities in the East, and the soldiers welcomed a chance to plunder the Mediterranean's greatest city and to avenge what they regarded as a century of Byzantine perfidy. Thus the Fourth Crusade captured not Jerusalem but Constantinople. Until 1261, the Eastern and Western churches were reunited under papal leadership, and substantial tracts of the Balkans fell to Western knights under a "Latin emperor" of Constantinople.

In later decades popes began to take a more active role in planning crusades. No pope wanted to lose control of a crusade as Innocent had done, and all popes saw that the liberation of Jerusalem required a solid base of operations in the eastern Mediterranean. Egypt was the objective of the Fifth (1218–1221) and Sixth (1248–1250) Crusades. Despite a few victories, the Crusaders could not win a secure base. No further crusades to the East were organized in the thirteenth century. In 1291 Acre, the last Crusader stronghold, fell, and the original crusading era ended.

During the crusading period the Holy Land was not the sole object of Crusaders' attentions. In about 1140 the pope preached a crusade against the Normans in southern Italy, and several popes in the thirteenth century, fearful of imperial encroachment, preached crusades against the Staufer dynasty in Italy. In 1147 the papacy authorized a crusade in the Baltic that opened nearly four centuries of German expansion into the pagan Slavic lands to the east of Saxony. In 1208 Innocent III proclaimed a crusade against the Albigensians in southwestern France.

A Balance Sheet   Why did the Crusades end? There are several reasons. By the late thirteenth century more violence was being directed inward against heretics and political foes of the papacy than outward against the alleged enemies of Christendom itself. As rulers became more sophisticated and controlled more territory, they had less interest in the intangible benefits of crusading, such as prestige. Whereas the cities of Italy once needed to open up Mediterranean ports, now they wished to secure comparative advantage over one another. The Christian ideals of poverty, charity, and service were incompatible with warfare. Literary images provide another insight into the decline of the Crusades. After 1300 we are less likely to read about a Christian knight fighting honorably for God and king than about a gentleman of manners seeking the favor of a fair lady.

Crusading was brutal. Soldiers and their clerical companions spent years away from their homes and families, endured scorching Mediterranean heat, and suffered shortages of food and basic supplies. The vulnerable crusader states never received enough settlers to be viable communities, and consequently intermarriage with locals was common and gradually produced a hybrid culture that was neither European nor Middle Eastern. Warfare was constant on all sides. When Crusaders conquered a town, they executed many locals. When Muslims recaptured a town, they did the same. The tremendous enthusiasm evident in 1095 could not be sustained over two centuries.

A balance sheet for the crusading movement as a whole reveals more losses than gains. The Crusades exported many violent men from Europe, but it is not clear that Europe became a less violent place. As might be expected, the Crusades devastated relations between Christian Europe and the Muslim world. The Fourth Crusade mortally wounded Byzantium and worsened the already tense standoff between the Catholic and Orthodox Churches. Crusading zeal was directed deliberately against heretics and coincidentally against Jews. The Jewish populations of several towns were massacred on the eve of the First and Second Crusades. The Crusades did not create anti-Semitism, but they aggravated it. Some women, particularly in France, from which the majority of all Crusaders came, may have enjoyed momentary benefits in terms of control of land, wealth, and people while their husbands were away. But the long-term trend in feudal society was disadvantageous to women, and the Crusades did not change that. Finally, the Crusades may have done as much to disrupt Mediterranean trade as to promote it. Italian urban rivalries took the place of Latin-Muslim-Byzantine ones. That a single new product, the apricot, entered Europe in the crusading era seems small reward for such a huge effort.

IMPORTANT EVENTS

862 Founding of Kiev

870–930 Settlement of Iceland

962 Imperial coronation of Otto I

987 Accession of Hugh Capet in France

988 Kievan Rus accept Orthodox Christianity

1016 Conquest of England by Cnut

1066 Norman Conquest of England

1072–1085 Pontificate of Gregory VII

1078 Decree against lay investiture

1085 Spanish reconquest of Toledo

1086 *Domesday Book*

1095–1099 First Crusade

1122 Concordat of Worms

1171 Henry II of England invades Ireland

1176 Battle of Legnano

1198–1216 Pontificate of Innocent III

1202–1204 French drive English out of Normandy

1203 Fourth Crusade

1212 Battles of Bouvines and Las Navas de Tolosa

1215 Magna Carta

1265 First Parliament in England

1294–1303 Quarrel between Boniface VIII and Philip IV

1295 Model Parliament

NOTES

1. Walter Map, *De nugis curialum,* 5.5, in John H. Mundy, *Europe in the High Middle Ages* (London: Longman, 1973), p. 387.
2. Slightly adapted from the *Gesta Francorum,* trans. August C. Krey, in *The First Crusade* (Princeton, N.J.: Princeton University Press, 1921), p. 257.

SUGGESTED READING

Bartlett, Robert. *The Making of Europe: Conquest, Colonization and Cultural Change, 950–1350.* 1993. An engaging account of the expansion and "Europeanization" of Europe.

Bisson, Thomas, ed. *Cultures of Power: Lordship, Status, and Process in Twelfth-Century Europe.* 1995. The thirteen sparkling essays in this book cover much of Europe and attempt to explain how power was actually wielded in a society in which states were just emerging.

Bloch, Marc. *Feudal Society.* Translated by L. A. Manyon. 2 vols. 1964. This best-known book by one of this century's greatest historians seeks to explain the total history of the post-Carolingian world in terms of the ideals and practices of feudalism.

Moore, Robert I. *The First European Revolution.* 2000. A distinguished historian offers the first comprehensive, synthetic treatment of the High Middle Ages in fifty years. Stimulating and readable.

Reynolds, Susan. *Fiefs and Vassals.* 1994. Brilliant, controversial, and difficult, this massive book challenges many long-standing ideas about feudalism.

———. *Kingdoms and Communities in Western Europe, 900–1300.* 2d ed. 1997. After exploring the kinds of legal notions that guided medieval community building, this lively book turns to communities themselves, ranging from the parish to the kingdom.

Riley-Smith, Jonathan, ed. *The Oxford Illustrated History of the Crusades.* 1997. A set of essays with lavish illustrations that explores almost every aspect of the Crusades and the world that produced them.

10

Medieval Civilization at Its Height, 900–1300

(Éditions Gaud)

Looking down the nave of Chartres Cathedral, built between 1192 and 1220, produces a number of somewhat contradictory sensations. The size and verticality; the play of light and dark; the amazing array of shapes, corners, and angles—all are a bit mysterious. They were meant to be. At the same time there is a logically ordered geometric elegance to the building that is plain to see. And this was intended, too.

The cathedral at Chartres aptly symbolizes the range of historical currents dominant in high medieval Europe. We saw in Chapter 9 that Europe was expanding economically, politically, and militarily. Like its greater context, this building is very large; the cathedrals built in the burgeoning cities of the twelfth and thirteenth centuries were larger than any that had been built since Justinian erected Hagia Sophia. The bishops of Chartres expended most of their considerable income—Chartres lies in France's richest grain-growing region—for some twenty years to build this church. Literally dozens of these great buildings were going up at the same time all over Europe, providing employment for thousands of ordinary workers and numerous master craftsmen. Nobles and townsfolk donated windows and other fixtures to the building, making the building itself an expression of the period's more complex society.

Chartres Cathedral is an excellent example of the Gothic style in architecture, medieval Europe's supreme architectural achievement. Gothic is one of two major stylistic innovations of this period. The other is Romanesque, a style that reached the summit of its beauty and power in the early twelfth century just as Gothic was about to appear. This change in architectural styles parallels others in the High Middle Ages. The Carolingian focus on grammar, on the most basic literary skills, gave way to an interest in logic. Intellectual problems that had in the past been solved by appeals to scriptural or patristic authority were now addressed by human reason. This produced a new style of intellectual endeavor called "Scholasticism." Monasteries and cathedrals housed schools in the Carolingian world, but by the thirteenth century the university had emerged as a higher kind of cultural institution.

Latin remained the dominant language of scholars, but almost everywhere the vernacular spoken languages were becoming graceful and effective tools for written communication. Religious themes were still foremost in writings of all kinds, but adventures, romances, and other works dedicated to secular themes were gaining in prominence. The Christian tradition still undergirded intellectual life, but that tradition was now spurred on to new heights of insight and expression by encounters with long-lost Greek texts and with the writings of Jewish and Muslim intellectuals. Look where you will, cultural life was richer and more complex than ever before.

The previous chapter concentrated on the economic foundations of society and on the ways in which people organized themselves politically. This chapter begins by introducing the increasingly complex social structures within which people lived and then turns to a study of what those people thought, said, and built.

THE TRADITIONAL ORDERS OF SOCIETY

After centuries of various experiments with ordering social relations after the end of the Roman Empire in the West, a new social order had evolved by 900 that was distinctively medieval. Alfred the Great (r. 871–899) of England once said that a kingdom needed "men of prayer, men of war, and men of work." In the tenth century two French bishops wrote lengthy works exploring this same theme. This three-way division reveals the way the elite looked at the world. It provided neat places for the clergy, warrior-aristocrats, and peasants. The clergy and the nobility agreed that they were superior to the "workers," but fierce controversies raged over whether ultimate leadership in society belonged to the "prayers" or the "fighters."

By the time this tripartite view of society was fully established in the West, it had begun to fit social realities less well. It excluded townspeople, who were becoming ever more important. Town residents worked for a living, of course, but only farmers were considered "workers." Alfred and the bishops did not speak about women, and they consciously excluded minorities, chiefly Jews. To form a full picture of Europe's increasingly intricate social relations, we begin with contemporary theoretical pronouncements and then look for the people whom the theoreticians neglected.

Those Who Pray: The Clergy

As the church promoted its own vision of the tripartite ordering of society, it assigned primacy to the prayers—its own leaders. Within the clergy, however, sharp disagreements arose over whether the leading prayers were the monks in the monasteries or the bishops in their cathedrals. Whereas in the Carolingian world the clergy served occasionally as an avenue of upward social mobility for talented outsiders, in the High Middle Ages church offices were usually reserved for the younger sons of the nobility. The church was always hierarchical in organization and outlook, so the increasingly aristocratic character of the church's leadership tended to reinforce those old tendencies.

In the aftermath of the Carolingian collapse, a great spiritual reform swept Europe. It began in 910 when Duke William of Aquitaine founded the monastery of Cluny in Burgundy on land that he donated. At a time when powerful local families dominated almost all monasteries, Cluny was a rarity because it was free of all lay and episcopal control and because it was under the direct authority of the pope. Cluny's abbots were among the greatest European statesmen of their day and became influential advisers to popes, French kings, German emperors, and aristocratic families.

In the tradition of the Carolingian monastic reforms, Cluny placed great emphasis on liturgical prayer. The monks spent long hours in solemn devotions and did little manual work. Because Cluniac prayer was thought to be especially efficacious, nobles all over Europe donated land to Cluny and placed local monasteries under Cluniac control. Many independent monasteries also appealed to Cluny for spiritual reform. By the twelfth century hundreds of monasteries had joined in a Cluniac order. Individual houses were under the authority of the abbot of Cluny, and their priors had to attend an annual assembly. Although the majority of houses reformed by Cluny were male, many convents of nuns also adopted Cluniac practices.

Cluny promoted two powerful ideas. One was that the role of the church was to pray for the world, not to be implicated deeply in it. The other was that freedom from lay control was essential if churches were to concentrate on their spiritual tasks.

The same spiritual forces that motivated the Cluniacs inspired Bishop Adalbero of Metz in 933 to promote the restoration of Benedictine practices in the dilapidated Lorraine monastery of Gorze. Customs at Gorze resembled those at Cluny, and they spread widely in Lorraine, Germany, and England. The Gorze reform was well received by kings and nobles; its aim was not so much to withdraw from the world as to improve it. Monks from the Gorze and Cluniac traditions bitterly condemned clerical immorality and inappropriate lay interference in the church. They preached against clerical marriage and simony, the buying and selling of church offices.

Reformers in the more ascetic eremitic tradition (see page 204) desired more profound changes. They criticized the monastery at Cluny, saying that it had become too opulent and successful, and the monastery at Gorze because it seemed too immersed in worldly affairs. A desire to build new communities according to their vision of the apostolic church, featuring a life of poverty, self-denial, and seclusion, captivated the ascetics. Thus the eleventh and early twelfth centuries saw a proliferation of both male and female experiments in eremitic monasticism. Other Europeans believed that the apostolic calling demanded not only an austere regimen of personal renunciation but also an active life of Christian ministry. Cathedral clergy, called canons, in particular, adapted the Rule of Saint Augustine so that they could live a communal life and also carry out priestly duties.

The greatest critics of the Cluniac tradition, and the real monastic elite of the early twelfth century, were the Cistercians. In 1098 Abbot Robert left his Burgundian monastery of Molesme because he believed it had abandoned the strict teachings of Saint Benedict. He founded a new monastery at Cîteaux in Burgundy. This house was to follow the Benedictine Rule literally and to refuse all secular entanglements: lands, rents, and servile dependents. So rigorous and poor was the community that it struggled until a charismatic young Burgundian nobleman named Bernard (1090–1153) joined in 1112. Three years later Bernard left to found a daughter house at Clairvaux, of which he remained abbot for the rest of his life. Through his writing, preaching, and personal example, Bernard dominated the religious life of Europe in his lifetime. By the end of the twelfth century there were about five hundred Cistercian (from the Latin for *Cîteaux*) monasteries in Europe, and Bernard's own Clairvaux had seven hundred monks. Initially the Cistercians wished to be an order of adult men. They successfully avoided admitting young boys, but by 1200 they had authorized about one hundred convents of Cistercian nuns.

And it was not just the Cistercians and the traditional Benedictines who attracted women. The twelfth century saw many new communities of women from England to eastern Europe. The age's growing prosperity and population contributed both potential nuns and healthy endowments, but the key factor was that women were responding to the spiritual forces of the age in the same way men were.

With the monastic clergy gaining so much in prestige and visibility, the episcopal clergy countered with its own view of society. Surely, the bishops agreed, spiritual, moral, and intellectual improvement were desirable. Likewise, it was time to end the grossest examples of lay interference in the church. But precisely because so many bishops came from great families and were so well connected, they were less inclined to be rigid about the line of demarcation between lay and clerical responsibilities. In Germany, for example, the king's chapel recruited young noblemen to train them as clerics and to inculcate in them the policies and ethos of the court. Many of these chaplains were appointed to bishoprics and then advanced the king's interests in their new ecclesiastical areas of authority. They were often men of spiritual depth and resented what they regarded as monastic carping about their worldliness. By the middle of the twelfth century bishops, and finally popes, had imposed on the church a view that monks belonged in their monasteries and that bishops should lead society.

It was always the special responsibility of the clergy to look after the moral order of society. In the turbulent world of gentlemen warriors, the church had its own ideas about what a perfect "fighter" should do. The English bishop and scholar John of Salisbury (d. 1180), reflecting on knighthood in the twelfth century, concluded that it existed "to protect the church, to attack infidelity, to reverence the priesthood, to protect the poor, to keep the peace, to shed one's blood and, if necessary, to lay down one's life for one's brethren."

Turning large numbers of violent young men into servants of the church was a tall order for the clergy, and they had only limited success. One strategy that worked was the creation of military orders. The Palestine-based Knights of St. John, or Hospitallers, and Knights of the Temple, or Templars, are the major examples, but others existed in Spain and Germany. The Hospitallers started near Jerusalem as a foundation under Benedictine auspices dedicated to charitable works and care of the sick. They evolved into a monastic order using a version of the Rule of Saint Benedict and devoted themselves to the defense of pilgrims to the Holy Land. The Templars were men living under religious rule and sworn to protect the small states created by the Crusaders (see pages 292–294). These military orders measured up very well to the clergy's idea of what a perfect knight should be.

The clergy could also regulate disputes in society. For example, when a community was divided by a difficult conflict that demanded resolution, it might turn to the *ordeal*—a judicial procedure that sought divine judgment by subjecting the accused to a physically painful or dangerous test. An accused person might walk a certain distance carrying hot iron or plunge a hand into a boiling cauldron to pluck out a pebble. The resulting wounds would be bandaged for a set time and then examined. If they were healing, the person was considered innocent; if festering, guilty. The clergy officiated at ordeals until the papacy forbade their participation in 1215.

Clergymen were also the conservators of the shrines where people gained special access to the holiness of the saints. The clergy wrote and preached about the miracles of the saints, and stories circulated through the church about relics, or artifacts associated with these martyrs. The shrines where relics were preserved attracted pilgrims seeking healing from illness, injury, or misfortune. The clergy thus played unique roles in forming and nurturing communities in the world and in interceding for this world with God in the next.

Those Who Fight: The Nobility

In recent years scholars have spilled a sea of ink trying to define the medieval nobility. The matter is important because even though the nobility constituted only a small minority of the total population, nobles were and expected to be the ruling class. To appreciate their crucial role, we need to consider the shape of the nobility and the nobles' lifestyle and ethos.

In English the word *noble* can be either an adjective or a noun. More commonly, it is an adjective, as in a "noble sentiment" or a "noble deed." Before the twelfth century the Latin *nobilis* was almost exclusively an adjective. The word pertained to certain desirable personal qualities. Then, gradually, the word became a noun and pertained to a certain kind of person.

What kind of person? In the ideal case a noble was a well-born, cultivated, office-holding soldier. In the earlier Middle Ages many men held offices without necessarily being considered noble. Virtually all free men were expected to be soldiers, but few of them ranked as nobles. It was in the century or so following the feudal revolution (see page 278) that these distinct elements were fused into a single social order.

In a world in which lords were everywhere extending their power, military prowess became more valuable. At the same time the need for horses and for more expensive arms and armor made it almost impossible for ordinary freemen to be soldiers. Likewise, ambitious lords who wished to expand their influence, and who were often, in an expanding economy, more prosperous than their forebears, were looking for ways to use their resources to gain followers. These trends came together as lords granted to their followers either military gear or lands, which would generate the income necessary to obtain arms and horses. We call those followers "vassals" and the lands they obtained "fiefs." Vassalage became a widespread institution all over Europe, and fief-holding became a normal accompaniment to vassalage. By contrast, in the Carolingian world vassalage was unusual and rarely connected with fief-holding.

Vassals and fiefs bring to mind the concept of *feudalism* or the term *feudal system*. As we saw in Chapter 9, England, France, and to a lesser degree Germany and Italy, were in some respects feudal realms. That is, lords, right up to the king, secured some personal and political services from vassals in return for material rewards, often landed estates called "fiefs." Today historians are reluctant to use the term *feudal system* because across Europe and through many centuries, there was nothing systematic about how services were obtained or discharged.

Contemporary sources often call vassals "knights." Knights rarely boasted high birth or venerable ancestry. Nor were they initially officeholders appointed by kings or

Courtly Love *This manuscript illumination from Heidelberg shows a fair lady arming her knight for battle, probably for a tournament, as other ladies watch from the walls above. In the age of chivalry, war could be bloody and brutal—or it could be romantic.* (Heidelberg, University Library/akg-images)

emperors. Moreover, they were not wealthy and could not sustain the kind of lavish lifestyle that one might expect from nobles. Across the eleventh and twelfth centuries knights saw their status change, in part because they aped the behavior of the nobles, who themselves accepted the necessity of military ability.

All over Europe, especially where royal power was ineffective, both knights and nobles secured tighter control of peasant labor. This process provided knights and nobles with the money to build castles and to acquire fine possessions. As governments expanded their competence, these nobles and knights often held high offices, or if they did not, they pressured kings to concede such offices to them. Lords also tended to gather their lands into coherent blocks and to name themselves after the castles they built on their lands. Families also began to produce genealogies tracing their ancestry to relatives in the distant past, and to kings if at all possible. At the same time families began to practice primogeniture—that is, reserving their lands, castles, and titles to the *primus genitus,* or "firstborn" son.

This allotment of the choicest inheritances to a shrinking group turned loose a large number of younger sons. Many of them entered the clergy, a tendency that helps to explain the rising aristocratic character of the church. It should be emphasized right away, however, that this was not a punishment. Sons were not "dumped" on the church. Clerical careers were prestigious and relatively comfortable. But more numerous than clerics were the young men who were without an estate and who lacked the means to secure a bride and to form a family of their own. It was from these men that vast crusading armies were recruited. These were also the men who traipsed about Europe looking for fame and fortune, or failing that, a lord to serve. Many of these "young" men were 30 or 40 years old. They were called young because they had not yet established themselves.

By 1200 the nobility was a group identified by the profession of arms, the holding of office, a consciousness of family traditions, and an elevated lifestyle. A specific ethos—chivalry—belonged to the nobility. Today chivalry is often thought of as either an elaborate code of conduct regulating relations between the sexes or the value system behind the literary image of dashing knights in shining armor saving damsels in distress from fire-breathing dragons. Actually its very name derives from *cheval,* French for "horse," the classic conveyance of a knight, or *caballarius* in Latin. Chivalry began as the code of conduct for mounted warriors.

Chivalry highly esteemed certain masculine, militant qualities. Military prowess was the greatest of chivalric virtues. A knight who was not a great warrior was useless. Literature of the time exalts the knight who slays fearsome beasts or the hero who single-handedly overwhelms impossible numbers of the enemy. Openhanded generosity was another key virtue. The truly noble person engaged in sumptuous display to manifest his power, to show concern for his dependents, and to enlarge his entourage. Medieval literature is full of rich banquets and stunning presents. In Anglo-Saxon England the king was called "the giver of rings." Knights were obsessed with their honor, their reputations. They sought glory, the better to win a lord or a bride or, if a lord already, to attract followers.

Chivalry also involved loyalty, the glue that held feudal society together. But we must take into account statements such as the following by a twelfth-century English historian, William of Malmesbury: "They [knights] are faithful to their lords, but swift to break faith. A breath of ill fortune and they are plotting treachery, a bag of money and their mind is changed." Knights, especially the "young," were loyal to their lords when they could be, but fundamentally they were loyal to themselves.

What role was left to noblewomen in a world of chivalry and lordship? By the late eleventh century three developments adversely affected the position of aristocratic women. First, the elaboration of the chivalric ethos defined most key social and political roles as military and "manly" and thereby excluded women. By the middle of the twelfth century it was rare for a woman to hold a castle and unheard-of for one to ride to arms. Second, the consolidation of lineages by aristocratic families accompanied a moral campaign by the church to promote monogamous, unbreakable marriages. This situation subordinated women's freedom in the marriage market to the dynastic and patrimonial demands of great families. Third, the spread of lordship, with its intricate network of personal and proprietary relationships based on military service, tended to deprive women of independent rights over land.

But every rule has its exceptions. As noble families married off fewer of their daughters to noblemen, "extra" daughters accounted in part for the dramatic increase in the number and size of convents. Convents of aristocratic nuns were places where women could be highly educated and almost entirely in control of their own affairs. Matilda, daughter of the German empress Adelaide, was abbess of Quedlinburg, mistress of vast estates in northern Germany, and a dominant figure in German politics. But knights looking for brides would often marry the younger daughters of noblemen, because if they could establish a household, any children born of that marriage could lay claim to the noble lineage of their maternal grandfathers.

Less predictably, Gaita, wife of a Norman prince in Italy, fought in helmet and armor alongside her husband, as did Duchess Agnes of Burgundy. And let us reflect on the career of Adela of Blois (ca. 1067–1137). She was the daughter of William the Conqueror, the wife of a powerful French count, and the mother of King Stephen I of England (see page 281). In addition to regularly accompanying her husband as he administered his county, Adela founded monasteries, promoted religious reform, hosted Pope Paschal II, helped to reconcile her brother Henry I with the archbishop of Canterbury (thus averting an English investiture controversy), issued formal legal judgments, held fairs, and skillfully negotiated the aristocratic politics of western France after her husband's death. Adela is unusual because we know so much about her. In other words, noblewomen in high medieval society may often have led interesting, active lives, but there are few surviving records to document this.

Those Who Work: The Peasants

The peasants were the "workers" in the tripartite model. An extremely diverse segment of society, "peasants" ranged from slaves to free persons of some means. Except in frontier zones, where victims were available and religious scruples diminished, slaves declined dramatically in numbers during the tenth and eleventh centuries (as illustrated by the shift in meaning of the classical Latin *servus* from "slave" to "serf"). Serfs, persons bound to the soil, constituted the majority of the peasants, although their legal and social statuses differed considerably from place to place. In the twelfth century serfdom was disappearing in France even as its terms were hardening in central and eastern Europe. Serfdom was a mixture of economic, legal, and personal statuses. The serf could be flogged in public, could be set upon by dogs, was excluded from many judicial proceedings, required approval to contract a marriage, and was denied the right to bear arms.

The tenth and eleventh centuries were decisive in the reshaping of rural society. As lordships of all kinds and sizes formed in the countryside, they drew communities of people. Castles were critical. Powerful men generally sited their castles in close proximity to wood, water, and iron. Sometimes a monastery, rural church, or graveyard also attracted a castle or else grew up near one and helped to anchor a site.

People from a fairly wide area settled in the vicinity of the castle. Many, originally free, commended themselves to the local lord by handing over their properties and receiving them back in return for rents or personal services. Other people fell into dependent status through military or economic misfortune. What eventually emerged was the manor, an institution best described as a powerful lord controlling the lives of an often large number of dependents. He required payments and services from them and regulated their ordinary disputes. His control was simultaneously public and private.

A minor castellan, or lord of a castle, might control only a small manor and would probably be the vassal of a great lord. A powerful landed lord, on the other hand, would generally control many manors and would often give some of them to retainers as fiefs. In other words, the reorganization of the countryside affected the nobility and the peasantry and created parallel sets of vertical bonds of association: feudal lords and vassals entered into political bonds; lords and peasants entered into economic bonds.

The structure of individual manors, and the dues owed by peasants, varied tremendously across Europe. Certain trends were fairly consistent, however. As the economy expanded, as trade brought more and different products into Europe, and as a more consciously aristocratic lifestyle spread, the nobility began to want disposable cash. Thus in many places corvées (labor services) were commuted into cash payments. Peasants were required to pay rent from their own holdings instead of working on the lord's lands. But lords still needed provisions, so they sometimes split peasant payments into cash and kind. Old forms of service could be wholly retained, involving many days per year of work on the lord's demesne, the portion of the manor the lord reserved for his own benefit. In such cases the lord could still extract money from his peasants by requiring them to use his mill and oven and then charging them gristing and kilning fees.

The trend everywhere, however, was for labor services to diminish. In one region in northern France, twelfth-century peasants owed only three corvées of two days' each per year for harvesting and haymaking. Elsewhere, peasants might still be required to haul crops to market or to keep roads, bridges, and buildings in repair. On many estates where the menfolk had been largely freed from corvées, the women might still have to work in the lord's house washing laundry, sewing, plucking fowl, cooking, minding dogs, and tending to other household chores.

In the expanding economy of the eleventh and twelfth centuries, the peasants grew more prosperous, and their lords constantly sought new ways to extract the fruits of that prosperity. Peasants thus began to band together to demand that "customs" be observed. These customs were more or less formal agreements spelling out the terms under which work and fees would be arranged. In general life improved for the peasants in terms of both legal status and living conditions.

The European village was a key product of the tenth and eleventh centuries. People who originally gathered together around a castle for security and livelihood began to form a durable human community. Their church and graveyard helped to reinforce the community by tying together the living and the dead and by giving the village a sense of memory and continuity. Peasants generally worked only 250 to 270 days per year, so they had a good deal of time for festivals and celebrations. Births, baptisms, betrothals, and deaths provided opportunities for the community to come together and affirm its mutual ties. Market days and sessions of the lord's court also assembled the village. Villagers needed to cooperate in many of the operations of daily life. They shared tools, plow teams, and wagons. They performed their corvées together. The peasants experienced much less social differentiation than the nobility, and so less tension.

The status of women in peasant society tended to be, in legal theory and in daily reality, the same as that of men at a time when the status of aristocratic women was fragile. Marriage contracts from northern Italy show that brides often entered marriages with a complement of valuable tools. This suggests that peasant women retained some control over their own personal property and also reminds us that the huge gains in rural productivity were almost certainly attributable in part to the work and ingenuity of women.

Those Left Out: Townspeople and Jews　The tripartite model excluded two important groups of people. The first neglected group consisted of the increasingly numerous citizens of Europe's growing towns. Obviously people in towns worked, but the prejudices of the aristocracy were rural, so the only "workers" deemed necessary to the smooth functioning of the social order were farmers. In the second group were Europe's principal religious minority, the Jews. Jews could be found almost everywhere, although they constituted only about 1 percent of the population as a whole and, outside of Rome and parts of Spain, formed no single community numbering more than 1,500 to 2,000.

The central factor in the growth of towns was the rise in the productivity and profitability of medieval agriculture. For the first time in history a regular and substantial farm surplus could support an urban population that did not produce its own food. Increased local exchange, coupled with the relentless growth of a money economy, meant there were fortunes to be made and cash to be spent. Some of that cash was spent on luxury and exotic products that increasingly became the objects of far-flung commercial networks. A good part of the cash was spent by rural nobles, who earned it from rents, booty, and the profits of the private exercise of public power. When those nobles moved into towns, they created opportunities for merchants, craftsmen, day laborers, domestic servants, and professional people such as notaries and lawyers. This was particularly true in Europe's most heavily urbanized regions: Flanders, southern France, and northern Italy. The key point is that the growth of the medieval city and of its human community began in the medieval countryside.

Town society was hierarchical, but its structures were new, ill defined, and flexible. Rich men built up bands of followers who supported them in urban politics, protected their neighborhoods, and occasionally raided the houses of their enemies in the next neighborhood. Relatives, friends, neighbors, people from a common rural district, or those engaged in similar trades tended to worship together in particular churches, observe certain festivals, and look after one another's families.

In the rapidly changing world of the tenth and eleventh centuries, towns provided numerous opportunities for women. In urban industries such as clothmaking, tanning, laundering, and brewing, women sometimes managed and even owned enterprises. Apart, perhaps, from finance and the law, distinctions between male and female roles were not as sharp in towns as in rural areas.

If urban men and all women stood in an ambiguous relationship to the ideals of the male, rural, aristocratic elite, we can hardly imagine what it must have been like for Jews. Jewish communities had existed in most European towns since antiquity. Then, because the Byzantine and Islamic worlds vacillated between persecution and toleration, many Jews migrated to western Europe, with the largest numbers settling in northern France and the German Rhineland. The Jewish community in England formed only around 1100. Paris had northern Europe's largest Jewish community, perhaps two thousand people in the twelfth century. Many cities had Jewish populations numbering two hundred to three hundred, but groups of forty or fifty were common. Although some Jews in Italy, Spain, and Germany owned farms and vineyards, most Jews settled in cities, where they could live and worship in community with other Jews. Urban clusters also provided strength in numbers for people who could at any moment fall victim to persecution and whose power was not based on landholding.

Three of the most important developments in high medieval Europe were disastrous for Jews. First, the growth of the European economy, with its attendant urban and commercial expansion, brought countless Christians into the practice of trade, an occupation dominated by Jews since Late Antiquity. As Jews were excluded from commercial opportunities, they were more and more confined to moneylending. Jews had been moneylenders before the economic surge of the High Middle Ages, but the expanding economy made financial operations more widespread than ever before. Given that, as we saw in Chapter 9, Christian moralists considered handling money to be the Devil's work, the visibility of Jews as moneylenders brought them much criticism, although they were never alone in this practice.

The second phenomenon that adversely affected Jews was the reform of the church. With so much attention being paid to the proper Christian life and the correct organization of the church, it was inevitable that more attention would be directed to the one prominent group in Western society that was not Christian.

Third, the Crusades unleashed vicious attacks on Jews. As crusading armies headed east in 1096, they visited unspeakable massacres on the Jewish communities of several German towns. This awful process was repeated on the eve of the Second Crusade in 1146–1147 and again just before the third in 1189. Popular frenzy identified the Jews as Christ-killers and equated them with Muslims as the enemies of Christianity. In fact, and despite grotesque and groundless stories about Jews kidnapping and ritually killing Christian children, Jews everywhere wished to live in peace with their Christian neighbors and to be left alone to observe their distinctive religious, dietary, and social customs.

The Jews were not without sympathetic champions, however. From the time of Gregory I (r. 590–604), the papacy urged peaceful coexistence and prayers for Jewish conversion. In the twelfth and thirteenth centuries popes forcefully reminded Christians that while converting Jews was highly desirable, Jews were to be tolerated and left in peace. The Carolingians protected the Jews, and some kings in succeeding centuries repeated or even expanded upon Carolingian legislation. Spanish Jews were taken under royal protection in reconquered areas in 1053, and Henry IV took German Jews under his protection in 1084. In England and France Jews enjoyed royal protection until the late twelfth century. Jews frequently served as royal advisers in Spain and were often entrusted with sensitive diplomatic missions elsewhere.

Despite such policies, Jews were vulnerable to attack at almost any time from people who simply disliked them or who owed them money. But in 1181 Philip II of France, always on the lookout for income, had his henchmen arrest Jews and confiscate their possessions. In 1182 he expelled them from the royal demesne. Across the thirteenth century French kings accorded the Jews less and less protection and often abused them financially. In 1306 Philip IV expelled the Jews from France after confiscating their goods. In England the story is much the same. The impecunious Henry II laid crushing taxes on the Jews in 1171. In 1189 in London and in 1190 in York, massive riots stirred by false rumors raged against the Jewish populations. In 1290 Edward I seized Jewish possessions and expelled Jews from the country. Royal protection of German Jews was reasonably effective until the death of Frederick II in 1250, after which time local princes often repudiated debts to Jewish lenders and appropriated Jewish property.

SOCIAL AND RELIGIOUS MOVEMENTS, CA. 1100–1300

Twelfth- and thirteenth-century Europe witnessed several social movements unlike any that had occurred before. Spurred by increasingly intrusive governments, economic dislocation, and spiritual turmoil, they involved large numbers of people; cut across lines of gender, wealth, status, and occupation; and appeared in many places. Most of these movements had cohesive beliefs, even ideologies, and well-determined goals. They are the first large-scale social movements in European history.

Heretics and Dissidents　　The canon lawyer Gratian (see page 314) defined *heresy* as a situation in which "each man chooses for himself the teaching he believes to be the better one"—that is, he ignores official doctrines. For Gratian and his like-minded contemporaries, faith was not an individual matter. Unity of belief was crucial in a catholic ("universal") Christian Europe. In the twelfth century, the church reacted ever more strictly to challenges to its teachings or to its exclusive right to teach. The effort by the church to define its law, theology, and bureaucratic procedures with greater precision drew lines more sharply than ever before between what was and was not acceptable.

Heretics did not see themselves as secessionists from the true church. Quite the contrary, they saw themselves as its only representatives. Church teachings always encountered a degree of popular skepticism. Not everyone believed, for example, that Jesus was born of a virgin or that he was true God and true man. But such doubts had not previously led to mass defections. Before the middle of the twelfth century, challenges to the church came from men—as far as we can tell the ringleaders were all men—who saw themselves as inspired reformers.

Tanchelm of Antwerp preached between 1100 and 1115 in the Netherlands. He scandalized the mainstream by calling churches brothels and clerics whores. He rejected the sacraments and the payment of tithes. Although Tanchelm was radical and pugnacious, his ideas constituted a fairly coherent program of criticism. Like many others, he was concerned about the immorality and wealth of the church. But Tanchelm and his followers went even further. The heretic distributed his nail and hair clippings as relics of a sort, and in a bizarre public ceremony he "married" a statue of the Virgin Mary. Across the twelfth century church orthodoxy was challenged by others whose influence seems to have been local. What is interesting is how numerous, and similar, they all were.

Coherent movements of much larger proportions emerged later in the century. In 1173 Waldo, a rich merchant of Lyon, decided to sell all his property, give the proceeds to the poor, and embrace a life of poverty and preaching. Waldo was motivated by the same quest for the apostolic life that had animated the eremitic movement of the eleventh century. But there was a difference: he was a layman. Waldo attracted many followers (known as Waldensians), and in 1179 Pope Alexander III (r. 1159–1181) scrutinized him closely, found his beliefs to be essentially correct, and approved his vow of poverty. But the pope commanded Waldo to preach only when invited to do so by bishops. The bishops, jealous about their own power, extended no such invitations.

Waldo and his "Poor Men of Lyon" went right on preaching and in 1184 were formally declared heretics. Until this point it was not their ideas so much as their appropriation of a clerical duty, preaching, that had set the church against them. From this time on, however, the Waldensians became more radical in their attacks. In about 1204 one group of Waldensians was reconciled to the Catholic Church, but the majority, who had spread all over southern France and Italy, into Germany, and as far away as Poland, remained estranged. Waldensian communities exist to this day.

The most serious of the popular heretical movements was Catharism (from the Greek *katharos,* meaning "pure"). Because there were numerous Cathars near the southern French town of Albi, the whole movement is sometimes called "Albigensian." In fact, Cathars could be found all over Europe, although they did cluster in northern Italy and southern France. Cathars were the religious descendants of Mani (see page 180), a third-century Persian who taught an extreme dualism that featured polarities in almost all things: good-evil, love-hate, flesh-spirit. Extreme Cathars abstained from flesh in all ways: they were vegetarians and renounced sexual intercourse so as not to produce offspring—that is, more flesh. Probably radiating from Bulgaria, Cathar ideas had spread widely in the West by the 1140s. Catharism attracted many converts when Nicetas, the Cathar bishop of Constantinople, visited northern Italy and southern France between 1166 and 1176. People of every station joined the new church, which, in its own view, was the only true church.

The Catholic Church sent isolated preachers against the Cathars, but with little success. In 1198 and 1203, Pope Innocent III organized systematic preaching tours in southern France, but these, too, lacked solid results, and in 1208 the pope's legate was murdered by a supporter of the count of Toulouse, who was sympathetic to the Cathars. The killing led to the launching of the Albigensian Crusade, a loosely structured military action that lasted into the 1260s. Although the crusade itself was largely over by the 1220s, violence against Albigensians sputtered for decades: a massacre in 1244 and inquisitorial campaigns in 1246 and again in 1256 to 1257. Isolated resisters struggled on into the fourteenth century.

Albigensians denounced the clergy of their day as rich and corrupt. These teachings attracted urban dwellers who resented the wealth and pretensions of the clergy—the same people who followed Waldo. Nobles may have been drawn to the movement because it gave them opportunities to take possession of extensive tracts of church lands, something the investiture controversy had denied them. In addition, embracing Catharism may have been a way for nobles to resist the increasing encroachment of the government of far-off Paris. The Albigensians also attracted many women. Unlike the Catholic Church, which denied clerical, preaching, and teaching offices to women, the heretical sects tended to permit women to hold leading roles.

The Albigensians, like the Waldensians, were driven by the same spiritual zeal and desire for ecclesiastical reform that moved many of their contemporaries. They differed from other would-be reformers in that they did not seek to reform the Catholic Church from within but departed from it or insisted that they alone represented it. Thus these heretical movements marked the first serious challenge to the ideology of a uniformly "catholic" Christendom since Late Antiquity.

Reform from Within: The Mendicant Orders
Traditional monastic orders continued to win adherents, but their interpretation of the apostolic life meant ascetic withdrawal from the world, not pastoral work and preaching. Laymen who wished both to embrace poverty and to preach fell under the suspicion of the ecclesiastical authorities. Early in the thirteenth century a new movement arose, the mendicants (literally, beggars). Mendicants were men who aimed to preach, to be poor, and to create formal but noncloistered religious orders. Though similar to the heretics in many ways, they submitted willingly to ecclesiastical authority.

The mendicant phenomenon began when Francis of Assisi (1181–1226), the son of a rich Italian merchant, decided to renounce the wealth and status that were his birthright. He carried out his renunciation in a most public display before the bishop of Assisi in 1206. Francis had gradually grown tired of a life of ease and luxury, but he also experienced a blinding moment of spiritual insight when, by chance, his eyes fell on the passage in the Scriptures in which Christ commanded the rich young ruler, "Go, sell all you have, and follow me." Francis stripped himself naked so that "naked he might follow the naked Christ."

For a few years Francis wandered about Italy begging for his meager sustenance, repairing churches, caring for the sick, and preaching repentance to all who would listen. By 1210 he had attracted many followers, and together they set out to see Innocent III to win approval. After considering the matter for a while, Innocent decided to approve the new order of friars (that is "brothers," from the Latin *fratres*) as long as they would accept monastic tonsure—a ritual haircut signifying submission—profess obedience to the pope, and swear obedience to Francis. The pope was genuinely won over by Francis himself, but he also sensed that by permitting the formation of the Franciscan order, he could create a legitimate and controllable repository for the explosive spiritual forces of the age.

Francis prepared a simple Rule based on his understanding of the scriptural ideals of poverty, preaching, and service. Alarmed by the vagueness of the first Rule and by the extraordinary influx of new members, the papal curia in 1223 prevailed on Francis to submit a revision that stressed order, a hierarchy of officials, and a novitiate—a regularized period of training for new members. Somewhat disappointed by this regulated formality, Francis withdrew more and more from the world and lived reclusively in the hills near Assisi.

The Parting of Mary from the Apostles   *Duccio di Buoninsegna lived from the middle of the thirteenth century to 1318 or 1319. He did his finest work in Siena, including a huge altarpiece, one of whose panels depicts the touching scene of Mary taking leave of the apostles just before her death. Note the clever way Duccio has arranged the figures and how he balances Saint Paul, standing in the doorway, with Mary, reclining on the bed.* (Scala/Art Resource, NY)

After Francis died, the issues of property, power, education, and ordination provoked deep controversies within his order. Usually called "Franciscan," Francis's order is technically the "Friars Minor." The movement had begun among laymen, but over time more Franciscan brothers became ordained priests. Franciscans established schools in most great cities, and by the middle of the thirteenth century some of Europe's greatest intellects were Franciscans. This prominence, like the sacramental power of ordination, was a kind of wealth that Francis had wished to avoid. The real issue of wealth, however, turned on the possession of property. Francis had aimed for both personal and corporate poverty. In the 1230s papal legislation had alleviated strict poverty by permitting the order to acquire property to support its work. Nevertheless, the issue of property continued to spark controversy among the Franciscans.

Of the nine or ten mendicant orders that developed, the other major one was the Dominican, a product of very different experiences than the Franciscan. Its founder, Dominic de Guzman (1170–1221), was the son of a Spanish nobleman. He became a priest and later a cathedral canon. While traveling, he saw firsthand the Albigensian heresy in southern France, and in 1206 he went to Rome to seek permission to preach against the heretics. The Albigensian Crusade began in 1208, but Dominic's methods were those of persuasion, not coercion.

Albigensian criticisms of the ignorance, indifference, and personal failings of the clergy could never be applied to Dominic and his fellow preachers. Dominic and his followers were supported enthusiastically by the bishop of Toulouse, who saw how useful these zealous preachers of unblemished lives could be. In 1215 Dominic, with his bishop's assistance, attempted to form a new order, but by that time Rome had forbidden the creation of new orders for fear of heresy or uncontrollable diversity. Thus Dominic's "Order of Preachers" (the proper name for the "Dominicans") adopted the Rule of Saint Augustine, which many communities of cathedral canons had been using since the eleventh century.

In 1217 Dominic presided at the first general meeting of the order. The Dominicans decided to disperse, some going to Paris, some (including Dominic) to Rome, some to other cities in Europe. Henceforth the order saw its mission as serving the whole church. Dominican schools were set up all over Europe, and the order acquired a reputation for learning and scholarship. The Dominicans were voluntarily poor, but the order was never rent by a controversy over property as the Franciscans were. Dominic's was a vision of personal, not corporate, poverty. Likewise, as a preaching order, the Dominicans had to be learned and ordained. Franciscan misgivings on these issues did not touch them.

Both the Franciscan and Dominican orders reflected a widespread desire to emulate the apostolic life of the early church by poverty and preaching. Both submitted to legitimate authority. Francis's religious vision of charity and service was the product of a heartfelt need for repentance and renewal. This concern for the soul often caused Franciscans to serve as missionaries. Dominic set out to save the church from its enemies. He desired preachers who were sufficiently learned that they could combat the errors of heretics. Both men saw the need for exemplary lives. Francis was a more charismatic figure than Dominic, and his apostolate to the urban poor was more compelling. By 1300 Franciscan houses outnumbered Dominican by 3 to 1. The mendicants were the greatest spiritual force in high medieval Europe.

Communities of Women

The religious forces that attracted men drew women as well. Traditional orders, however, tended to be hostile toward women. Cluniacs and Cistercians struggled to keep women out of their ranks. The wandering preachers of the twelfth century, without exception, acquired women as followers, but the usual results were either segregation of the women in cloisters or condemnation of the whole movement.

In 1212 Francis attracted the aristocrat Clare of Assisi (1194–1253), who was fleeing from an arranged marriage. She wanted to live the friars' life of poverty and preaching, and Francis wanted to assist her. Aware that the sight of women begging or preaching would be shocking, in 1215 he gave Clare and his other female followers their own rule. Clare became abbess of the first community of the "Poor Clares." Though cloistered and forbidden to preach, the Clares lived lives of exemplary austerity and attracted many adherents.

Beguines were communities of women who lived together, devoted themselves to charitable works, but did not take vows as nuns. The Beguine movement grew from the work in Nivelles, near Liège, of Mary of Oignies (ca. 1177–1213). She was drawn to the ideals of voluntary poverty and service to others. So strong was the pull that she renounced her marriage, gave away all her goods, worked for a while in a leper colony, and thought of preaching against the Cathars. Instead, she formed a community.

Groups of Beguines appeared all over the Low Countries, western Germany, and northern France. This was the first exclusively women's movement in the history of Christianity. Beguines sometimes vowed poverty and sometimes did not. They sometimes cloistered themselves into communities and sometimes taught and served the poor and outcast. They neither challenged the officials and teachings of the church nor demanded a right to preach. As laywomen, they did not give rise to scandal as noncloistered nuns would have. They were content to have power over their own lives and communities but not seek a voice in the wider world around them.

Thirteenth-century Europe knew more female than male mystics, and female mysticism tended to focus on Jesus, especially on His presence in the Eucharist. This is the first religious devotion that can be shown to have been more common to women than to men. Most of the mystics were either nuns or Beguines. As the clergy was defining its own prerogatives more tightly, and excluding women more absolutely from the exercise of formal public power, female communities provided a different locus for women's activity.

Women who spent their lives in community with other women reveal, in their writings, none of the sense of moral and intellectual inferiority that was routinely attributed to women by men and often by women themselves. Women who were in direct spiritual communion with God acquired, as teachers, mediators, and counselors in their communities, power that they simply could not have had outside those settings.

LATIN CULTURE: FROM SCHOOLS TO UNIVERSITIES

The dynamism so evident in the economic, social, and political life of Europe is just as apparent in cultural life. As in the late antique and Carolingian periods, courts and churches were the greatest patrons of artists and authors. But in this age of expansion the number and geographic spread of such patrons increased dramatically. By 1150 the church comprised 50 percent more bishoprics and about three times as many monasteries as it had in 900. In 1300 monarchies reigned in many places—Scandinavia and the Slavic world, for example—where none had existed in 900. In addition to an increase in the sheer amount of cultural activity, the years between 900 and 1300 also witnessed innovations. Logic replaced grammar at the heart of the school curriculum. Latin letters remained ascendant, but literature in many vernacular (native) languages began to appear in quantity and quality. Romanesque art and architecture were fresh and original interpretations of their Carolingian ancestors. Europe's incipient urbanization produced the first stirrings of a distinctively urban culture. In one of those cities, Paris, a new kind of academic institution emerged—the university—which was arguably the period's greatest legacy to the modern world.

The Carolingian Legacy

Cultural life depends on both creative geniuses and generous patrons. Political dislocation and constant attacks in the ninth and tenth centuries initially deprived schools and masters of the Carolingian patronage that they had enjoyed for a century or more. The Carolingians left firm enough foundations in a few centers for intellectual life to continue, but the scale of activity between 900 and 1050 was smaller than before. Three examples serve to capture the spirit of the age that set the stage for the High Middle Ages.

Gerbert of Aurillac (940–1003) was the most distinguished intellect of his age. He left his home in Aquitaine to study in Spain and Italy before settling in Reims, in northern France, where he was a teacher and then briefly a bishop. He attracted the attention of the emperor Otto III and spent some time at the German court, earning appointments as abbot of Bobbio, bishop of Ravenna, and, finally, pope. Gerbert followed Carolingian tradition in being a collector of manuscripts and critic of texts, but he departed from older traditions in his interest in mathematics and in his study of logic—the formal rules of reasoning that, in the Western tradition, trace back over many thinkers to Aristotle (see pages 90–92).

Fulbert of Chartres (960–1028), Gerbert's finest pupil, elevated the cathedral school of Chartres to the paramount place in academic Europe. Fulbert wrote letters in elegant Latin and composed fine poems. He carried on his master's literary interests more than his scientific ones, and well into the twelfth century Chartres remained a major center of literary studies.

Another figure of interest is the aristocratic German nun Roswitha of Gandersheim (d. 970). She wrote poems on saints and martyrs, as well as a story about a priest who sold his soul to the devil. In her mature years, Roswitha wrote Latin plays in rhymed verse based on the Roman writer Terence. In these plays she refashioned tales from Roman and biblical history to convey moral truths.

The Study of Law   Law was a field of major innovation. The increasing sophistication of urban life demanded a better understanding of law. The growing responsibilities of the church called for orderly rules, and the church's frequent quarrels with secular rulers demanded careful delineations of rights and responsibilities. Governments issued more laws and regulations than at any time since antiquity.

In about 1012 Burchard, the bishop of Worms, produced a collection of canon law that was influential for more than a century and heightened reformers' awareness of the law of the church. By midcentury scholars studying canon law in Italy and France helped to promote the papal view of reform. In Bologna, Irnerius (d. ca. 1130), a transplanted German and protégé of Emperor Henry V, began teaching Roman law from the law code of Justinian (see pages 214–216). This legal work culminated in the publication in 1140 of the *Decretum* of the Bolognese monk Gratian. The most comprehensive and systematic book of canon law yet written, Gratian's work remained authoritative for centuries.

Throughout the twelfth century canon lawyers studied and wrote commentaries on Gratian's *Decretum*. These legists are called "decretists." Gratian had systematically collected earlier papal *decretals* (official pronouncements), but popes continued to issue them. Several collections of these new decretals were prepared in the thirteenth century, and the scholars who studied these later decrees are called "decretalists." The church thus produced a vast corpus of law and legal commentary.

Law was by no means confined to the church. England was precocious in creating a common law, a single law applied uniformly in its courts. But English law was based on the careful accumulation of legal decisions—or precedents—and not on the routine application of the provisions of a law code. There were many law codes elsewhere. Alfonso X of Castile issued the *Siete Partidas,* a comprehensive law code largely reliant on Roman law. Prince Iaroslav (d. 1054) is reputed to have issued the first version of the laws of Kievan Rus. Iaroslav's laws were written in Old Russian, but they drew heavily on the laws and legal traditions of neighboring peoples. Byzantine law was revised under the Macedonian dynasty.

Greek, Arab, and Jewish Contributions Norman and German settlement in southern Italy and Sicily, the Reconquista in Spain, the Crusades, and the creation of Italian communities in many Mediterranean cities brought European thinkers face-to-face with the intellectual traditions of Classical Greece, Islam, and medieval Judaism. Between 1100 and 1270 almost the whole corpus of Aristotle's writings, virtually unknown in the West for a millennium, became available. Arab commentaries on Aristotle, as well as Jewish philosophical and theological works, began to circulate. The presence of all these texts and currents of thought was decisive in expanding the range and raising the level of Western thought.

Prior to about 1100 only a few of Aristotle's writings, primarily some of his early writings on logic, had been available in the West. Gradually scholars recovered Aristotle's full treatment of logic, then his scientific writings, and finally his studies of ethics and politics. Aristotle's books posed a number of problems for Christian scholars. If knowledge is a good thing and good things are gifts of God, how did a pagan get so smart? Is it possible that faith is unnecessary to knowledge? What relationship exists between faith and reason? Aristotle taught that the universe is eternal and mechanistic. His thought left no room for creation or for the continuing role of a Creator. For Christian thinkers Aristotle asked questions that demanded answers: Were the Scriptures true? Did God create the world as Genesis said? Did God continue to intervene in this world?

Between 750 and 900, mainly in Iran, a group of Arabic-speaking Christians began translating into Arabic the Greek texts of Aristotle as well as the more than fifteen thousand pages of commentary on Aristotle that had been produced between about A.D. 100 and 600. These translators were Monophysite Christians chased out of Syria by the emperor Heraclius when he conquered the area from the Persians (see page 233). This flood of material inspired generations of Arab scholars to tackle the thought of the man often called simply "the Philosopher."

Two major Arab thinkers were particularly influenced by the vast Aristotelian corpus. Ibn-Sina (980–1037), called Avicenna in the West, was drawn to the fundamental problem of how to understand the relationship between objects that exist in the world and the knowledge of those objects that is formed and held in the human mind. Ibn Rushd (1126–1198), called Averroes, wrote no fewer than thirty-eight commentaries on the works of Aristotle, and at least fifteen of these were translated into Latin in the thirteenth century. Among many contributions, Averroes particularly tried to clarify the relationship between truths acquired through the exercise of reason and truths that depend on divine revelation. Although his exact meaning remains controversial, his contemporaries and many later scholars understood him to teach the "double truth": Truths about the natural world are more or less accessible to everyone depending on a

Muslim Scholars in a Garden *From a thirteenth-century Iraqi manuscript, this picture shows literary men in a pleasure garden. Beasts are driving a water wheel to refresh them, and a lute player accompanies their poetry with music.* (Bibliothèque nationale de France)

person's intellectual ability. Revealed truths, however, are available only to the most enlightened.

Spain and northern France were both important centers of Jewish thought. In Spain some Jewish thinkers also grappled with Aristotle. Solomon ibn Gebirol (1021–1070), called Avicebron, wrote *The Fountain of Life*, a treatise that attempted to reconcile Aristotle with the Jewish faith by finding a role for God in communicating knowledge to every human mind. The greatest of all medieval Jewish thinkers, Moses ben Maimon (1135–1204), called Maimonides, wrote *A Guide for the Perplexed*. The perplexed he had in mind were those who had trouble reconciling the seemingly opposed claims of reason and faith. Maimonides taught a doctrine very close to Averroes's double truth.

Solomon ben Isaac (1040–1105), called Rashi, was educated in Jewish schools in the Rhineland and then set up his own school in Troyes. He became the most learned biblical and Talmudic scholar of his time, indeed one of the wisest ever. The Talmud was a detailed and erudite commentary on the scriptural studies of the ancient rabbis. It existed in two collections made in the fifth century, one in Palestine and one in Babylon. Later in the twelfth century Rashi's grandsons carried on his work and earned great fame on their own. Christian scholars who wished to know the exact meaning of passages in the Bible sometimes consulted them.

From Persia to Spain to France, then, countless thinkers were engaged in serious reflection on the mechanics of knowing, the nature of reality, the relationship between reason and faith, and the meaning and significance of revelation. In the years just around 1100 Latin Christian scholars began to encounter this torrent of thought and writing.

The Development of Western Theology Carolingian schools had focused on grammar—that is, on the basic foundations of language. Gradually logic supplanted grammar at the center of both intellectual interests and school curricula. Problems inside Europe initiated this shift, but soon the external influences we just described increased its scope. Eventually the wider application of logic produced a new intellectual style and also evoked bitter criticisms.

Berengar (ca. 1000–1088), master of the school of Tours, wrote a treatise that denied Christ's presence in the Eucharist—the Communion bread and wine received by Catholics and Orthodox Christians in the celebration of the mass. This position was heretical. Ordinarily churchmen would have refuted Berengar simply by quoting various passages from the Scriptures or from the writings of the Church Fathers, along with conciliar pronouncements about the consecrated elements. The evidence, however, was ambiguous. Berengar's claim was finally proved false, at least to the satisfaction of his opponents, by Lanfranc, archbishop of Canterbury during the reign of William the Conqueror. Lanfranc used Aristotelian logical argumentation to dispose of Berengar's heretical arguments.

Anselm (ca. 1033–1109), Lanfranc's successor as archbishop of Canterbury, developed an ingenious logical proof for the existence of God. The French theologian and philosopher Peter Abelard (1079–1142) used logic to reconcile apparent contradictions in the Scriptures and in the writings of the Church Fathers. We must not suppose that Anselm and Abelard were skeptics. Anselm's motto was "Faith seeking understanding." For him logic was the servant of divine truth. He would have agreed completely with Abelard's assessment that "faith has no merit with God when it is not the testimony of divine truth that leads us to it, but the evidence of human reason."

For conservatives such as Bernard of Clairvaux (see page 300) and Hildegard of Bingen (1098–1179), however, faith and immediate divine inspiration were primary. To them logical approaches to divine truth were the height of arrogance. Hildegard—well educated, musically gifted, and knowledgeable in medical matters—was perhaps the most profound psychological thinker of her age. More than anyone before her, Hildegard opened up for discussion the feminine aspects of divinity. She, like Bernard, believed that God was to be found deep within the human spirit, not in books full of academic wrangling.

The future lay with Anselm and Abelard, however. Anselm was the most gifted Christian thinker since Augustine. He wrote distinguished works on logic, and his theological treatise *Why God Became Man* (ca. 1100) served for three hundred years as the definitive philosophical and theological explanation of the incarnation of Christ, the central mystery of the Christian faith.

Peter Abelard was a more colorful figure. He argued rudely and violently with all his teachers, though in the end he was probably more intelligent than any of them. He rose to a keener understanding of Aristotle than anyone in centuries, and he developed a sharper sense of both the power and the limitations of language than anyone since the Greeks. He concerned himself with ethics, too, and was one of the first writers to see intention as more important than simple action.

Abelard seduced and then secretly married Heloise, one of his pupils and the daughter of an influential Paris churchman. Heloise's relatives castrated Abelard for his refusal to live openly with his wife. Abelard then arranged for Heloise to enter a convent, and he joined a monastic community, where he continued writing and teaching. The two carried on a voluminous correspondence that reveals Heloise as a first-rate philosophical thinker and one of her age's most knowledgeable connoisseurs of Classical literature. Some of Abelard's more imaginative ideas earned him formal ecclesiastical condemnations in 1121 and 1140. He popularized the schools of Paris, however, and attracted to them promising scholars from all over Europe.

Abelard and several of his contemporaries engaged in one of the first widespread intellectual debates in Western history, the quarrel over "universals." *Universal* is the philosophical name for a concept that applies to more than one seemingly related object. The dispute over universals went to the heart of people's understanding of reality, their sense of the limitations of human reason, and their awareness of problems of language.

To illustrate: May we agree that you are reading a book right now? May we further agree that the book you are reading is not identical to any other book on your bookshelf? And may we go one step further and agree that no book on your bookshelf is exactly like any other book on that shelf? So, why do we call all of these objects books? "Book" is here the universal that we are trying to understand.

A medieval "realist," whose thought may be traced back to Plato, would say that there is a concept, let us call it "bookness," that exists in our minds before we ever encounter any particular object that we label a book. Just as no book is ever identical to any other, so too no specific book is a perfect representation of that concept "bookness." The concept is fully real, and all representations of it in the world are mere hints, suggestions of a more perfect reality.

A medieval "nominalist," on the contrary, would say that "book" is merely a name (*nomen* in Latin, whence nominalism) that we apply to objects that we deem to bear sufficient similarity to one another that they can be adequately captured by one name. But only each particular book is fully real.

Problems aplenty surround the quarrel over universals: Is reality purely an intellectual proposition, or is reality a quality of existence in the world? How does the mind acquire knowledge of the universal? How does the mind know to which objects to apply the universal? What specific differences exist between objects to which the same name is applied?

With the emergence of the problem of universals, we enter fully into a new intellectual approach that has long been called "Scholasticism." This word has come to have many different meanings, but at the most basic level it describes a movement that attempted to show that Christian theology is inherently rational, that faith and reason need not be contradictory or antithetical. Scholasticism also implies a certain systematization of thought. Gratian's attempt to organize all of canon law rationally and systematically was a Scholastic exercise. Twelfth-century biblical scholars tried to produce a single, systematic commentary on the Bible. In 1160 Peter Lombard produced the *Four Books of Sentences*, a comprehensive treatment of all of Christian theology.

Thomas Aquinas (1225–1274) was the greatest of the Scholastics, the most sensitive to Greek and Arab thought, and the most prolific medieval philosopher. A Dominican friar, Thomas was educated at Naples, Cologne, and Paris. Apart from brief service at the papal court, he spent the years after 1252 teaching and writing in Paris. His two most famous works are the *Summa Contra Gentiles* and the *Summa Theologiae*. A *summa* is an encyclopedic compendium of carefully arrayed knowledge on a particular subject. One might think of Gratian's and Peter Lombard's works as precursors to the great summas of the thirteenth century. Thomas's first summa addresses natural truth—that is, the kinds of things that any person can know through the operation of reason. His second summa is a summation of the revealed truths of the Christian faith.

Thomas's works are distinctive for two reasons. First, no one before him had so rigorously followed the dialectical method of reasoning through a whole field of knowledge, not just a particular problem. For thousands of pages Thomas poses a question, suggests answers, confronts the answers with objections, refutes the objections, and then draws a conclusion. Then he repeats the process. Second, Thomas carefully distinguishes between two kinds of truths. On the one hand are *natural truths,* truths (even theological ones) that anyone can know (or so Thomas thought)—for example, that God exists. On the other hand are *revealed truths,* truths that can be known (if not understood) only through faith in God's revelation—for example, the Trinity or the incarnation of Christ. Thomas maintains that natural and revealed truths simply cannot contradict one another because God is ultimately the source of both. If a natural truth—for example, Aristotle's contention that the world is eternal—appears to contradict a revealed truth, the natural truth is wrong. Thomas was accused by some contemporaries of applying reason too widely, and after his death some of his ideas were condemned by the church. But he actually steered a middle path between intellectual extremes. In this respect Thomas was like Maimonides and Averroes.

The University

In the early decades of the twelfth century students gathered wherever famous teachers might be found. Such teachers—figures like Peter Abelard—clustered in a few centers, and the students congregated there as well. The last decades of the twelfth century saw a swarm of masters and students in Paris. Like members of secular guilds (see page 265), the masters organized. The University of Paris was the result of their efforts. By 1300 universities had formed elsewhere in France, as well as in Italy, England, and western Germany.

Several forces drove masters to organize. They wanted to negotiate with the bishop's chancellor, the traditional head of all schools in an episcopal city. They wanted to regulate the curriculum that students followed and to prescribe the requirements for entry into their own ranks. They also desired to set the fees to be charged for instruction. By 1209 the bishop of Paris, the pope, and the king of France had granted formal recognition to the university.

In Bologna the university developed a little differently. Here the students came primarily to study law, after already acquiring a basic education. These law students were usually older and more affluent than students elsewhere, and foreign to Bologna. Consequently, in Bologna the university arose from a guild of students who united to set standards in fees and studies and to protect themselves against unscrupulous masters.

Women and Medicine in Twelfth-Century Salerno

Late in the twelfth century an anonymous author compiled three lengthy medical texts into one that came to be called the "Trotula." The second of these treatises, "On the Cures of Women," was almost certainly written by a woman named Trota. For centuries scholars argued that a woman could not have written the widely disseminated Trotula because women could neither study nor teach in the Salerno schools. Absolutely nothing is known about Trota herself, but her text presents an intriguing question: How was she able to acquire vast learning in the Greek, Arab, and Persian medical traditions? Perhaps Trota "practiced" medicine. Whatever the case, most of her text involves either physical appearance or problems connected with menstruation and childbirth. Trota's treatise put her ahead of her time, but just maybe there were other women like her, concealed by ignorance and prejudice.

There are some women who, when they come to their time of menstruation, have either no or very few menses. For these, we proceed thus. Take root of the red willow with which large wine jars are tied and clean them well of the exterior bark, and, having pulverized them, mix them with wine or water and cook them, and in the morning give them in a potion when it has become lukewarm.

To those giving birth with difficulty we give aid in this manner. We should prepare a bath and we put the woman in it, and after she leaves let there be a fumigation of spikenard and similar aromatic substances. For strengthening and for opening the birth canal, let there be sternutatives [substances that induce sneezing] of white hellebore well ground into a powder. For just as Copho

Universities were known for certain specializations: Paris for arts and theology, Bologna for law, Salerno in Italy and Montpellier in France for medicine, Oxford for mathematical and scientific subjects. Still, the basic course of study was similar. At Paris a young scholar came to the city, found lodgings where he could, and attempted to find a master who would guide him through the arts curriculum. These boys might be in their early teens or several years older, depending on their earlier educations and financial resources. The arts course, which was the prerequisite to all higher faculties, usually lasted from four to six years. The bachelor's degree was a license to teach, but a bachelor who wished to teach in a university needed to go on for a master's degree. The master's degree required at least eight years of study (including the baccalaureate years), which culminated in a public oral examination. Some masters went on to become doctors in theology, law, or medicine. A doctorate required ten to fifteen years of study. Medieval academicians were immensely learned.

Student life was difficult. In many ways students were always foreigners. Although their presence in a town enhanced its prestige, townspeople exploited them by charging exorbitant prices for food and rent. Students' own behavior was not always above [a twelfth-century Salerno medical teacher] says, the organs are shaken and the uterus ruptures and thus the fetus is brought out and comes out.

For making the face red, take root of red and white bryony and clean it and chop it finely and dry it. Afterward, powder it and mix it with rose water, and with cotton or a very fine cloth we anoint the face and it induces redness. For the woman having a naturally white complexion, we make a red color if she lacks redness, so that with a kind of fake or cloaked whiteness a red color will appear as if it were natural.

For freckles of the face which appear by accident, take root of bistort and reduce it to powder, and cuttlefish bones and frankincense, and from all these things make a powder. And mix with a little water and smear it, rubbing, on the (face) in the morning . . . until you have removed the freckles.

An ointment for whitening the face. Take two ounces of the very best white lead, let them be ground; afterward let them be sifted through a cloth, and that which remains in the cloth, let it be thrown out. Let it be mixed in with rainwater and let it cook until the consumption of the water, which can be recognized when we see it almost completely dried out. Then let it be cooled. And when it is dried out and cooled, let rose water be added, and again boil it until it becomes hard and thick, so that from it very small pills can be formed. And when you wish to be anointed, take one pill and liquefy it in the hand with water and then rub it well on the face, so that the face will be dried. Then let it be washed with pure water, and this will last for eight days.

Source: Monica H. Green, ed. and trans., *The Trotula: A Medieval Compendium of Women's Medicine* (Philadelphia: University of Pennsylvania Press, 2001), pp. 117–119, 139, 141, 163. Reprinted by permission of the University of Pennsylvania Press.

reproach. There was surely some truth in the frequently lodged charge that students were noisy, quarrelsome, given to drinking, and excessively fond of prostitutes. England's Oxford and Cambridge were unique in always providing residential colleges for students; Paris got one later, and the mendicants often established houses of study. Typically, though, students were on their own.

Students had to work very hard. The arts curriculum demanded a thorough acquaintance with all the famous texts of grammar, logic, and rhetoric. Higher studies added more Aristotle, particularly his philosophical writings. In theology the students had to master the Scriptures, the principal biblical commentaries from patristic times to the present, and the *Four Books of Sentences*. In medicine the ancient writings of Galen and Hippocrates were supplemented by Arab texts as well as by observation and experimentation.

The basic method of teaching provides yet another definition of Scholasticism— that is, the method of studying in the schools. The teacher started by reciting a short piece of a set text, carried on with the presentation and discussion of many authoritative commentaries on that text, and concluded with his own explanations. The teacher then presented another passage of the set text and repeated the whole process. This education focused on standard books and accepted opinions and required students to remember large amounts of material. The curriculum nevertheless produced thinkers of prodigious originality.

In principle, universities were open to free men, but in practice they were restricted to those who had the means to attend them. Women were not accepted at universities, either as students or as teachers. It was generally thought, by men, that learning made women insubordinate. Lacking the required education, women were denied entry into the learned professions of theology, law, and medicine, despite the fact that many rural and some urban medical practitioners were women. Nevertheless, women commonly possessed and transmitted knowledge of both folk remedies and scientific medicine. Trota of Salerno, who probably lived in the twelfth century, wrote a knowledgeable treatise, *On the Care of Women*. Documents from medieval Naples record the names of twenty-four women surgeons between 1273 and 1410. How these women were educated is utterly unknown.

THE VERNACULAR ACHIEVEMENT

A major achievement of high medieval civilization, from Iceland to Kievan Rus, was the appearance of rich literatures in native tongues. Vernacular, from the Latin *vernaculus*, meaning "home-born" or "domestic," is the name for the languages other than Latin—say, English or French. Although Latin remained the language of the clerical elite, writers of vernacular prose and poetry produced some of the greatest works in Western literature.

Literatures and Languages
The number of people who could speak, read, or write Latin was always a minority in western Europe, just as native Greek-speakers were a minority in Byzantium. As Latin, beginning in Late Antiquity, slowly evolved into the Romance (from Roman) languages, people who used what eventually became French, Italian, and Spanish had some advantages over the people in Celtic, Germanic, or Slavic lands, where the languages bore no obvious relationship to Latin. Persons who spoke Old French in their towns and villages would have had an easier time learning Latin than people who spoke Irish or Polish. Nevertheless, vernacular literatures began to appear at roughly the same time all over Europe, between about 800 and 1000.

Of course, many writers continued to use Latin for several centuries. University scholars continued to compose their learned treatises in the ancient tongue, but now often in a style that was less ornate than before. Most law books and public documents were still in Latin, but in a "vulgar" Latin that was reasonably close to the vernacular in areas where Romance languages were spoken. Technical manuals—on farming and animal husbandry, on warfare and armaments, or on law and government—were prepared in Latin, too, but again in a style that was far more accessible than that of their ancient models. Popular literature—poetry, history and biography, and romance and adventure—was still often written in Latin. Some of this material was serious, but some breathed a light and carefree spirit. The anonymous German known as the Archpoet (d. 1165) wrote poems about drinking and womanizing. These lines are typical of his work:

In the public house to die
Is my resolution;
Let wine to my lips be nigh
At life's dissolution:
That will make the angels cry,
With glad elocution
"Grant this drunkard, God on high,
Grace and Absolution!"[1]

No less insouciant were the authors of biting satires such as the anonymous *The Gospel According to the Silver Marks,* which parodies the wealth and greed of the papal curia. But after 1200 this fresh spirit was largely confined to writings in the vernacular. For after that year Latin was rarely used as the language for serious, original literary compositions.

The literary masterpieces of the High Middle Ages are almost entirely written in vernacular languages. The epic poem *Beowulf* is the first classic of English literature. We do not know who wrote it or when it was written. Scholars formerly assigned it to the eighth century, but they now usually place it later, in the ninth or possibly the tenth century. The story focuses on three great battles fought by the hero, Beowulf. The first two are against the monster Grendel and Grendel's mother, who have been harrying the kingdom of an old ally of Beowulf's family; the third is against a dragon. *Beowulf* is a poem of adventure and heroism, of loyalty and treachery. It treats lordship, friendship, and kinship. Themes of good and evil resound throughout. The poem is barely Christian but nevertheless deeply moral. It speaks, in a mature, vigorous, and moving language, to and for the heart of a warrior society.

Beowulf is the best-known Anglo-Saxon work but by no means the only one. One of the Viking attacks that led to the undoing of Ethelred II was commemorated in *The Battle of Maldon.* Several volumes of elegiac and lyric poetry, mostly on religious themes, also survive. And Anglo-Saxon writers produced chronicles, legal materials and charters, and at least one large collection of homilies.

Some fragments of poetry in Old French survive from the ninth century, but the great *chansons de gestes* ("songs of deeds," or celebrations of the great) appeared in the eleventh century. Undoubtedly they were transmitted orally for a long time before they were written down. The best is the *Song of Roland,* written around 1100. In 778 as Charlemagne's army was returning from Spain, Basques raided the baggage train and killed Count Roland. By 1100 this obscure event, long kept alive in oral traditions, had been transformed into a heroic struggle between Charlemagne and his retinue and an army of countless thousands of "paynim," who are crude caricatures of Muslims.

Like *Beowulf,* the *Song of Roland* is a story about loyalty and treachery, bravery in the face of insuperable odds, and the kindness and generosity of leaders. Both take us into a man's chivalric world, where females are all but absent. The two works do not show us personal hopes, fears, or motivations. What pours forth is the communal ethos and the dominant values of the elite, male social group. Although *Beowulf* is lightly clothed in Christianity, the *Song of Roland* is thickly vested in the faith.

The heroic epic tradition that *Beowulf* and the *Song of Roland* represent did not disappear as the Middle Ages unfolded, but literary energies were applied in new directions. Southern France, in the middle and late twelfth century, added something new to Western literature: the love lyrics of the troubadours. This poetry, composed by both men and women, profoundly influenced an age and created the literary movement that has long been called "courtly love." Chivalry was initially a code for men interacting with other men. In the world of courtly love, chivalry became an elaborate set of rules governing relations between men and women.

Courtly love had several sources. The classical poet Ovid (43 B.C.–?A.D. 17), who wrote *The Art of Love*, a manual of seduction, was one. Another was the lyrical poetry of Muslim Spain. Ironically, feudal values such as loyalty and service played a critical role as men became, in effect, love vassals. Platonic ideas made some contribution, too, particularly the notion that any love in this world could be only a pale imitation of real love. The courtly poets sang of *fin'amours*, a pure love in contrast to the mere lust of the masses. A lover cherished an unattainable lady. He would do anything for the merest display of pleasure or gratitude on her part, as we see in these lines from Bernart de Ventadorn, court poet of the counts of Toulouse in the late twelfth century:

> Down there, around Ventadorn, all my friends
> have lost me, because my lady does not love me;
> and so, it is right that I never go back there again,
> because always she is wild and morose with me.
> Now here is why the face she shows me is gloomy and full of anger:
> because my pleasure is in loving her and I have settled down to it.
> She is resentful and complains for no other reason.[2]

Male troubadours placed women on pedestals and, in ballads, worshiped them from afar. Women troubadours took a different line. Women's poems were more realistic, human, and emotionally satisfying. Castellozza (b. ca. 1200), the southern French wife of a Crusader, idealized not at all when she wrote these lines:

> Friend, if you had shown consideration,
> meekness, candor and humanity,
> I'd have loved you without hesitation,
> but you were mean and sly and villainous.

And she did not assign the active role exclusively to the man:

> Handsome friend, as a lover true
> I loved you, for you pleased me,
> But now I see I was a fool,
> for I've barely seen you since.[3]

Count William IX of Poitou (1071–1127) was among the first of the troubadours, and his daughter, Eleanor of Aquitaine, brought the conventions of this poetry and point of view to the French and Angevin courts. She and her daughters were the greatest literary patrons of the late twelfth century. The wives of kings and nobles who were frequently away from home maintained stunning courts and cultivated vernacular literature.

The courtly literature of northern France owed much to the troubadour tradition of the south but broke new ground in both forms and content. The romance and the lay were the chief new forms. Both drew on Classical literature, the heroic Germanic past, and the Arthurian legends of the Celtic world to create stories of love and adventure. The romance usually develops a complex narrative involving several major characters over a long time. The lay is brief and focuses on a single incident. The most famous twelfth-century writer of romance was Chrétien de Troyes (1135–1183), the court writer of Marie of Champagne, the daughter of Eleanor of Aquitaine. The greatest writer of lays was Marie de France, who wrote at the Angevin court in the 1170s.

The romances and lays explore the contradictions and tensions in a variety of human relationships. Loyalty and honor make frequent appearances. Lancelot, a paragon of knightly virtue, desperately loves his lord Arthur's wife, Guinevere. What is he to do? How can he be loyal to his lord, to his love, and to himself? What will he do when a single course of action brings both honor and dishonor? In the epics speeches are made to swords, to horses, or sometimes to no one in particular; the points being made are universalized. In the romances credible human beings struggle to resolve powerful and conflicting emotional and moral dilemmas.

Slavic literatures began with the missionaries Cyril and Methodius (see pages 252–253), who developed both a language, Church Slavonic, and a script, Glagolitic. The Glagolitic script was modified into the Cyrillic, which was adopted by all the Slavic peoples who embraced Orthodoxy and remains in use today. The earliest writing in the Slavic languages was religious: biblical translations, saints' lives, and selections from the Church Fathers. Historical writings and imaginative literature, such as the *Tale of Igor*, made their appearance in Kievan Rus in the twelfth century. The latter work, a semilegendary account of Prince Igor and his many battles, is reminiscent of the *chansons des gestes*.

The Scandinavians who settled Iceland produced a diverse literature. They created law books, detailed accounts of their settlements, and a mighty saga tradition. *Saga* means "things said," and it is almost certainly the case that the greatest sagas were oral tales long before they were written down between about 1150 and 1350. Sagas fall into two categories: Historical sagas blend fact and fiction to praise the deeds of the great heroes of the Viking age. Family sagas mix history and myth to relate the stories of the great families who settled Iceland.

France led the way in the production of vernacular literature, but French models did not inspire slavish imitation. This is seen most clearly in the work of the master of all vernacular writers, Dante Alighieri (1265–1321). Dante began as a poet in *la dolce stil nuova*, "the sweet new style," which came from France and captivated Italians. But he moved beyond it in many ways. Dante was a man of extraordinarily wide learning and reading. He served Florence in public capacities and became an exile amid political strife. He wrote a long treatise in defense of the empire—or, really, against the secular rule of the church. But he is best known for one of the masterpieces of world literature, *The Divine Comedy*.

The secret of the *Comedy*'s success is not easy to grasp. It is a long and difficult poem, but it is also humorous, instructive, and moving. In an exquisitely beautiful Italian, Dante took the most advanced theology and philosophy of his time, the richest poetic traditions, a huge hoard of stories, many contemporary events, and a lot of common sense and wove them into an allegorical presentation of the journey of the whole human race and of the individual lives of all people.

Accompanied by the Roman poet Virgil (see page 167), Dante travels through Hell and Purgatory, commenting along the way on the condition of the people he meets. Then, because Virgil is a pagan and only Dante's true love can accompany Dante into paradise, Beatrice, the love of Dante's youth, joins him for a visit to Heaven. The poet's central metaphor is love; the love he feels for Beatrice symbolizes the love God feels for the world. Dante canvasses humanity from the pits of Hell, which he reserved for traitors, to the summit of Paradise, where a man inspired by pure love might, despite his sinfulness, dare to look into the face of God.

Although the romances and lays were by no means the exclusive preserve of the elite, very little is known about popular literature. Two exceptions are the mystery play and women's devotional writing. Mystery plays made their first appearance in the eleventh century. The liturgy of the church, which formally re-enacted the life of Christ, was confined to the clergy. But this limitation did not prevent troupes of actors from staging, on church porches or village greens, scenes from the life of Christ in simple, direct language. By the twelfth and thirteenth centuries guilds in many towns sponsored the production of plays commemorating the Christian mysteries. Such plays served as both a form of popular entertainment and a device for teaching elementary Christian ideas. The female religious movements of the age gave rise to prose and verse works in various vernaculars. Mechtild of Magdeburg (1210–1280), a German Beguine, wrote *The Flowering Light of Divinity,* a mystical, allegorical account of the marriage between God and a spiritual woman. The vernaculars opened avenues of expression to women, who were normally denied Latin learning.

Innovations in Architecture

Romanesque, "in the Roman style," is a term that was coined in the nineteenth century to characterize the architecture and, to a lesser extent, the painting of the period between the waning of Carolingian art and the full emergence of Gothic art in the late twelfth century. Today scholars view the Romanesque style as a transition between Carolingian and Gothic.

At several places in Ottonian Germany, a return of political stability led to the construction of churches. Ducal dynasties and women of the imperial family were among the most generous patrons. Pride in their Carolingian inheritance and their new imperial dignity led the Germans to a distinctive architectural style marked by very thick

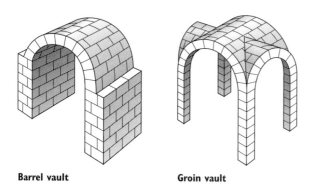

Barrel vault   **Groin vault**

The Structure of Romanesque Architecture

The basic structural element of Romanesque architecture was the barrel vault, which, when two were joined at right angles, formed a groin vault. These vaults produced great height and strength but gave buildings a massive, fortresslike appearance. *(Source: Anne Shaver-Crandell,* The Middle Ages. *Copyright © 1982 Cambridge University Press. Reprinted with permission of Cambridge University Press.)*

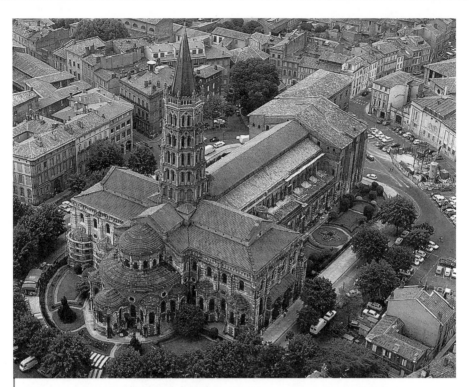

Romanesque Exterior, Saint Sernin, Toulouse   *This fortresslike church (ca. 1080–1120) was paid for by the offerings of pilgrims on their way to shrines in Spain. Its massive walls and numerous colonnades are typical of Romanesque architecture. The form of the building suggests the cross of Christ.*   (Jean Dieuzaid, Toulouse)

walls, alternating piers and columns in the nave, and galleries. As this architectural style spread all over Europe in the eleventh century, it produced true Romanesque, a style that differed from Roman and Carolingian styles mainly in the greater internal height and space made possible by vaulting. To the rectangular elegance of the classical basilica and the height of the Carolingian westworks (see page 251), Romanesque builders added a refined verticality.

Among the distinctive features of Romanesque churches were their wall paintings and frescoes, sculpture, reliquaries, pulpits, and baptisteries—in short, their exuberant decoration and ornament. Europe's growing wealth and sophistication, and the pride of the church's aristocratic patrons, are very much in evidence. Especially in the south of France, the façades of Romanesque churches provided space for sculpture. The tympanum above the doors, a space seen by all who entered, was a favored location. Large-scale sculpture made a comeback after its almost total absence in the early Middle Ages.

It is surely no coincidence that Gothic art and architecture emerged just as the West was absorbing the rediscovery of Euclid's mathematical writings and applying the intensely ordered logic of Aristotle to everything from legal problems to theological mysteries. One of the most familiar images of the Middle Ages is the inspiringly beautiful Gothic cathedral. It is thus ironic that the word *Gothic* first appeared in the sixteenth

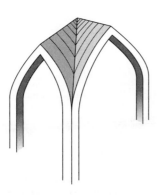

The Structure of Gothic Architecture

The adoption of pointed arches, an import from the Islamic world, let Gothic builders join structures of identical height but different widths. The resulting structures were high, light, airy, and visually interesting. *(Source: Anne Shaver-Crandell,* The Middle Ages. *Copyright © 1982 Cambridge University Press. Reprinted with permission of Cambridge University Press.)*

century as a term of derision for what was then regarded as an outmoded style so ugly that only the horrible conquerors of Rome, the Goths, could have been responsible for it. The name stuck, but today it simply identifies a period in European architecture, sculpture, and painting that began in the middle of the twelfth century and that in some places lasted until the early sixteenth century.

Gothic is a French invention. It was Abbot Suger (1085–1151) of Saint-Denis, a monastery outside Paris, who, in rebuilding his basilica beginning in 1135, consciously sought a new style. He desired to achieve effects of lightness, almost weightlessness, in the stonework of his church and to admit large amounts of light to create a dazzling and mysterious aura on the inside. The Bible often uses images of light to refer to God, and Suger wished to give expression to those images in the house of God for which he was responsible.

Suger produced something startlingly original by combining a number of elements that had long been in use—three in particular: A *pointed arch* is more elegant than a round one; it also permits the joining of two arches of identical height but different widths, which, in turn, permits complex shapes and sizes. The *ribbed vault* is lighter and more graceful than the barrel and groin vaults characteristic of Romanesque architecture; it also exerts less stress and facilitates experimentation with shapes. Finally, *point support*—basically, the support of structural elements at only certain points—permits the replacement of heavy, stress-bearing walls with curtains of stained glass. The points of support might be massive internal piers or intricate skeletal frameworks, called *buttresses,* on the outside of the church.

These three elements—pointed arch, ribbed vault, and point support—produce a building that is characterized by verticality and translucency. Everything seems to spring upward, and stone surfaces appear so frequently punctured by light as almost to disappear altogether. The desired, and achieved, effect is one of harmony, order, and mathematical precision.

The Gothic style soon spread in central and northern France. The cathedral of Notre-Dame of Paris was built beginning in the 1150s, and the royal portal at Chartres Cathedral was reconstructed after 1145. Gothic churches could be huge. The interior of Notre-Dame, for example, is 493 feet long and 107 feet high. To avoid a sense of sheer mass, Gothic builders used triple or quadruple elevations inside the buildings and took advantage of point support to pierce the walls at frequent intervals with stained glass windows. Exterior surfaces were broken up with windows, sculptures, colonnades, and towers. No opportunity was missed to create visual interest and complexity.

The thirteenth century was the most mature period for French Gothic architecture and also the time when Gothic spread most widely throughout Europe. Its popularity may be attributed to the superiority of French masons and stonecutters and also to the tremendous prestige of French culture. By 1300 distinctive Gothic traditions shaped the urban landscape in almost all parts of Europe from Iceland to Poland.

IMPORTANT EVENTS

ca. 900 *Beowulf*

910 Foundation of Cluny

940–1003 Gerbert of Aurillac

960–1028 Fulbert of Chartres

d. 970 Roswitha of Gandersheim

1000–1088 Berengar of Tours

ca. 1033–1109 Anselm of Canterbury

ca. 1050–1150 Emergence of the Romanesque

1079–1142 Peter Abelard

1184 Waldensians declared heretics

1090–1153 Bernard of Clairvaux

1098 Foundation of Cîteaux

1098–1179 Hildegard of Bingen

ca. 1100 *Song of Roland*

1135–1183 Chrétien de Troyes

1170–1221 Dominic de Guzman

ca. 1177–1213 Mary of Oignies

1181–1226 Francis of Assisi

1194–1253 Clare of Assisi

1208 Albigensian Crusade launched

1210–1280 Mechtild of Magdeburg

1225–1274 Thomas Aquinas

1265–1321 Dante Alighieri

NOTES

1. John Addington Symonds, *Wine, Women and Song: Medieval Latin Students' Songs* (reprint, New York: Cooper Square, 1966), p. 69.
2. Frederick Goldin, *Lyrics of the Troubadours and Trouvères: An Anthology and a History* (New York: Doubleday, 1973), p. 135.
3. Meg Bogin, *The Women Troubadours* (New York: Norton, 1976), p. 69.

SUGGESTED READING

Bony, Jean. *French Gothic Architecture of the Twelfth and Thirteenth Centuries.* 1983. Huge, clearly presented, and magnificently illustrated, this is a browser's book as well as a sustained essay by a master of his subject.

Bouchard, Constance B. *Strong of Body, Brave and Noble: Chivalry and Society in Medieval France.* 1998. A superb summation of the social and cultural history of the medieval aristocracy.

Bynum, Caroline Walker. *Jesus as Mother: Studies in the Spirituality of the High Middle Ages.* 1982. A collection of sparkling essays by a major historian that makes the feminine in religious thought accessible, even central, to any discussion of medieval religion.

Colish, Marcia. *Medieval Foundations of the Western Intellectual Tradition.* 1997. The first original and comprehensive history of medieval thought in a generation.

Grundmann, Herbert. *Religious Movements in the Middle Ages.* 1995. Translated into English sixty years after its appearance in German, this book has lost none of its interest or explanatory power.

Jaeger, C. Stephen. *Ennobling Love: In Search of a Lost Sensibility.* 1999. A beautiful and moving interpretation of the love literature of the High Middle Ages and of its philosophical and theological dimensions.

Lambert, Malcolm. *Medieval Heresy: Popular Movements from the Gregorian Reform to the Reformation.* 3d ed. 2002. Brilliant and readable, this book is the best history of medieval heresy ever written and one of the best books on medieval religion generally.

Southern, R. W. *Scholastic Humanism and the Unification of Europe.* 1995. A truly brilliant overview of twelfth-century culture by its greatest twentieth-century student.

Crisis and Recovery in Late Medieval Europe, 1300–1500

11

(Staatliche Museen zu Berlin, Preussischer Kulturbesitz Kunstgewerbemuseum/ Bildarchiv Preussischer Kulturbesitz/Art Resource, NY. Photo: Mues-Funke)

In the fourteenth century, Europeans sang an old Franciscan hymn, "Day of Wrath, Day of Burning." Its verses described the fear and disorder that would accompany the end of the world and God's judgment of the saved and the damned. That hymn could well have been in the mind of the painter of the facing illustration. When countless Europeans, such as these poor souls beneath the winged angel of death, fell victim to epidemic disease, many people thought they knew why. The illustrator seems to believe it was God's judgment against sinners, including these gamblers sickened by the angel's plague-tipped arrows. The flood, fire, and pestilence that ravaged late medieval Europe were thought to be premonitions of the breakdown of the world and a time of judgment.

The late Middle Ages (ca. 1300–1500) are often described as a period of continued crisis and decline that put an end to the growth and expansion of the previous three centuries. In truth, however, the years of crisis in the fourteenth and early fifteenth centuries gave way to a dramatic economic, social, and political recovery in the fifteenth century. The cultural and intellectual changes that accompanied the crisis and recovery are the focus of Chapter 12, "The Renaissance."

Military, political, religious, economic, and social crises burdened Europe in the fourteenth and early fifteenth centuries. Between 1337 and 1453 France and England fought a war that touched most of the states of western Europe. The Hundred Years' War, as it has come to be known, was fought primarily over English claims to traditionally French lands. Problems were not confined to England and France. Aristocrats in many parts of Europe challenged the hereditary rights of their rulers. In the towns of Germany and Italy patrician classes moved to reduce the influence of artisans and laborers in government, instituting oligarchies or even aristocratic lordships in place of more democratic governments.

Questions of power and representation also affected the Christian church as ecclesiastical claims to authority came under attack. Secular governments challenged church jurisdictions. Disputed papal elections led to the so-called Great Schism, a split between rival centers of control in Rome and Avignon (a city in what is now the south of France). In the aftermath of the crisis, the papacy was forced to redefine its place in both the religious life and the political life of Europe.

A series of economic and demographic shocks worsened these political and religious difficulties. Part of the problem was structural: the population of Europe had grown too large to be supported by the resources available. Famine and the return of the plague in 1348 sent the economy into long-term decline. In almost every aspect of political, religious, and social life, then, the fourteenth and early fifteenth centuries marked a pause in the growth and consolidation that had characterized the earlier medieval period.

Yet out of the crises a number of significant changes emerged. By 1500 the European population and economy were again expanding. England and France emerged strengthened by military and political conflicts. And the consolidation of the Spanish kingdoms, the Ottoman Empire, and the states of eastern Europe altered the political and social makeup of Europe. None of the transformations could have been predicted in 1300 as Europe entered a religious, political, and social whirlwind.

THE CRISIS OF THE WESTERN CHRISTIAN CHURCH

Early in the fourteenth century the Christian church endured a series of crises that instigated a debate about the nature of church government and the role of the church in society. First the popes and their entourages abandoned their traditional residences in central Italy and moved to Avignon, an imperial enclave in the south of modern France. Then, in the wake of a disputed election, two and later three rivals claimed the papal throne. Simultaneously, the church hierarchy faced challenges from radical reformers who wished to change it. At various times all the European powers became entangled in the problems of the church. By the mid-fifteenth century the papacy realized that it needed a stronger, independent base. Papal recovery in the fifteenth century was predicated on political power in central Italy.

The Babylonian Captivity, 1309–1377   The Christian church was in turmoil as a result of an attack on Pope Boniface VIII (r. 1294–1303) by King Philip IV (r. 1285–1314) of France. The king attempted to kidnap Boniface, intending to try him for heresy because of the pope's challenges to the king's authority within his own kingdom. The outstanding issues revolved around the powers of the pope and the responsibilities of the clergy to political leaders. It was, in fact, largely because of tensions with the northern kingdoms that the French archbishop of Bordeaux was elected Pope Clement V (r. 1305–1314). Clement chose to remain north of the Alps in order to seek an end to warfare between France and England and to protect, to the extent possible, the wealthy religious order of the Knights of the Temple, or Templars (see page 301), which Philip was in the process of suppressing. Clement also hoped to prevent the king from carrying through his threatened posthumous heresy trial of Boniface. After the death of Boniface it was clear that the governments of Europe had no intention of recognizing papal political authority as absolute.

Clement's pontificate marked the beginning of the so-called Babylonian Captivity, a period during which the pope resided almost continuously outside of Italy. In 1309 Clement moved the papal court to Avignon, on the Rhône River in a region that was still part of the Holy Roman Empire—the name that by the fourteenth century was given to the medieval empire whose origin reached back to Charlemagne. His successor, Pope John XXII (r. 1316–1334), set the tone for the brilliant papal court. To celebrate the marriage of his grandniece in 1324, for example, he ordered a wedding feast during which the numerous guests consumed 4,012 loaves of bread, 8¾ oxen, 55¼ sheep, 8 pigs, 4 boars, and vast quantities of fish, capons, chickens, partridges, rabbits, ducks, and chickens. The repast was topped off with 300 pounds of cheese, 3,000 eggs, and assorted fruits. The guests washed down this feast with about 450 liters of wine.

The papacy and its new residence in Avignon became a major religious, diplomatic, and commercial center. The size of the court changed as dramatically as its venue: although the thirteenth-century papal administration required only two hundred or so officials, the bureaucracy in Avignon grew to about six hundred. It was not just the pope's immediate circle that expanded the population of Avignon. Artists, writers, lawyers, and merchants from across Europe were drawn to the new center of administration and hub of patronage. Kings, princes, towns, and ecclesiastical institutions needed representatives at the papal court. Papal administrators continued to intervene actively in local ecclesiastical affairs, and the pope's revenues from annates (generally a portion of the first year's revenues from an ecclesiastical office granted by papal letter), court fees, and provisioning charges continued to grow.

Not everyone approved of this situation. It was the Italian poet and philosopher Francesco Petrarch (1304–1374) who first referred to the Avignon move as a "Babylonian Captivity of the papacy." Recalling the account in the Hebrew Bible of the exile of the Israelites and New Testament images of Babylon as the center of sin and immorality, he complained of

> [an] unholy Babylon, Hell on Earth, a sink of iniquity, the cesspool of the world. There is neither faith, nor charity, nor religion, nor fear of God, nor shame, nor truth, nor holiness, albeit the residence . . . of the supreme pontiff should have made it a shrine and the very stronghold of religion.[1]

To Petrarch and others the exile of the papacy epitomized all that was wrong with the church. Many people renowned for their piety, including women such as Saint Catherine of Siena and Saint Bridget of Sweden, appealed to the pope to return to simpler ways and to Rome, his episcopal city.

The Great Schism, 1378–1417   In 1377 Pope Gregory XI (r. 1370–1378) bowed to critics' pressure and did return to Rome. He was shocked by what he found: churches and palaces in ruin and the city violent and dangerous. By the end of 1377 he had resolved to retreat to Avignon, but he died a few months later. In a tumultuous election during which the Roman populace entered the Vatican Palace and threatened to break into the conclave itself, the cardinals finally elected a compromise candidate acceptable to both the French cardinals and the Roman mob. Urban VI (r. 1378–1389) may have been electable, but he was also violent, intemperate, and eager to reduce the privileges of the clerical hierarchy. In response, the French cardinals questioned the legitimacy of the election, which they came to believe had been conducted under duress. Within months they deposed Urban and elected in his place a French cardinal who took the name Clement VII (r. 1378–1394). Urban responded by denouncing the cardinals and continuing to rule in Rome. The church now had two popes.

After some hesitation Western Christians divided into two camps, initiating the Great Schism, a period of almost forty years during which no one knew for sure who was the true pope. This was a deadly serious issue for all. The true pope had the right to appoint church officials, decide important moral and legal issues, and allow or forbid taxation of the clergy by the state. Each side found ready supporters among the states of Europe; however, support for one pope or the other often had more to do with political rivalries than with religious convictions. The two sides largely mirrored the political tensions in Europe. France and those governments most closely allied with it—Burgundy, Savoy, Naples, Scotland, and Castile—tended to support Clement, who eventually resettled in Avignon. The English, together with most Italian governments, the German Empire, Scandinavia, Hungary, Portugal, and Poland, supported Urban, the pope in Rome.

The crisis gave impetus to new discussions about church government: Should the pope be considered the sole head of the church? Debates within the church followed lines of thought already expressed in the towns and kingdoms of Europe. Representative bodies—the English Parliament, the French Estates General, the Swedish Riksdag—already claimed the right to act for the realm, and in the city-states of Italy ultimate authority was thought to reside in the body of citizens. Canon lawyers and theologians similarly argued that authority resided in the whole church, which had the right and duty to come together in council to correct and reform the church hierarchy. Even the

Gregory XI Returns to Rome *This highly stylized painting conveys the hopes of European Christians when Gregory XI returned from Avignon in 1377. Saint Catherine of Siena, who had pleaded for the pope's return, is seen in the foreground.* (Scala/Art Resource, NY)

most conservative of these "conciliarists" agreed that the "universal church" had the right to respond in periods of heresy or schism. More radical conciliarists argued that the pope as bishop of Rome was merely the first among equals in the church hierarchy and that he, like any other bishop, could be corrected by a gathering of his peers—that is, by an ecumenical council.

The rival popes found themselves under increased pressure to end the schism. The issue seemed on its way to resolution when the two parties agreed to meet in northern Italy in 1408. In the end, though, the meeting never took place, and in retrospect many doubted whether either party had been negotiating in good faith. In exasperation the cardinals, the main ecclesiastical supporters of the rival popes, called a general council in Pisa, which deposed both popes and elected a new one. Since the council lacked the power to force the rivals to accept deposition, the result was that three men now claimed to be the rightful successor of Saint Peter. Conciliarists, by themselves, could not mend the split in the church.

Resolution finally came when the Holy Roman emperor Sigismund (r. 1411–1437) forced the diplomatically isolated third papal claimant, John XXIII (r. 1410–1415), to call a general council of the church. The council, which met from 1414 to 1417 in the German imperial city of Constance, could never have succeeded without Sigismund's support. At one point he forced the council to remain in session even after Pope John had fled the city in an attempt to end deliberations.

Heresy and the Council of Constance, 1414–1418   Sigismund hoped that a council could help him heal deep religious and civil divisions in Bohemia, the most important part of his family's traditional lands. Bohemia and its capital, Prague, were Czech-speaking. But Prague was also the seat of the Luxemburg dynasty of German emperors and the site of the first university in German or Slavic lands. Religious and theological questions quickly became entangled with the competing claims of Czech and German factions. The preaching and teaching of the Czech reformer Jan Hus (ca. 1370–1415) were at the center of the debate. As preacher in the Bethlehem Chapel in Prague from 1402 and eventually as rector of the university, Hus was the natural spokesman for the non-German townspeople in Prague and the Czech faction at the university. His criticisms of the church hierarchy, which in Prague was primarily German, fanned into flames the smoldering embers of Czech national feeling. It was Sigismund's hope that a council might clarify the orthodoxy of Hus's teachings and heal the rift within the church of Bohemia.

The council's response to the theological crisis was based on the church's experience with heresy over the previous forty years, primarily the teachings of John Wyclif (1329–1384). In the 1370s Wyclif, an Oxford theologian and parish priest, began to criticize in increasingly angry terms the state of the clergy and the abuses of the church hierarchy. By 1387 his ideas had been declared heretical and his followers were hunted out. Wyclif's most dangerous criticism was his denial of the priest's indispensable position as an intermediary between God and believers. Wyclif believed that the church could be at once a divine institution and an earthly gathering of individuals. Thus, in his opinion, individual Christians need not unquestioningly obey the pronouncements of the church hierarchy. Final authority lay only in the Scriptures, insisted Wyclif, who sponsored the first translations of the Bible into English. He gathered about himself followers called "Lollards," who emphasized Bible reading and popular piety; some even supported public preaching by women. According to one disciple, "Every true man and woman being in charity is a priest."[2] Because of their attacks on the ecclesiastical hierarchy, Lollards were popular among the nobility of England, and especially at the court of Richard II during the 1390s. In the first two decades of the fifteenth century, however, their influence waned.

Wyclif's influence continued on the Continent, especially in the circle of Jan Hus and the Czech reformers. While Hus disagreed with some of Wyclif's more radical ideas, he also attacked clerical power and privileges. By 1403 the German majority in the university had condemned Hus's teaching as Wycliffite, thus initiating almost a decade of struggle between Czechs and Germans, Hussites and Catholics. This was the impasse that Sigismund hoped the Council of Constance could settle. Accordingly, he offered a suspicious Hus a safe conduct pass to attend the council. When Hus arrived, it became clear that the councilors and Hus himself were in no mood to compromise. The council revoked the pledge of safe conduct and ordered Hus to recant his beliefs. He refused. The council condemned him as a heretic and burned him at the stake on July 6, 1415.

Far from ending Sigismund's problems with the Bohemians, the actions of the council provided the Czechs with a martyr and hero. The execution of Hus provoked a firestorm of revolution in Prague. Czech forces roundly defeated an imperial army sent in to restore order. The Hussite movement gathered strength and spread throughout Bohemia. Moderate Hussites continued Hus's campaign against clerical abuses and claimed the right to receive both the bread and the wine during the sacrament of Communion. Radical Hussites argued that the true church was the community of spiritual men and women; they had no use for ecclesiastical hierarchy of any kind. The German emperors were unable to defeat a united Hussite movement. In 1433 a new church council and moderate Hussites negotiated an agreement that allowed the Hussites to continue some of their practices, including receiving both bread and wine at Communion, while returning to the church. Radical Hussites refused the compromise, and the war dragged on until 1436. Bohemia remained a center of religious dissent, and the memory of Hus's execution at a church council would have a chilling effect on discussions of church reform during the Reformation in the sixteenth century.

The Reunion and Reform of the Papacy, 1415–1513   To most of the delegates at the Council of Constance, the reunion and reform of the papacy were more important than the issue of heresy. And as we will see, the crisis of the schism brought in its aftermath a transformed Christian church.

After initially agreeing to abdicate if his rivals did the same, John changed his mind and fled from Constance. Sigismund recaptured him and returned him to the council, where he was deposed. Pope Gregory XII (r. 1406–1415), the Roman pope, realizing he had lost all his support, resigned—after himself calling the council, as a rightful pope should do. Benedict III (r. 1394–1417), the pope in Avignon, refused to resign and he also was deposed. Finally, in 1417, the council elected a Roman nobleman as Pope Martin V (r. 1417–1431).

The council justified its actions in what was perhaps its most important decree, *Haec sancta synodus* ("This sacred synod"): "This sacred synod of Constance . . . declares . . . that it has its power immediately from Christ, and that all men, of every rank and position, including even the pope himself are bound to obey it in those matters that pertain to the faith."[3] Popes could no longer expect to remain unchallenged if they made claims of absolute dominion, and ecclesiastical rights and jurisdictions increasingly were matters for negotiation.

Critics agreed that the pope no longer behaved like the "Servant of the Servants of Christ" but instead acted like the "Lord of Lords." Cardinals claimed to represent the church at large as counterweights to papal abuse, but as the nobility of the church, they and other members of the hierarchy required the income from multiple offices to maintain their presence at the papal court. Both the cardinals and the popes viewed any reforms to the present system as potential threats to their ability to function. The council, however, recognized the need for further reforms. A second reform council met at Basel from 1431 to 1449, but with modest results. The council again tried to reduce papal power, but this time it received little support from European governments.

Because of the continuing conciliarist threat, the papacy needed the support of the secular rulers of Europe. Thus the papacy was forced to accept compromises on the issues of reform, on ecclesiastical jurisdictions and immunities, and on papal revenues. Various governments argued that it was they, and not the pope, who should be responsible for ecclesiastical institutions and jurisdictions within their territories.

Lay rulers focused on several issues. They wanted church officials in their territories to belong to local families. They wanted ecclesiastical institutions to be subject to local laws and administration. And by the 1470s it was clear that they wanted to have local prelates named as cardinal-protectors. These were not churchmen who could serve the church administration in Rome; rather they functioned as mediators between local governments and the papacy. The most famous of these new political cardinals was Thomas Wolsey of England (ca. 1470–1530), who was an important supporter of King Henry VII and chancellor of England under Henry VIII.

The reunited papacy had to accept claims it would have staunchly opposed a century earlier. One of the most important of these was the Pragmatic Sanction of Bourges of 1438. The papacy was unable to protest when the French clergy, at the urging of the king, abolished papal rights to annates, limited appeals to the papal court, and reduced papal rights to appoint clergy within France without the approval of the local clergy or the Crown. Similar concessions diminished church authority throughout Europe. Perhaps the most momentous was a bull (official papal document) issued in 1478 by Pope Sixtus IV (r. 1471–1484) that allowed Ferdinand and Isabella of Aragon and Castile to institute a church court, the Spanish Inquisition, under their own auspices (see page 365).

With reduced revenues from legal fees, annates, and appointments, the popes of the fifteenth century were forced to derive more and more of their revenue and influence from the Papal States. By 1430 the Papal States accounted for about half of the annual income of the papacy. Papal interests increasingly centered on protecting the papacy's influence as a secular ruler of a large territory in central Italy. Thus the papacy had to deal with many of the same jurisdictional, diplomatic, and military challenges that faced other medieval governments.

WAR AND THE STRUGGLE OVER POLITICAL POWER, 1300–1450

A lawyer who served King Philip IV of France (r. 1285–1314) observed that "everything within the limits of his kingdom belongs to the lord king, especially protection, high justice and dominion."[4] Royal officials in England and France generally believed that "liberties"—that is, individual rights to local jurisdictions—originated with the king. These ideas were the result of several centuries of centralization of political power in royal hands. At almost the same time, however, an English noble challenged royal claims on his lands, saying, "Here, my lords, is my warrant," as he brandished a rusty long sword. "My ancestors came with William the Bastard [that is, William the Conqueror, in 1066] and conquered their lands with the sword, and by the sword I will defend them against anyone who tries to usurp them."[5] The views of the royal lawyer and the feisty earl exemplify the central tension over power in the late Middle Ages. The struggle over political power was played out in the context of the Hundred Years' War, which affected not just England and France but also most of western Europe, especially Italy. In England and France the crisis led to strengthened monarchies. In Italy, however, public power resided more and more in local entities.

[handwritten: Italy → local entities - power]
[handwritten: Hundred Yrs War → strengthened P. of Monarchs]

England, France, and the Hundred Years' War, 1337–1453

In the twelfth and thirteenth centuries centralization of royal power in England and France had proceeded almost without interruption. In the fourteenth century matters changed in both countries. Questions of the nature of royal power, common responsibility, and hereditary rights to rule challenged the power of the English and French monarchs.

[handwritten: 1300's - power of Monarchs = challenged]

In England fears arising from the growing power of the English crown and the weakness of a gullible king brought issues to a head during the reign of Edward II (r. 1307–1327). By the early fourteenth century, resident justices of the peace (JPs) were replacing the expensive and inefficient system of traveling justices. In theory, the JPs were royal officials doing the king's bidding, but this was often not the case in reality. These unpaid local officials were modestly well-to-do gentry who were often clients of local magnates. Justices were known to use their offices to carry out local vendettas and feuds and to protect the interests of the wealthy and powerful.

[handwritten: protect interests of wealthy]

The barons, the titled lords of England, were interested in controlling more than just local justices. Fearing that Edward II would continue many of the centralizing policies of his father, the barons passed reform ordinances in 1311 limiting the king's right to wage war, leave the realm, grant lands or castles, or appoint chief justices and chancellors without the approval of Parliament, which they dominated. Special taxes or

[handwritten: reforms limiting kings power]

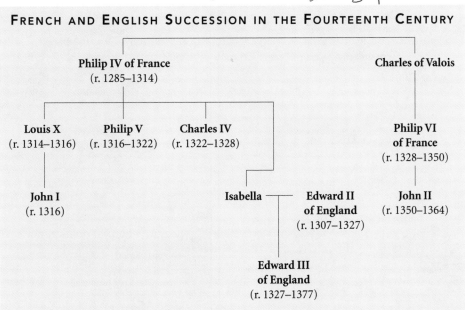

FRENCH AND ENGLISH SUCCESSION IN THE FOURTEENTH CENTURY

Philip IV of France (r. 1285–1314)

Charles of Valois

Louis X (r. 1314–1316)   Philip V (r. 1316–1322)   Charles IV (r. 1322–1328)

Philip VI of France (r. 1328–1350)

John I (r. 1316)

Isabella ⎯ Edward II of England (r. 1307–1327)

John II (r. 1350–1364)

Edward III of England (r. 1327–1377)

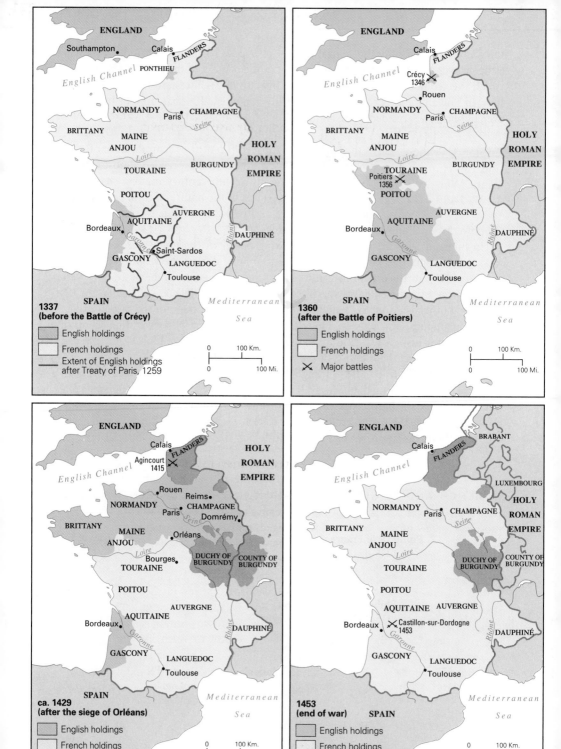

1337
(before the Battle of Crécy)

ENGLAND
Southampton Calais FLANDERS
PONTHIEU
English Channel
NORMANDY CHAMPAGNE
Paris
Seine
BRITTANY
MAINE HOLY
ANJOU ROMAN
Loire EMPIRE
TOURAINE BURGUNDY
POITOU
AUVERGNE
Bordeaux AQUITAINE DAUPHINÉ
Garonne *Rhône*
GASCONY Saint-Sardos
LANGUEDOC
Toulouse
SPAIN *Mediterranean*
Sea

English holdings
French holdings
Extent of English holdings
after Treaty of Paris, 1259

0   100 Km.
0   100 Mi.

1360
(after the Battle of Poitiers)

ENGLAND
Calais FLANDERS
Crécy
1346
English Channel
Rouen
NORMANDY CHAMPAGNE
Paris
Seine HOLY
BRITTANY ROMAN
MAINE EMPIRE
ANJOU
Loire BURGUNDY
TOURAINE
Poitiers Poitiers
1356
POITOU
AUVERGNE
AQUITAINE
Bordeaux DAUPHINÉ
Garonne *Rhône*
GASCONY
LANGUEDOC
Toulouse
SPAIN *Mediterranean*
Sea

English holdings
French holdings
✕ Major battles

0   100 Km.
0   100 Mi.

ca. 1429
(after the siege of Orléans)

ENGLAND
Calais FLANDERS HOLY
Agincourt ROMAN
1415 EMPIRE
English Channel
Rouen
Reims
NORMANDY CHAMPAGNE
Paris Domrémy
Seine
BRITTANY Orléans
MAINE
ANJOU DUCHY OF COUNTY OF
Loire BURGUNDY BURGUNDY
Bourges
TOURAINE
POITOU
AUVERGNE
AQUITAINE
Bordeaux DAUPHINÉ
Garonne *Rhône*
GASCONY
LANGUEDOC
Toulouse
SPAIN *Mediterranean*
Sea

English holdings
French holdings
Burgundian lands allied
with England to 1435
✕ Major battle

0   100 Km.
0   100 Mi.

1453
(end of war)

ENGLAND BRABANT
Calais FLANDERS
LUXEMBOURG
English Channel
HOLY
NORMANDY ROMAN
Paris CHAMPAGNE EMPIRE
Seine
BRITTANY
MAINE
ANJOU DUCHY OF COUNTY OF
Loire BURGUNDY BURGUNDY
TOURAINE
POITOU
AQUITAINE AUVERGNE
Bordeaux Castillon-sur-Dordogne DAUPHINÉ
1453
Garonne *Rhône*
GASCONY
LANGUEDOC
Toulouse
Mediterranean
SPAIN *Sea*

English holdings
French holdings
Burgundian lands reconciled
with France after 1435
✕ Last battle

0   100 Km.
0   100 Mi.

subsidies were to be paid to the public Exchequer rather than into the king's private treasury. Some of these ordinances were later voided, but the tradition of parliamentary consent remained a key principle of English constitutional history.

The baronial influence grew because Edward II was a weak and naive king, easily influenced by court favorites. After a humiliating defeat at the hands of the Scots at the Battle of Bannockburn (1314), his position steadily deteriorated until he was deposed in 1327 by a coalition of barons led by his wife, Queen Isabella. After a short regency, their son Edward III (r. 1327–1377), assumed the throne. He was a cautious king, ever aware of the violence and rebelliousness of the baronage.

French kings seemed significantly more powerful in the early fourteenth century. A complex succession crisis, however, made clear the limits of French kingship. In 1328 the direct Capetian line, which had sired the kings of France since the election of Hugh Capet in 987, finally died out. The last Capetians did produce daughters, but by the fourteenth century many argued that according to custom the French crown should pass through the male line only. Thus the French nobility selected as king Philip of Valois (Philip VI; r. 1328–1350), a cousin of the last king through the male line (Charles IV; r. 1322–1328). He was chosen in preference to the daughters of the last Capetian kings and, more significantly, in preference to King Edward III of England, whose mother, Isabella, was the daughter of King Philip IV (r. 1285–1314).

Controversy over succession was just one of the disputes between the French and English. An even longer-standing issue was the status of lands within France that belonged to the English kings. In 1340, climaxing a century of tensions over English possessions in France, Edward III of England formally claimed the title "King of France," and the Hundred Years' War was on.

The war was marked by quick English raids and only occasional pitched battles. With a population of about 16 million, France was far richer and more populous than England. On at least one occasion the French managed to field an army of over 50,000; the English mustered only 32,000 at most. These armies were easily the largest ever assembled by a medieval European kingdom. In almost every engagement the English were outnumbered. Their strategy, therefore, was to avoid pitched battles except on the most advantageous terms. Edward III engaged in extremely destructive raids, hoping to lure the French into ill-considered attacks. The English stole what they could, destroyed what they could not steal, and captured enemy knights to hold for ransom.

The war can be divided into four stages. The first stage (1337–1360) was characterized by a rapid series of English assaults and victories. The few pitched battles, including Crécy (1346) and Poitiers (1356), show how Edward's strategy worked. In these cases the English gathered their forces in careful defensive positions and took advantage of an individualistic French chivalric ethos according to which, in the words of one knight, "who does the most is worth the most." The key to the English defensive position was the use of longbowmen and cannon. As French knights labored up a hill in a

England and France in the Hundred Years' War

The succession of maps depicts both why hit-and-run tactics worked for the English early in the war and why the English were ultimately unable to defeat the French and take control of all of France.

vain attempt to reach the English lines, they were met with withering fire. The longbow was developed in Wales, and the English perfected its use in numerous border wars with the Scots. Arrows from the longbow had more penetrating power than a bolt from a crossbow, and the longbow could be fired much more rapidly. Gunpowder and cannon probably arrived in the West from China in the late thirteenth century. Both the French and the English adopted firearms. Although there is a debate over how effective they were, when used in combination with the longbow, they effectively disrupted and scattered advancing troops.

In the second stage of the war (1360–1396), French forces responded more cautiously to the English tactics and slowly regained much of the territory they had lost. But during this stage, the disruptions and expenses of war placed a huge burden on both French and English society. In the confusion and unrest following the French disaster at Poitiers in 1356, Étienne Marcel, provost (director) of the merchants of Paris, mobilized a protest movement designed to reduce royal and aristocratic power. This revolution seemed too radical to conservative townspeople in the provinces, and Marcel's only allies were bands of rebellious countrymen roaming the region around Paris. These rebels, and eventually Marcel himself, were isolated and then defeated by aristocratic armies.

England was soon rocked by unrest as well. The Rising of 1381 is often called the Peasants' Revolt, despite the fact that townsfolk as well as peasants participated. Already England seethed with unrest as a result of the plague (see pages 347–349) and landlord claims for traditional dues. But the final straw was a poll tax levied to pay for the war. Commoners responded with violent protests. The heart of the uprising was a revolt by rural peasants and artisans in the southeast, primarily in Kent and Essex. Popular armies led by Wat Tyler (d. 1381) converged on London in June 1381. Tyler was murdered during a dramatic meeting with Richard II outside London, and a reaction against the rebels quickly ensued.

The rest of Richard's reign was anything but tranquil. Recognizing the dangers of noble influence, Richard tried to insulate himself from the peers of the realm by choosing advisers from the lesser nobility and the middle classes as well as from the peerage. The result was increasing tensions with the peers and charges that Richard's rule was tyrannical. Simmering discontent boiled over, and leaders of the peers captured Richard and forced him to abdicate in 1399. Parliament then elected as king Henry IV (r. 1399–1413), the first ruler from the House of Lancaster. Richard died in prison under mysterious circumstances in 1400.

A fateful shift occurred in the third stage of the war (1396–1422). King Charles VI (r. 1380–1422) of France suffered bouts of insanity throughout his long reign, which made effective French government almost impossible. The English king Henry V (r. 1413–1422) renewed his family's claim to the French throne. At Agincourt in 1415 the English (led by Henry himself) again enticed a larger French army into attacking an English position fortified by longbows and cannon. By the terms of the Treaty of Troyes (1420), Charles VI's son (the future Charles VII) was declared illegitimate and disinherited; Henry married Catherine, the daughter of Charles VI, and he was declared the legitimate heir to the French throne. A final English victory seemed assured, but both Charles VI and Henry V died in 1422, leaving Henry's infant son, Henry VI (r. 1422–1461), to inherit both thrones.

The kings' deaths ushered in the final stage of the Hundred Years' War (1422–1453), the French reconquest. In 1428 military and political power seemed firmly in the hands of the English and the great aristocrats. Yet in a stunning series of events the French were able to reverse the situation.

In 1429, with the aid of the mysterious Joan of Arc (d. 1431), the French king, Charles VII, was able to raise the English siege of Orléans and begin the reconquest of the north of France. Joan was the daughter of prosperous peasants from an area of Burgundy that had suffered under the English and their Burgundian allies. Like many late medieval mystics, she reported regular visions of divine revelation. Her "voices" told her to go to the king and assist him in driving out the English. Dressed as a man, she was Charles's most charismatic and feared military leader. With Joan's aid, the king was crowned in the cathedral at Reims, the traditional site of French coronations. Joan was captured during an audacious attack on Paris itself and eventually fell into English hands. Because of her "unnatural dress" and her claim to divine guidance, she was condemned and burned as a heretic in 1431. A heretic only to the English and their supporters, Joan almost instantly became a symbol of French resistance. Pope Calixtus III reversed the condemnation in 1456, and Joan was canonized in 1920. The heretic became Saint Joan, patron of France.

Despite Joan's capture, the French advance continued. By 1450 the English had lost all their major centers except Calais. In 1453 the French armies captured the fortress of Castillon-sur-Dordogne in what was to be the last battle of the war. There was no treaty, only a cessation of hostilities.

The war touched almost every aspect of life in western Europe: political, religious, economic, and social. It ranged beyond the borders of France as Scotland, Castile, Aragon, and German principalities were at various times drawn into the struggle. French and English support for rival popes prevented early settlement of the Great Schism in the papacy (see pages 334–336). Further, the war caused a general rise in the level of violence in society. As Henry V casually observed, "War without fire is as bland as sausages without mustard."[6] And because of the highly profitable lightning raids, this war was never bland. During periods of truce many soldiers simply ranged through France, pillaging small towns and ravaging the countryside. Others went in search of work as mercenaries, especially in Germany, Poland, and Italy. Truces in France did not necessarily mean peace in Europe.

Italy

Compared with France and England, fourteenth- and fifteenth-century Italy was a land of cities. In northern Europe a town of over 20,000 or 30,000 people was unusual; only Paris and London boasted more than 100,000 people in the fourteenth century. Yet at one time or another in the late Middle Ages, Milan, Venice, Florence, and Naples all had populations near or exceeding 100,000, and countless other Italian towns boasted populations of well over 30,000. Unlike northern European states with their kings or emperors, however, the Italian peninsula lacked a unifying force. The centers of power were in Italy's flourishing cities. Political life revolved around the twin issues of who should dominate city governments and how cities could learn to coexist peacefully.

By the late thirteenth century, political power in most Italian towns was divided among three major groups. First was the old urban nobility that could trace its wealth back to grants of property and rights from kings, emperors, and bishops in the tenth and eleventh centuries. Second was the merchant families who had grown wealthy in the twelfth and thirteenth centuries as Italians led the European economic expansion into the Mediterranean. Third, challenging these entrenched urban groups, were the modest artisans and merchants who had organized trade, neighborhood, or militia groups and referred to themselves as the *popolo*, or "people." Townspeople gathered together in factions based on wealth, family, profession, neighborhood, and even systems of clientage that reached back into the villages from which many of them had come. "War and hatred have so multiplied among the Italians," observed one Florentine, "that in every town there is a division and enmity between two parties of citizens."

Riven with factions, townspeople often would turn control of their government over to a *signor*, a "lord" or "tyrant," often a local noble with a private army. Once firmly in power, the tyrant often allowed the government to continue to function as it had, requiring only that he control all major political appointments. The process might appear democratic, but it represented a profound shift in power. The transformation was clear in Mantua, where, according to one chronicler, "[Pinamonte Bonacolsi (d. 1293)] usurped the lordship of his city and expelled his fellow-citizens and occupied their property. . . . He was feared like the devil."[7] In the case of Milan, the noble Viscontis used support from the emperor Henry VII (r. 1308–1313) to drive their opponents out of the city. Eventually granted Milan and its territories as a duchy, the Viscontis, and later their Sforza successors, made marriage alliances with the French crown and created a splendid court culture. In a series of wars between the 1370s and 1450s, the dukes of Milan expanded their political control throughout most of Lombardy, Liguria, and, temporarily, Tuscany. The Viscontis maintained control of the city and much of the region of Lombardy until the last scion of the family died in 1447.

The great republics of Venice and Florence escaped domination by signori, but only by undertaking significant constitutional change. In both republics political life had been disrupted by the arrival of immigrants and by the demands of recently enriched merchants and speculators for a voice in government. In 1297, reacting to increased competition for influence, the Venetian government enacted a reform that would come to be known as the "Closing of the Grand Council." The act enlarged to about eleven hundred the number of families eligible for public office, but its eventual effect was to freeze out subsequent arrivals from ever rising to elite status. The Venetian patriciate became a closed urban nobility. Political, factional, and economic tensions were hidden beneath a veneer of serenity as Venetians developed a myth of public-spirited patricians who governed in the interests of all the people, leaving others free to enrich themselves in trade and manufacture.

In Florence the arguments over citizenship and the right of civic participation disrupted public life. Violent wealthy families, immigrants, and artisans of modest background were cut off from civic participation. A series of reforms culminating in the Ordinances of Justice of 1293 to 1295 restricted political participation in Florence to members in good standing of certain merchant and artisan guilds. Members of violence-prone families were defined as *Magnate* (literally, "the powerful") and disqualified from holding public office. In spite of the reforms, political power remained concentrated in the hands of the great families, whose wealth was based primarily on banking and mercantile investments. These families used their political influence and economic power to dominate Florentine life.

The Journey of the Magi

The story of the journey of the Magi to Bethlehem to find the baby Jesus seemed a perfect image of the power and wisdom of rulers. This painting (a detail) of the Magi was commissioned for the private chapel of Cosimo de' Medici, the de facto ruler of Florence. (Palazzo Medici Riccardi, Florence/Scala/Art Resource, NY)

[handwritten margin notes: Political power limited still to families (wealthy + named), merchant + artisan guilds — power still in hands of few despite reform + huge controversy]

[handwritten note below image: Power in grasp of influential patricians]

There were short-lived attempts to reform the system and extend the rights of political participation to include the more modest artisans and laborers. The most dramatic was in 1378 when the Ciompi, unskilled workers in Florence's woolen industry, led a popular revolution hoping to expand participation in government and limit the authority of the guild masters over semiskilled artisans and day laborers. They created new guilds to represent the laborers who had no voice in government. Barely six weeks after the Ciompi insurrection, however, wealthy conservatives began a reaction suppressing, exiling, or executing the leaders of the movement and eventually suppressing the new guilds. Political and economic power was now even more firmly in the grip of influential patricians.

Following a crisis in 1434 brought on by war and high taxes, virtual control of Florentine politics fell into the hands of Cosimo de' Medici, the wealthiest banker in the city. From 1434 to 1494, Cosimo; his son, Piero; his grandson, Lorenzo; and Lorenzo's son dominated the government in Florence. Although the Medicis were always careful to pay homage to Florentine republican traditions, their control was virtually as complete as that of the lords of towns such as Ferrara and Milan.

Indeed, by the middle of the fifteenth century little differentiated the republics—Florence and Venice—from cities such as Milan and Mantua, where lords held sway. Although Florentines maintained that they intervened to protect Florentine and Tuscan "liberty" when the Viscontis of Milan threatened Tuscany and central Italy, their interests went beyond simple defense. Relations among the great cities of Milan, Venice, Florence, Rome, and Naples were stabilized by the Peace of Lodi and the creation of the Italian League in 1454. In response to endemic warfare in Italy and the looming threat of the Ottoman Turks in the eastern Mediterranean (see page 358), the five powers agreed to the creation of spheres of influence that would prevent any one of them from expanding at the expense of the others.

The limits of these territorial states became clear when King Charles VIII of France invaded Italy in 1494 to assert his hereditary claim to the kingdom of Naples. The French invasion touched off a devastating series of wars called the Habsburg-Valois Wars (1496–1559). French claims were challenged by the Habsburg emperors and also by the Spanish, who themselves made claims on southern Italy and much of Lombardy. The cost of prolonged warfare kept almost all governments in a state of crisis. Unrest brought on by the invasion even allowed Pope Alexander VI (r. 1492–1503) to attempt to create a state for his son, Cesare Borgia (1475–1507), in central Italy.

In Florence the wars destroyed the old Medici-dominated regime and brought in a new republican government. Anti-Medici efforts were initially led by the popular Dominican preacher Girolamo Savonarola (1452–1498). In the constitutional debates after 1494, Savonarola argued that true political reform required a sweeping purge of the evils of society. Gangs of youth flocked to his cause, attacking prostitutes and homosexuals. Many of his followers held "bonfires of vanities," burning wigs, silks, and other luxuries. In 1498, when his followers had lost influence in the government, Savonarola was arrested, tortured, and executed.

In spite of republican reforms, new fortresses, and a citizen militia, the Florentine government was unable to defend itself from papal and imperial armies. In 1512 the Habsburg emperor restored Medici control of Florence. The Medicis later became dukes and then grand dukes of Tuscany. The grand duchy of Tuscany remained an independent, integrated, and well-governed state until the French Revolution of 1789. Venice also managed to maintain its republican form of government and its territorial state until the French Revolution, but like the grand dukes of Tuscany, the governors of Venice were no longer able to act independently of the larger European powers.

The Habsburg-Valois Wars ended with the Treaty of Cateau-Cambrésis in 1559, which left the Spanish kings in control of Milan, Naples, Sardinia, and Sicily. Thus the Spanish dominated Italy, but without the centralizing control typical of England and France. Venice, Tuscany, the Papal States and even lesser republics and principalities retained significant influence, as Italy remained a land of regional governments.

ECONOMY AND SOCIETY

After nearly three centuries of dramatic growth, Europe in 1300 was seriously overpopulated, with estimates ranging from about 80 million to as high as 100 million. In

[handwritten: 1300's]

[handwritten: Europe overpopulated — had famine/war → affects trade]

some parts of Europe, population would not be this dense again until the late eighteenth century. Opportunities dwindled because of overpopulation, famine, war, and
epidemic, which also brought changes in trade and commerce. As the population began *[handwritten: affected]*
to decline, this trend, along with deflation and transformed patterns of consumption, *[handwritten: agriculture]*
affected agriculture, which was still the foundation of the European economy. Recov-
ery from all these crises altered the structure and dynamics of families, the organization of work, and the culture in many parts of Europe.

[handwritten: affected structure of families, org. of work, culture]

**Plague and Demo-
graphic Crisis**   People in many parts of Europe were living on the edge of disaster in 1300. Given the low level of agricultural technology
and the limited amount of land available for cultivation, it became increasingly difficult for the towns and countryside to feed and support the
growing population. The nature of the problem varied from place to place. *[handwritten: Not enough food]*

Growing numbers of people competed for land to farm and for jobs. Farm sizes
declined throughout Europe as parents tended to divide their land among their children. Rents for farmland increased as landlords found that they could play one land-
hungry farmer against another. Competition for jobs kept wages low, and when taxes
were added to high rents and low wages, many peasants and artisans found it difficult
to marry and raise families. Thus, because of reduced opportunities brought on by
overpopulation, poor townspeople and peasants tended to marry late and have small
families. *[handwritten: ↑ married late + had small families]*

More dramatic than this crisis of births were the deadly famines that occurred in
years of bad harvests. The great famine of 1315 to 1322 marks a turning point in the
economic history of Europe. Wet and cold weather repeatedly ruined crops in much of
northern Europe. Food stocks were quickly exhausted, and mass starvation followed.
People died so quickly, English chroniclers reported, that survivors could not keep up
with the burials. At Ypres, in Flanders, 2,800 people (about 10 percent of the population) died in just six months. And shortages continued. Seven other severe famines
were reported in the south of France or Italy during the fourteenth century.

If Europe's problem had merely been one of famine brought on by overpopulation,
rapid recovery should have been possible. But the difficulties of overpopulation were
exacerbated by war and plague. As noted previously, the devastation of cities and the
countryside was a common tactic in the Hundred Years' War. It was also typical of the
local wars in parts of Spain, Germany, and especially Italy. The destruction of trees and
vineyards and the theft of livestock made it difficult for rural populations to survive.
Then, in 1348, the Black Death, or "the great Mortality" as contemporaries called it,
struck Europe. *[handwritten: overpopulation + war + plague = disaster!]*

Today there is no consensus as to what caused the Black Death. In the early twentieth century, after the bacillus that causes bubonic plague was identified by French and
Japanese physicians in Hong Kong, it was assumed that bubonic plague was the cause.
Subsequently, there have been controversial claims that DNA fragments of bubonic
plague have been found in mass graves. Yet bubonic plague usually travels slowly and
infects a relatively small portion of a given population. By contrast, the Black Death
seemed to race across Europe, wiping out entire families and infecting whole cities. Because of this evidence, some historical epidemiologists have speculated that the cause
may actually have been anthrax or a "hemorrhagic plague" similar to the Ebola virus.

[handwritten margin: # famine of 1315-1322 = turning point in economic history.]

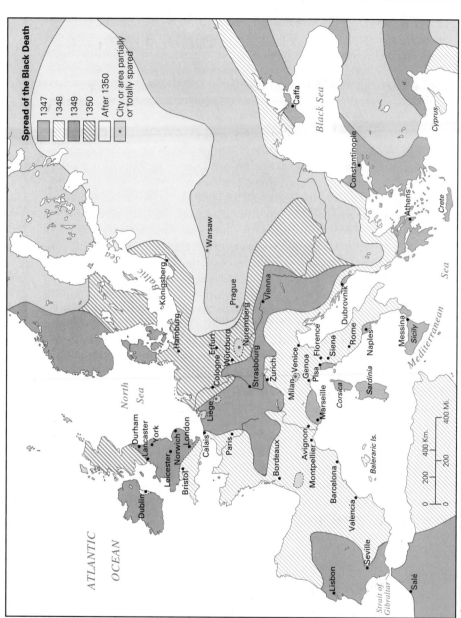

The Progress of the Black Death The Black Death did not advance evenly across Europe; rather, as is clear from the dates at which it struck various regions, it followed the main lines of trade and communication.

Although the historical identification of the Black Death remains controversial, contemporaries had little doubt about where the disease came from. Genoese traders, they believed, contracted the plague in Caffa, on the Black Sea coast. Infected sailors carried the disease south into Egypt and west into Sicily, then on to Genoa and Venice. From there it followed established trade routes first into central Italy; later to the south of France, the Low Countries, and England; and finally, through the North and Baltic Seas, into Germany and the Slavic lands to the east.

Mortality rates varied, but generally 60 percent or more of those infected died. In the initial infestation of 1348 to 1351, 25 to 35 percent of Europe's population may have died. In some of Europe's larger cities the death rate may have been as high as 60 percent. In Florence, for example, the population probably declined from about 90,000 to about 50,000 or even less. And the nearby town of Siena likely fared even worse, with the town and its suburbs losing 55 percent of their people. The shock and disruption were immense. Governments in some towns simply ceased to function at the height of the epidemic. Chroniclers reported that no one could be found to care for the sick or bury the dead. Although abandonment of the sick was probably more a fear than a reality, the epidemic nonetheless significantly disrupted daily life.

Just as areas were rebounding from the initial outbreak of the plague, it returned between 1360 and 1363, and then for three centuries thereafter almost no generation could avoid it. It has been calculated that in central Italy, where the best records are available, the plague returned on average every eleven years between 1350 and 1400. Less is known about the plague in Muslim lands and in the eastern Mediterranean, but the situation seems to have been similar to the European experience. Because the plague tended to carry off the young, the almost generational return of the disease accounts for the depressed population levels found in many parts of Europe until the late fifteenth century and in western Asia until the late seventeenth or eighteenth century.

Lacking an understanding of either contagion or infection, fourteenth-century doctors depended on traditional theories inherited from the Greeks, especially the work of Galen, to treat the plague. In Galenic medicine good health depended on the proper balance of bodily and environmental forces; it could be upset by corrupt air, the movement of planets, and even violent shifts in emotions. Yet in the fifteenth and sixteenth centuries, as the rhythms of the infestations became clearer, towns and, later, territorial governments perceived the contagious nature of the disease. Officials instituted increasingly effective quarantines and embargoes to restrict the movement of goods and people from areas where the plague was raging. Some argue that this innovative effort at public health regulation probably explains the disappearance of the plague from western Europe by the early eighteenth century.

Alongside medical theory, however, another class of explanations developed. Taking a lead from miracle stories in which Jesus linked illness and sin, many Christians considered the Black Death a signal of the Last Judgment, or at least a sign of the severe judgment of God on a sinful world. Given that view, a traditional, and logical, religious response was to urge various moral reforms and penitential acts, such as charitable gifts, special prayers, and holy processions. Many Muslim theologians also concluded that "the plague is part of Allah's punishment." Women were often thought to be a source of moral pollution and hence one of the causes of God's wrath. In Muslim Egypt, women were ordered off the streets; in Christian Europe prostitutes were driven out of towns.

A movement of penitents called "flagellants" arose in Hungary and spread quickly into Germany and across France and the Low Countries. In an imitation of Christ's life and sufferings, they sought to atone in their own bodies for the sins of the world. Following an ancient Christian tradition, they ritually beat (flagellated) themselves between the shoulders with metal-tipped whips. Through their processions and sufferings, these pilgrims hoped to bring about a moral and religious transformation of society. The arrival of flagellants was often an occasion for an end of feuds and political violence within a community. But their arrival just as often was an occasion for political and even religious unrest. Authorities recognized the flagellants and the leaders of the religious riots as dangerous and drove them from towns.

In a quest for a purer, truly Christian society, the flagellants brought suspicion on all those who were not Christian or who were otherwise suspect. Some parts of Europe witnessed murderous attacks on outsiders, especially lepers and Jews, who were suspected of spreading the contagion in an attempt to bring down Latin Christendom. These attacks probably have more to do with tensions and fears already existing in parts of Europe than with the provocations of the flagellants. Like many other anti-Semitic myths, the rumors of wells poisoned by Jews seemed to arise in the south of France and spread in their most virulent forms to German towns along the Rhine. In Strasbourg attacks on Jews preceded the arrival of the plague. Except in a few districts, officials opposed attacks on Jews, lepers, and heretics. Doctors and churchmen often observed that Jews were unlikely culprits, since the plague claimed Jewish as well as Christian victims.

It was a commonplace among contemporary chroniclers that "so many did die that everyone thought it was the end of the world." Yet it was the very young, the elderly, and the poor—those least likely to pay taxes, own shops, or produce children—who were the most common victims. And even in towns such as Florence, where mortality rates were extraordinarily high, recovery from the initial epidemic was rapid. Government offices were closed at most for only a few weeks; markets reopened as soon as the death rate began to decline; and within two years tax receipts were back at preplague levels. Below the surface, however, famine, warfare, plague, and population decline fueled the economic and social transformations of the late Middle Ages.

Trade and Agriculture

In the aftermath of plague, the economy of Europe changed in a number of profound ways. Disruptions brought on by population decline were accompanied by changes in the basic structure of economic life. In particular, Italy's domination of the European economy was challenged by the growth of trade and manufacturing in many other parts of Europe. Further, Italian bankers came to face competition from equally astute local bankers.

Discussions of the economy must begin with Italy because it was the key point of contact between Europe and the international economy. In 1300 Italian merchants sold woolens produced in Flanders and Italy to Arab traders in North Africa, who sold them along the African coast and as far south as the Niger Delta. The Italians used the gold that they collected in payment to buy spices and raw materials in Byzantium, Egypt, and even China. They resold these highly prized goods in the cities and at regional fairs of northern Europe. Italian traders also sold spices, silks, and other luxuries throughout Europe, from England to Poland.

Because of their expertise in moving bullion and goods and their ready sources of capital, Italian merchants, such as the Ricciardis of Lucca who flourished in England, were ideal bankers and financial advisers to the popes and European rulers, who appreciated sources of ready capital. In time of war rulers tended to trade the rights to various revenues to Italian bankers, who had cash at hand. Merchants from Cremona, Genoa, Florence, and Siena forged commercial agreements with the kings of France, Aragon, and Castile, and with the papacy.

→ Medici Bank of Florence

The most powerful bank in fifteenth-century Europe was the Medici bank of Florence. Founded in 1397 by Giovanni de' Medici (1360–1429), the bank grew quickly _even to Pope_ because of its role as papal banker. Medici agents transferred papal revenues from all parts of Europe to Rome and managed papal alum mines, which provided an essential mineral to the growing cloth industry. Cosimo de' Medici (1389–1464), Giovanni's son and successor, transformed the enterprise into a series of bilateral partnerships with easily controlled junior partners in other parts of Europe. In this way he avoided the problem of supervision and control that plagued other banks, whose partners were equal and free to speculate and invest as they wished. _Spread bank + partners._

The dramatic career of the Frenchman Jacques Coeur (1395?–1456) demonstrates that by the mid-fifteenth century, Italian merchants were not the only Europeans who understood international trade. After making a fortune trading in southern France, Coeur managed the French royal mint and became the financial adviser of King Charles VII (r. 1422–1461). He put the French monarchy back on a solid financial footing after the Hundred Years' War, becoming in the process the wealthiest individual in France. Not surprisingly, his wealth and influence earned him jealous enemies, who tried to bring him down with outrageous claims: he was accused of murdering the king's mistress, trading with Muslims, and stealing royal funds. In 1451 his property was confiscated, and he was jailed for a short time. He later led a papal expedition against the Turks in the Aegean, where he died.

By 1500 Italians faced increased competition from local merchants throughout Europe. From as early as the late thirteenth century, trade along the North and Baltic Seas in northern Europe was dominated by the Hanseatic League, an association of over a hundred trading cities centered on the German city of Lübeck. By the late fourteenth and early fifteenth centuries, the Hansa towns controlled grain shipments from eastern Europe to England and Scandinavia. The league's domination waned in the second half of the fifteenth century, however, as Dutch, English, and even southern German merchants gained shares of the wool, grain, and fur trades. Towns in the eastern Baltic found that their interests no longer coincided with those of the towns in western Germany that made up the Hanseatic League. Wroclaw (in modern Poland) signaled the nature of the change when it resigned from the league in 1474 to expand trade connections with the southern German towns.

In contrast to the Hanseatic League of towns, merchants in southern Germany adopted Italian techniques of trade, manufacture, and finance to expand their influence throughout central Europe. German merchants regularly bought spices in the markets of Venice and distributed them in central and eastern Europe. By the fifteenth century the townspeople of southern Germany also produced linen and cotton cloth, which found ready markets in central and eastern Europe.

The Fugger family of Augsburg in southern Germany, the most prosperous of the German commercial families, exemplifies the variety of activities undertaken by south

German merchants. Hans Fugger (1348–1409) moved to Augsburg from a nearby village in the 1360s and quickly established himself as a weaver and wool merchant. By the 1470s Hans's grandson, Jacob Fugger (1459–1525), was a dominant figure in the spice trade and also participated in a number of unusually large loans to a succession of German princes. The Fuggers became leaders in the Tyrolean silver-mining industry, which expanded dramatically in the late fifteenth century. And in the early sixteenth century they handled all transfers of money from Germany to the papacy. Jacob Fugger's wealth increased fourfold between 1470 and 1500. The Fuggers were indispensable allies of the German emperors. Jacob himself ensured the election of Charles V as Holy Roman emperor in 1519, making a series of loans that allowed Charles to buy the influence that he needed to win election.

As wealthy as the great merchants were, in most parts of Europe prosperity was still tied to agriculture and the production of food grains. In northern and western Europe foodstuffs were produced on the manorial estates of great churchmen and nobles. These estates were worked by a combination of farmers paying rents, serfs who owed a variety of labor services, and day laborers who were hired during planting and harvesting. In the face of a decimated population, landlords and employers found themselves competing for the reduced number of laborers who had survived the plague. In 1351 the English crown issued the Statute of Laborers, which pegged wages and the prices of commodities at preplague levels. According to the statute, regulation was necessary because laborers "withdrew themselves from serving great men and others unless they have living [in food] and wages double or treble of what they were [before the plague]." This statute and similar ones passed in other parts of Europe were dead letters. So long as population levels remained low, landowners were unable to keep wages low and rents high.

Cloth manufacture, not agriculture, was the part of the European economy that changed most dramatically in the late Middle Ages. First in Flanders, then later in England, Germany, and the rest of Europe, production shifted from urban workshops to the countryside. Industries in rural areas tended to be free of controls on quality or techniques. Rural production, whether in Flanders, England, or Lombardy, became the most dynamic part of the industry.

Rural cloth production, especially in southwestern Germany and parts of England, was organized through the putting-out system. Merchants who owned the raw wool contracted with various artisans in the city, suburbs, or countryside—wherever the work could be done most cheaply—to process the wool into cloth. Rural manufacture was least expensive because it could be done as occasional or part-time labor by farmers, or by their wives or children, during slack times of the day or season. Because production was likely to be finished in the countryside (beyond guild supervision), the merchant was free to move the cloth to wherever it could most easily and profitably be sold; guild masters had no control over price or quality.

Two other developments also changed the woolen trade of the fifteenth century: the rise of Spain as an exporter of unprocessed wool and the emergence of England, long recognized as a source of prime wool, as a significant producer of finished cloth. Spain was an ideal region for the pasturing of livestock. By the fifteenth century highly prized Spanish wool from merino sheep was regularly exported to Italy, Flanders, and England. By 1500 over three million sheep grazed in Castile alone, and revenues from duties on wool formed the backbone of royal finance.

In England, in contrast, economic transformation was tied to cloth production. During the fifteenth century England reduced its export of its high-quality raw wool and began instead to export its own finished cloth. In 1350 the English exported just over 5,000 bolts of cloth. By the 1470s exports had risen to 63,000 bolts, and they doubled again by the 1520s. The growth of cloth exports contributed enormously to the expansion of London. During the fourteenth and fifteenth centuries English commerce became increasingly controlled by London merchant-adventurers. Soon after 1500 over 80 percent of the cloth for export passed through the hands of the Londoners. This development, coupled with the rise of London as a center of administration and consumption, laid the foundation for the economic and demographic growth that would make London the largest and most prosperous city in western Europe by the eighteenth century.

All these patterns of economic change in the fifteenth century challenged customs and institutions by admitting new entrepreneurs into the marketplace. But Europe was still a conservative society in which social and political influence was more prized than economic wealth. Patricians in many European towns acted to dampen competition and preserve traditional values. Great banking families such as the Medicis of Florence tended to avoid competition and concentrations of capital. They did not try to drive their competitors out of business because the leaders of rival banks were their political and social peers. In northern Europe, governments in towns such as Leiden restricted the concentration of resources in the hands of the town's leading cloth merchants. Their aim was to ensure full employment for the town's laborers, political power for the guild masters, and social stability in the town.

Full employment was not just for men. Although men had controlled the guilds and most crafts in the thirteenth and early fourteenth centuries, women's guilds existed in several European cities, including Paris and Cologne. In Italy some women could be found among the more prosperous crafts. Women often practiced their trades in the context of the family. In Cologne, for instance, women produced the linen yarn and silk cloths that their husbands sold throughout Europe. Speaking of the silkmakers of Cologne, a report noted that "the women are much more knowledgeable about the trade than are the men." Unlike southern Europe, where women had no public roles, some northern towns apparently allowed women's guilds to protect their members' activities as artisans and even peddlers. Because they often worked before marriage, townswomen in northern Europe tended to marry at a later age than did women in Italy. Many women earned their own marriage dowries. Since they had their own sources of income and often managed the shop of a deceased husband, women could be surprisingly independent. They were consequently under less pressure to remarry at the death of a spouse. Although their economic circumstances varied considerably, up to a quarter of the households in northern towns such as Bern and Zurich were headed by women. Many of them were widows, but many others, perhaps a third, were women who had never married.

The fifteenth century brought new restrictions to women's lives. In England brewing ale had been a highly profitable part-time activity that women often combined with the running of a household. Ale was usually produced in small batches for household use, and whatever went unconsumed would be sold. The introduction of beer changed matters. Because hops were added as a preservative during brewing, beer was easier to produce, store, and transport in large batches. Beer brewing became a lucrative full-time

Women at Work *Although guild records tend to ignore the contributions of women, many women worked in their husbands' shops. In this miniature a woman is selling jewelry. Widows often managed the shops they inherited.* (Bibliothèque nationale de France)

women were being artisans, etc. single, earning $
or later b/came dishonorable.

trade, reducing the demand for the alewife's product and providing work for men as brewers. At the same time the rights of women to work in urban crafts and industries were reduced. Wealthy fathers became less inclined to allow wives and daughters to work outside the home. Guilds banned the use of female laborers in many trades and severely limited the rights of widows to supervise their spouses' shops. For reasons that are not entirely clear, journeymen—employees of guild masters who themselves hoped to become masters—objected to working alongside women. These complaints may have come from workers who realized that their status as employees was permanent instead of a temporary stage before promotion to master. By the early sixteenth century journeymen in Germany considered it "dishonorable" for a woman, even the master's wife or daughter, to work in a shop.

Despite the narrowing of economic opportunities for women, the overall economic prospects of peasants and laborers improved. Lower rents and increased wages in the wake of the plague meant a higher standard of living for small farmers and laborers. Before the plague struck in 1348, most poor Europeans had subsisted on bread or grain-based gruel, consuming meat, fish, and cheese only a few times a week. A well-off peasant in England had lived on a daily ration of about two pounds of bread and a cup or two of oatmeal porridge washed down with three or four pints of ale. Poorer peasants generally drank water except on very special occasions. After the plague laborers were more prosperous. Adults in parts of Germany may have consumed nearly a liter of wine, a third of a pound of meat, and a pound or more of bread each day. Elsewhere people could substitute an equivalent portion of beer, ale, or cider for the wine. Hard times for landlords were good times for peasants and day laborers.

Hard times for landlord = good for peasants + laborers

Landlords in England responded to the shortage of labor by converting their lands to grazing in order to produce wool for the growing textile market. In parts of Italy landlords invested in canals, irrigation, and new crops in order to increase profits. In eastern Germany and Poland landlords were able to take advantage of political and social unrest to force tenants into semi-free servile status. This so-called second serfdom created an impoverished work force whose primary economic activity was in the lord's fields, establishing commercial grain farming. Increasingly in the second half of the century grains cultivated in Poland and Prussia found their way to markets in England and the Low Countries. Europe east of the Elbe River became a major producer of grain, but at a heavy social cost.

lost 1/3 of urban pop. to plague

The loss of perhaps a third of the urban population to the plague had serious consequences in the towns of Europe. Because of lower birthrates and higher death rates, late medieval towns needed a constant influx of immigrants to expand or even to maintain their populations. These immigrants did not find life in the cities easy, however. Citizenship in most towns was restricted to masters in the most important guilds, and local governments were in their hands, if not under their thumbs. In many towns citizens constructed a system of taxation that worked to their own economic advantage and fell heavily on artisans and peasants living in territories controlled by the towns. Unskilled laborers and members of craft guilds depended for their economic well-being on personal relationships with powerful citizens who controlled the government and the markets. Peace and order in towns and in the countryside required a delicate balance of the interests of the well-to-do and the more humble. When that balance was shattered by war, plague, and economic depression, the result was often a popular revolt, such as the Ciompi insurrection of 1378 in Florence and the Rising of 1381 in England.

constant influx of immigrants

Citizenship restricted to masters

Popular Revolt = result of war plague + economic depression — breaking peace order + balance of govt. + personal relationships

taxation fell mostly on artisans + peasants.

THE CONSOLIDATION OF THE LATE MEDIEVAL GOVERNMENTS, 1450–1500

By 1500 it seemed that the French royal lawyer's claim that all within the kingdom belonged to the king was finally accepted. With the exception of Italy and Germany, strong central governments recovered from the crises of war and civil unrest that wracked the fourteenth and fifteenth centuries. The Hundred Years' War and the resulting disorganization in France and England seemed to strike at the heart of the monarchies. But through the foundation of standing armies and the careful consolidation of power in the royal court, both countries seemed stronger and more able to defend themselves in the second half of the century. And as the Italians learned in the wars following the French invasion of 1494, small regional powers were no match for the mighty monarchies.

France, England, and Scandinavia

In France recovery from a century of war was based on a consolidation of the monarchy's power. A key to French military successes had been the creation of a paid professional army, which replaced the feudal host and mercenary companies of the fourteenth century. Charles VII created Europe's first standing army, a cavalry of about eight thousand nobles under the direct control of royal commanders. Charles also expanded his judicial claims. He and his son, Louis XI (r. 1461–1483), created new provincial *parlements,* or law courts, at Toulouse, Grenoble, Bordeaux, and Dijon. They also required that local laws and customs be registered and approved by the parlements.

A second key to maintaining royal influence was the rise of the French court as a political and financial center. Through careful appointments and judicious offers of annuities and honors, Charles VII and Louis XI drew the nobility to the royal court and made the nobles dependent on it. "The court," complained a frustrated noble, "is an assembly of people who, under the pretense of acting for the good of all, come together to diddle each other; for there's scarcely anyone who isn't engaged in buying and selling and exchanging . . . and sometimes for their money we sell them our . . . humanity."[8] One of Louis XI's advisers noted that Charles VII never had revenues greater than 18,000 francs in a single year but that Louis collected 4.7 million. By 1500 France had fully recovered from the crisis of war and was once again a strong and influential state.

The fate of the English monarchy was quite different. Henry VI (r. 1422–1461) turned out to be weak-willed, immature, and prone to bouts of insanity—inherited, perhaps, from his French grandfather, Charles VI (see page 342). The infirmity of Henry VI and the loss of virtually all French territories in 1453 led to factional battles known as the Wars of the Roses—the red rose symbolized Henry's House of Lancaster, the white the rival House of York. Edward of York eventually deposed Henry and claimed the Crown for himself as Edward IV (r. 1461–1483). He faced little opposition because few alternatives existed. English public life was again thrown into confusion, however, at Edward's death. The late king's brother, Richard, duke of Gloucester, claimed the protectorship over the 13-year-old king, Edward V (r. April–June 1483), and his younger brother. Richard seized the boys, who were placed in the Tower of London and never seen again. He proclaimed himself king and was crowned Richard III (r. 1483–1485). He withstood early challenges to his authority but in 1485 was killed in the Battle of Bosworth Field, near Coventry, by Henry Tudor, a leader of the Lancastrian faction. Henry married Elizabeth, the surviving child of Edward IV. Symbolically at least, the struggle between the rival claimants to the Crown appeared over.

Like his predecessor, Edward IV, Henry VII (r. 1485–1509) recognized the importance of avoiding war and taxation. Like the French kings, he created a patronage network of local officials to secure allies for his dynasty. Royal power, however, was not based on a transformation of the institutions of government. Following Edward's example, Henry controlled local affairs through the traditional system of royal patronage. He also imitated Edward in emphasizing the dignity of the royal office. Though careful with his funds, he was willing to buy jewels and clothing if they added to the brilliance of his court. As one courtier summed up his reign, "His hospitality was splendidly generous. . . . He knew well how to maintain his majesty and all which pertains to kingship." Henry solidified ties with Scotland and Spain by marrying his daughter, Margaret Tudor, to James IV of Scotland and his sons, Arthur and (after Arthur's death) Henry, to Catherine of Aragon, daughter of the Spanish rulers Ferdinand and Isabella.

The English monarchy of the late fifteenth century departed little from previous governments. The success of Henry VII was based on several factors: the absence of powerful opponents; lower taxation thanks to twenty-five years of peace; and the desire, shared by ruler and ruled alike, for an orderly realm built on the assured succession of a single dynasty.

In the fourteenth and fifteenth centuries the Scandinavian kingdoms of Denmark, Sweden, and Norway lay open to economic and political influences from Germany. German merchants traded throughout the area and completely controlled access to the important port of Bergen in Norway. German nobles sought to influence northern political life, especially in Denmark. The Scandinavian aristocracy, however, especially in Denmark, remained wary of German interests. Alert to outside pressures, Scandinavian elites tended to marry among themselves and forge alliances against the Germans.

Public authority varied greatly across Scandinavia. In Norway, Denmark, and Sweden the power of the king was always mediated by the influence of the council, made up of the country's leading landowners. Power was based on ownership or control of lands and rents. All the Scandinavian countries were home to a significant class of free peasants, and they were traditionally represented in the Riksdag in Sweden and the Storting in Norway, popular assemblies that had the right to elect kings, authorize taxes, and make laws. Scandinavians spoke similar Germanic languages and were linked by close social and economic ties. Thus it is not surprising that the crowns of the three kingdoms were joined during periods of crisis. In 1397 the dowager queen Margaret of Denmark was able to unite the Scandinavian crowns by the Union of Kalmar, which would nominally endure until 1523.

Eastern Europe and Russia

Two phenomena had an especially profound effect on the governments of eastern Europe. One was the emergence of a newly important ruling dynasty. The other was the decline of Mongol, or Tatar, influence in the region. Since the thirteenth century much of eastern Europe had been forced to acknowledge Tatar dominion and pay annual tribute. Now the Tatar subjugation was challenged and finally ended.

As in much of Europe, political power was segmented and based on personal relationships between family members, communities, clients, and friends. Life in the East was further complicated by the mix of languages, cultures, and religions. Native Catholic and Orthodox populations were further diversified in the fourteenth century by the arrival of Muslims in the Balkans and Ashkenazi Jews throughout most of the region. Escaping growing persecution, the Ashkenazim migrated to Poland, Lithuania, and Ruthenian lands (parts of modern Russia), where they lived under their own leaders and followed their own laws.

This mix of cultures and religions played a role in the growth of new states. Under the pretext of converting their pagan neighbors to Christianity, the mostly German Teutonic Knights sought to expand eastward against the kingdom of Poland and the Lithuanian state. They were thwarted, however, by a profound dynastic shift. In 1386 Grand Duke Jagiello (r. 1377–1434) of Lithuania converted to Catholic Christianity and married Hedwig, the daughter and heir of King Louis of Poland (r. 1370–1382). The resulting dynastic union created a state with a population of perhaps six million that reached from the Baltic nearly to the Black Sea. Polish-Lithuanian power slowed and finally halted the German advance to the east. Most serious for the Teutonic

Knights was their defeat in 1410 at Tannenberg, in Prussia, by a Polish-Lithuanian army led by Jagiello's cousin, Prince Vytautus of Lithuania. The Polish-Lithuanian union was only dynastic. The descendants of Jagiello, called Jagiellonians, had no hereditary right to rule Poland, and the Lithuanians opposed any Polish administrative influence in their lands. Yet because of Jagiellonian power, the Poles continued to select them as kings. At various times Jagiellonians also sat on the thrones of Bohemia and Hungary.

Poland and Lithuania remained more closely tied to western Europe than to the Russian East. They tended to be Catholic rather than Orthodox Christians. They wrote in a Roman rather than a Cyrillic script. And their political institutions resembled those of western Europe. Polish nobles managed to win a number of important concessions, the most significant being freedom from arbitrary arrest and confinement. This civil right was secured in Poland well before the more famous English right of habeas corpus. It was during this period, and under the influence of the Polish kings, that Cracow emerged as the economic and cultural center of Poland. Cracow University was founded in 1364 in response to the foundation of Prague University by the emperor Charles IV in 1348. After the dynastic union of Poland and Lithuania, Polish language and culture increasingly influenced the Lithuanian nobility. This union laid the foundation for the great Polish-Lithuanian commonwealth of the early modern period.

Lithuania had never been conquered by the Tatars, and its expansion contributed to the decline of Tatar power. The rise of Moscow, however, owed much to the continuing Tatar domination. Since the Mongol invasions in the thirteenth century, various towns and principalities of Kievan Rus had been part of a Tatar sphere of influence. This primarily meant homage and payment of an annual tribute.

A key to the emergence of Moscow occurred when Ivan I (r. 1328–1341), Prince of Moscow, was named Grand Prince and collector of tribute from the other Russian princes. Not for nothing was he called "the Moneybag." It was during this same period that the head of the Russian Orthodox Church was persuaded to make his home in Moscow. And in 1367 the princes began to rebuild the Kremlin walls in stone.

The decisive change for Moscow, however, was the reign of Ivan III (r. 1462–1505). By 1478 Ivan III, called "Ivan the Great," had seized the famed trading center of Novgorod. Two years later he was powerful enough to renounce Mongol overlordship and refuse further payments of tribute. After his marriage to an émigré Byzantine princess living in Rome, Ivan began to call himself "Tsar" (Russian for "Caesar"), implying that in the wake of the Muslim conquest of Constantinople, Moscow had become the new Rome.

The Ottoman Empire

The eastern Mediterranean region was a politically tumultuous area in the fourteenth century, when the Ottoman Turks were first invited into the Balkans by the hard-pressed Byzantine emperor. Early in the fifteenth century the Turks were only one, and perhaps not even the greatest, of the Balkan threats to the Byzantine Empire and the other Balkan states. Hungarians, Venetians, and Germans also competed for influence in this volatile area. Individuals and groups added to the turmoil by expediently switching their political allegiances and even their religions. In the 1420s, for example, as the Turks and the Hungarians fought for influence in Serbia, the Serbian king moved easily from alliance with one to alliance with the other. Elites often retained their political and economic influence by changing religion. The Christian aristocracy of late-fifteenth-century Bosnia, for example, was welcomed into Islam and instantly created a cohesive elite fighting force for the Turks. Conversely, as Turkish power in Albania grew, one noble, George Castriota (d. 1467), known by his Turkish name Skanderbeg, reconverted to Christianity and became a leading figure in the resistance to the Turks. Only after his death were the Turks able to integrate Albania into their empire.

An Ottoman victory over a Christian crusading army at Varna, on the Black Sea coast, in 1444 changed the dynamics and virtually sealed the fate of Constantinople. It was only a matter of time before the Turks took the city. When Mehmed II (r. 1451–1481) finally turned his attention to Constantinople in 1453, the siege of the city lasted only fifty-three days. Turkish artillery breached the walls before a Venetian navy or a Hungarian army could come to the city's defense. The destruction of the last vestiges of the Roman imperial tradition that reached back to the emperor Augustus sent shock waves through Christian Europe and brought forth calls for new crusades to liberate the East from the evils of Islam. It also stirred anti-Christian feelings among the Turks. The rise of the Ottoman Turks transformed eastern Europe and led to a profound clash between Christian and Muslim civilizations.

After the fall of Constantinople the Turks worked to consolidate their new territories. Through alliance and conquest Ottoman hegemony extended through Syria and Palestine and by 1517 to Egypt. Even the Muslim powers of North Africa were nominally under Turkish control. In short order they expanded to the west and north, seizing Croatia, Bosnia, Dalmatia, Albania, eastern Hungary, Moldavia, Bulgaria, and Greece. Turkish strength was based on a number of factors. The first was the loyalty and efficiency of the sultan's crack troops, the Janissaries. These troops were young boys forcibly taken from the subject Christian populations, trained in the Turkish language and customs, and converted to Islam. Although they functioned as special protectors of the Christian community from which they were drawn, they were separated from it by their new faith. Because the Turkish population viewed them as outsiders, they were particularly loyal to the sultan.

The situation of the Janissaries underlines a secondary explanation for Ottoman strength: the unusually tolerant attitudes of Mehmed, who saw himself not only as the greatest of the *ghazi* (crusading warriors who were considered the "instruments of Allah") but also as emperor, heir to Byzantine and ancient imperial traditions. Immediately after the conquest of Constantinople he repopulated the city with Greeks, Armenians, Jews, and Muslims. Mehmed especially welcomed Sephardic Jews from Spain and Portugal to parts of his empire. Thessalonica (Salonika), for example, was second only to Amsterdam as a Sephardic Jewish center until the community was destroyed in World War II. Religious groups in the cities lived in separate districts centered on a church or synagogue, and each religious community retained the right to select its own leaders. Mehmed made Constantinople the capital of the new Ottoman Empire. And by building mosques, hospitals, hostels, and bridges, he breathed new life into the city, which he referred to as Istanbul—that is, "the city." In the fifty years following the conquest, the population of the city grew an extraordinary 500 percent, from about 40,000 to over 200,000, making it the largest city in Europe, as it had been in Late Antiquity.

At a time when Christian Europe seemed less and less willing to tolerate non-Christian minorities, the Ottoman Empire's liberal attitude toward outsiders seemed striking. Muslims and non-Muslims belonged to the same trade associations and

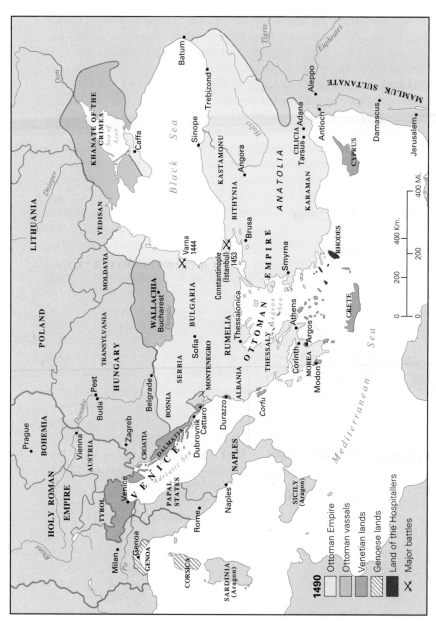

Turkey and Eastern Europe With the conquest of Constantinople, Syria, and Palestine, the Ottoman Turks controlled the eastern Mediterranean and dominated Europe below the Danube River. The Holy Roman emperors, rulers of Italy, and kings of Spain had to be concerned about potential invasions by land or by sea.

traveled throughout the empire. Mehmed had no qualms about making trade agreements with the Italian powers in an attempt to consolidate his control. And in Serbia, Bulgaria, Macedonia, and Albania he left in place previous social and political institutions, requiring only loyalty to his empire.

Mehmed had to tread carefully, though, because the Turks had a number of powerful enemies. Serious problems, for example, surfaced during the reign of Mehmed's son, Bayazid (r. 1481–1512). Following Turkish tradition, Mehmed had not chosen a successor but let his sons fight for control. Normally the successful claimant achieved the throne by doing away with his closest relatives. Bayazid's brother, Jem, however, fled into the protective custody of Christian powers, where he spent the rest of his life. In times of crisis kings and popes would threaten to foment rebellion in Ottoman lands by releasing him. Bayazid also had to worry about the Mamluk Turks, who controlled Egypt and Syria, and the new Safavid dynasty in Persia. Although both were Muslim,

The Siege of Constantinople

The siege of Constantinople by the Turks required the attackers to isolate the city both by sea and by land. This miniature from the fifteenth century shows the Turkish camps, as well as the movements of Turkish boats, completing the isolation of the city. (Bibliothèque nationale de France)

they were willing to join with various Christian states to reduce the power of the Ottomans. Only in the second decade of the sixteenth century, after Bayazid's son, Selim (r. 1512–1520), had defeated the Persians and the Mamluks, were the Ottomans finally safe from attack from the east or south.

The Union of Crowns in Spain

While expanding across the Mediterranean, the Turks came in contact with the other new state of the fifteenth century, the newly unified kingdom of Spain. As in Poland-Lithuania, the Spanish monarchy was only a dynastic union. In 1469 Ferdinand, heir to the kingdom of Aragon and Catalonia, married Isabella, daughter of the king of Castile. Five years later Isabella became queen of Castile, and in 1479 Ferdinand took control of the kingdom of Aragon. This union of Crowns eventually would lead to the creation of a united Spain, but true integration was still a distant dream in 1469.

The permanence of the union was remarkable because the two kingdoms were so different. Castile was a much larger and more populous state. It had taken the lead in the Reconquista, the fight begun in the eleventh century to reclaim Iberia from Muslim rule. As a result, economic power within Castile was divided among the groups most responsible for the Reconquista: military orders and nobles. The military orders of Calatrava, Santiago, and Alcantara were militias formed by men who had taken a religious vow similar to that taken by a monk, with an added commitment to fight against the enemies of Christianity. In the course of the Reconquista, the military orders assumed control of vast districts. Lay nobles who aided in the Reconquista also held large tracts of land and proudly guarded their independence.

Castile's power stemmed from its agrarian wealth. During the Reconquista Castilians took control of large regions and turned them into ranges for grazing merino sheep, producers of the prized merino wool exported to the markets of Flanders and Italy (see page 352). To maximize the profits from wool production, the kings authorized the creation of the Mesta, a brotherhood of sheep producers. The pastoral economy grew to the point that by the early sixteenth century Castilians owned over three million sheep.

Economic power in Castile lay with the nobility, but political power rested with the monarch. Because the nobility was largely exempt from taxation, nobles ignored the Cortes, the popular assembly, which could do little more than approve royal demands. The towns of Castile were important only as fortresses and staging points for militias rather than as centers of trade and commerce.

The kingdom of Aragon was dramatically different. The center of the kingdom was Barcelona, an important trading center in the Mediterranean. In the fourteenth and fifteenth centuries the kings of Aragon concentrated their efforts on expanding their influence in the Mediterranean, especially south of France and Italy. By the middle of the fifteenth century the Aragonese empire included the kingdom of Naples, Sicily, the Balearic Islands, and Sardinia.

The power of the Aragonese king, in sharp contrast to the Castilian monarchy, was limited because the Crown was not unified. The ruler was king in Aragon and Navarre but only count in Catalonia. Aragon, Catalonia, and Valencia each maintained its own Cortes. In each area the traditional nobility and the towns had a great deal more influence than did their counterparts in Castile. The power of the Cortes is clear in the coronation oath taken by the Aragonese nobility: "We who are as good as you and together are more powerful than you, make you our king and lord, provided that you observe our laws and liberties, and if not, not."[9] The distinction between Aragon and Castile could not be stronger.

Initially the union of the crowns of Aragon and Castile did little to unify the two monarchies. Nobles fought over disputed boundaries, and Castilian nobles felt exploited by Aragonese merchants. Trade duties and internal boundaries continued to be disputed. The two realms even lacked a treaty to allow for the extradition of criminals from one kingdom to the other. Castilians never accepted Ferdinand as more than their queen's consort. After the death of Isabella in 1504 he ruled in Castile only as regent for his infant grandson, Charles I (r. 1516–1556). "Spain" would not emerge in an institutional sense until the late sixteenth century.

Nonetheless, the reign of Isabella and Ferdinand marked a profound change in politics and society in the Iberian kingdoms and in Europe in general. Ferdinand and Isabella married their daughter Joanna, to Philip of Habsburg in 1496 to draw the Holy Roman Empire into the Italian wars brought on by the French invasion (see page 346). The marriage of their daughter Catherine of Aragon to Prince Arthur of England in 1501 was designed to obtain yet another ally against the French. Those two marriages would have momentous consequences for European history in the sixteenth century.

The reign of Ferdinand and Isabella is especially memorable because of the events of 1492. In January of that year a crusading army conquered Granada, the last Muslim stronghold in Iberia. In March Ferdinand and Isabella ordered the Jews of Castile and Aragon to convert or leave the kingdom within four months. In April Isabella issued her commission authorizing Christopher Columbus "to discover and acquire islands and mainland in the Ocean Sea" (see pages 415–416).

The conquest of Granada and the expulsion of the Jews represented a radical shift in the Spanish mentality. Until the beginning of the fifteenth century Spain maintained a level of religious tolerance unusual in Christendom. In the fourteenth century perhaps 2 percent of the population of Iberia was Jewish, and the Muslim population may have been as high as 50 percent. The various groups were inextricably mixed. The statutes of the Jewish community in Barcelona were written in Catalan, a Spanish dialect, rather than in Hebrew. *Maranos,* Jewish converts to Christianity, and *moriscos,* Muslim converts, mixed continuously with Christians and with members of their former religions. It was difficult at times to know which religion these converts, or *conversos,* actually practiced. One surprised northern visitor to Spain remarked that one noble's circle was filled with "Christians, Moors, and Jews and he lets them live in peace in their faith."

This tolerant mingling of Christians, Muslims, and Jews had periodically occasioned violence. All three communities, in fact, preferred clear boundaries between the groups. In 1391, however, a series of violent attacks had long-lasting and unfortunate effects on Iberian society. An attack on the Jews of Seville led to murders, forced conversions, and suppression of synagogues throughout Spain. In the wake of the assault, large portions of the urban Jewish population either converted to Christianity or moved into villages away from the large commercial cities. The Jewish population in Castile may have declined by a fourth. Although the anti-Jewish feelings were expressed in religious terms, the underlying cause was anger over the economic prominence of some Jewish or converso families. After 1391 anti-Jewish feeling increasingly became racial. As one rebel said, "The converso remains a Jew and therefore should be barred from public office."[10]

Hostility and suspicion toward Jews grew throughout the fifteenth century until Ferdinand and Isabella concluded that the only safe course was to order all Jews to accept baptism. Jews who would not convert would have to leave the kingdom within four months. The order was signed on March 31, 1492, and published in late April after an unsuccessful attempt by converso and Jewish leaders to dissuade the monarchs from implementing it.

Many Jews could not dispose of their possessions in the four months allowed and so chose to convert and remain. But it is estimated that about ten thousand Jews left Aragon and that even more left Castile. Many moved to Portugal and then to North

Interrogating a Jew *In 1492 Jews faced the order to convert or leave the kingdom of Spain.* (Museo de Zargoza)

[handwritten: expulsion of Jews expanded to Muslims]

Africa. Some went east to Istanbul or north to the Low Countries. A number of others moved to the colonies being established in the New World in the vain hope of avoiding the Inquisition, which was already underway when the expulsion order was issued (see below). In 1504 the expulsion order was extended to include all Muslims.

The economic and social costs of the expulsion were profound. Not every Muslim or Jew was wealthy and cultured, but the exiles did include many doctors, bankers, and merchants. Spanish culture, long open to influences from Muslim and Jewish sources, became narrower and less willing to accept new ideas. After the expulsion a chasm of distrust opened between the "Old Christians" and the "New Christians"—that is, those newly converted. As early as the first decades of the fifteenth century, some religious orders had refused to accept "New Christians." They required that their members demonstrate *limpieza de sangre,* a purity of blood. By 1500 the same tests of blood purity became prerequisites for holding most religious and public offices. Thus by the end of the fifteenth century the Iberian kingdoms had created more powerful, unified governments, but at a terrible cost to the only portion of Christendom that had ever practiced religious tolerance.

[handwritten: powerful, unified govt. → but horrible religious tolerance]

Complaints that led to the expulsion arose from a variety of sources. The fact that many of the most important financiers and courtiers were Jews or conversos bred jealousies and tensions among the communities. All three religious communities favored distinct dress and identifying behaviors. Old Christians seemed concerned that many of the conversos might reconvert to Judaism, and the fear of reconversion, or "judaizing," led many to advocate the institution of the Spanish Inquisition.

Inquisitions were well known in many parts of Europe, but the Spanish Inquisition was unique because in 1478 Pope Sixtus IV placed the grand inquisitor under the direct control of the monarchs. Like most Christian rulers, Ferdinand and Isabella believed that uniform Christian orthodoxy was the only firm basis for a strong kingdom. Inquisitors attacked those aspects of converso tradition that seemed to make the conversos less than fully Christian. They were concerned that many conversos and maranos had converted falsely and were secretly continuing to follow Jewish or Muslim rituals—a fear that some recent scholars have argued was unfounded.

[handwritten margin: Inquisition → kingdom → uniform than Orthodoxy]

Because its administration, finances, and appointments were in Spanish, not papal, hands, the Spanish Inquisition quickly became an important instrument for the expansion of state power. Many inquisitors used their offices to attack wealthy or politically important converso families not just to drive them from public life but also to fill the royal treasury, which was where the estates of those judged guilty wound up. "This inquisition is as much to take the conversos' estates as to exalt the faith," concluded one despairing conversa woman.[11]

[handwritten margin: everyone must be fully Xtian]

[handwritten: Inquisition exalts the faith + takes estates → gain land + $ for govt]

The Limits of Consolidation: Germany

The issue of central versus local control played a key role in German affairs as well. The Holy Roman Empire of the late Middle Ages was dramatically different from the empire of the early thirteenth century. Emperors generally were unable to claim lands and preside over jurisdictions outside Germany. And within Germany power shifted eastward. Imperial power had previously rested on lands and castles in southwestern Germany. These strongholds melted away as emperors willingly pawned and sold traditional crown lands in order to build up the holdings of their own families.

Germany b/came a loose collection of territories

Emperor Henry VII (r. 1308–1313) and his grandson, Charles IV (r. 1347–1378), for example, liquidated imperial lands west of the Rhine in order to secure the House of Luxemburg's claims to the crown of Bohemia and other lands in the east. The Habsburgs in Austria, the Wittelsbachs in Bavaria, and a host of lesser families staked out power bases in separate parts of the empire. As a result, Germany unraveled into a loose collection of territories. And more seriously, the power of each emperor depended almost entirely on the wealth and power of his dynastic lands.

wealth + power of lands determined dynasty

The power of regional authorities in the empire was further cemented by the so-called Golden Bull of 1356, the most important constitutional document of late medieval German history. In it Charles IV declared that henceforth the archbishops of Cologne, Mainz, and Trier, plus the secular rulers of Bohemia, the Rhenish Palatinate, Saxony, and Brandenburg, would be the seven electors responsible for the choice of a new emperor. He further established that the rulers of these seven principalities should

Golden Bull of 1356 – 7 electors to choose new emperor + have full jurisdictional rights

IMPORTANT EVENTS

1303	Pope Boniface VIII attacked at Anagni and dies
1305	Election of Pope Clement V
1309	Clement V moves papal court to Avignon; beginning of Babylonian Captivity
1337	Beginning of Hundred Years' War between England and France
1348–1351	Black Death
1356	German emperor issues Golden Bull
1378	Great Schism
1381	English Rising
1397	Union of Kalmar unites Denmark, Norway, and Sweden
1410	Battle of Tannenberg
1414–1417	Council of Constance
1415	Battle of Agincourt
1420	Treaty of Troyes
1431	Execution of Joan of Arc
1438	Pragmatic Sanction of Bourges
1453	End of the Hundred Years' War
	Ottoman Turks conquer Constantinople
1469	Marriage of Ferdinand and Isabella unites kingdoms of Aragon and Castile
1480	Ivan III ends Tatar overlordship of Moscow
1485	Tudor dynasty established in England
1492	Spanish conquest of Granada
	Jews expelled from Spanish lands
	Columbus commissioned to discover new lands
1494	Charles VIII invades Italy

pol. power-territory princes

have full jurisdictional rights within their territories. The Golden Bull acknowledged the power of regional princes, but it did nothing to solve the inherent weakness of an electoral monarchy. Between 1273 and 1519 Germany elected fourteen emperors from six different dynasties, and only once, in 1378, did a son follow his father. The contrast between Germany and the monarchies of Iberia, France, and England is striking. By 1350 Germany had no hereditary monarchy, no common legal system, no common coinage, and no representative assembly. Political power rested in the hands of the territorial princes.   *Germ. = no hereditary monarchy/no common legal system*

Territorial integration was least effective in what is now Switzerland, where a league of towns, provincial knights, and peasant villages successfully resisted a territorial prince. The Swiss Confederation began modestly enough in 1291 as a voluntary association to promote regional peace. By 1410 the confederation had conquered most of the traditionally Habsburg lands in the Swiss areas. By the 1470s the Swiss had invented the myth of William Tell, the fearless woodsman who refused to bow his head to a Habsburg official, as a justification for their independent and anti-aristocratic traditions. Though still citizens of the Holy Roman Empire, the Swiss maintained an independence similar to that of the princes. Their expansion culminated with the Battle of Nancy in Lorraine in 1477, when the Swiss infantry defeated a Burgundian army and killed Charles the Bold, the duke of Burgundy. From then on "turning Swiss" was a common threat made by German towns and individuals who hoped to slow territorial centralization.

NOTES

1. Quoted in Guillaume Mollat, *The Popes at Avignon, 1305–1378* (London: Thomas Nelson, 1963), p. 112.

2. Quoted in Mary Aston, *Lollards and Reformers: Images and Literacy in Late Medieval Religion* (Ronceverte, W.V.: Hambledon, 1984), p. 60.

3. Quoted in Francis Oakley, *The Western Church in the Later Middle Ages* (Ithaca, N.Y.: Cornell University Press, 1979), pp. 65–66.

4. Quoted in Charles T. Wood, *Joan of Arc and Richard III* (New York: Oxford University Press, 1988), pp. 56–57.

5. Quoted in Michael T. Clanchy, "Law, Government, and Society in Medieval England," *History* 59 (1974): 75.

6. A. Buchon, *Choix des Chroniques* (Paris, 1875), p. 565, as quoted in John Gillingham and J. C. Holt, eds., *War and Government in the Middle Ages* (Totowa, N.J.: Barnes & Noble, 1984), p. 85.

7. Salimbene de Adam, quoted in John Larner, *Italy in the Age of Dante and Petrarch, 1215–1380* (New York: Longman, 1980), p. 141.

8. Quoted in Peter Shervey Lewis, *Later Medieval France: The Polity* (New York: Macmillan, 1968), p. 15.

9. Quoted in Angus MacKay, *Spain in the Middle Ages: From Frontier to Empire, 1000–1500* (London: Macmillan, 1977), p. 105.

10. Quoted in Angus MacKay, "Popular Movements and Pogroms in Fifteenth-Century Spain," *Past & Present* 55 (1972): 52.

11. Haim Beinart, ed., *Records of the Trials of the Spanish Inquisition in Ciudad Real,* vol. 1, trans. Duane Osheim (Jerusalem: Israel Academy of Sciences and Humanities, 1974), p. 391.

SUGGESTED READING

Bennett, Judith, and Amy Froide, eds. *Singlewomen in the European Past*. 1999. The medieval essays in this collection are especially good on working women.

Cohn, Samuel K., Jr. *The Black Death Transformed*. 2002. The most recent study of the plague in medieval Europe. In a closely argued analysis, Cohn concludes that the Black Death was not bubonic plague.

Duffy, E. *Saints & Sinners: A History of the Popes*. 1997. An excellent introduction to the papacy by a leading historian. The sections on the late Middle Ages are clear and balanced.

Dyer, C. *Making a Living in the Middle Ages: The People of Britain, 850–1520*. 2002. A masterful and accessible survey of the economic history of England that is especially good on rural life.

Guenée, B. *States and Rulers in Later Medieval Europe*. Translated by Juliet Vale. 1985. The best general introduction to the nature of government in the late Middle Ages. It introduces recent trends in historical research.

Inalcik, H. *The Ottoman Empire: The Classical Age, 1300–1600*. 1973. A general discussion of the growth of the Ottoman state by Turkey's best medieval historian.

Keen, Maurice H. *English Society in the Later Middle Ages, 1348–1500*. 1990. A general introduction to late medieval England that covers culture and religion as well as politics.

Nicholas, D. *The Transformation of Europe, 1300–1600*. 1999. A comprehensive survey of politics and society in Europe between 1300 and 1600; includes coverage of Scandinavia and the Slavic lands as well as northwestern Europe.

Oakley, Francis. *The Western Church in the Later Middle Ages*. 1979. The best general history of the church in the late Middle Ages. Oakley gives superior treatments of the Great Schism and conciliarism.

Warner, Marina. *Joan of Arc: The Image of Female Heroism*. 1981. An excellent and quite readable book that emphasizes the conflicting religious and political opinions about "the Maid."

The Renaissance 12

The painting above, *School of Athens* by Raphael (1483–1520), was commissioned for the Stanze, the papal apartments in the Vatican. At the center Plato and Aristotle advance through a churchlike hall, surrounded by the great thinkers and writers of the ancient world. But Raphael portrayed more than just ancient wisdom. The figure of Plato is, in fact, a portrait of Leonardo da Vinci. A brooding Michelangelo leans on a marble block in the foreground. In a companion painting on the opposite wall, Raphael depicted a gathering of the greatest scholars of Christendom. In this way he brought together Christian and classical, writers and artists, and captured the entire cultural reform plan of the Renaissance.

The revival these paintings celebrate was a response to the religious, social, economic, and political crises discussed in the previous chapter. Italians, and later Europeans generally, found themselves drawn to imitate Roman literature, ethics, and politics. The ideas of antiquity seemed to offer an opportunity to perfect the theological ideas about moral and political life current in the earlier Middle Ages.

Renaissance Italians wrote of themselves and their contemporaries as having "revived" arts, "rescued" painting, and "rediscovered" classical authors. They even coined the phrases "Dark Ages" and "Middle Ages" to describe the period that separated the Roman Empire from their own times. They believed that their society saw a new age, a rebirth of culture. And to this day we use the French word for "rebirth," *renaissance*, to describe the period of intense creativity and change from 1300 to 1500 not just in Italy but in all of Europe.

This view comes to us primarily from the work of the nineteenth-century Swiss historian Jacob Burckhardt. In his book *The Civilization of the Renaissance in Italy* (1860) he argued that Italians were the first individuals to recognize the state as a moral structure free from the restraints of religious or philosophical traditions. Burckhardt believed that individuals are entirely free. Their success or failure depends on personal qualities of creative brilliance rather than on family status, religion, or guild membership. Burckhardt thought he saw in Renaissance Italy the first signs of the romantic individualism and nationalism that characterized the modern world.

In fact, as brilliant as Renaissance writers and artists were, they do not represent a radical shift from the ideas or values of previous medieval culture. As we have seen, there were no "Dark Ages." Although the culture of Renaissance Europe was in many aspects new and innovative, it had close ties both to the ideas of the High Middle Ages and to traditional Christian values.

How, then, should we characterize the Renaissance in Europe? The Renaissance was an important cultural movement that aimed to reform and renew by imitating what the reformers believed were classical and early Christian traditions in art, education, religion, and political life. Italians, and then other Europeans, came to believe that the social and moral values, as well as the literature, of classical Greece and Rome offered the best formula for changing their own society for the better. This enthusiasm for a past culture became the vehicle for changes in literature, education, and art that established cultural standards that were to hold for the next five hundred years.

HUMANISM AND CULTURE IN ITALY
1300–1500

Italians turned to models from classical antiquity in their attempts to deal with current issues of cultural, political, and educational reform. A group of scholars who came to be known as humanists began to argue the superiority of the literature, history, and politics of the past. As humanists discovered more about ancient culture, they were able to understand more clearly the historical context in which Roman and Greek writers and thinkers lived. And by the early sixteenth century their debates on learning, civic duty, and the classical legacy had led them to a new vision of the past and a new appreciation of the nature of politics.

The Emergence of Humanism

Humanism initially held greater appeal in Italy than elsewhere in Europe because the culture in central and northern Italy was significantly more secular and more urban than the culture of much of the rest of Europe. Members of the clergy were not likely to dominate government and education in Italy. Quite the reverse: Boards dominated by laymen had built and were administering the great urban churches of Italy. Religious hospitals and charities were often reorganized and centralized under government control. In 1300 four cities in Italy (Milan, Venice, Florence, and Naples) had populations of about 100,000, and countless others had populations of 40,000 or more. By contrast, London, which may have had a population of 100,000, was the only city in England with more than 40,000 inhabitants. Even the powerful Italian aristocracy tended to live at least part of the year in towns and conform to urban social and legal practices.

Differences between Italy and northern Europe are also apparent in the structure of local education. In northern Europe education was organized to provide clergy for local churches. In the towns of Italy education was much more likely to be supervised by town governments to provide training in accounting, arithmetic, and the composition of business letters. Public grammar masters taught these basics, and numerous private masters and individual tutors were prepared to teach all subjects. Giovanni Villani, a fourteenth-century merchant and historian, described Florence in 1338 as a city of about 100,000 people in which perhaps as many as 10,000 young girls and boys were completing elementary education and 1,000 were continuing their studies to prepare for careers in commerce. Compared with education in the towns of northern Europe, education in Villani's Florence seems broad-based and practical.

Logic and Scholastic philosophy (see pages 318–319) dominated university education in northern Europe in the fourteenth and fifteenth centuries but had less influence in Italy, where education focused on the practical issues of town life rather than on theological speculation. Educated Italians of this period were interested in the *studia humanitatis*, which we now call humanism. By *humanism*, Italians meant rhetoric and literature—the arts of persuasion. Poetry, history, letter writing, and oratory based on standardized forms and aesthetic values consciously borrowed from ancient Greece and Rome were the center of intellectual life. In general, fourteenth-century Italians were suspicious of ideological or moral programs based on philosophical arguments or religious assumptions about human nature.

Italian towns were the focus of theorizing about towns as moral, religious, and political communities. Writers wanted to define the nature of the commune—the town government. Moralists often used "the common good" and "the good of the commune" as synonyms. By 1300 it was usual for towns to celebrate the feast days of their patron saints as major political as well as religious festivals. And town governments often supervised the construction and expansion of cathedrals, churches, and hospitals as signs of their wealth and prestige.

Literature of the early fourteenth century tended to emphasize the culture of towns. The most famous and most innovative work of the fourteenth century, *The Decameron* by Giovanni Boccaccio (1313–1375), pondered moral and ethical issues, but in the lively context of Italian town life. Boccaccio hoped the colorful and irreverent descriptions of contemporary Italians, which make his *Decameron* a classic of European literature, would also lead individuals to understand both the essence of human nature and the folly of human desires. The plot involves a group of privileged young people who abandon friends and family during the plague of 1348 to go into the country, where on successive days they mix feasting, dancing, and song with one hundred tales of love, intrigue, and gaiety. With its mix of traditional and contemporary images, Boccaccio's book spawned numerous imitators in Italy and elsewhere. Many credit him with popularizing a new, secular spirit. But the point too often missed by Boccaccio's imitators was, as he himself said, that "to have compassion for those who suffer is a human quality which everyone should possess."

The majority of educated Italians in the early fourteenth century, such as Boccaccio, were not particularly captivated by thoughts of ancient Rome. Italian historians chose to write the histories of their hometowns. Most, including Giovanni Villani of Florence, were convinced that their towns could rival ancient Rome. Theirs was a practical world in which most intellectuals were men trained in notarial arts—the everyday skills of oratory, letter writing, and the recording of legal documents.

Early Humanism   The first Italians who looked back consciously to the literary and historical examples of ancient Rome were a group of northern Italian lawyers and notaries who imitated Roman authors. These practical men found Roman history and literature more stimulating and useful than medieval philosophy. Writers such as Albertino Mussato of Padua (1262–1329) adopted classical styles in their poetry and histories. Mussato used his play *The Ecerinis* (1315) to tell of the fall of Can Grande della Scala, the tyrannical ruler of Verona (d. 1329), and to warn his neighbors of the dangers of tyranny. From its earliest the classical revival in Italy was tied to issues of moral and political reform.

This largely emotional fascination for the ancient world was transformed into a literary movement for reform by Francesco Petrarch (1304–1374), who popularized the idea of mixing classical moral and literary ideas with the concerns of the fourteenth century. Petrarch was the son of an exiled Florentine notary living at the papal court in Avignon. Repelled by the urban violence and wars he had experienced on his return to Italy, Petrarch was highly critical of his contemporaries: "I never liked this age," he once confessed. He criticized the papacy in Avignon, calling it the "Babylonian Captivity" (see pages 333–334); he supported an attempt to resurrect a republican government in Rome; and he believed that imitation of the actions, values, and culture of the ancient Romans was the only way to reform his sorry world.

Petrarch believed that an age of darkness—he coined the expression "Dark Ages"— separated the Roman world from his own time and that the separation could be overcome only through a study and reconstruction of classical values: "Once the darkness has been broken, our descendants will perhaps be able to return to the pure, pristine radiance."[1] Petrarch's program, and in many respects the entire Renaissance, involved first of all a reconstruction of classical culture, then a careful study and imitation of the classical heritage, and finally a series of moral and cultural changes that went beyond the mere copying of ancient values and styles.

Petrarch labored throughout his life to reconstruct the history and literature of Rome. He learned to read and write classical Latin. While still in his twenties he discovered, reorganized, and annotated fragments of Livy's *Roman History,* an important source for the history of Republican Rome. His work on Livy was merely the first step. In the 1330s he discovered a number of classical works, including orations and letters by Cicero, the great philosopher, statesman, and opponent of Julius Caesar (see pages 158–160). Cicero's letters to his friend Atticus were filled with gossip, questions about politics in Rome, and complaints about his forced withdrawal from public life. They create the portrait of an individual who was much more complex than the austere philosopher of medieval legend.

Petrarch's humanism was not worldly or secular; he was and remained a committed Christian. He recognized the tension between the Christian present and pagan antiquity. "My wishes fluctuate and my desires conflict, and in their struggle they tear me apart," he said.[2] Yet he prized the beauty and moral value of ancient learning. He wrote *The Lives of Illustrious Men,* biographies of men from antiquity whose thoughts and actions he deemed worthy of emulation. To spread humanistic values he issued collections of his letters, written in classically inspired Latin, and his Italian poems. He believed that study and memorization of the writings of classical authors could lead to the internalization of the ideas and values expressed in those works, just as a honeybee drinks nectar to create honey. He argued that the ancient moral philosophers were superior to the Scholastic philosophers, whose work ended with the determination of truth, or correct responses. "The true moral philosophers and useful teachers of the virtues," he concluded, "are those whose first and last intention is to make hearer and reader good, those who do not merely teach what virtue and vice are but sow into our hearts love of the best . . . and hatred of the worst."[3]

Humanistic Studies   Petrarch's articulation of humanism inspired a broad-based transformation of Italian intellectual life that affected discussions of politics, education, literature, and philosophy. His style of historical and literary investigation of the past became the basis for a new appreciation of the present.

Petrarch's program of humanistic studies became especially popular with the wealthy oligarchy who dominated political life in Florence. The Florentine chancellor Coluccio Salutati (1331–1406) and a generation of young intellectuals who formed his circle evolved an ideology of civic humanism. Civic humanists wrote letters, orations, and histories praising their city's classical virtues and history. In the process they gave a practical and public meaning to the Petrarchan program. Civic humanists argued, as had Cicero, that there was a moral and ethical value intrinsic to public life. In a letter to a friend, Salutati wrote that public life is "something holy and holier than idleness in [religious] solitude." To another he added, "The active life you flee is to be followed both as an exercise in virtue and because of the necessity of brotherly love."[4]

More than Petrarch himself, civic humanists desired to create and inspire men of virtue who could take the lead in government and protect their fellow citizens from lawlessness and tyranny. In the early years of the fifteenth century civic humanists applauded Florence for remaining a republic of free citizens rather than falling under the control of a lord, like the people of Milan, whose government was dominated by the Viscontis (see page 344). In his *Panegyric on the City of Florence* (ca. 1405) Leonardo

Isabella d'Este *As part of the program to revive ancient Roman practices, Italian rulers had medals struck containing their own images. This image of Isabella was meant to celebrate the woman herself and the fact that her husband held the imperial office of marquis.* (Kunsthistorisches Museum, Vienna/Erich Lessing/ Art Resource, NY)

Bruni (ca. 1370–1444) recalled the history of the Roman Republic and suggested that Florence could re-create the best qualities of the Roman state. To civic humanists, the study of Rome and its virtues was the key to the continued prosperity of Florence and similar Italian republics.

One of Petrarch's most enthusiastic followers was Guarino of Verona (1374–1460), who became the leading advocate of educational reform in Renaissance Italy. After spending five years in Constantinople learning Greek and collecting classical manuscripts, he became the most successful teacher and translator of Greek literature in Italy. Greek studies had been advanced by Manuel Chrysoloras (1350–1415), who, after his arrival from Constantinople in 1397, taught Greek for three years in Florence. Chrysoloras was later joined by other Greek intellectuals, especially after the fall of Constantinople to the Turks in 1453. Guarino built on this interest.

Guarino emphasized careful study of grammar and memorization of large bodies of classical history and poetry. He was convinced that through a profound understanding of Greek and Latin literature and a careful imitation of the style of the great authors, a person could come to exhibit the moral and ethical values for which Cicero, Seneca, and Plutarch were justly famous. Although it is unclear whether Guarino's style of education had such results, it did provide a thorough education in literature and oratory. In an age that admired the ability to speak and write persuasively, the new style of humanistic education pioneered by Guarino spread quickly throughout Europe. The elegy spoken at Guarino's funeral sums up Italian views of humanistic education as well as the contribution of Guarino himself: "No one was considered noble, as leading a blameless life, unless he had followed Guarino's courses."

Guarino's authority spread quickly. One of his early students, Vittorino da Feltre (1378–1446), was appointed tutor at the Gonzaga court of Mantua. Like Guarino, he emphasized close literary study and careful imitation of classical authors. But the school he founded, the Villa Giocosa, was innovative because he advocated games and exercises as well as formal study. In addition, Vittorino required that bright young boys from poor families be included among the seventy affluent students normally resident in his school. Vittorino was so renowned that noblemen from across Italy sent their sons to be educated at the Villa Giocosa.

Humanistic education had its limits, however. Leonardo Bruni of Florence once composed a curriculum emphasizing literature and moral philosophy for a young woman to follow. But, he suggested, there was no reason to study rhetoric: "For why should the subtleties of . . . rhetorical conundrums consume the powers of a woman, who never sees the forum? . . . The contests of the forum, like those of warfare and battle, are the sphere of men."[5] To what extent did women participate in the cultural and artistic movements of the fourteenth and fifteenth centuries? Was the position of women better than it had been previously? The current of misogyny—the assumption that women were intellectually and morally weaker than men—continued during the Renaissance, but it was not unopposed.

During the fifteenth century many women did learn to read and even to write. Religious women and wives of merchants read educational and spiritual literature. Some women needed to write in order to manage the economic and political interests of their families. Alessandra Macinghi-Strozzi of Florence (1407–1471), for example, wrote numerous letters to her sons in exile describing her efforts to find spouses for her children and to influence the government to end their banishments.

Yet many men were suspicious of literate women. Just how suspicious is evident in the career of Isotta Nogarola of Verona (b. 1418), one of a number of fifteenth- and sixteenth-century Italian women whose literary abilities equaled those of male humanists. Isotta quickly became known as a gifted writer, but men's response to her work was mixed. One anonymous critic suggested that it was unnatural for a woman to have such scholarly interests and accused her of equally unnatural sexual interests. Guarino of Verona himself wrote to her warning that if she was truly to be educated, she must put off female sensibilities and find "a man within the woman."[6]

The problem for humanistically educated women was that society provided no acceptable role for them. A noblewoman such as Isabella d'Este (see page 398), wife of the duke of Mantua, might gather humanists and painters around her at court, but it was not generally believed that women themselves could create literary works of true merit. When women tried, they were usually rebuffed and urged to reject the values of civic humanism and to hold instead to traditional Christian virtues of rejection of the world. In other words, a woman who had literary or cultural interests was expected to enter a convent. That was a friend's advice to Isotta Nogarola. It was wrong, he said, "that a virgin should consider marriage, or even think about that liberty of lascivious morals."[7] Throughout the fifteenth and early sixteenth centuries some women in Italy and elsewhere in Europe learned classical languages and philosophy, but they became rarer as time passed. The virtues of humanism were public virtues, and Europeans of the Renaissance remained uncomfortable with the idea that women might act directly and publicly.

The Transformation of Humanism   The fascination with education based on ancient authorities was heightened by the discovery in 1416, in the Monastery of Saint Gall in Switzerland, of a complete manuscript of

Transformation of knowledge re. Donation (handwritten margin note)

Quintilian's *Institutes of Oratory*, a first-century treatise on the proper education for a young Roman patrician. The document was found by Poggio Bracciolini (1380–1459), who had been part of the humanist circle in Florence. The discovery was hardly accidental. Like Petrarch, the humanists of the fifteenth century scoured Europe for ancient texts to read and study. In searching out the knowledge of the past, these fifteenth-century humanists made a series of discoveries that changed their understanding of language, philosophy, and religion. Their desire to imitate led to a profound transformation of knowledge.

A Florentine antiquary, Niccolò Niccoli (1364–1437), coordinated and paid for much of this pursuit of "lost" manuscripts. A wealthy bachelor, Niccolò spent the fortune he had inherited from his father by acquiring ancient statuary, reliefs, and, most of all, books. When he died, his collection of more than eight hundred volumes of Latin and Greek texts became the foundation of the humanist library housed in the Monastery of San Marco in Florence. Niccolò had specified that all his books "should be accessible to everyone," and humanists from across Italy and the rest of Europe came to Florence to study his literary treasures. Niccolò's library prompted Pope Nicholas V (r. 1447–1455) to begin the collection that is now the Apostolic Library of the Vatican in Rome. The Vatican library became a lending library, serving the humanist community in Rome. Similar collections were assembled in Venice, Milan, and Urbino. The Greek and Latin sources preserved in these libraries allowed humanists to study classical languages in a way not possible before.

The career of Lorenzo Valla (1407–1457) illustrates the transformation that took place in the fifteenth century as humanism swept Europe. Valla was born near Rome and received a traditional humanistic education in Greek and Latin studies. He spent the rest of his life at universities and courts lecturing on philosophy and literature. Valla's studies had led him to understand that languages change with time—that they, too, have a life and a history. In 1440 he published a work called *On the Donation of Constantine*, which purported to record the gift by the emperor Constantine (r. 311–337) of jurisdiction over Rome and the western half of the empire to the pope when the imperial capital was moved to Constantinople (see page 195). In the High and late Middle Ages the papacy used the document to defend its right to political dominion in central Italy. The donation had long been criticized by legal theorists, who argued that Constantine had no right to make it. Valla went further and attacked the legitimacy of the document itself. Because of its language and form, he argued, it could not have been written at the time of Constantine:

> Through his [the writer's] babbling, he reveals his most impudent forgery himself. . . . Where he deals with the gifts he says "a diadem . . . made of pure gold and precious jewels." The ignoramus did not know that the diadem was made of cloth, probably silk. . . . He thinks it had to be made of gold, since nowadays kings usually wear a circle of gold set with jewels.[8]

Valla was correct; the *Donation* was an eighth-century forgery.

Valla later turned his attention to the New Testament. Jerome (331–420) had put together the Vulgate edition of the Bible in an attempt to create a single accepted Latin version of the Hebrew Bible and the New Testament (see page 220). In 1444 Valla published his *Annotations on the New Testament*. In this work he used his training in classical languages to correct Jerome's standard Latin text and to show numerous instances of mistranslations. His annotations on the New Testament were of critical importance to humanists outside Italy and were highly influential during the Protestant Reformation.

The transformation of humanism exemplified by Valla was fully expected by some Florentines. They anticipated that literary studies would lead eventually to philosophy. In 1456 a young Florentine began studying Greek with just such a change in mind. Supported by the Medici rulers of Florence, Marsilio Ficino (1433–1499) began a daunting project: to translate the works of Plato into Latin and to interpret Plato in light of Christian doctrine and tradition.

Ficino believed that Platonism, like Christianity, demonstrated the dignity of humanity. He wrote that everything in creation was connected along a continuum ranging from the lowliest matter to the person of God. The human soul was located at the midpoint of this hierarchy and was a bridge between matter and God. True wisdom, and especially experience of the divine, could be gained only through contemplation and love. According to Ficino, logic and scientific observation did not lead to true understanding, for humans know logically only what they can define in human language; individuals can, however, love things, such as God, that they are not fully able to comprehend.

Ficino's belief in the dignity of man was shared by Giovanni Pico della Mirandola (1463–1494), who proposed to debate with other philosophers nine hundred theses dealing with the nature of man, the origins of knowledge, and the uses of philosophy. Pico extended Ficino's idea of the hierarchy of being, arguing that humans surpassed even the angels in dignity. Angels held a fixed position in the hierarchy, just below God. In contrast, humans could move either up or down in the hierarchy, depending on the extent to which they embraced spiritual or worldly interests. Pico further believed that he had proved that all philosophies contain at least some truth. He was one of the first humanists to learn Hebrew and to argue that divine wisdom could be found in Jewish mystical literature. Along with others, he studied the Jewish Cabala, a collection of mystical and occult writings that humanists believed dated from the time of Moses. Pico's adoption of the Hebrew mystical writings was often controversial in the Jewish community as well as among Christians.

Pico's ideas were shared by other humanists, who contended that an original divine illumination—a "Pristine Theology," they called it—preceded even Plato and Aristotle. These humanists found theological truth in what they believed was ancient Egyptian, Greek, and Jewish magic. Ficino himself popularized the *Corpus Hermeticum* (the Hermetic collection), an amalgam of magical texts of the first century A.D. that was mistakenly thought to be the work of an Egyptian magician, Hermes Trismagistos. They assumed Hermes wrote during the age of Moses and Pythagoras. Like many mystical writings of the first and second centuries, Hermetic texts explained how the mind could influence and be influenced by the material and celestial worlds.

Along with exploring Hermetic magic, many humanists of the fifteenth and sixteenth centuries investigated astrology and alchemy. All three systems posit the existence of a direct, reciprocal connection between the cosmos and the natural world. In the late medieval and Renaissance world astrological and alchemical theories seemed reasonable. By the late fifteenth century many humanists assumed that personality was profoundly affected by the stars and that the heavens were not silent regarding human affairs. It was not by accident that for a century or more after 1500 astrologers were official or unofficial members of most European courts.

Interest in alchemy was equally widespread though more controversial. Alchemists believed that everything was made of a primary material and that therefore it was possible to transmute one substance into another. The most popular variation, and the one most exploited by hucksters and frauds, was the belief that base metals could be turned into gold. The hopes of most alchemists, however, were more profound. They were convinced that they could unlock the explanation of the properties of the whole cosmos. On a personal and religious level, as well as on a material level, practitioners hoped to make the impure pure. The interest in understanding and manipulating nature that lay at the heart of Hermetic magic, astrology, and alchemy was an important stimulus to scientific investigations and, ultimately, to the rise of modern scientific thought.

Humanism and Political Thought

The humanists' plan to rediscover classical sources meshed well with their political interests. "One can say," observed Leonardo Bruni, "that letters and the study of the Latin language went hand in hand with the condition of the Roman republic." Petrarch and the civic humanists believed that rulers, whether in a republic or a principality, should exhibit all the classical and Christian virtues of faith, hope, love, prudence, temperance, fortitude, and justice. A virtuous ruler would be loved as well as obeyed. The civic humanists viewed governments and laws as essentially unchanging and static. They believed that when change does occur, it most likely happens by chance—that is, because of fortune (the Roman goddess Fortuna). Humanists believed that the only protection against chance is true virtue, for the virtuous would never be dominated by fortune. Thus, beginning with Petrarch, humanists advised rulers to love their subjects, to be magnanimous with their possessions, and to maintain the rule of law. Humanistic tracts of the fourteenth and fifteenth centuries were full of classical and Christian examples of virtuous actions by moral rulers.

The French invasions of Italy in 1494 (see pages 345–346) and the warfare that followed called into question many of the humanists' assumptions about the lessons and virtues of classical civilization. Francesco Guicciardini (1483–1540), a Florentine patrician who had served in papal armies, suggested that, contrary to humanistic hopes, history held no clear lessons. Unless the causes of separate events were identical down to the smallest detail, he said, the results could be radically different. An even more thorough critique was offered by Guicciardini's friend and fellow Florentine, Niccolò Machiavelli (1469–1527). In a series of writings Machiavelli developed what he believed was a new science of politics. He wrote *Discourses on Livy*, a treatise on military organization, a history of Florence, and even a Renaissance play titled *The Mandrake Root*. He is best remembered, however, for *The Prince* (1513), a small tract numbering fewer than a hundred pages.

Machiavelli felt that his contemporaries paid too little heed to the lessons to be learned from history. Thus in his discourses on Livy he comments on Roman government, the role of religion, and the nature of political virtue, emphasizing the sophisticated Roman analysis of political and military situations. A shortcoming more serious than ignorance of history, Machiavelli believed, was his contemporaries' ignorance of the true motivations for people's actions. His play *The Mandrake Root* is a comedy about the ruses used to seduce a young woman. In truth, however, none of the characters is fooled. All of them, from the wife to her husband, realize what is happening but use the seduction to their own advantage. In the play Machiavelli implicitly challenges the humanistic assumption that educated individuals will naturally choose virtue over vice. He explicitly criticizes these same assumptions in *The Prince*. Machiavelli holds the contrary view: that individuals are much more likely to respond to fear and that power rather than rhetoric makes for good government.

Machiavelli's use of the Italian word *virtù* led him to be vilified as amoral. Machiavelli deliberately chose a word that meant both "manliness" or "ability" and "virtue as a moral quality." Earlier humanists had restricted *virtù* to the second meaning, using the word to refer to upright qualities such as prudence, generosity, and love. Machiavelli tried to show that in some situations these "virtues" could have violent, even evil, consequences. If, for example, a prince was so magnanimous in giving away his wealth that he was forced to raise taxes, his subjects might come to hate him. Conversely, a prince who, through cruelty to the enemies of his state, brought peace and stability to his subjects might be obeyed and perhaps even loved by them. A virtuous ruler must be mindful of the goals to be achieved—that is what Machiavelli really meant by the phrase often translated as "the ends justify the means."

Machiavelli expected his readers to be aware of the ambiguous nature of virtue— whether understood as ability or as morality. "One will discover," he concludes, "that something which appears to be a virtue, if pursued, will end in his destruction; while some other thing which seems to be a vice, if pursued, will result in his safety and his well-being."[9]

Like Guicciardini, Machiavelli rejected earlier humanistic assumptions that one needed merely to imitate the great leaders of the past. Governing is a process that requires different skills at different times, he warned: "The man who adapts his course of action to the nature of the times will succeed and, likewise, the man who sets his course of action out of tune with the times will come to grief."[10] The abilities that enable a prince to gain power may not be the abilities that will allow him to maintain it.

With the writings of Machiavelli humanistic ideas of intellectual, moral, and political reform came to maturation. Petrarch and the early humanists believed fully in the powers of classical wisdom to transform society. Machiavelli and his contemporaries admitted the importance of classical wisdom but also recognized the ambiguity of any simplistic application of classical learning to contemporary life.

THE ARTS IN ITALY, 1250–1550

Townspeople and artists in Renaissance Italy shared the humanists' perception of the importance of classical antiquity. Filippo Villani (d. 1405), a wealthy Florentine from an important business family, wrote that artists had recently "reawakened a lifeless and almost extinct art." In the middle of the fifteenth century the sculptor Lorenzo Ghiberti concluded that with the rise of Christianity "not only statues and paintings [were destroyed], but the books and commentaries and handbooks and rules on which men relied for their training." Italian writers and painters themselves believed that the recovery of past literary and artistic practices was essential if society was to recover from the "barbarism" that they believed characterized the recent past.

The Renaissance of the arts is traditionally divided into three periods. In the early Renaissance artists imitated nature; in the middle period they rediscovered classical

Giotto's Naturalism *Later painters praised the naturalistic emotion of Giotto's painting. In this detail from the Arena Chapel, Giotto portrays the kiss of Judas, one of the most dramatic moments in Christian history.* (Scala/Art Resource, NY)

ideas of proportion; in the High Renaissance artists were "superior to nature but also to the artists of the ancient world," according to the artist and architect Giorgio Vasari (1511–1574), who wrote a famous history of the eminent artists of his day.

The Artistic Renaissance

The first stirrings of the new styles can be found in the late thirteenth century. The greatest innovator of that era was Giotto di Bondone of Florence (ca. 1266–1337). Although Giotto's background was modest, his fellow citizens, popes, and patrons throughout Italy quickly recognized his skill. He traveled as far south as Rome and as far north as Padua painting churches and chapels. According to later artists and commentators, Giotto broke with the prevailing stiff, highly symbolic style and introduced lifelike portrayals of living persons. He produced paintings of dramatic situations, showing events located in specific times and places. The frescoes of the Arena Chapel in Padua (1304–1314), for example, recount episodes in the life of Christ. In a series of scenes leading from Christ's birth to his crucifixion, Giotto situates his actors in towns and countryside in what appears to be actual space. Even Michelangelo, the master of the High Renaissance, studied Giotto's painting. Giotto was in such demand throughout Italy that his native Florence gave him a public appointment so that he would be required by law to remain in the city.

Early in the fifteenth century Florentine artists devised new ways to represent nature that surpassed even the innovations of Giotto. The revolutionary nature of these artistic developments is evident from the careers of Lorenzo Ghiberti (1378–1455), Filippo Brunelleschi (1377–1446), and Masaccio (born Tomasso di ser Giovanni di Mone, 1401–ca. 1428). Their sculpture, architecture, and painting began an ongoing series of experiments with the representation of space through linear perspective. Perspective is a system for representing three-dimensional objects on a two-dimensional plane. It is based on two observations: (1) as parallel lines recede into the distance, they seem to converge; and (2) a geometric relationship regulates the relative sizes of objects at various distances from the viewer. Painters of the Renaissance literally found themselves looking at their world from a new perspective.

In 1401 Ghiberti won a commission to design door panels for the baptistery of San Giovanni in Florence. He was to spend the rest of his life working on two sets of bronze doors on which were recorded the stories of the New Testament (the north doors) and the Old Testament (the east doors). Ghiberti used the new techniques of linear perspective to create a sense of space into which he placed his classically inspired figures. Later, in the sixteenth century, Michelangelo remarked that the east doors were worthy to be the "Doors of Paradise," and so they have been known ever since.

In the competition for the baptistery commission, Ghiberti had beaten the young Filippo Brunelleschi, who, as a result, gave up sculpture for architecture and later left Florence to study in Rome. While in Rome he is said to have visited and measured surviving examples of classical architecture—the artistic equivalent of humanistic literary research. According to Vasari, he was capable of "visualizing Rome as it was before the fall." Brunelleschi's debt to Rome is evident in his masterpiece, Florence's foundling hospital. Built as a combination of hemispheres and cubes and resembling a Greek stoa or an arcaded Roman basilica, the long, low structure is an example of how profoundly different Renaissance architecture was from the towering Gothic of the Middle Ages. But his experience in Rome was also critical to his famous plan for constructing a dome over the Cathedral of Santa Maria del Fiore in Florence.

In the first decade of the fifteenth century, many commentators believed that painting would never be as innovative as either sculpture or architecture. They knew of no classical models that had survived for imitation. Yet the possibilities in painting became apparent in 1427 with the unveiling of Masaccio's *Trinity* in the Florentine Church of Santa Maria Novella. Masaccio built on revolutionary experiments in linear perspective to create a painting in which a flat wall seems to become a recessed chapel. The space created is filled with the images of Christ crucified, the Father, and the Holy Spirit.

In the middle years of the fifteenth century, artists came to terms with the innovations of the earlier period. In the second half of the fifteenth century, however, artists such as the Florentine Sandro Botticelli (1445–1510) added a profound understanding of classical symbolism to the technical innovations of Masaccio and Brunelleschi. Botticelli's famous *Primavera* (*Spring*, 1478), painted for a member of the Medici family, is filled with Neo-Platonic symbolism concerning truth, beauty, and the virtues of humanity.

Brunelleschi's Dome

The construction of a dome over the Cathedral of Santa Maria del Fiore in Florence was acknowledged to be one of the most influential accomplishments of the Renaissance, combining Florentine and medieval traditions of building with ideas based on a study of the past. A dome, with a diameter of about 180 feet and weighing 2,500 tons, was impossible to build using traditional construction methods. Filippo Brunelleschi solved the problem of supporting the double domes during construction by using a complex pattern of brickwork, such that each layer of the dome was locked into and braced by the preceding layer. As important as the technical innovations were, historians are interested in the significance given to Brunelleschi's achievement by his fellow Florentines. This late-fifteenth-century portrait makes clear how Florentines understood his accomplishment and by extension how they thought the old and the new had to be combined.

And [Filippo Brunelleschi] decided that while he looked at the sculpture of the ancients . . . to rediscover the fine and highly skilled method of building and the harmonious proportions of the ancients and how they might, without defects, be employed with convenience and economy. Noting the great and complex elements making up these matters—which had nevertheless been resolved—did not make him change his mind about understanding the methods and means they used. . . . He saw ruins—both standing and fallen down for some reason or other—which had been vaulted in various ways. He considered the methods of centering the vaults and other systems of support, how they could be dispensed with and what method had to be used, and when—because of the size of the vault or for other reasons—armatures could not be used. . . . In many places [Filippo] had excavations made in order to see the junctures of the membering of the buildings and their type—whether square, polygonal, completely round, oval or whatever. When possible they estimated the height [by measuring] from base to base for the height and similarly [they estimated the heights of] the entablatures

and roofs from the foundations. . . . [Filippo was called to a meeting to discuss the proposed vaulted dome of Florence's new cathedral.] That the vault had to be supported with centering was taken for granted by all the masters except Filippo. . . . [He was asked to demonstrate his system in the construction of a chapel.] And so he did. . . . Fixed at the lowest side is a cane or pole that circles upward, gradually narrowing as the cane or pole presses constantly on the bricks . . . on the unfixed side until it is enclosed. . . . Finally after other experiments . . . , he was asked about the procedure [for vaulting] such a great thing without centering, with a double vault and a lantern appropriate to such a large building. . . . Filippo reasoned orally with great conscientiousness and precision, and finally he was requested to put down in writing the method of keeping it steady and firm so that it would not slip.

Source: Antonio di Tuccio Manetti, The Life of Brunelleschi, ed. Howard Saalmon and trans. Catherine Enggass, published at University Park by The Pennsylvania State University Press, 1970, pp. 50, 52, 66, 68, 70. Copyright © 1970 by The Pennsylvania State University. Reproduced by permission of the publisher.

The high point in the development of Renaissance art came at the beginning of the sixteenth century in the work of several masters throughout Italy. Artists in Venice learned perspective from the Florentines and added their own tradition of subtle coloring in oils. The works of Italian artists were admired well beyond the borders of Italy. Even Sultan Mehmed II of Constantinople valued Italian painters.

The work of two Florentines, Leonardo da Vinci (1452–1519) and Michelangelo Buonarroti (1475–1564), best exemplifies the sophisticated heights that art achieved early in the sixteenth century. Leonardo, the bastard son of a notary, was raised in the village of Vinci outside of Florence. Cut off from the humanistic milieu of the city, he desired above all else to prove that his artistry was the equal of his formally schooled social superiors. In his notebooks he confessed, "I am fully conscious that, not being a literary man, certain presumptuous persons will think they may reasonably blame me, alleging that I am not a man of letters."[11] But he defended his lack of classical education by arguing that all the best writing, like the best painting and invention, is based on the close observation of nature. Close observation and scientific analysis made Leonardo's work uniquely creative in all these fields. Leonardo is famous for his plans, sometimes prophetic, for bridges, fortresses, submarines, and airships. There seemed

The Pietà　*Michelangelo sculpted three versions of Mary holding the crucified Jesus. This late, unfinished work reveals Michelangelo's desire to show the suffering of Christ.* (Scala/Art Resource, NY)

to be no branch of learning in which he was not interested. In painting he developed chiaroscuro, a technique for using light and dark in pictorial representation, and showed aerial perspective. He painted horizons as muted, shaded zones rather than with sharp lines. "I know," he said, "that the greater or less quantity of air that lies between the eye and the object makes the outlines of that object more or less distinct."[12] It was Leonardo's analytical observation that had the greatest influence on his contemporaries.

Michelangelo, however, was widely hailed as the capstone of Renaissance art. In the words of a contemporary, "He alone has triumphed over ancient artists, modern artists and over Nature itself." In his career we can follow the rise of Renaissance artists from the ranks of mere craftsmen to honored creators, courtiers who were the equals of the humanists—in fact, Michelangelo shared Petrarch's concern for reform and renewal in Italian society. We can also discern the synthesis of the artistic and intellectual transformations of the Renaissance with a profound religious sensitivity.

The importance of Michelangelo's contribution is obvious in two of his most important works: the statue *David* in Florence and his commissions in the Sistine Chapel of the Vatican in Rome. From his youth Michelangelo had studied and imitated antique sculpture, to the point that some of his creations were thought by many actually to be antiquities. He used his understanding of classical art in *David* (1501). Florentines recalled David's defeat of the giant Goliath, saving Israel from almost certain conquest by the Philistines. *David* thus became a symbol of the youthful Florentine republic struggling to maintain its freedom against great odds. As Vasari noted, "Just as David had protected his people and governed them justly, so whoever ruled Florence should vigorously defend the city and govern it with justice."[13]

Michelangelo was a committed republican and Florentine, but he spent much of his life working in Rome on a series of papal commissions. In 1508 he was called by Pope Julius II (r. 1503–1513) to work on the ceiling of the Sistine Chapel. Michelangelo spent four years decorating the ceiling with hundreds of figures and with nine scenes from the Book of Genesis, including the famous *Creation of Adam*. In the late 1530s, at the request of Pope Clement VII (r. 1523–1534), he completed *The Last Judgment*, which covers the wall above the altar. In that painting the techniques of perspective and the conscious recognition of debts to classical culture recede into the background as the artist surrounds Christ in judgment with saints and sinners. In the hollow, hanging skin of flayed Saint Bartholomew we can detect a psychological self-portrait of an artist increasingly concerned with his own spiritual failings.

Michelangelo's self-portrait reminds us that the intellectual content of the artist's work is one of its most enduring traits. He was a Platonist who believed that the form and beauty of a statue are contained, buried, in the stone itself. The artist's job is to peel away excess material and reveal the beauty within. As he noted in one of his poems, sculpting is a process not unlike religious salvation:

> Just as by carving . . . we set
> Into hard mountain rock
> A living figure
> Which grows most where the stone is most removed;
> In like manner, some good works . . .
> Are concealed by the excess of my very flesh.[14]

Art and Patronage [handwritten: Art Communicated social, political, +spiritual values]   The religious passion of Michelangelo's poetry indicates one of the reasons that art was so popular in Renaissance Italy. Art, like poetry, provided symbols and images through which Italians could reason about the most important issues of their communities. Italians willingly spent vast sums on art because of its ability to communicate social, political, and spiritual values.

Italy in the fourteenth and fifteenth centuries was unusually wealthy relative to the towns and principalities of northern Europe. Despite the population decline caused by plague and the accompanying economic dislocations, per person wealth in Italy remained quite high. Because of banking, international trade, and even service as mercenaries, Italians, and particularly Florentines, had money to spend on arts and luxuries. Thus the Italians of the Renaissance, whether as public or private patrons, could afford to use consumption of art as a form of competition for social and political status. [handwritten: consumption of art affected social + political status]

It was not just the elite who could afford art. Surprisingly modest families bought small religious paintings, painted storage chests, and decorative arts. Moralists advised families to buy small paintings of the Virgin Mary or the baby Jesus. Families also bought small paintings of saints considered special to their town or family. Wealthy and modest families alike bought brightly decorated terra-cotta pitchers, platters, and plates. Decorative arts were a critical social marker for families at all levels. Thus the market for art steadily increased in the fourteenth and fifteenth centuries, as did the number of shops and studios in which artists could be trained.

Artists in the modern world are accustomed to standing outside society as critics of conventional ideas. In the late Middle Ages and Renaissance, artists were not alienated commentators. In 1300 most art was religious in subject, and public display was its purpose. Throughout Europe art fulfilled a devotional function. Painted crucifixes, altarpieces, and banners were often endowed as devotional or penitential objects. The Arena Chapel in Padua, with its frescoes by Giotto, was funded by a merchant anxious to pay for some of his sins.

In the late Middle Ages and Renaissance, numerous paintings and statues throughout Italy (and much of the rest of Europe) were revered for their miraculous powers. During plague, drought, and times of war people had recourse to the sacred power of the saints represented in these works of art. The construction of the great churches of the period was often a community project that lasted for decades, even centuries. The city council of Siena, for example, voted to rebuild its Gothic Cathedral of Saint Mary, saying that the Blessed Virgin "was, is and will be in the future the head of this city" and that through veneration of her "Siena may be protected from harm." Accordingly, although the subject of art was clearly and primarily religious, the message was bound up in the civic values and ideas of the fourteenth and fifteenth centuries.

The first burst of artistic creativity in the fourteenth century was paid for by public institutions. Communal governments built and redecorated city halls to house government functionaries and to promote civic pride. Most towns placed a remarkable emphasis on the beauty of the work. Civic officials often named special commissions to consult with a variety of artists and architects before approving building projects. Governments, with an eye to the appearance of public areas, legislated the width of streets, height limits, and even the styles of dwelling façades. [handwritten: artistic creativity ⇒ public institutions]

The series of paintings called the *Good Government of Siena* illustrates the use of art to communicate political ideas. Painted in the first half of the fourteenth century by

Ambrogio Lorenzetti (ca. 1300–1348), *Good Government* combines allegorical representations of Wisdom and the cardinal virtues on one wall with realistic street scenes of a well-ordered Siena on an adjacent wall. Across from the scenes of good government are its opposite, graphic representations of murder, rape, and general injustice and mayhem. In this ambitious work, with its specific scenes and unmistakable tone, the government broadcast a clear political message in realistic brushstrokes. The popular preacher San Bernardino of Siena (1380–1444) reinforced the point of Lorenzetti's painting: "To see Peace depicted is a delight and so it is a shame to see War painted on the other wall." And Bernardino's sermon reminded listeners of the conclusions they should draw: "Oh my brothers and fathers, love and embrace each other . . . give your aid to this toil which I have undertaken so gladly, to bring about love and peace among you."[15]

Public art in Florence was often organized and supported by various guild organizations. Guild membership was a prerequisite for citizenship, so guildsmen set the tone in politics as well as in the commercial life of the city. Most major guilds commissioned sculpture for the Chapel of Or San Michele, a famous shrine in the grain market (its painting of the Virgin Mary was popularly thought to have wonderworking powers) and seat of the Guelf Party, the city's most powerful political organization. Guilds took responsibility for building and maintaining other structures in the city as well. Guildsmen took pride in creating a beautiful environment, but as the clothmakers' decision to supervise the baptistery shows, the work reflected not only on the city and its patron saint but also on the power and influence of the guild itself.

The princes who ruled outside the republics of Italy often had similarly precise messages that they wished to communicate. Renaissance popes embarked on a quite specific ideological program in the late fifteenth century to assert their dual roles as spiritual leaders of Christendom and temporal lords of a central Italian state (see pages 398–399). Rulers such as the Este dukes of Ferrara and the Sforza dukes of Milan constructed castles within their cities or hunting lodges and villas in the countryside and adorned them with pictures of the hunt or murals of knights in combat—scenes that emphasized their noble virtues and their natural right to rule.

By the mid-fifteenth century patrons of artworks in Florence and most other regions of Italy were more and more likely to be wealthy individuals. Many of the patrons who commissioned and oversaw artists were women. Women paid for the construction of convents and chapels. In many cases their patronage can simply be understood as an extension of their families, but in many other cases it was not. One woman who had lived for years as a concubine of a merchant in Florence used her dead lover's bequest to commission a painting titled *Christ and the Adultress*, making clear that even women in her situation could hope for God's mercy.

Republics, in which all families were in principle equal, initially distrusted the pride and ambition implied by elaborate city palaces and rural villas. By the middle of the fifteenth century, however, such reserve was found in none but the most conservative republics, such as Venice and Lucca. Palaces, gardens, and villas became the settings in which the wealthy could entertain their peers, receive clients, and debate the political issues of the day. The public rooms of these *palazzos* were decorated with portraits, gem collections, rare books, ceramics, and statuary. Many villas and palaces included private chapels. In the Medici palace in Florence, for example, the chapel is the setting for a painting of the Magi (the three wise men who came to worship the infant Jesus) in which the artist, Benozzo Gozzoli (1420–1498), used members of the Medici family as models for the portraits of the Magi and their entourage (see the painting on page 345). The Magi, known to be wise and virtuous rulers, were an apt symbol for the family that had come to dominate the city.

Artists at princely courts were expected to work for the glory of their lord. Often the genre of choice was the portrait. One of the most successful portraitists of the sixteenth century was Sofonisba Anguissola (1532–1625). Anguissola won renown as a prodigy because she was female and from a patrician family; one of her paintings was sent to Michelangelo, who forwarded it to the Medici in Florence. Since women would never be allowed to study anatomy, Anguissola concentrated her talents on portraits and detailed paintings of domestic life. Later she was called to the Spanish court, where the king, queen, and their daughter sat for her. She continued to paint after her marriage and return to Italy. Even in her nineties she welcomed painters from all parts of Europe to visit and discuss techniques of portraiture.

THE SPREAD OF THE RENAISSANCE, 1350–1536

By 1500, the Renaissance had spread from Italy to the rest of Europe. Well beyond the borders of the old Roman Empire, in Prague and Cracow, for example, one could find a renewed interest in classical ideas about art and literature. As information about the past and its relevance to contemporary life spread, however, the message was transformed in several important ways. Outside Italy, Rome and its history played a much less pivotal role. Humanists elsewhere in the West were interested more in religious than in political reform, and they responded to a number of important local interests. Yet the Renaissance notion of renewal based on a deep understanding and imitation of the past remained at the center of the movement. The nature of the transformation will be clearer if we begin by considering the nature of vernacular literatures before the emergence of Renaissance humanism.

Vernacular Literatures The humanistic movement was not simply a continuation of practical and literary movements. The extent of its innovation will be clearer if we look briefly at the vernacular literatures (that is, written in native languages, rather than Latin) of the fourteenth and fifteenth centuries.

As in Italy, fourteenth-century writers elsewhere were not immediately drawn to classical sources. Boccaccio's work, for example, influenced another vernacular writer, Geoffrey Chaucer (ca. 1343–1400), the son of a London burgher, who served as a diplomat, courtier, and member of Parliament. In addition to the pervasive French influence, Chaucer read and studied Boccaccio. Chaucer's most famous work, *The Canterbury Tales,* consists of stories told by a group of thirty pilgrims who left the London suburbs on a pilgrimage to the shrine of Saint Thomas Becket at Canterbury Cathedral. The narrators and the stories themselves describe a variety of moral and social types, creating an acute, sometimes bitter, portrait of English life. The Wife of Bath is typical of Chaucer's pilgrims: "She was a worthy woman all her life, husbands at the churchdoor she had five." After describing her own marriages she observes that marriage is a proper way to achieve moral perfection, but it can be so only if the woman is master.

Although Chaucer's characters present an ironic view of the good and evil that characterize society, Chaucer's contemporary, William Langland (ca. 1330–1400), took a decidedly more serious view of the ills of English life. Whereas Boccaccio and Chaucer all told realistic tales about life as it truly seemed to be, Langland used the traditional allegorical language (that is, symbolic language in which a place or person represents an idea) of medieval Europe. In *Piers Plowman* Langland writes of people caught between the "Valley of Death" and the "Tower of Truth." He describes the seven deadly sins that threaten all of society and follows with an exhortation to do better. Both Chaucer and Langland expected that their audiences would immediately recognize commonly held ideas and values.

Despite the persistence of old forms of literature, new vernacular styles arose, although they still dealt with traditional values and ideas. Throughout Europe many writers directly addressed their cares and concerns. Letters like those of the Paston family in England or Alessandra Macinghi-Strozzi in Italy described day-to-day affairs of business, politics, and family life. Letters dictated and sent by Saint Catherine of Siena and Angela of Foligno offered advice to the troubled. Small books of moral or spiritual writings were especially popular among women readers in the fourteenth and fifteenth centuries, among them *The Mirror for Simple Souls* by Marguerite of Porete (d. 1310). Though Marguerite was ultimately executed as a heretic, her work continued to circulate anonymously. Her frank descriptions of love, including God's love for humans, inspired many other writers in the fourteenth and fifteenth centuries. Less erotic but equally riveting was the memoir of Margery Kempe, an alewife from England, who left her husband and family, dressed in white (symbolic of virginity), and joined other pilgrims on trips to Spain, Italy, and Jerusalem.

One of the most unusual of the new vernacular writers was Christine de Pizan (1369–1430), the daughter of an Italian physician at the court of Charles V of France. When the deaths of her father and husband left her with responsibility for her children and little money, she turned to writing. From 1389 until her death, she lived and wrote at the French court. She is perhaps best known for *The Book of the City of the Ladies* (1405). In it she added her own voice to what is known as the *querelle des femmes,* the "argument over women." Christine wrote to counter the prevalent opinions of women as inherently inferior to men and incapable of moral judgments. She argued that the problem was education: "If it were customary to send daughters to school like sons, and if they were then taught the natural sciences, they would learn as thoroughly and understand the subtleties of all the arts and sciences as well as sons." Christine described in her book an ideal city of ladies in which prudence, justice, and reason would protect women from ignorant male critics.

All these vernacular writings built on popular tales and sayings as well as on traditional moral and religious writings. Unlike the early humanists, the vernacular writers saw little need for new cultural and intellectual models.

The Impact of Printing

The spread of humanism beyond Italy was aided greatly by the invention of printing. In the fifteenth century the desire to own and to read complete texts of classical works was widespread, but the number of copies was severely limited by the time and expense of hand-copying, collating, and checking manuscripts. Poggio Bracciolini's letters are filled with complaints about the time and expense of reproducing the classical manuscripts he had discovered. One copy he had commissioned was so inaccurate and illegible as to be nearly unusable. Traveling to repositories and libraries was often easier than creating a personal library. It was rarely possible for someone who read a manuscript once to obtain a complete copy to compare with other works.

The invention of printing with movable lead type changed things dramatically. Although block printing had long been known in China and was a popular way to produce playing cards and small woodcuts in Europe, only with the creation of movable type by Johann Gutenberg in the 1450s did printing become a practical way to produce books. Between 180 and 200 copies of the so-called Gutenberg Bible were printed in 1452 and 1453. It was followed shortly by editions of the Psalms. By 1470 German printing techniques had spread to Italy, the Low Countries, France, and England. It has been estimated that by 1500 a thousand presses were operating in 265 towns. The output of the early presses was extremely varied, ranging from small devotional books and other popular and profitable literature to complete editions of classical authors and their humanistic and theological texts.

Printing allowed for the creation of agreed-upon standard editions of works in law, theology, philosophy, and science. Scholars in different parts of the European world could feel fairly confident that they and their colleagues were analyzing identical texts. Similarly, producing accurate medical and herbal diagrams, maps, and even reproductions of art and architecture was easier. Multiple copies of texts also made possible the study of rare and esoteric literary, philosophical, and scientific works. An unexpected result of the print revolution was the rise of the printshop as a center of culture and communication. The printers Aldus Manutius (1450–1515) in Venice and Johannes Froben (d. 1527) in Basel were humanists. Both invited humanists to work in their shops editing their texts and correcting the proofs before printing. Printshops became a natural gathering place for clerics and laymen. Thus they were natural sources of humanist ideas and later, in the sixteenth century, of Protestant religious programs.

Humanism Outside Italy

As the influence of the humanist movement extended beyond Italy, the interests of the humanists changed. Although a strong religious strain infused Italian humanism, public life lay at the center of Italian programs of education and reform. Outside Italy, however, moral and religious reform formed the heart of the movement. Northern humanists wanted to renew Christian life and reinvigorate the church. Critics of the church complained that the clergy were wealthy and ignorant and that the laity were uneducated and superstitious. To amend those failings, northern humanists were involved in building educational institutions, in unearthing and publishing texts by Church Fathers, and in chronicling local customs and history. The works of the two best-known humanists, Thomas More and Desiderius Erasmus, present a sharp critique of contemporary behavior and, in the case of Erasmus, a call to a new sense of piety. The religious views of Erasmus were so influential that northern humanism has generally come to be known as "Christian humanism."

The intellectual environment into which humanism spread from Italy had changed significantly since the thirteenth century. The universities of Paris and Oxford retained the status they had acquired earlier but found themselves competing with a host of new

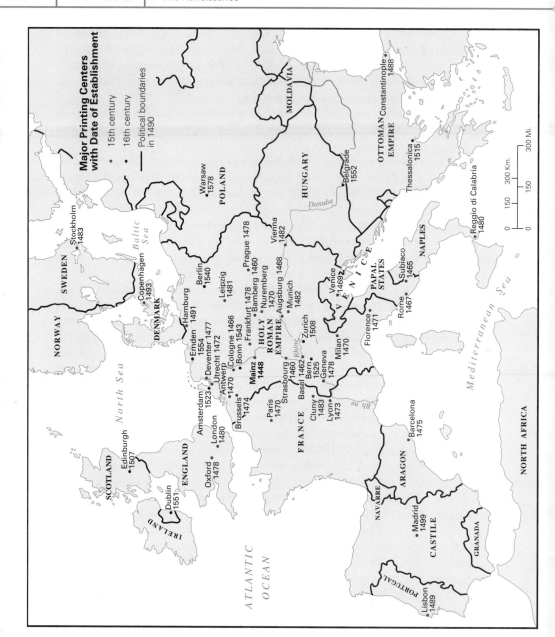

Major Printing Centers with Date of Establishment

- 15th century
- 16th century
— Political boundaries in 1490

NORWAY

SWEDEN
Stockholm 1483

DENMARK
Copenhagen 1493

Baltic Sea

POLAND
Warsaw 1578

MOLDAVIA

HUNGARY
Danube
Belgrade 1552

OTTOMAN EMPIRE
Constantinople 1488
Thessalonica 1515

Berlin 1540

Hamburg 1491

Leipzig 1481

Prague 1478

Vienna 1482

Emden 1554

Deventer 1477

Cologne 1466

Nuremberg 1470

Bamberg 1460

Frankfurt 1478

Augsburg 1468

Munich 1482

NAPLES

Subiaco 1465

Reggio di Calabria 1480

Bonn 1543

HOLY ROMAN EMPIRE

Mainz 1448

Zurich 1508

PAPAL STATES

Rome 1467

Utrecht 1472

Antwerp 1470

Strasbourg 1460

Basel 1462

Bern

Venice 1469

VENICE

Amsterdam 1523

Brussels 1474

Paris 1470

Cluny 1483

Geneva 1478

Milan 1470

Florence 1471

NORTH SEA

London 1480

Oxford 1478

ENGLAND

SCOTLAND
Edinburgh 1507

IRELAND
Dublin 1551

FRANCE

Lyon 1473

Barcelona 1475

ARAGON

NAVARRE

Madrid 1499

CASTILE

GRANADA

PORTUGAL
Lisbon 1489

ATLANTIC OCEAN

Mediterranean Sea

NORTH AFRICA

Rhine

Rhône

0   150   300 Km.
0   150   300 Mi.

The Spread of Printing

Printing technology moved rapidly along major trade routes to the most populous and prosperous areas of Europe. The technology was rapidly adopted in peripheral areas as well as in highly literate centers such as the Low Countries, the Rhine Valley, and northern Italy.

foundations. Like Paris, almost all had theological faculties dominated by Scholastically trained theologians. Nevertheless, the new foundations often had chairs of rhetoric, or "eloquence," which left considerable scope for those who advocated humanistic learning. These new universities, from Cracow (1367) to Uppsala in Sweden (1477), also reflected the increased national feeling in various regions of Europe. The earliest university in the lands of the German Empire, the Charles University in Prague (1348), was founded at the request of emperor Charles IV, whose court was in Prague. The foundation of a new university at Poszony (1465) by Johannes Vitéz was part of a cultural flowering of the Hungarian court at Buda. A supporter of King Matthias Corvinus, Vitéz corresponded with Italian humanists, collected manuscripts, and tried to recruit humanist teachers to come to Buda. The universities in Vienna (1365), Aix (1409), Louvain (1425), and numerous other cities owed their foundations to the pride and ambition of local rulers.

The humanists associated with the new universities were often educated in Italy, but they brought a new perspective to their work. Humanists in Sweden wrote histories of the Goths, celebrating the contributions of Germans to European culture. Polish humanists wrote similarly, in one case trying to define where in eastern Europe one could draw the line between Europe and Asia.

Humanists on faculties of law at French universities used humanistic techniques of historical and linguistic study. Italian-trained French lawyers introduced what came to be called the "Gallican style" of jurisprudence. Because legal ideas, like language, changed over time, they argued that Roman law had to be studied as a historically created system and not as an abstract and unchanging structure. Humanists like Guillaume Budé (1468–1540) moved from the study of law to considerations of Roman coinage, religion, and economic life in order to better understand the formation of Roman law. The desire to understand the law led other humanist-legists to add the study of society in ancient Gaul to their work on Rome, and then to examine the law of other societies as well.

The new universities often became centers of linguistic studies. Humanistic interest in language inspired the foundation of "trilingual" colleges in Spain, France, and the Low Countries to foster serious study of Hebrew, Greek, and Latin. Like Italian humanists, other humanists believed that knowledge of languages would allow students to understand more clearly the truths of Christianity. Typical of this movement was the archbishop of Toledo, Francisco Jiménez de Cisneros (1436–1517), who founded the University of Alcalá in 1508 with chairs of Latin, Greek, and Hebrew. He began the publication of a vast new edition of the Bible, called the "Polyglot ("many tongue") Bible" (1522) because it had parallel columns in Latin, Greek, and, where appropriate, Hebrew. Unlike Valla, Jiménez intended his translations not to challenge the Vulgate but merely to clarify its meaning. The university and the Bible were part of an effort to complete the conversion of Muslims and Jews and to reform religious practices among the old Christians.

To these humanists, the discovery and publication of early Christian authors seemed critical to any reform within the church. Jacques Lefèvre d'Étaples (1455–1536) of France was one of the most famous and influential of these humanistic editors of early Christian texts. After 1500 he concentrated on editing the texts of the early Church Fathers. The true spirit of Christianity, he believed, would be most clear in the works and lives of those who had lived closest to the age of the apostles. Christian humanists inspired by Lefèvre became key players in the later Reformation movements in France. Lefèvre's faith in the value of classical languages was shared by John Colet (1467–1519) of England, founder of St. Paul's School in London. He instituted a thorough program of teaching Latin and Greek aimed at creating scholars who would have access to the earliest Christian writings.

Tensions between the humanists and the advocates of Scholastic methods broke out over the cultural and linguistic studies that formed the heart of the humanist program. Taking to heart the humanistic belief that all philosophies and religions, not just Christianity, contained universal moral and spiritual truths, Johannes Reuchlin (1455–1522) of Württemberg embarked on a study of the Cabala. Johannes Pfefferkorn, a Dominican priest and recent convert from Judaism, attacked Reuchlin's use of Jewish traditions in the study of Christian theology. Sides were quickly drawn. The theological faculties of the German universities generally supported Pfefferkorn. The humanists supported Reuchlin. In his own defense Reuchlin issued *The Letters of Illustrious Men*, a volume of correspondence he had received in support of his position. This work gave rise to one of the great satires of the Renaissance, *The Letters of Obscure Men* (1516), written by anonymous authors and purporting to be letters from various narrow-minded Scholastics in defense of Pfefferkorn. Although the debate arose over the validity of Hebraic studies for Christian theology and not over humanistic ideas of reform or wisdom, it indicates the division between the humanists and much of the Scholastic community. Many people initially misunderstood the early controversies of the Protestant Reformation as a continuation of the conflicts between humanists and Scholastic theologians over the uses of Hebrew learning.

| Thomas More and Desiderius Erasmus | The careers of two humanists in particular exemplify the strength—and the limits—of the humanistic movement outside Italy: Sir Thomas More (1478–1535) of London and Desiderius Erasmus (1466–1536) of Rotterdam. Their careers |

developed along very different paths. More was educated at St. Anthony's School in London and became a lawyer. He translated Lucan and wrote a humanistic history of Richard III while pursuing his public career. He is most famous for his work *Utopia* (1516), the description of an ideal society located on the island of Utopia (literally, "nowhere") in the newly explored oceans. This powerful and contradictory work comprises two volumes. Book I is a debate over the moral value of public service between Morus, a well-intentioned but practical politician, and Hythloday, a widely traveled idealist. Morus tries to make the bureaucrat's argument about working for change from within the system. Hythloday rejects the argument out of hand. Thomas More himself seems to have been unsure at that time about the virtues of public service. He was of two minds, and the debate between Morus and Hythloday reflects his indecision. As part of his critique of justice and politics in Europe, Hythloday describes in Book II the commonwealth of Utopia, in which there is no private property but strict equality of possessions, and, as a result, harmony, tolerance, and little or no violence.

Since the publication of *Utopia* debates have raged about whether More, or anyone, could ever really hope to live in such a society. Some scholars have questioned how seriously More took this work—he seems to have written the initial sections merely to

amuse friends. Yet whatever More's intentions, Utopia's society of equality, cooperation, and acceptance continues to inspire social commentators.

Ironically, More, like his creation Morus, soon found himself trying to work for
justice within precisely the sort of autocratic court that Hythloday criticized. Not long
after the completion of *Utopia* More entered the service of King Henry VIII (r. 1509–
1547), eventually serving as chancellor of England. As a staunch Catholic and royal official More never acted on utopian principles of peace and toleration. He was, in fact,
responsible for the persecution of English Protestants in the years before the king's
break with Rome (see page 454). More's opposition to Henry's divorce and repudiation
of papal authority, and his refusal to acknowledge Henry as the head of the English
church, led him to resign his offices. He was eventually imprisoned and beheaded.
More's writing was a stinging critique of political values. He implied that society could
be reformed, yet in the period after 1521 his humanism and his vision of Utopia had no
influence on his own public life.

Unlike More, who was drawn to the power of king and pope, Erasmus always
avoided working for authorities. Often called the "Prince of Humanists," he was easily
the best-known humanist of the early sixteenth century. He was born the illegitimate
son of a priest in the Low Countries. Forced by relatives into a monastery, he disliked
the conservative piety and authoritarian discipline of traditional monastic life. Once
allowed out of the monastery to serve as an episcopal secretary, he never returned. He
lived and taught in France, England, Italy, and Switzerland. Of all the humanists it was
Erasmus who most benefited from the printing revolution. The printer Aldus Manutius invited him to live and work in Venice, and he spent the last productive years of his
life at Johannes Froben's press in Basel. He left the city only when Protestant reformers
took control of the city government.

Over a long career Erasmus brought out repeated editions of works designed to educate Christians. His *Adages,* first published in 1500, was a collection of proverbs from
Greek and Roman sources. The work was immensely popular, and Erasmus repeatedly
issued expanded editions. He tried to present Greek and Roman wisdom that would
illuminate everyday problems. *The Colloquies* was a collection of popular stories, designed as primers for students, that taught moral lessons even as they served as examples of good language. His ironic *Praise of Folly* (1511) was dedicated to Thomas More.
An oration by Folly in praise of folly, it is satire of a type unknown since antiquity.
Folly's catalog of vices includes everyone from the ignoramus to the scholar. But more
seriously Erasmus believed, as Saint Paul had said, that Christians must be "fools for
Christ." In effect, human existence is folly. Erasmus's Folly first made an observation
that Shakespeare would refine and make famous: "Now the whole life of mortal men,
what is it but a sort of play in which . . . [each person] plays his own part until the director gives him his cue to leave the stage."[16]

Erasmus's greatest contributions to European intellectual life were his edition of
and commentaries on the New Testament. His was a critical edition of the Greek text
and a Latin translation independent of the fourth-century Latin Vulgate of Jerome.
Unlike Jiménez, Erasmus corrected parts of the Vulgate. He rejected the authority of
tradition, saying, "The sin of corruption is greater, and the need for careful revision by
scholars is greater also, where the source of corruption was ignorance."[17] What was
revolutionary in his edition was his commentary, which emphasized the literal and

historical recounting of human experiences. Erasmus's Bible was the basis of later vernacular translations of Scripture during the Reformation.

Underlying Erasmus's scholarly output was what he called his "Philosophy of Christ." Erasmus was convinced that the true essence of Christianity was to be found in the life and actions of Christ. Reasonable, self-reliant, truly Christian people did not need superstitious rituals or magic. In his *Colloquies* he tells of a terrified priest who during a shipwreck promised everything to the Virgin Mary if only she would save him from drowning. But, Erasmus observed, it would have been more practical to start swimming!

Erasmus believed that a humanistic combination of classical and Christian wisdom could wipe away violence, superstition, and ignorance. Unlike More, Erasmus never abandoned the humanistic program. Yet his philosophy of Christ, based on faith in the goodness and educability of the individual, was swamped in the 1520s and 1530s by the sectarian claims of both Protestants and Catholics. Although Erasmus's New Testament was influential in the Reformation, his calls for reforms based on tolerance and reason were not.

Renaissance Art in the North

In the early fifteenth century, while Brunelleschi and Masaccio were revolutionizing the ways in which Italian artists viewed their world, artists north of the Alps, especially in Flanders, were making equally striking advances in the ways they painted and sculpted. Artistic innovation in northern Europe began with changes tied closely to the world of northern courts; only later did artists take up the styles of the Italian Renaissance. Northerners took Italian Renaissance art and fit it to a new environment.

Northern art of the late fourteenth and fifteenth centuries changed in two significant ways. In sculpture the long, austere, unbroken vertical lines typical of Gothic sculpture gave way to a much more complex and emotional style. In painting Flemish artists moved from ornate, vividly colored paintings to experiments with ways to create a sense of depth. Artists strove to paint and sculpt works that more faithfully represented reality. The sculptures of Claus Sluter (1350–1406), carved for a family chapel of the Burgundian dukes at Champmol, captured a lifelike drama unlike the previous Gothic sculpture. Court painters such as Jan van Eyck (ca. 1390–1441), in miniatures, portraits, and altar paintings, also moved away from a highly formalized style to a careful representation of specific places. In van Eyck's portrait of the Italian banker and courtier Giovanni Arnolfini and his bride, the image of the painter is reflected in a small mirror behind the couple, and above the mirror is written, "Jan van Eyck was here, 1434." Whereas Italians of the early fifteenth century tried to re-create space through linear perspective, the Flemish used aerial perspective, softening colors and tones to give the illusion of depth.

The influence of Renaissance styles in the north of Europe dates from the reign of the French king Francis I (r. 1515–1547), when Italian artists in significant numbers traveled north. Francis invited Italian artists to his court—most notably Leonardo da Vinci, who spent his last years in France. The most influential of the Italian-style creations in France was doubtless Francis's château Fontainebleau, whose decorations contained mythologies, histories, and allegories of the kind found in the Italian courts. Throughout the sixteenth century Italianate buildings and paintings sprang up throughout Europe.

Van Eyck: The Arnolfini Wedding   *Careful observation of people and places was typical of the new art of both northern and southern Europe. Van Eyck seems to have re-created this scene to the smallest detail. His own image appears in the mirror on the wall.* (Reproduced by Courtesy of the Trustees, The National Gallery, London)

Perhaps the most famous artist who traveled to Italy, learned Italian techniques, and then transformed them to suit the environment of northern Europe was Albrecht Dürer of Nuremberg (1471–1528). Son of a well-known goldsmith, Dürer became a painter and toured France and Flanders learning the techniques popular in northern Europe. Then in 1494 he left Nuremberg on the first of two trips to Italy, during which he sketched Italian landscapes and studied the work of Italian artists, especially in Venice. What he learned in Italy, combined with the friendship of some of Germany's leading humanists, formed the basis of Dürer's works, which blended northern humanistic interests with the Italian techniques of composition and linear perspective. Dürer worked in charcoal, watercolors, and paints, but his influence was most widely spread through his numerous woodcuts covering classical and contemporary themes. His woodcut *Whore of Babylon,* prepared in the context of the debate over the reform of the church, is based on sketches of Venetian prostitutes completed during his first visit to Italy.

Numerous other artists and engravers traveled south to admire and learn from the great works of Italian artists. The engravings they produced and distributed back home made the southern innovations available to those who would never set foot in Italy. In fact, some now lost or destroyed creations are known only through the copies engraved by northern artists eager to absorb Italian techniques.

THE RENAISSANCE AND COURT SOCIETY

The educational reforms of the humanists and the innovations in the arts between 1300 and 1550 provided an opportunity for rulers and popes alike to use culture to define and celebrate their authority. Art, literature, and politics merged in the brilliant life of the Renaissance Italian courts, both secular and papal. To understand fully the Renaissance and its importance in the history of Europe, we need to examine the uses of culture by governments, specifically investigating the transformation of European ideas about service at court during the fourteenth and fifteenth centuries. We will take as a model the politics and cultural life at one noble court: the court of the Gonzaga family of Mantua. Then we will see how the Renaissance papacy melded the secular and religious aspects of art, culture, and politics in its glittering court in Rome. Finally, we will discuss the development of the idea of the Renaissance gentleman and courtier made famous by Baldassare Castiglione, who was reared at the Gonzaga court.

The Elaboration of the Court

The courts of northern Italy took an interest in the cultural and artistic innovations of the Renaissance artists and humanists inspired by classical civilization, and they closely imitated many of the values and new styles that were developing in the courts of northern Europe, such as the court of Burgundy. Throughout Europe attendance at court became increasingly important to members of the nobility as a source of revenue and influence. Kings and the great territorial lords were equally interested in drawing people to their courts as a way to influence and control the noble and the powerful.

Rulers in most parts of Europe instituted monarchical orders of knighthood to reward allies and followers. The most famous in the English-speaking world was the Order of the Garter, founded in 1349 by King Edward III. The orders were but one of the innovations in the organization of the court during the fourteenth and fifteenth centuries. The numbers of cooks, servants, huntsmen, musicians, and artists employed at court jumped dramatically in the late Middle Ages. In this expansion the papal court was a model for the rest of Europe. The popes at Avignon in the fourteenth century already had households of nearly six hundred persons. If all the bureaucrats, merchants, local officials, and visitors who continually swarmed around the elaborate papal court were also counted, the number grew even larger.

Courts were becoming theaters built around a series of widely understood signs and images that the ruler could manipulate. Culture was meant to reflect the reputation of the ruler. On important political or personal occasions, rulers organized jousts or tournaments around themes drawn from mythology. The dukes of Milan indicated the relative status of courtiers by inviting them to participate in particular hunts or jousts. They similarly organized their courtiers during feasts or elaborate entries into the towns and cities of their realms.

The late fourteenth and fifteenth centuries were periods of growth in the political and bureaucratic power of European rulers. The increasingly elaborate and sumptuous courts were one of the tools that rulers used to create a unified culture and ideology. At the court of the Gonzagas in Mantua, one of the most widely known of the fifteenth-century courts, the manipulation of Renaissance culture for political purposes was most complete.

**The Court
of Mantua**

The city of Mantua, with perhaps 25,000 inhabitants in 1500, was small compared with Milan or Venice—the two cities with which it was most commonly allied. Located in a rich farming region along the Po River, Mantua did not have a large merchant or manufacturing class. Most Mantuans were involved in agriculture and regional trade in foodstuffs. The town had been a typical medieval Italian city-state until its government was overthrown by the noble Bonacolsi family in the thirteenth century. The Bonacolsis in turn were ousted in a palace coup in 1328 by their former comrades, the Gonzagas, who ruled the city until 1627.

The Gonzagas faced problems typical of many of the ruling families in northern Italy. The state they were creating was relatively small, their right to rule was not very widely recognized, and their control over the area was weak. The first step for the Gonzagas was to construct fortresses and fortified towns that could withstand foreign enemies. The second step was to gain recognition of their right to rule. In 1329 they were named imperial vicars, or representatives in the region. Later, in 1432, they bought the title "marquis" from the emperor Sigismund for the relatively low price of £12,000—equivalent to a year's pay for their courtiers. By 1500 they had exchanged that title for the more prestigious "duke."

Presiding over a strategic area between the Milanese and Venetian states, the Gonzagas maintained themselves through astute diplomatic connections with other Italian and European courts and through service as well-paid mercenaries in the Italian wars of the fifteenth and sixteenth centuries. Marquis Lodovico (d. 1478) served the Venetians, the Milanese, the Florentines, and even the far-off Neapolitans. With considerable understatement, Lodovico concluded, "We have worn armor for a long time."

The family's reputation was enhanced by Gianfrancesco (d. 1444) and Lodovico, who brought the Renaissance and the new court style to Mantua. By 1500 as many as eight hundred or more nobles, cooks, maids, and horsemen may have gathered in the court. Critics called them idlers, "who have no other function but to cater to the tastes of the Duke." It was under the tutelage of the Gonzagas that Vittorino da Feltre created his educational experiment in Villa Giocosa, which drew noble pupils from throughout Italy. It would be hard to overestimate the value for the Gonzagas of a school that attracted sons of the dukes of Urbino, Ferrara, and Milan and of numerous lesser nobles. The family also called many artists to Mantua. Lodovico invited Antonio Pisano, called Pisanello (ca. 1415–1456), probably the most famous court artist of the fifteenth century. Pisanello created a series of frescoes on Arthurian themes for the Gonzaga palace. In these frescoes Lodovico is portrayed as a hero of King Arthur's Round Table.

The Gonzagas are best known for their patronage of art with classical themes. Leon Battista Alberti redesigned the façade of the Church of Sant'Andrea for the Gonzagas in the form of a Roman triumphal arch. The church, which long had been associated with the family, became a monument to the Gonzaga court just as the Arch of Constantine in Rome had celebrated imperial power a thousand years earlier. In the 1460s Lodovico summoned Andrea Mantegna (1441–1506) to his court. Trained in Padua and Venice, Mantegna was at that time the leading painter in northern Italy. His masterwork is the *Camera degli Sposi* (literally, "the room of the spouses"), completed in 1474. It features family portraits of Lodovico Gonzaga and his family framed in imitations of Roman imperial portrait medallions. One scene shows Lodovico welcoming his son, a newly appointed cardinal, back from Rome—proof to all of the new status of the Gonzagas.

The Gonzaga court, like most others, was both public and private. On the one hand, finances for the city, appointments to public offices, and important political decisions were made by the men who dominated the court. On the other hand, as the prince's domestic setting, it was a place where women were expected to be seen and could exert their influence. Women were thus actively involved in creating the ideology of the court. Through the patronage of classical paintings, often with moral and political messages, wives of princes helped make the court better known and more widely accepted throughout Italy and Europe.

The arrival of Isabella d'Este (1494–1539) at court as the wife of Francesco Gonzaga marked the high point of the Renaissance in Mantua. Isabella had received a classical education at Ferrara and maintained an interest in art, architecture, and music all her life. As a patron of the arts, she knew what she wanted. Isabella was also an accomplished musician, playing a variety of string and keyboard instruments. She and others of the Gonzaga family recruited Flemish and Italian musicians to their court. By the end of the sixteenth century Mantua was one of the most important musical centers of Europe. One festival brought twelve thousand visitors to the city. Later it would be in Mantua that Claudio Monteverdi (1567–1643) wrote works that established the genre of opera.

In the fourteenth century Petrarch had complained that however enjoyable feasting in Mantua might be, the place was dusty, plagued by mosquitoes, and overrun with frogs. By the end of the fifteenth century the Gonzagas had secured for themselves and their city a prominent place on the Italian, and the European, stage.

| The Renaissance Papacy | The issues of power and how it is displayed had religious as well as secular dimensions. After its fourteenth- and fifteenth-century struggles over jurisdiction, the papacy found itself reduced in many respects to the status of an Italian Renaissance court. But popes needed to defend their primacy within the church from conciliarists, who had argued that all Christians, including the pope, were bound to obey the commands of general councils. The ideological focus of the revived papacy was Rome. |

The first step in the creation of a new Rome was taken by Pope Nicholas V (r. 1446–1455), a cleric who had spent many years in the cultural environment of Renaissance Florence. Hoping to restore Rome and its church to their former glory, Nicholas and his successors patronized the arts, established a lively court culture, and sponsored numerous building projects. Nicholas was an avid collector of ancient manuscripts that seemed to demonstrate the intellectual and religious primacy of Rome. He invited numerous artists and intellectuals to the papal court, including the Florentine architect and writer Leon Battista Alberti (1404–1472). On the basis of his research in topography and reading done in Rome, Alberti wrote his treatise *On Architecture* (1452), the most important work on architecture produced during the Renaissance. It was probably under Alberti's influence that Nicholas embarked on a series of ambitious urban renewal projects in Rome, which included bridges, roads, and a rebuilt Saint Peter's Basilica.

The transformation of Rome had an ideological purpose. As one orator proclaimed, "Illuminated by the light of faith and Christian truth, [Rome] is destined to be the firmament of religion . . . , the secure haven for Christians."[18] Thus the papal response to critics was to note that Rome and its government were central to political and religious life in Christendom. By reviving the style and organization of classical antiquity, the church sought to link papal Rome to a magnificent imperial tradition reaching back to Augustus and even to Alexander the Great. To papal supporters only one authority could rule the church. Early tradition and the continuity of the city itself, they assumed, demonstrated papal primacy.

One particular monument in Rome captures most vividly the cultural, religious, and ideological program of the papacy: the Sistine Chapel in the Vatican Palace. The chapel is best known for the decoration of the ceiling by the Florentine artist Michelangelo (see page 384) and for the striking images in his painting of the Last Judgment. The chapel, however, was commissioned by Pope Sixtus IV in 1475. It was to be an audience chamber in which an enthroned pope could meet the representatives of other states. In addition, it was expected that the college of cardinals would gather in the chapel for the election of new popes.

The decorations done before Michelangelo painted the ceiling reflect the intellectual and ideological values that Sixtus hoped to transmit to the churches and governments of Christendom. Along the lower sidewalls are portraits of earlier popes, a feature typical of early Roman churches. More significant are two cycles of paintings of the lives of Moses and Christ, drawing parallels between them. To execute the scenes Sixtus called to Rome some of the greatest artists of the late fifteenth century: Sandro Botticelli, Domenico Ghirlandaio, Luca Signorelli, and Pietro Perugino. The works illustrate the continuity of the Old Testament and New Testament and emphasize the importance of obedience to the authority of God. The meaning is most obvious in Perugino's painting of Saint Peter receiving the keys to the Kingdom of Heaven from Christ. The allusion is to Matthew 16:18: "Thou art Peter and upon this rock I shall build my church." The keys are the symbol of the claim of the pope, as successor to Saint Peter, to have the power to bind and loose sinners and their punishments.

Directly across from Perugino's painting is Botticelli's *The Judgment of Corah*, which portrays the story of the opponent who challenged the leadership of Moses and Aaron while the Israelites wandered in the wilderness. Corah and his supporters, according to Numbers 16:33, fell live into Hell. Various popes recalled the fate of Corah and the rebels. The pope was bound to oppose the council, Pope Eugenius argued, "to save the people entrusted to his care, lest together with those who hold the power of the council above that of the papacy they suffer a punishment even more dire than that which befell Corah."[19]

The effects of Renaissance revival were profound. Rome grew from a modest population of about 17,000 in 1400 to 35,000 in 1450. By 1517 the city had a population of over 85,000, five times its population at the end of the Great Schism. The papal program was a success. Rome was transformed from a provincial town to a major European capital, perhaps the most important artistic and cultural center of the sixteenth century. Visitors to the Sistine Chapel, like visitors to the papal city itself, were expected to leave with a profound sense of the antiquity of the papal office and of the continuity of papal exercise of religious authority. Because the building and decorating were being completed as the Protestant Reformation was beginning in Germany, some historians have criticized the expense of the political and cultural program undertaken by the Renaissance popes. But to contemporaries on the scene, the work was a logical and necessary attempt to strengthen the church's standing in Christendom.

Castiglione and the European Gentleman

Renaissance ideas did not just spread in intellectual circles. They also were part of the transformation of the medieval knight into the early modern "gentleman." In 1528 Baldassare Castiglione (1478–1529) published *The Book of the Courtier*. The work, which describes the ideal behavior of a courtier, was based on Castiglione's own distinguished career serving in Italian courts. Set at the court of Urbino, the book chronicles a series of fictional discussions over the course of four nights in March 1507. Among the participants are the duchess of Urbino, Elizabeth Gonzaga; her lady-in-waiting; and a group of humanists, men of action, and courtiers. In four evenings members of the circle try to describe the perfect gentleman of court. In the process they debate the nature of nobility, humor, women, and love.

Castiglione describes, in many respects, a typical gathering at court, and the discourses reflect contemporary views of relations between men and women. The wives of princes were expected to be organizers of life at court but also paragons of domestic virtues. Thus in this book the women organize the discussion, and the men discuss. Although the women direct and influence the talk by jokes and short interventions, they cannot afford to dominate the debate: "[Women] must be more circumspect, and more careful not to give occasion for evil being said of them . . . for a woman has not so many ways of defending herself against false calumnies as a man has."[20]

The topics of such discussions were not randomly chosen. Castiglione explains that he wished "to describe the form of courtiership most appropriate for a gentleman living at the courts of princes." Castiglione's popularity was based on his deliberate joining of humanistic ideas and traditional chivalric values. Although his topic is the court with all its trappings, he tells his readers that his models for the discussion were Greek and Latin dialogues, especially those of Cicero and Plato. As a Platonist he believed that all truly noble gentlemen have an inborn quality of "grace." It has to be brought out, however, just as Michelangelo freed his figures from stone. Castiglione held that all moral and courtly virtues exist in tension with their opposites: "no magnanimity without pusillanimity." With numerous examples of good and bad in the world, wisdom can be revealed only through careful imitation, for like the classical authors favored by humanists, Castiglione advises, "He who lacks wisdom and knowledge will have nothing to say or do."[21]

What struck Castiglione's readers most was his advice about behavior. Francesco Guicciardini of Florence once remarked, "When I was young, I used to scoff at knowing how to play, dance, and sing, and other such frivolities. . . . I have nevertheless seen from experience that these ornaments and accomplishments lend dignity and reputation even to men of good rank."[22] Guicciardini's comment underlines the value that readers found in Castiglione's work. Grace may be inbred, but it must be brought to the attention of those who control the court. Courtiers should first of all study the military arts. They have to fight, but only on occasions when their prowess will be noticed. Castiglione adds practical advice about how to dress, talk, and participate in music and dancing: never leap about wildly when dancing as peasants might, but dance only with an air of dignity and decorum. Castiglione further urges the courtier to be careful in dress: the French are "overdressed"; the Italians too quickly adopt the most recent and colorful styles. Reflecting political as well as social realities, Castiglione advises black or dark colors, which "reflect the sobriety of the Spaniards, since external appearances often bear witness to what is within."

According to Castiglione, the courtier must take pains "to earn that universal regard which everyone covets." Too much imitation and obvious study, however, lead to affectation. Castiglione counsels courtiers to carry themselves with a certain diffidence or unstudied naturalness (*sprezzatura*) covering their artifice. Accomplished courtiers should exhibit "that graceful and nonchalant spontaneity (as it is often called) . . . so that those who are watching them imagine that they couldn't and wouldn't even know how to make a mistake." Thus Castiglione's courtier must walk a fine line between clearly imitated and apparently natural grace.

Castiglione's book was an immediate success and widely followed even by those who claimed to have rejected it. By 1561 it was available in Spanish, French, and English translations. The reasons are not difficult to guess. It was critical for the courtier "to win for himself the mind and favour of the prince," and even those who disliked music, dancing, and light conversation learned Castiglione's arts "to open the way to the favour of princes." Many of the courtly arts that Castiglione preached had been traditional for centuries. Yet Castiglione's humanistic explanations and emphasis on form, control, and fashion had never seemed so essential as they did to the cultured gentlemen of the courts of the Renaissance and early modern Europe.

IMPORTANT EVENTS

1304–1314 Giotto paints Arena Chapel in Padua

1345 Petrarch discovers Cicero's letters to Atticus

1348–1350 Boccaccio, *The Decameron*

1393–1400 Chaucer, *The Canterbury Tales*

1401 Ghiberti wins competition to cast baptistery doors, Florence

1405 Christine de Pizan, *The Book of the City of the Ladies*

1427 Unveiling of Masaccio's *Trinity*

1434 Van Eyck, *The Arnolfini Wedding*

1440 Valla, *On the Donation of Constantine*

1440s Da Feltre establishes Villa Giocosa in Mantua

1450s Gutenberg begins printing with movable metal type

1460 Gonzaga invites Mantegna to Mantua

1475 Pope Sixtus IV orders construction of Sistine Chapel

1494 Dürer begins first trip to Venice

1511 Michelangelo, *David*

Erasmus, *The Praise of Folly*

1513 Machiavelli, *The Prince*

1516 More, *Utopia*

1527 Castiglione, *The Book of the Courtier*

NOTES

1. Quoted in J. B. Trapp, ed., *Background to the English Renaissance* (London: Gray-Mills Publishing, 1974), p. 11.
2. Quoted in N. Mann, *Petrarch* (Oxford: Oxford University Press), p. 67.
3. Petrarch, "On His Own Ignorance and That of Many Others," in *The Renaissance Philosophy of Man,* ed. Ernst Cassirer, Paul Oskar Kristeller, and John H. Randall (Chicago: University of Chicago Press, 1948), p. 105.
4. Quoted in Benjamin G. Kohl and Ronald G. Witt, *The Earthly Republic* (Philadelphia: University of Pennsylvania Press, 1978), p. 11.
5. Quoted in M. L. King, *Women of the Renaissance* (Chicago: University of Chicago Press, 1991), p. 194.
6. Quoted ibid., p. 222.
7. Quoted ibid., p. 198.
8. K. R. Bartlett, *The Civilization of the Italian Renaissance* (Lexington, Mass.: D. C. Heath, 1992), p. 314.
9. Quoted in *The Portable Machiavelli,* ed. and trans. Peter Bondanella and Mark Musa (New York: Penguin, 1979), p. 128.
10. Quoted ibid., p. 160.
11. Quoted in *The Notebooks of Leonardo da Vinci,* ed. J. P. Richter, vol. 1 (New York: Dover, 1883 and 1970), p. 14.
12. Quoted ibid., p. 129.
13. Giorgio Vasari, *The Lives of the Artists,* trans. George Bull (Baltimore: Penguin, 1965), p. 338.
14. Julia Bondanella and Mark Musa, eds., *The Italian Renaissance Reader* (New York: Meridian Books, 1987), p. 377.
15. I. Origo, *The Merchant of Prato: Francesco di Marco Datini, 1335–1410* (New York: Knopf, 1957), pp. 155–156.
16. Quoted in A. Rabil, Jr., *Renaissance Humanism: Foundations, Forms, and Legacy,* vol. 2 (Philadelphia: University of Pennsylvania Press, 1988), p. 236.
17. Quoted ibid., p. 229.
18. Raffaele Brandolini, quoted in Charles L. Stinger, *The Renaissance in Rome* (Bloomington: Indiana University Press, 1985), p. 156.
19. Quoted in Leopold D. Ettlinger, *The Sistine Chapel Before Michelangelo* (Oxford: Oxford University Press, 1965), p. 105.
20. Quoted in R. M. San Juan, "The Court Lady's Dilemma: Isabella d'Este and Art Collecting in the Renaissance," *Oxford Art Journal* 14 (1991): 71.
21. Unless otherwise noted, quotes from Castiglione are from Baldassare Castiglione, *The Book of the Courtier,* trans. George Bull (Baltimore: Penguin, 1967).
22. Quoted in R. W. Hanning and D. Rosand, eds., *Castiglione: The Ideal and the Real in Renaissance Culture* (New Haven, Conn.: Yale University Press, 1983), p. 17.

SUGGESTED READING

Brown, Alison. *The Renaissance.* 2d ed. 1999. An excellent short introduction to Renaissance art and culture designed for those with little or no background in the field.

Burke, Peter. *The European Renaissance: Centres and Peripheries.* 1998. A broad account of Renaissance cultural movements in Europe.

————. *The Fortunes of the Courtier: The European Reception of Castiglione's Cortegiano.* 1995. A well-written survey of the influence of Castiglione's ideas.

Goldthwaite, Richard. *Wealth and the Demand for Art in Italy, 1300–1600.* 1993. A thoughtful essay about the social and economic influences on the creation and patronage of art.

Goodman, A., and A. Mackay, eds. *The Impact of Humanism.* 1990. A volume of basic surveys of the arrival of Italian humanistic ideas in the various lands of Europe.

Hale, John R. *The Civilization of Europe in the Renaissance.* 1994. A beautifully written survey of the culture of Europe in the fifteenth to seventeenth centuries.

King, M. L. *Women of the Renaissance.* 1991. A survey of the social, economic, and cultural experience of women during the Renaissance.

Stinger, Charles L. *The Renaissance in Rome.* 1985. An engaging survey of the vibrant cultural life at the papal court and in the city during the Renaissance.

Welch, E. S. *Art and Society in Italy, 1350–1500.* 1997. A well-written, well-illustrated discussion of the social context in which artists worked.

Witt, R. G. *"In the Footsteps of the Ancients": The Origins of Humanism from Lovato to Bruni.* 2000. The definitive work on European humanism and the cultural connections between Italy and France.

13

European Overseas Expansion to 1600

veyotlıpan.

oncāqna qmacaq̃y

(Trans. no. V/C 31[2].
Courtesy Department of
Library Sciences, American
Museum of Natural
History)

Hernán Cortés's march in 1519 through the Valley of Mexico toward Tenochtitlán, the Aztec capital, was recorded not only in Spaniards' journals but also by local witnesses. In the native portrayal shown here, an elegantly garbed Mexica leader brings food and supplies to Cortés. Behind the adventurer are his own Spanish soldiers and his native allies. Many native peoples saw the Spanish as their defenders against the Aztecs, their harsh, recently arrived overlords. The woman standing next to Cortés is Malintzin (who later adopted the Spanish name Doña Marina). She was an Aztec noblewoman traded by her stepfather to the Maya and eventually given to Cortés. As a translator and interpreter, she was an essential ally during the conquest of Mexico.

The image, with its baskets of bread, meats, and fodder, is part of a pictograph telling the story of Cortés in the Nahuatl language of the Mexica peoples. The arrival of the Spanish began a cultural exchange between the Spanish and the peoples of the Americas that was more complex than even they initially imagined. The picture captures the contradictory aspects of European contact with Asia and the Americas. Europeans called it discovery, but they were entering sophisticated, fully functioning political and cultural worlds. Doña Marina's presence also reminds us of a more general truth—that without allies, pilots, and interpreters among the native peoples, Europeans would have been lost both in the New World and in the Old.

Cortés's meeting with the Mexica peoples was part of a program of European overseas expansion that began in the last decade of the fifteenth century and would eventually carry Europeans to every part of the world. It would change how Europeans thought of themselves and how they understood their own connections to the rest of the world. Their expansion unified the "Old World" continents of Asia, Africa, and Europe with a "New World"—the Americas and the islands of the Pacific. Accounts of contacts between the Old World and the New are influenced, perhaps more than any other episode of Western history, by the perspectives of the writers and the readers.

Those who focus on the transfer of European religion and culture view exploration and settlement as marking the creation of a new world with new values. However, the descendants of the native peoples who greeted the newly arriving Europeans—the Amerindians and the Aborigines, Maori, and Polynesians of the Pacific islands—remind us that the outsiders brought modern warfare and epidemic diseases that virtually destroyed indigenous cultures.

Spain sent its explorers west because the Portuguese already controlled the eastern routes to Asia around the African coast and because certain technological innovations made long open-sea voyages possible. Thus, as those who celebrate European expansion have said, the story includes national competition, the development of navigational techniques, and strategic choices.

Finally, the Europeans overthrew the great empires of the Aztecs and the Inca, but the transfer of European culture was never as complete as the Europeans thought or expected. As our image suggests, the language and customs of the conquered peoples, blanketed by European language and law, survived, though the lands colonized by the Europeans would never again be as they had been before their encounter with the Old World.

THE EUROPEAN BACKGROUND, 1250–1492

By 1400 Europeans already had a long history of connections with Africa and Asia. They regularly traded with Arabs in North Africa, traveled through the Muslim lands on the eastern edge of the Mediterranean, and eventually reached India, China, and beyond. After 1400, however, Europeans developed the desire and the ability to travel overseas to distant lands in Africa and Asia. Three critical factors behind the exploratory voyages of the fifteenth and early sixteenth centuries were technology, curiosity and interest, and geographic knowledge. A series of technological innovations made sailing far out into the ocean less risky and more predictable than it had been. The writings of classical geographers, myths and traditional tales, and merchants' accounts of their travels fueled popular interest in the East and made ocean routes to the East seem safe and reasonable alternatives to overland travel.

| Lands Beyond Christendom | Medieval Europeans knew there were lands to their west. Irish monks and Norse settlers traveled there. Indeed, by the late ninth century Norse sailors, primarily Norwegians, had con- |

structed boats combining oars and sails with strong-keeled hulls, which they used to travel to Iceland, Greenland, and eventually Vinland—the coast of Labrador and New-foundland. The Norse traveled in families. A woman named Gudridr gave birth to a son in North America before returning to Iceland and eventually going on a pilgrimage to Rome. Although the settlements in North America and Greenland ultimately failed, the Norse were followed by English, French, and Spanish fishermen who regularly visited the rich fishing grounds off North America.

The Greeks and Romans had cultivated contacts with the civilizations of Asia and Africa, and despite the nation-building focus of the Middle Ages, interest in the lands beyond Christendom had never been lost. In the thirteenth and fourteenth centuries European economic and cultural contacts with these lands greatly increased. The rising volume of trade between Europe and North Africa brought with it information about the wealthy African kingdoms of the Niger Delta. The Mongols in the thirteenth century allowed European merchants and missionaries to travel along trade routes extending all the way to China, opening regions formerly closed to them by hostile Muslim governments.

Trade in the Mediterranean also kept Christians and Muslims, Europeans and North Africans in close contact. Europeans sold textiles to Arab traders, who carried them across the Sahara to Timbuktu, where they were sold for gold bullion from the ancient African kingdoms of Ghana and Mali, located just above the Niger River. European chroniclers recorded the pilgrimage to Mecca of Mansa Musa, the fabulously wealthy fourteenth-century emperor of Mali. Italian merchants tried unsuccessfully to trade directly with the African kingdoms, but Muslim merchants prevented any permanent contact.

Europeans enjoyed more successful trade connections farther east. The discovery in London of a brass shard inscribed with a Japanese character attests to the breadth of connections in the early fourteenth century. After the rise of the Mongols, Italian merchants regularly traveled east through Constantinople and on to India and China. By the fourteenth century they knew how long travel to China might take and the probable expenses along the way. European intellectuals also maintained an interest in the lands beyond Christendom. They had read the late classical and early medieval authors who described Africa, the Indies, and China.

The work of the greatest of the classical geographers, Ptolemy of Alexandria (ca. A.D. 127–145), was known only indirectly until the early fifteenth century, but medieval thinkers read avidly and speculated endlessly about the information contained in the works of authors from Late Antiquity. For instance, one author reported that snakes in Calabria, in isolated southern Italy, sucked milk from cows and that men in the right circumstances became wolves—the earliest mention of werewolves. By the twelfth century fictitious reports circulated widely in the West of a wealthy Christian country in the East or possibly in Africa. Chroniclers at that time talked of Prester John, who some thought was a wealthy and powerful descendant of the Magi, the wise men from the East who Scripture says visited the baby Jesus. The legend of the kingdom of Prester John probably reflects some knowledge of the Christian groups living near the shrine of Saint Thomas in India or the kingdom of Ethiopia. In the fifteenth century European Christians looked to Prester John for aid against the rising Turkish empire.

Tales of geographic marvels are epitomized by *The Travels of Sir John Mandeville*, a book probably written in France but purporting to be the observations of a knight from St. Albans, just north of London. Mandeville says that he left England in 1322 or 1323 and traveled to Constantinople, Jerusalem, Egypt, India, China, Persia, and Turkey. Sir John describes the islands of wonders, inhabited by dog-headed humans, one-eyed giants, headless men, and hermaphrodites. Less fantastically, Mandeville reports that the world could be, and in fact had been, circumnavigated. He adds that the lands south of the equator, the Antipodes, were habitable.

More reliable information became available in the thirteenth century, largely because of the arrival of the Mongols. Jenghiz Khan and his descendants created an empire that reached from eastern Hungary to China (see page 289). This *pax Mongolica*, or area of Mongol-enforced peace, was a region in which striking racial and cultural differences were tolerated. In the 1240s and 1250s a series of papal representatives traveled to the Mongol capital at Karakorum near Lake Baikal in Siberia. The letters of these papal ambassadors, who worked extensively to gain converts and allies for a crusade against the Turks, were widely read and greatly increased accurate knowledge about Asia. Other missionaries and diplomats journeyed to the Mongol court, and some continued farther east to India and China. By the early fourteenth century the church had established a bishop in Beijing.

Italian merchants followed closely on the heels of the churchmen and diplomats. The pax Mongolica offered the chance to trade directly in Asia and the adventure of visiting lands known only from travel literature. In 1262 Niccolo and Maffeo Polo embarked from Venice on their first trip to China. On a later journey they took Niccolo's son, Marco (1255–1324). In all they spent twenty-four years in China. Marco dictated an account of his travels to a Pisan as they both languished as prisoners of war in a Genoese jail in 1298. It is difficult to know how much of the text represents Marco's own observations and how much is chivalric invention by the Pisan. Some modern commentators have even speculated that Marco himself never traveled to China. His contemporaries, however, had no doubts. The book was an immediate success even among Venetians, who could have exposed any fraud. Christopher Columbus himself owned and extensively annotated a copy of Marco Polo's *Travels*, which combines a merchant's observations of ports, markets, and trade with an administrator's eye for people and organizations.

By 1300 a modest community of Italians had settled in China. By the late thirteenth and fourteenth centuries Italian traders were traveling directly to the East in search of Asian silks, spices, pearls, and ivory. They and other European merchants could consult the *Handbook for Merchants* (1340) compiled by the Florentine Francesco Pegalotti, which described the best roads, the most hospitable stopping points, and the appropriate freight animals for a trip to the East. Fragmentary reports of Europeans in the Spice Islands (also known as the Moluccas), Japan, and India indicate that many Europeans other than merchants traveled simply for the adventure of visiting new lands.

Navigational Innovations

The invention of several navigational aids in the fourteenth and fifteenth centuries made sailing in open waters easier and more predictable. Especially important was the fly compass, consisting of a magnetic needle attached to a paper disk (or "fly"). The simple compass had been invented in China and was known in Europe by the late twelfth century, but because it was not initially marked off in degrees, it was only a rudimentary aid to navigation. By 1500 astrolabes and other devices enabling sailors to use the positions of the sun and stars to assist in navigation had also become available. An astrolabe allowed sailors to measure the altitude of the polestar in the sky and thereby calculate the latitude, or distance north or south of the equator, at which their ship was sailing. Still, until the general adoption of charts marked with degrees of latitude, most navigators relied on the compass, experience, and instinct—dead reckoning.

The most common Mediterranean ship of the late Middle Ages was a galley powered by a combination of sails and oars. Such a vessel was able to travel quickly and easily along the coast, but it was ill-suited for sailing the open seas. Throughout the Mediterranean shipbuilders experimented with new designs, and during the fifteenth century the Portuguese and Spanish perfected the caravel and adapted the European full-rigged ships. Large, square sails efficiently caught the wind and propelled these ships forward, and smaller triangular sails (lateens) allowed them to tack diagonally across a headwind, virtually sailing into the wind.

By the 1490s the Portuguese and Spanish had developed the ships and techniques that would make long open-sea voyages possible. What remained was for Europeans, especially the Portuguese and Spanish, to conclude that such voyages were both necessary and profitable.

The Revolution in Geography

The situation changed significantly over the course of the fourteenth century. With the conversion of the Mongols to Islam, the breakdown of Mongol unity, and the subsequent rise of the Ottoman Turks, the highly integrated and unusually open trade network fell apart. The caravan routes across southern Russia, Persia, and Afghanistan were abruptly closed to Europeans. Western merchants once again became dependent on Muslim middlemen.

The reports of travelers, however, continued to circulate long after the trade routes shut down, contributing to a veritable revolution in geography in the decades before the Portuguese and Spanish voyages.

In 1375 Abraham Cresques, a Jewish mathematician from the Mediterranean island of Majorca, produced what has come to be known as the *Catalan World Atlas*. He combined the traditional medieval *mappa mundi* (world map) with a Mediterranean *portolan*. The mappa mundi often followed the O-T form—that is, a circle divided into three parts representing Europe, Africa, and Asia, the lands of the descendants of Noah. Jerusalem—the heart of Christendom—was always at the center of the map. What the map lacked in accuracy, it made up in symbolism. The portolan, in contrast, was entirely practical. Sailors valued it because of its accurate outline of coasts, complete with sailing instructions and reasonable portrayals of ports, islands, and shallows along with general compass readings. The *Catalan World Atlas* largely holds to the portolan tradition but has more correct representations of the lands surrounding the Mediterranean.

In the fifteenth century, following Ptolemy's suggestions, mapmakers began to divide their maps into squares marking lines of longitude and latitude. This format made it possible to show with some precision the contours of various lands and the relationships between landmasses. Numerous maps of the world were produced in this period. The culmination of this cartography was a globe constructed for the city of Nuremberg in 1492, the very year Columbus set sail. From these increasingly accurate maps it has become possible to document the first exploration of the Azores, the Cape Verde Islands, and the western coast of Africa.

After his voyages Columbus observed that maps had been of no use to him. True enough. But without the accumulation of knowledge by travelers and the mingling of that knowledge with classical ideas about geography, it is doubtful whether Columbus or the Portuguese seaman Vasco da Gama would have undertaken—or could have found governments willing to support—the voyages that so dramatically changed the relations between Europe and the rest of the world.

PORTUGUESE VOYAGES OF EXPLORATION, 1350–1515

Portugal, a tiny country on the edge of Europe, for a short time led the European overseas expansion. Portuguese sailors were the first Europeans to perfect the complex techniques of using the winds and currents of the South Atlantic, especially along the western coast of Africa. Portugal's experience reflects the range of options open to Europeans as they extended their influence into new areas. As the Portuguese moved down the African coast, and later as they tried to compete commercially in Asia, they adapted traditional Mediterranean cultural and commercial attitudes to fit the new environment in which they found themselves. In some areas the Portuguese created networks of isolated naval and trading stations to control the movement of goods. In other areas they attempted to create substantial colonies, inhabited by Portuguese settlers. In still other areas they introduced plantation slavery to create commercial products for the international market. Spain and the other European states would use these same strategies in Asia and the New World as they expanded their economic and political interests overseas.

The Early Voyages   Portugal, like other late medieval European states, hoped that exploration and expansion would lead to "gold and Christians." The search for Christians was accelerated in the fifteenth century by the growing power of the Ottoman Turks. Europeans increasingly desired an alliance with the mythical Christian kingdoms of the East to open a second front against the militant Turks. Further, rediscovering the "lost" Christians and reclaiming Jerusalem fed Christian expectations that they were living in the last days before Christ's return.

For the Portuguese, facing the Atlantic and insulated from a direct Turkish threat, the lure of gold was always mixed with their religious motives. The nearest source of gold was well known to late medieval Christians: the African kingdoms of the Niger Delta. The problem for European traders and their governments was that commercial contacts with this wealthy region remained controlled by the Muslim Berber merchants

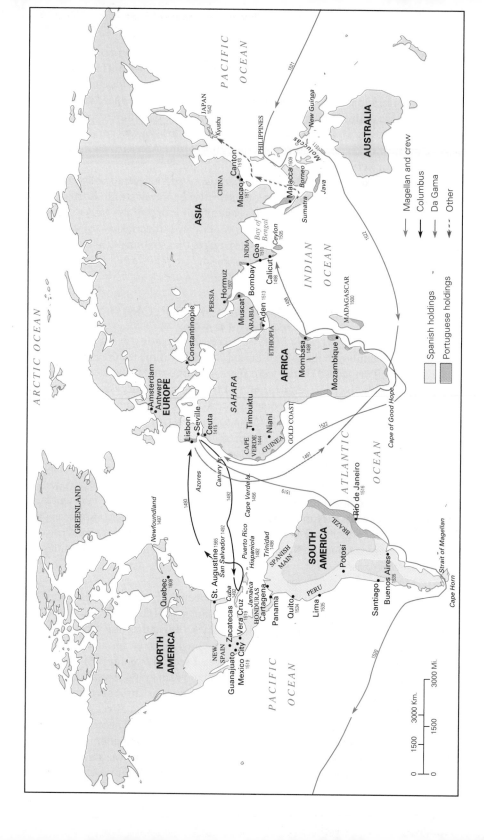

ARCTIC OCEAN

GREENLAND

NORTH
AMERICA

Newfoundland
1497

Quebec
1608

St. Augustine 1565
San Salvador 1492
Puerto Rico
1492
Hispaniola
1492
Cuba
1492
Jamaica
1492

NEW
SPAIN
Guanajuato Zacatecas Vera Cruz
Mexico City 1519
1519

HONDURAS
Cartagena

Panama

Quito
1534

PERU
Lima
1535

Santiago
1535

PACIFIC

OCEAN

1493
1492

Azores

Canary Is.

Cape Verde Is.
1456

SPANISH
MAIN

Trinidad
1498

1519

Buenos Aires
1535

SOUTH
AMERICA

Potosí

BRAZIL

Rio de Janeiro
1516

ATLANTIC

OCEAN

1497

1522

Cape of Good Hope

Strait of Magellan

Cape Horn

1520

EUROPE

Amsterdam
Antwerp

Lisbon
Seville
Ceuta
1415

Constantinople

SAHARA

CAPE
VERDE

Timbuktu
1444

Niani

GUINEA

GOLD COAST

Timbuktu

AFRICA

ETHIOPIA

Mombasa
1498

Mozambique

MADAGASCAR
1500

PERSIA

Hormuz
1507

Muscat

ARABIA

Aden 1513

Bombay

Goa 1510

Calicut
1498

INDIA

Ceylon
1505

Bay of
Bengal

INDIAN

OCEAN

ASIA

CHINA

Macao
1557

Canton
1513

JAPAN
1542

Kyushu

PHILIPPINES

Malacca 1511

Sumatra

Borneo

Java

Moluccas

New Guinea

1521

1522

AUSTRALIA

PACIFIC

OCEAN

Magellan and crew
Columbus
Da Gama
Other

Spanish holdings

Portuguese holdings

0   1500   3000 Km.

0   1500   3000 Mi.

of North Africa. The Portuguese and Spanish hoped to break the monopoly by taking control of the North African coast or by means of a flanking movement along the western coast of Africa.

Actual exploration of the Atlantic had begun long before Europeans recognized the extent of the Turkish threat. By 1350 the Madeiras and the Canaries, groups of islands off the western coast of Africa, regularly were included on European maps. By about 1365 Portuguese, Spanish, and probably French sailors were visiting the Canary Islands. By 1400 the Azores, a chain of islands one-third of the way across the Atlantic, were known and from early in the fifteenth century were routine ports of call for Portuguese ships. These voyages were no mean feat, calling for sophisticated ocean sailing out of sight of land for weeks at a time.

In the second decade of the fifteenth century the Portuguese expansion began in earnest with the capture of the Muslim port of Ceuta on the coast of Morocco. From then on, the Portuguese, led by Prince Henry "the Navigator" (1394–1460), younger son of King John I (r. 1385–1433), moved steadily down the western coast of Africa. Contemporaries reported that Prince Henry was intent on reaching the "River of Gold"—that is, the Gold Coast of Africa and the Niger Delta. To accomplish this, he directed efforts to colonize the Canaries (which eventually were lost to the Spanish), the Azores, and Madeira, the largest of the Madeira Islands. He also sponsored a series of expeditions down the African coast, reaching Senegal and the Cape Verde Islands by 1444. The Portuguese quickly established trading stations in the region and soon were exporting gold and slaves to Lisbon.

The islands off the coast of Africa were uninhabited, except for the Canaries, which the Portuguese tried unsuccessfully to keep from the Spanish. Thus the Portuguese could not merely plant trading communities within a larger population, for the Azores and Madeira had no native population. As a result, by the early 1440s the Portuguese were bringing sheep, seed, and peasants to these hitherto unoccupied islands, and the Crown was granting extensive lordships to encourage reluctant nobles to relocate to the Azores. The islanders survived largely by exporting sheep and grain to Iberia.

A significant transformation occurred on Madeira in the 1440s, when the Portuguese introduced sugar cane to the island. Sugar production was capital- and labor-intensive. A great many workers were needed to cut the cane, and expensive mills and lengthy processing were required to extract and produce sugar. On Madeira most of the work was done by Portuguese peasants. But when the Portuguese extended sugar cultivation to the newly discovered and colonized Cape Verde Islands in the 1460s, they found that Portuguese peasants would not work voluntarily in the sultry equatorial climate. Soon the Portuguese introduced a slave-based plantation system to maximize production and profits.

Slaves imported from the Black Sea areas had been used in agriculture since the introduction of sugar cultivation into the Mediterranean in the thirteenth century. The Portuguese had been trading in slaves along the western coast of Africa since the

World Exploration, 1492–1535

The voyages of Columbus, da Gama, and Magellan charted the major sea-lanes that became essential for communication, trade, and warfare for the next three hundred years.

1440s—the date from which black slaves appear in Lisbon. African slaves, along with slaves from northern and eastern Europe, could be found in Italy and throughout the Mediterranean in the fifteenth century, most often as domestics or laborers in small enterprises. Not since Roman times, however, had slave-based industries developed on the scale of the Portuguese sugar plantations. Sugar production in the New World would be modeled on the plantation system perfected by the Portuguese on their island colonies in the Atlantic.

The Search for a Sea Route to Asia   Until the middle of the fifteenth century the Niger Delta remained the focus of Portuguese interest. Only after securing control of the western coast of Africa did the Portuguese look seriously at sailing around Africa and discovering a sea route to Asia.

The fifteenth-century sailors who first tried to sail down the coast of Africa faced enormous difficulties. Water and wind currents tend to move in clockwise and counterclockwise circles against which it is difficult for a sail-powered ship to make progress. Winds near the equator generally blow from the east; farther north and south, the westerlies prevail. Some zones, in certain seasons, are pockets of stillness—called doldrums—with few breezes to propel ships. A navigator had to find winds and currents moving in the direction he wished to travel. Sailing directly from port to port was virtually impossible.

Knowledge of winds and currents allowed Bartholomeu Dias (1450?–1500) to explore the coast of southern Africa in 1487. He followed the traditional Portuguese routes until southeasterly winds forced him to sail south and west, almost to the Brazilian and Argentine coasts. Then he was able to ride the westerlies well past the southern tip of Africa, where he turned north. On his return he sighted what he called the "Cape of Storms," later renamed the "Cape of Good Hope" by the Portuguese king. Dias had perfected the techniques for searching out currents in the Southern Hemisphere and opened the way to India.

A decade after Dias's return from the Cape of Good Hope, Vasco da Gama (1460?–1524) set sail on a voyage that would take him to Calicut on the western coast of India. Using the information gathered from countless navigators, travelers, and even spies sent into East Africa, da Gama set sail in 1497 with four square-rigged, armed caravels and over 170 men. He had been provided with maps and reports that indicated what he might expect to find along the eastern coast of Africa. He also carried textiles and metal utensils, merchandise of the type usually traded along the western coast of Africa. This was a trading mission and in no sense a voyage of discovery.

Da Gama followed established routes beyond the Cape of Good Hope and into the Indian Ocean. He traveled up the coast until he reached Malindi in Mozambique, where he secured an Arab pilot who taught him the route to Calicut. Although the goods the Portuguese traders presented were not appropriate for the sophisticated Asian market, da Gama did manage to collect a cargo of Indian spices, which he brought back to Portugal, arriving in 1499. From that pioneering voyage until the Portuguese lost their last colonies in the twentieth century (Goa, 1961; Mozambique, 1975), Portugal remained a presence in the Indian Ocean.

The Portuguese in Asia   Trade in the Indian Ocean was nominally controlled by Muslims, but in fact a mixture of ethnic and religious groups—

Portuguese in India *This watercolor by a Portuguese traveler shows the varied peoples and customs and the great wealth to be found in India. Europeans were fascinated by all that seemed different from their own world.* (Biblioteca Casanatense, Rome. Photo: Humberto Nicoletti Serra)

including Muslims, Hindus, Chinese, Jains, and Nestorian Christians—participated in the movement of cottons, silks, and spices throughout the region. There were numerous small traders, as well as prosperous long-distance merchants with connections reaching into Central Asia, Africa, and China.

Less than a century before Vasco da Gama's arrival, the Chinese seaman Zheng He made a series of voyages into the Indian Ocean. In 1405 he led a huge armada of 317 ships and over 27,000 sailors on an expedition designed to expand the trade and political influence of Ming China. He would make six subsequent trips before a new emperor, intent on concentrating his resources on China's internal development, ended the ventures. With the retreat of the Chinese, trade returned to its previous patterns.

The hodgepodge of trade reflected the political situation. Vasco da Gama's arrival coincided with the rise of the Moguls, Muslim descendants of Jenghiz Khan. By 1530 they had gained control of most of northern India, and during the sixteenth century their influence increased in the south. The wealth and security of the Moguls depended on landed power. They generally left traders and trading ports to themselves. Throughout the sixteenth century the Moguls remained tolerant of India's religious, cultural, and economic diversity. Neither Muslim nor Hindu powers initially considered the Portuguese an unusual threat.

Asians may not have worried much about the Portuguese because at first there were so few of them. Vasco da Gama arrived with only three ships. And the subsequent fleet of Pedro Alvares Cabral carried only fifteen hundred men. In the 1630s, after more than a century of emigration, probably no more than ten thousand Portuguese were scattered from modern Indonesia to the east coast of Africa. In addition to government officials, Portuguese settlers were likely to be petty traders, local merchants, and poorly paid mercenaries.

The problem for the Portuguese was that their numbers were so few and their trade goods had so little value in sophisticated, highly developed Asian markets. In most cases they bought spices, textiles, and dyes with gold and silver brought from mines in central Europe and the New World. In response to this difficult situation, they created a seaborne "trading-post empire"—an empire based on control of trade rather than on colonization. It was, in fact, a model that fit well with their crusading experience in North Africa and their desire to push back Muslim control.

Portugal's commercial empire in the East was based on fortified, strategically placed naval bases. As early as Vasco da Gama's second expedition in 1502, the Portuguese bombarded Calicut and defeated an Arab fleet off the coast of India. This encounter set the stage for Portugal's most important imperial strategist, Alfonso d'Albuquerque (1453–1515), governor-general of Portuguese colonies in India. He convinced the monarchy that the key to dominance in the region was the creation of fortified naval bases commanding the Bay of Bengal and thereby controlling access to the coveted Spice Islands. By 1600 the Portuguese had built a network of naval bases that reached from Mozambique and Mombasa on the east coast of Africa to Goa on the west coast of India and the island of Macao off southeastern China.

The Portuguese established a royal trading firm, the Casa da India, to manage the booming market in cinnamon, ginger, cloves, mace, and a variety of peppers. Although their control was far from total, the Portuguese did become significant exporters of spices to Europe. More significant was the creation of the Portuguese Estado da India, or India office, to oversee Portuguese naval forces, administer ports, and regulate maritime trade. Under the Portuguese system all merchants were expected to acquire export licenses and to ship products through Portuguese ports. Asians often found it more convenient to cooperate than to resist, and most agreed to pay for export licenses and trade through Portuguese ports. They even found it expedient to ship in European-style vessels and to use Portuguese as the language of commerce.

Spanish Voyages of Exploration, 1492–1522

Spanish overseas expansion seems a logical continuation of the centuries-long Reconquista (see pages 285–286). In 1492 Castile was finally able to conquer the last Muslim kingdom of Granada and unify all of Iberia, with the exception of Portugal, under a single monarchy. Initially, in 1479, the Spanish kingdoms had agreed to leave the exploration and colonization of the African coast to the Portuguese, yet they watched nervously as the Portuguese expanded their African contacts. Portuguese successes led Castilians to concentrate their efforts on what came to be called the "Enterprise of the Indies"—that is, the conquest and settlement of Central and South America.

The sailing and exploring necessary to compete with the Portuguese produced critical information about ocean winds and currents and facilitated later voyages. They also established the basic approaches that the Spanish would follow in their exploration, conquest, and colonization of the lands where they dropped anchor.

| The Role of Columbus | The story of the enterprise begins with Christopher Columbus (1451–1506), a brilliant seaman, courtier, and self-promoter who has become a symbol of European expansion. Columbus, |

however, was not a bold pioneer who fearlessly did what no others could conceive of doing. He benefited from long-standing interests in the world beyond European shores.

Columbus was born into a modest family in Genoa and spent his early years in travel and in the service of the Castilian and Portuguese crowns. His vision seems to have been thoroughly traditional and medieval. He knew the medieval geographic speculations inherited from Arab and ultimately Classical Greek sources. Medieval seafarers did not fear a flat earth; rather, the concern was whether a ship could cover the vast distances necessary to sail west to Asia. Studying information in *Imago Mundi* (*Image of the World*, 1410), by the French philosopher Pierre d'Ailly (1350–1420), Columbus convinced himself that the distance between Europe and Asia was much less than it actually is. D'Ailly's estimate put the east coast of Asia within easy reach of the western edge of Europe. "This sea is navigable in a few days if the wind is favorable," d'Ailly concluded.

D'Ailly's theories seemed to be confirmed by the work of the Florentine mathematician Paolo Toscanelli. Columbus knew of Toscanelli's calculations and even revised them downward. From his own study he concluded that the distance from the west coast of Europe to the east coast of Asia was about 5,000 miles, instead of the actual 12,000. Columbus's reading of traditional sources put Japan in the approximate location of the Virgin Islands. (It is not surprising that Columbus remained convinced that the Bahamas were islands just off the coast of Asia.) When Amerindians told him of Cuba, he concluded that it "must be Japan according to the indications that these people give of its size and wealth."[1]

On the basis of first-century descriptions Columbus assured Spanish authorities that King Solomon's mines were only a short distance west of his newly discovered islands. In addition to finding the gold of Solomon, Columbus expected that by sailing farther west he could fulfill a series of medieval prophecies that would lead to the conversion of the whole world to Christianity. This conversion, he believed, would shortly precede the Second Coming of Christ. In Columbus's own view, then, his voyages were epochal not because they were ushering in a newer, more empirical world but because they signaled the fulfillment of history, God's plan for redemption.

Columbus's enthusiasm for the venture was only partially shared by the Spanish monarchs, Ferdinand and Isabella. Vasco da Gama had been well supplied with a flotilla of large ships and a crew of over 170 men, but Columbus sailed in 1492 with three small vessels and a crew of 90. Da Gama carried extra supplies and materials for trade and letters for the rulers he knew he would meet. Columbus had nothing similar in his sea chest. His commission did authorize him as "Admiral of Spain" to take possession of all he should find, but royal expectations do not seem to have been great.

Yet on October 12, about ten days later than he had expected, Columbus reached landfall on what he assumed were small islands in the Japanese chain. He had actually landed in the Bahamas. Because Columbus announced to the world that he had arrived in the Indies, the indigenous peoples have since been called "Indians" and the islands are called the "West Indies."

Columbus reported to the Spanish monarchs that the inhabitants on the islands were friendly and open to the new arrivals. He described a primitive, naked people eager, he believed, to learn of Christianity and European ways. Indeed, the Tainos, or Arawaks, whom he had misidentified, did live simple, uncomplicated lives. The islands easily produced sweet potatoes, maize, beans, and squash, which along with fish provided an abundant diet. Initially these people shared their food and knowledge with the newcomers, who they seem to have thought were sky-visitors.

The Spanish, for their part, praised the Tainos. The visitors generally believed that they had discovered a compliant, virtuous people who, if converted, would be exemplars of Christian virtues to Europeans. Columbus himself observed:

> They are very gentle and do not know what evil is; nor do they kill others, nor steal; and they are without weapons. They say very quickly any prayer that we tell them to say, and they make the sign of the cross, †. So your Highnesses ought to resolve to make them Christians.[2]

The Spanish authorities changed their opinion quickly. The settlers Columbus left at his fortress set an unfortunate example. They seized food stocks, kidnapped women, and embarked on a frenzied search for gold. Those who did not kill one another were killed by the Tainos.

During succeeding voyages, Columbus struggled to make his discoveries the financial windfall he had promised the monarchs. He was utterly unable to administer this vast new land. He quickly lost control of the colonists and was forced to allow the vicious exploitation of the island population. He and other Spanish settlers claimed larger and larger portions of the land and required the Indians to work it. Islands that easily supported a population of perhaps a million natives could not support those indigenous peoples and the Spanish newcomers and still provide exports to Spain. Scholars have estimated that the native population of the islands may have fallen to little more than thirty thousand by 1520, largely because of diseases (see pages 428–429). By the middle of the sixteenth century the native population had virtually disappeared.

Columbus remained convinced that he would find vast fortunes just over the horizon. But he found neither the great quantities of gold he promised nor a sea passage to Asia. With the islands in revolt and his explorations seemingly going nowhere, the Spanish monarchs stripped Columbus of his titles and commands. Once he was returned to Spain in chains. Even after his final transatlantic trip, he continued to insist that he had finally found either the Ganges River of India or one of the rivers that according to the Hebrew Bible flow out of the earthly paradise. Although Columbus died in 1506 rich and honored for his discoveries, he never gained all the power and wealth he had expected. He remained frustrated and embittered by the Crown's refusal to support one more voyage, during which he expected to find the mainland of Asia.

In 1501, after sailing along the coast of Brazil, the Florentine geographer Amerigo Vespucci (1451–1512) drew the obvious conclusion from the information collected by Columbus's explorations. He argued that Columbus had discovered a new continent unknown to the classical world. These claims were accepted by the German mapmaker Martin Waldseemüller, who in 1507 honored Amerigo's claim by publishing the first map showing "America."

Columbus's
Successors
Columbus's explorations set off a debate over which nations had the right to be involved in trade and expansion. Portuguese claims were based on a papal bull of 1481, issued by Pope Sixtus IV (r. 1471–1484), that granted Portugal rights to all lands south of the Canaries and west of Africa. After Columbus's return, the Spaniards lobbied one of Sixtus's successors, Alexander VI (r. 1492–1503), whose family, the Borgias, was from the kingdom of Aragon. In a series of bulls Pope Alexander allowed the Spanish to claim all lands lying 400 miles or more west of the Azores. Finally, in the Treaty of Tordesillas (1494), Spain and Portugal agreed that the line of demarcation between their two areas should be drawn 1,480 miles west of the Azores. The treaty was signed just six years before Pedro Alvares Cabral (1467–1520) discovered the coast of Brazil. Thus the Spanish unwittingly granted the Portuguese rights to Brazil.

Adventurers and explorers worried little about the legal niceties of exploration. Even as Columbus lay dying in 1506, others, some without royal permission, sailed up and down the eastern coasts of North and South America. Amerigo Vespucci traveled on Spanish vessels as far as Argentina, while Spanish explorers sailed among the islands of the Caribbean and along the coast of the Yucatán Peninsula. Vasco Nuñez de Balboa (1475–1519) crossed the Isthmus of Panama in 1513 and found the Pacific Ocean exactly where the natives living in the region said it would be.

The most important of the explorations that Columbus inspired was the voyage undertaken by Ferdinand Magellan in 1519. Although his motives are unclear, Magellan

Colonial Seaport
Travelers to the new world tried to convey what they saw as important about the lands they visited. In this image, the artist emphasizes a mercantile harbor and its connection to the interior.
(The Pierpont Morgan Library/ Art Resource, NY)

(1480?–1521) may have planned to complete Columbus's dream of sailing to the Indies. By the 1510s mariners and others understood that the Americas were a new and hitherto unknown land, but they did not know what lay beyond them or what distance separated the Americas from the Spice Islands of Asia. After sailing along the well-known coastal regions of South America, Magellan continued south, charting currents and looking for a passage into the Pacific. Late in 1520 he beat his way through the dangerous straits (now the Strait of Magellan) separating Tierra del Fuego from the mainland. These turbulent waters marked the boundary of the Atlantic and Pacific Oceans. It took almost four months to travel from the straits to the Philippines. The crew suffered greatly from scurvy and a shortage of water and at times had to eat the rats aboard ship to survive. One crew member reported, "We ate biscuit, which was no longer biscuit, but powder of biscuit swarming with worms, for they had eaten the good."[3] Nevertheless, Magellan managed to reach the Philippines by March 1521. A month later he was killed by natives.

Spanish survivors in two remaining ships continued west, reaching the Moluccas, or Spice Islands, where they traded merchandise that they had carried along for a small cargo of cloves. A single surviving ship continued around Africa and back to Spain, landing with a crew of 15 at Cádiz in September 1522, after a voyage of three years and the loss of four ships and 245 men. Magellan completed and confirmed the knowledge of wind and ocean currents that European sailors had been accumulating. One of his sailors wrote of him, "More accurately than any man in the world did he understand sea charts and navigation."[4] The way was now open for the vast expansion of Europeans and European culture into all parts of the world.

Spanish adventurers were not the only ones to follow in Columbus's wake. The French and the English concentrated their explorations farther north. Building on a tradition of fishing off the coast of Newfoundland, English sailors under the command of John Cabot (1450?–1499?) sighted Newfoundland in 1497, and later voyages explored the coast as far south as New England. Cabot initiated an intense period of English venturing that would lead to an unsuccessful attempt to found a colony on Roanoke Island in 1587 and eventually to a permanent settlement at Jamestown in 1607. French expeditions followed Cabot to the north. In 1534 Jacques Cartier (1491–1557) received a royal commission to look for a northern passage to the East. He was the first European to sail up the St. Lawrence River and began the process of exploration and trading that would lead to a permanent presence in Canada beginning in the early seventeenth century. But British and French settlements in the New World came later. The sixteenth century belonged to the Spanish.

SPAIN'S COLONIAL EMPIRE, 1492–1600

Spanish penetration of the New World was a far cry from the model of the Portuguese in Asia. The Spaniards established no complex network of trade and commerce, and no strong states opposed their interests. A "trading-post empire" could not have worked in the New World. To succeed, the Spaniards needed to colonize and reorganize the lands they had found.

Between 1492 and 1600 almost 200,000 Spaniards immigrated to the New World. "New Spain," as they called these newly claimed lands, was neither the old society transported across the ocean nor an Amerindian society with a thin veneer of Spanish and European culture. To understand the history of New Spain it is essential to grasp what it replaced, and how: the Spaniards overthrew two major civilizations and created new institutions in the wake of conquest. The whole story is not conquest and extermination—many of the Spanish attempted to secure fair treatment for the indigenous peoples who were now part of the Spanish Empire.

The Americas Before the European Invasion
The Spaniards and later their European peers entered a world vastly different from their own. It was a world formed by two momentous events—one geological, the other anthropological. The first was the creation of the continents of North and South America. The Americas, along with Africa and the Eurasian landmass, were once part of a single supercontinent. The breakup of this supercontinent left the Americas, Africa, and Eurasia free to evolve in dramatically different ways. The continental breakup occurred millions of years ago, long before the appearance of human beings and many other forms of mammalian life.

The second momentous event was the peopling of the Americas. Some migrants may have come over the seas. Most, though, arrived thanks to a temporary rejoining of the Americas to the Eurasian landmass by land and ice bridges that allowed Asians to cross over what is now the Bering Strait to the Americas in the period between 30,000 and 10,000 B.C. Their timing had a great impact. They arrived in the Americas long before the beginnings of the Neolithic agricultural revolution, which involved the domestication of numerous plants and animals. The agricultural revolution in the Americas occurred around 3000 B.C., perhaps six thousand years after similar developments in the Old World. The peoples of the Americas created complex societies, but those societies lacked large domesticated meat or pack animals (the llama was the largest), iron, other hard metals, and the wheel.

Nonetheless, by the time of Columbus's arrival, relatively populous societies were living throughout North and South America. Population estimates for the two continents range from 30 million to 100 million—the lower figure is probably more accurate. North America saw the development of complex Mound Builder societies in the East and along the Mississippi River and pueblo societies in the deserts of the American Southwest. But the greatest centers of Amerindian civilization were in central and coastal Mexico and in the mountains of Peru.

In the late fifteenth century, as the cultural collision approached, the two most powerful centers were the empires of the Aztecs and the Inca. When the collection of tribes now known as the "Aztec" (or Mexica) peoples appeared in central Mexico in the early fourteenth century, they found an already flourishing civilization concentrated around the cities and towns dotting the Valley of Mexico. Through conquest the Aztecs united the many Nahuatl-speaking groups living in the valley into a confederation centered in Tenochtitlán, a city of perhaps 200,000 people built on an island in Lake Texcoco. In early-sixteenth-century Europe only London, Constantinople, and Naples would have been as large as the Aztec capital. It literally rose out of the water of Lake Texcoco. Only Venice could have equaled the sight. The whole valley supported an unusually high

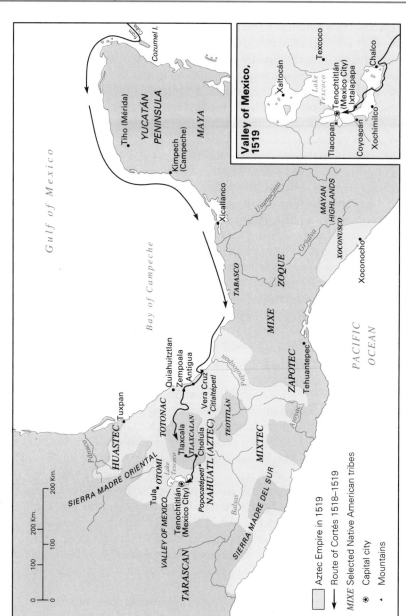

Mexico and Central America

The Valley of Mexico was a populous region of scattered towns, most of which were part of the Aztec Empire. As Cortés marched inland from Vera Cruz toward the valley, he passed through lands that for generations had been in an almost constant state of war with the Aztecs.

population of about a million. Using canals along the edge of the lake and other canals in Tenochtitlán itself, merchants easily moved food, textiles, gold and silver ornaments, jewels, and ceremonial feathered capes into the city markets. Spaniards later estimated that fifty thousand or more people shopped in the city on market days.

Religion was integral to the Aztecs' understanding of their empire. They believed that the world was finite and that they lived in the last of five empires. It was only regular human sacrifice to Huitzilopochtli that allowed the world to continue: the hearts of victims were necessary to sustain their god, to ensure that the sun would rise each morning. Thus life for the Aztecs required a relentless parade of death.

Tenochtitlán was the center of an imperial culture based on tribute. Towns and villages under Aztec control owed ongoing allotments of food and precious metals to the Aztecs. To emphasize that Aztec power and dominance were complete, the Aztecs not only collected vast quantities of maize, beans, squash, and textiles but demanded payment in everything down to centipedes and snakes. The most chilling tribute, however, was in humans for sacrifice. When the wars of expansion that had provided prisoners came to an end, the Aztecs and their neighbors fought "flower wars"—highly ritualized battles to provide prisoners to be sacrificed. Five thousand victims were sacrificed at the coronation of Moctezuma II (r. 1502–1520) in 1502. Even more, reportedly twenty thousand, were sacrificed at the dedication of the great temple of Huitzilopochtli in Tenochtitlán.

Aztec society maintained a perpetual state of war with the peoples beyond the mountains that ringed the Valley of Mexico—especially the people along the Caribbean

Aztec Warrior   *This water-color, by a Mexican artist who was trained in European painting, depicts a pre-Aztec ruler. The dress and the stone-edged sword would have been typical of the Aztecs, too.*
(Bibliothèque nationale de France)

coast. Given this constant state of war, plus the heavy burdens in tribute placed on the nearby subject cities, it is no wonder that the Aztecs were obsessed by the contingencies of life. At the end of each calendar cycle of fifty-two years, all fires in the empire were extinguished until fire-priests ascertained that the world would continue. And the Aztec world did continue until August 1523 (see page 424).

The other great Amerindian empire of the fifteenth century, the empire of the Inca, was also of recent origin. During the fifteenth century the Inca formed efficient armies and expanded their control beyond the central highlands of Peru. Fifteen thousand miles of roads and a sophisticated administrative system allowed the Inca to create a state that extended from modern-day Ecuador to Chile. As they expanded, they demanded political control and tribute but seem to have been tolerant of local traditions and language. The Inca perfected systems of irrigation and bridge-building initiated by earlier inhabitants of the region. The empire, centered on the city of Cuzco high in the mountains of Peru, was able to sustain a population that may have reached 10 million by the end of the fifteenth century.

Human sacrifice, though not unknown to the Inca people, was not an essential part of their religious life. Their state was unsettled, however, by increasingly harsh tax exactions. Under the Inca system the title Paca Inca, or "Great Inca," was inherited by the eldest son of the ruler's principal wife. The ruler's wealth, however, was retained by the rest of his family, who maintained the court as if the ruler still lived. Thus each new ruler needed money to finance the creation of an entirely new court, and taxes were not only high but continuously climbing.

Both great Amerindian empires, despite their brilliance, rested on uneasy conquests. Subject groups would be willing allies for any invader.

The Spanish Conquests   Hernán Cortés (1485–1546) was ambitious to make something of himself in the New World. Of a poor but aristocratic background from the Extremadura region of southwestern Spain, he had gone to the West Indies in 1504 to seek his fortune in the service of the governor of Cuba. The governor gave him a commission to lead an expeditionary force to investigate reports of a wealthy and prosperous mainland Indian civilization. From the beginning Spanish authorities seem to have distrusted Cortés's aims. In fact, he departed hastily from Cuba to evade formal notification that the governor had revoked his commission because of insubordination.

Cortés landed in Mexico at the site of the city he would name Vera Cruz ("True Cross") early in 1519 with a tiny command of five hundred men, sixteen horses, eleven ships, and a few pieces of artillery. Aided by a devastating outbreak of smallpox and Amerindian peoples happy to shake off Aztec control, Cortés and his troops managed to destroy the network of city-states dominated by the Aztecs of Tenochtitlán in two years and lay claim to the Valley of Mexico for the king of Spain. The manner in which Cortés explained and justified his mission can serve as a model against which to measure the adventures of other sixteenth-century Europeans in the Americas.

Cortés, like Machiavelli (see pages 378–379), believed in the power of truly able leaders (men of *virtù*) to overcome chance through bold acts. Even so, an attempt to capture a city of 200,000 with an army of 500 appears more foolhardy than bold. Cortés seems to have attempted it simply because he found himself with very little choice. With his commission revoked by the governor of Cuba, Cortés arrived on the mainland as a rebel against both the governor of Cuba and the king of Spain. He burned his ships in Vera Cruz harbor, making clear to all his men that there was no turning back. Much of what he did and said concerning the great Aztec Empire was an attempt to justify his initial act of insubordination and win back royal support. He quickly found allies among native groups who, for their own reasons, wished to see the Aztec Empire destroyed. The allied forces moved toward Tenochtitlán.

Cortés was greatly aided by fortune in the form of Malintzin, a Mexica woman who after her conversion to Christianity called herself Doña Marina (ca. 1501–1550). Malintzin was Cortés's interpreter and, later, his mistress. Without her, one of Cortés's followers recalled, "we could not have understood the language of New Spain and Mexico." Her story illustrates many of the complex interactions at play in sixteenth-century Mexico. Born a noble Aztec, she was sold by her stepfather and mother, ending up in the hands of the Maya. They gave her, along with twenty other women, to Cortés. Knowing both the Maya and Mexica languages, and quickly learning Spanish, she was the one person who could mediate between Spaniard and native. She changed her name to the Spanish Doña Marina and was baptized as a Christian. After bearing Cortés a son, she finished her life in Spain as the wife of a Spanish gentleman. Like many of the natives who felt no affection for the Aztecs of Tenochtitlán, she did not find it difficult to aid the Spaniards.

Despite the help of Malintzin and Spaniards who had previously lived with the natives, the meeting of Aztecs and Spaniards demonstrated the breadth of the chasm separating the Old World and the New. At first the Aztec king Moctezuma was unconcerned about the coming of the Spaniards. Later he seems to have attempted to buy them off. And finally he and his successors fought desperately to drive them out of Tenochtitlán. The Aztecs' indecision was caused in large part by the fact that in neither words nor gestures did the two groups speak the same language. Hearing that the Spaniards were on the march, Moctezuma sent ambassadors bearing gold, silver, and other costly gifts, which they presented in a most humble fashion to the Spaniards. To a modern ear the gifts sound like (and have often been interpreted to be) desperate attempts to buy off the invaders. To Cortés, or any European or Asian resident of the Old World, such gifts were a sign of submission. But to Moctezuma and most Amerindians the giving of gifts with great humility by otherwise powerful and proud people could be a show of wealth and status. Seen in that light, Moctezuma's lavish gifts and apparent humility were probably meant to demonstrate the superiority of his civilization, and Cortés's acceptance of the gifts seemed to indicate his recognition of his own inferior status.

Spaniards later claimed that Moctezuma was confounded by the sudden appearance of these peoples from the East. Cortés himself reported to the king of Spain that when he first met Moctezuma, the Aztec leader said, "We have always held that those who descended from [the god Quetzalcoatl] would come and conquer this land and take us as his vassals." Later Spaniards explained that the Aztecs believed that Quetzalcoatl, the serpent-god symbolically conquered by Huitzilopochtli, had traveled to the east, promising one day to return and reclaim his lands, thus ending Aztec rule. The Spaniards believed that Moctezuma's ambivalence toward them was rooted in his belief in that myth.

Neither story holds up in light of the evidence. There is no surviving preconquest source for Moctezuma's supposed confession, and the myth of the return of Quetzalcoatl was first recorded in Spanish, not Mexica, sources long after the conquest. In truth, neither Cortés nor historians can satisfactorily explain in Western terms Moctezuma's initial response to the Spaniards. Cortés took the Aztec leader captive in 1521 and began what would be a two-year battle to take control of the capital and its empire. Although weakened by the arrival of smallpox and other virulent Old World diseases, the Aztecs continued to fight even as more and more of the subject peoples joined the Spanish besiegers. The Spaniards cut off food and water to Tenochtitlán, but still the Aztecs fought.

Different understandings of the rules of war, different traditions of diplomacy, and different cultures prevented the Aztecs and Cortés from reaching any understanding. The peoples of the Valley of Mexico tried to take captives to be sacrificed in temples. The Spaniards, to Aztec eyes, killed indiscriminately and needlessly on the battlefield. Cortés later complained of the Aztecs' refusal to negotiate: "We showed them more signs of peace than have ever been shown to a vanquished people." Thus, to end a war that neither side could resolve in any other way, in August 1523 Cortés and his allies completely destroyed the garden city of Tenochtitlán.

Cortés's recurring insubordination was an unfortunate model. His own lieutenants later rebelled against his control and attempted to create their own governments as they searched for riches and El Dorado, a mythical city of gold. Later adventurers marched throughout the North American Southwest and Central and South America following rumors of hidden riches. Using private armies and torturing native peoples, veterans of Cortés's army and newly arrived speculators hoped to find wealth that would allow them to live like nobles on their return to Spain. Like Cortés, they claimed to be acting for the monarchy and the church, but in fact they expected that success would justify their most vicious acts.

Francisco Pizarro (1470–1541) was the most successful of the private adventurers. Poor and illegitimate at birth, he arrived in the Americas ambitious for riches and power. After serving in Balboa's army, participating in several slaving expeditions, and helping to found Panama City, Pizarro was prosperous but still not wealthy. Rumors of Inca wealth filtered through to Central America. Pizarro and a partner resolved in 1530 to lead an expedition down the west coast of South America in search of the Inca capital. Benefiting from disorganization caused by a smallpox epidemic and ensuing civil war, Pizarro was able to find local sympathizers.

Like Cortés, he used numerous Indian allies in his most important battles. Aided by Amerindians eager to throw off Inca domination, he captured and executed the Paca Inca and conquered the capital of Cuzco by 1533. He later built a new capital on the coast at Lima, from which he worked to extend his control over all of the old Inca Empire. Pizarro and his Spanish partners seized vast amounts of gold and silver from the Inca. The Spanish eventually found silver mines at Potosí, which would be a critical source of revenue for the Spanish monarchy. Resistance to Spanish rule continued into the 1570s, when the last of the independent Inca strongholds was finally destroyed.

Colonial Organization

The Spanish crown needed to create a colonial government that could control the actions of its headstrong adventurers and create an orderly economy. Although the Spaniards proclaimed that they would "give to those strange lands the form of our own [land]," the resulting political and economic organization of the new Spanish possessions was a curious mixture of old and new.

The head of the administration was the monarchy. As early as the reigns of Ferdinand and Isabella, Spanish monarchs had tried to curb the excesses of the explorers and conquerors who traveled in their name. Isabella initially opposed the enslavement of Amerindians and any slave trade in the new lands. Further, the monarchs promoted a broad-based debate about the rights of Amerindians and the nature of religious conversion. It was royal policy that native rights, even the right not to become Christian, were to be protected. Mexicans had to accept missionaries, but they did not have to convert. Royal control, however, was limited by the sheer distance between the court and the new provinces. It could easily take two years for a royal response to a question to arrive at its destination. Things moved so slowly that as one viceroy ruefully noted, "If death came from Madrid, we should all live to a very old age." Given the difficulties of communication, the powers of local administrators had to be very broad.

By 1535 Spanish colonial administration was firmly established in the form it would retain for the next two hundred years. The king created the Council of the Indies, located at court, eventually in Madrid, which saw to all legal and administrative issues pertaining to the new possessions. The new territories themselves were eventually divided into the viceroyalty of Mexico (primarily Central America and part of Venezuela) and the viceroyalty of Peru.

In Spain, Castilian conquerors completely dominated newly won lands, but in New Spain royal administrators created Indian municipalities, or districts, in which Spaniards had no formal right to live or work. Government in these municipalities remained largely in the hands of preconquest native elites. Throughout the sixteenth century, official documents in these communities continued to be written in Nahuatl, the Aztec language. These native communities were, however, fragile. Colonists and local administrators often interfered in the hope of gaining control.

The Colonial Economy

The problem that most plagued the government was the conquerors' desire for laborers to work on the lands and in the mines that they had seized. From Columbus's first visit the Spanish adopted a system of forced labor developed in Spain. A colonist called an *encomendero* was offered a grant, or *encomienda*, of a certain number of people or tribes who were required to work under his direction. The Spanish government expected that the encomendero was to be a protector of the conquered peoples, someone who would Christianize and civilize them. In theory, Indians who voluntarily agreed to listen to missionaries or to convert to Christianity could not be put under the control of an encomendero. If they refused, however, the Spaniards believed they had the right of conquest. In many areas encomenderos allowed life to continue as it had, simply collecting traditional payments that the preconquest elites had claimed. In other cases, where the subject peoples were forced into mining districts, the conditions were brutal. The treatment of native peoples was "more unjust and cruel," one reformer concluded, "than Pharaoh's oppression of the Jews."

The pressures exerted by the encomenderos were worsened by the precipitous fall in the indigenous population. Old World diseases such as smallpox and measles swept

Caribbean Sugar Plantation *The production of sugar from cane was easily industrialized and centralized. Missing from this depiction of the process are the supervisors who would have overseen the slaves at every step.* (Courtesy of the John Carter Brown Library at Brown University)

through peoples with no previous exposure to them (see pages 428–429). In central Mexico, where we know most about population changes, the preconquest population was at least 10 million to 12 million and may have been twice that. By the mid-sixteenth century, the native population may have declined to just over 6 million, and it probably plunged to less than 1 million early in the seventeenth century before beginning to grow again.

A large population was essential to the Spanish and the Portuguese when they introduced the Old World plantation system to the New World. The Caribbean islands and Brazil were ideal for the production of sugar—a commercial crop in great demand throughout Europe. At first plantations and mines were worked by Amerindians, but when their numbers shrank, the Spanish and Portuguese imported large numbers of slaves from Africa.

Africans had participated in the initial stages of the conquest. Some had lived in Spain and become Christian; indeed, Amerindians called them "black whitemen." Most Africans, however, were enslaved laborers. African slaves were in Cuba by 1518; they labored in the mines of Honduras by the 1540s. After the 1560s the Portuguese began mass importations of African slaves into Brazil to work on the sugar plantations. It has been estimated that 62,500 slaves were brought into Spanish America and 50,000 into Brazil during the sixteenth century. By 1810, when the movement to abolish the slave trade began to gather momentum, almost 10 million Africans had been involuntarily transported to the New World to work the fields and mines on which the colonial economy depended.

The conquerors had hoped to find vast quantities of wealth that they could take back to the Old World. In the viceroyalty of Mexico the search for El Dorado remained largely unsuccessful. The discovery in 1545 of the silver mines at Potosí in Peru, however, fulfilled the Spaniards' wildest dreams. Between 1550 and 1650 the Spanish probably sent back to Spain 181 tons of gold and 16,000 tons of silver, one-fifth of which was paid directly into the royal treasury.

The tonnage of precious metals was so great that the French scholar Jean Bodin (see page 505) held this infusion of wealth responsible for the rampant inflation that disrupted the European economy in the late sixteenth century. Although Bodin overestimated the European-wide effect of the precious metals on prices, the flood of silver and gold did have a significant impact on the Continent. The treasure represents one-quarter of the income of King Philip II of Spain in the 1560s and made him the richest monarch in Europe. The New World bonanza funded Spanish opposition to the Protestant Reformation and Spain's attempts to influence the politics of most of its neighbors. And the Spanish coins, the *reales* and *reales a ocho* (the "pieces of eight" prized by English pirates), became the common coin of European traders and even Muslim and Hindu traders in the Indian Ocean. In a world with limited commercial credit, the Spanish treasure allowed for the beginnings of a truly integrated system of world trade.

The Debate over Indian Rights

To most conquerors the ruthless pursuit of wealth and power needs little justification, but the more thoughtful among the Spaniards were uneasy. "Tell me," demanded Friar Antonio Montesinos in 1511, "by what right or justice do you hold these Indians in such cruel and horrible slavery? By what right do you wage such detestable wars on these people who lived idly and peacefully in their own lands?"[5]

Initially the conquerors claimed the right to wage a just war of conquest if Amerindians refused to allow missionaries to live and work among them. Later, on the basis of reports of human sacrifice and cannibalism written by Columbus and other early explorers, Europeans concluded that the inhabitants of the New World rejected basic natural laws. Juan Gines de Sepulveda, chaplain of King Charles I of Spain, argued in 1544 that the idolatry and cannibalism of the Indians made them, in Aristotle's terms, natural slaves—"barbarous and inhuman peoples abhorring all civil life, customs and virtue." People lacking "civil life" and "virtue" clearly could not be allowed self-government. Other writers commented that nakedness and cannibalism were both signs of the lack of "civility" among the Amerindians. Sepulveda implied that Indians were merely "humanlike," not necessarily human.

Franciscan and Dominican missionaries were especially vocal opponents of views such as Sepulveda's. To these missionaries the Indians initially seemed innocent and ideal subjects for conversion to the simple piety of Christ and his first apostles. In their eyes Indians were like children who could be converted and led by example and, where necessary, by stern discipline. The simple faith of the newly Christian native peoples was to be an example, the missionaries believed, for the lax believers of old Europe. These mendicants saw themselves as advocates for Indians; they desired to protect the natives from the depredations of the Spanish conquerors and the corruptions of European civilization.

The most eloquent defender of Indian rights was Bartolomé de Las Casas (1474–1566), a former encomendero who became a Dominican missionary and eventually bishop of Chiapas in southern Mexico. Las Casas passionately condemned the violence and brutality of the Spanish conquests. In a famous debate with Sepulveda, Las Casas rejected the "humanlike" argument. "All races of the world are men," he declared. All are evolving along a historical continuum. It was wrong, he added, to dismiss any culture or society as outside or beyond natural law. Like all other peoples, Indians had reason. That being the case, even the most brutal could be civilized and Christianized, but by conversion, not coercion. In the view of Las Casas, the argument for natural slavery was indefensible.

King Charles accepted Las Casas's criticisms of the colonial administration. In 1542 he issued "New Laws" aimed at ending the virtual independence of the most adventurous encomenderos. He further abolished Indian slavery and greatly restricted the transfer of encomiendas. We should have no illusion, however, that these measures reflected a modern acceptance of cultural pluralism. The very mendicants who protected the Indians assumed that Westernization and Christianization would quickly follow mercy. When it did not, as during revolts in the 1560s, the mendicants themselves sometimes reacted with a puzzled sense of anger, frustration, and betrayal.

THE COLUMBIAN EXCHANGE

The conquerors, adventurers, and traders who completed the expansion begun by the voyages of Christopher Columbus and Vasco da Gama profoundly altered the Old World and the New. A system of world trade had been in place before 1492, but now, as the Spanish proclaimed, Europe and especially Spain were at the center of economic and political life. As the Spanish and other Europeans moved throughout the world, they carried with them religions, ideas, people, plants, animals, and diseases—forever uniting the Old World and the New. This blending of cultures is known as the "Columbian Exchange."

Disease   Columbus and those who followed him brought not only people to the New World but also numerous Old World diseases. "Virgin-soil" epidemics—that is, epidemics of previously unknown diseases—are invariably fierce. Although the New World may have passed syphilis to Spain, from which it quickly spread throughout the Old World, diseases transferred from the Old World to the New were much more virulent than syphilis. Smallpox spread from Cuba to Mexico as early as 1519. It was soon followed by diphtheria, measles, trachoma, whooping cough, chickenpox, bubonic plague, malaria, typhoid fever, cholera, yellow fever, scarlet fever, amoebic dysentery, influenza, and some varieties of tuberculosis. Disease served as the silent ally of the conquerors. At critical points during the conquest of Tenochtitlán, smallpox was raging in the Aztec population. The disease later moved along traditional trade networks. An epidemic shortly before Pizarro's expedition to Peru carried off the Paca Inca and may have contributed to the unrest and civil war that worked to the advantage of the invaders.

Lacking sources, historians cannot trace accurately the movement of epidemic diseases or their effects on New World populations, yet many archaeologists and historians remain convinced that Old World diseases moved north from Mexico and ravaged and disrupted Amerindian populations in eastern North America long before the arrival of European immigrants. In most of the New World 90 percent or more of the native population was destroyed by wave after wave of previously unknown afflictions. Explorers and colonists did not enter an empty land but rather an *emptied* one.

It was at least partially because of disease that both the Spanish and the Portuguese needed to import large numbers of African slaves to work their plantations and mines. With the settlement of southeastern North America, plantation agriculture was extended to include the production of tobacco and later cotton. As a result of the needs of plantation economies and the labor shortages caused by epidemics, African slaves were brought in by the thousands, then hundreds of thousands. In the Caribbean and along the coasts of Central and South America, the Africans created an African Caribbean or African American culture that amalgamated African, European, and American civilizations.

Plants and Animals It became increasingly clear to the Spaniards that the New World had been completely isolated from the Old. The impact of Old World peoples on native populations was immediately evident to all parties. But scholars have recently argued that the importation of plants and animals had an even more profound effect than the arrival of Europeans. The changes that began in 1492 created "Neo-Europes" in what are now Canada, the United States, Mexico, Argentina, Australia, and New Zealand. The flora and fauna of the Old World, accustomed to a relatively harsh, competitive environment, found ideal conditions in the new lands. Like the rabbits that overran the Canary Islands and eventually Australia, Old World plants and animals multiplied, driving out many New World species.

The most important meat and dairy animals in the New World today—cattle, sheep, goats, and pigs—are imports from Europe. Sailors initially brought pigs or goats aboard ship because they were easily transportable sources of protein. When let loose on the Caribbean islands, they quickly took over. The spread of horses through what is now Mexico, Brazil, Argentina, the United States, and Canada was equally dramatic. To the list of domesticated animals can be added donkeys, dogs, cats, and chickens. The changes these animals brought were profound. Cattle, pigs, and chickens quickly became staples of the New World diet. Horses enabled Amerindians and Europeans to travel across and settle on the vast plains of both North and South America.

The flora of the New World was equally changed. Even contemporaries noted how Old World plants flourished in the New. By 1555 European clover was widely distributed in Mexico—Aztecs called it "Castilian grass." Other Old World grasses, as well as weeds such as dandelions, quickly followed. Domesticated plants, including apples, peaches, and artichokes, spread rapidly and naturally in the hospitable new environment. Early in the twentieth century it was estimated that only one-quarter of the grasses found on the broad prairies of the Argentine pampas were native before the arrival of Columbus. Studies of plant life in California, Australia, and New Zealand offer much the same results. The Old World also provided new and widely grown small grains such as oats, barley, and wheat.

The exchange went both ways. Crops from the New World also had an effect on the Old. By the seventeenth century maize (or American corn), potatoes, and sweet potatoes had significantly altered the diets of Europe and Asia and supported the dramatic population growth that invigorated Italy, Ireland, and Scandinavia. With the addition of the tomato in the nineteenth century, much of the modern European diet became dependent on New World foods. The new plants and new animals, as well as the social and political changes initiated by the Europeans, pulled the Old World and the New more closely together.

Culture

One reason for the accommodation between the Old World and the New was that the Europeans and Amerindians tended to interpret conquest and cultural transformation in the same way. The peoples living in the Valley of Mexico believed that their conquest was fated by the gods and that their new masters would bring in new gods. The Spaniards' beliefs were strikingly similar, based on the revelation of divine will and the omnipotence of the Christian God. Cortés, by whitewashing former Aztec temples and converting native priests into white-clad Christian priests, was in a way fulfilling the Aztecs' expectations about their conqueror.

Acculturation was also facilitated by the Spanish tendency to place churches and shrines at the sites of former Aztec temples. The shrine of the Virgin of Guadalupe (on the northern edge of modern Mexico City), for example, was located on the site of the temple of the goddess Tonantzin, an Aztec fertility-goddess of childbirth and midwives. The shrine of Guadalupe is a perfect example of the complex mixture of cultures. The shrine initially appealed to *creoles*—people of mixed Spanish and Mexican descent. In the seventeenth century and after, it came to symbolize the connection of poor Mexicans to Christianity and was a religious rallying point for resisting state injustices.

The colonists tended to view their domination of the New World as a divine vindication of their own culture and civilization. During the sixteenth century they set about remaking the world they had found. In the century after the conquest of Mexico, Spaniards founded 190 new cities in the Americas. Lima, Bogota, and many others were proudly modeled on and compared with the cities of Spain. In 1573 King Philip II (r. 1556–1598) established ordinances requiring all new cities to be laid out on a uniform grid with a main plaza, market, and religious center. The new cities became hubs of social and political life in the colonies. In these cities religious orders founded colleges for basic education much like the universities they had organized in the Old World. In the aftermath of conquest there were schools to teach Spanish, the liberal arts, and trades to the Amerindian population. By midcentury, however, the urban colleges were primarily for the mestizo and Spanish population. In 1551 the Crown authorized the first universities in the New World. The universities in Mexico City and Lima mirrored the great Spanish university in Salamanca, teaching law and theology to the colonial elites. Colonists attempted to re-create in all essentials the society of Spain.

IMPORTANT EVENTS

ca. 1400 Portuguese reach Azores

1444 Prince Henry "the Navigator" discovers Cape Verde Islands

1487 Dias becomes first European to sail around Cape of Good Hope

1492 Columbus reaches New World

1494 Treaty of Tordesillas

1497 Da Gama sails to India around Cape of Good Hope

Cabot sights Newfoundland

1501 Vespucci concludes Columbus discovered a new continent

1507 Waldseemüller issues the first map showing "America"

1510 Portuguese capture Goa

1513 Balboa becomes first European to see Pacific Ocean

1519–1522 Magellan's expedition sails around the world

1519–1523 Cortés conquers the Aztecs, destroys Tenochtitlán

1533 Pizarro conquers Cuzco, the Inca capital

1534 Cartier discovers St. Lawrence River

1542 Charles V issues "New Laws"

1545 Spanish discover Potosí silver mines

The experience of the Spanish and Portuguese in the sixteenth century seemed confirmed by the later experiences of the French and English in the seventeenth century. In seventeenth-century New England the English Puritan John Winthrop concluded, "For the natives, they are nearly all dead of smallpox, so as the Lord hath cleared our title to what we possess."[6] A seventeenth-century French observer came to a similar conclusion: "Touching these savages, there is a thing that I cannot omit to remark to you, it is that it appears visibly that God wishes that they yield their place to new peoples."[7] Political philosophers believed that in the absence of evidence that the indigenous people were improving the land, the rights to that land passed to those who would make the best use of it. Thus colonists believed that they had divine and legal sanction to take and to remake these new lands in a European image.

NOTES

1. Quoted in William D. Phillips, Jr., and Carla Rahn Phillips, *The Worlds of Christopher Columbus* (Cambridge: Cambridge University Press, 1992), p. 163.

2. Quoted ibid., p. 166.

3. Quoted in J. H. Parry, ed., *The European Reconnaissance: Selected Documents* (New York: Harper & Row, 1968), p. 242.

4. Quoted in Alfred W. Crosby, *Ecological Imperialism: The Biological Expansion of Europe, 900–1900* (Cambridge: Cambridge University Press, 1986), p. 125.

5. Quoted in Mark A. Burkholder and Lyman L. Johnson, *Colonial Latin America* (Oxford: Oxford University Press, 1990), p. 29.

6. Quoted in Crosby, p. 208.

7. Quoted ibid., p. 215.

8. Quoted in Maria Parker Pascua, "Ozette: A Makah Village in 1491," *National Geographic* (October 1991), p. 53.

SUGGESTED READING

Burkholder, Mark A., and Lyman L. Johnson. *Colonial Latin America.* 1990. A thorough introduction to the conquest and colonization of Central and South America by the Spanish and Portuguese.

Clendinnen, Inga. *Aztecs: An Interpretation.* 1991. A dramatic, beautifully written essay on the Aztecs that shows how daily life, religion, and imperialism were linked.

Crosby, A. W. *Ecological Imperialism: The Biological Expansion of Europe, 900–1900.* 1986. A discussion of how migrating peoples carried plants, animals, and diseases; includes excellent maps and illustrations.

Curtin, P. *The Tropical Atlantic in the Age of the Slave Trade.* 1991. An introductory pamphlet that is an excellent first work for students interested in the history of slavery and the movement of peoples from Africa to the New World.

Friedman, John Block, and Kristen Mossler Figg, eds. *Trade, Travel, and Exploration in the Middle Ages.* 2000. This encyclopedia includes discussions of the earliest stage of European expansion, especially contacts with Asia.

Mills, Kenneth, and William B. Taylor, eds. *Colonial Latin America: A Documentary History.* 1998. This engaging collection of primary documents and short essays also includes unique discussions of contemporary maps and drawings.

Phillips, J. R. S. *The Medieval Expansion of Europe.* 1988. The best survey of European interest in and knowledge of the world beyond Christendom; especially good on European travelers to the East in the thirteenth century.

Phillips, William D., Jr., and Carla Rahn Phillips. *The Worlds of Christopher Columbus.* 1992. Though written for a popular audience, this is an excellent survey of Columbus and his voyages and an up-to-date summary of recent work on Columbus, maritime technology, and Spanish colonial interests.

Scammell, Geoffrey. *The First Imperial Age: European Overseas Expansion, 1400–1715.* 1989. As the title implies, this is an introductory survey of European colonial interests through the early eighteenth century, with the Spanish and Portuguese explorations discussed in the context of later French and English experiences.

Subrahmanyam, S. *The Portuguese Empire in Asia, 1500–1700: A Political and Economic History.* 1993. A thoughtful introduction to Portuguese expansion by a renowned Indian economic historian.

14

The Age of the Reformation

(Institut Amatller d'Art Hispanic)

El Greco's *The Burial of the Count de Orgaz* encapsulates the hopes and contradictions of the age of the Reformation. El Greco ("the Greek") first learned to paint on the island of Crete, then studied and worked in Venice and Rome before settling in Spain. This painting expresses the medieval Christian understanding of a good death. We see a saintly knight surrounded by clergy and witnesses as his soul (in the form of a cloud-wrapped body) is commended to Christ. But El Greco (1541–1614) painted during a period of social, political, and religious turmoil, when medieval assumptions about the nature of salvation were being challenged by religious reformers.

If we look more closely at the painting, we can see what El Greco and Roman Catholic Christians wished to emphasize. The two figures holding the count's body are Saint Stephen, the first Christian martyr, and Saint Augustine, perhaps the most important of the early Church Fathers. They represent the continuity of the Christian tradition. But just as important is the heavenly hierarchy of saints and angels reaching from the count upward to Christ. At the very top are Saint John and Saint Mary, who are interceding with Christ for the count's soul. The hierarchy of saints and intercessors so vividly painted by El Greco represents one of the clearest differences between the two contending visions of Christian life and society. Most reformers rejected the idea that salvation depended on the intervention of others, no matter how saintly. Salvation was a simpler process. The hierarchy of saints and angels depicted by El Greco seemed unnecessary.

The crisis of the Reformation began with a challenge to the religious authority of the papacy. Debates over the power and authority of the church that raged during this period, however, did not occur in a political vacuum. Support for the old church was an issue of state that profoundly affected the exercise of political authority in the Holy Roman Empire. In England and Scandinavia, in contrast, monarchs viewed the church as a threat to strong royal government, and reformers soon found themselves with royal patrons. Elsewhere, especially in eastern Europe, no strong central governments existed to enforce religious unity, and so a variety of Christian traditions coexisted.

By the second half of the sixteenth century political and religious authorities concentrated their energies on a process of theological definition and institutionalization that led to the formation of the major Christian religious denominations we know today. They created Roman Catholic, Anglican, Reformed (Calvinist), and Lutheran churches as clearly defined confessions, with formally prescribed religious beliefs and practices.

An important aspect of the reform movement was the emphasis on individual belief and religious participation. Far from freeing the individual, however, the Christian churches of the late sixteenth century all emphasized correct doctrine and orderliness in personal behavior. Although early Protestants rejected a system that they accused of oppressing the individual, the institutions that replaced the old church developed their own traditions of control. The increased moral control held by churches accompanied and even fostered the expansion of state power that would characterize the late sixteenth and seventeenth centuries.

THE REFORMATION MOVEMENTS, CA. 1517–1545

In 1517 Martin Luther, a little-known professor of theology in eastern Germany, launched a protest against practices in the late medieval church. Luther's criticisms struck a responsive chord with many of his contemporaries and led to calls for reform across much of Europe. All the reformers, even the most radical, shared with Luther a sense that the essential sacramental and priestly powers claimed by the late medieval church were illegitimate. These reformers initially had no intention of forming a new church; they simply wanted to return Christianity to what they believed was its earlier, purer form. Although their various protests resulted in the creation of separate and well-defined religious traditions, the differences among the reformers became clear only in the second half of the sixteenth century. Thus it is appropriate to speak of "Reformation movements" rather than a unified Protestant Reformation.

We call the men and women who joined these new churches "Protestants," but the reformers tended to think of themselves as "evangelical reformed Christians." The word *evangelical* derived from *evangel* (literally, "good news"), the New Testament Gospel. They were evangelical in the sense that they believed that authority derived from the Word of God, the Bible. They were reformed Christians because their aim was to restore Christianity to the form they believed it exhibited in the first centuries of its existence.

The Late Medieval Context Although reformers claimed religious life was in decline before the Reformation, medieval Christianity was, in fact, flourishing. Questions of an individual's salvation and personal relationship to God and to the Christian community remained at the heart of religious practice and theological speculation. Nominalist theologians, the leading thinkers of the late Middle Ages, rejected the key assumption of previous Scholastics—that moral life was circumscribed by universal ideas and generally applicable rules. In the words of William of Ockham (ca. 1285–1347), "No universal reality exists outside the mind." Truth was to be found in daily experience or in revealed Scripture, not in complex logical systems. At the heart is Ockham's method—known as "Ockham's razor"—the observation that what can be explained simply "is vainly explained by assuming more."

Nominalist theologians dismissed ponderous systems of logic, but they held on to the traditional rituals and beliefs that tied together the Christian community. They believed in a holy covenant in which God would save those Christians who, by means of the church's sacraments and through penitential acts, were partners in their own salvation. Foremost among the penitential acts was the feeding of "Christ's Poor," especially on important feast days. The pious constructed and supported hospices for travelers and hospitals for the sick. Christians went on pilgrimages to shrines such as the tomb of Saint Thomas Becket in Canterbury or the Church of Saint James of Compostela in Spain. They also built small chapels, called chantry chapels, for the sake of their own souls. To moralists work itself was in some sense a penitential and ennobling act.

The most common religious practice of the late Middle Ages was participation in religious brotherhoods. Urban brotherhoods were usually organized around a craft guild or neighborhood; rural brotherhoods were more likely to include an entire village or parish. Members vowed to attend monthly meetings, to participate in processions on feast days, and to maintain peaceful and charitable relations with fellow members.

The most typical religious feast was that of *Corpus Christi* (the "Body of Christ"). The feast celebrated and venerated the sacrament of the mass and the ritual by which the bread offered to the laity became the actual body of Christ. Corpus Christi was popular with the church hierarchy because it emphasized the role of the priest in the central ritual of Christianity. The laity, however, equated Corpus Christi with the body of citizens who made up the civic community.

Kingdoms, provinces, and towns all venerated patron saints who, believers thought, offered protection from natural as well as political disasters. At the pinnacle were royal saints such as Edward of England, Louis of France, and Olaf of Norway. Festivals in honor of the saints were major events in towns or kingdoms. The most revered saint in the late Middle Ages was the Virgin Mary, the mother of Jesus. The most popular new pilgrimage shrines in the north of Europe were dedicated to the Virgin. It was she, townspeople believed, who protected them from invasion, plague, and natural disasters. In such a society it was impossible to distinguish between religion and society, church and state.

Women played a prominent role in late medieval religious life. Holy women who claimed any sort of moral standing often did so because of visions or prophetic gifts such as knowledge of future events or discernment of the status of souls in Purgatory. Reputations for sanctity provided a profound moral authority. The Italian Blessed Angela of Foligno (ca. 1248–1309) had several visions and became the object of a large circle of devoted followers. She was typical of a number of late medieval religious women who on the death of a spouse turned to religion. They tended to gather "families" around them, people whom they described as their spiritual "fathers" or "children." They offered moral counsel and boldly warned businessmen and politicians of the dangers of lying and sharp dealings. "Oh my sons, fathers, and brothers," counseled Angela, "see that you love one another . . . [and] likewise unto all people."[1]

In the late Middle Ages religious houses for women probably outnumbered those for men. For unmarried or unmarriageable (because of poverty or disabilities) daughters, convents provided an economical, safe, and controlled environment. Moralists denounced the dumping of women in convents: "They give [unmarriageable daughters] to a convent, as if they were the scum and vomit of the world," Saint Bernardino of Siena (1380–1444) concluded. The general public, however, believed that well-run communities of religious women promoted the spiritual and physical health of the general community. In a society in which women were not allowed to control their own property and, except among the nobility, lacked a visible role in political and intellectual life, a religious vocation may have had a compelling appeal. At the least it permitted women to define their own religious and social relationships. Well-to-do or aristocratic parents also appreciated the fact that the traditional gift that accompanied a daughter entering a religious house was much smaller than a dowry.

Some women declined to join convents, which required vows of chastity and obedience to a Rule and close male supervision. They could be found among the many pilgrims who visited local shrines, the great churches of Rome, or even the holy city of Jerusalem. Many other women chose to live as anchoresses, or recluses, in closed cells beside churches and hospitals or in rooms in private homes. Men and women traveled from all parts of England seeking the counsel of the Blessed Julian of Norwich (d. after 1413), who lived in a tiny cell built into the wall of a parish church.

The most controversial group of religious women were the Beguines, who lived in communities without taking formal vows and often with minimal connections to the local church hierarchy. By the early fifteenth century Beguines were suspect because clerics believed that these independent women rejected traditional religious cloistering and the moral leadership of male clergy; consequently, it was thought, they were particularly susceptible to heresy. Critics maintained that unsupervised Beguines held to

Crowning with Thorns *Late medieval Christians meditated on Christ's sufferings and preferred images like this one that shows a tortured Christ living in their own time.* (Courtesy, Augustiner Chorherrenstift, Herzogenburg. Photo: Fotostudio Wurst Erich)

what was called the "Heresy of the Free Spirit," a belief that one who had achieved spiritual perfection was no longer capable of sin. Fantastic rumors of sexual orgies, spread by fearful clerical opponents, quickly brought suspect women before local church authorities. Although some Beguines may have held such a belief in spiritual perfection, the majority certainly did not. Even so, they were feared by an ecclesiastical hierarchy that distrusted independence.

A more conservative movement for renewal in the church was the Brothers and Sisters of the Common Life, founded by the Dutchman Geert Groote (1340–1384). A popular preacher and reformer, Groote gathered male and female followers into quasi-monastic communities at Deventer in the Low Countries. Eventually a community of Augustinian canons was added at Windsheim. Brothers and Sisters of the Common Life supported themselves as book copyists and teachers in small religious schools. Members of these communities followed a strict, conservative spirituality that has come to be known as the *devotio moderna,* or "modern devotion." Although they called themselves "modern," their piety was traditional. Their ideas are encapsulated in *The Imitation of Christ,* a popular work of traditional monastic spirituality written by Thomas à Kempis (ca. 1380–1471), a canon of Windsheim. They advocated the contrary ideals of fourteenth-century religious life: broader participation by the laity and strict control by clerical authorities.

Religious life in the late medieval period was broadly based and vigorous. Theologians, laypeople, and popular preachers could take heart that they were furthering their own salvation and that of their neighbors. Thus the Reformation of the sixteenth century involved more than simple moral change.

Martin Luther and the New Theology   Martin Luther (1483–1546) eventually challenged many of the assumptions of late medieval Christians. He seemed to burst onto the scene in 1517, when he objected to the way in which papal indulgences—that is, the remission of penalties owed for sins—were being bought and sold in the bishopric of Brandenburg. Luther's father, a miner from the small town of Mansfeld, had hoped that his son would take a degree in law and become a wealthy and prestigious lawyer. Luther chose instead to enter a monastery and eventually become a priest.

Throughout his life Luther seems to have been troubled by a sense of his own sinfulness and unworthiness. According to late medieval theology, the life of a Christian was a continuing cycle of sin, confession, contrition, and penance, and the only way to achieve salvation was to have confessed all one's sins and at least begun a cycle of penance at the time of one's death. Christians lived in fear of dying suddenly, unconfessed. The purchase of indulgences, membership in penitential brotherhoods, ritualized charity, and veneration of popular saints were seen as ways to acquire merit in the eyes of God.

Luther came to believe that the church's requirement that believers achieve salvation by means of confession, contrition, and penance made too great a demand on the faithful. Instead, Luther said, citing the New Testament, salvation (or justification) was God's gift to the faithful. Luther's belief is known as "justification by faith." Acts of charity were important products resulting from God's love, but in Luther's opinion, they were not necessary for salvation. Late in his life Luther explained how he came by these ideas:

> Though I lived as a monk without reproach, I felt that I was a sinner before God with an extremely disturbed conscience. I could not believe that he was placated by my [acts of penance]. I did not love, yes, I hated the righteous God who punishes sinners. At last, by the mercy of God, I gave context to the words, namely, "In it the righteousness of God is revealed, as it is written, 'He who through faith is righteous shall live.'" There I began to understand that the righteous lives by a gift of God, namely by faith. Here I felt that I was altogether born again and had entered paradise itself through open gates.[2]

Although Luther recalled a sudden, dramatic revelation, it now seems clear that his insight developed slowly over the course of his academic career and during his defense of his teachings. Nonetheless, his recollection conveys a sense of the novelty of his theology and suggests why his attack on the late medieval church proved to be so much more devastating than the complaints of earlier critics.

Others had complained of impious priests, an unresponsive bureaucracy, and a church too much involved in matters of government, but the theology that Luther developed struck at the doctrinal foundations of the church itself. Luther separated justification from acts of sanctification—from the good works or charity expected of all

Christians. In Luther's theology the acts of piety so typical of the medieval church were quite unnecessary for salvation because Christ's sacrifice had brought justification once and for all. Justification came entirely from God and was independent of human works. Luther argued that the Christian was at the same time sinner and saved, so the penitential cycle and careful preparation for a "good death" were, in his opinion, superfluous.

Luther also attacked the place of the priesthood in the sacramental life of the church and, by extension, the power and authority a church might claim in public life. The church taught that, through the actions of ordained priests, Christ was really present in the bread and wine of the sacrament of Holy Communion. Luther agreed that the sacrament transformed the bread and wine into the body and blood of Christ, but he denied that priests had a role in the transformation. Priests, in Luther's view, were not mediators between God and individual Christians. John Wyclif and Jan Hus (see page 336) had argued against the spiritual authority of unworthy priests. Luther, however, challenged the role of all clergy, and of the institutional church itself, in the attainment of salvation. Thus he argued for a "priesthood of all believers."

In the years before 1517 Luther's views on salvation and his reservations about the traditional ways of teaching theology attracted little interest outside his own university. Matters changed, however, when he questioned the sale of indulgences. Indulgences were often granted as rewards for pilgrimages or for noteworthy acts of charity or sacrifice. The papacy frequently authorized the sale of indulgences to pay various expenses. Unscrupulous priests often left the impression that purchase of an indulgence freed a soul from Purgatory. After getting no response to his initial complaints, Luther made his "Ninety-five Theses" public. He probably posted his document on the door of the Wittenberg Castle church, the usual way to announce topics for theological debates. His text created a firestorm when it was quickly translated and printed throughout German-speaking lands. His charges against the sale of indulgences encapsulated German feelings about unworthy priests and economic abuses by the clergy. Luther was acclaimed as the spokesman of the German people.

In a debate with a papal representative in Leipzig in 1519, Luther was forced to admit that in some of his positions he agreed with the Czech reformer Jan Hus, who had been burned at the stake as a heretic in 1415. In the Leipzig debate and in hearings the following year, Luther responded to his critics and tried to explain more fully the nature of the changes he advocated. Three tracts were especially important. In *Address to the Christian Nobility of the German Nation* Luther urged the princes to reject papal claims of temporal and spiritual authority. In *On the Babylonian Captivity of the Church* he argued for the principle of *sola scriptura*—that is, church authority had to be based on biblical teachings. In *On Christian Freedom* he explained clearly his understanding of salvation: "A Christian has all he needs in faith and needs no works to justify him." Luther was speaking of spiritual freedom from unnecessary ritual, not social or political freedom. This distinction would later be crucial to Luther's opposition to political and economic protests by peasants and artisans.

In 1520 Pope Leo X (r. 1513–1521) condemned Luther's teachings and gave him sixty days to recant. Luther refused to do so and publicly burned the papal letter. In 1521 Emperor Charles V called an imperial diet, or parliament, at Worms to deal with the religious crisis. Charles demanded that Luther submit to papal authority. Luther, however, explained that religious decisions must be based on personal experience and conscience, as both were informed by a study of Scripture:

> Unless I am convicted by the testimony of Scripture or by clear reason, for I do not trust either in the Pope or in councils alone, since it is well known that they have often erred and contradicted themselves, I cannot and will not retract anything, for it is neither safe nor right to go against conscience. I cannot do otherwise, here I stand, may God help me. Amen.[3]

The emperor and his allies stayed firmly in the papal camp, and the excommunicated Luther was placed under an imperial ban—that is, declared an outlaw. As Luther left the Diet of Worms, friendly princes took him to Wartburg Castle in Saxony, where they could protect him. During a year of isolation at Wartburg, Luther used Erasmus's edition of the Greek New Testament as the basis of a translation of the New Testament into German, which became an influential literary as well as religious work.

The Reformation of the Communities
Luther challenged the authority of the clerical hierarchy and called on laypeople to take responsibility for their own salvation. His ideas spread rapidly in the towns and countryside of Germany because he and his followers took advantage of the new technology of printing. Perhaps 300,000 copies of his early tracts were published in the first years of the protest. Luther's claim that the Scriptures must be the basis of all life and his appeal to the judgment of the laity made sense to the men and women in towns and villages, where councils of local people were accustomed to making decisions based on ideas of the common good. It is also true that townspeople and villagers saw religious and civic life as being inextricably interconnected. For them the notion of a religiously neutral act was unthinkable.

The impact of Luther's ideas quickly became evident. If the active intercession of the clergy was not necessary for the salvation of individuals, then, according to Luther's followers, there was no reason for the clergy to remain unmarried and celibate, nor for men and women to cloister themselves in monasteries and convents. Also, maintained Luther's partisans, the laity's participation in the sacrament of the Eucharist need not be restricted. Thus the priest must distribute wine to the congregants along with the bread. With the spread of Luther's ideas came the end of a very visual part of clerical power. Because Luther's followers believed that penitential acts were not prerequisites for salvation, they tended to set aside the veneration of saints and give up pilgrimages to the shrines and holy places all over Europe.

Many historians have referred to the spread of these reform ideas as the "Reformation of the Common Man." In Strasbourg, Nuremberg, Zurich, and other towns ideas about the primacy of the Bible and attacks on clerical privilege were spread by "people's priests." These individuals were hired by the town government to preach and teach, and to care for the souls in the community. Many of the most famous reformers initially gained a following through preaching. The message seems to have spread especially quickly among artisan and mercantile groups, which put pressure on town governments to press for reform. Agitation was often riotous. One resident of Augsburg exposed himself during a church service to protest what he believed was an evil and idolatrous service. Women on both sides of the reform stepped out of traditional roles,

Legend:

- Signatories to initial Protestation
- Cities where reform movement failed or was suppressed
- Other cities and towns of the Reformation
- Boundary of the Holy Roman Empire

Reform in Germany, 1517–1555

The pattern of religious reform in Germany was complex. Although some territorial princes, such as the dukes of Bavaria, rejected the reform, most free towns, particularly those in the southwest, adopted it.

in which they were seen as subservient. For instance, a "common man" was understood to be the sturdy bulwark of the sacred community, but a "common woman" was a prostitute. Even women tended to accept these stereotypes. Nonetheless, aristocratic women such as Margaret of Angoulême in France (see page 458) supported and protected reformers. Other women wrote tracts advocating reform or defending the old order, and still others used shovels and rakes to defend religious values.

The process of reform in Zurich is instructive. In 1519 the people's priest of Zurich was Huldrych Zwingli (1484–1531), son of a rural official from a nearby village. After a university education he became a typical late medieval country priest, right down to his publically acknowledged mistress. Yet after experiences as a military chaplain and an acquaintance with the humanist writings of Erasmus, Zwingli began to preach strongly biblical sermons. In 1522 he defended a group of laymen who protested by breaking the required Lenten fast. Later in the same year he requested episcopal permission to marry. Early in 1523 he led a group of reformers in a public debate over the nature of the church. The city council declared in favor of the reformers, and Zurich became in effect a Protestant city.

Unlike Luther, Zwingli believed that reform should be a communal movement—that town governments should take the lead in bringing reform to the community. Zwingli explained that the moral regeneration of individuals was an essential part of God's salvation. In the years following 1523 the reformers restructured church services, abolishing the mass. They also removed religious images from churches and suppressed monastic institutions. Zwingli further disagreed with Luther about the nature of the sacrament of Holy Communion. Whereas Luther, like Catholic theologians, accepted that Christ was truly present in the bread and wine, Zwingli argued that Christ's presence was merely spiritual—that the bread and wine only signified Christ. This disagreement created within the reform movement a division that made a common response to papal or imperial pressure difficult.

The reform message spread from towns into the countryside, but often with effects that the reformers did not expect or desire. Luther thought his message was a spiritual and theological one. Many peasants and modest artisans, however, believed that Luther's message of biblical freedom carried material as well as theological meaning.

In many parts of Germany villagers and peasants found themselves under increasing pressure from landlords and territorial princes. Taking advantage of changed economic and political conditions, these lords were intent on regaining claims to ancient manorial rights, on suppressing peasant claims to use common lands, and on imposing new taxes and tithes. Like townspeople, peasants saw religious and material life as closely connected. They argued that new tithes and taxes not only upset tradition but violated the Word of God. Using Luther's argument that authority should be based on the Scriptures, peasants from the district of Zurich, for example, petitioned the town council in 1523 and 1524, claiming that they should not be required to pay tithes on their produce because there was no biblical justification for doing so. Townsmen rejected the peasants' demand, noting that although the Bible did not stipulate such payments, it also did not forbid them. Accordingly, the peasants should make them "out of love"—that is, because they were traditional.

Demands that landlords and magistrates give up human ordinances and follow "Godly Law" soon turned to violence. Peasants, miners, and villagers in 1524 and 1525 participated in a series of uprisings that began on the borderlands between Switzerland and Germany and spread throughout southwestern Germany, upper Austria, and even northern Italy. Bands of peasants and villagers, perhaps a total of 300,000 in the empire, revolted against their seigneurial lords or even their territorial overlords.

Luther initially counseled landlords and princes to redress the just grievances. As reports of riots and increased violence continued to reach Wittenberg, however, Luther condemned the rebels as "mad dogs" and urged that they be suppressed. Territorial princes and large cities quickly raised armies to meet the threat. The peasants were defeated and destroyed in a series of battles in April 1525. When it became clear that the reformers were unwilling to follow the implications of their own theology, villagers and peasants lost interest in the progress of the reform. As a townsman of Zurich commented, "Many came to a great hatred of the preachers, where before they would have bitten off their feet for the Gospel."[4]

John Calvin and the Reformed Tradition

The revolts of 1524 and 1525 demonstrated the mixed messages traveling under the rubric "true" or "biblical" religion. In the 1530s the theological arguments of the reformers began to take on a greater clarity, mostly because of the Franco-Swiss reformer John Calvin (1509–1564). Calvin had a humanistic education in Paris and became a lawyer before coming under the influence of reform-minded thinkers in France. In 1534 he fled from Paris as royal pressures against reformers increased. He arrived in Geneva in 1536, where he would remain, except for a short exile, until the end of his life.

Because of Geneva's central location and the power of Calvin's theology, it quickly came to rival Wittenberg as a source of Protestant thought. Reformed preachers moved easily from Geneva to France, Scotland, England, and the Low Countries, carrying with them Calvin's ideas about salvation and the godly. Until the end of his life Calvin was a magnet drawing people interested in reform.

The heart of Calvin's appeal lay in his formal theological writings. In 1536 he published the first of many editions of the *Institutes of the Christian Religion,* which was to become the summa of Reformed theology. In it Calvin laid out a doctrine of the absolute power of God and the complete depravity and powerlessness of humanity.

Like Luther, Calvin viewed salvation as a mysterious gift from God. Yet Calvin differed from Luther in a crucial aspect. Salvation was by grace, but it was part of a progressive sanctification. This was a critical difference, for Luther did not believe that human behavior could be transformed. We are, he said, "simultaneously justified and sinners." By contrast, Calvin believed that there could be no salvation "if we do not also live a holy life." Thus the religious behavior of the individual and the community was an essential gift of justification. As a result, Calvin believed that it was the church's duty to promote moral progress. Public officials were to be "vicars of God." They had the power to lead and correct both the faithful and the unregenerate sinners who lived in Christian communities. In his years in Geneva Calvin tried to create a "Christian Commonwealth," but Geneva was far from a theocracy. Calvin's initial attempts to create a Christian community by requiring public confession and allowing church leaders to discipline sinners were rejected by Geneva's city council, which exiled Calvin in 1538.

On his return in 1541 he sought to institute church reforms modeled on those he had observed in the Protestant city of Strasbourg. Calvin's Reformed church hierarchy was made up of four offices: preachers, teachers, deacons, and elders. Preachers and teachers saw to the care and education of the faithful. Deacons, as in the early church, were charged with attending to the material needs of the congregation. Elders—the true leaders of the Genevan church—were selected from the patriciate who dominated the civil government of the city. Thus it makes as much sense to speak of a church governed by the town as a town dominated by the church. The elders actively intervened

Iconoclasm *Calvinists believed that Christians had to live in communities in which "true religion" was practiced. Iconoclasts (image smashers) cleansed churches of all paintings and statuary that might lead people back to the worship of idols—that is, the medieval cult of saints. This illustration shows just how organized iconoclasm really was.* (The Fotomas Index, U.K.)

in education, charity, and attempts to regulate prostitution. Consistories, or church courts, made up of preachers and community elders who enforced community moral and religious values, became one of the most important characteristics of Reformed (Calvinist) communities.

Most reformers accepted a commonplace medieval idea that since salvation depended on God's gift of grace, God in effect "predestined" some people to be saved. They differed on whether this meant that God predestined others to damnation. Luther argued that Christians could never know why some people were saved and others were not. Calvin, however, believed that God's power was such that "eternal life is foreordained for some, eternal damnation for others."

Calvin suggested that the elect, those predestined for salvation, would benefit from "signs of divine benevolence," an idea that would have a profound impact on the Calvinist understanding of the relationship of wealth to spiritual life. Calvin believed that good works and a well-ordered society were the result of God's grace. By the seventeenth century many followers of Calvin in Europe's commercial centers believed that the elect had a duty to work in the secular world and that wealth accumulated in business was a sign of God's favor. It was an idea nicely adapted to the increasingly wealthy society of early modern Europe.

That connection between salvation and material life, however, lay in the future. The aspect of election that most interested Calvin was the creation of a truly Christian community by the elect. To accomplish this, Reformed churches—that is, those that took their lead from Zwingli and Calvin, purged themselves of any manifestation of "superstition." Like Zwinglians, they rejected the idea that Christ was really present in the sacrament of Holy Communion. They rejected the role of saints. They removed from their churches and destroyed paintings and statuary that they believed were indications of idolatry.

Reformed churchmen reacted promptly and harshly to events that seemed to threaten either church or state. The most famous episode involved the capture, trial, and execution of Michael Servetus (1511–1553), a Spanish physician and radical theologian who rejected traditional doctrines such as the Trinity and specifically criticized many of Calvin's teachings in the *Institutes*. After corresponding with Servetus for a time, Calvin remarked that if Servetus were in Geneva, "I would not suffer him to get out alive." After living in various parts of Europe, Servetus eventually did come anonymously to Geneva. He was recognized and arrested. Calvin was as good as his word. After a public debate and trial Servetus was burned at the stake for blaspheming the Trinity and the Christian religion. Calvin's condemnation of Servetus was all too typical of Christians in the sixteenth century. Lutherans, Calvinists, and Catholics all believed that protection of true religion required harsh measures against the ignorant, the immoral, and the unorthodox. All too few would have said, as the humanist reformer Sebastion Castellio did, "To burn a heretic is not to defend a doctrine, but to burn a man."[5]

The Radical Reform of the Anabaptists Michael Servetus was but one of a number of extremists who claimed to be carrying out the full reform implied in the teachings of Luther, Zwingli, and Calvin. Called "Anabaptists" (or "rebaptizers" because of their rejection of infant baptism) or simply "radicals," they tended to take biblical commands more literally than the mainline reformers. They represented a broad social movement dominated by peasants and modest townspeople. They were more interested in behavior and community standards than in learned theological arguments. They believed that only adults should be baptized, and then only after confession of sin. They believed that Christians should live apart in communities of the truly redeemed. Thus they refused to take civil oaths or hold public office, for to do so would be to compromise with unreformed civil society.

The earliest of the radicals allied themselves with the rebels of 1524 and 1525. Thomas Müntzer (1490–1525) was an influential preacher who believed in divine revelation through visions and dreams. His visions told him that the poor were the true elect and that the end of the world was at hand. An active participant in the uprisings of 1525, Müntzer called on the elect to drive out the ungodly. After the defeat of the rebels, he was captured and executed by the German princes.

Other radicals, such as the revolutionaries who took control of the northern German city of Münster, rejected infant baptism, adopted polygamy, and proclaimed a new "Kingdom of Righteousness." The reformers of Münster instituted the new kingdom in the city by rebaptizing those who joined their cause and expelling those who opposed them. They abolished private property rights in Münster and instituted new laws concerning morality and behavior. Leadership in the city eventually passed to a

The Hutterite Community

Peter Riedemann (1506–1556), a founding member of the Hutterites, was captured and imprisoned several times for his Anabaptist beliefs. In his Confession of Faith, written as an explanation to his jailers, Riedemann lays out a vision of the simple Christian community that still remains central to Hutterites and Moravians throughout the world. The confession begins with an explanation of the Apostles' Creed, then discusses the nature of salvation and the structure of the Christian community. This excerpt highlights some of the distinctive features of the Hutterites.

Community of Goods

All believers have fellowship in holy things, that is, in God. . . . Just as Christ has nothing for himself, . . . no members of Christ's body should possess any gift for themselves or for their own sake. . . . Community of goods applies to both spiritual and material gifts. All of God's gifts, not only the spiritual but also the temporal, have been given so that they not be kept but be shared with each other. Therefore, the fellowship of believers should be visible not only in spiritual but also in temporal things. . . .

Separation from the World

God has chosen this church for himself and separated the members from all peoples, so that they might serve him with one mind and heart. . . . We have left the gatherings of profane and impure people, and we wish that everyone would do the same. . . . If some will not repent and will not keep the true ordinances of God, but remain in sin, we must let them go their way and leave them to God.

Warfare

Christ . . . has prepared a kingdom for himself . . . therefore all worldly warfare

tailor, Jan of Leiden (d. 1535), who proclaimed himself the new messiah and lord of the world. The Anabaptists were opposed by the prince-bishop of Münster, the political and religious lord of the city. After a sixteen-month siege, the bishop and his allies recaptured the city in 1535. Besieging forces massacred men, women, and children. Jan of Leiden was captured and executed by mutilation with red-hot tongs.

With the destruction of the Münster revolutionaries in 1535, the Anabaptist movement turned inward. Under leaders such as Menno Simons (1495–1561), who founded the Mennonites, and Jakob Hutter (d. 1536), who founded the Hutterian Brethren, or Hutterites, they rejected their predecessors' violent attempts to establish truly holy cities. To varying degrees they also rejected connections with civil society, military service, and even civil courts. They did, however, believe that their own communities were exclusively of the elect. They tended to close themselves off from outsiders and enforce a strict discipline over their members. The elders of these communities were empowered to excommunicate or "shun" those who violated the groups' precepts. Anabaptist communities have proved unusually durable. Hutterite and Mennonite comin this kingdom has come to an end. . . . Therefore Christians should not take part in war, nor should they use force for the purpose of vengeance.

Church Discipline

Paul says, "Put away the evil that is among you" [I Corinthians 5:13]. . . . That is why we admonish one another, warning and rebuking each other persistently. . . . A different method is used for major sins. . . . Such a person is separated from the church without admonition. . . . When a person is banned, we have no fellowship with him and nothing to do with him so that he may become ashamed . . . in the hope that the sinner will be moved to return all the more quickly to God. If that does not happen, the church remains pure and is innocent of his sin. . . . When a person is excluded, we have no fellowship with that person until there is true repentance, . . . until he has received from the church the good report of a truly repentant life.

Adornment

First, we say with Peter that the adornment of Christians does not consist in outward show, such as jewelry, fine clothing, or similar trappings. . . . The only thing they should learn from the children of the world is diligence. In order to please each other, worldly people are diligent to dress and to adorn themselves to the very utmost in accordance with the fashion of the land in which they live. . . . Christians should adorn themselves . . . so as to please God, who dwells in heaven.

Source: Peter Riedemann's Hutterite Confession of Faith, ed. and trans. John J. Friesen, pp. 119–123, 134–135, 152–155. Herald Press, Scottsdale, PA 15683. All rights reserved.

munities continue to exist in western Europe, North America, and parts of the former Soviet Union.

Like Luther, all of the early reformers appealed to the authority of the Bible in their attacks on church tradition. Yet in the villages and towns of Germany and Switzerland, many radicals were prepared to move far beyond the positions Luther had advocated. When they did so, Luther found himself in the odd position of appealing for vigorous action by the very imperial authorities whose previous inaction had allowed his own protest to survive.

THE EMPIRE OF CHARLES V (R. 1519–1556)

Luther believed that secular authorities should be neutral in religious matters. In his eyes the success of the early Reformation was simply God's will:

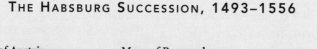

THE HABSBURG SUCCESSION, 1493–1556

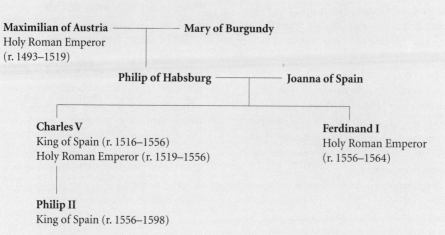

Maximilian of Austria — **Mary of Burgundy**
Holy Roman Emperor
(r. 1493–1519)

Philip of Habsburg — **Joanna of Spain**

Charles V
King of Spain (r. 1516–1556)
Holy Roman Emperor (r. 1519–1556)

Ferdinand I
Holy Roman Emperor
(r. 1556–1564)

Philip II
King of Spain (r. 1556–1598)

> I simply taught, preached and wrote God's Word; otherwise I did nothing. And while I slept or drank Wittenberg beer with my friends, the Word so greatly weakened the Papacy that no prince or emperor ever inflicted such losses on it.[6]

Luther's belief in the Word of God was absolute, yet he must have known, even as he drank his beer, that the Holy Roman emperor could have crushed the reform movements if he had been able to enforce imperial decrees. But attempts to resolve religious conflict became entangled with attempts to hold together the family lands of the Habsburg emperor and with political rivalries among the various German princes. The eventual religious settlement required a constitutional compromise that preserved the virtual autonomy of the great princes of Germany. Charles had dreamed of using his imperial office to restore and maintain the political and religious unity of Europe. The political realities of sixteenth-century Europe, however, made nobles afraid of the emperor even when he tried to preserve the unity of the church.

Imperial Challenges

Emperor Charles V (r. 1519–1556) was the beneficiary of a series of marriages that, in the words of his courtiers, seemed to re-create the empire of Charlemagne. From his father, Philip of Habsburg, he inherited claims to Austria, the imperial crown, and Burgundian lands that included the Low Countries and the county of Burgundy. Through his mother, Joanna, the daughter of Ferdinand and Isabella of Spain, Charles became heir to the kingdoms of Castile, Aragon, Sicily, Naples, and Spanish America. During the Italian wars of the early sixteenth century Charles's holdings in Italy expanded to include the duchy of Milan and most of the rest of Lombardy. By 1506 he was duke in the Burgundian lands, in 1516 he became king of Aragon and Castile, and in 1519 he was elected Holy Roman emperor. Every government in Europe had to deal with one part or another of Charles's empire. His chancellor enthused, "[God] has set you on the way

The Capture of Belgrade, 1521 *During the sixteenth century Ottoman Turks dominated the Balkans militarily and were a significant force in European diplomacy. They were masters of coordinated attacks combining artillery and infantry.* (Bildarchiv d. ONB, Wien)

towards a world monarchy, towards the gathering of all Christendom under a single shepherd."

Charles seems to have sincerely desired such a world monarchy, but he faced challenges in each of the areas under his control. In Castile, for example, grandees, townspeople, and peasants felt they had grounds for complaint. They objected that taxes were too heavy and that Charles disregarded the Cortes and his natural advisers, the old nobility. But most of all they complained that too many of his officials were foreigners whom he had brought with him from his home in Flanders. Protests festered in the towns and villages of Castile and finally broke out into a revolt called the *Comunero* (townsmen's or citizens') movement. Between 1517 and 1522, when religious reform was making dramatic advances in Germany, many of the most important towns of Spain were in open rebellion against the Crown. Charles's forces eventually took control of the situation, and by 1522 he had crushed the Comuneros. But in the critical years between 1522 and 1530 he was careful to spend much of his time in his Spanish kingdoms.

Charles's claims in Italy, as well as in the Pyrenees and the Low Countries, brought him into direct conflict with the Valois kings of France. In the critical 1520s the Habsburgs and the Valois fought a series of wars (see page 346). Charles dramatically defeated the French at Pavia in northern Italy in 1525, sacked and occupied Rome in 1527, and became the virtual arbiter of Italian politics. The volatile situation in Italy made for cynical alliances. In the course of the struggle the Catholic Francis I of France, whose title was "the Most Christian King," found it to his advantage to ally himself with

Charles's most serious opponents, the Protestants and the Turks. Francis demonstrated the truth of Machiavelli's dictum that private virtues play a small role in political and diplomatic life. The Habsburg-Valois Wars dragged on until, in exhaustion, the French king Henry II (r. 1547–1559) and the Spanish king Philip II (r. 1556–1598) signed the Treaty of Cateau-Cambrésis in 1559 (see page 346).

Charles was not the only ruler to claim the title "emperor" and a succession reaching back to the Roman Empire. After the conquest of Constantinople in 1453, the sultan of the Ottoman Turks began to refer to himself as "the Emperor." After consolidating control of Constantinople and the Balkans, Turkish armies under the command of the emperor Suleiman (r. 1520–1566), known as "the Magnificent," resumed their expansion to the north and west. After capturing Belgrade, Turkish forces soundly defeated a Hungarian army at the Battle of Mohács in 1526. Charles appealed for unity within Christendom against the threat. Even Martin Luther agreed that Christians should unite during invasion.

Suleiman's army besieged Vienna in 1529 before being forced to retreat. The Turks also deployed a navy in the Mediterranean and, with French encouragement, began a series of raids along the coasts of Italy and Spain. The Turkish fleet remained a threat throughout the sixteenth century. The reign of Suleiman marked the permanent entry of Turkey into the European military and diplomatic system. Turkish pressure was yet another reason Charles was unable to deal with German Protestants in a direct and uncompromising way.

German Politics   The political configuration of Germany had an ongoing influence on the course of religious reform. In 1500 Germany was much less centralized than France or England. The emperor's claims in most areas amounted to the right to collect modest taxes on households and individuals, a court of high justice, and the authority to proclaim imperial truces. Yet the empire lacked a unified legal system, and the emperor himself had only one vote on the imperial council. In many respects political centralization and innovation were characteristics of individual territories, not of the empire as a whole. The power of the emperor depended on his relations with the towns and princes of Germany.

In the first years after Luther issued his "Ninety-five Theses," he was defended by the elector Frederick of Saxony, who held a key vote in Charles's quest for election as Holy Roman emperor. As long as Frederick protected Luther, imperial officials had to proceed against the reformer with caution. When Luther was outlawed by the imperial Diet of Worms in 1521, Frederick and many other princes and towns refused to enforce the edict against him and his followers unless their own grievances against the emperor and their complaints about the church were taken up at the same time. At the Diet of Speyer in 1526, delegates passed a resolution empowering princes and towns to settle religious matters in their territories as they saw it. In effect, this resolution legitimated the reform in territories where authorities chose to follow the new teachings and presaged the final religious settlement in Germany.

German princes took advantage of the emperor's relative powerlessness and made choices reflecting a complex of religious, political, and diplomatic issues. Electoral Saxony and ducal Saxony, the two parts of the province of Saxony, split over the issue of reform. Electoral Saxony, Luther's homeland, was Lutheran. Ducal Saxony was strongly

Catholic. Especially in the autonomous towns many decisions about religion were often made with one eye on the choices made by neighbors and competitors.

Some rulers acted in ways that were even more consciously cynical and self-serving. The grand master of the religious order of the Teutonic Knights, Albrecht von Hohenzollern (1490–1568), who controlled the duchy of Prussia, renounced his monastic vows. Then, at the urging of Luther and other reformers, he secularized the order's estates (that is, he transferred them from church to private ownership), which then became East Prussia, hereditary lands of the Hohenzollern family. In other territories rulers managed to claim the properties of suppressed religious orders. Even when, as in the case of Count Philip of Hesse (1504–1567), much of the revenue from secularization was used to create hospitals and an organized system of charity, the reforming prince was still enriched.

Some rulers found their personal reservations about Luther reinforced by their fears of popular unrest. Luther's call for decisions based on personal conscience seemed to the dukes of Bavaria, for example, to repudiate princely authority and even to provoke anarchy. In the confused and fluid situation of the 1520s and 1530s, imperial interests were never the primary issue.

The Religious Settlement With the fading of the Turkish threat on Vienna in 1529, Charles V renewed his pressure on the German principalities at a meeting of the imperial diet at Augsburg in 1530. It was for this diet that Philip Melanchthon (1497–1560), Luther's closest adviser, prepared the Augsburg Confession, which would become the basic statement of the Lutheran faith. Melanchthon hoped that the document would form the basis of compromise with Catholic powers, but that possibility was rejected out of hand by the imperial party. Charles aimed to affirm his strength in Germany by forcing the princes to end the reform movement and enforce bans on Luther's teachings.

The Protestant princes responded by forming the League of Schmalkalden. At first the founders of the league claimed that they were interested in protecting Lutheran preaching, but the league quickly developed as a center of opposition to imperial influence in general. Eventually Charles and a group of allied princes managed to defeat the league at the Battle of Mühlberg in 1547. The emperor was unable to continue pressure on the Protestants, however, because he had depended on the support of some Protestant princes in his battles with the league. As a result, even after military defeat, the Protestant princes were able to maintain religious autonomy. In the religious Peace of Augsburg of 1555, the emperor formally acknowledged the principle that sovereign princes could choose the religion to be practiced in their territories—*cuius regio, eius religio* ("whose territory, his religion"). There were limits, however: leaders had only two choices—remain under papal authority or adopt the Augsburg Confession outlined by Melanchthon. Reformed churches associated with Zwingli or Calvin were not legally recognized.

Shortly after the settlement, Charles abdicated his Spanish and imperial titles. Exhausted by years of political and religious struggle, he ceded the imperial crown to his brother, Ferdinand (r. 1556–1564). He transferred his possessions in the Low Countries, Spain, Italy, and the New World to his son, Philip II (r. 1556–1598). Charles had believed his courtiers when they had compared his empire to that of the ancient Romans.

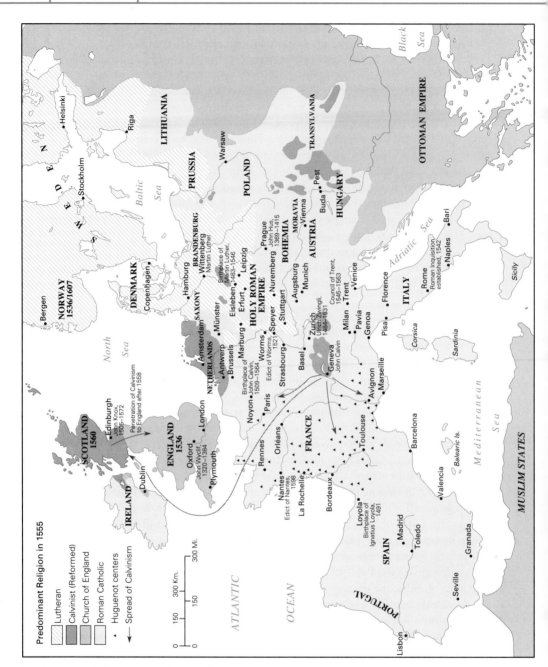

Catholics and Protestants in 1555

At the time of the Peace of Augsburg, Christendom in western Europe was divided into three major groups. Lutheran influence was largely confined to parts of Germany and Scandinavia, while Calvinist influence was strong in Switzerland, Scotland, the Low Countries, and parts of France. Most of the West remained within the Roman Catholic Church.

He had accepted that his duty as emperor was to unite Christendom under one law and one church. But in no part of his empire did he ever command the authority that would have allowed him to unite his lands politically, let alone to re-establish religious unity. Following his abdication Charles retired to a monastery in Spain, where he died in 1558.

THE ENGLISH REFORMATION, 1520–1603

The Reformation in England is often called a monarchical Reformation. In contrast with Germany, where reform occurred in spite of imperial opposition, in England the Crown instituted the reform. As in Germany, however, institutional change in the church followed from both secular issues and reform ideas. In England an initially hostile monarch began to tolerate reform when he perceived the papacy as an unbiblical, tyrannical force blocking essential state policy. Although reformers were active in England, their success depended entirely on royal support. And by the middle of the sixteenth century, it was royal interest in compromise that brought a settlement that left England a curious hybrid of reformed and traditional religious practices.

Henry VIII and the Monarchical Reformation
England was closely tied to Germany. Since the twelfth century large numbers of German merchants had lived and traded in England, and Cologne was home to a considerable English community. Anglo-German connections became especially significant during the Reformation. Reformers from Wittenberg and other Protestant towns had contact with English merchants from London who traded and traveled on the Continent. One reformer, William Tyndale (ca. 1494–1536), served as a bridge between the Continent and England. He had a humanistic education in classical languages and began working on a translation of the Bible in the 1520s. Forced to flee London by the church hierarchy, he visited Luther in Wittenberg before settling in Antwerp, where he completed his English New Testament. By 1526 copies of his translation and his religious tracts flooded England. By the 1520s Lutheran influence was noticeable in London and Cambridge. There is still debate about just how strong this early influence was. To some extent the ground may have been prepared for the reformers by the few surviving Lollards (see page 360), who tended to be literate and were an ideal market for Tyndale's English Bible and his numerous reformist tracts. But religious brotherhoods, lay piety, and traditional forms of penance remained an important part of religious life. If reform was to succeed, it required support from the king.

Henry VIII (r. 1509–1547) began his reign as a popular and powerful king. Handsome, athletic, and artistic, he seemed to be the ideal ruler. Henry took an interest in theology and humanistic culture. At first he was quite hostile to Luther's reform ideas and wrote *Defense of the Seven Sacraments,* which earned him the title "Defender of the Faith" from a grateful Pope Leo X. Throughout his life Henry remained suspicious of many Protestant ideas, but he led the initial phase of the break with the papacy because of his political problems with the highly orthodox Holy Roman emperor Charles V. The first phase of the English Reformation was thus monarchical.

Henry VII had initiated closer relations with Spain when he married his eldest son, Arthur, Prince of Wales, to Ferdinand of Aragon's daughter, Catherine. After Arthur's death the future Henry VIII was married to his brother's widow in 1509. Henry VIII later tried to further the Anglo-imperial alliance when he arranged a treaty by which the emperor Charles V, who was Catherine of Aragon's nephew, agreed to marry Henry's daughter, Mary Tudor. But by the late 1520s the Anglo-imperial alliance fell apart when Charles, responding to Spanish pressures, renounced the proposed marriage and instead married a Portuguese princess.

Henry's relations with Charles were further hampered by what the English called "the King's Great Matter"—that is, his determination to divorce Catherine. Recalling the unrest of the Wars of the Roses (see page 356), Henry believed that he needed a son to ensure that the Tudors could maintain control of the English crown. By 1527 Henry and Catherine had a daughter, Mary, but no living sons. Henry became convinced that he remained without a male heir because, by biblical standards, he had committed incest by marrying his brother's widow. As Leviticus 20:21 says, "If a man takes his brother's wife, it is impurity; they shall remain childless." Henry desired an annulment. Unfortunately for him, Leo X's successor, Pope Clement VII (r. 1523–1534), was a virtual prisoner of imperial troops who had recently sacked Rome and taken control of most of Italy. As long as Charles supported Catherine of Aragon and his forces occupied Rome, a papal annulment was out of the question.

The king's advisers quickly divided into two camps. Sir Thomas More, humanist writer (see pages 392–394), royal chancellor and staunch Catholic, urged the king to continue his policy of negotiation with the papacy and his efforts to destroy the growing Protestant party. Until his resignation in 1532, More led royal authorities in a vigorous campaign against the dissemination of the newly translated Tyndale Bible and against the spread of Protestant ideas. More was opposed and eventually ousted by a radical party of Protestants led by Thomas Cranmer (1489–1556) and Thomas Cromwell (1485?–1540), who saw in the king's desire for a divorce an effective wedge to pry Henry out of the papal camp. Cromwell, who eventually replaced More as chancellor, advised the king that the marriage problem could be solved by the English clergy without papal interference.

Between 1532 and 1535 Henry and Parliament took a number of steps that effectively left the king in control of the church in England. Early in 1533 Cranmer was named archbishop of Canterbury. Later that year Parliament ruled that appeals of cases concerning wills, marriages, and ecclesiastical grants had to be heard in England. In May an English court annulled the king's marriage to Catherine. Four months later Henry's new queen, Anne Boleyn, gave birth to a daughter, Elizabeth.

After the split began, the king started to seize church properties. Parliamentary action culminated in the passage of the Act of Supremacy in 1534, which declared the king to be "the Protector and only Supreme Head of the Church and the Clergy of England." Henry meant to enforce his control by requiring a public oath supporting the act. Sir Thomas More refused to take the oath and was arrested, tried, and executed for treason. In some respects Parliament had acted as an instrument of reform, in the manner of the German and Swiss town councils that moderated debates over church reform. In England, however, Parliament and perhaps a majority of the laity perceived this reform primarily as a political issue.

Cromwell and Cranmer had hoped to use "the King's Great Matter" as a way to begin a Lutheran-style reform of the church. But, though separated from the papal party, Henry remained suspicious of religious change. He complained of radicals who "do wrest and interpret and so untruly allege [novel understandings of Scripture] to subvert and overturn as well the sacraments of Holy Church as the power and authority of princes and magistrates." Between 1534 and Henry's death in 1547, neither the Protestant nor the Catholic party was able to gain the upper hand at court or at Canterbury. Substantive changes in the English church would be made by Henry's children.

Reform and Counter-Reform Under Edward and Mary
Prince Edward, Henry's only surviving son in 1547, was born to Henry's third wife, Jane Seymour. He was only 10 years old when his father died. By chance Edward Seymour, who was Prince Edward's uncle, and the Protestant faction were in favor at the time of Henry's death. Seymour was named duke of Somerset and Lord Protector of the young King Edward VI (r. 1547–1553). Under Somerset the Protestants were able to make significant changes in religious life in England. Edward completed the "dissolution of the monasteries"—the process of confiscating properties belonging to chapels and shrines—that his father had begun. In an act of great symbolic meaning, priests were legally allowed to marry; many had already done so. Finally, Archbishop Cranmer introduced the first edition of the English *Book of Common Prayer* in 1549. The publication updated some late medieval English prayers and combined them with liturgical and theological ideas taken from Luther, Zwingli, and Calvin. In its beautifully expressive English, it provided the laity with a primer on how to combine English religious traditions with reform theology. Later, continental Protestants were named to teach theology at Oxford and Cambridge. If Edward had not died of tuberculosis in 1553, England's reform would have looked very much like the movement in Switzerland and southern Germany.

Protestant reformers attempted to prevent Mary Tudor (r. 1553–1558), Henry's Catholic daughter, from claiming the throne, but Mary and the Catholic party quickly took control of the court and the church. Mary immediately declared previous reform decrees to be void. Cardinal Reginald Pole (1500–1558), who had advocated reform within the Catholic Church, became the center of the Catholic restoration party in Mary's England. Pole rooted out Protestants within the church. More than eight hundred gentlemen, clerics, and students fled England for Protestant havens on the Continent. Some officials, including Cranmer, chose to remain and paid with their lives. In all, three hundred Protestants, mostly artisans and laborers, were tried and executed by church courts, earning the queen her nickname, "Bloody Mary."

The policies of the queen brought about an abrupt return of the English church to papal authority. Most of the English quickly and easily returned to traditional Roman religious practices. Statues were removed from hiding and restored to places of honor in churches and chapels. Although conclusive evidence is lacking, the queen's initial successes may indicate that the Reformation was not broadly supported by the people. In fact, the restoration of Catholicism by Mary might have worked had the queen not died after little more than six years on the throne. At her death the final settlement of the reform in England was far from certain.

The Elizabethan Settlement
Queen Elizabeth (r. 1558–1603), daughter of Anne Boleyn, succeeded to the throne at the death of her half sister. The reign of Elizabeth was one of the most enigmatic and successful of English history. At home she managed to gain control of the various political and religious factions in the country, and abroad she exploited the rivalries of a variety of

international powers to her own advantage. She seems to have clearly recognized the necessity of striking a balance between opposing forces.

Her first pressing task was to effect a religious settlement. Early in her reign she twice left church services at the elevation of the bread by the priest. Since in Catholic thought it was this action of the priest that made Christ present in the bread, she was indicating symbolically her opposition to a purely Catholic understanding of the sacraments. In the next few years she continued to work for the restoration of many features of her father's and her half brother's reforms. In 1559 the new Act of Supremacy and an Act of Uniformity reinstituted royal control of the English church and reestablished uniform liturgical and doctrinal standards. The *Book of Common Prayer* composed by Cranmer was brought back, and final changes were made in the liturgy.

Protestants had hoped for a complete victory, but the "Elizabethan Settlement" was considerably less than that. Although figures are lacking, it is likely that a large portion of the English population did not support a return to Henry's and Edward's reforms. After making clear her significant differences with Rome, Elizabeth confounded her most fervent Protestant supporters by offering a number of concessions to Anglo-Catholics. She remained celibate, and she ordered the Anglican clergy to do the same—

The Queen in Parliament
This image was meant to show the willingness of Parliament to support the queen, a key element of the Elizabethan Settlement. (Bibliothèque nationale de France)

although she could do little to prevent clerical marriage. More important, she and her closest advisers allowed a great variety of customs and practices favored by Anglo-Catholics. These matters, the queen's supporters argued, were not essential to salvation, and thus individuals could be allowed to choose. Many of the prayers in the *Book of Common Prayer,* for example, seemed "papist" to the most radical Protestants. Similarly, many of the traditional clerical vestments and altar furnishings remained unchanged. Elizabeth probably knew that the Protestants had no alternative but to support her and thus felt free to win back the support of the Anglo-Catholics.

Toward the end of Elizabeth's reign Richard Hooker (1554–1600) published his *Laws of Ecclesiastical Polity,* which provides an excellent description of the Anglican (English) Church born of the Elizabethan Settlement. England, Hooker maintains, had its own way of handling religious affairs. Theologically it represented a middle ground between the traditions cultivated by the Roman church and the more radically biblical religion favored by the Lutherans of Germany and the Calvinists of Switzerland. The Church of England moderated Luther's and Calvin's absolute reliance on Scriptures with history and tradition. In areas where tradition was strong, processions and other pre-Reformation traditions continued to animate village life. In other areas more austere reformed practices were likely to predominate.

France, Scandinavia, and Eastern Europe, 1523–1560

In England and in the empire of Charles V, the success of the new religious reforms depended greatly on the political situation. It would be naive to conclude, as Luther claimed, that "the Word did everything." Yet this complex religious reform movement cannot be reduced to the politics of kings and princes. The issues will be clearer if we survey politics and reform in the rest of Europe, noting whether and to what extent the new ideas took root. In France, for example, the widespread, popular support of the old religion limited the options of the country's political leaders. Similarly, in northern Europe religious reform was an issue of both popular feeling and royal politics.

France   Luther's work, and later the ideas of the urban reformers of southwestern Germany and Switzerland, passed quickly into France. Geneva is in a French-speaking area close to the French border. It, like Strasbourg, was easy for French Protestants to reach. Perhaps because of France's proximity to the Calvinists in French-speaking Switzerland or because of the clarity and power of Calvin's *Institutes,* French Protestants, known as Huguenots, were tied more closely to the Calvinists of Geneva than to the Lutherans of Germany.

It is difficult, however, to know how many French Christians were Protestants. At the height of the Reformation's popularity Protestants probably represented no more than 10 percent of the total population of France. It has been estimated that Protestant congregations numbered about 2,100 in the 1560s—in a country that had perhaps 32,000 traditional parishes. Protestants seem to have comprised a diverse mix that included two of the three most important noble families at court: the Bourbon and Montmorency families. Clerics interested in moral reform and artisans who worked at new trades, such as the printing industry, also made up a significant portion of the converts. Perhaps reflecting the numerous printers and merchants in their numbers, Protestants tended to be of higher than average literacy. The Protestant population was spread throughout the country. Protestants were particularly well represented in towns and probably constituted a majority in the southern and western towns of La Rochelle, Montpellier, and Nîmes. Paris was the one part of the realm in which they had little influence, and their absence in the capital may have been their undoing.

The conservative theologians of the Sorbonne in Paris were some of Luther's earliest opponents. They complained that many masters at the University of Paris were "Lutheran." As early as 1523 Parisian authorities seized and burned books said to be by Luther. But as in Germany, there was no clear understanding of who or what a Lutheran was. The Sorbonne theologians were also suspicious of a number of "pre-reformers," including the humanistic editor Jacques Lefèvre d'Étaples (1455–1536; see pages 391–392), who late in life had come to an understanding of justification quite like Luther's. Others were clerics intent on religious reform within the traditional structures. Unlike Luther and the French Protestants, these pre-reformers did not challenge the priests' relationship to the sacraments. They were interested in the piety and behavior of churchmen. They never challenged the role of the clergy in salvation. King Francis's own sister, Margaret of Angoulême (1492–1549), gathered a group of religious persons, including several reformers, at her court. But Margaret herself urged that theology be left to scholars; she believed that the laity should stick to simple pieties. Like Margaret, most French Christians had no clear sense that Protestant teachings required a complete break with medieval Christian traditions.

Like previous French kings, Francis I (r. 1515–1547) hoped to extend royal jurisdictions in France and make France an international power. Engaged in the seemingly intractable wars with the Habsburgs, Francis generally ignored religious questions. In 1525 he was taken captive in the wake of a military disaster at Pavia in Lombardy. He was held prisoner for nearly a year, during which time conservatives at the Sorbonne and in Paris moved actively against suspected Protestants. Francis was not initially opposed to what seemed to be moral reform within the church. His own view was that the king's duty was to preserve order and prevent scandal, and at first carrying out that duty meant protecting reformers whom the conservative militants persecuted. The king feared disorder more than he feared religious reform.

On October 18, 1534, however, Francis's attitude changed when he and all Paris awoke to find the city littered with anti-Catholic placards containing, in the words of the writers, "true articles on the horrible, great and insufferable abuses of the Papal Mass." The response of the Parisians was outrage. They attacked foreigners, especially those who by dress or speech seemed "Lutheran"—that is, German or Flemish. Several months later Francis led a religious procession through Paris in honor of the Blessed Sacrament. The "Affair of the Placards" changed Francis's ideas about the sources of disorder. Opposition to traditional religious practices became more difficult and more dangerous. John Calvin himself was forced to leave Paris, and eventually France, because he feared persecution. Between 1534 and 1560 some ten thousand Protestants fled France, many joining Calvin in Geneva.

By the middle of the sixteenth century it was clear that neither Protestant nor Catholic factions would be able to control religious and political life in France. Francis I died in 1547, and the stage was set for a series of destructive factional struggles over religion and political power that would continue for the rest of the century (see Chapter 15).

Scandinavia
All of Scandinavia became Lutheran. Initial influences drifted north from Germany, carried by Hanseatic merchants and students who had studied at the universities of northern Germany. Yet the reform in Sweden and Denmark even more than in England was monarchical. In both Scandinavian kingdoms the kings began with an attack on the temporal rights and properties of the church. Changes in liturgy and practice came later as reformers gained royal protection.

Since 1397 all Scandinavia had been united in theory in the Union of Kalmar (see page 357). But early in the sixteenth century the last pretenses of unity were shattered. Christian I of Denmark (r. 1513–1523) invaded Sweden and captured Stockholm, the capital. So great was his brutality that within a few years Gustav Vasa, a leading noble, was able to secure the loyalty of most of the Swedes and in 1523 was elected king of Sweden. Gustav's motto was "All power is of God." Like Henry VIII of England, Gustav (r. 1523–1560) moved carefully in an attempt to retain the loyalty of as many groups as possible. Although he never formally adopted a national confession of faith, the Swedish church and state gradually took on a more Lutheran character. In an effort to secure royal finances, the Riksdag, or parliament, passed the Vasteras Ordinances, which secularized ecclesiastical lands and authorized the preaching of the "Pure Word of God." Olaus Petri (1493–1552), Sweden's principal reform preacher, was installed by royal order in the cathedral of Stockholm.

In Denmark the reformers also moved cautiously. Frederick I (r. 1523–1533) and his son, Christian III (r. 1534–1559), continued the policy of secularization and control that Christian I had initiated. Danish kings seemed interested in reform as a diplomatic means of attack on the Roman church. It seems that in Denmark the old religion simply suffered from a sort of royal indifference. The kings tended to support reformers as a way to attack the political power of the bishops. The Danes finally accepted the Augsburg Confession, which was becoming the most widely accepted exposition of Lutheran belief, in 1538. The transformation of practice proceeded slowly over the next decades.

In the frontier regions of Scandinavia—Finland, Iceland, and Norway—the reform was undertaken as a matter of royal policy. Initially only a handful of local reformers introduced and proselytized the new theology and practice. In many regions resistance to the Reformation continued for several generations. One valley hidden in the mountains of western Norway continued to follow the old religion for three centuries after its contacts with Rome had been severed.

Eastern Europe
In some respects there was less opposition to the expansion of Protestantism in eastern Europe. The result was the creation of a unique religious culture. The church hierarchy was not in a position to enforce orthodoxy. Some rulers were indifferent to religious debates, as were the Muslim Ottoman Turks, who controlled much of eastern Hungary and what is now Romania. Other rulers whose societies already contained Orthodox and Catholic Christians, as well as Muslims and Jews, offered toleration because they could ill afford to alienate any portion of their subject populations.

Protestant ideas initially passed through the German communities of Poland and the trading towns along the Baltic coast. But in the 1540s Calvinist ideas spread quickly among the Polish nobles, especially those at the royal court. Given the power and influence of some of the noble families, Catholics were unable to suppress the various secret Calvinist congregations. During the first half of the sixteenth century Protestantism became so well established in Poland that it could not be rooted out. Throughout the sixteenth century Protestantism remained one of the rallying points for those opposed to the expansion of royal power.

The situation was much the same in Hungary and Transylvania. Among German colonists, Magyars, and ethnic Romanians there were numerous individuals who were interested first in Luther's message and later in Calvin's revisions of the Reformed theology. The situation was exacerbated after the Turkish victory at Mohács in 1526, which destroyed the traditional political and religious elite of Hungary. Because no one could hope to enforce uniformity, some cities adopted a moderate Lutheran theology, and others followed a Calvinist confession. By the 1560s the Estates (representative assemblies) of Transylvania had decreed that four religions were to be tolerated—Catholic, Lutheran, Reformed (Calvinist), and Unitarian. Further, when various radical groups migrated from the west in search of toleration, they were able to create their own communities in Slavic and Magyar areas.

The Reformation was to have virtually no influence farther to the east, in Russia. The Orthodox Church in Russia was much more firmly under government control than was the church in the West. The Russian church followed the traditions of the Greek church, and Western arguments over justification made little sense in Orthodox churches. Given the historic suspicion of the Orthodox churches toward Rome, the Russians were more tolerant of contacts with the Protestants of northern Europe, but there would be no theological innovation or reform in sixteenth-century Russia.

THE LATE REFORMATION, CA. 1545–1600

In the first half of the sixteenth century Catholics applied the term *Lutheran* to anyone who was anticlerical. As Francesco Guicciardini (1483–1540), a papal governor in central Italy, remarked:

> I know of no one who loathes the ambition, the avarice, and the sensuality of the clergy more than I. . . . In spite of all this, the positions I have held under several popes have forced me, for my own good, to further their interests. Were it not for that, I should have loved Martin Luther as much as myself—not so that I might be free of the laws based on Christian religion as it is generally interpreted and understood; but to see this bunch of rascals get their just deserts, that is, to be without vices or without authority.[7]

Guicciardini's remarks catch both the frustration many Christians felt toward the traditional church and the very real confusion over just what it was that Luther had said. In parts of Germany by the late 1520s and across Europe by the 1550s, political and religious leaders attempted to explain to the people just what *Lutheran, Reformed (Calvinist),* and *Catholic* had come to mean. It was only in the second half of the sixteenth century that these terms came to have any clarity. After the middle of the sixteenth century it was true that along with theological and political changes, the Reformation represented a broad cultural movement.

The profound changes that began in the sixteenth century continued into the seventeenth. People began to sort out what it meant to belong to one church instead of to another. Central governments supported religious authorities who desired religious uniformity and control over individual Christians. In all parts of Europe, religious behavior changed. Both Protestants and Catholics became more concerned with the personal rather than the communal aspects of Christianity. After the sixteenth century the nature of Christianity and its place in public life, whether in Protestant or in Catholic countries, differed profoundly from Christianity in the Middle Ages.

Catholic Reform, 1512–1600   Historians commonly speak of both a movement for traditional reform and renewal within the Catholic Church, and a "Counter-Reformation," which was a direct response to and rejection of the theological positions championed by the Protestants. It is certainly true that one can categorize certain acts as clearly challenging the Protestants. However, to do so is to miss the point that the energetic actions of the Roman Catholic Church during the sixteenth century both affirmed traditional teachings and created new institutions better fitted to the early modern world.

The idea of purer, earlier church practices to which the "modern" church should return had been a commonplace for centuries. The great ecumenical Council of Constance early in the fifteenth century had called for "reform in head and members" (see pages 337–338). In 1512, five years before Luther made his public protests, Pope Julius II (r. 1503–1513) convened another ecumenical council, the Fifth Lateran Council (1513–1517), which was expected to look into the problems of nonresident clergy, multiple benefices, and a host of other issues. This tradition of moral reform was especially strong in Spain, Portugal, and Italy, lands whose political rulers were either indifferent or opposed to Protestant reforms.

The desire for reform along traditional lines was deeply felt within the Catholic Church. In the wake of the sack of Rome by imperial troops in 1527, one Roman cardinal, Bishop Gian Matteo Giberti of Verona (1495–1543), returned to his diocese and began a thoroughgoing reform. He conducted visitations of the churches and other religious institutions in Verona, preached tirelessly, worked hard to raise the educational level of his clergy, and required that priests live within their parishes. Giberti believed that morally rigorous traditional reform and renewal could counter the malaise he perceived. Other reforming bishops could be found throughout Catholic Europe.

New religious foundations sprang up to renew the church. The Spanish mystic Teresa of Avila (1515–1582) reflected the thinking of many when she lamented, "No wonder the Church is as it is, when the religious live as they do." Members of the new orders set out to change the church through example. The Florentine Filippo Neri (1515–1595) founded the Oratorian order, so named because of the monks' habit of leading the laity in prayer services. Filippo was joined in his work by Giovanni Palestrina (ca. 1525–1594), who composed music for the modest but moving prayer gatherings in Rome. Palestrina's music combined medieval plainchants with newer styles of polyphony, creating complex harmonies without obscuring the words and meaning of the text. The popularity of the Oratorians and their services can be measured in part by the fact that oratories, small chapels modeled on those favored by Filippo, remain to this day important centers of the musical life in the city of Rome.

The Catholic reform of the sixteenth century, however, was better known for its mystical theology than for its music. In Italy and France, but especially in Spain, a profusion of reformers chose to reform the church through austere prayer and contemplative devotions. Teresa of Avila, who belonged to a wealthy converso family (see pages 363–365), led a movement to reform the lax practices within the religious houses of Spain. Famed for her rigorous religious life, her trances, and her raptures, Teresa animated a movement to reform the order of Carmelite nuns in Spain. Because of her writings about her mystical experiences she was named a "Doctor of the Church," a title reserved for the greatest of the church's theologians.

The most important of the new religious orders was the Society of Jesus, or Jesuits, founded in 1534 by Ignatius Loyola (1491–1556). A conservative Spanish nobleman, Loyola was wounded and nearly killed in battle. During a long and painful rehabilitation he continuously read accounts of the lives of the saints. After recovering he went on a pilgrimage and experienced a profound conversion.

Loyola initially meant to organize a missionary order directed at converting the Muslims. The structure of his order reflected his military experience. It had a well-defined chain of command leading to the general of the order and then to the pope. To educate and discipline the members, Loyola composed *Spiritual Exercises,* emphasizing the importance of obedience. He encouraged his followers to understand their own attitudes, beliefs, and even lives as less important than the papacy and the Roman church. If the church commands it, he concluded, "I will believe that the white object I see is black." He prohibited Jesuits from holding any ecclesiastical office that might compromise their autonomy. After papal approval of the order in 1540, the Jesuits directed their activities primarily to education in Catholic areas and reconversion of Protestants.

Throughout Europe Jesuits gained fame for their work as educators of the laity and as spiritual advisers to the political leaders of Catholic Europe. In the late sixteenth and early seventeenth centuries they were responsible for a number of famous conversions, including that of Christina (1626–1689), the Lutheran queen of Sweden, who abdicated her throne in 1654 and spent the rest of her life in Rome. Jesuits were especially successful in bringing many parts of the Holy Roman Empire back into communion with the papacy. They have rightly been called the vanguard of the Catholic reform movement.

Catholic reformers were convinced that one of the reasons for the success of the Protestants was that faithful Christians had no clear guide to orthodox teachings. The first Catholic response to the reformers was to try to separate ideas they held to be correct from those they held to be incorrect. Successive popes made public lists of books and ideas that they considered to be in error. The lists were combined into the *Index of Prohibited Books* in 1559. The climate of suspicion was such that the works of humanists such as Erasmus were prohibited alongside the works of Protestants such as Martin Luther. In times of religious tensions, the *Index* could be vigorously enforced. In general, however, it did little to inhibit the circulation of books and ideas. It was finally suppressed in 1966.

A Marian Shrine

Shrines, such as this one in Regensburg dedicated to the Virgin Mary, remained important centers of Catholic piety. As we see here, shrines drew large crowds made up of individuals and religious groups who came in search of spiritual and physical healing. (Foto Marburg/Art Resource, NY)

During the first half of the sixteenth century Catholics joined Protestants in calls for an ecumenical council that all believed would solve the problems dogging the Christian church. But in the unsettled political and diplomatic atmosphere that lasted into the 1540s, it was impossible to find any agreement about where or when a universal council should meet. Finally, in 1545, at a time when the hostilities between the Valois and Habsburgs had cooled, Pope Paul III (r. 1534–1549) was able to convene an ecumenical council in the city of Trent, a German imperial city located on the Italian side of the Alps.

It is difficult to overemphasize the importance of the Council of Trent. It marked and defined Roman Catholicism for the next four hundred years. Reformers within the Catholic Church hoped that it would be possible to create a broadly based reform party within the church and that the council would define theological positions acceptable to the Protestants, making reunion possible. Unfortunately for the reformers, conservatives quickly took over the papal-controlled council.

The Council of Trent sat in three sessions between 1545 and 1563. The initial debates were clearly meant to mark the boundaries between Protestant heresy and the orthodox positions of the Catholic Church. In response to the Protestant emphasis on the

Scriptures, the council said that the church always recognized the validity of traditional teaching and understanding. Delegates rejected the humanists' work on the text of the Bible, declaring that the Latin Vulgate edition compiled by Jerome in the late fourth century was the authorized text. In response to the widely held Protestant belief that salvation came through faith alone, the council declared that good works were not merely the outcome of faith but prerequisites to salvation. The council rejected Protestant positions on the sacraments, the giving of wine to the laity during Holy Communion, the marriage of clergy, and the granting of indulgences.

Protestant critics often point to these positions as evidence that the work of the council was merely negative. To do so, however, is to ignore the many ways in which the decrees of the council were an essential part of the creation of the Roman Catholic Church that would function for the next four centuries. The delegates at Trent generally felt that the real cause behind the Protestant movement was the lack of leadership and supervision within the church. Many of the acts of the council dealt with that issue.

First, the council affirmed apostolic succession—the idea that the authority of a bishop is transmitted through a succession of bishops, ultimately leading back through the popes to Saint Peter. Thus the council underlined the ultimate authority of the pope in administrative as well as theological matters. The council ordered that local bishops should reside in their dioceses; that they should establish seminaries to see to the education of parish clergy; and that, through regular visitation and supervision, they should make certain that the laity participated in the sacramental life of the church. In the final sessions of the council the nature of the Roman Catholic Church was summed up in the Creed of Pius IV, which like the Lutheran Augsburg Confession expressed the basic position of the church.

Confessionalization The labors of the Jesuits and the deliberations of the Council of Trent at midcentury proved that reconciliation between the Protestant reformers and the Catholic Church was not possible. Signs of the separation include the flight of several important Protestant religious leaders from Italy in the late 1540s and the wholesale migration of Protestant communities from Modena, Lucca, and other Italian towns to France, England, and Switzerland. These actions signify the beginnings of the theological, political, and social separation of "Protestant" and "Catholic" in European society. Further, the states of Europe saw themselves as the enforcers of religious uniformity within their territories. It is from this time forward that denominational differences become clearer.

The theological separation was marked in a number of concrete and symbolic ways. Churches in which both bread and wine were distributed to the laity during the sacrament of Holy Communion passed from Catholic to Protestant. Churches in which the altar was moved forward to face the congregation but the statuary was retained were likely to be Lutheran. Churches in which statues were destroyed and all other forms of art were removed were likely to be Reformed (Calvinist), for Calvin had advised that "only those things are to be sculpted or painted which the eye is capable of seeing; let not God's majesty, which is far above the perception of the eyes, be debased through unseemly representations."[8] Even matters such as singing differentiated the churches. Although the Calvinist tradition tended to believe that music, like art, drew the Christian away from consideration of the word, Luther believed that "next to the

Word of God, music deserves the highest praise." Lutherans emphasized congregational singing and the use of music within the worship service. Countless pastors in the sixteenth and seventeenth centuries followed Luther in composing hymns and even theoretical tracts on music. This tradition would reach its zenith in the church music of Johann Sebastian Bach (1685–1750), most of whose choral works were composed to be part of the normal worship service.

Music had played an important role in Catholic services since well before the Reformation. It was really architecture that distinguished Catholic churches from Protestant churches in the late sixteenth and seventeenth centuries. In Rome the great religious orders built new churches in the baroque style (see page 504). Baroque artists and architects absorbed all the classical lessons of the Renaissance and then went beyond them, sometimes deliberately violating them. Baroque art celebrates the supernatural, the ways in which God is not bound by the laws of nature. Whereas Renaissance art was meant to depict nature, baroque paintings and sculpture seem to defy gravity. The work celebrates the supernatural power and splendor of the papacy. This drama and power are clear in the construction of the Jesuit Church of the Gesu in Rome and even more so in Gianlorenzo Bernini's (1598–1680) throne of Saint Peter, made for Saint Peter's Basilica in the Vatican. The construction of baroque churches, first in Spain and Italy but especially in the Catholic parts of Germany, created yet another boundary between an austere Protestantism and a visual and mystical Catholicism.

The Regulation of Religious Life   Because of the continuing religious confusion and political disorder brought on by the reforms, churchmen, like state officials, were intent on maintaining religious order within their territories by requiring what they understood to be the practice of true Christianity. In an ironic twist, both Protestant and Catholic authorities followed much the same program. In both camps regulation of religion became a governmental concern. Religious regulation and state power grew at the same time. This true religion was much less a public and communal religion than medieval Christianity had been. Medieval Christians had worried greatly about public sins that complicated life in a community. In the age of confessionalization theologians—both Protestant and Catholic—became preoccupied with the moral status and interior life of individuals. Sexual sins and gluttony now seemed more dangerous than economic sins such as avarice and usury. Even penance was understood less as a "restitution" that would reintegrate the individual into the Christian community than as a process of coming to true contrition for one's sins.

The changed attitude toward penance made the sense of Christian community less important and left individuals isolated and more subject to the influence of the church and secular authorities. In all parts of Europe officials were consumed with the control and supervision of the laity.

All of the major religious groups in the late sixteenth century emphasized education, right doctrine, and social control. In Catholic areas it was hoped that a renewed emphasis on private confession by the laity would lead to a proper understanding of doctrine. During this period Charles Borromeo, archbishop of Milan (1538–1584), introduced the private confessional box, which isolated priest and penitent from the prying ears of the community. This allowed confessors the time and opportunity to instruct individual consciences with care. As early as the 1520s some Lutheran princes had begun visitations to ensure that the laity understood basic doctrine.

Churchmen in both Protestant and Catholic areas used catechisms—handbooks containing instruction for the laity. The first and most famous was by Luther himself. Luther's *Small Catechism* includes the Lord's Prayer, Ten Commandments, and Apostles' Creed, along with simple, clear explanations of what they mean. More than Catholic rulers, Protestant rulers used church courts to enforce discipline within the community. Churchmen began to criticize semireligious popular celebrations such as May Day, harvest feasts, and the Feast of Fools, whose origins lay in popular myths and practices that preceded Christianity. Such observances were now scorned for encouraging superstition and mocking the social and political order with, for example, parodies of ignorant clergy and foolish magistrates.

Religious authorities were also concerned by what seemed to be out-of-control mysticism and dangerous religious practices, especially among women. The impact of the Reformation on the status of women has often been debated. The Protestant position is that the Reformation freed women from the cloistered control of traditional convents. Further, the Protestant attack on state-controlled prostitution reduced one of the basest forms of exploitation. To the realists who argued that young, unmarried men would always need sexual outlets, Luther replied that one cannot merely substitute one evil practice for another. Critics of the Reformation counter that a convent was one of very few organizations that a woman could administer and direct. Women who took religious vows, Catholics point out, could engage in intellectual and religious pursuits

IMPORTANT EVENTS

1513–1517 Fifth Lateran Council meets to consider reform of the Catholic Church

1517 Luther makes public his "Ninety-five Theses"

1518 Zwingli is appointed people's priest of Zurich

1520 Pope Leo X condemns Luther's teachings

1521 Luther appears at the Diet of Worms

1524–1525 Peasant revolts in Germany

1527 Imperial troops sack Rome

1530 Melanchthon composes the Augsburg Confession summarizing Lutheran belief

1534 Calvin flees Paris

Loyola founds the Society of Jesus

1535 Anabaptist community of Münster is destroyed

1536 Calvin arrives in Geneva and publishes *Institutes of the Christian Religion*

1545–1563 Council of Trent meets to reform Catholic Church

1555 Emperor Charles V accepts the Peace of Augsburg

1559 Parliament passes Elizabethan Act of Supremacy and Act of Uniformity similar to those enjoyed by men. The destruction of religious houses for women, Catholics argue, destroyed one of the few alternatives that women had to life in an authoritarian, patriarchal society.

In fact, in the late sixteenth and early seventeenth centuries both Protestant and Catholic authorities viewed with suspicion any signs of religious independence by women. In the first years of the Reformation some women did leave convents, eager to participate in the reform of the church. Early in the 1520s some women wrote tracts concerning the morality of the clergy. And for a time women served as deacons in some Reformed (Calvinist) churches. Yet like the female witches discussed in Chapter 15, these religious women seemed somehow dangerous. Lutheran and Calvinist theologians argued that a woman's religious vocation should be in the Christian care and education of her family. And even the most famous of the sixteenth- and seventeenth-century female Catholic mystics were greeted with distrust and some hostility. Religious women in Catholic convents were required to subordinate their mysticism to the guidance they received from male spiritual advisers. Calvinist theologians exhibited similar suspicions toward the theological and spiritual insights of Protestant women. For the laity in general and for women in particular, the late Reformation brought increased control by religious authorities.

NOTES

1. Angela of Foligno, *The Book of Divine Consolation of the Blessed Angel of Foligno,* trans. Mary G. Steegmann (New York: Cooper Square Publishers, 1966), p. 260.
2. Martin Luther, *Works,* vol. 34 (Philadelphia: Muhlenberg Press, 1960), pp. 336–337.
3. Quoted in Steven Ozment, *The Age of Reform, 1250–1550* (New Haven, Conn.: Yale University Press, 1980), p. 245.
4. Quoted in Robert W. Scribner, *The German Reformation* (London: Macmillan, 1986), p. 32.
5. Quoted in Carter Lindberg, *The European Reformations* (New York: Blackwell Publishers, 1996), p. 269.
6. Quoted in Euan Cameron, *The European Reformation* (Oxford: Clarendon Press, 1991), pp. 106–107.
7. Francesco Guicciardini, *Maxims and Reflections (Ricordi),* trans. Mario Domandi (Philadelphia: University of Pennsylvania Press, 1965), p. 48.
8. Quoted in Lindberg, p. 375.

SUGGESTED READING

Bennedict, Philip. *Christ's Churches Purely Reformed: A Social History of Calvinism.* 2002. A magisterial survey of the Reformed (Calvinist) tradition that emphasizes the dynamics of religious communities.

Bireley, Robert. *The Refashioning of Catholicism: A Reassessment of the Counter Reformation.* 1999. A well-written survey that places the Roman Catholic Church in the context of political, social, and religious developments between 1450 and 1600.

Cameron, Euan. *The European Reformation.* 1991. The best recent history of the Reformation, emphasizing the common principles of the major reformers.

Dickens, Arthur G. *The English Reformation.* 1991. A classic, clear discussion of English religion, emphasizing the popular enthusiasm for reform, which Dickens believes was connected to the earlier Lollard movements.

Haigh, Christopher, ed. *The English Reformation Revised.* 1987. A collection of essays criticizing Dickens's thesis on the popular basis of reform in England; the introduction is especially useful for following what is still an important debate over reform.

Hillerbrand, Hans J., ed. *The Oxford Encyclopedia of the Reformation.* 1996. An essential source on almost all topics of sixteenth-century history; the entries are accessible and up-to-date.

McGrath, Alister E. *A Life of John Calvin: A Study in the Shaping of Western Culture.* 1990. An excellent biography emphasizing the denitive role of Calvin's religious thought.

Oberman, Heiko. *Luther: Man Between God and the Devil.* 1989. A brilliant, beautifully written essay connecting Luther to prevailing late medieval ideas about sin, death, and the Devil.

Oberman, Heiko, Thomas Brady, and James Tracy, eds. *Handbook of European History, 1400–1600: Late Middle Ages, Renaissance, and Reformation.* 1994–1995. A collection of excellent introductory studies of political, religious, and social life.

Pettegree, Andrew, ed. *The Reformation World.* 2000. A demanding but very comprehensive survey of the most recent work on the Reformation.

15

Europe in the Age of Religious Wars, 1560–1648

(Detail, *La Saint-Barthelemy*, entre 1572 et 1584, Huile sur bois, 94 cm x 154 cm, Musée Cantonal des Beaux-Arts, Lausanne)

Three well-dressed gentlemen stand over a mutilated body; one of them holds up the severed head. Elsewhere sword-wielding men engage in indiscriminate slaughter, even of babies. Corpses are piled up in the background. This painting memorializes the grisly events of August 24, 1572. A band of Catholic noblemen accompanied by the personal guard of the king of France had hunted down a hundred Protestant nobles, asleep in their lodgings in and around the royal palace, and murdered them in cold blood. The king and his counselors had planned the murders as a preemptive political strike because they feared that other Protestant nobles were gathering an army outside Paris. But the calculated attack became a general massacre when ordinary Parisians, overwhelmingly Catholic and believing they were acting in the king's name, turned on their neighbors. About three thousand Protestants were slain in Paris over the next three days.

This massacre came to be called the Saint Bartholomew's Day Massacre for the Catholic saint on whose feast day it fell. Though particularly horrible in its scope, the slaughter was not unusual in the deadly combination of religious and political antagonisms it reflected. Religious conflicts were by definition intractable political conflicts since virtually every religious group felt that all others were heretics who could not be tolerated and must be eliminated. Rulers of all faiths looked to divine authority and religious institutions to uphold their power.

In the decades after 1560 existing political tensions contributed to instability and violence, especially when newly reinforced by religious differences. Royal governments continued to consolidate authority, but resistance to royal power by provinces, nobles, or towns accustomed to independence now might have a religious sanction. Warfare over these issues had consumed the Holy Roman Empire in the first half of the sixteenth century. The conflict had now spilled over into France and the Netherlands and threatened to erupt in England. In the early seventeenth century the Holy Roman Empire once again was wracked by a war simultaneously religious and political in origin. Regardless of its roots, warfare itself had become more destructive than ever before thanks to innovations in military technology and campaign tactics. Tensions everywhere were also worsened by economic changes, especially soaring prices and grinding unemployment.

A period of tension, even extraordinary violence, in political and social life, the era of the late sixteenth and early seventeenth centuries was also distinguished by great creativity in some areas of cultural and intellectual life. The plays of Shakespeare, for example, mirrored the passions but also reflected on the dilemmas of the day and helped to analyze Europeans' circumstances with a new degree of sophistication.

ECONOMIC CHANGE AND SOCIAL TENSIONS

Religious strife, warfare, and economic change disrupted the everyday lives of whole communities as well as individuals in the late sixteenth and early seventeenth centuries. Wars were devastating to many areas of western Europe and contributed to especially severe economic decline in parts of the Low Countries (the Netherlands), France, and the Holy Roman Empire. But other factors, most notably a steady rise in prices, also played a role in the dramatic economic and social changes of the century after 1550. A series of economic changes altered power relations in cities, in the countryside, and in the relationship of both to central governments. Ordinary people managed their economic difficulties in a variety of ways: they sought new sources of work; they protested against burdensome taxes; sometimes they found scapegoats for their distress among their neighbors.

Economic Trans-formation and the New Elites

The most obvious economic change was an unrelenting rise in prices, which resulted in the concentration of wealth in fewer and fewer hands. Sixteenth-century observers attributed rising prices to the inflationary effects of the influx of precious metals from Spanish territories in the New World. Historians now believe that European causes may also have helped trigger this "price revolution." Steady population growth caused a relative shortage of goods, particularly food, and the result was higher prices. Both the amount and the effect of price changes were highly localized, depending on factors such as the structure of local economies and the success of harvests. Between 1550 and 1600, however, the price of grain may have risen between 50 and 100 percent, and sometimes more, in cities throughout Europe—including eastern Europe, the breadbasket for growing urban areas to the west. Wages did not keep pace with prices; historians estimate that wages lost between one-tenth and one-fourth of their value by the end of the century. The political and religious struggles of the era thus took place against a background of increasing want, and economic distress was often expressed in both political and religious terms.

These economic changes affected the wealthy as well as the poor. During this period monarchs were making new accommodations with the hereditary aristocracy—with the Crown usually emerging stronger, if only through concessions to aristocrats' economic interests. Underlying this new symbiosis of monarchy and traditional warrior-nobles were the effects of the widespread economic changes. These changes would eventually blur lines between the old noble families and the new elites and would simplify power relationships within the state. Conditions in the countryside, where there were fewer resources to feed more mouths, grew less favorable. But at the same time, more capital became available to wealthy urban or landholding families to invest in the countryside, by buying land outright on which to live like gentry or by making loans to desperate peasants. This capital came from profits from expanded production and trade and was also an effect of the scarcity of land as population and prices rose. Enterprising landholders raised ground rents wherever they could, or they converted land to the production of wool, grain, and other cash crops destined for distant markets.

As a result, a stratum of wealthy, educated, and socially ambitious "new gentry," as these families were called in England, began growing and solidifying. Many of the men of these families were royal officeholders. Where the practice existed, many bought titles outright or were granted nobility as a benefit of their offices. They often lent money to royal governments. The monumental expense of wars made becoming a lender to government, as well as to individuals, an attractive way to live off personal capital.

No one would have confused this up-and-coming gentry with warrior-aristocrats from old families, but the social distinctions between them are less important (to us) than what they had in common: legal privilege, the security of landownership, a cooperative relationship with the monarchy. Monarchs deliberately favored the new gentry as counterweights to independent aristocrats.

City governments also changed character as wealth accumulated in the hands of formerly commercial families. Town councils became dominated by successive generations of privileged families, now more likely to live from landed than from commercial wealth. By the beginning of the seventeenth century traditional guild control of government had been subverted in many places. Towns became more closely tied to royal interests by means of the mutual interests of Crown and town elites. The long medieval tradition of towns serving as independent corporate bodies had come to an end.

Economic Change and the Common People

The growth of markets around Europe and in Spanish possessions overseas, as well as population growth within Europe, had a marked effect on patterns of production and the lives of artisans and laborers. Production of cloth on a large scale for export, for example, now required huge amounts of capital—much more than a typical guild craftsman could amass. Cloth production was increasingly controlled by new investor-producers with enormous resources and access to distant markets. These entrepreneurs bought up large amounts of wool and hired it out to be cleaned, spun into thread, and woven into cloth by wage laborers in urban workshops or by pieceworkers in their homes. Thousands of women and men in the countryside around urban centers helped to support themselves and their families in this way.

The new entrepreneurs had sufficient capital entirely to bypass guild production. In towns guilds still regulated most trades but could not accommodate the numbers of artisans who sought to join them. Fewer and fewer apprentices and journeymen could expect to become master artisans. The masters began to treat apprentices virtually as wage laborers, at times letting them go during slow periods. The household mode of production, in which apprentices and journeymen had worked and lived side by side with the master's family, also began to break down, with profound economic, social, and political consequences.

One of the first reflections of the dire circumstances faced by artisans was an attempt to reduce competition at the expense of the artisans' own mothers, sisters, daughters, and sons. Increasingly, widows were forbidden to continue practicing their husbands' enterprises, though they headed from 10 to 15 percent of households in many trades. Women had traditionally learned and practiced many trades but rarely followed the formal progress from apprenticeship to master status. A woman usually combined work of this kind with household production, with selling her products and those of her husband, and with bearing and nursing children. Outright exclusion of women from guild organization appeared as early as the thirteenth century but now began regularly to appear in guild statutes. In addition, town governments tried to restrict women's participation in work such as selling in markets, which they had long dominated. Even midwives had to defend their practices, even though as part of housewifery women were expected to know about herbal remedies and practical medicine. Working women thus began to have difficulty supporting themselves if single or widowed and difficulty supporting their children. In the changing position of such women we can see the distress of the entire stratum of society that they represent.

Wealth in the countryside was also becoming more stratified. Population growth caused many peasant farms to be subdivided for numerous children, creating tiny plots that could not support the families who lived on them. Countless peasants lost what lands they had to wealthy investors—many of them newly wealthy gentry—who lent them money for renting more land or for purchasing seed and tools, and then reclaimed the land when the peasants failed to repay. Other peasants were simply unable to rent land as rents rose. To survive, some sought work as day laborers on the land of rich landlords or more prosperous farmers. But with the shrinking opportunities for farming, this option became less feasible. Many found their way to cities, where they swelled the ranks of the poor. Others, like some of their urban counterparts, coped by becoming part of the newly expanding network of cloth production, combining spinning and weaving with subsistence farming. However, one bad harvest might send them out on the roads begging or odd-jobbing; many did not long survive such a life.

In eastern Europe peasants faced other dilemmas, for their lands had a different relationship to the wider European economy. The more densely urbanized western Europe, whose wealth controlled the patterns of trade, sought bulk goods, particularly grain, from eastern Germany, Poland, and Lithuania. Thus there was an economic incentive for landowners in eastern Europe to bind peasants to the land just as the desire of their rulers for greater cooperation had granted the landlords more power. Serfdom now spread in eastern Europe, while precisely the opposite condition—a more mobile labor force—grew in the West.

Coping with Poverty and Violence

The common people of Europe did not submit passively to either the economic difficulties or the religious and political crises of their day. Whatever their religion, common people took the initiative in attacking members of other faiths to rid their communities of them. Heretics were considered to be spiritual pollution that might provoke God's wrath, and ordinary citizens believed that they had to eliminate heretics if the state failed to do so. Common people, as well as elites and governments, were thus responsible for the violence that sometimes occurred in the name of religion.

Ordinary people fought in wars not only from conviction but also from the need for self-defense and from economic choice. It was ordinary people who defended the walls of towns, dug siege works, and manned artillery batteries. Although nobles remained military leaders, armies consisted mostly of infantry made up of common people, not mounted knights. Women were part of armies, too. Much of the day-to-day work of finding food and firewood, cleaning guns, and endlessly repairing inadequate clothing was done by women looking after their husbands and lovers among the troops.

Many men joined the armies and navies of their rulers because, given the alternatives, the military seemed a reasonable way of life. Landless farm hands, day laborers, and out-of-work artisans found the prospect of employment in the army attractive enough to outweigh the dangers of military life. Desertion was common; nothing more than the rumor that a soldier's home village was threatened might prompt a man to abandon his post. Battle-hardened troops could threaten their commanders not only with desertion but with mutiny. A mutiny of Spanish soldiers in 1574 was a well-organized affair, for example, somewhat like a strike. Occasionally mutinies were brutally suppressed; more often they were successful and troops received some of their back wages.

Townspeople and country people participated in riots and rebellions to protest their circumstances when the situation was particularly dire or when other means of action had failed. The devastation of religious war led to both peasant rebellions and urban uprisings. Former soldiers, prosperous farmers, or even noble landlords whose economic fortunes were tied to peasant profits might lead rural revolts. Urban protests could begin spontaneously when new grievances worsened existing problems. In 1585 food riots in Naples were provoked not simply by a shortage of grain but also by a government decision to raise the price of bread during the shortage. Rebels sometimes seized property—for example, they might distribute looted bread among themselves—and occasionally killed officials. Their protests rarely generated lasting political change and were usually brutally quashed.

Governments at all levels tried to cope with the increasing problem of poverty by changing the administration and scale of poor relief. In both Catholic and Protestant Europe caring for the poor became more institutionalized and systematic, and more removed from religious impulses. In the second half of the sixteenth century, governments established public almshouses and poorhouses to dispense food or to care for orphans or the destitute in towns throughout Catholic and Protestant Europe. Initially these institutions reflected an optimistic vision of an ideal Christian community attentive to material want. But by 1600 the charitable distribution of food was accompanied by attempts to distinguish "deserving" from "undeserving" poor, by an insistence that the poor work for their ration of food, and even by an effort to compel the poor to live in almshouses and poorhouses.

These efforts were not uniformly successful. Begging was outlawed by Catholic and Protestant city governments alike, but never thoroughly suppressed. Catholic religious orders and parishes often resisted efforts at regulating their charitable work—even when they were imposed by Catholic governments. Nonetheless, the trend was clear. From viewing poverty as a fact of life and as an occasional lesson in Christian humility, European elites were beginning to see it as a social problem. And they saw the poor as people in need of control and institutional discipline.

| The Hunt for Witches | Between approximately 1550 and 1650 Europe saw a dramatic increase in the persecution of women and men for witchcraft. |

Approximately one hundred thousand people were tried and about sixty thousand executed. The surge in witch-hunting was closely linked to communities' religious concerns and also to the social tensions that resulted from economic difficulties.

Certain types of witchcraft had long existed in Europe. So-called black magic of various kinds—one peasant casting a spell on another peasant's cow—had been common since the Middle Ages. What now made the practice seem particularly menacing, especially to elites, were theories linking black magic to Devil worship. Catholic leaders and legal scholars began to advance such theories in the fifteenth century, and by the late sixteenth century both Catholic and Protestant elites viewed a witch not only as someone who might cast harmful spells but also as a heretic.

The impetus for most individual accusations of witchcraft came from within the communities where the "witch" lived—that is, from common people. Usually targeted were solitary or unpopular people whose difficult relationships with fellow villagers made them seem likely sources of evil. Often such a person had practiced black magic (or had been suspected of doing so) for years, and the villagers took action only when faced with a community crisis, such as an epidemic.

The majority of accused witches were women. Lacking legal, social, and political resources, women may have been more likely than men to use black magic for self-protection or advancement. Women's work often made them vulnerable to charges of witchcraft since families' food supplies and routine medicines passed through women's hands. The deaths of young children or of domestic animals, such as a milk cow, were among the most common triggers for witchcraft accusation. The increase in poverty during the late sixteenth and early seventeenth centuries made poor women frequent targets of witch-hunts. It was easier to find such a woman menacing—and to accuse her of wrongdoing—than to feel guilty because of her evident need.

Both Christian dogma and humanistic writing portrayed women as morally weaker than men and thus more susceptible to the Devil's enticements. Writings on witchcraft described Devil worship in sexual terms, and the prosecution of witches had a voyeuristic, sexual dimension. The bodies of accused witches were searched for the "Devil's mark"—a blemish thought to be Satan's imprint. In some regions women accounted for 80 percent of those prosecuted and executed. A dynamic of gender stereotyping was not always at work, however; in other regions prosecutions were more evenly divided between men and women, and occasionally men made up the majority of those accused.

Because they were often prompted by village disasters or tragedies, individual accusations of witchcraft increased in these decades in response to the crises that beset many communities. In addition, isolated accusations often started localized frenzies of active hunting for other witches. Dozens of "witches" might be identified and executed before the whirlwind subsided. These more widespread hunts were driven in part by the anxieties of local elites about disorder and heresy and were facilitated by contemporary legal procedures that they applied. These procedures permitted lax rules of evidence and the use of torture to extract confessions. Torture or the threat of torture led most of those accused of witchcraft to "confess" and to name accomplices or other "witches." In this way a single initial accusation could lead to dozens of prosecutions. In regions where procedures for appealing convictions and sentences were fragile or nonexistent, witch-hunts could expand with alarming speed. Aggressive hunts were common, for example, in the small principalities and imperial cities of the Holy Roman Empire, which were largely independent of higher political authority.

The widespread witch-hunts virtually ended by the late seventeenth century, in part because the intellectual energies of elites shifted from religious to scientific thought. The practice of witchcraft continued among common folk, although accusations of one neighbor by another never again reached the level of these crisis-ridden decades.

IMPERIAL SPAIN AND THE LIMITS OF ROYAL POWER

To contemporary observers, no political fact of the late sixteenth century was more obvious than the ascendancy of Spain. Philip II (r. 1556–1598) ruled Spanish conquests in the New World as well as wealthy territories in Europe, including the Netherlands and parts of Italy. Yet imperial Spain did not escape the political, social, and religious turmoil of the era. Explosive combinations of religious dissent and political disaffection led to revolt against Spain in the Netherlands. This conflict revealed the endemic tensions of sixteenth-century political life: nobles, towns, and provinces trying to safeguard remnants of medieval autonomy against efforts at greater centralization—with the added complications of economic strain and religious division. The revolt also demonstrated the material limits of royal power, since even with treasure from the American conquests pouring in, Philip could at times barely afford to keep armies in the field. As American silver dwindled in the seventeenth century, Philip's successors faced severe financial and political strains even in their Spanish domains.

The Revolt of the Netherlands

Philip's power stemmed in part from the far-flung territories he inherited from his father, the Habsburg king of Spain and Holy Roman emperor Charles V: Spain, the Low Countries (the Netherlands), the duchy of Milan, the kingdom of Naples, the conquered lands in the Americas, and the Philippine Islands in Asia. (Control of Charles's Austrian lands had passed to his brother, Ferdinand, Philip's uncle.) Treasure fleets bearing precious metals from the New World began to reach Spain regularly during Philip's reign. Spain was now the engine powering a trading economy unlike any that had existed in Europe before. To supply its colonies Spain needed timber and other shipbuilding materials from the hinterlands of the Baltic Sea. Grain from the Baltic fed the urban populations of Spain (where wool was the principal cash crop) and the Netherlands, while the Netherlands, in turn, was a source of finished goods, such as cloth. The major exchange point for all of these goods was the city of Antwerp in the Netherlands, the leading trading center of all of Europe by 1550.

The Netherlands were the jewel among Philip's European possessions. These seventeen provinces (constituting mostly the modern nations of Belgium and the Netherlands) had been centers of trade and manufacture since the twelfth century. In the fourteenth and fifteenth centuries they had enjoyed political importance and a period of cultural innovation under the control of the dukes of Burgundy. By the time Philip inherited the provinces from his father, a sort of federal system of government had evolved to accommodate the various centers of power. Each province had an assembly (Estates) in which representatives of leading nobility and towns authorized taxation, but each also acknowledged a central administration in Brussels that represented Philip. Heading the council of state in Brussels was a governor-general, Philip's half sister, Margaret of Parma.

Philip's clumsy efforts to adjust this distribution of power in his favor pushed his subjects in the Netherlands into revolt. Though conscientious to a fault, Philip was a rigid, unimaginative man. Born and raised in Spain, he had little real familiarity with the densely populated, linguistically diverse Netherlands, and he never visited there after 1559. Early in Philip's reign, tensions in the Netherlands arose over taxation and Spanish insistence on maintaining tight control. Bad harvests and commercial disruptions occasioned by wars in the Baltic region in the 1560s depressed the Netherlands' economy and made it difficult for the provinces to pay taxes demanded by Spain. When the Peace of Cateau-Cambrésis of 1559 brought an end to the long struggle between the Habsburgs and the Valois kings of France, the people of the Netherlands had reason to hope for lower taxes and reduced levels of Spanish control, yet neither was forthcoming. Indeed, Philip had named to the council of state officials who were Spaniards themselves or had close ties to the Spanish court, bypassing local nobles who had fought for Philip and his father before 1559 and who expected positions of influence in his government.

Philip only added to the economic and political discontent by unleashing an invigorated repression of heresy. Unlike his father, Philip directed the hunt for heretics not

Philip II in 1583
Dressed in the austere black in fashion at the Spanish court, Philip holds a rosary and wears the Order of the Golden Fleece, an order of knighthood, around his neck. At age 56 Philip has outlived four wives and most of his children.
(Museo del Prado, Madrid)

just at lower-class dissenters but also at well-to-do Calvinists—followers of the French Protestant religious reformer John Calvin—whose numbers were considerable. Punishment for heresy now included confiscation of family property along with execution of the individual. By 1565 municipal councils in the Netherlands were routinely refusing to enforce Philip's religious policies, believing that urban prosperity—as well as their personal security—depended on restraint in the prosecution of heresy. Leading nobles also stopped enforcing the policies on their estates.

Encouraged by greater tolerance, Protestants by 1566 had begun to hold open-air meetings and attract new converts in many towns. In a series of actions called the "iconoclastic fury," townsfolk around the provinces stripped Catholic churches of the relics and statues deemed idolatrous by Calvinist doctrine. At the same time, reflecting the economic strain of these years, some townsfolk rioted to protest the price of bread. One prominent nobleman warned Philip, "All trade has come to a standstill, so that there are 100,000 men begging for their bread who used to earn it . . . which is [important] since poverty can force people to do things which otherwise they would never think of doing."[1]

In early 1567 armed bands of Calvinist insurgents seized two towns in the southern Netherlands by force of arms in hopes of stirring a general revolt that would secure freedom of worship. Margaret of Parma quelled the uprisings by rallying city governments and loyal nobles, now fearful for their own property and power. But by then, far away in Spain, a decision had been made to send in the Spanish duke of Alba with an army of ten thousand men.

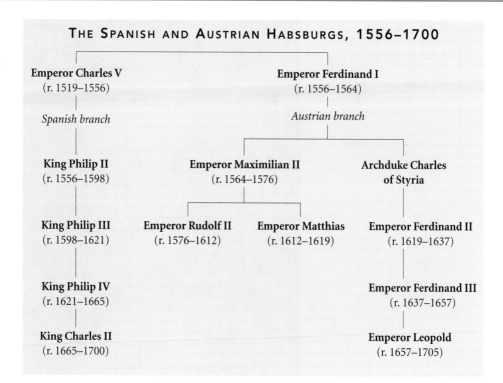

THE SPANISH AND AUSTRIAN HABSBURGS, 1556–1700

Emperor Charles V
(r. 1519–1556)

Spanish branch

King Philip II
(r. 1556–1598)

King Philip III
(r. 1598–1621)

King Philip IV
(r. 1621–1665)

King Charles II
(r. 1665–1700)

Emperor Ferdinand I
(r. 1556–1564)

Austrian branch

Emperor Maximilian II
(r. 1564–1576)

Archduke Charles
of Styria

Emperor Rudolf II
(r. 1576–1612)

Emperor Matthias
(r. 1612–1619)

Emperor Ferdinand II
(r. 1619–1637)

Emperor Ferdinand III
(r. 1637–1657)

Emperor Leopold
(r. 1657–1705)

Alba arrived in August 1567 and, to bolster his own shaky standing at the Spanish court, acted more like a conqueror than a peacemaker. He billeted troops in friendly cities, established new courts to try rebels, arrested thousands of people, executed about a thousand rebels (including Catholics as well as prominent Protestants), and imposed heavy new taxes to support his army. Thus Alba repeated every mistake of Spanish policy that had triggered rebellion in the first place.

Margaret of Parma resigned in disgust and left the Netherlands. Protestants from rebellious towns escaped into exile, where they were joined by nobles who had been declared traitors for resisting Alba's extreme policies. The most important of these was William of Nassau, prince of Orange (1533–1584), whose lands outside the Netherlands, in France and the Holy Roman Empire, lay beyond Spanish reach and so could be used to finance continued warfare against Spain. A significant community with military capability began to grow in exile.

In 1572 ships of exiled Calvinist privateers known as the "Sea Beggars" began preying on Spanish shipping and coastal fortresses from bases in the northern provinces. These provinces, increasingly Calvinist, became the center of opposition to the Spanish, who concentrated their efforts against rebellion in the wealthier southern provinces. Occasionally the French and English lent aid to the rebels.

The war in the Netherlands was a showcase for the new and costly technology of warfare in this period. Many towns were (or came to be, as a consequence of the revolt) equipped with "bastions," newly designed walled defenses that could resist artillery fire;

The Netherlands, 1559–1609

The seventeen provinces of the Netherlands were strikingly diverse politically, economically, and culturally. Like his father, Philip was, technically, the ruler of each province separately— that is, he was count of Flanders, duke of Brabant, and so forth.

United Provinces as of 1609

Spanish Netherlands

Truce line, 1609

North Sea

GRONINGEN
FRIESLAND
DRENTHE
•Amsterdam OVERIJSSEL
HOLLAND UTRECHT GELDERLAND
Brill • •Utrecht
•Rotterdam
DUCHY •OF BRABANT GELDERLAND
Bruges• •Antwerp HOLY
Ghent• *Scheldt*
FLANDERS
•Ypres •Brussels
ARTOIS LIMBOURG ROMAN
Valenciennes BISHOPRIC
Cambrai HAINAUT NAMUR OF LIÈGE
•Cateau-Cambrésis EMPIRE
DUCHY OF LUXEMBOURG
FRANCE *Meuse* *Rhine*

| 0 | 50 | 100 Km. |
| 0 | 50 | 100 Mi. |

such cities could not be taken by storm. Where bastions had been built, military campaigns consisted of grueling sieges, skirmishes in surrounding areas for control of supplies, and occasional pitched battles between besiegers and forces attempting to break the siege. Vast numbers of men were required both for effective besieging forces and for garrisoning the many fortresses that controlled the countryside and defended access to major towns.

In an attempt to supply the Netherlands with seasoned veterans and materiel from Spain and Spanish territories in Italy, the Spanish developed the "Spanish Road," an innovative string of supply depots where provisions could be gathered in advance of troops marching to the Netherlands. Maintaining its large armies, however, taxed Spain's resources to the breaking point. Even with American silver at hand, Philip could at times barely afford to keep armies in the field. Inevitably, large numbers of troops also exhausted the countryside, and both soldiers and civilians suffered great privations. On occasion Spanish troops reacted violently to difficult conditions and to delayed pay (American treasure dwindled badly between 1572 and 1578). In 1576 Spanish troops sacked the hitherto loyal city of Antwerp and massacred about eight thousand people. This event was bitterly remembered afterward as the "Spanish Fury."

The massacre prompted leaders in the southern provinces to raise their own armies to protect themselves against the Spanish. Late in 1576 they concluded an alliance with William of Orange and the northern rebels. But the northern and southern provinces were increasingly divided by religion, and their differences were skillfully exploited by Philip's new commander, Margaret's son Alexander Farnese, duke of Parma. With galleons from America filling the king's coffers again, Parma wooed the Catholic elites of the southern provinces back into loyalty to Philip, in return for promises to respect their provincial liberties and safeguard their property from troops.

In 1579 the northern provinces united in a defensive alliance, the Union of Utrecht, against the increasingly unified south. Parma's forces could not surmount the natural barrier of the Rhine River that bisects the Low Countries or meet the increasing costs of siege warfare in waterlogged terrain, particularly as Spain diverted money to conflicts with England in 1588 and France after 1589. In 1609 a truce was finally concluded between Spain and the northern provinces. This truce did not formally recognize the "United Provinces" as an independent entity, though in fact they were. The modern nations of Belgium (the Spanish provinces) and the Netherlands are the distant result of this truce.

The independent United Provinces (usually called, simply, the Netherlands) was a fragile state, an accident of warfare at first. But commercial prosperity began to emerge as its greatest strength. Much of the economic activity of Antwerp had shifted north to Amsterdam in the province of Holland because of fighting in the south and a naval blockade of Antwerp by rebel ships. Philip's policies had created a new enemy nation and had enriched it at his expense.

The Failure of the Invincible Armada The revolt of the Netherlands had lured Spain into wider strategic involvement, particularly against England. Spain and England had a common foe in France and common economic interests, and Philip had married Mary Tudor, the Catholic queen of England (r. 1553–1558). Even after Mary's death and the accession of her Protestant half sister, Queen Elizabeth (r. 1558–1603), Spanish-English relations remained cordial. Relations started to sour, however, when Elizabeth began tolerating the use of English ports by the rebel Sea Beggars and authorizing attacks by English privateers on Spanish treasure fleets. In response Spain supported Catholic resistance to Elizabeth within England, including plots to replace her on the throne with her Catholic cousin, Mary, Queen of Scots. Greater Spanish success in the Netherlands, raids by the Spanish and English on each other's shipping, and Elizabeth's execution of Mary in 1587 prompted Philip to order an invasion of England. A fleet (*armada*) of Spanish warships sailed in 1588.

"The enterprise of England," as the plan was called in Spain, represented an astounding logistical effort. The Armada was supposed to clear the English Channel of English ships in order to permit an invading force—troops under Parma in the Netherlands—to cross on barges. The sheer number of ships required for the undertaking—about 130—meant that some, inevitably, were slower supply ships, or vessels designed for the more protected waters of the Mediterranean. The English also had the advantage in arms, since they had better long-range artillery and better-trained gunners.

When the Armada entered the Channel on July 29, the English harassed the Spanish with artillery from a distance without sustaining much damage themselves. Parma could not get his men readied on their barges quickly enough once the fleet's presence in the Channel had been confirmed by messenger, nor could the fleet protect itself while waiting offshore. On the night of August 7 the English launched eight fire ships—burning vessels set adrift to deliver arson—into the anchored Spanish fleet. At dawn on the next day, they attacked the weakened fleet off Gravelines, sank many ships, and dispersed what remained.

The Battle at Gravelines was the first major artillery battle by sailing ships and helped set the future course of naval warfare. It was a disaster for Philip's hopes and for thousands of sailors and soldiers in Spanish pay. Many of the surviving ships sank in bad weather or were forced into hostile harbors as the Armada sailed for home around the northern tip of the British Isles. Less than half of Philip's great fleet made it back to Spain.

Successes at Home and Around the Mediterranean Despite his bountiful overseas empire and his preoccupation with the Netherlands, many of Philip's interests still centered on the Mediterranean. Spain and the kingdom of Naples had exchanged trade for centuries. Newer ties had been forged with the duchy of Milan and the city-state of Genoa, whose bankers were financiers to the Spanish monarchy. It was in his kingdoms of Spain and their Mediterranean sphere of interest that Philip made his power felt more effectively, though not without effort.

Philip's father, Charles V, had tried to secure the western Mediterranean against the Turks and their client states along the African coast, but it was under Philip that the Turkish challenge in the western Mediterranean receded. The Spanish allied temporarily with the papacy and Venice—both were concerned with Turkish naval power in the Mediterranean—and their combined navies inflicted a massive defeat on the Turkish navy at Lepanto, off the coast of Greece, in October 1571. The Turks remained the leading power in the eastern Mediterranean, but their ability to threaten Spain and Spanish possessions in the West was over.

To Philip and his advisers, the Turks represented a potential internal threat as well, since it was feared that they might incite rebellion among his Muslim subjects. These were the nominally Christian descendants of the Muslims of Granada, who had been conquered by the Spanish in 1492. Called *moriscos,* they had been forced to convert to Christianity in 1504 or be expelled from Spain. Yet no serious effort had been made to teach them Christian beliefs in their own language (Arabic), and they had not been assimilated into Spanish society. Philip inaugurated a new wave of persecution and provoked a massive rebellion by the moriscos that began on Christmas Day in 1568. The revolt took two years to suppress. After it was crushed, the moriscos of Granada were forcibly exiled and dispersed farther north in Spain.

Philip's power in each of his Spanish kingdoms was limited by the traditional privileges of towns, nobility, and clergy. In Aragon, for example, he could raise revenues only by appealing to local assemblies, the Cortes. Philip made significant inroads into Aragonese independence by the end of his reign, however. Noble feuds and peasant rebellions in Aragon during the 1580s provided a pretext for sending in veteran troops from the Netherlands campaigns to establish firmer royal control. Philip was successful in the long run in Aragon, as he had not been in the Netherlands, because he used adequate force but tempered it afterward with constitutional changes that were cleverly moderate. He cemented the peace by appearing in Aragon in person, in the words of a contemporary, "like a rainbow at the end of a storm."[2]

In Castile, the arid kingdom in the center of the Iberian Peninsula, the king was able to levy taxes with greater ease but only because of concessions that gave nobles

The Battle of Lepanto *On October 7, 1571, vessels of the Holy League (Spain, Venice, and the papacy) defeated the Ottoman fleet off the coast of Greece. It was the last great battle between galleys—the oared warships that had dominated Mediterranean waters since ancient times. The Ottomans never again contested for power in the western Mediterranean, but they rebounded to eclipse Venice in the east.* (Courtesy, National Maritime Museum)

undisputed authority over their peasants. Philip established his permanent capital, Madrid, and his principal residence, the Escorial, there. The Spanish Empire became more and more Castilian as the reign progressed, with royal advisers and counselors increasingly drawn only from the Castilian elite. Yet the rural economy of Castile was stunted by the dual oppression of landholders and royal tax collectors.

Philip also invaded and annexed Portugal in 1580, temporarily unifying the Iberian Peninsula. The annexation was ensured by armed force but had been preceded by careful negotiation to guarantee that Philip's claim to the throne—through his mother—would find some support within the country. When Philip died in 1598, he was old and ill, a man for whom daily life had become a painful burden. His Armada had been crushed; the Netherlands had slipped through his fingers. Yet he had learned from his mistakes and had been more successful, by his own standards, in other regions that he ruled.

Spain in Decline, 1600–1648	Spain steadily lost ground economically and strategically after the turn of the century. Imports of silver declined. The American mines were exhausted, and the natives forced to work in

them were decimated by European diseases and brutal treatment. Spain's economic health was further threatened by the very success of its colonies: local industries in the Americas began to produce goods formerly obtained from Spain. The increasing presence of English, French, and Dutch shipping in the Americas provided colonists with rival sources for the goods they needed. Often these competitors could offer their goods more cheaply than the Spanish, for Spanish productivity was low and prices were high because of the inflationary effects of the influx of precious metals.

Spain renewed hostilities with the United Provinces in 1621, after the truce of 1609 had expired. Philip IV (r. 1621–1665) also aided his Habsburg cousins in the Thirty Years' War in the Holy Roman Empire (see pages 493–495). Squeezed for troops and revenue for these commitments, other Spanish territories revolted. The uprisings reflected both economic distress and unresolved issues of regional autonomy. Castile bore the brunt of the financial support of the state. The chief minister to Philip IV, Gaspar de Guzmán, Count Olivares (1587–1645), was an energetic Castilian aristocrat determined to distribute the burdens of government more equitably among the various regions of Spain. His policies provoked rebellions in Catalonia and Portugal.

In Catalonia, a province of the kingdom of Aragon, the revolt began as a popular uprising against the billeting of troops. At one point Catalan leaders invited French troops to defend them and solemnly transferred their loyalty to the French king in the hope that he would respect their autonomy. Spain resumed control only in 1652, after years of military struggle and promises to respect Catalan liberties.

In Portugal a war of independence began in 1640, also launched by popular revolt. The Spanish government tried to restore order with troops under the command of a leading Portuguese prince, John, duke of Braganza. The duke, however, was the nearest living relative to the last king of Portugal, and he seized this opportunity to claim the crown of Portugal for himself. Although war dragged on until 1668, the Portuguese under John IV (r. 1640–1656) succeeded in winning independence from Spain.

As a result of these uprisings, Count Olivares resigned in disgrace in 1643. In 1647 upheaval would shake Spain's Italian possessions of Sicily and Naples. By midcentury Spain had lost its position as the pre-eminent state in Europe.

RELIGIOUS AND POLITICAL CONFLICT IN FRANCE AND ENGLAND

In the second half of the sixteenth century France was convulsed by civil war that had both religious and political causes. Although a temporary resolution was achieved by 1598, the kingdom was still divided by religion and by military and political challenges to royal authority. England, in contrast, was spared political and religious upheaval in the second half of the century, in part because of the talents and long life of its ruler, Elizabeth I. But in the seventeenth century constitutional and religious dissent began to reinforce each other in new ways and dramatically threatened royal power.

The French Religious Wars, 1562–1598

Civil war wracked France from 1562 until 1598. As in the Netherlands, the conflicts in France had religious and political origins and international ramifications. The French monarch, like Philip, was unable to monopolize military power. In 1559 the king of France, Henry II (r. 1547–1559), had concluded the Peace of Cateau-Cambrésis with Philip II, ending the Habsburg-Valois Wars, but had died in July of that year from wounds suffered at a tournament held to celebrate the new treaty. His death was a political disaster. Great noble families vied for influence over his 15-year-old son, Francis II (r. 1559–1560). The queen mother, Catherine de' Medici (1519–1589), worked carefully and intelligently to balance the nobles' interests. She gained greater authority when, in late 1560, the sickly Francis died and was succeeded by his brother, Charles IX—a 10-year-old for whom Catherine was officially the regent. But keeping the conflicts among the great courtiers from boiling over into civil war proved impossible.

In France, as elsewhere, noble conflict invariably had a violent component. Noblemen carried swords and daggers and were accompanied by armed entourages. Although they relied on patronage and army commands from the Crown, the Crown depended on their services. Provincial landholdings, together with the royal offices they enjoyed, afforded enough resources to support private warfare, and the nobles assumed the right to wage it.

In addition, religious tension was rising throughout France. (Henry II had welcomed the 1559 treaty in part because he wanted to turn his attention to "heresy.") Public preaching by and secret meetings of Protestants (known as "Huguenots" in France) were causing unrest in towns. At court members of leading noble families—including the Bourbons, who were princes of royal blood—had converted to Protestantism and worshiped openly in their rooms in the palace. In 1561 Catherine convened a national religious council, known as the Colloquy of Poissy, to reconcile the two faiths. When it failed, she chose provisional religious toleration as the only practical course and issued a limited edict of toleration in the name of the king in January 1562.

The edict led only to further unrest. Ignoring its restrictions, Protestants armed themselves, while townspeople of both faiths insulted and attacked one another at worship sites and religious festivals. In March 1562 the armed retainers of a Catholic duke killed a few dozen Protestants gathered in worship at Vassy, near one of the duke's estates. The killing, in bringing the military power of the nobility to bear on the broader problem of religious division, sparked the first of six civil wars. In some ways the initial conflict was decisive. The Protestant army lost the principal pitched battle of the war in December 1562. This defeat checked the growth of the Protestant movement by reducing the appeal of the movement to nobles. The peace edict granted in 1563 curtailed the reach of the Huguenot movement; the limited rights granted to Protestants in the Crown's edict made it difficult for Protestants in towns—where the vast majority of them lived—to worship. But if the Protestants were not powerful enough to win, neither were they weak enough to be decisively beaten.

The turning point most obvious to contemporaries came a decade later. The Protestant faction was still represented at court by the Bourbon princes and by the very able and influential nobleman Gaspard de Coligny, related to the Bourbons by marriage. Coligny was pressing the king for a war against Spain in order to aid Protestant rebels in the Netherlands. Opposed to entanglement in another war against Spain and alarmed by rumors of Huguenot armies massing outside Paris, Charles IX (r. 1560–1574) and his mother authorized royal guards to murder Coligny and other Protestant leaders on August 24, 1572—Saint Bartholomew's Day. Coligny's murder touched off a massacre of Protestants throughout Paris and, once news from Paris had spread, throughout the kingdom.

The Saint Bartholomew's Day Massacre revealed the degree to which religious differences had strained the fabric of community life. Neighbor murdered neighbor in an effort to rid the community of heretical pollution; bodies of the dead, including Coligny's, were mutilated. Gathered in the south of France, the remaining Huguenot forces vowed "never [to] trust those who have so often and so treacherously broken faith and the public peace."[3] Huguenot writers published tracts arguing that royal power was by nature limited and that rebellion was justified against tyrants who overstepped their legitimate authority.

Further war produced the inevitable truces and limited toleration, but many Catholics also renounced reconciliation. Some noblemen formed a Catholic league to fight in place of the weakened monarchy. Charles's brother, Henry III (r. 1574–1589), was another king of limited abilities. Middle-aged, Henry had no children. The heir to his throne was the Protestant Henry of Navarre, and the assumption of the throne by a Protestant was unimaginable to the zealous Catholic faction at court and to many ordinary Catholics. By the end of Henry III's reign, the king had almost no royal authority left to wield. He was forced to cooperate with first one of the warring parties and then another. In December 1588 he resorted to murdering two courtiers who led the ultra-Catholic faction; in turn he was murdered by a priest in early 1589.

Henry of Navarre, the Bourbon prince who became Henry IV (r. 1589–1610), had to fight for his throne. He faced Catholic armies now subsidized by Philip II of Spain, an extremist Catholic city government in Paris, and subjects who were tired of war but mainly Catholic, and he could count on only meager support from Protestants abroad. Given these obstacles, the politically astute Henry agreed to convert to Catholicism.

After his conversion in 1593, the wars continued for a time, but after thirty years of civil strife many of Henry's subjects believed that only rallying to the monarchy could save France from chaos. Nobles grew increasingly disposed, for both psychological and practical reasons, to cooperate with the Crown. Service to a successful king could be a source of glory, and Henry was personally esteemed because he was a talented general and brave, gregarious, and charming. The nobility forced the citizens of Paris and other cities to accept Henry's authority. The civil war period thus proved to be an important phase in the incremental accommodation of the nobility to the power of the state.

In April 1598 Henry granted toleration for the Huguenot minority in a royal edict proclaimed in the city of Nantes. The Edict of Nantes was primarily a repetition of provisions from the most generous edicts that had ended the various civil wars. Nobles were allowed to practice the Protestant faith on their estates; townspeople were granted more limited rights to worship in selected towns in each region. Protestants were also guaranteed rights of self-defense—specifically, the right to maintain garrisons in about two hundred towns. About half of these garrisons would be paid for by the Crown.

The problem was that the Edict of Nantes, like any royal edict, could be revoked by the king at any time. Moreover, the provision allowing Protestants to keep garrisoned towns reflected concessions to Protestant aristocrats, who could support their followers by paid garrison duty. It also reflected the assumption that living peacefully amid religious diversity might prove to be impossible. Thus, although Henry IV ended the French religious wars, he had not solved the problem of religious and political division within France.

The Consolidation of Royal Authority in France, 1598–1643

During Henry IV's reign, France recovered from the long years of civil war. Population and productivity began to grow; the Crown encouraged internal improvements to facilitate commerce. Henry's chief minister, Maximilien de Béthune, duke of Sully (1560–1641), increased royal revenue by nibbling away at traditional local self-government and control of taxation. He succeeded in creating a budget surplus and in extending mechanisms of centralized government.

Yet Henry's regime was stable only in comparison with the preceding years of civil war. The power of the great nobility had not been definitively broken. Moreover, the king had agreed to a provision, known as the *paulette* (named for the functionary who first administered it), that allowed royal officeholders not merely to own their offices but also to pass on those offices to their heirs in return for the payment of an annual fee. Primarily a device to raise revenue after decades of civil war, the paulette also helped cement the loyalty of royal bureaucrats at a critical time, particularly that of the royal judges of the supreme law court, the Parlement of Paris, who had recently agreed to register the Edict of Nantes only under duress. However, the paulette made royal officeholders largely immune from royal control since their posts were now in effect property, like the landed property of the traditional nobility.

In 1610 a fanatical Catholic assassinated Henry IV. Henry's death brought his 9-year-old son, Louis XIII (r. 1610–1643), to the throne with Louis's mother, Marie de' Medici, serving as regent. Marie was disgraced when her unpopular leading minister— resented for monopolizing patronage—was assassinated with Louis's approval in 1617.

Four years later Louis faced a major rebellion by his Huguenot subjects in southwestern France. Huguenots felt that Louis's recent marriage to a Spanish princess and other ominous policies meant that royal support for toleration was wavering. Certain Huguenot nobles initiated fighting as a show of force against the king. The wars persisted, on and off, for eight years, as the French royal troops, like the Spanish in the Netherlands, had difficulty breaching the defenses of even small fortress towns. The main Huguenot stronghold was the well-fortified port city of La Rochelle, which had grown wealthy from European and overseas trade. Not until the king took the city, after a siege lasting more than a year and costing thousands of lives, did the Protestants accept a peace on royal terms.

The Peace of Alais (1629) reaffirmed the policy of religious toleration but rescinded the Protestants' military and political privileges. It was a political triumph for the Crown because it deprived French Protestants of the means for further rebellion while reinforcing their dependence on the Crown for religious toleration. Most of the remaining great noble leaders began to convert to Catholicism.

The Peace of Alais was also a personal triumph for the king's leading minister, who crafted the treaty and who had directed the bloody siege that made it possible. Armand-Jean du Plessis (1585–1642), Cardinal Richelieu, came from a provincial noble family and rose in the service of the queen mother. He was admired and feared for his skill in the political game of seeking and bestowing patronage—a crucial skill in an age when elites received offices and honors through carefully cultivated relationships at court. His control of many lucrative church posts gave him the resources to build up a large network of clients. He and the king—whose sensitive temperament Richelieu handled adeptly—formed a lasting partnership that had a decisive impact not only on French policy but also on the entire shape of the French state.

Richelieu favored an aggressive foreign policy to counter what he believed still to be the greatest threat to the French crown: the Spanish Habsburgs. When war resumed between the Netherlands and Spain after their truce expired in 1621 (see page 496), Richelieu sent troops to attack Spanish possessions in Italy. In the 1630s, with the king's full confidence, he superintended large-scale fighting against Spain in the Netherlands itself, as well as in Italy, and he began subsidizing Swedish and German Protestant armies fighting the Habsburgs in Germany.

Richelieu's policies were opposed by many people, who saw taxes double, then triple, in just a few years. Many courtiers and provincial elites favored keeping a tenuous peace with Spain, a fellow Catholic state, and objected to alliances with German Protestants. They were alarmed by the increasing taxes and by the famine, disease, and, above all, the revolts that accompanied the peasants' distress. Their own status was also directly threatened by Richelieu's monopoly of royal patronage and by his creation of new offices, which diluted and undermined their power. In 1632, for example, Richelieu created the office of *intendant*. Intendants had wide powers for defense and administration in the provinces that overrode the established bureaucracy.

By 1640 Richelieu's ambitious foreign policy seemed to be bearing fruit. The French had won territory along their northern and eastern borders by their successes against Habsburg forces. But when Richelieu and Louis XIII died within five months of each other, in December 1642 and May 1643, Richelieu's legacy was tested. Louis XIII was succeeded by his 5-year-old son, and the warrior-nobility, as well as royal bureaucrats, would waste little time before challenging the Crown's new authority.

Precarious Stability in England: The Reign of Elizabeth I, 1558–1603 England experienced no civil wars during the second half of the sixteenth century, but religious dissent challenged the stability of the monarchy. In Elizabeth I (r. 1558–1603), England—in stark contrast to France—possessed an able and long-lived ruler. Elizabeth was well educated in the humanistic tradition and was already an adroit politician at the age of 25, when she acceded to the throne at the death of her Catholic half sister, Mary Tudor (r. 1553–1558).

Elizabeth faced the urgent problem of reaching a policy of consensus in religious matters. Her father, Henry VIII (r. 1509–1547), had broken away from the Catholic Church for political reasons but had retained many Catholic doctrines and practices. A Calvinist-inspired Protestantism had been prescribed for the Church of England by the advisers of Henry's successor, Elizabeth's young half brother, Edward VI (r. 1547–1553). True Catholicism, such as Mary had tried to reimpose, was out of the question. The Roman church had never recognized Henry VIII's self-made divorce and thus regarded Elizabeth as a bastard with no right to the throne.

Elizabeth adopted a cleverly moderate solution and used force, where necessary, to maintain it. In 1559 Parliament passed a new Act of Supremacy, which restored the monarch as head of the Church of England. Elizabeth dealt with opposition to the act by arresting bishops and lords whose votes would have blocked its passage by Parliament. Elizabeth and most of her ministers, all moderate realists, were willing to accept some flexibility in personal belief. For example, the official prayer book in use in Edward's day was revised to include elements of both traditional and radical interpretations of Communion. But church liturgy, clerical vestments, and, above all, the hierarchical structure of the clergy closely resembled Catholic practices. The Act of Uniformity required all worship to be conducted according to the new prayer book. Although uniformity was required in worship, Elizabeth was careful, in her words, not to "shine beacons into her subjects' souls."

Elizabeth I: The Armada Portrait *Both serene and resolute, Elizabeth is flanked by "before" and "after" glimpses of the Spanish fleet; her hand rests on the globe in a gesture of dominion that also memorializes the circumnavigation of the globe by her famous captain, Sir Francis Drake, some years before.* (By kind permission of His Grace the Duke of Bedford and the Trustees of the Bedford Estates. Copyright © His Grace the Duke of Bedford and the Trustees of the Bedford Estates.)

Catholicism continued to be practiced, especially by otherwise loyal nobility and gentry in the north of England, who worshiped privately on their estates. But priests returning from exile beginning in the 1570s, most newly imbued with the proselytizing zeal of the Counter-Reformation (the Catholic response to the Protestant Reformation), practiced it more visibly and were zealously prosecuted for their boldness. In the last twenty years of Elizabeth's reign, approximately 180 Catholics were executed for treason, two-thirds of them priests. (By 1585 being a Catholic priest in itself was a crime.)

In the long run, the greater threat to the English crown came from the most radical Protestants in the realm, known (by their enemies initially) as Puritans. Puritanism was a broad movement for reform of church practice along familiar Protestant lines: an emphasis on Bible reading, preaching, and private scrutiny of conscience; a de-emphasis on institutional ritual and clerical authority. Most Puritans had accepted Elizabeth's religious compromise for practical reasons but grew increasingly alienated by her insistence on clerical authority and her refusal to change any elements of the original religious settlement. A significant Presbyterian underground movement began to form among them. Presbyterians wanted to dismantle the episcopacy—the hierarchy of priests and bishops—and to govern the church instead with councils, called "presby-teries," that included lay members of the congregation. Laws were passed late in the queen's reign to enable the Crown to prosecute more easily, and even to force into exile, anyone who attended "nonconformist" (non-Anglican) services.

The greatest challenge Elizabeth faced from Puritans came in Parliament, where they were well represented by many literate gentry. Parliament met only when called by the monarch, and in theory members could merely voice opinions and complaints. Initiating legislation and prescribing policy were beyond its purview. However, only Parliament could vote taxes. Further, since it had in effect helped constitute royal authority by means of the two Acts of Supremacy, Parliament's supposedly consultative role had been expanded by the monarchy itself. During Elizabeth's reign, Puritans capitalized on Parliament's enlarged scope, using meetings to press for further religious reform. In 1586 they went so far as to introduce bills calling for an end to the episcopacy and the Anglican prayer book. Elizabeth had to resort to imprisoning one Puritan leader to end debate on the issue and on Parliament's right to address it.

Also during Elizabeth's reign, efforts at English expansion in the New World began, in the form of unsuccessful attempts at colonization and successful raids on Spanish possessions. However, the main focus of her foreign policy remained Europe itself. Elizabeth, like all her forebears, felt her interests tightly linked to the independence of the Netherlands, whose towns were a major outlet for English wool. Philip II's aggressive policy in the Netherlands increasingly alarmed her, especially in view of France's weakness. She began to send small sums of money to the rebels and allowed their ships access to southern English ports, from which they could raid Spanish-held towns on the Netherlands' coast. In 1585, in the wake of the duke of Parma's successes against the rebellions, she committed troops to help the rebels.

Her decision was a reaction not only to the threat of a single continental power dominating the Netherlands but also to the threat of Catholicism. From 1579 to 1583 the Spanish had helped the Irish fight English domination and were involved in several plots to replace Elizabeth with her Catholic cousin, Mary, Queen of Scots. These threats occurred as the return of Catholic exiles to England peaked. The victory over the Spanish Armada in 1588 was quite rightly celebrated, for it ended any Catholic threat to Elizabeth's rule.

The success against the Armada has tended to overshadow other aspects of Elizabeth's foreign policy, particularly with regard to Ireland. Since the twelfth century an Anglo-Irish state dominated by great princely families had been loosely supervised from England, but most of Ireland remained under the control of Gaelic chieftains. Just as Charles V and Philip II attempted to tighten their governing mechanisms in the Netherlands, so did Henry VIII's minister, Thomas Cromwell, streamline control of outlying areas such as Wales and Anglo-Ireland. Cromwell proposed that the whole of Ireland be brought under English control partly by the established mechanism of feudal ties: the Irish chieftains were to pay homage as vassals to the king of England.

Under Elizabeth this legalistic approach gave way to virtual conquest. Elizabeth's governor, Sir Henry Sidney, appointed in 1565, inaugurated a policy whereby Gaelic lords, by means of various technicalities, could be entirely dispossessed of their lands. Any Englishman capable of raising a private force could help enforce these dispossessions and settle his conquered lands as he saw fit. This policy provoked stiff Irish resistance, which was viewed as rebellion and provided the rationale for further military action, more confiscations of lands, and more new English settlers. Eventually the Irish, with Spanish assistance, mounted a major rebellion, consciously Catholic and aimed against the "heretic" queen. The rebellion gave the English an excuse for brutal suppression and massive transfers of lands to English control. The political domination of the Irish was complete with the defeat, in 1601, of the Gaelic chieftain Hugh O'Neill, lord of Tyrone, who had controlled most of the northern quarter of the island. Although the English were unable to impose Protestantism on the conquered Irish, to Elizabeth and her English subjects the conquests in Ireland seemed as significant as the victory over the Spanish Armada.

The English enjoyed relative peace at home during Elizabeth's reign. However, her reign ended on a note of strain. The foreign involvements, particularly in Ireland, had been very expensive. Taxation granted by Parliament more than doubled during her reign, and local taxes further burdened the people. Price inflation related to government spending, social problems caused by returned unemployed soldiers, and a series of bad harvests heightened popular resentment against taxation. Despite her achievements, therefore, Elizabeth passed two problems on to her successors: unresolved religious tensions and financial instability. Elizabeth's successors would also find in Parliament an increasing focus of opposition to their policies.

Rising Tensions in England, 1603–1642

In 1603 Queen Elizabeth died, and James VI of Scotland, the Protestant son of Mary, Queen of Scots, ascended to the English throne as James I (r. 1603–1625). Religious tensions between Anglicans and Puritans were temporarily quieted under James because of a plot, in 1605, by Catholic dissenters. The Gunpowder Plot, as it was called, was a conspiracy to blow up the palace housing both king and Parliament at Westminster. Protestants of all stripes once again focused not on their differences but on their common enemy, Catholics.

Financial problems were James's most pressing concern. Court life became more elaborate and an increasing drain on the monarchy's resources. James's extravagance was partly to blame for his financial problems, but so were pressures for patronage from courtiers. Added to the debts left from the Irish conflicts and wars with Spain were new military expenses as James helped defend the claims of his daughter and her husband, a German prince, to rule Bohemia (see page 496).

To raise revenue without Parliament's consent, James relied on sources of income that the Crown had enjoyed since medieval times: customs duties, wardship (the right to manage and liberally borrow from the estates of minor nobles), and the sale of monopolies, which conveyed the right to be sole agent for a particular kind of goods. To rebuild his treasury James increased the number of monopolies for sale and even created a new noble title—baronet—which he sold to socially ambitious commoners.

The monopolies were widely resented. Merchants objected to the arbitrary restriction of production and trade; common people found that they could no longer afford certain ordinary commodities, such as soap. Resentments among the nobility were sharpened, and general criticism of the court escalated, as James indulged in extreme favoritism of certain courtiers, including the corrupt George Villiers (1592–1628), duke of Buckingham, who served as the king's first minister.

When James summoned Parliament to ask for funds in 1621, Parliament used the occasion to protest court corruption and the king's financial measures. The members revived the medieval procedure of impeachment and removed two royal ministers from office. In 1624, still faced with expensive commitments to Protestants abroad and in failing health, James again called Parliament, which voted new taxes but also openly debated the wisdom of the king's foreign policy.

Tensions between Crown and Parliament increased under James's son, Charles I (r. 1625–1649). One reason was the growing financial strain of foreign policy as well as the policies themselves. Charles declared war on Spain and supported the Huguenot rebels in France. Many wealthy merchants opposed this aggressive foreign policy because it disrupted trade. In 1626 Parliament was dissolved without granting any monies, in order to stifle its objections to royal policies. Instead, Charles levied a forced loan and did not hesitate to imprison gentry who refused to lend their money to the government.

Above all, Charles's religious policies were a source of controversy. Charles was personally inclined toward "high church" practices: an emphasis on ceremony and sacrament reminiscent of Catholic ritual. He also was a believer in Arminianism, a school of thought that rejected the Calvinist notion that God's grace cannot be earned, and hence emphasized the importance of the sacraments and the authority of the clergy. Charles's attempt to fashion the Church of England into an instrument that would reflect and justify royal claims to power put him on a collision course with gentry and aristocrats who leaned toward Puritanism.

Charles's views were supported by William Laud (1573–1645), archbishop of Canterbury from 1633 and thus leader of the Church of England. He tried to impose changes in worship, spread Arminian ideas, and censor opposing views. He also challenged the redistribution of church property, which had occurred in the Reformation of the sixteenth century, and thereby alienated the gentry on economic as well as religious grounds.

Charles's style of rule worsened religious, political, and economic tensions. Cold and intensely private, he did not inspire confidence or have the charm or the political skills to disarm his opponents. His court was ruled by formal protocol, and access to the king was highly restricted—a serious problem in an age when proximity to the monarch was a guarantee of political power.

Revenue and religion dominated debate in the Parliament of 1628–1629, which Charles had called, once again, to get funds for his foreign wars. In 1628 Parliament presented the king with a document called the Petition of Right, which protested his financial policies as well as arbitrary imprisonment. (Seventeen members of Parliament had been imprisoned for refusing loans to the Crown.) Though couched conservatively as a restatement of customary practice, the petition in fact claimed a tradition of expanded parliamentary participation in government. Charles dissolved Parliament in March 1629, having decided that the money he might extract was not worth the risk.

For eleven years Charles ruled without Parliament. When he was forced by necessity to summon it again in 1640, the kingdom was in crisis. Royal finances were in desperate straits, even though Charles had pressed collection of revenues far beyond traditional bounds. In 1634, for example, he had revived annual collection of "ship money"—a medieval tax levied on coastal districts to help support the navy during war. England, however, was not at war at that time, and the tax was levied not only on seaports but on inland areas, too.

The immediate crisis in 1640—and the reason for Charles's desperate need for money—was a rebellion in Scotland. Like Philip II in the Netherlands, Charles tried to rule in Scotland through a small council of men who did not represent the local elite. Worse, he also tried to force his "high church" practices on the Scots. The Scottish Church had been more dramatically reshaped during the Reformation and now was largely Presbyterian in structure. The result of Charles's policies was riots and rebellion. Unable to suppress the revolt in a first campaign in 1639, Charles was forced to summon Parliament to obtain funds to raise a more effective army.

But the Parliament that assembled in the spring of 1640 provided no help. Instead, members questioned the war with the Scots and other royal policies. Charles's political skills were far too limited for him to re-establish a workable relationship with Parliament under the circumstances. Charles dissolved this body, which is now known as the "Short Parliament," after just three weeks. Even more stinging than Charles's dissolution of the Parliament was the lack of respect he had shown the members: a number of them were harassed or arrested. Mistrust fomented by the eleven years in which Charles had ruled without Parliament thus increased.

Another humiliating and decisive defeat at the hands of the Scots later in 1640 made summoning another Parliament imperative. Members of the "Long Parliament" (it sat from 1640 to 1653) took full advantage of the king's predicament. Charles was forced to agree not to dissolve or adjourn Parliament without the members' consent and to summon Parliament at least every three years. Parliament abolished many of his unorthodox and traditional sources of revenue and impeached and removed from office his leading ministers, including Archbishop Laud. The royal commander deemed responsible for the Scottish fiasco, Thomas Wentworth, earl of Strafford, was executed without trial in May 1641.

The execution of Strafford shocked many aristocrats in the House of Lords (the upper house of Parliament), as well as some moderate members of the House of Commons. Meanwhile, Parliament began debating the perennially thorny religious question. A bare majority of members favored abolition of Anglican bishops as a first step in thoroughgoing religious reform. Working people in London, kept apprised of the issues by the regular publication of parliamentary debates, demonstrated in support of that majority. Moderate members of Parliament, in contrast, favored checking the king's power but not upsetting the Elizabethan religious compromise.

An event that unified public and parliamentary opinion at a crucial time—a revolt against English rule in Ireland in October 1641—temporarily eclipsed these divisions and once again focused suspicion on the king. The broad consensus of anti-Catholicism once again became the temporary driving force in politics. Fearing that Charles would use Irish soldiers against his English subjects, Parliament demanded that it have control of the army to put down the rebellion. In November the Puritan majority introduced a document known as the "Grand Remonstrance," an appeal to the people and a long catalog of parliamentary grievances against the king. It was passed by a narrow margin, further setting public opinion in London against Charles. The king's remaining support in Parliament eroded in January 1642 when he attempted to arrest five leading members on charges of treason. The five escaped, and the stage was set for wider violence. The king withdrew from London, unsure he could defend himself there, and began to raise an army. In mid-1642 the kingdom stood at the brink of civil war.

RELIGIOUS AND POLITICAL CONFLICT IN CENTRAL AND EASTERN EUROPE

The Holy Roman Empire enjoyed a period of comparative quiet after the Peace of Augsburg halted religious and political wars in 1555. The 1555 agreement, which permitted rulers of the various states within the empire to impose either Catholicism or Lutheranism in their lands, proved to be a workable solution, for a time, to the problem of religious division. By the early seventeenth century, however, fresh causes of instability brought about renewed fighting. One factor was the rise of Calvinism, for which no provision had been necessary in 1555. Especially destabilizing was the drive by the Austrian Habsburgs to reverse the successes of Protestantism both in their own lands and in the empire at large and to solidify their control of their diverse personal territories. The result was a devastating conflict known as the Thirty Years' War (1618–1648).

Like conflicts elsewhere in Europe, the Thirty Years' War reflects religious tensions, regionalism versus centralizing forces, and dynastic and strategic rivalries between rulers. The war was particularly destructive because of the size of the armies and the degree to which army commanders evaded control by the states for which they fought. As a result of the war, the empire was eclipsed as a political unit by the regional powers that composed it. Meanwhile, a Polish state resembling the Habsburg territories in its regional diversity remained the dominant state in northeastern Europe. But it would soon face challenges, particularly from a powerful new state being crafted in Russia.

Fragile Peace in the Holy Roman Empire, 1556–1618 The Austrian Habsburgs ruled over a diverse group of territories in the Holy Roman Empire, as well as northwestern Hungary. On his abdication in 1556, Emperor Charles V granted Habsburg lands in central Europe to his brother, Ferdinand (see the chart on page 478), who had long been the actual ruler there in Charles's stead. On Charles's death in 1558, Ferdinand was duly crowned emperor.

Though largely contiguous, Ferdinand's territories comprised independent duchies and kingdoms, each with its own institutional structure, and included speakers of Italian, German, and Czech, plus a few other languages. The non-German lands of Bohemia (the core of the modern Czech Republic) and Hungary had been distinct kingdoms since the High Middle Ages. Both states bestowed their crowns by election and had chosen Ferdinand, the first Habsburg to rule them, in separate elections in the 1520s and 1530s. Most of Hungary was now under Ottoman domination, but Bohemia, with its rich capital, Prague, was a wealthy center of population and culture.

Unlike the Netherlands, these linguistically and culturally diverse lands were still governed by highly decentralized institutions. Moreover, unlike their Spanish cousins, the Austrian Habsburgs made no attempt to impose religious uniformity in the late sixteenth century. Ferdinand was firmly Catholic but tolerant of reform efforts within the church. Both he and his son, Maximilian II (r. 1564–1576), believed that an eventual

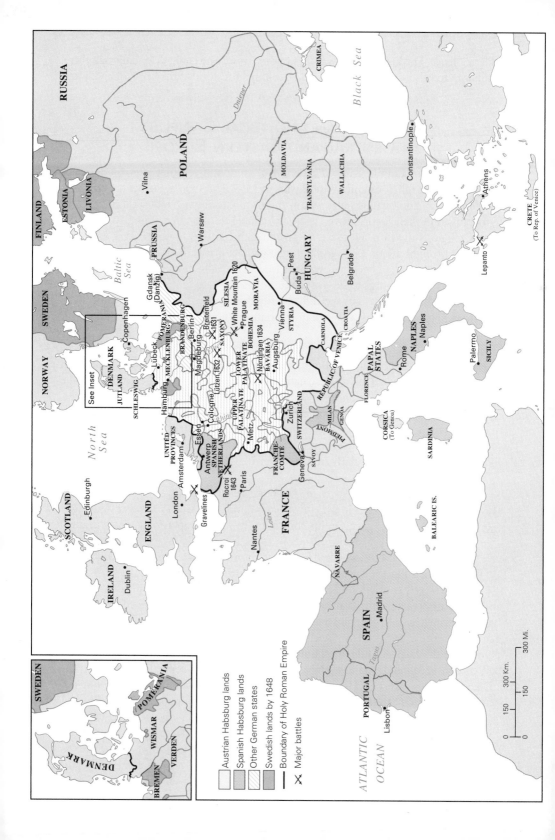

RUSSIA

FINLAND

SWEDEN

NORWAY

ESTONIA

LIVONIA

• Vilna

POLAND

CRIMEA

Black Sea

MOLDAVIA

TRANSYLVANIA

WALLACHIA

• Constantinople

Athens •

CRETE
(To Rep. of Venice)

Baltic Sea

• Warsaw

PRUSSIA

HUNGARY

Gdansk
(Danzig)

POMERANIA

Pest •

Belgrade •

NAPLES

Copenhagen •

Lübeck •

MECKLENBURG

BRANDENBURG

• Berlin

SILESIA

White Mountain 1620

Buda •

CROATIA

Naples •

See Inset

DENMARK

• Hamburg

Breitenfeld
× 1631

SAXONY

MORAVIA

• Prague

BOHEMIA

Vienna •

STYRIA

CARNIOLA

Palermo •

SICILY

Rome •

PAPAL
STATES

JUTLAND

SCHLESWIG

Magdeburg •

Lützen 1632 ×

LOWER
PALATINATE

× Nördlingen 1634

BAVARIA
Augsburg •

REPUBLIC OF VENICE

FLORENCE

Milan •

Genoa •

North
Sea

UNITED
PROVINCES

Essen •

Cologne •
Rhine

UPPER
PALATINATE

Metz •

Zurich •

SWITZERLAND

Geneva •

PIEDMONT

SAVOY

CORSICA
(To Genoa)

SARDINIA

SCOTLAND

Edinburgh •

Antwerp •

Amsterdam •

SPANISH
NETHERLANDS

Rocroi
1643 ×

FRANCHE-
COMTÉ

ENGLAND

London •

× Gravelines

Paris •

IRELAND

Dublin •

Nantes •

Loire

FRANCE

NAVARRE

BALEARIC IS.

ATLANTIC
OCEAN

PORTUGAL

SPAIN

• Madrid

Tagus

Lisbon •

Lepanto ×

Austrian Habsburg lands

Spanish Habsburg lands

Other German states

Swedish lands by 1648

Boundary of Holy Roman Empire

× Major battles

0   150   300 Km.

0   150   300 Mi.

Inset:

SWEDEN

POMERANIA

WISMAR

DENMARK

BREMEN

VERDEN

reunion of the Catholic and Protestant faiths might be possible. During his reign Maximilian worked to keep religious peace in the empire as a whole and granted limited rights of worship to Protestant subjects within his ancestral lands (separate territories more or less equivalent to modern Austria in extent). Catholicism and many strands of Protestantism flourished side by side in Maximilian's domains, above all in Hungary and, especially, Bohemia, which had experienced its own religious reform movement under Jan Hus in the fifteenth century.

Maximilian's son, Rudolf II (r. 1576–1612), shared the religious style of his father and grandfather. He was an energetic patron of the arts and humanist education and sponsored the work of scientists. Yet Rudolf was a weak leader politically and was challenged by his brother and ambitious cousins for control both of Habsburg lands and the empire itself. Meanwhile, the resurgence of Catholicism in the wake of the Council of Trent (1545–1563) had begun to shift the religious balance. Members of the Jesuit order arrived in Habsburg lands in the reign of Maximilian. Tough-minded and well trained, they established Catholic schools and became confessors and preachers to the upper classes. Self-confident Catholicism emerged as one form of cultural identity among the German-speaking ruling classes, and thus as a religious impetus to further political consolidation of all the Habsburg territories.

Resurgent Catholicism was evident, too, in the empire as a whole, where certain princes were confident they might now eliminate Protestantism, as their ancestors had failed to do. In the face of this challenge, certain Protestant princes formed a defensive pact known as the Evangelical Union in 1608. In response Catholic princes formed an alliance, the Holy League, the next year. A major war between the two alliances over a disputed territory was narrowly averted the following year. Like the English under Elizabeth, Habsburg subjects and peoples in the empire had enjoyed a period of calm in political and religious matters. Now, as in England, the stage was set for conflict of both kinds.

The Thirty Years' War, 1618–1648 The Thirty Years' War was touched off in 1618 by a revolt against Habsburg rule in the kingdom of Bohemia. Bohemia was populous and prosperous; Rudolf II had made its bustling capital, Prague, his imperial capital. Its powerful and diverse Protestant community had wrested formal recognition of its right to worship from Rudolf and his younger brother, Matthias (r. 1612–1619).

Matthias was quickly succeeded by his cousin Ferdinand II (r. 1619–1637), who was the ideal Counter-Reformation prince and unlikely to honor these agreements. Educated by the Jesuits, Ferdinand sincerely believed that reimposing Catholicism was his Christian duty; he once stated that he would "sooner beg than rule over heretics."[4] He had virtually eliminated Protestantism, by persuasion as well as by compulsion, in the small duchy in southern Austria he had governed before assuming the throne.

Europe During the Thirty Years' War, 1618–1648

The Thirty Years' War was fought largely within the borders of the Holy Roman Empire. It was the result of conflicts within the empire as well as the meddling of neighbors for their own strategic advantages.

Ferdinand would not tolerate the political independence of nobles and towns in Bohemia or the religious pluralism that independence defended. As Philip II had done in the Netherlands, Ferdinand appointed a regency council to govern in his name. That council enforced unpopular policies: the right to build new Protestant churches was denied, Bohemian crown lands were given to the Catholic Church, and non-Catholics were barred from serving in government.

On May 23, 1618, delegates to a Protestant assembly that had unsuccessfully petitioned Ferdinand to end his violations of earlier guarantees marched to the palace in Prague where the royal officials met. After a confrontation over their demands, the delegates "tried" the officials on the spot for treason and, literally, threw them out of the palace window. The incident became known as the "Defenestration of Prague" (from the Latin *fenestra,* or "window"). (The officials' lives were saved only because they fell into a pile of refuse in the moat.) The rebels proceeded to set up their own government.

This upstart Bohemian government officially deposed Ferdinand and elected a new Protestant king in 1619: Frederick, elector of the Palatinate and a Calvinist prince. His election had implications for the Holy Roman Empire as a whole because his role as leader of the territories in west-central Germany called the Lower and Upper Palatinate conveyed the right to be one of the seven electors who chose the emperor.

Emboldened by these events, Protestant subjects in other Habsburg lands asked for guarantees of freedom of worship similar to those enjoyed by Protestants in Bohemia. Other princes saw their chance to make political gains. For example, rival claimants to Habsburg rule in Hungary took up arms against Ferdinand.

The revolt in Bohemia set off a wider war because foreign rulers also felt their interests to be involved. The English king, James I, supported Frederick because Frederick was married to his daughter. Spain's supply routes north from Italy to the Netherlands passed next to Frederick's lands in western Germany. France's first interest was its rivalry with Spain; thus France kept its eye on the border principalities that were strategically important to Spain. In addition, France desired to keep Protestant as well as Catholic princes within the empire strong enough to thwart Austrian Habsburg ambitions. Thus, from the outset, the war was a conflict not only over the Habsburgs' power in their own lands but also over the balance of religious and political power in the empire and in Europe.

Ferdinand secured aid from the Catholic duke of Bavaria and from his cousin, King Philip III (r. 1598–1621) of Spain, by promising them Frederick's lands in the Palatinate. By the fall of 1620 a Catholic army was closing in on Bohemia. On November 8, on a hillside near Prague, the Catholic force faced a Bohemian army that had received little aid from its Protestant allies. The Battle of White Mountain was a complete Catholic victory.

Despite the rout, fighting did not cease but instead became more widespread. The truce between Spain and the Netherlands, established in 1609, expired in 1621, and the nearby Lower Palatinate, now in Spanish hands, offered a staging point for Spanish forces and thus threatened the peace in that corner of the empire. Claiming to be a Protestant champion, the Protestant king of Denmark, Christian IV (r. 1588–1648), who was also duke of Holstein in northern Germany, sought to conquer additional German territory. His goals were to gain greater control over profitable German Baltic seaports and to defend himself against any Catholic attempt to seize northern German territory. Christian received little help from fellow Protestants, however. The Dutch were busy with Spain, the English were wary of fighting after Frederick's defeat, and Denmark's regional rivals, the Swedes, were uninterested in furthering Danish ambitions in the Baltic.

The confusing blend of politics and religion that motivated the Protestant rulers was also evident on the Catholic side. When imperial forces defeated Christian's armies in 1626, Catholic princes became alarmed at the possibility of greater imperial power in northern Germany. Led by the duke of Bavaria, they arranged a truce that resulted in Denmark's withdrawal from the fighting on relatively generous terms. At the same time, Protestants outside Bohemia saw the potential consequences of imperial victory and took up arms. As his armies defeated Christian, Ferdinand issued new edicts that in effect voided the religious settlement in place since 1555. His victorious armies brutally enforced his edicts wherever they passed.

Christian's rival, Gustav Adolf, king of Sweden (r. 1611–1632), now assumed the role of Protestant leader. An innovative military leader, Gustav Adolf hoped to gain territory along the Baltic seacoast, but personal aggrandizement also was one of his goals. His campaigns were capped by a victory over an imperial army at Breitenfeld, in Saxony, in 1631. After he was killed in battle in 1632, however, the tide turned in favor of Ferdinand's forces. A decisive imperial victory over a combined Swedish and German Protestant army at Nördlingen in 1634 led to the Peace of Prague (1635), a general peace treaty favorable to Catholics.

The Peace of Prague brought only a temporary peace, however, because Ferdinand died shortly thereafter and French involvement increased now that other anti-Habsburg forces had been eclipsed. France tried to seize imperial territory along its own eastern border and generously subsidized continued fighting within the empire by channeling monies to Protestant princes and mercenaries there. The fighting dragged on. By the end of the Thirty Years' War order had disintegrated so completely in the wake of the marauding armies that both staunchly Catholic rulers and firmly Protestant ones allied with religious enemies to safeguard their states.

A comprehensive peace treaty became possible when France withdrew its sponsorship of the fighting in order to concentrate on its conflict with Spain. The French wanted only a workable balance of power in the empire, which was achieved once they and their allies convincingly defeated imperial forces in 1645. More urgent to the French was the continued rivalry with the Spanish Habsburgs for control of territory along France's eastern and northern borders and in Italy. A defeat by France in the Spanish Netherlands in 1643 had convinced Spain to concentrate on that rivalry, too, and fighting between them continued separately until 1659. Negotiations for peace had begun in 1643 among war-weary states of the empire and resulted in a group of agreements known as the Peace of Westphalia in 1648.

The Effects of the War

The Thirty Years' War ruined the economy and decimated the population in many parts of the empire and had long-term political consequences for the empire as a whole. One reason for the war's devastation was a novel application of firepower to warfare that increased both the size of armies and their deadly force in battle. This was the use of volley fire, the arrangement of foot soldiers in parallel lines so that one line of men could fire

The Horrors of War   *This painting by a seventeenth-century artist depicts an attack on a supply convoy by opposing troops. Control of supplies to feed and equip the increasing numbers of troops was one of the most important aspects of warfare.*   (Staatsgalerie Aschaffenburg [Schloss], Bayerische Staatsgemäldesammlungen/Godwin Alfen-ARTOTHEK)

while another reloaded. This tactic, pioneered in the Netherlands around the turn of the century, was further refined by Gustav Adolf of Sweden. Gustav Adolf amassed large numbers of troops and increased the rate of fire so that a virtually continuous barrage was maintained. He also used maneuverable field artillery to protect the massed infantry from cavalry charges.

Following Gustav Adolf's lead, armies of all the major states adopted these new offensive tactics. But defensive expertise—as in holding fortresses—also remained important, and pitched battles, such as at Nördlingen in 1634, still tended to be part of sieges. The costs in resources and human life of this kind of warfare reached unheard-of dimensions. Popular printed literature and court drama both condemned the horrors of the war.

Where fighting had been concentrated, as in parts of Saxony, between one-third and one-half of the inhabitants of rural villages and major towns may have disappeared. Many starved, were caught in the fighting, or were killed by marauding soldiers. The most notorious atrocity occurred in the aftermath of the siege of Magdeburg in 1631. After the city surrendered to besieging Catholic forces, long-deprived soldiers ate and drank themselves into a frenzy, raped and killed indiscriminately, and set fires that destroyed the town. Some victims of war migrated to other regions in search of peaceful conditions and work. Some joined the armies in order to survive. Others formed armed bands to fight off the soldiers or to steal back enough goods to live on.

Compounding these effects of war were the actions of armies hired by enterprising mercenary generals for whom loyalty to the princes who paid them took a back seat to personal advancement. They contracted to provide, supply, and lead troops and thus were more willing than the princes would have been to allow troops to live "economically" on plunder. States thus managed to field large armies but had not yet evolved the mechanisms fully to fund, and thus control, them.

The Peace of Westphalia, which ended fighting in the empire, was one of the most important outcomes of the war. The various treaties composing the peace effectively put an end to religious war in the empire. Calvinism was recognized as a tolerated religion. The requirement that all subjects must follow their ruler's faith was retained, but some leeway was allowed for those who now found themselves under new rulers.

In political matters the treaties reflected some of the recent successes of the Swedes by granting them territory on the Baltic coast. France gained the important towns of Metz, Toul, and Verdun on its eastern border. Spain formally recognized the independence of the Netherlands.

The most important political outcome of the peace was a new balance of power in the empire. Most of the major Catholic and Protestant rulers extended their territories at the expense of smaller principalities and cities. The son of Frederick, Protestant king of Bohemia, received back the smaller of the two Palatine territories that his father had held. The Upper Palatinate—as well as the right to be a new elector of the emperor—was given to the powerful duke of Bavaria. The principalities within the empire were acknowledged, in the peace, to be virtually autonomous, both from the emperor and from one another. In addition, the constitution of the empire was changed to make it very difficult for one prince or a group of princes to disrupt the peace in their own interests. As a result, the agreements at Westphalia were the beginning of one hundred years of peace within the Holy Roman Empire.

Another outcome was that the Habsburgs, though weakened as emperors, were strengthened as rulers of their own hereditary lands on the eastern fringes of the empire. Except in Hungary, Protestantism—and its contrary political baggage—had been eliminated early in the wars, and the peace did not alter these circumstances. The Habsburgs moved their capital back to Vienna from Prague, and the government of their hereditary lands gained in importance as administration of the empire waned.

Stability and Dynamism in Eastern Europe   On the southern frontier of Austrian Habsburg lands, the empire of the Ottoman Turks continued to control southeastern Europe in the late sixteenth and early seventeenth centuries. The Ottoman state had reached the practical limits of its expansion with the conquests of Suleiman I (r. 1520–1566), known to Europeans as "the Magnificent." Sporadic fighting between the Ottomans and the Habsburgs continued in Hungary, which the Ottomans largely controlled, but the fighting there was secondary to the Ottomans' rivalry with the Safavid rulers of Persia. The Ottomans succeeded in extending their territory eastward into modern Iraq, Azerbaijan, and Georgia at Safavid expense. Despite the Ottomans' many commitments and a succession of weak rulers, their presence in southeastern Europe remained secure, partly because they respected the cultural and religious diversity of their Christian subjects. Aristocratic and regional independence were factors, too: Christian princes, particularly in the Hungarian borderlands, found distant Turkish overlords more palatable than closer Habsburg ones. The naval defeat at Lepanto in 1571 (see page 481) had been a setback for the Ottomans, but they quickly rebuilt their fleet and re-established supremacy in the eastern Mediterranean.

Ottoman power was a constant presence in European affairs, but a more dynamic state in the late sixteenth century was the newly proclaimed empire in Russia. Through the late Middle Ages Muscovite princes had accumulated land and authority as they vied for pre-eminence with other principalities after the decline of Kievan Rus (modern Ukraine). Ivan III (r. 1462–1505) absorbed neighboring Russian principalities and ended Moscow's subservience to Mongol overlords. He then took the title of "Tsar," Russian for "Caesar." In 1547 his grandson, Ivan IV (r. 1533–1584), was officially proclaimed "Tsar of All the Russias" and became the first ruler to routinely use the title. For Russians this title placed Ivan IV in higher esteem than the neighboring Polish-Lithuanian and Swedish kings.

Ivan's use of the title reflects his imperial intentions, as he continued Moscow's push south, into lands that were once part of Kievan Rus, and east, against the Tatar states of Astrakhan, Kazan, and Sibir (Siberia). Within his expanding empire Ivan ruled as an autocrat. The practice of gathering tribute money for Mongol overlords had concentrated many resources in the hands of Muscovite princes. Ivan was able to bypass noble participation and intensify the centralization of government by creating ranks of officials loyal only to him. Part of his authority stemmed from his personality. He was willing, perhaps because of mental imbalance, to use ruthless methods—including torture and the murder of thousands of subjects—to enforce his will.

Ivan came to be called "the Terrible," from a Russian word meaning "awe-inspiring." Although a period of disputed succession to the throne known as the "Time of Troubles" followed Ivan's death in 1584, the foundations of the large and cohesive state he had built survived until a new dynasty of rulers was established in the seventeenth century.

Checking Russian expansion to the west was the commonwealth of Poland-Lithuania, a large, multi-ethnic state at the height of its power. The duchy of Lithuania had conquered the territories known as Ruthenia (comprising most of modern Belarus and Ukraine) in the fourteenth century. Then in 1386 a marriage had brought the duchy of Lithuania and the kingdom of Poland under a joint ruler. Like the union of Castile and Aragon in Spain, the union of Poland and Lithuania was initially only dynastic. But two hundred years later, in 1569, they were brought under a single set of institutions by the Treaty of Lublin. Even so, the two states retained distinct traditions. Poles spoke Polish, a Slavic language, and were primarily Catholic, although there were also large minorities of Protestants, Orthodox Christians, and Jews in Poland. Lithuanians, whose language was only distantly related to the Slavic languages, were mostly Catholic as well, although Orthodox Christianity predominated among the Ruthenians, who spoke a Slavic language related to both Russian and Polish. Poland-Lithuania was unusual among European states in that religious toleration was a long-standing practice and was even enshrined in law in 1573.

Valuable resources such as grain, timber, and other naval stores passed through Polish-controlled ports on the Baltic Sea on their way to western Europe. Poland itself also became an increasingly important source of grain for Spanish, French, and English cities. Russia and Sweden, however, challenged Polish control of the lucrative Baltic coast. Polish forces were able to defeat efforts by Ivan the Terrible to control Livonia (modern Latvia), with its important port of Riga, and briefly placed a Polish claimant on the Russian throne during the Time of Troubles. They were not as successful against the Swedes, who, under the expansionist Gustav Adolf, took Riga and the Baltic coast to its north in 1621 (as part of the same drive for Baltic territory that lay behind his involvement in the Thirty Years' War). The Turks also were a constant threat to Poland-Lithuania on its southern border.

In addition to the foreign challenges it faced by virtue of its geography, Poland-Lithuania had internal weaknesses. It was a republic of the nobility, with a weak elected king at its head. (The elective crown was a tradition that had developed over centuries when the throne had been contested by rival claimants from within Poland or from other states.) The great nobles, whose fortunes increased with the grain trade, ran the affairs of state through the national parliament, the Sejm, as well as local assemblies and various lifelong offices. They drastically limited the ability of the Crown to tax and to grant new titles of nobility, as was the practice throughout Europe. These limitations meant that the king could not reward and reinforce the loyalty of wealthy gentry or the small numbers of urban elites so that they might be a counterweight to noble power. Limited funds also meant that the Polish crown would be hard put to defend its vast territories later in the seventeenth century.

WRITING, DRAMA, AND ART IN AN AGE OF UPHEAVAL

Both imaginative literature and speculative writing, such as political theory, bear the stamp of their times. In the late sixteenth and early seventeenth centuries, political speculation often concerned questions of the legitimacy of rulers and of the relationship of political power to divine authority—urgent problems in an age when religious division threatened the very foundations of states. Authors and rulers alike often relied on still-prevalent oral modes of communication to convey their ideas. Indeed, some of the greatest literature and some of the most effective political statements of the period were presented as drama and not conveyed in print. Nevertheless, literacy continued to spread and led to greater opportunities for knowledge and reflection. The medium of print became increasingly important to political life. In the visual arts, the dramatic impulse was wedded to religious purposes to create works that conveyed both power and emotion.

Literacy and Literature Traditional oral culture changed slowly under the impact of the spread of printing, education, and literacy. Works of literature from the late sixteenth and early seventeenth centuries incorporate material from traditional folktales, consciously reflecting the coexistence of oral and literate culture. In *Don Quixote*, by Spain's Miguel de Cervantes (1547–1616), the title character and his companion, Sancho Panza, have a long discussion about oral and literate traditions. The squire Panza speaks in the style that was customary in oral culture—a rather roundabout and repetitive style, which enabled the speaker and listener to remember what was said. Much of the richness of *Don Quixote* is due to the interweaving of prose styles and topical concerns from throughout Cervantes' culture—from the oral world of peasants to the refined world of court life. Yet the perspective that enabled Cervantes to accomplish this rich portrayal came from his own highly developed literacy and the awareness of language that literacy made possible.

The spread of education and literacy in the late sixteenth century had a dramatic impact on attitudes toward literature and on literature itself. The value of education—particularly of the continuing humanist recovery of ancient wisdom—was reflected in much of the literature of the period. Writers found in humanistic education a vision of what it meant to be cultivated and disciplined men of the world. This vision provided the beginnings of a new self-image for members of the warrior class.

It is customary to regard the French author Michel de Montaigne (1533–1592) as the epitome of the reflective—and, more important, the *self*-reflective—gentleman. Montaigne was a judge in the parlement (law court) of Bordeaux. In 1570 he resigned from the court and retired to his small château, where he wrote his *Essais* (from which we derive the word *essays*), a collection of short reflections that were revolutionary in both form and content. Montaigne invented writing in the form of a sketch, an "attempt" (the literal meaning of *essai*) that enabled him to combine self-reflection with formal analysis.

Montaigne's reflections range from the destructiveness of the French civil wars to the consequences of European exploration of the New World. Toward all of these events and circumstances, Montaigne was able to achieve an analytic detachment remarkable for his day. For example, he noted an irony in Europeans labeling New World peoples "savages," given Europeans' seemingly endless and wanton violence against those "savages" and one another. Owing to the spread of printing and literacy, Montaigne had—in addition to his own effort and the resources of leisure—a virtually unparalleled opportunity to reflect on the world through reading the wide variety of printed texts available to him. For the first time it was possible for a leisured lay reader to consider and compare different events, values, and cultures.

Montaigne's essays also reveal a distancing from himself. This distancing was another result of literacy—not simply the ability to read and write but the capacity to enjoy long periods of solitude and reflection in the company of other solitary, bookbound voices. Montaigne's works mark the beginning of what we know as the "invention" of private life, in which an individual is known more by internal character and personality traits than by social role and past behavior.

The works of the great English poet and playwright William Shakespeare (1564–1616) are still compelling to us because of the profundity of the questions he asked about love, honor, and political legitimacy, but he asked these questions in terms appropriate to his own day. One of his favorite themes—evident in *Hamlet* and *Macbeth*—is the legitimacy of rulers. He was at his most skilled, perhaps, when exploring the contradictions in values between the growing commercial world he saw around him and the older, seemingly more stable world of feudal society. Subtle political commentary distinguishes Shakespeare's later plays, written near and shortly after the death of Queen Elizabeth in 1603, when political and economic problems were becoming increasingly visible and troublesome. Shakespeare explored not only the duties of rulers but also the rights of their subjects. In *Coriolanus* he portrays commoners as poor but neither ignorant nor wretched; they are in fact fully rational and capable of analyzing their situation—perhaps more capable, Shakespeare hints, than their ruler is. The play is safely set in ancient Rome, but the social and political tensions it depicts clearly applied to the Elizabethan present.

Shakespeare, Cervantes, and other writers of their day were also representatives of what were starting to be self-consciously distinct national literatures. The spread of humanism added a historical dimension to their awareness of their own languages and to their distinct subject matter: each one's own society and its past. This kind of self-consciousness is evident in Shakespeare's historical plays, such as *Henry V* and *Richard II*. In *Richard II* he depicts the kingdom in terms that reflect the Elizabethan sense of England as a separate and self-contained nation:

> This royal throne of kings, this scept'red isle,
> This earth of majesty, this seat of Mars,
> This other Eden, demi-paradise,
> This fortress built by Nature for herself
> Against infection and the hand of war,
> This happy breed of men, this little world,
> This precious stone set in the silver sea . . .
> This blessed plot, this earth, this realm, this England . . .
> (*Richard II*, act 2, sc. 1, lines 40–50)[5]

The Great Age of Theater

Shakespeare's extraordinary career was possible because his life coincided with the rise of professional theater. In the capitals of England and Spain professional theaters first opened in the 1570s. Some drama was produced at court or in aristocratic households, but most public theaters drew large and very mixed audiences, including the poorest city dwellers. Playwrights, including Shakespeare, often wrote in teams under great pressure to keep acting companies supplied with material. The best-known dramatist in Spain, Lope de Vega (1562–1635), wrote more than fifteen hundred works on a wide range of topics. Although religious themes remained popular in Spanish theater, as an echo of medieval drama, most plays in England and Spain treated secular subjects and, as in *Coriolanus*, safely disguised political commentary.

Over time theater became increasingly restricted to aristocratic circles. In England Puritan criticism of the "immorality" of public performance drove actors and playwrights to seek royal patronage. The first professional theater to open in Paris, in 1629, as political and religious turmoil quieted, quickly became dependent on Cardinal Richelieu's patronage. Inevitably, as court patronage grew in importance, the wide range of subjects treated in plays began to narrow to those of aristocratic concern, such as family honor and martial glory. These themes are depicted in the works of the Spaniard Pedro Calderón (1600–1681), who wrote for his enthusiastic patron, Philip IV, and of the

Frenchman Pierre Corneille (1606–1684), whose great tragedy of aristocratic life, *Le Cid*, was one of the early successes of the seventeenth-century French theater.

Drama's significance as an art form is reflected in its impact on the development of music: the opera, which weds drama to music, was invented in Italy in the early seventeenth century. The first great work in this genre is generally acknowledged to be *Orfeo* (*Orpheus*, 1607) by Claudio Monteverdi (1567–1643). Opera, like drama, reflected the influence of humanism in its secular themes and in its emulation of Greek drama, which had used both words and music. The practice of music itself changed under the dramatic impulse. Monteverdi was the first master of a new musical style known as "monody," which emphasizes the progression of chords. Monodic music is inherently dramatic, creating a sense of forward movement, expectation, and resolution.

Sovereignty in Ceremony, Image, and Word

Whether produced on a public stage or at court or in a less formal setting, drama was a favored method of communication in this era because people responded to and made extensive use of the spoken word. Dramatic gesture and storytelling to get a message across were commonplace and were important components of politics.

What we might call "street drama" was an ordinary occurrence. When great noble governors entered major towns, such as when Margaret of Parma entered Brussels, a solemn yet ostentatious formal "entry" was often staged. The dignitary would ride through the main gate, usually beneath a canopy made of luxurious cloth. The event might include staged tableaux in the town's streets, with costumed townspeople acting out brief symbolic vignettes, such as David and Goliath, and it might end with an elaborate banquet. A remnant of these proceedings survives today in the ceremony by which distinguished visitors are given "the keys to the city," which, in the sixteenth century, really were functional.

Royalty made deliberate and careful use of dramatic ceremony. Royal entries into towns took on an added weight, as did royal funerals and other such occasions. These dramas reinforced political and constitutional assumptions in the minds of witnesses and participants. Thus over time we can see changes in the representations of royal power. In France, for example, the ritual entry of the king into Paris had originally stressed the participation of the leading guilds, judges, and administrators, symbolizing their active role in governing the city and the kingdom. But in the last half of the sixteenth century the procession began to glorify the king alone. Speculation about and celebration of power, as well as dramatic emotion, also occurred in the visual arts—most notably in painting and architecture, in the style now known as "baroque." Baroque style was a new kind of visual language that could project power and grandeur and simultaneously engage viewers' senses.

The very fact that rulers experimented self-consciously with self-representation suggests that issues pertaining to the nature and extent of royal power were profoundly important and far from settled. Queen Elizabeth I had the particular burden of assuming the throne in a period of great instability. Hence she paid a great deal of attention to the image of herself that she conveyed in words and authorized to be fashioned in painting. Elizabeth styled herself variously as mother to her people and as a warrior-queen (drawing on ancient myths of Amazon women). She made artful use of the image of her virginity to buttress each of these images—as the wholly devoted, self-sacrificing mother (which, of course, had religious tradition behind it) or as an androgynous ruler, woman but doing the bodily work of man.

More formal speculation about constitutional matters also resulted from the tumult of the sixteenth and seventeenth centuries. As we have seen, the Protestant faction in France advanced an elaborate argument for the limitation of royal power. Alternative theories enhancing royal authority were offered, principally in support of the Catholic position though also simply to buttress the beleaguered monarchy itself. The most famous of these appeared in *The Six Books of the Republic* (1576), by the legal scholar Jean Bodin (1530–1596). Bodin was a Catholic but offered a fundamentally secular perspective on the purposes and source of power within a state. His special contribution was a vision of a truly sovereign monarch. Bodin offered a theoretical understanding that is essential to states today and is the ground on which people can claim rights and protection from the state—namely, that there is a final sovereign authority. For Bodin that authority was the king. He recognized that in practice royal power was

IMPORTANT EVENTS

1556–1598 Reign of Philip II

1558–1603 Reign of Elizabeth I

1559 Act of Supremacy (England)

1562–1598 Religious wars in France

1565 Netherlands city councils and nobility ignore Philip II's law against heresy

1566 Calvinist "iconoclastic fury" begins in the Netherlands

1567 Duke of Alba arrives in the Netherlands

1571 Defeat of Turkish navy at Lepanto

1576 Sack of Antwerp

1579 Union of Utrecht

1588 Defeat of Spanish Armada

1589–1610 Reign of Henry IV

1598 Edict of Nantes (France)

1609 Truce between Spain and the Netherlands is declared

1618–1648 Thirty Years' War

1620 Catholic victory at Battle of White Mountain

1621 Truce between Spain and the Netherlands expires; war between Spain and the Netherlands begins

1629 Peace of Alais

1631 Swedes under Gustav Adolf defeat imperial forces

1635 Peace of Prague

1640–1653 "Long Parliament" in session in England

1648 Peace of Westphalia

constrained by limitations, but he was intrigued more by the theoretical grounding for royal authority than by its practical application.

Contract theory devised by French Protestants to legitimize resistance to the monarchy had to be abandoned when Henry IV granted toleration to the Huguenots in 1598. In England theoretical justification of resistance to Charles I was initially limited to invoking tradition and precedent. Contract theory, as well as other sweeping claims regarding subjects' rights, would be more fully developed later in the century.

Bodin's theory of sovereignty, however, was immediately echoed in other theoretical works, most notably that of Hugo Grotius (1583–1645). A Dutch jurist and diplomat, Grotius developed the first principles of modern international law. He accepted the existence of sovereign states that owed no loyalty to higher authority (such as the papacy) and thus needed new principles to govern their interactions. His major work, *De Jure Belli ac Pacis* (*On the Law of War and Peace*, 1625), was written in response to the turmoil of the Thirty Years' War. Grotius argued that relations between states could be based on respect for treaties voluntarily reached between them. In perhaps his boldest move he argued that war must be justified, and he developed criteria to distinguish just from unjust wars.

NOTES

1. Geoffrey Parker, *The Dutch Revolt* (London: Penguin, 1985), p. 288, n. 5.
2. Quoted in A. W. Lovett, *Early Habsburg Spain, 1517–1598* (Oxford: Oxford University Press, 1986), p. 212.
3. Quoted in R. J. Knecht, *The French Wars of Religion, 1559–1598* (London: Longman, 1989), p. 109.
4. Quoted in Jean Berenger, *A History of the Habsburg Empire, 1273–1700*, trans. C. A. Simpson (London and New York: Longman, 1990), p. 239.
5. *The Riverside Shakespeare*, ed. G. Blakemore Evans, 2d ed. (Boston: Houghton Mifflin, 1997), p. 855. Copyright © 1997 by Houghton Mifflin Company. Reprinted by permission of the publisher.

SUGGESTED READING

Berenger, Jean. *A History of the Habsburg Empire, 1273–1700,* trans. C. A. Simpson. 1990. A detailed treatment of Habsburg rule in the Holy Roman Empire and in their own principalities. Considers economic and cultural changes as well as political ones.

Bonney, Richard. *The European Dynastic States, 1494–1660.* 1991. A rich survey of the period that is solid on eastern as well as western Europe. Written from an English point of view, it does not consider England as part of Europe.

Eagleton, Terry. *William Shakespeare.* 1986. A brief and highly readable interpretation of Shakespeare that emphasizes the tensions in the plays caused by language and by ideas from the new world of bourgeois commercial life.

Edwards, Philip. *The Making of the Modern English State.* 2001. A readable survey of political and religious developments in England that incorporates much new scholarship.

Holt, Mack P. *The French Wars of Religion, 1562–1629.* 1995. An up-to-date synthesis that evaluates social and political context while not slighting the importance of religion.

Lynch, John. *Spain, 1516–1598: From Nation-State to World Empire.* 1991. A survey covering the reign of Philip II by a leading scholar of Spanish history.

Parker, Geoffrey. *The Military Revolution.* 1988; and Black, Jeremy. *A Military Revolution?* 1991. Two works that disagree about the nature and extent of the changes in military practices and their significance for military, political, and social history. Black tries to refute claims of a dramatic military "revolution."

Parker, Geoffrey. *The Dutch Revolt.* 2d ed. 1985. The best survey of the revolt available in English.

Wiesner, Merry. *Women and Gender in Early Modern Europe.* 1993. Discusses all aspects of women's experience, including their working lives.

16

Europe in the Age of Louis XIV, ca. 1640–1715

(Scala/Art Resource, NY)

This portrait of King Louis XIV of France as a triumphant warrior was one of hundreds of such images of the king that decorated his palace at Versailles and other sites around his kingdom—where they made his subjects aware of his presence, regardless of whether he was in residence. Louis is dressed as a Roman warrior, and his power is represented by a mixture of other symbols—Christian and pagan, ancient and contemporary. An angel crowns him with a victor's laurel wreath and carries a banner bearing the image of the sun. In his hand Louis holds a marshal's baton—a symbol of military command—covered with the royal emblem of the fleur-de-lys. In the background, behind the "Roman" troops following Louis, is an idealized city.

These trappings symbolized the significant expansion of royal power during Louis's reign. He faced down the challenges of warrior-nobles, suppressed religious dissent, and tapped the nation's wealth to wage a series of wars of conquest. A period of cultural brilliance early in his reign and the spectacle of an elaborate court life crowned his achievements. In his prime, his regime was supported by a consensus of elites; such harmony was made possible by the lack of institutional brakes on royal authority. However, as his attention to symbolism suggests, Louis's power was not unchallenged. By the end of the Sun King's reign the glow was fading: France was struggling under economic distress brought on by the many wars fought for his glory and had missed opportunities for commercial success abroad. Elites throughout France who had once accepted, even welcomed, his rule became trenchant critics, and common people outright rebels.

After the Thirty Years' War, vigorous rulers in central and eastern Europe undertook a program of territorial expansion and state building that led to the dominance in the region of Austria, Brandenburg-Prussia, and Russia. The power of these states derived, in part, from the economic relationship of their lands to the wider European economy. In all the major states of continental Europe, princely governments were able to monopolize military power for the first time, in return for economic and political concessions to noble landholders. In England, by contrast, the Crown faced rebellion by subjects claiming religious authority and political legitimacy for their causes. Resistance to the expansion of royal authority, led by Parliament, resulted in the execution of the king and the establishment of a short-lived republic, the Commonwealth. Although the monarchy was restored, the civil war had long-term consequences for royal power in England.

The seventeenth century also witnessed a dynamic phase of European expansion overseas, following on the successes of the Portuguese and the Spanish in the fifteenth and sixteenth centuries. Eager migrants settled in the Americas in ever increasing numbers, while forced migrants—enslaved Africans—were transported by the thousands to work on the profitable plantations of European colonizers. Aristocrats, merchants, and peasants back in Europe jockeyed to take advantage of—or to mitigate the effects of—the local political and economic impact of Europe's expansion.

FRANCE IN THE AGE OF ABSOLUTISM

Absolutism is a term often used to describe the extraordinary concentration of power in royal hands achieved by the kings of France, most notably Louis XIV (r. 1643–1715), in the seventeenth century. Louis continued the expansion of state power begun by his father's minister, Cardinal Richelieu (see pages 386–387). The extension of royal power, under Louis as well as his predecessor, was accelerated by the desire to sustain an expensive and aggressive foreign policy. The policy itself was partly traditional—fighting the perpetual enemy, the Habsburgs, and seeking military glory—and partly new—expanding the borders of France. Louis XIV's successes in these undertakings made him both envied and emulated by other rulers: the French court became a model of culture and refinement. But increased royal authority was not accepted without protest: common French people as well as elites dug in their heels.

The Last Challenge to Absolutism: The Fronde, 1648–1653 Louis came to the throne as a 5-year-old child in 1643. Acting as his regent, his mother, Anne of Austria (1601–1666), had to defuse a serious challenge to royal authority during her son's minority. Together with her chief minister and personal friend, Cardinal Jules Mazarin (1602–1661), she faced opposition from royal bureaucrats and the traditional nobility as well as the common people.

Revolts against the concentration of power in royal hands and against the exorbitant taxation that had prevailed under Louis's father began immediately. In one province a group of armed peasants cornered the intendant and forced him to agree to lower taxes; elsewhere provincial parlements tried to abolish special ranks of officials, especially the intendants, created by Richelieu. In 1648, after several more years of foreign war and the financial expedients to sustain it, the most serious revolt began, led by the Parlement of Paris and the other sovereign law courts in the capital.

The source of the Parlement's leverage over the monarchy was its traditional right to register laws and edicts, which amounted to judicial review. Now the Parlement, as a guardian of royal authority, attempted to extend this power by debating and even initiating government policy. The sovereign courts sitting together drew up a reform program abolishing most of the machinery of government established under Richelieu and calling for consent to future taxation. The citizens of Paris rose to defend the courts when royal troops were sent against them in October.

Mazarin was forced to accept the proposed reform of government, at least in theory. He also had to avert challenges by great nobles for control of the young king's council. Civil war waxed and waned around France from 1648 to 1653. The main combatants were conventionally ambitious great nobles, but reform-minded urban dwellers often made common cause with them, to benefit from their military power. Meanwhile, middling nobles in the region around Paris began to devise a thoroughgoing reform program and to prepare for a meeting of the Estates General—a representative assembly—to enact it.

These revolts begun in 1648 were derided with the name "Fronde," which was a popular children's game. However, the Fronde was not child's play; it constituted a serious challenge to the legacy of royal government as it had developed under Richelieu. It ended without a noteworthy impact on the growth of royal power for several reasons. First, Mazarin methodically regained control of the kingdom through armed force and artful concessions to individual aristocrats, who were always eager to trade their loyalty for the fruits of royal service. Meanwhile, the Parlement of Paris, as well as many citizens of the capital, welcomed a return to royal authority when civil war caused starvation as well as political unrest.

Moreover, the Parlement of Paris was a law court, not a representative assembly. Its legitimacy derived from its role as upholder of royal law, and it could not, over time, challenge the king on the pretext of upholding royal tradition in his name. Parlementaires tended to see the Estates General as a rival institution and helped quash the proposed meeting of representatives. Above all, they wanted to avert reforms such as the abolition of the paulette, a fee guaranteeing the hereditary right to royal office (see page 486).

Unlike in England, there was in France no single institutional focus for resistance to royal power. A strong-willed and able ruler, as Louis XIV proved to be, could obstruct or override challenges to royal power, particularly when he satisfied the ambitions of aristocrats and those bureaucrats who profited from the expansion of royal power. Moreover, the young Louis had been traumatized by the uprisings of the Fronde and grew up determined never to allow another such challenge to his absolute sovereignty.

France Under Louis XIV, 1661–1715 Louis XIV fully assumed control of government at Mazarin's death in 1661. It was a propitious moment. The Peace of the Pyrenees in 1659 had ended in France's favor the wars with Spain that had dragged on since the end of the Thirty Years' War. As part of the peace agreement, Louis married a Spanish princess, Maria Theresa. In the first ten years of his active reign Louis achieved a degree of control over the mechanisms of government unparalleled in the history of monarchy in France or anywhere else in Europe. Louis was extremely vigorous and proved a diligent king. He put in hours a day at a desk while sustaining the ceremonial life of the court, with its elaborate hunts, balls, and other public events.

Louis did not invent any new bureaucratic devices but rather used existing ranks of officials in new ways that increased government efficiency and further centralized control. He radically reduced the number of men in his High Council, the advisory body closest to the king, to include only three or four great ministers of state affairs. This intimate group, with Louis's active participation, handled all policymaking. The ministers of state, war, and finance were chosen exclusively from non-noble men of bourgeois background whose training and experience fitted them for such positions. Jean-Baptiste Colbert (1619–1683), perhaps the greatest of them, served as minister of finance and supervised most domestic policy from 1665 until his death. He was from a merchant family and had served for years under Mazarin.

Several dozen other officials, picked from the ranks of up-and-coming lawyers and administrators, drew up laws and regulations and passed them to the intendants for execution at the provincial level. Sometimes these officials at the center were sent to the provinces on short-term supervisory missions. The effect of this system was to bypass many entrenched provincial bureaucrats, particularly those known as tax farmers. Tax farmers were freelance businessmen who bid for the right to collect taxes in a region in return for a negotiated fee they paid to the Crown. The Crown, in short, did not control its own tax revenues. The money Louis's regime saved by the more efficient collection of taxes (revenues almost doubled in some areas) enabled the government to streamline the bureaucracy: dozens of the offices created over the years to bring cash in were bought back by the Crown from their owners.

The system still relied on the bonds of patronage and personal service—political bonds borrowed from aristocratic life. Officials rose through the ranks by means of service to the great, and family connection and personal loyalty still were essential. Of the seventeen different men who were part of Louis XIV's High Council during his reign, five were members of the Colbert family, for example. In the provinces important local families vied for minor posts, which at least provided prestige and some income.

Further benefits of centralized administration can be seen in certain achievements of the early years of Louis's regime. Colbert actively encouraged France's economic development. He reduced the internal tolls and customs barriers, which were relics of medieval decentralization—for example, the right of a landholder to charge a toll on all boats along a river under his control. He encouraged industry with state subsidies and protective tariffs. He set up state-sponsored trading companies—the two most important being the East India Company and the West India Company, established in 1664.

Mercantilism is the term historians use to describe the theory behind Colbert's efforts. This economic theory stressed self-sufficiency in manufactured goods, tight control of trade to foster the domestic economy, and the absolute value of bullion. Both capital for development—in the form of hard currency, known as bullion—and the amount of world trade were presumed to be limited in quantity. Therefore state intervention in the form of protectionist policies was believed necessary to guarantee a favorable balance of payments.

This static model of national wealth did not wholly fit the facts of growing international trade in the seventeenth century. Nevertheless, mercantilist philosophy was helpful to France. France became self-sufficient in the all-important production of woolen cloth, and French industry expanded notably in other sectors. Colbert's greatest success was the systematic expansion of the navy and merchant marine. By 1677 the navy had increased almost sixfold, to 144 ships. By the end of Louis XIV's reign the French navy was virtually the equal of the English navy.

Colbert and the other ministers began to develop the kind of planned government policymaking that we now take for granted. Partly by means of their itinerant supervisory officials, they tried to formulate and execute policy based on carefully collected information. How many men of military age were available? How abundant was this year's harvest? Answers to such questions enabled not only the formulation of economic policy but also the deliberate management of production and services to achieve certain goals—above all, the recruitment and supply of the king's vast armies.

Beginning in 1673 Louis tried to bring the religious life of the realm more fully under royal control, claiming for himself—with mixed success—some of the church revenues and powers of ecclesiastical appointment that still remained to the pope. Partly to bolster his position with the pope, he also began to attack the Huguenot community in France. First he offered financial inducements for conversion to Catholicism. Then he took more drastic steps, such as destroying Protestant churches and quartering troops in Huguenots' homes to force them to convert. In 1685 he declared that France would no longer abide any Protestant community, and he revoked the Edict of Nantes. A hundred thousand Protestant subjects—including some six hundred army and navy officers—refused even nominal conversion to Catholicism and chose to emigrate.

Meanwhile, Louis faced resistance to his claims against the pope from within the ranks of French clergy. These churchmen represented a movement within French Catholicism known as Jansenism, after Cornelius Jansen, a professor of theology whose writings were its inspiration. Jansenists practiced an austere style of Catholic religiosity that, in its notions about human will and sinfulness, was akin to some Protestant doctrine. Louis was suspicious of Jansenism because its adherents included many of his political enemies, particularly among families of parlement officials. Louis was wary of any threat to the institutional—or symbolic—unity of his regime, such as Protestants and Jansenists represented. At the end of Louis's long reign another pope obligingly declared many Jansenist doctrines to be heretical as part of a compromise agreement with Louis on matters of church governance and finance. Louis's efforts to exert greater control over the church had brought him modest practical gains, but at the price of weakening the religious basis of his authority in the eyes of many sincere Catholics.

By modern standards the power of the Crown was still greatly limited. The "divine right" of kingship, a notion formulated by Louis's chief apologist, Bishop Jacques Bossuet (1627–1704), did not mean unlimited power to rule; rather it meant that hereditary monarchy was the divinely ordained form of government, best suited to human needs. *Absolutism* was not ironfisted control of the realm but rather the successful focusing of energy, loyalties, and symbolic authority in the Crown. The government functioned well in the opening decades of Louis's reign because his role as the focal point of power and loyalty was both logical, after the preceding years of unrest, and skillfully exploited. Much of the glue holding together the absolutist state lay in informal mechanisms such as patronage and court life, as well as in the traditional hunt for military glory—all of which Louis amply supplied.

The Life of the Court

An observer comparing the lives of prominent noble families in the mid-sixteenth and mid-seventeenth centuries would have noticed striking differences. By the second half of the seventeenth century, most sovereigns or territorial princes had the power to crush revolts, and the heirs of the feudal nobility had to accommodate themselves to the increased power of the Crown. The nobility relinquished its former independence but retained economic and social supremacy and, as a consequence, considerable political clout. Nobles also developed new ways to symbolize their privilege by means of cultural refinement. This process was particularly dramatic in France as a strong Crown won out over a proud nobility.

One sign of Louis's success in marshaling the loyalty of the aristocracy was the brilliant court life that his regime sustained. No longer able to wield independent political power, aristocrats lived at court whenever they could. There they endlessly jostled for patronage and prestige—for commands in the royal army and for honorific positions at court itself. A favored courtier might, for example, participate in the elaborate daily *lever* (arising) of the king; he might be allowed to hand the king his shirt—a demeaning task, yet a coveted one for the attention by the king that it implied and guaranteed. Courtiers now defended their honor with private duels, not warfare, and more routinely relied on elegant ceremonial, precise etiquette, and clever conversation to demarcate their political and social distinctiveness.

As literacy became more widespread and the power of educated bureaucrats of even humble origin became more obvious, nobles from the traditional aristocracy began increasingly to use reading and writing as a means to think critically about their behavior—in the case of men, to re-imagine themselves as gentlemen rather than warriors. Noblewomen and noblemen alike began to reflect on their new roles in letters, memoirs, and the first novels. A prominent theme of these works is the increasing necessity for a truly private life of affection and trust, with which to counterbalance the public façade necessary to an aspiring courtier. The most influential early French novel

The Château of Versailles *This view of the central section of the palace is taken from the gardens. The reflecting pools you see here are on the first level of an immense terraced garden that, to someone exiting the château, seems to stretch to the horizon. The apparent openness of the king's residence (notice the rows of floor-length windows on the ground floor) is in stark contrast to a fortified castle and was a dramatic statement of a new kind of royal power.* (Château de Versailles, France/Peter Willi/The Bridgeman Art Library)

was *The Princess of Cleves* by Marie-Madeleine Pioche de la Vergne (1634–1693), best known by her title, Madame de Lafayette. Mme. de Lafayette's novel treats the particular difficulties faced by aristocratic women who, without military careers to bring glory and provide distraction, were more vulnerable than men to gossip and slander at court and more trapped by their arranged marriages.

Louis XIV's court is usually associated with the palace he built at Versailles, southwest of Paris. Some of the greatest talent of the day worked on the design and construction of Versailles from 1670 through the 1680s. It became a masterpiece of luxurious but restrained baroque style—a model for royal and aristocratic palaces throughout Europe for the next one hundred years.

Before Louis's court in his later years withdrew to Versailles, it traveled among the king's several châteaux around the kingdom, and in this itinerant period of the reign, court life was actually at its most creative and productive. These early years of Louis's personal reign were the heyday of French drama. The comedian Jean-Baptiste Poquelin, known as Molière (1622–1673), impressed the young Louis with his productions in the late 1650s and was rewarded with the use of a theater in the main royal palace in Paris. Like Shakespeare earlier in the century, Molière explored the social and political tensions of his day. He satirized the pretensions of the aristocracy, the social climbing of the bourgeoisie, and the self-righteous piety of clerics. Some of his plays were banned from performance, but most were not only tolerated but extremely popular with the elite audiences they mocked. Their popularity is testimony to the confidence of Louis's regime in its early days.

Also popular at court were the tragedies of Jean Racine (1639–1699), who was to the French theater what Shakespeare was to the English: the master of poetic language. His plays, which treat familiar classical stories, focus on the emotional and psychological lives of the characters and often stress the unpredictable, usually unhappy, role of fate, even among royalty. The pessimism in Racine foreshadowed the less successful second half of Louis's reign.

The Burdens of War and the Limits of Power

Wars initiated by Louis XIV dominated the attention of most European states in the second half of the seventeenth century. Louis's wars sprang from traditional causes: the importance of the glory and dynastic aggrandizement of the king and the preoccupation of the aristocracy with military life. But if Louis's wars were spurred by familiar concerns about territorial and economic advantage, they were far more demanding on state resources than any previous wars.

In France and elsewhere the size of armies grew markedly. And with the countryside still smarting from the rampaging armies of the Thirty Years' War, so did the need for greater management of troops. Louis XIV's victories in the second half of the century are partly traceable to his regime's attention to the bureaucratic tasks of recruitment, training, and supply, which together constituted another phase of the "military revolution." The new offensive tactics developed during the Thirty Years' War (see page 497) changed the character of armies in ways that demanded more resources for training. A higher proportion of soldiers became gunners, and their effectiveness lay in how well they operated as a unit. Armies began to train seriously off the field of battle because drill and discipline were vital to success. France was the first to provide its soldiers with uniforms, which boosted morale and improved discipline. The numbers of men on the battlefield increased somewhat as training increased the effectiveness of large numbers of infantry, but the total numbers of men in arms supported by the state at any time increased dramatically once the organization to support them was in place. Late in the century France kept more than 300,000 men in arms when at war (which was most of the time).

Louis's first war, in 1667, reflects the continuing French preoccupation with Spanish power on French frontiers. Louis invoked rather dubious dynastic claims to demand from Spain lands in the Spanish Netherlands and the large independent county on France's eastern border called the Franche-Comté. After a brief conflict, the French obtained only some towns in the Spanish Netherlands by the terms of the Treaty of Aix-la-Chapelle. Louis had already begun to negotiate with the Austrian Habsburgs over the eventual division of Spanish Habsburg lands, for it seemed likely that the Spanish king, Charles II (r. 1665–1700), would die without an heir. So, for the moment, Louis was content with modest gains at Spain's expense, confident that he would get much more in the future.

Louis's focus then shifted to a new enemy, the Dutch. The Dutch had been allied with France since the beginning of their existence as provinces in rebellion against Spain. The French now turned against the Dutch for reasons that reflect the growth of the international trading economy: Dutch dominance of seaborne trade. The French at first tried to offset the Dutch advantage in trade with tariff barriers against Dutch goods. But confidence in the French army led Louis's generals to urge action against the vulnerable Dutch lands. "It is impossible that his Majesty should tolerate any longer the insolence and arrogance of that nation," rationalized the usually pragmatic Colbert in 1670.[1]

The Dutch War began in 1672, with Louis personally leading one of the largest armies ever fielded in Europe—perhaps 120,000 men. At the same time, the Dutch were challenged at sea by England. The English had fought the Dutch over trade in the 1650s; now Louis secretly sent the English king, Charles II, a pension to secure an alliance against the Dutch.

At first the French were spectacularly successful against the tiny Dutch army. However, the Dutch opened dikes and flooded the countryside, and what had begun as a rout became a soggy stalemate. Moreover, the Dutch were beating combined English and French forces at sea and were gathering allies who felt threatened by Louis's aggression. The French soon faced German and Austrian forces along their frontier, and by 1674 the English had joined the alliance against France as well.

Nonetheless, the French managed to hold their own, and the Peace of Nijmegen in 1678 gave the illusion of a French victory. Not only had the French met the challenge of an enemy coalition, but Spain ceded them further border areas in the Spanish Netherlands as well as control of the Franche-Comté.

Ensconced at Versailles since 1682, Louis seemed to be at the height of his powers. Yet the Dutch War had in fact cost him more than he had gained. Meeting the alliance against him had meant fielding ever increasing numbers of men. Internal reforms in government and finance ended under the pressure of paying for war, and old financial expedients of borrowing money and selling privileges were revived. Other government obligations, such as encouraging overseas trade, were neglected. Colbert's death in 1683 dramatically symbolized the end of an era of innovation in the French regime.

Louis's unforgiving Dutch opponent, William of Orange, king of England from 1689 to 1702, renewed and stirred up anti-French alliances. The war, now known as the Nine Years' War, or King William's War, was touched off late in 1688 by French aggression—an invasion of Germany to claim an inheritance there. In his ongoing dispute with the pope, Louis seized the papal territory of Avignon in southern France. Boldest of all, he helped the exiled Catholic claimant to the English crown mount an invasion to reclaim his throne.

A widespread war began with all the major powers—Spain, the Netherlands, England, Austria, the major German states—ranged against France. The French also carried the fighting abroad by seizing English territory in Canada. As with the Dutch War, the Nine Years' War was costly and, on most fronts, inconclusive. This time, though, there was no illusion of victory for Louis. In the Treaty of Ryswick (1697) Louis gave up most of the territories in Germany, the Spanish Netherlands, and northern Spain that he managed to occupy by war's end. Avignon went back to the pope, and Louis relinquished his contentious claim to papal revenues. The terrible burden of war taxes combined with crop failures in 1693 and 1694 caused widespread starvation in the countryside. French courtiers began to criticize Louis openly.

The final major war of Louis's reign, called the War of the Spanish Succession, broke out in 1701. In some ways it was a straightforward dynastic clash between France and its perennial nemesis, the Habsburgs. Both Louis and Habsburg Holy Roman emperor Leopold I (r. 1657–1705) hoped to claim for their heirs the throne of Spain, left open at the death in 1700 of the last Spanish Habsburg, Charles II. Leopold represented the Austrian branch of the Habsburg family (see page 478), but Charles II bequeathed the throne to Louis's grandson, Philip of Anjou, by reason of Louis's marriage to the Spanish princess Maria Theresa. Philip quickly proceeded to enter Spain and claim his new kingdom. War was made inevitable when Louis renounced one of the conditions of Charles's will: Philip's accession to the throne of Spain, Louis insisted, did not preclude his becoming king of France as well. This declaration was an act of sheer belligerence, for Philip was only third in line for the French throne. The Dutch and English responded to the prospect of so great a disruption of the balance of power in Europe by joining the emperor in a formal Great Alliance in 1701. The Dutch and English also wanted to defend their colonial interests since the French had already begun to profit from new trading opportunities with the Spanish colonies.

Again the French fought a major war on several fronts on land and at sea. Again the people of France felt the cost in crushing taxes worsened by harvest failures. Major revolts inside France forced Louis to divert troops from the war. For a time it seemed that the French would be soundly defeated, but they were saved by the superior organization of their forces and by dynastic accident: unexpected deaths in the Habsburg family meant that the Austrian claimant to the Spanish throne suddenly was poised to inherit rule of Austria and the empire as well. The English, more afraid of a revival of unified Habsburg control of Spain and Austria than of French domination of Spain, quickly called for peace negotiations.

The Peace of Utrecht in 1713 resolved long-standing political conflicts and helped to set the agenda of European politics for the eighteenth century. Philip of Anjou was recognized as Philip V, the first Bourbon king of Spain, but on the condition that the Spanish and French crowns would never be worn by the same monarch. To maintain the balance of power against French interests, the Spanish Netherlands and Spanish territories in Italy were ceded by a second treaty in 1714 to Austria, which for many decades would be France's major continental rival. The Peace of Utrecht also marked the beginning of England's dominance of overseas trade and colonization. The French gave to England lands in Canada and the Caribbean and renounced any privileged relationship with Spanish colonies. England was allowed to control the highly profitable slave trade with Spanish colonies.

Louis XIV had added small amounts of strategically valuable territory along France's eastern border, and a Bourbon ruled in Spain. But the costs in human life and resources were great for the slim results achieved. Moreover, the army and navy had swallowed up capital that might have fueled investment and trade; strategic opportunities overseas were lost, never to be regained. Louis's government had been innovative in its early years but remained constrained by traditional ways of imagining the interest of the state.

English Civil War and Its Aftermath

In England, unlike in France, a representative institution—Parliament—became an effective, permanent brake on royal authority. The process by which Parliament gained a secure role in governing the kingdom was neither easy nor peaceful, however. As we saw in Chapter 15, conflicts between the English crown and its subjects, culminating in the Crown-Parliament conflict, concerned control over taxation and the direction of religious reform. Beginning in 1642 England was beset by civil war between royal and parliamentary forces. The king was eventually defeated and executed, and for a time the monarchy was abolished altogether. It was restored in 1660, but Parliament retained a crucial role in governing the kingdom—a role that was confirmed when, in 1688, it again deposed a monarch whose fiscal and religious policies became unacceptable to its members.

Civil War and Regicide, 1642–1649 Fighting broke out between the armies of Charles I and parliamentary armies in the late summer of 1642. The Long Parliament (see page 492) continued to represent a broad coalition of critics and opponents of the monarchy, ranging from aristocrats concerned primarily with abuses of royal prerogative to radical Puritans eager for thorough religious reform and determined to defeat the king. Fighting was halfhearted initially, and the tide of war at first favored Charles.

In 1643, however, the scope of the war broadened. Charles made peace with Irish rebels and brought Irish troops to England to bolster his armies. Parliament in turn sought military aid from the Scots in exchange for promises that Presbyterianism would become the religion of England. Meanwhile, Oliver Cromwell (1599–1658), a Puritan member of the Long Parliament and a cavalry officer, helped reorganize parliamentary forces. The eleven-hundred-man cavalry trained by Cromwell and known as the "Ironsides," supported by parliamentary and Scottish infantry, defeated the king's troops at Marston Moor in July 1644. The victory made Cromwell famous.

Shortly afterward Parliament further improved its forces and created the New Model Army, rigorously trained like Cromwell's Ironsides. Sitting members of Parliament were barred from commanding troops; hence upper-class control of the army was reduced. This army played a decisive role not only in the war but also in the political settlement that followed the fighting.

The New Model Army won a convincing victory over royal forces at Naseby in 1645. In the spring of 1646 Charles surrendered to a Scottish army in the north. In January 1647 Parliament paid the Scots for their services in the war and took the king into custody. In the negotiations that followed, Charles tried to play his opponents off against one another, and, as he had hoped, divisions among them widened.

Most members of Parliament were Presbyterians, Puritans who favored a strongly unified and controlled state church along Calvinist lines. They wanted peace with the king in return for acceptance of the new church structure and parliamentary control of standing militias for a specified period. They did not favor expanding the right to vote or other dramatic constitutional or legal change. These men were increasingly alarmed by the rise of sectarian differences and the actual religious freedom that many ordinary people were claiming for themselves. With the weakening of royal authority and the disruption of civil war, censorship was relaxed, and public preaching by ordinary men and even women who felt divinely inspired was becoming commonplace.

Above all, Presbyterian gentry in Parliament feared more radical groups in the army and in London who had supported them up to this point but who favored more thoroughgoing reform. Most officers of the New Model Army, such as Cromwell, were

Independents, Puritans who favored a decentralized church, a degree of religious toleration, and a wider sharing of political power among men of property, not just among the very wealthy gentry. In London a well-organized artisans' movement known as the "Levellers" favored universal manhood suffrage, law reform, better access to education, and decentralized churches—in short, the separation of political power from wealth and virtual freedom of religion. Many of the rank and file of the army were deeply influenced by Leveller ideas.

In May 1647 the majority in Parliament voted to offer terms to the king and to disband the New Model Army—without first paying most of the soldiers' back wages. This move provoked the first direct intervention by the army in politics. Representatives of the soldiers were chosen to present grievances to Parliament; when this failed, the army seized the king and, in August, occupied Westminster, Parliament's meeting place. Independent and Leveller elements in the army debated the direction of possible reform to be imposed on Parliament.

In November Charles escaped from his captors and raised a new army among his erstwhile enemies, the Scots, who were also alarmed by the growing radicalism in England. Civil war began again early in 1648. Although it ended quickly with a victory by Cromwell and the New Model Army in August, the renewed war further hardened political divisions and enhanced the power of the army. The king was widely blamed for the renewed bloodshed, and the army did not trust him to keep any agreement he might now sign. When Parliament, still dominated by Presbyterians, once again voted to negotiate with the king, army troops under Colonel Thomas Pride prevented members who favored Presbyterianism or the king from attending sessions. The "Rump" Parliament that remained after "Pride's Purge" voted to try the king. A hasty trial ensued, and Charles I was executed for "treason, tyranny and bloodshed" against his people on January 30, 1649.

The Interregnum, A Commonwealth—a republic—was declared. Executive
1649–1660 power resided in a council of state. The House of Lords having been abolished, legislative power resided in the one-chamber Rump Parliament. Declaring a republic proved far easier than running one, however. The execution of the king shocked most English and Scots and alienated many elites from the new regime. The legitimacy of the Commonwealth government would always be in question.

The tasks of making and implementing policy were hindered by the narrow political base on which the government now rested. Excluded were the majority of the reformist gentry who had been purged from Parliament. Also excluded were the more radical Levellers; Leveller leaders in London were arrested when they published tracts critical of the new government. Within a few years many disillusioned Levellers would join a new religious movement called the Society of Friends, or Quakers, which espoused complete religious autonomy. Quakers declined all oaths or service to the state, and they refused to acknowledge social rank.

Above all, the new government was vulnerable to the power of the army, which had created it. In 1649 and 1650 Cromwell led expeditions to Ireland and Scotland, partly for sheer revenge and partly to put down resistance to Commonwealth authority. In Ireland Cromwell's forces acted with shameful ruthlessness. English control there was

The Putney Debates

In October 1647 representatives of the Leveller movement in the army ranks confronted Independents—largely comprising the officer corps—in formally staged debates in a church at Putney, outside London. In this exchange, the Leveller representative, Thomas Rainsborough, advocates universal manhood suffrage, whereas Cromwell's fellow officer, Henry Ireton, argues for a more restricted franchise. The staging of the debates reflects the importance of the army in deciding the scope of constitutional change in England at this moment of extraordinary political fluidity. Even more important were the views that were aired at the debates, which had in common the assertion that government should exist only by the consent of the governed. These ideas became reality very slowly. The poorest men (and all women) did not get the vote in Britain until the twentieth century.

Rainsborough: . . . Really I think that the poorest he that is in England hath a life to live as the greatest he; and therefore truly, sir, I think it's clear, that every man that is to live under a government ought first by his own consent to put himself under that government; and I do think that the poorest man in England is not at all bound in a strict sense to that government that he hath not had a voice to put himself under; and I am confident that, when I have heard the reasons against it, that something will be said to answer those reasons, insomuch that I should doubt whether I was an Englishman or no, that should doubt of these things.

Ireton: . . . I think that no person hath a right to an interest or share in the disposing of the affairs of the kingdom, and in determining or choosing those that shall determine what laws we shall be ruled by here, no person hath a right to this that hath not a permanent fixed interest in this kingdom, and those per-

strengthened by more dispossession of Irish landholders, which also served to pay off the army's wages. Meanwhile, Parliament could not agree on systematic reforms, particularly the one reform Independents in the army insisted on: more broadly based elections for a new Parliament. Fresh from his victories, Cromwell led his armies to London and dissolved Parliament in the spring of 1652.

In 1653 a cadre of army officers drew up the "Instrument of Government," England's first and only written constitution. It provided for an executive, the Lord Protector, and a Parliament to be based on somewhat wider male suffrage. Cromwell was the natural choice for Lord Protector, and whatever success the government of the Protectorate had was due largely to him.

Cromwell was an extremely able leader who was not averse to compromise. Although he had used force against Parliament in 1648, he had worked hard to reconcile the Rump Parliament and the army before marching on London in 1652. He believed sons together are properly the represented of this kingdom, who taken together, and consequently are to make up the representers of this kingdom, are the representers, who taken together do comprehend whatsoever is of real or permanent interest in the kingdom, and I am sure there is otherwise (I cannot tell what), otherwise any man can say why a foreigner coming in amongst us, or as many as will be coming in amongst us, or by force or otherwise settling themselves here, or at least by our permission having a being here, why they should not as well lay claim to it as any other. We talk of birthright. Truly birthright there is thus much claim: men may justly have by birthright, by their very being born in England, that we should not seclude them out of England. That we should not refuse to give them air and place and ground, and the freedom of the highways and other things, to live amongst us, not any man that is born here, though he in birth, or by his birth there come nothing at all that is part of the permanent interest of this kingdom to him. That I think is due to a man by birth. But that by a man's being born here he shall have a share in that power that shall dispose of the lands here, and of all things here, I do not think it a sufficient ground, but I am sure if we look upon that which is the utmost, within man's view, of what was originally the constitution of this kingdom, upon that which is most radical and fundamental, and which if you take away, there is no man hath any land, any goods, you take away any civil interest, and that is this: that those that choose the representers for the making of laws by which this state and kingdom are to be governed, are the persons who taken together, do comprehend the local interest of this kingdom; that is, the persons in whom all land lies, and those in corporations in whom all trading lies. This is the most fundamental constitution of this kingdom, and which if you do not allow, you allow none at all.

Source: G. E. Aylmer, ed., *The Levellers in the English Revolution* (Ithaca, N.Y.: Cornell University Press, 1975), pp. 100–101. Copyright Thames & Hudson Ltd. Reprinted by kind permission of Thames & Hudson Ltd., London.

in a state church, but one that allowed for control, including choice of minister, by local congregations. He also believed in toleration for other Protestant sects, as well as for Catholics and Jews, as long as no one disturbed the peace.

As Lord Protector, Cromwell oversaw impressive reforms in law that testify to his belief in the limits of governing authority. For example, contrary to the practice of his day, he opposed capital punishment for petty crimes. The government of the Protectorate, however, accomplished little given Parliament's internal divisions and opposition to Cromwell's initiatives. The population at large still harbored royalist sympathizers; after a royalist uprising in 1655, Cromwell divided England into military districts and vested governing authority in army generals.

In the end the Protectorate could not survive the strains over policy and the challenges to its legitimacy. When Cromwell died of a sudden illness in September 1658, the Protectorate did not long survive him. In February 1660 the decisive action of one army

Popular Preaching in England *Many women took advantage of the collapse of royal authority to preach in public—a radical activity for women at the time. This print satirizes the Quakers, a religious movement that attracted many women.* (Mary Evans Picture Library)

general enabled all the surviving members of the Long Parliament to rejoin the Rump. The Parliament summarily dissolved itself and called for new elections. The newly elected Parliament recalled Charles II, son of Charles I, from exile abroad and restored the monarchy. The chaos and radicalism of the late civil war and "interregnum"—the period between reigns, as the years from 1649 to 1660 came to be called—now spawned a conservative reaction.

The Restoration, 1660–1685

Charles II (r. 1660–1685) claimed his throne at the age of 30. He had learned from his years of uncertain exile and from the fate of his father. He did not seek retribution but rather offered a general pardon to all but a few rebels (mostly those who had signed his father's death warrant), and he suggested to Parliament a relatively tolerant religious settlement that would include Anglicans as well as Presbyterians. He was far more politically adept than his father and far more willing to compromise.

That the re-established royal government was not more tolerant than it turned out to be was not Charles's doing but Parliament's. During the 1660s, the "Cavalier" Parliament, named for royalists in the civil war, passed harsh laws aimed at religious dissenters. Anglican orthodoxy was reimposed, including the re-establishment of bishops and the Anglican *Book of Common Prayer*. All officeholders and clergy were required to swear oaths of obedience to the king and to the established church. As a result, hundreds were forced out of office and pulpits. Holding nonconformist religious services became illegal, and Parliament passed a "five-mile" act to prevent dissenting ministers from traveling near their former congregations. Property laws were tightened and the criminal codes made more severe.

The king's behavior in turn began to mimic prerevolutionary royalist positions. Charles II began to flirt with Catholicism, and his brother and heir, James, openly converted. Charles promulgated a declaration of tolerance that would have included Catholics as well as nonconformist Protestants, but Parliament would not accept it. Anti-Catholic feeling still united all Protestants. In 1678 Charles's secret treaties with the French became known (see page 516), and rumors of a Catholic plot to murder Charles and reimpose Catholicism became widespread. No evidence of any plot was ever unearthed, although thirty-five people were executed for alleged participation. Parliament focused its attention on anti-Catholicism, passing the Test Act, which barred all but Anglicans from public office. As a result, the Catholic James was forced to resign as Lord High Admiral.

When Parliament moved to exclude James from succession to the throne, Charles dissolved it. A subsequent Parliament, worried by the specter of a new civil war, backed down. But the legacy of the civil war was a potent one. First, despite the harsh laws, to silence all dissent was not possible. After two decades of religious pluralism and broadly based political activity, it was impossible to reimpose conformity; well-established communities of various sects and self-confidence bred vigorous resistance. The clearest reflection of the legacy of events was the power of Parliament. Though reluctant to press too far, Parliament had tried to assert its policies against the desires of the king.

Nevertheless, by the end of his reign Charles was financially independent of Parliament, thanks to increased revenue from overseas trade and secret subsidies from France, his recent ally against Dutch trading rivals. This financial independence and firm political tactics enabled Charles to regain, and retain, a great deal of power. If he had been followed by an able successor, Parliament might have lost a good measure of its confidence and independence. But his brother James's reign and its aftermath further enhanced Parliament's power.

The Glorious Revolution, 1688

When James II (r. 1685–1689) succeeded Charles, Parliament's royalist leanings were at first evident. James was granted customs duties for life and was also given funds to suppress a rebellion by one of Charles's illegitimate sons. James did not try to impose Catholicism on England as some had feared, but he did try to achieve toleration for Catholics in two declarations of indulgence in 1687 and 1688. However admirable his goal—toleration—he had essentially changed the law of the realm without Parliament's consent and further undermined his position with heavy-handed tactics. When several leading Anglican bishops refused to read the declarations from their pulpits, he had them imprisoned and tried for seditious libel. However, a sympathetic jury acquitted them.

James also failed because of the coincidence of other events. In 1685, at the outset of James's reign, Louis XIV of France had revoked the Edict of Nantes. The possibility that subjects and monarchs in France and, by extension, elsewhere could be of different faiths seemed increasingly unlikely. Popular fears of James's Catholicism were thus heightened early in his reign, and his later declarations of tolerance, though benefiting

Protestant dissenters, were viewed with suspicion. In 1688 not only were the Anglican bishops acquitted but the king's second wife, who was Catholic, gave birth to a son. The birth raised the specter of a Catholic succession.

In June 1688, to put pressure on James, leading members of Parliament invited William of Orange, husband of James's Protestant daughter, Mary, to come to England. William mounted an invasion that became a rout when James refused to defend his throne. James simply abandoned England and went to France. William called Parliament, which declared James to have abdicated and offered the throne jointly to William and Mary. With French support James eventually invaded Ireland in 1690—bound for Westminster—but was defeated by William at the Battle of Boyne that year.

The substitution of William (r. 1689–1702) and Mary (r. 1689–1694) for James, known as the "Glorious Revolution," was engineered by Parliament and confirmed its power. Parliament presented the new sovereigns with a Declaration of Rights upon their accession and, later that year, with a Bill of Rights that defended freedom of speech, called for frequent Parliaments, and required subsequent monarchs to be Protestant. The effectiveness of these documents was reinforced by Parliament's power of the purse. Parliament's role in the political process was ensured by William's interests in funding his ambitious military efforts, particularly the Netherlands' ongoing wars with France.

The issues that had faced the English since the beginning of the century were common to all European states: religious division and elite power, fiscal strains and resistance to taxation. Yet the cataclysmic events in England—the interregnum, the Commonwealth, the Restoration, the Glorious Revolution—had set it apart from other states. Consequently, the incremental assumption of authority by a well-established institution, Parliament, made challenge of the English monarchy more legitimate and more effective.

NEW POWERS IN CENTRAL AND EASTERN EUROPE

By the end of the seventeenth century three states dominated central and eastern Europe: Austria, Brandenburg-Prussia, and Russia. After the Thirty Years' War the Habsburgs' dominance in the splintering empire waned, and they focused on expanding and consolidating their power in their hereditary possessions. Brandenburg-Prussia, in northeastern Germany, emerged from obscurity to rival the Habsburg state. The rulers of Brandenburg-Prussia had gained lands in the Peace of Westphalia, and astute management transformed their relatively small and scattered holdings into one of the most powerful states in Europe. Russia's new stature in eastern Europe resulted in part from the weakness of its greatest rival, Poland, and the determination of one leader, Peter the Great, to assume a major role in European affairs. Sweden controlled valuable Baltic territory through much of the century but eventually was also eclipsed by Russia as a force in the region.

The internal political development of these states was dramatically shaped by their relationship to the wider European economy: they were sources of grain and raw materials for the more densely urbanized West. The development of and the competition among states in central and eastern Europe were closely linked to developments in western Europe.

<table>
<tr><td>The Consolidation
of Austria</td><td>The Thirty Years' War (see pages 495–497) weakened the Habsburgs as emperors but strengthened them in their own lands.</td></tr>
</table>

The main Habsburg lands in 1648 were a collection of principalities comprising modern Austria, the kingdom of Hungary (largely in Turkish hands), and the kingdom of Bohemia. In 1714 Austria acquired the Spanish Netherlands, which were renamed the Austrian Netherlands. Although language and ethnic differences prevented an absolutist state along French lines, Leopold I (r. 1657–1705) instituted political and institutional changes that enabled the Habsburg state to become one of the most powerful in Europe through the eighteenth century.

Much of the coherence that already existed in Leopold's lands had been achieved by his predecessors in the wake of the Thirty Years' War. The lands of rebels in Bohemia had been confiscated and redistributed among loyal, mostly Austrian, families. In return for political and military support for the emperor, these families were given the right to exploit their newly acquired land and the peasants who worked it. The desire to recover population and productivity after the destruction of the Thirty Years' War gave landlords further incentive to curtail peasants' autonomy, particularly in devastated Bohemia. Austrian landlords throughout the Habsburg domains provided grain and timber for the export market and foodstuffs for the Austrian armies, while elite families provided the army with officers. This political-economic arrangement provoked numerous serious peasant revolts, but the peasants were not able to force changes in a system that suited both the elites and the central authority.

Although Leopold had lost much influence within the empire itself, an imperial government made up of various councils, a war ministry, financial officials, and the like still functioned in his capital, Vienna. Leopold worked to extricate the government of his own lands from the apparatus of imperial institutions, which were staffed largely by Germans more loyal to imperial than to Habsburg interests. In addition, Leopold used the Catholic Church as an institutional and ideological support for the Habsburg state.

Leopold's personal ambition was to re-establish devout Catholicism throughout his territories. Acceptance of Catholicism became the litmus test of loyalty to the Habsburg regime, and Protestantism vanished among elites. Leopold encouraged the work of Jesuit teachers and members of other Catholic orders. These men and women helped staff his government and administered religious life down to the most local levels.

Leopold's most dramatic success, as a Habsburg and a religious leader, was his reconquest of the kingdom of Hungary from the Ottoman Empire. Since the mid-sixteenth century the Habsburgs had controlled only a narrow strip of the kingdom. Preoccupied with countering Louis XIV's aggression, Leopold did not himself choose to begin a reconquest. His centralizing policies, however, alienated nobles and townspeople in the portion of Hungary he did control, as did his repression of Protestantism, which had flourished in Hungary. Hungarian nobles began a revolt, aided by the Turks, aiming for a reunited Hungary under Ottoman protection.

The Habsburgs emerged victorious in part because they received help from the Venetians, the Russians, and especially the Poles, whose lands in Ukraine were threatened by the Turks. The Turks overreached their supply lines to besiege Vienna in 1683.

When the siege failed, Habsburg armies slowly pressed east and south, recovering Buda, the capital of Hungary, in 1686 and Belgrade (modern Serbia) in 1688. The Danube basin lay once again in Christian hands. The Treaty of Carlowitz ended the fighting in 1699, after the first conference where European allies jointly dictated terms to a weakening Ottoman Empire. Austria's allies had also gained at the Ottomans' expense: the Poles recovered the threatened Ukraine, and the Russians gained a vital foothold on the Black Sea.

Leopold gave land in the reclaimed lands to Austrian officers who he believed were loyal to him. The traditions of Hungarian separatism, however, were strong, and the great magnates—whether they had defended the Habsburgs against Turkish encroachment or guarded the frontier for Turkish overlords—retained their independence. The peasantry, as elsewhere, suffered a decline in status as a result of the Crown's efforts to ensure the loyalty of elites. In the long run Hungarian independence weakened the Habsburg state, but in the short run Leopold's victory over the Turks and the recovery of Hungary itself were momentous events, confirming the Habsburgs as the preeminent power in central Europe.

The Rise of Brandenburg-Prussia

Three German states, in addition to Austria, gained territory and stature after the Thirty Years' War: Bavaria, Saxony, and Brandenburg-Prussia. By the end of the seventeenth century the strongest was Brandenburg-Prussia, a conglomeration of small territories held, by dynastic accident, by the Hohenzollern family. The two principal territories were electoral Brandenburg, in northeastern Germany, with its capital, Berlin, and the duchy of Prussia, a fief of the Polish crown along the Baltic coast east of Poland proper. In addition, the Hohenzollerns ruled a handful of small principalities near the Netherlands. The manipulation of resources and power that enabled these unpromising lands to become a powerful state was primarily the work of Frederick William, known as "the Great Elector" (r. 1640–1688).

Frederick William used the occasion of a war to effect a permanent change in the structure of government. He took advantage of a war between Poland and its rivals, Sweden and Russia (described in the next section), to win independence for the duchy of Prussia from Polish overlordship. When his involvement in the war ended in 1657, he kept intact the general war commissariat, a combined civilian and military body that had efficiently directed the war effort, bypassing traditional councils and representative bodies. He also used the standing army to force the payment of high taxes. Most significantly, he established a positive relationship with the Junkers, hereditary landholders, which ensured him both revenue and loyalty. He agreed to allow the Junkers virtually total control of their own lands in return for their agreement to support his government—in short, they surrendered their accustomed political independence in exchange for greater economic and social power over the peasants who worked their lands.

Peasants and townspeople were taxed, but nobles were not. The freedom to control their estates led many nobles to invest in profitable agriculture for the export market. The peasants were serfs who received no benefits from the increased productivity of the land. Frederick William further enhanced his state's power by sponsoring state industries. These industries did not have to fear competition from urban producers because the towns had been frozen out of the political process and saddled with heavy taxes. Though an oppressive place for many Germans, Brandenburg-Prussia attracted many skilled refugees, such as Huguenot artisans fleeing Louis XIV's France.

Bavaria and Saxony, in contrast to Brandenburg-Prussia, had vibrant towns, largely free peasantries, and weaker aristocracies but were relative nonentities in international affairs. Power on the European stage depended on military force. Such power, whether in a large state like France or in a small one like Brandenburg-Prussia, usually came at the expense of the people.

Competition Around the Baltic: The Decline of Poland and the Zenith of Swedish Power

The rivers and port cities of the Baltic coast were conduits for the growing trade between the Baltic hinterland and the rest of Europe. In 1600 a large portion of the Baltic hinterland lay under the control of Poland-Lithuania, a vast and diverse state at the height of its power, but one that would prove an exception to the pattern of expanding royal power in the seventeenth century. Wars in the middle of the century were extremely destructive in regard not only to lives and property but also, unlike in neighboring Prussia, to the coherence of the state as well.

Internal strains began to mount in Poland-Lithuania in the late sixteenth century. The spread of the Counter-Reformation, encouraged by the Crown, created tensions with both Protestant and Orthodox subjects in the diverse kingdom. The greatest source of political instability was the power of landholding nobles, whose fortunes grew as Poland became the granary of western Europe. Impoverished peasants were bound to the land, and lesser gentry, particularly in the Ruthenian lands of Lithuania, were shut out of political power by Polish aristocrats. In Ukraine communities of Cossacks, nomadic farmer-warriors, grew as Polish and Lithuanian peasants fled harsh conditions to join them. The Cossacks had long been tolerated because they served as a military buffer against the Ottoman Turks to the south, but now Polish landlords wanted to reincorporate the Cossacks into the profitable political-economic system they controlled.

In 1648 the Polish crown faced revolt and invasion that it could not fully counter. The Cossacks led a major uprising, which included Ukrainian gentry as well as peasants. The Cossacks held their own against the Polish armies. Meanwhile, the Crown's efforts to reach a peace agreement were blocked by the noble landlords against whom the revolt had been directed. In 1654 the Cossacks tried to assure their autonomy by transferring their allegiance to Moscow. They became part of a Russian invasion of Poland-Lithuania that by the next year had engulfed much of the eastern half of the dual state. At the same time, Poland's perennial rival, Sweden, seized central Poland in a military campaign marked by extreme brutality. Many Polish and Lithuanian aristocrats continued to act like independent warlords and cooperated with the invaders to preserve their own local power.

Operating with slim resources, Polish royal armies eventually managed to recover much territory—most important, the western half of Ukraine. But the invasions and subsequent fighting were disastrous. These wars were afterward referred to as "the deluge," and with good reason. The population of Poland declined by as much as 40 percent, and vital urban economies were in ruins. The Catholic identity of the Polish heartland had been a rallying point for resistance to the Protestant Swedes and the Orthodox Russians, but the religious tolerance that had distinguished the Polish kingdom

Map legend:
- Prussian territory in 1640
- Prussian acquisitions in 1688
- Russian territory in 1693
- Seized by Peter the Great from Sweden, 1694–1725
- Austrian territory by 1699
- Ottoman Empire in 1699
- Boundary of the Holy Roman Empire

New Powers in Central and Eastern Europe, to 1725

The balance of power in central and eastern Europe shifted with the strengthening of Austria, the rise of Brandenburg-Prussia, and the expansion of Russia at the expense of Poland and Sweden.

and had been mandated in its constitution was now abandoned. In addition, much of its recovery of Lithuanian territory was only nominal.

The elective Polish crown passed in 1674 to the military hero Jan Sobieski (r. 1674–1696), known as "Vanquisher of the Turks" for his role in raising the siege of Vienna in 1683. Given Poland's internal weakness, however, Sobieski's victories in the long run helped the Ottomans' other foes—Austria and Russia—more than they helped the Poles. Moreover, though a brilliant tactician, he was a master of an increasingly outmoded form of warfare that was almost wholly reliant on cavalry. He was unable to force reforms that would have led to increased royal revenue and a more up-to-date royal army. After his death Poland would be vulnerable to the political ambitions of its more powerful neighbors. Augustus II of Saxony (r. 1697–1704, 1709–1733) dragged Poland back into war, from which Russia would emerge the clear winner in the power struggle in eastern Europe.

The Swedes, meanwhile, had successfully vied with the Poles and other competitors for control of the lucrative Baltic coast. Swedish efforts to control Baltic territory began in the sixteenth century, first to counter the power of its perennial rival, Denmark, in the western Baltic. It then competed with Poland to control Livonia (modern Latvia), whose principal city, Riga, was an important trading center for goods from both Lithuania and Russia. By 1617, under Gustav Adolf, the Swedes gained the lands to the north surrounding the Gulf of Finland (the most direct outlet for Russian goods), and in 1621 they displaced the Poles in Livonia itself. Swedish intervention in the Thirty Years' War came when imperial successes against Denmark both threatened the Baltic coast and created an opportunity to strike at Sweden's old enemy. The Treaty of Westphalia (1648) confirmed Sweden's earlier gains and added control of further coastal territory, mostly at Denmark's expense.

The port cities held by Sweden were profitable but simply served to pay for the costly wars necessary to seize and defend them. Indeed, Sweden's efforts to hold Baltic territory were driven by dynastic and strategic needs as much as economic objectives. The ruling dynasty struggled against Denmark's control of western Baltic territory in order to safeguard its independence from the Danes, who had ruled the combined kingdoms until 1523. Similarly, competition with Poland for the eastern Baltic was part of a dynastic struggle after 1592. Sigismund Vasa, son of the king of Sweden, had been elected king of Poland in 1587 but also inherited the Swedish throne in 1592. Other members of the Vasa family fought him successfully to regain rule over Sweden and extricate Swedish interests from Poland's continental preoccupations. Although Sigismund ruled Poland until his death in 1632, a Vasa uncle replaced him on the Swedish throne in 1604.

The one permanent gain that Sweden realized from its aggression against Poland in the 1650s was the renunciation of the Polish Vasa line to any claim to the Swedish crown. Owing to its earlier gains, Sweden reigned supreme on the Baltic coast until the end of the century, when it was supplanted by the powerful Russian state.

Russia Under Peter the Great
The Russian state expanded dramatically through the sixteenth century under Ivan IV and weathered the period of disputed succession known as the "Time of Troubles" (see pages 499–501). The foundations of the large and cohesive state laid by Ivan enabled Michael Romanov to rebuild autocratic government with ease after being chosen tsar in 1613.

Peter the Great *This portrait by a Dutch artist captures the tsar's "westernizing" mission by showing Peter in military dress according to European fashions of the day.* (Rijksmuseum-Stichting, Amsterdam)

The Romanovs were an eminent aristocratic family related to Ivan's. Michael (r. 1613–1645) was selected to rule by an assembly of aristocrats, gentry, and commoners who were more alarmed at the civil wars and recent Polish incursions than at the prospect of a return to strong tsarist rule. Michael was succeeded by his son, Alexis (r. 1645–1676), who presided over the extension of Russian control to eastern Ukraine in 1654 following the wars in Poland and developed an interest in cultivating relationships with the West.

Shifting the balance of power in eastern Europe and the Baltic in Russia's favor was also the work of Alexis's son, Peter I (r. 1682–1725), "the Great." Peter accomplished this by military successes against his enemies and by forcibly reorienting Russian government and society toward involvement with the rest of Europe.

Peter was almost literally larger than life. Nearly 7 feet tall, he towered over most of his contemporaries and had physical and mental energy to match his size. He set himself to learning trades and studied soldiering by rising through the ranks of the military like a common soldier. He traveled abroad to learn as much as he could about western European economies and governments. He wanted the revenue, manufacturing output, technology and trade, and, above all, up-to-date army and navy that other rulers enjoyed. In short Peter sought for Russia a more evolved state system because of the strength it would give him.

Immediately on his accession to power, Peter initiated a bold series of changes in Russian society. His travels had taught him that European monarchs coexisted with a privileged but educated aristocracy and that a brilliant court life symbolized and reinforced their authority. So he set out to refashion Russian society in what amounted to an enforced cultural revolution. He provoked a direct confrontation with Russia's traditional aristocracy over everything from education to matters of dress. He elevated numerous new families to the ranks of gentry and created an official ranking system for the nobility to encourage and reward service to his government.

Peter's effort to reorient his nation culturally, economically, and politically toward Europe was most apparent in the construction of the city of St. Petersburg on the Gulf of Finland, which provided access to the Baltic Sea. In stark contrast to Moscow, dominated by the medieval fortress of the Kremlin and churches in the traditional Russian style, St. Petersburg was a modern European city with wide avenues and palaces designed for a sophisticated court life.

Although Peter was highly intelligent, practical, and determined to create a more productive and better-governed society, he was also cruel and authoritarian. Peasants already were bearing the brunt of taxation, but their tax burden worsened when they were assessed arbitrarily by head and not by output of the land. The building of St. Petersburg cost staggering sums in both money and workers' lives. Peter's entire reform system was carried out tyrannically; resistance was brutally suppressed. Victims of Peter's oppression included his son, Alexis, who died after torture while awaiting execution for questioning his father's policies.

Peter faced elite as well as populist rebellions against the exactions and the cultural changes of his regime. The most serious challenge was the revolt in 1707 of the Cossacks in the Don River region against the regime's tightened controls. A major reason for the high cost of Peter's government to the Russian people was his ambition for territorial gain—hence his emphasis on an improved, and costly, army and navy. Working side by side with workers and technicians, many of whom he had recruited while abroad, Peter created the Russian navy from scratch. At first ships were built in the south to contest Turkish control of the Black Sea. Later they were built in the north to secure and defend the Baltic. Peter also modernized the Russian army by employing tactics, training, and discipline he had observed in the West. He introduced military conscription and munitions plants. By 1709 Russia was able to manufacture most of the up-to-date firearms its army needed.

Russia waged war virtually throughout Peter's reign. Initially with some success, he struck at the Ottomans and their client state in the Crimea. Later phases of these conflicts brought reverses, however. Peter was spectacularly successful against his northern competitor, Sweden, for control of the weakened Polish state and the Baltic Sea. The conflicts between Sweden and Russia, known as the Great Northern War, raged from 1700 to 1709 and, in a less intense phase, lasted until 1721. By the Treaty of Nystadt in 1721, Russia gained its present-day territory in the Gulf of Finland near St. Petersburg, plus Livonia and Estonia. These acquisitions gave Russia a secure window on the Baltic and, in combination with its gains of Lithuanian territory earlier in the century, made Russia the pre-eminent Baltic power, at Sweden's and Poland's expense.

THE EXPANSION OF OVERSEAS TRADE AND SETTLEMENT

By the beginning of the seventeenth century competition from the Dutch, French, and English was disrupting the Spanish and Portuguese trading empires in Asia and the

New World. During the seventeenth century European trade and colonization expanded and changed dramatically. The Dutch not only became masters of the spice trade but broadened the market to include many other commodities. In the Americas a new trading system linking Europe, Africa, and the New World came into being with the expansion of tobacco and, later, sugar production. French and English colonists began settling in North America in increasing numbers. By the end of the century trading and colonial outposts around the world figured regularly as bargaining chips in disagreements between European states. More important, overseas trade had a crucial impact on life within Europe: on patterns of production and consumption, on social stratification, and on the distribution of wealth.

The Growth of Trading Empires: The Success of the Dutch
By the end of the sixteenth century the Dutch and the English were making incursions into the Portuguese-controlled spice trade with areas of India, Ceylon, and the East Indies. Spain had annexed Portugal in 1580, but the drain on Spain's resources from its wars with the Dutch and French prevented Spain from adequately defending its enlarged trading empire in Asia. The Dutch and, to a lesser degree, the English rapidly supplanted Portuguese control of this lucrative trade.

The Dutch were particularly well placed to be successful competitors in overseas trade. They already dominated seaborne trade within Europe, including the most important long-distance trade, which linked Spain and Portugal—with their wine and salt, as well as spices, hides, and gold from abroad—with the Baltic seacoast, where these products were sold for grain and timber produced in Germany, Poland-Lithuania, and Scandinavia. The geographic position of the Netherlands and the fact that the Dutch consumed more Baltic grain than any other area, because of their large urban population, help to explain their dominance of this trade. In addition, the Dutch had improved the design of their merchant ships to maximize their profits. By 1600 they were building the *fluitschip* (flyship) to transport cargo economically; it was a vessel with a long, flat hull, simple rigging, and cheap construction.

The Dutch were successful in Asia because of institutional as well as technological innovations. In 1602 the Dutch East India Company was formed. The company combined government management of trade, typical of the period, with both public and private investment. In the past groups of investors had funded single voyages or small numbers of ships on a one-time basis. The formation of the Dutch East India Company created a permanent pool of capital to sustain trade. After 1612 investments in the company were negotiable as stock. These greater assets allowed proprietors to spread the risks and delays of longer voyages among larger numbers of investors. In addition, more money was available for warehouses, docks, and ships. The English East India Company, founded in 1607, also supported trade, but more modestly. It had one-tenth the capital of the Dutch company and did not use the same system of permanent capital held as stock by investors until 1657. The Bank of Amsterdam, founded in 1609, became the depository for the bullion that flowed into the Netherlands with the flood of trade. The bank established currency exchange rates and issued paper money and instruments of credit to facilitate commerce.

A dramatic expansion of trade with Asia resulted from the Dutch innovations, so much so that by 1650 the European market for spices was glutted, and traders' profits had begun to fall. To control the supply of spices, the Dutch seized some of the areas where they were produced. The Dutch and English further responded to the oversupply of spices by diversifying their trade. The proportion of spices in cargoes from the East fell from about 70 percent at midcentury to just over 20 percent by the century's end. New consumer goods such as tea, coffee, and silk and cotton fabrics took their place. The demand of ordinary people for inexpensive yet serviceable Indian cottons grew steadily. Eventually the Dutch and the English, alert for fresh opportunities in the East, entered the local carrying trade among Asian states. Doing so enabled them to make profits even without purchasing goods, and it slowed the drain of hard currency from Europe—currency in increasingly short supply as silver mines in the Americas were depleted.

The "Golden Age" of the Netherlands The prosperity occasioned by the Netherlands' "mother trade" within Europe and its burgeoning overseas commerce helped foster social and political conditions unique among European states. The concentration of trade and shipping sustained a healthy merchant oligarchy and also an extensive and prosperous artisanal sector. Disparities of wealth were smaller here than anywhere else in Europe. The shipbuilding and fishing trades, among others, supported large numbers of workers with a high standard of living for the age.

The Netherlands appeared to contemporaries to be an astonishing exception to the normal structures of politics. Political decentralization in the Netherlands persisted. The Estates General (representative assembly) for the Netherlands as a whole had no independent powers of taxation. Each of the seven provinces retained considerable autonomy. Wealthy merchants in the Estates of the province of Holland, in fact, constituted the government for the entire nation for long periods because of Holland's economic dominance. The head of government was the executive secretary, known as the pensionary, of Holland's Estates.

Holland's only competition in the running of affairs came from the House of Orange, aristocratic leaders of the revolt against Spain (see pages 477–480). They exercised what control they had by means of the office of *stadholder*—a kind of military governorship—to which they were elected in individual provinces. Their principal interest was the traditional one of military glory and self-promotion. Therein lay a portion of their influence, for they continued to lead the defense of the Netherlands against Spanish attempts at reconquest until the Peace of Westphalia in 1648 and against French aggression after 1672. Their power also came from their status as the only counterweight within the Netherlands to the dominance of Amsterdam's (in Holland) mercantile interests. Small towns dependent on land-based trade or rural areas dominated by farmers and gentry looked to the stadholders of the Orange family to defend their interests.

As elsewhere, religion was a source of political conflict. The stadholders and the leading families of Holland, known as regents, vied for control of the state church. Pensionaries and regents of Holland generally favored a less rigid and austere form of Calvinism than did the stadholders. Their view reflected the needs of the diverse urban communities of Holland, where thousands of Jews, as well as Catholics and various Protestants, lived. Foreign policy was also disputed: Hollanders desired peace in order to foster commerce, whereas stadholders willingly engaged in warfare for territory and dynastic advantage.

These differences notwithstanding, Dutch commercial dominance involved the Netherlands in costly wars throughout the second half of the century. Between 1657

Vermeer: The Soldier and the Laughing Girl
This is an early work by one of the great artists of the Dutch "Golden Age." Dutch art was distinguished by its treatment of common, rather than heroic, subjects. The masterful use of light and perspective in paintings such as this one would not be equaled until the invention of photography. (Copyright The Frick Collection, New York)

and 1660 the Dutch defended Denmark against Swedish ambitions in order to safeguard the sea-lanes and port cities of the Baltic. More costly conflicts arose because of rivalry with the more powerful England and France. Under Cromwell the English attempted to close their ports to the Dutch carrying trade. In 1672 the English under Charles II allied with the French, assuming that together they could destroy Dutch power and perhaps even divide the Netherlands' territory between them. The Dutch navy, rebuilt since Cromwell's challenge, soon forced England out of the alliance.

Owing largely to the land war with France, the Estates in Holland lost control of policy to William of Nassau (d. 1702), prince of Orange after 1672. William drew the Netherlands into his family's long-standing close relationship with England. Like other members of his family before him, William had married into the English royal family: his wife was Mary, daughter of James II.

Ironically, after William and Mary assumed the English throne, Dutch commerce suffered more in alliance with England than in its previous rivalry. William used Dutch resources for the land war against Louis XIV and reserved for the English navy the fight at sea. By the end of the century Dutch maritime strength was being eclipsed by English sea power.

The Growth of Atlantic Colonies and Commerce

In the seventeenth century the Dutch, the English, and the French joined the Spanish as colonial and commercial powers in the Americas. The Spanish colonial empire, in theory a trading system closed to outsiders, was in fact vulnerable to incursion by other European traders. Spanish treasure fleets were themselves a glittering attraction. In 1628, for example, a Dutch captain seized the entire fleet. But by then Spain's goals and those of its competitors had begun to shift. The limits of an economy based on the extraction, rather than the production, of wealth became clear with the declining output of the Spanish silver mines during the 1620s. In response the Spanish and their Dutch, French, and English competitors expanded the production of the cash crops of tobacco, dyestuffs, and, above all, sugar.

The European demand for tobacco and sugar, both addictive substances, grew steadily in the seventeenth century. The plantation system—the use of forced labor to produce cash crops on vast tracts of land—had been developed on Mediterranean islands in the Middle Ages by European entrepreneurs, using slaves procured in Black Sea ports by Venetian and Genoese traders. Sugar production by this system had been established on Atlantic islands, such as the Cape Verde Islands, using African labor, and then in the Americas by the Spanish and Portuguese. Sugar production in the New World grew from about 20,000 tons in 1600 to about 200,000 tons by 1770.

In the 1620s, while the Dutch were exploiting Portuguese weakness in the Eastern spice trade, they were also seizing sugar regions in Brazil and replacing the Portuguese in slaving ports in Africa. The Portuguese were able to retake most of their Brazilian territory in the 1650s. But the Dutch, because they monopolized the carrying trade, were able to become the official supplier of slaves to Spanish plantations in the New World and the chief supplier of slaves as well as other goods to most other regions. The Dutch were able to make handsome profits dealing in human cargo until the end of the seventeenth century, when they were supplanted by the British.

The Dutch introduced sugar cultivation to the French and English after learning it themselves in Brazil. Sugar plantations began to supplant tobacco cultivation, as well as subsistence farming, on the Caribbean islands the English and French controlled. Beginning in the late sixteenth century English and French seamen had seized island territories to serve as provisioning stations and staging points for raids against or commerce with Spanish colonies. Some island outposts had expanded into colonies and attracted European settlers—some, as in North America, coming as indentured servants—to work the land. Sugar cultivation, though potentially more profitable than tobacco, demanded huge outlays of capital and continual supplies of unskilled labor, and it drastically transformed the settlements' characters. Large plantations owned by wealthy, often absentee landlords and dependent on slave labor replaced smaller-scale independent farming. The most profitable sugar colonies were, for the French, the islands of Martinique and Guadeloupe and, for the English, Barbados and Jamaica.

Aware of the overwhelming Spanish territorial advantage in the New World, and yet still hoping for treasures such as the Spanish had found, the English, French, and Dutch were also eager to explore and settle North America. From the early sixteenth century on, French, Dutch, English, and Portuguese seamen had fished and traded off Newfoundland. By 1630 small French and Scottish settlements in Acadia (near modern Nova Scotia) and on the St. Lawrence River and English settlements in Newfoundland were established to systematically exploit the timber, fish, and fur of the north Atlantic coasts.

In England rising unemployment and religious discontent created a large pool of potential colonists, some of whom were initially attracted to the Caribbean. The first of

Sugar Manufacture in Caribbean Colonies *Production of sugar required large capital outlays, in part because the raw cane had to be processed quickly, on-site, to avoid spoilage. This scene depicts enslaved workers operating a small sugar mill on the island of Barbados in the seventeenth century. In the background a press crushes the cane; in the foreground the juice from the cane is boiled down until sugar begins to crystallize.* (Mary Evans Picture Library)

the English settlements to endure in what was to become the United States was established at Jamestown, named for James I, in Virginia in 1607. ("Virginia," named for Elizabeth I, the "Virgin Queen," was an extremely vague designation for the Atlantic coast of North America and its hinterland.)

The Crown encouraged colonization, but a private company similar to those that financed long-distance trade was established to organize the enterprise. The directors of the Virginia Company were London businessmen. Investors and would-be colonists purchased shares. Shareholders among the colonists could participate in a colonial assembly, although the governor appointed by the company was the final authority.

The colonists arrived in Virginia with ambitious and optimistic instructions. They were to open mines, establish profitable cultivation, and search for sea routes to Asia. But at first they struggled merely to survive. The indigenous peoples in Virginia, unlike those in Spanish-held territories, were not organized in urbanized, rigidly hierarchical societies that, after conquest, could provide the invaders with a labor force. Indeed, much of the local native population was quickly wiped out by European diseases. The introduction of tobacco as a cash crop a few years later saved the colonists economically—although the Virginia Company had already gone bankrupt and the Crown had assumed control of the colony. With the cultivation of tobacco, the Virginia colony, like the Caribbean islands, became dependent on forced, eventually slave, labor.

Among the Virginia colonists were impoverished men and women who came as servants indentured to those who had paid their passage—that is, they were bound by contract to pay off their debts by several years of labor. Colonies established to the north, in what was called "New England," also drew people from the margins of English society. Early settlers there were religious dissidents. The first to arrive were the Pilgrims, who arrived at Plymouth (modern Massachusetts) in 1620. They were a community of religious Separatists who had originally immigrated to the Netherlands from England for freedom of conscience.

Following the Pilgrims came Puritans escaping escalating persecution under Charles I. The first, in 1629, settled under the auspices of another royally chartered company, the Massachusetts Bay Company. Among their number were many prosperous Puritan merchants and landholders. Independence from investors in London allowed them an unprecedented degree of self-government once the Massachusetts Bay colony was established.

Nevertheless, the colonies in North America were disappointments to England because they generated much less wealth than expected. Shipping timber back to Europe proved too expensive, although New England forests did supply some of the Caribbean colonists' needs. The fur trade became less lucrative as English settlement pushed the Native Americans who did most of the trapping west and as French trappers to the north encroached on the trade. Certain colonists profited enormously from the tobacco economy, but the mother country did so only moderately because the demand in Europe for tobacco never grew as quickly as the demand for sugar. The English settlements did continue to attract more migrants than other colonizers' outposts. By 1640 Massachusetts had some fourteen thousand European inhabitants. Through most of the next century the growth of colonial populations in North America would result in an English advantage over the French in control of New World territory.

The French began their settlement of North America at the same time as the English, in the same push to compensate for their mutual weakness vis-à-vis the Spanish. The French efforts, however, had very different results, owing partly to the sites of their settlements but mostly to the relationship between the mother country and the colonies. The French hold on territory was always tenuous because of the scant number of colonists who could be lured from home. There seems to have been less economic impetus for colonization from France than from England. And after the French crown took over the colonies, any religious impetus evaporated, for only Catholics were allowed to settle in New France. Moreover, control by the Crown forced a traditional hierarchical political organization on the French colonies. A royal governor directed the colony, and large tracts of land were set aside for privileged investors. Thus North America offered little to tempt French people of modest means who were seeking a better life.

The first successful French colony was established in Acadia in 1605. This settlement was an exception among the French efforts because it was founded by Huguenots, not by Catholics. A few years later the explorer Samuel de Champlain (1567?–1635) navigated the St. Lawrence River and founded Quebec City (1608). He convinced the royal government, emerging from its preoccupations with religious wars at home, to promote the development of the colony. French explorers went on to establish Montreal, farther inland on the St. Lawrence (1642), and to explore the Great Lakes and the Mississippi River basin.

The English and French in North America, ca. 1700

By 1700 a veritable ring of French-claimed territory encircled the coastal colonies of England. English-claimed areas, however, were more densely settled and more economically viable.

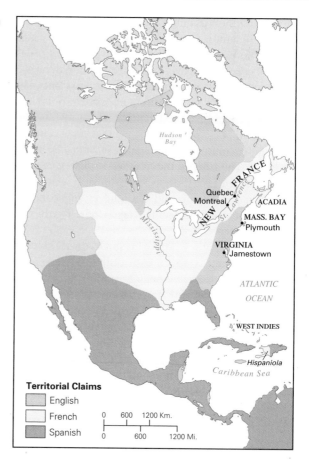

Territorial Claims
- English
- French
- Spanish

0   600   1200 Km.

0   600   1200 Mi.

Such investment as the French crown was able to attract went into profitable trade, mainly in furs, and not into the difficult business of colonization. French trappers and traders who ventured into wilderness areas were renowned for their hardiness and adaptability, but they did not bring their families and establish settled, European-style towns. Quebec remained more of a trading station, dependent on shipments of food from France, than a growing urban community. Added to the commercial dimension of New France was the church's interest: much of the energy of French colonization was expended by men and women of religious orders—the "Black Robes"—bringing their zeal to new frontiers. By the middle of the seventeenth century all of New France had only about three thousand European inhabitants.

The seeming weakness of the French colonial effort in North America was not much noticed at the time. French and English fishermen, trappers, and traders competed intensely, and the French often reaped the greater share of profits, owing to their closer ties with Native American trading systems. Outright battles occasionally erupted between English and French settlements. But for both England and France the major profits and strategic interests in the New World lay to the south, in the Caribbean. The Dutch experience reveals the degree to which North America, for all colonial powers, was of secondary importance to the plantation profits farther south. In 1624 the Dutch founded a trading center, New Amsterdam, at the site of modern-day New York City. Fifty years later they relinquished New Amsterdam—the cornerstone of their northern enterprise—to the English in return for recognition of the Dutch claims to sugar-producing Guiana (modern Suriname) in South America.

Consequently, by far the largest group of migrants to European-held territories in the Americas were forced migrants: African men and women sold into slavery and transported across the Atlantic to work the plantations established by Europeans. A conservative estimate is that approximately 1.35 million Africans were forcibly transported as slave labor to the New World during the seventeenth century.

The Beginning of the End of Traditional Society

Within Europe the economic impact of overseas trade was profound. Merchants and investors in a few of Europe's largest cities reaped great profits. Mediterranean ports such as Venice, once the heart of European trade, did not share in the bonanza from the new trade with Asia or the Americas. Atlantic ports such as Seville, through which most Spanish commerce with the New World flowed, and, above all, Amsterdam began to flourish. The population of Amsterdam increased from about 30,000 to 200,000 in the course of the seventeenth century.

All capital cities, however, not just seaports, grew substantially during the 1600s. Increasing numbers of government functionaries, courtiers and their hangers-on, and people involved in trade lived and worked in capital cities. These cities also grew indirectly from the demand such people generated for services and products, ranging from fashionable clothing to exotic foodstuffs. For the first time cities employed vast numbers of country people. Perhaps as much as one-fifth of the population of England passed through London at one time or another, creating the mobile, volatile community so active in the English civil war and its aftermath.

The economy became more productive and flexible as it expanded, but social stratification intensified. Patterns of consumption in cities reflected the economic gulfs between residents. Most people could not afford to buy imported pepper or sugar. Poverty increased in cities, even in vibrant Amsterdam, because cities attracted people fleeing rural unemployment with few skills and fewer resources. As growing central governments heaped tax burdens on peasants, many rural people were caught in a cycle of debt; the only escape was to abandon farming and flock to cities.

Peasant rebellions occurred throughout the century as a result of depressed economic conditions and heavy taxation, reflecting the expansion of royal power and expensive royal military ambitions. Some small-scale revolts involved direct action, such as seizing the tax collector's grain or stopping the movement of grain to the great cities. Urban demand often caused severe food shortages in rural areas in western Europe, despite the booming trade in grain with eastern Europe via the Baltic.

The typical peasant revolt in western Europe during the seventeenth century, however, was directed against escalating taxation. Tax rebellions often formed spontaneously, perhaps as tax officials passed through a village, but they were not mere chaotic gatherings of rabble. Country folk were accustomed to defending themselves as communities—against brigands and marauding soldiers, for example. Local gentry or prosperous farmers who ordinarily fulfilled the function of local constable led such revolts from time to time, convinced that they represented the legitimate interests of the

IMPORTANT EVENTS

1602 Dutch East India Company formed

1607 Jamestown colony founded in Virginia

1608 Champlain founds Quebec City

1613 Michael becomes first Romanov tsar in Russia

1620 Pilgrims settle at Plymouth (Massachusetts)

1642–1648 Civil war in England

1643 Louis XIV becomes king of France

1648–1653 Fronde revolts in France

1649 Execution of Charles I

1649–1660 English Commonwealth

1659 Peace of the Pyrenees

1660 Monarchy restored in England

1661 Louis XIV assumes full control of government

1672–1678 Dutch War

1682 Peter the Great becomes tsar of Russia

1685 Edict of Nantes revoked

1688 Glorious Revolution

1699 Treaty of Carlowitz

1700–1721 Great Northern War

1701–1714 War of the Spanish Succession

1713 Peace of Utrecht

1715 Death of Louis XIV

community against rapacious officials higher up. The scale of peasant violence meant that thousands of troops sometimes had to be diverted from a state's foreign wars. As a matter of routine, soldiers accompanied tax officials and enforced collection all over Europe. Thus, as the ambitions of rulers grew, so too did the resistance of ordinary people to the exactions of the state.

NOTES

1. Quoted in D. H. Pennington, *Europe in the Seventeenth Century,* 2d ed. (London: Longman, 1989), p. 508.

SUGGESTED READING

Collins, James B. *The State in Early Modern France.* 1995. An up-to-date synthesis by one of the leading scholars of French absolutism.

Howard, Michael. *War in European History.* 1976. A general study of warfare emphasizing the relationship between war making and state development.

Ingrao, Charles. *The Habsburg Monarchy, 1618–1815.* 1994. A treatment of the Austrian Habsburgs that stresses the distinctiveness of the Habsburg state.

Kishlansky, Mark. *A Monarchy Transformed.* 1996. The most recent full scholarly treatment of political events in England.

Musgrave, Peter. *The Early Modern European Economy.* 1999. A recent survey of the scholarship on the expanding European economy.

Oakley, Stewart P. *War and Peace in the Baltic, 1560–1790.* 1992. An excellent survey of the Baltic region in the early modern period.

Pennington, D. H. *Europe in the Seventeenth Century.* 2d ed. 1989. A general history of the century.

Riasanovsky, Nicolas V. *A History of Russia.* 6th ed. 2000. A reliable and readable survey of Russian history from medieval times; includes an extensive bibliography of major works available in English.

Schama, Simon. *The Embarrassment of Riches: An Interpretation of Dutch Culture in the Golden Age.* 1997. An innovative study of Dutch culture that explores the social and psychological tensions created by its growing wealth in the seventeenth century.

Wolf, Eric R. *Europe and the People Without History.* 1982. A survey of European contact with and conquest of peoples after 1400; includes extensive treatments of non-European societies and detailed explanations of the economic and political interests of the Europeans.

A Revolution
in World-View

(Réunion des Musées
Nationaux/Art
Resource, NY)

The year is 1649. Queen Christina of Sweden welcomes us
with her gaze and her gesture to witness a science lesson
at her court. Her illustrious instructor, the French philosopher René Descartes, clutches a compass and points to an
astronomical drawing. The young queen, twenty-three years
old at the time, was already well known as a patron of artists
and scholars. Christina had invited Descartes to her court be-

cause of his achievements in physics and philosophy. This painting depicts the fact that during Christina's lifetime, new theories in the field of astronomy revolutionized the sciences and required new definitions of matter to explain them. Descartes earned famed both for his novel theories about matter and for his systematic approach to the application of human reason to understanding the universe. This painting celebrates both Descartes's work and Christina's sponsorship of it.

The revolution within the sciences had been initiated in the sixteenth century by the astronomical calculations and hypotheses of Nicholas Copernicus, who posited that the earth moves around the sun. The work of the Italian mathematician and astronomer Galileo Galilei, as well as others, added evidence to support this hypothesis. Their work overturned principles of physics and philosophy that had held sway since ancient times. Later generations of scientists and philosophers, beginning with Descartes, labored to construct new principles to explain the way the physical universe behaves. The readiness of scientists, their patrons, and educated laypeople to push Copernicus's hypothesis to these conclusions came from several sources: their exposure to the intellectual innovations of Renaissance thought, the intellectual challenges and material opportunities represented by the discovery of the New World, and the challenge to authority embodied in the Reformation. Also, the new science offered prestige and technological advances to the rulers, such as Christina, who sponsored it.

By the end of the seventeenth century a vision of an infinite but orderly cosmos appealing to human reason had, among educated Europeans, largely replaced the medieval vision of a closed universe centered on the earth and suffused with Christian purpose. Religion became an increasingly subordinate ally of science as confidence in an open-ended, experimental approach to knowledge came to be as strongly held as religious conviction. It is because of this larger shift in world-view, not simply because of particular scientific discoveries, that the seventeenth century may be labeled the era of the Scientific Revolution.

Because religious significance had been attached to previous explanations and religious authority defended them, the new astronomy automatically led to an enduring debate about the compatibility of science and religion. But the revolution in world-view was not confined to astronomy or even to science generally. As philosophers gained confidence in human reason and the intelligibility of the world, they turned to new speculation about human affairs. They began to challenge traditional justifications for the hierarchical nature of society and the sanctity of authority just as energetically as Copernicus and his followers had overthrown old views about the cosmos.

THE REVOLUTION IN ASTRONOMY, 1543–1632

The origins of the seventeenth-century revolution in world-view lie, for the most part, in developments in astronomy. Because of astronomy's role in the explanations of the world and human life that had been devised by ancient and medieval scientists and philosophers, any advances in astronomy were bound to have widespread intellectual repercussions. By the early part of the seventeenth century fundamental astronomical beliefs had been successfully challenged. The consequence was the undermining of both the material (physics) and the philosophical (metaphysics) explanations of the world that had been standing for centuries.

The Inherited World-View and the Sixteenth-Century Context

Ancient and medieval astronomy accepted the perspective on the universe that unaided human senses support—namely, that the earth is fixed at the center of the universe and the celestial bodies rotate around it. The regular movements of heavenly bodies and the obvious importance of the sun for life on earth made astronomy a vital undertaking for both scientific and religious purposes in many ancient societies. Astronomers in ancient Greece carefully observed the heavens and learned to calculate and to predict the seemingly circular motion of the stars and the sun about the earth. The orbits of the planets were more difficult to explain, for the planets seemed to travel both east and west across the sky at various times and with no regularity that could be mathematically understood. Indeed, the very word *planet* comes from a Greek word meaning "wanderer."

We now know that all the planets simultaneously orbit the sun at different speeds in paths that are at different distances from the sun. The relative positions of the planets constantly change; sometimes other planets are "ahead" of the earth and sometimes "behind." In the second century A.D. the Greek astronomer Ptolemy attempted to explain the planets' occasional "backward" motion by attributing it to "epicycles"—small circular orbits within the larger orbit. Ptolemy's mathematical explanations of the imagined epicycles were extremely complex, but neither Ptolemy nor medieval mathematicians and astronomers were ever able fully to account for planetary motion.

Ancient physics, most notably the work of the Greek philosopher Aristotle (384–322 B.C.), explained the fact that some objects (such as cannonballs) fall to earth but others (stars and planets) seem weightless relative to earth because of their composition: different kinds of matter have different inherent tendencies and properties. In this view all earthbound matter (like cannonballs) falls because it is naturally attracted to earth—heaviness being a property of earthbound things.

In the Christian era the Aristotelian explanation of the universe was infused with Christian meaning and purpose. The heavens were said to be made of different, pure matter because they were the abode of the angels. Both the earth and the humans who inhabited it were changeable and corruptible. Yet God had given human beings a unique and special place in the universe, which was thought to be a closed world with the stationary earth at the center. Revolving around the earth in circular orbits were the sun, moon, stars, and planets. The motion of all lesser bodies was caused by the rotation of all the stars together in the vast crystal-like sphere in which they were embedded.

A few ancient astronomers theorized that the earth moved about the sun. Some medieval philosophers also adopted this heliocentric thesis (*helios* is the Greek word for "sun"), but it remained a minority view because it seemed to contradict both common sense and observed data. The sun and stars *appeared* to move around the earth with great regularity. Moreover, how could objects fall to earth if the earth was moving beneath them? Also, astronomers detected no difference in angles from which observers on earth viewed the stars at different times. Such differences would exist, they thought, if the earth changed positions by moving around the sun. It was inconceivable that the universe could be so large and the stars so distant that the earth's movement would produce no measurable change in the earth's position with respect to the stars.

Several conditions of intellectual life in the sixteenth century encouraged new work in astronomy and led to the revision of the earth-centered world-view. The most important was the work of Renaissance humanists in recovering and interpreting ancient texts. Now able to work with new Greek versions of Ptolemy, mathematicians and astronomers noted that his explanations for the motion of the planets were imperfect and not simply inadequately transmitted, as they had long believed. Also, the discovery of the New World dramatically undercut the assumption that ancient knowledge was superior. The existence of the Americas specifically undermined Ptolemy's authority once again, for it disproved many of the assertions in his *Geography*, which had just been recovered in Europe the previous century.

The desire to explain heavenly movements better was still loaded with religious significance in the sixteenth century and was heightened by the immediate need for reform of the Julian calendar (named for Julius Caesar). Ancient observations of the movement of the sun, though remarkably accurate, could not measure the precise length of the solar year. By the sixteenth century the cumulative error of this calendar had resulted in a change of ten days: the spring equinox fell on March 11 instead of March 21. An accurate and uniform system of dating was necessary for all rulers and their tax collectors and recordkeepers. And because the calculation of the date of Easter was at stake, a reliable calendar was the particular project of the church.

Impetus for new and better astronomical observations and calculations arose from other features of the intellectual and political landscape as well. Increasingly, as the century went on, princely courts became important sources of patronage for and sites of scientific activity. Rulers eager to buttress their own power by symbolically linking it to dominion over nature sponsored investigations of the world, as Ferdinand and Isabella had so successfully done, and displayed the marvels of nature at their courts. Sponsoring scientific inquiry also yielded practical benefits: better mapping of the ruler's domains and better technology for mining, gunnery, and navigation.

Finally, schools of thought fashionable at the time, encouraged by the humanists' critique of received tradition, hinted at the possibilities of alternative physical and metaphysical systems. The ancient doctrine of Hermeticism (named for the mythical originator of the ideas, Hermes Trismegistos), revived since the Renaissance, claimed that matter is universally imbued with divine (or magical) spirit. Drawing on Hermeticism was Paracelsianism, named for the Swiss physician Philippus von Hohenheim (1493–1541), who called himself Paracelsus (literally "beyond Celsus," an acclaimed Roman physician whose works had just been recovered). Paracelsus scoffed at the notion that ancient authorities were the final word on the workings of nature. "He who is born in imagination," he wrote, "discovers the latent forces of nature."[1] Paracelsus offered an alternative to accepted medical theory, put forth by the physician Galen (ca. 131–201), the premier medical authority of antiquity, now as revered as Aristotle. Galen believed that an imbalance of bodily "humors" caused illness. Paracelsus substituted a theory of chemical imbalance that was a forerunner of modern understandings of pathology. He was wildly popular wherever he taught because of the success of his treatments of illness and his willingness to lecture openly to laymen.

Neo-Platonism, another school of thought, had a more systematic and far-reaching impact. Neo-Platonism was a revival, primarily in Italian humanist circles, of certain aspects of Plato's thought. It contributed directly to innovation in science because it emphasized the abstract nature of true knowledge and thus encouraged mathematical investigation. This provided a spur to astronomical studies, which, since ancient times, had been concerned more with mathematical analysis of heavenly movements than with physical explanations for them. Also, like Hermeticism and Paracelsianism, Neo-Platonism had a mystical dimension that fostered creative speculation about the nature of matter and the organization of the universe. Neo-Platonists were particularly fascinated by the sun as a symbol of the one divine mind or soul at the heart of all creation.

The Copernican Challenge

Nicholas Copernicus (1473–1543), son of a German merchant family in Poland, pursued wide-ranging university studies in philosophy, law, astronomy, mathematics, and medicine—first in Cracow in Poland and then in Bologna and Padua in Italy. In Italy he was exposed to Neo-Platonic ideas. He took a degree in canon (church) law in 1503 and became a cathedral canon (a member of the cathedral staff) in the city of Frauenburg (modern Poland), where he pursued his own interests in astronomy while carrying out administrative duties. When the pope asked Copernicus to assist with the reform of the Julian calendar, he replied that reform of the calendar required reform in astronomy. His major work, *De Revolutionibus Orbium Caelestium* (*On the Revolution of Heavenly Bodies,* 1543), was dedicated to the pope in the hopes that it would help with the task of calendar reform—as indeed it did. The Gregorian calendar, issued in 1582 during the pontificate of Gregory XIII (r. 1572–1585), was based on Copernicus's calculations.

Copernicus postulated that the earth and all the other planets orbit the sun. He did not assert that the earth does in fact move around the sun but offered the heliocentric system as a mathematical construct, useful for predicting the movements of planets, stars, and the sun. However, he walked a thin line between making claims for a mathematical construct on the one hand and physical reality on the other. Scholars now believe that Copernicus was himself persuaded that the heliocentric theory was correct. He had searched in ancient sources for thinkers who believed the earth moved. Other astronomers familiar with his work and reputation urged him to publish the results of his calculations. But not until 1542, twelve years after finishing the work, did he send *De Revolutionibus* to be published. He received a copy just before his death the next year.

By affirming the earth's movement around the sun while also salvaging features of the old system, Copernicus faced burdens of explanation not faced by Ptolemy. For example, Copernicus still assumed that the planets traveled in circular orbits, so he was forced to retain some epicycles in his schema to account for the circular motion. In general, however, the Copernican account of planetary motion was simpler than the Ptolemaic account. It appealed to other astronomers of the age because it was useful and because it highlighted the harmony of heavenly motion, which remained a fundamental physical and metaphysical principle. Inaccessible except to other astronomers, Copernicus's work only slowly led to conceptual revolution, as scientists worked with his calculations and assembled other evidence to support the heliocentric theory.

The most important reason that fundamental conceptual change followed Copernican theory so gradually was that Copernicus did not resolve the physical problems his ideas raised. If Copernicus were right, the earth would have to be made of the same material as other planets. How, then, would Copernicus explain the motion of objects on earth—the fact that they fall to earth—if it was not in their nature to fall toward the heavy, stationary earth? In Copernicus's system, the movement of the earth caused the *apparent* motion of the stars. But if the stars did not rotate in their crystalline sphere, what made all other heavenly bodies move?

Copernicus was not as troubled by these questions as we might expect him to be. Since ancient times, mathematical astronomy—the science of measuring and predicting the movements of heavenly bodies—had been far more important than, and had proceeded independently of, physical explanations of observed motion. Nevertheless, as Copernicus's own efforts to support his hypothesis reveal, his theories directly contradicted many of the supposed laws of motion. The usefulness of his theories to other astronomers meant that the contradictions between mathematical and physical models for the universe would have to be resolved. Copernicus himself might be best understood as the last Ptolemaic astronomer, working within inherited questions and with known tools. His work itself did not constitute a revolution, but it did initiate one.

The First Coperni-can Astronomers In the first generation of astronomers after the publication of *De Revolutionibus* in 1543 we can see the effects of Copernicus's work. His impressive computations rapidly won converts among fellow astronomers. Several particularly gifted astronomers continued to develop the Copernican system. Thus, by the second quarter of the seventeenth century, they and many others accepted the heliocentric theory as a reality and not just as a useful mathematical fiction. The three most important astronomers to build on Copernican assumptions, and on the work of one another, were the Dane Tycho Brahe (1546–1601), the German Johannes Kepler (1571–1630), and the Italian Galileo Galilei (1564–1642).

Like generations of observers before him, Tycho Brahe had been stirred by the majesty of the regular movements of heavenly bodies. After witnessing a partial eclipse of the sun, he abandoned a career in government befitting his noble status and became an astronomer. Brahe was the first truly post-Ptolemaic astronomer because he was the first to improve on the data that the ancients and all subsequent astronomers had used. Ironically, no theory of planetary motion could have reconciled the data that Copernicus had used: they were simply too inaccurate, based as they were on naked-eye observations, even when errors of translation and copying, accumulated over centuries, had been corrected.

In 1576 the king of Denmark showered Brahe with properties and pensions enabling him to build an observatory, Uraniborg, on an island near Copenhagen. At Uraniborg Brahe improved on ancient observations with large and very finely calibrated instruments that permitted precise measurements of celestial movements by the naked eye. His attention to precision and frequency of observation produced results that were twice as accurate as any previous data had been.

As a result of his observations, Brahe agreed with Copernicus that the various planets did rotate around the sun, not around the earth. He still could not be persuaded that the earth itself moved, for none of his data supported such a notion. Brahe's lasting and crucial contribution was his astronomical data. They would become obsolete as soon as data from telescopic observations were accumulated about a century later. But in the meantime they were used by Johannes Kepler to further develop Copernicus's model and arrive at a more accurate heliocentric theory.

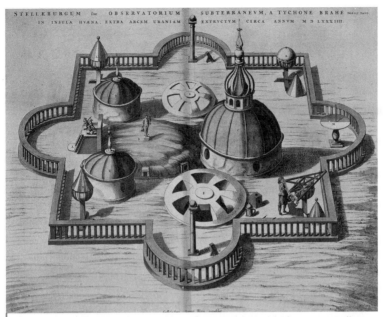

STELLÆBURGUM sive OBSERVATORIUM SUBTERRANEVM, A TYCHONE BRAHE Nobili Dano
IN INSULA HVÆNA, EXTRA ARCEM URANIAM EXTRVCTVM, CIRCA ANNVM M D LXXXIIII.

Tycho Brahe's Observatory   *A gifted artist and craftsman as well as an astronomer, Brahe gathered the best talent, including German instrument makers and Italian architects, to build his state-of-the-art observatory near Copenhagen. Brahe named the complex Uraniborg, for Urania, the muse of astronomy.*   (The Fotomas Index, U.K.)

Kepler was young enough to be exposed to Copernican ideas from the outset of his raining, and he quickly recognized in Brahe's data the means of resolving the problems in Copernican analysis. Though trained in his native Germany, Kepler went to Prague, where Brahe spent the last years of his life at the court of the Holy Roman emperor after a quarrel with the Danish king. There Kepler became something of an apprentice to Brahe. After Brahe's death in 1601, Kepler kept his mentor's records of astronomical observations and continued to work at the imperial court as Rudolf II's court mathematician.

Kepler's contribution to the new astronomy, like that of Copernicus, was fundamentally mathematical. In it we can see the stamp of the Neo-Platonic conviction about the purity of mathematical explanation. Kepler spent ten years working to apply Brahe's data to the most intricate of all the celestial movements—the motion of the planet Mars—as a key to explaining all planetary motion. Mars is close to the earth, but its orbital path is farther from the sun. This combination produces very puzzling and dramatic variations in the apparent movement of Mars to an earthly observer.

The result of Kepler's work was laws of planetary motion that, in the main, are still in use. First, Kepler eliminated the need for epicycles by correctly asserting that planets follow elliptical and not circular orbits. Elliptical orbits could account, both mathematically and visually, for the motion of the planets when combined with Kepler's second law, which describes the *rate* of a planet's motion around its orbital path. Kepler noted that the speed of a planet in its orbit slows proportionally as the planet's distance from the sun increases. A third law demonstrates that the distance of each planet from the sun and the time it takes each planet to orbit the sun are in a constant ratio.

Kepler's work was a breakthrough because it mathematically confirmed the Copernican heliocentric hypothesis. In so doing, the work directly challenged the ancient world-view, in which heavenly bodies constantly moved in circular orbits around a stationary earth. Hence Kepler's laws invited speculation about the properties and movements of heavenly and terrestrial bodies alike. A new physics would be required to explain the novel motion that Kepler had posited. Kepler himself, in Neo-Platonic fashion, attributed planetary motion to the sun: "[The sun] is a fountain of light, rich in fruitful heat, most fair, limpid and pure . . . called king of the planets for his motion, heart of the world for his power. . . . Who would hesitate to confer the votes of the celestial motions on him who has been administering all other movements and changes by the benefit of the light which is entirely his possession?"[2]

| Galileo and the Triumph of Copernicanism | Galileo Galilei holds a pre-eminent position in the development of astronomy because, first, he provided compelling new evidence to support Copernican theory and, second, he contributed to the development of a new physics—or, more precisely, mechanics—that could account for the movements of bodies in new terms. In |

short he began to close the gap between the new astronomy and new explanations for the behavior of matter. Just as important, his efforts to publicize his findings and his condemnation by the church spurred popular debate about Copernican ideas in literate society and helped to determine the course science would take.

Galileo's career also illustrates, in dramatic fashion, the dependence of scientists on and their vulnerability to patronage relationships. Born to a minor Florentine noble family, Galileo began studying medicine at the nearby University of Pisa at the age of 17 but became intrigued by problems of mechanics and mathematics. He began studying those disciplines at Pisa under the tutelage of a Florentine court mathematician and became a lecturer in mathematics there in 1589, at age 25, after publishing promising work in mechanics. Three years later, well-connected fellow mathematicians helped him secure a more lucrative and prestigious professorship at the University of Padua, where Copernicus had once studied. Galileo skillfully cultivated the learned Venetian aristocrats (Venice ruled Padua at this time) who controlled academic appointments and secured renewals and salary raises over the next eighteen years.

During his years at Pisa and Padua, Galileo pursued his revolutionary work in mechanics, although he did not publish the results of his experiments until much later. Galileo's principal contribution to mechanics lay in his working out of an early theory of inertia. As a result of a number of experiments with falling bodies (balls rolling on carefully constructed inclines—not free-falling objects that, according to myth, he dropped from the Leaning Tower of Pisa), Galileo ventured a new view of what is "natural" to objects. Galileo's view was that uniform motion is as natural as a state of rest. In the ancient and medieval universe, all motion needed a cause, and all motion could be explained in terms of purpose. "I hold," Galileo countered, "that there exists nothing in external bodies . . . but size, shape, quantity and motion."[3] Galileo retained the old assumption that motion was somehow naturally circular. Nevertheless, his theory was a crucial step in explaining motion according to new principles and in fashioning a world-view that accepted a mechanical universe devoid of metaphysical purpose.

The results of this work were, for the most part, not published until the end of his life. In the meantime, Galileo became famous for his astronomical observations, which he began in 1609 and which he parlayed into a position back at the Florentine court. Early that year Galileo learned of the invention of a primitive telescope (which could magnify distant objects only three times) and quickly improved on it to make the first astronomically useful instrument. In *Sidereus Nuncius* (*The Starry Messenger,* 1610) he described his scrutiny of the heavens with his telescope in lay language. He documented sighting previously undetectable stars, as well as moons orbiting the planet Jupiter. In another blow to ancient descriptions of the universe, he noted craters and other "imperfections" on the surface of the moon. Three years later he published his solar observations in *Letters on Sunspots.* Sunspots are regions of relatively cool gaseous material that appear as dark spots on the sun's surface. For Galileo sunspots and craters on the moon proved that the heavens are not perfect and changeless but rather are like the supposedly "corrupt" and changeable earth. His telescopic observations also provided further support for Copernican heliocentrism. Indeed, Galileo's own acceptance of Copernicanism can be dated to this point because magnification revealed that each heavenly body rotates on its axis: sunspots, for example, can be tracked across the visible surface of the sun as the sun rotates.

Galileo had already been approached by various Italian princes and in turn sought to woo their support with gifts of some of his earlier inventions, such as a military compass. He aimed his *Starry Messenger* at the Medici dukes of Florence, naming Jupiter's moons the "Medicean Stars" and publishing the work to coincide with the accession of the young Cosimo II, whom he had tutored as a youth. In 1610 he returned in triumph to his native Tuscany as court philosopher to the grand duke. Soon, however, his own fame and the increasing acceptance of Copernicanism, especially vindicated by his work on sunspots, aroused opposition. In 1615 Galileo was denounced to the Inquisition by a Florentine friar. After an investigation, the geokinetic theory (that the earth moves) was declared heretical, but Galileo himself was not condemned. He could continue to use Copernican theory, but only as a theory. Indeed, a number of the most fervent practitioners of the new science continued to be clergymen who followed Galileo's work with interest. A new pope, elected in 1623, was a Tuscan aristocrat and an old friend of Galileo. Galileo dedicated his work on comets, *The Assayer* (1624), to Urban VIII in honor of his election.

Now in his 60s, Galileo began to work on a book that summarized his life's work—*Dialogue on the Two Chief Systems of the World* (1632), structured as a conversation among three characters debating the merits of Copernican theory. Given the work's sensitive subject matter, Galileo obtained explicit permission from the pope to write it and cleared some portions with censors before publication. The work was the most important single source in its day for the popularization of Copernican theory, but it led to renewed concerns in Rome. Galileo had clearly overstepped the bounds of discussing Copernicanism in theory only and appeared to advocate it. Simplicio, the character representing the old world-view, was, as his name suggests, an example of ignorance, not wisdom.

Moreover, the larger political context affecting Galileo's patrons and friends had changed. The pope was being threatened by the Spanish and Austrian Habsburgs for his tepid support in the Thirty Years' War, in which Catholic forces were now losing to Protestant armies, and he could no longer be indulgent with his friend. (The pope tended to favor French foreign policy as a counterweight to the enormous power of the Habsburgs.) Galileo was forced to stand trial for heresy in Rome in 1633. When, in a kind of plea-bargain arrangement, he pled guilty to a lesser charge of inadvertently advocating Copernicanism, Pope Urban intervened to insist on a weightier penalty. Galileo's book was banned, he was forced to formally renounce his "error," and he was sentenced to house arrest. Galileo lived confined and guarded, continuing his investigations of mechanics, until his death seven years later.

THE SCIENTIFIC REVOLUTION GENERALIZED, CA. 1600–1700

Galileo's work found such a willing audience in part because Galileo, like Kepler and Brahe, was not working alone. Dozens of other scientists were examining old problems from the fresh perspective offered by the breakthroughs in astronomy. Some analyzed the nature of matter, now that it appeared that all matter in the universe was somehow the same despite its varying appearances. Many of these thinkers addressed the metaphysical issues that their investigations inevitably raised. They began the complex intellectual and psychological journey toward a new world-view, one that accepted the existence of an infinitely large universe of undifferentiated matter with no obvious place in it for humans.

The Promise of the New Science No less a man than Francis Bacon (1561–1626), lord chancellor of England during the reign of James I, wrote a utopian essay extolling the benefits of science for a peaceful society and for human happiness. In *New Atlantis,* published one year after his death, Bacon argued that science would produce "things of use and practice for man's life."[4] In *New Atlantis* and *Novum Organum* (1620) Bacon reveals his faith in science by advocating patient, systematic observation and experimentation to accumulate knowledge about the world. He argues that the proper method of investigation "derives axioms from . . . particulars, rising by gradual and unbroken ascent, so that it arrives at the most general axioms of all. This is the true way but untried."[5]

Bacon himself did not undertake experiments, although his widely read works were influential in encouraging both the empirical method (relying on observation and experimentation) and inductive reasoning (deriving general principles from particular facts). Indeed, Bacon was a visionary. Given the early date of his writings, it might seem difficult to account for his enthusiasm and confidence. In fact, Bacon's writings reflect the widespread interest and confidence in science within his elite milieu, an interest actively encouraged by the state. In another of his writings he argues that a successful state should concentrate on effective "rule in religion *and nature,* as well as civil administration."[6]

Bacon's pronouncements reflect the fact that an interest in exploring nature's secrets and exercising "dominion over nature" had become an indispensable part of

A Collection of Naturalia   *Displays of exotica, such as these specimens in Naples, symbolized the ruler's authority by suggesting his or her power over nature.*   (From Ferrante Imperato, *Dell' historia naturale . . . libri XXVIII*, Naples, Costantino Vitale, 1599. Typ 525 99.461. Department of Printing and Graphic Arts, Houghton Library, Harvard College Library)

princely rule. Princely courts were the main sources of financial support for science and the primary sites of scientific work during Bacon's lifetime. Part of the impetus for this development had come from the civic humanism of the Italian Renaissance, which had celebrated the state and service to it and had provided models both for educated rulers and for cultivated courtiers. Attention to science and to its benefits for the state also reflect the scope, and pragmatism, of princely resources and ambitions: the desire of rulers for technical expertise in armaments, fortification, construction, navigation, and mapmaking.

The promise of the New World and the drive for overseas trade and exploration especially encouraged princely support of scientific investigation. A renowned patron of geographic investigation, from mapmaking to navigation, was Henry, prince of Wales (d. 1612), eldest son of James I. Prince Henry patronized technical experts such as experienced gunners and seamen, as well as those with broader and more theoretical expertise. One geographer at his court worked on the vital problem of calculating longitude, sketched the moon after reading and emulating Galileo's work with the telescope, and, in the spirit of empiricism often associated with Bacon, compiled information about the new territory Virginia, including the first dictionary of any Native American language.

Science was an ideological as well as a practical tool for power. Most courts housed collections of marvels, specimens of exotic plants and animals, and mechanical contrivances. These demonstrated the ruler's interest in investigation of the world—in other words, his or her status as an educated individual. These collections and the work of court experts also enhanced the ruler's reputation as a patron and person of power. Galileo was playing off such expectations when he named his newly discovered moons of Jupiter "Medicean Stars." Like all patronage relationships, the status was shared by both partners; indeed, the attention of a patron was a guarantee of the researcher's scientific credibility.

By the beginning of the seventeenth century, private salons and academies where investigators might meet on their own were another significant milieu of scientific investigation. These, too, had their roots in the humanist culture of Italy, where circles of scholars without university affiliations had formed. Though also dependent on private resources, these associations were an important alternative to princely patronage, since a ruler's funds might wax and wane according to his or her other commitments. Private organizations could avoid the stark distinctions of rank that were inevitable at courts yet mimicked courts in the blend of scholars and educated courtiers they embraced. This more collegial but still privileged environment also fostered a sense of legitimacy for the science pursued there: legitimacy came from the recognition of fellow members and, in many cases, from publication of work by the society itself.

The earliest academy dedicated to scientific study was the *Accadèmia Segreta* (Secret Academy) founded in Naples in the 1540s. The members pursued experiments together in order, in the words of one member, "to make a true anatomy of the things and operations of nature itself."[7] During the remainder of the sixteenth century and on into the seventeenth, such academies sprang up in many cities. The most celebrated was the *Accadèmia dei Lincei*, founded in Rome by an aristocrat in 1603. Its most famous member, Galileo, joined in 1611. The name "Lincei," from *lynx*, was chosen because of the legendary keen sight of that animal, an appropriate mascot for "searchers of secrets."

Galileo's notoriety and the importance of his discoveries forced all such learned societies to take a stand for or against Copernicanism. Throughout the seventeenth century, specific investigation of natural phenomena would continue in increasingly sophisticated institutional settings. The flowering of scientific thought in the seventeenth century occurred because of the specific innovations in astronomy and the general spread of scientific investigation that had been achieved by the end of Bacon's life.

Scientific Thought in France: Descartes and a New Cosmology

Philosophers, mathematicians, and educated elites engaged in lively debate and practical investigation throughout Europe in the first half of the seventeenth century. In France the great questions about cosmic order were being posed, ironically, at a time of political disorder. The years following the religious wars saw the murder of Henry IV, another regency, and further civil war in the 1620s (see pages 485–487). In this environment questions about order in the universe and the possibilities of human knowledge took on particular urgency. It is not surprising that a Frenchman, René Descartes (1596–1650), created the first fully articulated alternative world-view.

Descartes's thinking was developed and refined in dialogue with a circle of other French thinkers. His work became more influential among philosophers and laypeople than the work of some of his equally talented contemporaries because of its thoroughness and rigor, grounded in Descartes's mathematical expertise, and because of his graceful, readable French. His system was fully presented in his *Discours de la méthode* (*Discourse on Method,* 1637). Descartes described some of his intellectual crises in his later work, *Meditations* (1641).

Descartes accepted Galileo's conclusion that the heavens and the earth are made of the same elements. In his theorizing about the composition of matter he drew on ancient atomic models that previously had not been generally accepted. His theory that all matter is made up of identical bits, which he named "corpuscles," is a forerunner of modern atomic and quantum theories. Descartes believed that all the different appearances and behaviors of matter (for example, why stone is always hard and water is always wet) could be explained solely by the size, shape, and motion of these "corpuscles." Descartes's was an extremely mechanistic explanation of the universe. It nevertheless permitted new, more specific observations and hypotheses and greater understanding of inertia. For example, because he re-imagined the universe as being filled with "corpuscles" free to move in any direction, "natural" motion no longer seemed either circular (Galileo's idea) or toward the center of the earth (Aristotle's idea). The new understanding of motion would be crucial to Isaac Newton's formulations later in the century.

In his various works Descartes depicts and then firmly resolves the crisis of confidence that the new discoveries about the universe had produced. The collapse of the old explanations about the world made Descartes and other investigators doubt not only what they knew but also their capacity to know anything at all. Their physical senses—which denied that the earth moved, for example—had been proved untrustworthy. Descartes's solution was to re-envision the human rational capacity, the mind, as completely distinct from the world—that is, as distinct from the human body—and the unreliable perceptions it offers the senses. In a leap of faith Descartes presumed that he could count on the fact that God would not have given humans a mind if that mind consistently misled them. For Descartes, God became the guarantor of human reasoning capacity, and humans were distinguished by that capacity. This is the significance of his famous claim "I think, therefore I am."

Descartes thus achieved a resolution of the terrifying doubt about the world—a resolution that exalted the role of the human knower. The Cartesian universe was one of mechanical motion, not purpose or mystical meaning, and the Cartesian human being was pre-eminently a mind that could apprehend that universe. In what came to be known as "Cartesian dualism," Descartes proposed that the human mind is detached from the world and yet at the same time can objectively analyze the world.

Descartes's ambitious view of human reason emphasizes deductive reasoning (a process of reasoning in which the conclusion follows necessarily from the stated premises), a natural consequence of his philosophical rejection of sense data. The limits of deductive reasoning for scientific investigation would be realized and much of Cartesian physics supplanted by the end of the century. Nevertheless, Descartes's assumption about the objectivity of the observer would become an enduring part of scientific practice. In Descartes's day the most radical aspect of his thought was the reduction of God to the role of guarantor of knowledge. Many fellow scientists and interested laypeople were fearful of Descartes's system because it seemed to encourage "atheism." In fact, a profound faith in God was necessary for Descartes's creativity in imagining his new world system—but the system did work without God.

Although Descartes would have been surprised and offended by charges of atheism, he knew that his work would antagonize the church. He moved to the Netherlands to study in 1628, and his *Discourse* was first published there. He had lived in the Netherlands and in Germany earlier in his life; fearful of the tense atmosphere during the renewed war against French Protestants, he now left France virtually for good. Unlike Galileo, Descartes enjoyed personal wealth that enabled him to travel widely, work in solitude, and sample the intellectual environment of courts and universities without depending on powerful patrons. Long residence in the Netherlands led him to advocate religious toleration late in his life. In 1649, at the urging of an influential friend with contacts at the Swedish court, Descartes accepted the invitation of Queen Christina to visit there. Christina was an eager but demanding patron, who required Descartes to lecture on scientific topics at 5:00 a.m. each day. The long hours of work and harsh winter weather took their toll on his health, and Descartes died of pneumonia after only a few months in Sweden.

A contemporary of Descartes, fellow Frenchman Blaise Pascal (1623–1662), drew attention in his writings and in his life to the limits of scientific knowledge. The son of a royal official, Pascal was perhaps the most brilliant mind of his generation. A mathematician like Descartes, he stressed the importance of mathematical representations of phenomena, built one of the first calculating machines, and invented probability theory. He also carried out experiments to investigate air pressure, the behavior of liquids, and the existence of vacuums.

Pascal's career alternated between periods of intense scientific work and religious retreat. Today he is well known for his writings justifying the austere Catholicism known as Jansenism (see page 512) and explored the human soul and psyche. His *Pensées* (*Thoughts,* 1657) consists of the published fragments of his defense of Christian faith, which remained unfinished at the time of his death. Pascal's appeal for generations after him may lie in his attention to matters of faith and of feeling. His most famous statement, "The heart has its reasons which reason knows not," can be read as a declaration of the limits of the Cartesian world-view.

Science and Revolution in England

The new science had adherents and practitioners throughout Europe by 1650. Dutch scientists in the commercial milieu of the Netherlands, for example, had the freedom to pursue practical and experimental interests. The Dutch investigator Christiaan Huygens (1629–1695) worked on a great variety of problems, including air pressure and optics. In 1657 he invented and patented the pendulum clock, the first device to measure accurately small units of time, essential for a variety of measurements.

England proved a unique environment for the development of science in the middle of the century. In a society torn by civil war, differing positions on science became part and parcel of disputes over Puritanism, church hierarchy, and royal power. Scientific investigation and speculation were spurred by the urgency of religious and political agendas. Scientific, along with political and religious, debate was generally encouraged by the collapse of censorship beginning in the 1640s.

During the 1640s natural philosophers with Puritan leanings were encouraged in their investigations by dreams that science, of the practical Baconian sort, could be the means by which the perfection of life on earth could be brought about and the end of history—the reign of the saints preceding the return of Christ—could be accelerated. Their concerns ranged from improved production of gunpowder (for the armies fighting against Charles I) to surveying and mapmaking. Perhaps the best-known member of this group was Robert Boyle (1627–1691). In his career we can trace the evolution of English science through the second half of the seventeenth century.

Boyle and his colleagues were theoretically eclectic, drawing on Cartesian mechanics and even Paracelsian chemical theories. They attacked the English university system, still under the sway of Aristotelianism, and proposed widespread reform of education. They were forced to moderate many of their positions, however, as the English civil wars proceeded. Radical groups such as the Levellers used Hermeticism and the related Paracelsianism as part of their political and religious tenets. The Levellers and other radical groups drew on the Hermetic notion that matter is imbued with divine spirit; they believed that each person was capable of divine knowledge and a godly life without the coercive hierarchy of church and state officials.

Boyle and his colleagues responded to these challenges. They gained institutional power, accepting positions at Oxford and Cambridge. They formed the core of the Royal Society of London, which they persuaded Charles II to recognize and charter on his accession to the throne in the Restoration of 1660. They worked to articulate a theoretical position that combined the orderliness of mechanism, a continued divine presence in the world, and a Baconian emphasis on scientific progress. This unwieldy set of notions was attractive to the educated elite of their day, who embraced the certainties of science but also clung to certain authoritarian aspects of the old Christian world-view.

Their most creative contribution, both to their own cause and to the advancement of science, was their emphasis on and refinement of experimental philosophy and practice. In 1660 Boyle published *New Experiments Physico-Mechanical.* The work describes the results of his experiments with an air pump he had designed, and it lays out general rules for experimental procedure. Descartes had accounted for motion by postulating that "corpuscles" of matter interact, thereby eliminating the possibility of a vacuum in nature. Recent experiments on air pressure suggested otherwise, however, and Boyle tried to confirm their findings with his air pump.

Boyle's efforts to demonstrate that a vacuum could exist—by evacuating a sealed chamber with his pump—were not successes by modern standards because they could not readily be replicated. Boyle tied the validity of experimental results to the agreement of witnesses to the experiment—a problematic solution, for only investigators sympathetic to his hypothesis and convinced of his credibility usually witnessed the results. In response to a Cambridge scholar who criticized his interpretation of one of his experiments, Boyle replied that he could not understand his critic's objections, "the experiment having been tried both before our whole society [the Royal Society of London], and very critically, by its royal founder, his majesty himself."[8] Rather than debate differing interpretations, Boyle appealed to the authority and prestige of the participants. In English science of the mid-seventeenth century, therefore, we have a further example of the fact that new truths, new procedures for determining truth, and new criteria for practitioners were all being established simultaneously.

The Newtonian Synthesis: The Copernican Revolution Completed

The Copernican revolution reached its high point with the work of the Englishman Isaac Newton (1643–1727), born one year almost to the day after Galileo died. Newton completed the new explanation for motion in the heavens and on earth that Copernicus's work had initiated and that Kepler, Galileo, and others had sought.

After a difficult childhood and an indifferent education, Newton entered Cambridge University as a student in 1661. Copernicanism and Cartesianism were being hotly debated, though not yet officially studied. Newton made use of Descartes's work in mathematics to develop his skill on his own, and by 1669 he had invented calculus. (He did not publish his work at the time, and another mathematician, Gottfried von Leibniz, later independently developed calculus and vied with Newton for credit.)

Newton was elected to a fellowship at Cambridge in 1667 and was made a professor of mathematics in 1669 at the recommendation of a retiring professor with whom he had shared his work on calculus. With less demanding teaching assignments, he was able to devote much of the next decade to work on optics—an important area of study for testing Descartes's corpuscular theory of matter.

In the 1680s Newton experienced a period of self-imposed isolation from other scientists after a particularly heated exchange with one colleague, provoked by Newton's difficult temperament. During this decade he returned to the study of alternative theories about matter. As a student at Cambridge he had been strongly influenced by the work of a group of Neo-Platonists who were critical of Cartesian dualism. This controversial theory posited God as a cause of all matter and motion but removed God, or any other unknown or unknowable force, as an explanation for the behavior of matter. The Neo-Platonists' concerns were both religious and scientific. As Newton says in some of his early writing while a student, "However we cast about we find almost no other reason for atheism than this [Cartesian] notion of bodies having . . . a complete, absolute and independent reality."[9]

Newton now read treatises in alchemy and Hermetic tracts and began to imagine explanations for the behavior of matter (such as for bits of cloth fluttered from a distance by static electricity) that Cartesian corpuscular theory could not readily explain. Precisely what the forces were that caused such behavior he was not sure, but his eclectic mind and his religious convictions enabled him to accept their existence.

It was this leap that allowed him to propose the existence of gravity—a mysterious force that accounts for the movements of heavenly bodies in the vacuum of space. Others had speculated about the existence of gravity; indeed, the concept of inertia as so far elaborated by Galileo, Descartes, and others suggested the need for the concept of gravity. Otherwise, if a planet were "pushed" (say, in Kepler's view, by the "motive force" of the sun), it would continue along that course forever unless "pulled back" by something else.

Newton's extraordinary contribution to a new mechanistic understanding of the universe was the mathematical computation of the laws of gravity and planetary motion, which he combined with a fully developed concept of inertia. In 1687 Newton published *Philosophia Naturalis Principia Mathematica* (*Mathematical Principles of Natural Philosophy;* usually called *Principia*). In this mathematical treatise—so intricate that it was baffling to laypeople, even those able to read Latin—Newton laid out his laws of motion and expressed them as mathematical theorems that can be used to test future observations of moving bodies. Then he demonstrated that these laws also apply to the solar system, confirming the data already gathered about the planets and even predicting the existence of an as yet unseen planet. His supreme achievement was his law of gravitation, with which he could predict the discovery of the invisible planet. This law states that every body, indeed every bit of matter, in the universe exerts over every other body an attractive force proportional to the product of their masses and inversely proportional to the square of the distance between them. Newton not only accounted for motion but definitively united heaven and earth in a single scheme and created a convincing picture of an orderly nature.

Neither Newton nor anyone else claimed that his theorems resolved all questions about motion and matter. Exactly what gravity is and how it operates were not clear, as they still are not. Newton's laws of motion are taught today because they still adequately account for most problems of motion. The fact that so fundamental a principle as gravity remains unexplained in no way diminishes Newton's achievement but is clear evidence of the nature of scientific understanding: science provides explanatory schemas that account for many—but not all—observed phenomena. No schema explains everything, and each schema contains open doorways that lead both to further discoveries and to blind alleys. Newton, for example, assumed that the forces that accounted for gravity would mysteriously work on metals so that, as alchemists predicted, they might "quickly pass into gold."[10]

After the publication of *Principia* Newton was more of a celebrated public figure than a practicing scientist. He helped lead resistance to James II's Catholicizing policies in the university, and he became the familiar of many other leading minds of his day, such as John Locke (see page 566). Newton became the president of the Royal Academy of Sciences in 1703 and was knighted in 1705, the first scientist to be so distinguished. By the end of his life universities in England were dominated by men who acclaimed and built on his work. The transformation of the institutional structure of science in England was complete.

Other Branches of Science   The innovations in astronomy that led to the new mechanistic view of the behavior of matter did not automatically spill over to other branches of science. In astronomy innovation came after the ancient and medieval inheritance had been fully assimilated and its errors disclosed. Other branches of science followed their own paths, though all were strongly influenced by the mechanistic world-view.

In chemistry the mechanistic assumption that all matter was composed of small, equivalent parts was crucial to understanding the properties and behaviors of compounds (combinations of elements). But knowledge of these small units of matter was not yet detailed enough to be of much use in advancing chemistry conceptually. Nevertheless, the flawed conceptual schema did not hold back all chemical discovery and development. Lack of understanding of gases, and of the specific elements in their makeup, for example, did not prevent the development and improvement of gunpowder. Indeed, unlike the innovations in astronomy, eventual conceptual innovation in chemistry and biology owed a great deal to the results of plodding experiment and the slow accumulation of data.

A conceptual leap forward was made in biology in the sixteenth and seventeenth centuries. Because biological knowledge was mostly a byproduct of the practice of medicine, biological studies remained very practical and experimental. The recent discovery of *On Anatomical Procedures*, a treatise by the ancient physician Galen, encouraged dissection and other practical research. Andreas Vesalius (1514–1564), in particular, made important advances by following Galen's exhortation to anatomical research. Born in Brussels, Vesalius studied at the nearby University of Louvain and then at Padua, where he was appointed professor of surgery. He ended his career as physician to Emperor Charles V and his son, Philip II of Spain. In his teaching at Padua Vesalius acted on the newly recovered Galenic teachings by doing dissections himself rather than giving the work to technicians. In 1543 he published versions of his lectures as an illustrated compendium of anatomy, *De Humani Corporis Fabrica* (*On the Fabric of the Human Body*).

The results of his dissections of human corpses, revealed in this work, demonstrated a number of errors in Galen's knowledge of human anatomy, much of which had been derived from dissection of animals. Neither Vesalius nor his immediate successors, however, questioned overall Galenic theory about the functioning of the human body, any more than Copernicus had utterly rejected Aristotelian physics.

The slow movement from new observation to changed explanation is clearly illustrated in the career of the Englishman William Harvey (1578–1657). Much like

Vesalius on Human Anatomy
The meticulous illustrations in Vesalius's work helped ensure its success. The medium of print was essential for accurate reproduction of scientific drawings. Note also the way the human body, in this drawing of musculature, is depicted as dominating the landscape. (Courtesy, Dover Publications)

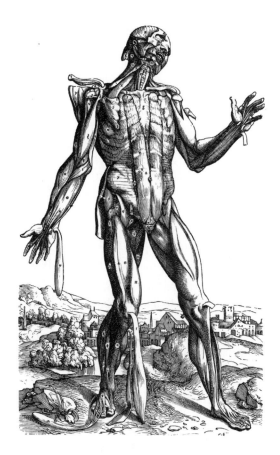

Vesalius, Harvey was educated first in his own land and then at Padua, where he benefited from the tradition of anatomical research. He also had a career as a practicing physician in London and at the courts of James I and Charles I.

Harvey postulated the circulation of the blood—postulated rather than discovered, because owing to the technology of the day, he could not observe the tiny capillaries where the movement of arterial blood into the veins occurs. After conducting vivisectional experiments on animals that revealed the actual functioning of the heart and lungs, he reasoned that circulation must occur. He carefully described his experiments and his conclusions in *Exercitatio Anatomica de Motu Cordis et Sanguinis in Animalibus* (1628), usually shortened to *De Motu Cordis* (*On the Motion of the Heart*).

Harvey's work challenged Galenic anatomy and, like Copernicus's discoveries, created new burdens of explanation. According to Galenic theory, the heart and lungs helped each other to function. The heart sent nourishment to the lungs through the pulmonary artery, and the lungs provided raw material for the "vital spirit," which the heart gave to the blood to sustain life. The lungs also helped the heart sustain its "heat." This heat was understood to be an innate property of organs, just as "heaviness," in traditional physics, had been considered an innate property of earthbound objects.

From his observations Harvey came to think of the heart in terms consonant with the new mechanistic notions about nature: as a pump to circulate the blood. But he adjusted, rather than abandoned, Galenic theories concerning "heat" and "vital spirit." The lungs had been thought to "ventilate" the heart by providing air to maintain "heat," just as a bellows aerates a fire. In light of his discovery of the pulmonary transit (that all of the blood is pumped through the lungs and back through the heart), Harvey suggested instead that the lungs carried out some of these functions for the blood, helping it to concoct the "vital spirit." Only in this sense did he think of the heart as a machine, circulating this life-giving material throughout the body.

Harvey's explanation of bodily functions in light of his new knowledge did not constitute a rupture with Galenic tradition. But by the end of his life Harvey's own adjustments of Galenic theory were suggesting new conceptual possibilities. His work inspired additional research in physiology, chemistry, and physics. Robert Boyle's efforts to understand vacuums can be traced in part to questions Harvey raised about the function of the lungs and the properties of air.

THE NEW SCIENCE: SOCIETY, POLITICS, AND RELIGION

Scientists wrestled with questions about God and human capacity every bit as intently as they attempted to find new explanations for the behavior of matter and the motion of the heavens. Eventually the profound implications of the new scientific world-view would affect thought and behavior throughout society. Once people no longer thought of the universe in hierarchical terms, they could question the hierarchical organization of society. Once people questioned the authority of traditional knowledge about the universe, the way was clear for them to begin to question traditional views of the state, the social order, and even the divine order. Such profound changes of perspective took hold very gradually, however. The advances in science did lead to revolutionary cultural change, but until the end of the seventeenth century traditional institutions and ideologies limited its extent.

The Beginnings of Scientific Professionalism

Institutions both old and new supported the new science developing in the sixteenth and seventeenth centuries. Some universities were the setting for scientific breakthroughs, but court patronage, a well-established institution, also sponsored scientific activity. The development of the Accadèmia dei Lincei, to which Galileo belonged, and other academies was a step toward modern professional societies of scholars, although these new organizations depended on patronage.

In England and France, royally sponsored scientific societies were founded in the third quarter of the century. The Royal Society of London, inaugurated in 1660, received royal recognition but no money and remained an informal institution sponsoring amateur scientific interests as well as specialized independent research. The Académie Royale des Sciences in France, established in 1666 by Jean-Baptiste Colbert, Louis XIV's minister of finance (see page 512), sponsored research and supported chosen scientists with pensions. These associations were extensions to science of traditional kinds of royal recognition and patronage. Thus the French Académie was well funded but tightly controlled by the government of Louis XIV, and the Royal Society of London received little of Charles II's scarce resources or precious political capital. Like the earlier academies, these royally sponsored societies published their fellows' work; in England the *Philosophical Transactions of the Royal Society* began in 1665.

The practice of seventeenth-century science took place in so many diverse institutions—academies, universities, royal courts—that neither *science* nor *scientist* was rigorously defined. Science as a discipline was not yet detached from broad metaphysical questions. Boyle, Newton, Pascal, and Descartes all concerned themselves with questions of religion, and all thought of themselves not as scientists but, like their medieval forebears, as natural philosophers. These natural philosophers were still members of an elite who met in aristocratic salons to discuss literature, politics, or science with equal ease and interest. Nevertheless, the beginnings of a narrowing of the practice of science to a tightly defined, truly professional community are evident in these institutions.

The importance of court life and patronage to the new science had at first enabled women to be actively involved. Women ran important salons in France; aristocratic women everywhere were indispensable sources of patronage for scientists; and women themselves were scientists, combining, as did men, science with other pursuits. Noblewomen and daughters of gentry families had access to education in their homes, and a number of such women were active scientists—astronomers, mathematicians, and botanists. The astronomer Maria Cunitz (1610–1664), from Silesia (a Habsburg-controlled province, now in modern Poland), learned six languages with the encouragement of her father, who was a medical doctor. Later she published a useful simplification of some of Kepler's mathematical calculations. Women from artisanal families might also receive useful training at home. Such was the case of the German entomologist Maria Sibylla Merian (1647–1717). Merian learned the techniques of illustration in the workshop of her father, an artist in Frankfurt. She later used her artistic training and her refined powers of observation to study and record the features and behaviors of insects and plants in the New World.

Margaret Cavendish, duchess of Newcastle (1623–1673), wrote several major philosophical works, including *Grounds of Natural Philosophy* (1668). She was a Cartesian but was influenced by Neo-Platonism. She believed matter to have "intelligence" and thus disagreed with Cartesian dualism, but she criticized fellow English philosophers on the grounds that, like Descartes, she distrusted sensory knowledge as a guide to philosophy.

Women were routinely accepted as members of Italian academies, but they were excluded from formal membership in the academies in London and Paris, although they could use the academies' facilities and received prizes from the societies for their work. One reason that women were barred was the purse: the amount of available patronage was limited, and coveted positions automatically went to men. Moreover, the hierarchical distinction signified by gender made the exclusion of women a useful way to define the academies as special and privileged.

Margaret Cavendish was aware of the degree to which her participation in scientific life depended on informal networks and on the resources available to her because of her aristocratic status. Women scientists from more modest backgrounds, without Cavendish's resources, had to fight for the right to employment as public institutions gained importance as settings for the pursuit of science. The German astronomer Maria Winkelman (1670–1720), for example, tried to succeed her late husband in an official position in the Berlin Academy of Sciences in 1710, after working as his unofficial partner during his tenure as astronomer to the academy. The academy withheld an official position from Winkelman after her husband's death, however, despite her experience and accomplishments (she had discovered a new comet, for example, in 1702). The secretary of the academy stated: "That she be kept on in an official capacity to work on the calendar or to continue with observations simply will not do. Already during her husband's lifetime the society was burdened with ridicule because its calendar was prepared by a woman. If she were now to be kept on in such a capacity, mouths would gape even wider."[11]

Winkelman worked in private observatories but was able to return to the Berlin Academy only as the unofficial assistant to her own son, whose training she herself had supervised. As the new science gained in prestige, women scientists often found themselves marginalized.

The New Science, the State, and the Church

The new natural philosophy had implications for traditional notions about the state. The new world-view that all matter was identical and answerable to discernible natural laws gradually undermined political systems resting on a belief in the inherent inequality of persons and on royal prerogative. By the middle of the eighteenth century a fully formed alternative political philosophy would argue for more "rational" government in keeping with the rational, natural order of things. But the change came slowly, and while it was coming, traditional rulers found much to admire and utilize in the new science.

Technological possibilities of the new science were very attractive to governments. Experiments with vacuum pumps had important applications in the mining industry, for example. Governments also sponsored pure, and not only applied, scientific research. A French naval expedition to Cayenne, in French Guiana, led to refinements of the pendulum clock but had as its main purpose progressive observations of the sun to permit the calculation of the earth's distance from the sun. Members of the elite saw the opportunity not only for practical advances but also for prestige and, most important, confirmation of the orderliness of nature. It is hard to overestimate the psychological impact and intellectual power of this fundamental tenet of the new science—namely, that nature is an inanimate machine that reflects God's design not through its purposes but simply by its orderliness. Thus, in the short run, the new science supported a vision of order that was very pleasing even to a monarch of absolutist pretensions such as Louis XIV.

As we have seen, scientists themselves flourished in close relationships with princes and actively sought their patronage for its many benefits. Christiaan Huygens left the Netherlands to accept the patronage of Louis XIV, producing in France some of his most important work in optics and mechanics. Huygens had learned from his father, secretary to the princes of Orange in the Netherlands, that a princely court not only offered steady support but also opened doors to other royal academies and salons. Huygens published some of his early research through the Royal Society in London, thanks to contacts his father had established. When Galileo left his position at Padua for the Medici court in Florence, he wrote to a friend, "It is not possible to receive a salary from a Republic [Venice] . . . without serving the public, because to get something from the public one must satisfy it and not just one particular person; . . . no one can exempt me from the burden while leaving me the income; and in sum I cannot hope for such a benefit from anyone but an absolute prince."[12]

Scientists and scientific thought also remained closely tied to religion in both practical and institutional ways during the seventeenth century. Both religion and the Catholic Church as an institution were involved with scientific advancement from the time of Copernicus. Copernicus himself was a cleric, as were many philosophers and scientists after him. This is not surprising, for most research in the sciences to this point had occurred within universities sponsored and staffed by members of religious orders, who had the education, time, and resources necessary for scientific investigation. Some of Descartes's closest collaborators were clerics, as were certain of Galileo's aristocratic patrons and his own protégés. Moreover, religious and metaphysical concerns were central to the work of virtually every scientist. The entire Cartesian edifice of reasoning about the world, for example, was grounded in Descartes's certainty about God. Copernicus, Kepler, Newton, and others perceived God's purpose in the mathematical regularity of nature.

The notion that religion was the opponent of science in this era is a result of Galileo's trial, and represents a distortion even of that event. It is true that the new astronomy and mechanics challenged traditional interpretations of Scripture, as well as the fundamentals of physics and metaphysics that were taught in universities. Thus, in its sponsorship of universities, the church was literally invested in the old view, even though individual clerics investigated and taught Copernican ideas.

The rigid response of the church hierarchy to Galileo is partially explained by the aftermath of the Protestant Reformation, which, in the minds of many churchmen—including Galileo's accusers and some of his judges—had demonstrated the need for a firm response to any challenge to the church's authority. Galileo seemed particularly threatening because he was well known, wrote for a wide audience, and, like the

Science and Royal Power   *This painting memorializes the founding of the French Académie des Sciences and the building of the royal observatory in Paris. Louis himself is at the center of the painting, reflecting the symbolic importance of royal power in the sponsorship of science.*   (Château de Versailles/Laurie Platt Winfrey, Inc.)

Protestants, presumed to interpret the Scriptures. Galileo may well have escaped punishment entirely had it not been for the political predicament faced by the pope coincident with his trial, however.

The condemnation of Galileo shocked many clerics, including the three who had voted for leniency at his trial. Clerics who were also scientists continued to study and teach the new science where and when they could. Copernicanism was taught by Catholic missionaries abroad. To be sure, Galileo's trial did have a chilling effect on scientific investigation in most Catholic regions of Europe. Investigators could and did continue their research, but many could publish results only by smuggling manuscripts to Protestant lands. Many of the most important empirical and theoretical innovations in science occurred in Protestant regions after the middle of the seventeenth century.

Protestant leaders, however, were also not initially receptive to Copernican ideas because they defied scriptural authority as well as common sense. In 1549 one of Martin Luther's associates wrote: "The eyes are witnesses that the heavens revolve in the space of twenty-four hours. But certain men, either from love of novelty or to make a display of ingenuity, have concluded that the earth moves. . . . Now it is want of honesty and decency to assert such notions publicly and the example is pernicious. It is part of a good mind to accept the truth as revealed by God and to acquiesce in it."[13]

Protestant thinkers were also as troubled as Catholics by the metaphysical dilemmas that the new theories seemed to raise. In 1611, one year after Galileo's *Starry Messenger* appeared, the English poet John Donne (1573–1631) reflected on the confusion that now reigned in human affairs, with the heavenly hierarchy dismantled:

> [The] new Philosophy calls all in doubt,
> The Element of fire is quite put out;
> The Sun is lost, and th'earth, and no man's wit
> Can well direct him where to look for it.
> . . . .
> Tis all in pieces, all coherence gone;
> All just supply, and all Relation:
> Prince, Subject, Father, Son, are things forgot,
> For every man alone thinks he hath got
> To be a Phoenix, and that then can be
> None of that kinde, of which he is, but he.[14]

The challenge of accounting in religious terms for the ideas of Copernicus and Descartes became more urgent for Protestants as the ideas acquired an anti-Catholic status after the trial of Galileo in 1633 and as they became common scientific currency by about 1640. A religious certainty about divine force that could account for the motion of bodies in a vacuum enabled Newton to develop his theories on motion and gravity. In short, religion did not merely remain in the scientists' panoply of explanations; it remained a fundamental building block of scientific thought and central to most scientists' lives, whether they were Catholic or Protestant.

The New Science and Human Affairs at the End of the Seventeenth Century

Traditional institutions and ideologies checked the potential effects of the new science for a time, but by the middle of the seventeenth century political theory was beginning to reflect the impact of the mechanistic world-view. Political philosophers began to doubt that either the world or human society was an organic whole in which each part was distinguished in nature and function from the rest. Thomas Hobbes, John Locke, and others recast the bonds that link citizens to one another and to their rulers.

Because of the political turmoil in England, Thomas Hobbes (1588–1679) spent much of his productive life on the Continent. After the beginnings of the parliamentary rebellion he joined a group of royalist émigrés in France. He met Galileo and lived for extended periods in Paris, in contact with the circle of French thinkers that included Descartes. Like Descartes, he theorized about the nature and behavior of matter and published a treatise on his views in 1655.

Hobbes is best known today for *Leviathan* (1651), his treatise on political philosophy. *Leviathan* applies to the world of human beings Hobbes's mostly Cartesian view of nature as composed of "self-motivated," atomlike structures. Hobbes viewed people as mechanistically as he viewed the rest of nature. In his view, people are made up of appetites of various sorts—the same kind of innate forces that drive all matter. The ideal state, he concluded, is one in which a strong sovereign controls the disorder that inevitably arises from the clash of desires. Unlike medieval philosophers, Hobbes did not draw analogies between the state and the human body (the king as head, judges and magistrates as arms, and so forth). Instead, he compared the state to a machine that "ran" by means of laws and was kept in good working order by a skilled technician—the ruler.

Hobbes's pessimism about human behavior and his insistence on the need for restraint imposed from above reflect, as does the work of Descartes, a concern for order in the wake of political turmoil. This concern was one reason he was welcomed into the community of French philosophers, who were naturally comfortable with royalty as a powerful guarantor of order. But Hobbes's work, like theirs, was a radical departure because it envisioned citizens as potentially equal and constrained neither by morality nor by natural obedience to authority.

Another Englishman, John Locke (1632–1704), offered an entirely different vision of natural equality among people and, consequently, of social order. Locke's major works, *Essay on Human Understanding* (1690) and *Two Treatises of Government* (1690), reflect the experimentalism of Robert Boyle, the systematizing rationality of Descartes, and other strands of the new scientific thought. In his *Essay* Locke provides a view of human knowledge more pragmatic and utilitarian than the rigorous mathematical model of certainty used by many other philosophers. He argues that human knowledge is largely the product of experience. He agrees with Descartes that reason orders and explains human experience, but unlike Descartes, he doubts that human reason had unlimited potential to comprehend the universe. Locke, however, offered a more optimistic vision of the possible uses of reason. Whereas Descartes was interested in mentally ordering and understanding the world, Locke was interested in actually functioning *in* the world.

Locke's treatises on government reflect his notion of knowledge based on experience, as well as his particular experiences as a member of elite circles following the Restoration in England. Trained in medicine, he served as personal physician and general political assistant to one of the members of Parliament most opposed to Charles II's pretensions to absolutist government. When James II acceded to the throne in 1685, Locke remained in the Netherlands, where he had fled to avoid prosecution for treason. He became an adviser to William of Orange and returned to England with William and Mary in 1688. Locke's view of the principles of good government came to reflect the pro-parliamentary stance of his political milieu.

Unlike Hobbes, Locke argued that people are capable of self-restraint and mutual respect in their pursuit of self-interest. The state arises, he believed, from a contract that individuals freely enter into to protect themselves, their property, and their happiness from possible aggression by others. They can invest the executive and legislative authority to carry out this protection in monarchy or any other governing institution, though Locke believed that the English Parliament was the best available model. Because sovereignty resides with the people who enter into the contract, rebellion against the abuse of power is justified. At the core of Locke's schema is thus a revolutionary vision of political society based on human rights.

Locke's experience as an English gentleman is apparent in his emphasis on private property, which he considered a fundamental human right. Nature, he believed, cannot benefit humankind unless it is worked by human hands, as on a farm, for example. Private ownership of property guarantees its productivity and entitles the owner to participate in Locke's imagined contract. Indeed, Locke's political vision is unequivocal, and unbending, on the nature of property. Locke even found a justification for slavery. He also did not consider women to be political beings in the same way as men. The family, he felt, is a separate domain from the state, not bound by the same contractual obligations.

Locke and many other seventeenth-century thinkers were unable to imagine a new physical or political reality without invoking a notion of gender as a "natural" principle of order and hierarchy. Although Margaret Cavendish (see page 562) and other women disputed the validity of such gender distinctions, men frequently used them. Locke's use of gender as an arbitrary organizing principle gave his bold new vision of rights for certain men a claim to being "natural." The use of gender-specific vocabulary to describe nature itself had the effect of making the new objective attitude toward the world seem "natural." Works by seventeenth-century scientists are filled with references to nature as a woman who must be "conquered," "subdued," or "penetrated."

Traditional gender distinctions limited and reinforced most facets of political thought, but in other areas the fact of uncertainty and the need for tolerance were embraced. Another of Locke's influential works was the impassioned *Letter on Toleration* (1689). In it he argues that religious belief is fundamentally private and that

IMPORTANT EVENTS

1543 Copernicus, *De Revolutionibus Orbium Caelestium*; Vesalius, *On the Fabric of the Human Body*

1576 Construction of Brahe's observatory begins

1603 Accadèmia dei Lincei founded in Rome

1609 Kepler's third law of motion

1610 Galileo, *The Starry Messenger*

1620 Bacon, *Novum Organum*

1628 Harvey, *On the Motion of the Heart*

1632 Galileo, *Dialogue on the Two Chief Systems of the World*

1633 Galileo condemned and sentenced to house arrest

1637 Descartes, *Discourse on Method*

1651 Hobbes, *Leviathan*

1660 Boyle, *New Experiments Physico-Mechanical*
Royal Society of London founded

1666 Académie Royale des Sciences founded in France

1686 Fontenelle, *Conversations on the Plurality of Worlds*

1687 Newton, *Principia* (*Mathematical Principles of Natural Philosophy*)

1690 Locke, *Two Treatises of Government and Essay on Human Understanding*

1702 Bayle, *Historical and Critical Dictionary*

only the most basic Christian principles need be accepted by everyone. Others went further than Locke by entirely removing traditional religion as necessary to morality and public order. Fostering this climate of religious skepticism were religious pluralism in England and the self-defeating religious intolerance of Louis XIV's persecution of Protestants.

Pierre Bayle (1647–1706), a Frenchman of Protestant origins, argued that morality can be wholly detached from traditional religion. Indeed, Bayle concluded, one need hardly be a Christian to be a moral being. Bayle cited as an example of morality the philosopher Baruch Spinoza (1632–1677), a Dutch Jew who had been cast out of his local synagogue for supposed atheism. Even so, Spinoza believed the state to have a moral purpose and human happiness to have spiritual roots.

Bayle's skepticism toward traditional knowledge was more wide-ranging than his views on religion. His best-known work, *Dictionnaire historique et critique* (*Historical and Critical Dictionary,* 1702), was a compendium of observations about and criticisms of virtually every thinker whose works were known at the time, including such recent and lionized figures as Descartes and Newton. Bayle was the first systematic skeptic, and he relentlessly exposed errors and shortcomings in all received knowledge. His works were very popular with elite lay readers.

Bayle's countryman Bernard de Fontenelle (1657–1757), secretary to the Académie des Sciences from 1699 to 1741, was the greatest popularizer of the new science of his time. His *Entretiens sur la Pluralités des Mondes* (*Conversations on the Plurality of Worlds,* 1686) was, as the title implies, an informally presented description of the infinite universe of matter. A great success, it went through numerous editions and translations. As secretary to the Académie, Fontenelle continued his work as popularizer by publishing descriptions of the work of the Académie's scientists. At his death (at age 99) in 1757, it was said that "the Philosophic spirit, today so much in evidence, owes its beginnings to Monsieur de Fontenelle."[15]

NOTES

1. Quoted in *Encyclopaedia Britannica,* 15th ed., vol. 9, p. 135.

2. Quoted in Thomas S. Kuhn, *The Copernican Revolution* (Cambridge, Mass.: Harvard University Press, 1985), p. 131.

3. Quoted in Margaret C. Jacob, *The Cultural Meaning of the Scientific Revolution* (Philadelphia: Temple University Press, 1988), p. 18.

4. Quoted ibid., p. 33.

5. Quoted in Alan G. R. Smith, *Science and Society in the Sixteenth and Seventeenth Centuries* (New York: Science History Publications, 1972), p. 72.

6. Quoted in Jacob, p. 32 (emphasis added).

7. Quoted in Bruce T. Moran, ed., *Patronage and Institutions: Science, Technology and Medicine at the European Court* (Rochester, N.Y.: Boyden Press, 1991), p. 43.

8. Quoted in Steven Shapin, *A Social History of Truth* (Chicago: University of Chicago Press, 1994), p. 298.

9. Quoted in Jacob, p. 89.

10. Quoted ibid., p. 25.

11. Quoted in Londa Schiebinger, *The Mind Has No Sex?* (Cambridge, Mass.: Harvard University Press, 1989), p. 92.

12. Quoted in Richard S. Westfall, "Science and Patronage," *ISIS* 76 (1985): 16.

13. Quoted in Kuhn, p. 191.

14. *Complete Poetry and Selected Prose of John Donne,* ed. John Hayward (Bloomsbury, England: Nonesuch Press, 1929), p. 365, quoted in Kuhn, p. 194.

15. Quoted in Paul Edwards, ed., *The Encyclopedia of Philosophy,* vol. 3 (New York: Macmillan, 1967), p. 209.

SUGGESTED READING

Biagioli, Mario. *Galileo, Courtier.* 1993. A study that stresses the power of patronage relations to shape scientific process.

Dear, Peter. *Revolutionizing the Sciences: European Knowledge and Its Ambitions, 1500–1700.* 2001. An excellent general overview of the era of the Scientific Revolution.

Kuhn, Thomas. *The Copernican Revolution.* 1985. A classic treatment of the revolution in astronomy that lucidly explains the Aristotelian world-view; to understand the Copernican revolution, start here.

Schiebinger, Londa. *The Mind Has No Sex?* 1989. An examination of the participation of women in the practice of science and an explanation of how science began to reflect the exclusion of women in its values and objects of study—above all, in its claims about scientific "facts" about women themselves.

Shapin, Steven, and Simon Schaffer. *Leviathan and the Air-Pump.* 1985. One of the most important studies of seventeenth-century science; traces the conflict between Cartesian science, as represented by Hobbes, and experimental science, in the work of Boyle; shows the relationship of Hobbes and Boyle to their respective contexts and the widespread philosophical implications of each school of thought.

Westfall, Richard S. *Never at Rest: A Biography of Isaac Newton.* 1993. A biography by one of the best-known historians of science.

18

Europe on the Threshold of Modernity, ca. 1715–1789

(G. Dagli Orti/The Art Archive)

Drinks are set before these gentlemen on their table, but something tells us this is more than just a social gathering. The men are absorbed in intense conversation. One man raises his hand, perhaps to emphasize his point, while another listens with a skeptical smirk. Several others eagerly follow their conversation. Other animated discussions go on at nearby tables. The setting depicted here was altogether new in the eighteenth century, when this picture was made, and a caption that originally accompanied the illustration speaks to its importance: "Establishment of the new philosophy: our cradle was the café."

Cafés were one of the new settings in which literate elites could discuss the "new philosophy"—what we now call Enlightenment philosophy—and could explore its implications for social and political life. Men gathered in clubs and cafés; women directed private gatherings known as salons. Both men and women read more widely than ever before. The Enlightenment was the extension into political and social thought of the intellectual revolution that had already occurred in the physical sciences. Hence it constituted a revolution in political philosophy, but it was also much more. The era witnessed the emergence of an informed body of public opinion, critical of the prevailing political system. The relationship between governments and the governed had begun to change: subjects of monarchs were becoming citizens of nations.

The notion that human beings, using their rational faculties, could not only understand nature but might also transform their societies was appealing to rulers as well, in part for the traditional reason—strengthening state power. Frederick the Great of Prussia, Catherine the Great of Russia, and other monarchs self-consciously tried to use Enlightenment precepts to guide their efforts at governing. They had mixed success because powerful interests opposed their efforts at reform and because, ultimately, their own hereditary and autocratic power was incompatible with Enlightenment perspectives.

Profound changes in economic and social life accompanied this revolution in intellectual and political spheres. Economic growth spurred population growth, which in turn stimulated industry and trade. The increasing economic and strategic importance of overseas colonies made them important focal points of international conflict. As the century closed, Europe was on the threshold of truly revolutionary changes in politics and production that had their roots in the intellectual, economic, and social ferment of eighteenth-century life.

THE ENLIGHTENMENT

The Enlightenment was an intellectual movement that applied to political and social thought the confidence in the intelligibility of natural law that Newton and other scientists had recently achieved. Following Descartes and Locke, Enlightenment thinkers believed that human beings could discern and work in concert with the laws of nature for the betterment of human life. Perhaps the most significant effect of this confidence was the questioning of traditional social and political bonds. A belief grew that society must be grounded on rational foundations to be determined by humans, not arbitrary foundations determined by tradition and justified by religious authority.

The Enlightenment was a social and cultural movement: Enlightenment thought was received and debated in the context of increasingly widespread publications and new opportunities for exchanging views in literary societies, salons, and cafés. This context shaped the potential radicalism of the Enlightenment by helping to ensure that informed public opinion would become a new force in political and cultural life. Given this broad base, Enlightenment thinking was certain to challenge the very foundations of social and political order.

Voltaire: The Quintessential Philosophe

A wide range of thinkers participated in the Enlightenment. In France they were known as *philosophes*, a term meaning not a formal philosopher but rather a thinker and critic. The most famous of the philosophes was Voltaire (1694–1778). A prolific writer, critic, and reformer, Voltaire was lionized by admirers throughout Europe, including several rulers. Born François-Marie Arouet to a middle-class family, he took the pen name Voltaire in 1718, after one of his early plays was a critical success. Like many philosophes, Voltaire moved in courtly circles but was often on its margins. His mockery of the regent for the young French king earned him a year's imprisonment in 1717, and an exchange of insults with a leading courtier some years later led to enforced exile in Great Britain for two years.

After returning from Britain, Voltaire published his first major philosophical work. *Lettres philosophiques* (*Philosophical Letters*, 1734) revealed the influence of his British sojourn and helped to popularize Newton's achievement. To confidence in the laws governing nature Voltaire added cautious confidence in humans' attempts to discern truth. From Locke's work (see pages 566–567) he was persuaded to trust human educability tempered by awareness of the finite nature of the human mind. These elements gave Voltaire's philosophy both its passionate conviction and its sensible practicality.

Voltaire portrayed Great Britain as a more rational society than France. He was particularly impressed with the relative religious and intellectual toleration evident across the Channel. The British government had a more workable set of institutions; the economy was less crippled by the remnants of feudal privilege, and education was not in the hands of the church. Voltaire was one of many French thinkers who singled out the Catholic Church as the archenemy of progressive thought. Philosophes constantly collided with the church's negative views of human nature and resented its control over most education and its still strong sway in political life. Typical of Voltaire's castigation of the church is his stinging satire of the clerics who condemned Galileo: "I desire that there be engraved on the door of your holy office: Here seven cardinals assisted by minor brethren had the master of thought of Italy thrown into prison at the age of seventy, made him fast on bread and water, because he instructed the human race."

After the publication of his audacious *Letters*, Voltaire was again forced into exile from Paris, and he resided for some years in the country home of a woman with whom he shared a remarkable intellectual and emotional relationship: Emilie, marquise du Châtelet (1706–1749). Châtelet was a mathematician and a scientist. She prepared a French translation of Newton's *Principia* while Voltaire worked at his accustomed variety of writing, which included a commentary on Newton's work. Because of Châtelet's tutelage, Voltaire became more knowledgeable about the sciences and more serious in his efforts to apply scientific rationality to human affairs. He was devastated by her sudden death in 1749.

Shortly afterward he accepted the invitation of the king of Prussia, Frederick II, to visit Berlin. His stay was stormy and brief because of disagreements with other court philosophers. He resided for a time in Geneva, until his criticisms of the city's moral codes forced yet another exile on him. He spent most of the last twenty years of his life at his estates on the Franco-Swiss border, where he could be relatively free from interference by any government. These were productive years. He produced his best-known satirical novelette, *Candide*, in 1758. It criticized aristocratic privilege and the power of clerics as well as the naiveté of philosophers who took "natural law" to mean that the world was already operating as it should.

Voltaire's belief that only by struggle are the accumulated habits of centuries overturned is also reflected in his political activity. He became involved in several celebrated legal cases in which individuals were pitted against the authority of the church, which was still backed by the authority of the state. In pursuit of justice in these cases and in relentless criticism of the church, Voltaire added a stream of straightforward political pamphlets to his literary output. He also worked closer to home, initiating agricultural reform on his estates and working to improve the status of peasants in the vicinity.

Voltaire died in Paris in May 1778, after a triumphal welcome for the staging of one of his plays. By then he was no longer leader of the Enlightenment in strictly intellectual terms. Thinkers and writers more radical than he had earned prominence during his long life and had dismissed some of his beliefs, such as the notion that a monarch could introduce reform. But Voltaire had provided a crucial stimulus to French thought with his *Philosophical Letters.* His importance lies also in his embodiment of the critical spirit of eighteenth-century rationalism: its confidence, its increasingly practical bent, its wit and sophistication. Until the end of his life, Voltaire remained a bridge between the increasingly diverse body of Enlightenment thought and the literate elite audience.

The Variety of Enlightenment Thought

Differences among philosophes grew as the century progressed. In the matter of religion, for example, there was virtual unanimity of opposition to the Catholic Church among French thinkers, but no unanimity about God. Voltaire was a theist—believing firmly in God, creator of the universe, but not a specifically Christian God. To some later thinkers, God was irrelevant—the creator of the world, but a world that ran continuously according to established laws. Some philosophes were atheists, arguing that a universe operating according to discoverable laws needs no higher purpose and no divine presence to explain, run, or justify its existence. In Protestant areas of Europe, in contrast to France, Enlightenment thought was often less hostile to Christianity.

Questions about social and political order, as well as about human rationality, also were pondered. Charles de Secondat (1689–1755), baron of Montesquieu, a French judge and legal philosopher, combined the belief that human institutions must be rational with Locke's assumption of human educability. Montesquieu's treatise *De L'Esprit des lois* (*The Spirit of the Laws,* 1748) was published in twenty-two printings within two years. In it Montesquieu maintained that laws were not meant to be arbitrary rules but derived naturally from human society: the more evolved a society was, the more liberal were its laws. This notion that progress is possible within society and government deflated Europeans' pretensions with regard to other societies, for a variety of laws could be equally "rational" given different conditions. Montesquieu is perhaps best known to Americans as the advocate of the separation of legislative, executive, and judicial powers that later became enshrined in the U.S. Constitution. To Montesquieu this scheme seemed to parallel in human government the balance of forces observable in nature; moreover, the arrangement seemed best to guarantee liberty.

Enlightenment philosophers also investigated the "laws" of economic life. In France economic thinkers known as *physiocrats* proposed ending "artificial" control over land use in order to free productive capacity and permit the flow of produce to market. Their target was traditional forms of land tenure, including collective control of village lands by peasants and seigneurial rights over land and labor by landlords. The freeing of restrictions on agriculture, manufacture, and trade was proposed by the Scotsman Adam Smith in his treatise *An Inquiry into the Nature and Causes of the Wealth of Nations* (1776).

Smith (1723–1790), a professor at the University of Glasgow, is best known in modern times as the originator of "laissez-faire" economics. *Laissez faire,* or "let it run on its own," assumes that an economy will regulate itself, without interference by government and, of more concern to Smith, without the monopolies and other economic privileges common in his day. Smith's schema for economic growth was not merely a rigid application of natural law to economics. His ideas grew out of an optimistic view of human nature and rationality that was heavily indebted to Locke. Humans, Smith believed, have drives and passions that they can direct and govern by means of reason and inherent mutual sympathy. Thus, Smith suggested, in seeking their own achievement and well-being, people are often "led by an invisible hand" simultaneously to benefit society as a whole.

Throughout the century, philosophers of various stripes disagreed about the nature and the limits of human reason. Smith's countryman and friend David Hume (1711–1776) was perhaps the most radical in his critique of the human capacity for knowing. He was the archskeptic, taking Locke's view of the limitations on pure reason to the point of doubting the efficacy of any sensory data. His major exposition of these views, *Essay Concerning Human Understanding* (1748), led to important innovations later in the century in the work of the German philosopher Immanuel Kant. At the time, though, Hume's arguments were almost contrary to the prevailing spirit that embraced empirical knowledge. Hume himself separated this work from his other efforts in moral, political, and economic philosophy, which were more in tune with contemporary views.

Mainstream confidence in empirical knowledge and in the intelligibility of the world is evident in the production of the *Encyclopédie (Encyclopedia).* This seventeen-volume compendium of knowledge, criticism, and philosophy was assembled by leading philosophes in France and published there between 1751 and 1765. The volumes were designed to contain state-of-the-art knowledge about arts, sciences, technology, and philosophy. The guiding philosophy of the project, set forth by its chief editor, Denis Diderot (1713–1784), was a belief in the advancement of human happiness through the advancement of knowledge. The *Encyclopedia* was a history of the march of knowledge as well as a compendium of known achievements. It was revolutionary in that it not only intrigued and inspired intellectuals but also assisted thousands of government officials and professionals.

The encyclopedia project illustrates the political context of Enlightenment thought as well as its philosophical premises. The Catholic Church placed the work on the *Index of Prohibited Books,* and the French government might have barred its publication but for the fact that the official who would have made the decision was himself drawn to Enlightenment thinking. Many other officials, however, worked to suppress it. By the late 1750s, losses in wars overseas had made French officials highly sensitive to political challenges of any kind. Thus, like Voltaire, the major contributors to the *Encyclo-*

pedia were admired by certain segments of the elite and persecuted by others in their official functions.

The *Encyclopedia* reflects the complexities and limitations of Enlightenment thought on another score—the position of women. One might expect that the Enlightenment penchant for challenging received knowledge and traditional hierarchies would lead to revised views of women's abilities and rights. Indeed, some contributors blamed women's inequality with men not on inherent gender differences but rather on the customs and laws that had kept women from education and the development of their abilities. However, other contributors blamed women, and not society, for their plight, or they argued that women had talents that fit them only for the domestic sphere.

Both positions were represented in Enlightenment thought as a whole. The assumption of the natural equality of all people provided a powerful ground for arguing the equality of women with men. Some thinkers, such as Mary Astell (1666–1731), challenged Locke's separation of family life from the public world of free, contractual relationships. "If absolute authority be not necessary in a state," she reasoned, "how comes it to be so in a family?" Most such thinkers advocated increased education for women, if only to make them more fit to raise enlightened children. By 1800 the most radical thinkers were advocating full citizenship rights for women and equal rights to property, along with enhanced education.

The best-known proponent of those views was an Englishwoman, Mary Wollstonecraft (1759–1797), who wrote *A Vindication of the Rights of Woman* (1792). She assumed that most elite women would devote themselves to domestic duties, but she argued that without the responsibilities of citizenship, the leavening of education, and economic independence, women could be neither fully formed individuals nor worthy of their duties. Working women, she concluded, needed these rights simply to survive.

A more limited view of women's capacities was one element in the influential work of Jean-Jacques Rousseau (1712–1778). Like Locke, Rousseau could conceive of the free individual only as male, and he grounded his scorn of the old order and his novel political ideas in an arbitrary division of gender roles. Rousseau's view of women was linked to a critique of the artificiality of elite, cosmopolitan society in which Enlightenment thought was then flourishing, and in which aristocratic women were fully involved. Rousseau believed in the educability of men but was as concerned with issues of character and emotional life as with cognitive knowledge. Society—particularly the artificial courtly society—was corrupting, he believed. The true citizen had to cultivate virtue and sensibility, not manners, taste, or refinement. Rousseau designated women as guarantors of the "natural" virtues of children and as nurturers of the emotional life and character of men—but not as fully formed beings in their own right.

Rousseau's emphasis on the education and virtue of citizens was the underpinning of his larger political vision, set forth in *Du Contrat social* (*The Social Contract*, 1762). He imagined an egalitarian republic—possible particularly in small states such as his native Geneva—in which men would consent to be governed because the government would determine and act in accordance with the "general will" of the citizens. The "general will" was not majority opinion but rather what each citizen *would* want if he were fully informed and were acting in accordance with his highest nature. The "general will" became apparent whenever the citizens met as a body and made collective decisions, and it could be imposed on all inhabitants. This was a breathtaking vision of

An Enlightenment Thinker Argues for the Equality of Women

Mary Wollstonecraft was not alone among thinkers in the eighteenth century to argue for the equality of women with men. She was more radical than most, however, when she argued that even to be good wives and mothers, women must be economically independent. She was extending to women the connection between independence and virtue that John Locke and Jean-Jacques Rousseau, among others, applied to men. Locke's and Rousseau's assumptions that only men could exercise political rights or be independent beings won out in the short term but have been vigorously contested since Wollstonecraft's day.

It is vain to expect virtue from women till they are in some degree independent from men; nay, it is vain to expect that strength of natural affection which would make them good wives and mothers. Whilst they are absolutely dependent on their husbands, they will be cunning, mean and selfish. . . . Yet whilst wealth enervates men, and women live, as it were, by their personal charms, how can we expect them to discharge those ennobling duties which equally require exertion and self-denial? . . . The society is not properly organized which does not compel men and women to discharge their respective duties, by making it the only way to acquire that countenance [respect] from their fellow creatures which every human being wishes some way to attain. . . .

But to render [woman] really virtuous and useful, she must not . . . want, individually, the protection of civil laws; she must not be dependent on her husband's bounty for her subsistence during his life or support after his death—for how can a being be generous who has nothing of its own? Or virtuous, who is not free? . . .

Business of various kinds they might likewise pursue, if they were educated in a more orderly manner. . . . Women would not then marry for a support, as men accept of places under government, and neglect the implied duties; nor would an attempt to earn their own subsistence . . . sink them almost to the level of those poor abandoned creatures who live by prostitution.

Source: Moira Ferguson, ed., *First Feminists: British Women Writers, 1578–1799* (Bloomington: Indiana University Press, 1985), pp. 423–429.

The Growth of the Book Trade   *Book ownership dramatically increased in the eighteenth century, and a wide range of secular works—from racy novelettes to philosophical tracts—was available in print. In this rendering of a bookshop, shipments of books have arrived from around Europe. Notice the artist's optimism in the great variety of persons, from the peasant with a scythe to a white-robed cleric, who are drawn to the shop by "Minerva" (the Roman goddess of wisdom).*   (Musée des Beaux-Arts de Dijon)

direct democracy—but one with ominous possibilities, for Rousseau rejected the institutional checks on state authority proposed by Locke and Montesquieu.

Rousseau's emphasis on private emotional life anticipated the romanticism of the early nineteenth century. It also reflected Rousseau's own experience as the son of a humble family, always sensing himself an outcast in the brilliant world of Parisian salons. He had a love-hate relationship with this life, remaining attached to several aristocratic women patrons even as he decried their influence. His own personal life did not match his prescriptions for others. He completely neglected to give his four children the nurture and education that he argued were vital; indeed, he abandoned them all to a foundling home. He was nevertheless influential as a critic of an elite society still dominated by status, patronage, and privilege. Rousseau's work reflects to an extreme degree the tensions in Enlightenment thought generally: it was part of elite culture as well as its principal critic.

The Growth of Public Opinion   It is impossible to appreciate the significance of the Enlightenment without understanding the degree to which it was a part of public life. Most of the philosophes were of modest origin. They influenced the privileged elite of their day because of the social and political environment in which their ideas were elaborated. Indeed, the clearest distinguishing feature of the Enlightenment may be the creation of an informed body of public opinion that stood apart from court society.

Increased literacy and access to books and other printed materials are an important part of the story. Perhaps more important, the kinds of reading that people favored began to change. We know from inventories made of people's belongings at the time of their deaths (required for inheritance laws) that books in the homes of ordinary people were no longer just traditional works such as devotional literature. Ordinary people now read secular and contemporary philosophical works. As the availability of such works increased, reading itself evolved from a reverential encounter with old ideas to a critical encounter with new ideas. Solitary reading for reflection and pleasure became more widespread.

Habits of reading and responding to written material changed not only because of these increased opportunities to read but also because of changes in the social environment. In the eighteenth century, forerunners of the modern lending libraries made their debut. In Paris, for a fee, one could join a *salle de lecture* (literally, a "reading room") where the latest works were available to any member. Booksellers, whose numbers increased dramatically, found ways to meet readers' demands for inexpensive access to reading matter. One might pay for the right to read a book in the bookshop itself. In short, new venues encouraged people to see themselves not just as readers but as members of a reading public.

Among the most famous and most important of these venues were the Parisian salons, regular gatherings in private homes, where Voltaire and others read their works in progress aloud and discussed them. Several Parisian women—mostly wealthy, but of modest social status—invited courtiers, bureaucrats, and intellectuals to meet in their homes at regular times each week. The *salonnières* (salon leaders) themselves read widely in order to facilitate the exchange of ideas among their guests. This mediating function was crucial to the success of the salons. Manners and polite conversation had been a defining feature of aristocratic life since the seventeenth century, but they had largely been means of displaying status and safeguarding honor. The leadership of the salonnières and the protected environment they provided away from court life enabled a further evolution of "polite society" to occur: anyone with appropriate manners could participate in conversation as an equal. The assumption of equality in turn enabled conversation to turn away from maintaining the status quo to questioning it.

The influence of salons was extended by the wide correspondence networks the salonnières maintained. Perhaps the most famous salonnière in her day, Marie-Thérèse Geoffrin (1699–1777) corresponded with Catherine the Great, the reform-minded empress of Russia, as well as with philosophes outside Paris and with interested would-be members of her circle. The ambassador of Naples regularly attended her salon while in Paris and exchanged weekly letters with her when home in Italy. He reflected on the importance of salon leaders such as Geoffrin when he wrote from Naples lamenting, "[Our gatherings here] are getting farther away from the character and tone of those of France, despite all [our] efforts. . . . There is no way to make Naples resemble Paris unless we find a woman to guide us, organize us, *Geoffrinise* us."[1]

Various clubs, local academies, and learned and secret societies, such as Masonic lodges, copied some features of the salons of Paris. Hardly any municipality was without a private society that functioned both as a forum for political and philosophical discussion and as an elite social club. Here mingled doctors, lawyers, local officials—some of whom enjoyed the fruits of the political system in offices and patronage. In Scotland universities were flourishing centers of Enlightenment thought, but political clubs in Glasgow and Edinburgh enriched debate and the development of ideas.

Ideas circulated beyond the membership of the multitude of clubs by means of print. Newsletters reporting the goings-on at salons in Paris were produced by some participants. Regularly published periodicals in Great Britain, France, and Italy also served as important means for the dissemination of enlightened opinion in the form of reviews, essays, and published correspondence. Some of these journals had been in existence since the second half of the seventeenth century, when they had begun as a means to circulate the new scientific work. Now subscribers included Americans anxious to keep up with intellectual life in Europe. Europeans who could not afford the annual subscriptions could peruse the journals in the newly opened reading rooms and libraries. In addition to newsletters and journals, newspapers, which were regularly published even in small cities throughout western and central Europe, circulated ideas.

In all these arenas Enlightenment ideas encouraged, and lent legitimacy to, a type of far-reaching political debate that had never before existed, except possibly in England during the seventeenth century. The greatest impact of the Enlightenment, particularly in France, was not the creation of any specific program for political or social change. Rather its supreme legacy was an informed body of public opinion that could generate change.

Art in the Age of Reason

The Enlightenment reverberated throughout all aspects of cultural life. Just as the market for books and the reading public expanded, so did the audience for works of art in the growing leisured urban circles of Paris and other great cities. The modern cultured public—a public of concertgoers and art gallery enthusiasts—began to make its first appearance and constituted another arena in which public opinion was shaped. The brilliant and sophisticated courts around Europe continued to sponsor composers, musicians, and painters by providing both patronage and audiences. Yet some performances of concerts and operas began to take place in theaters and halls outside the courts in venues more accessible to the public.

Beginning in 1737 one section of the Louvre palace in Paris was devoted annually to public exhibitions of painting and sculpture (though by royally sponsored and approved artists). In both France and Britain, public discussion of art began to take place in published reviews and criticisms: the role of art critic was born. Works of art were also sold by public means, such as auctions. As works became more available, demand grew and production increased.

In subject matter and style these various art forms exhibited greater variety than works in preceding centuries had shown. We can nevertheless discern certain patterns and tendencies in both the content and the form of eighteenth-century European art. Late baroque painters contributed to an exploration of private life and emotion sometimes called the "cult of sensibility." Frequently they depicted private scenes of upper-class life, especially moments of intimate conversation or flirtation.

The cult of sensibility was fostered by literature as well. The private life of emotion was nurtured by increased literacy, greater access to books, and the need to retreat from the elaborate artifice of court life. The novel became an increasingly important genre as a means of exploring social problems and human relationships. In English literature the novels of Samuel Richardson (1689–1761)—*Pamela* (1740) and *Clarissa* (1747–1748)—explored personal psychology and passion. Other novelists, such as Daniel Defoe in *Robinson Crusoe* (1717), used realism for purposes of social commentary.

Rousseau followed Richardson's lead in structuring his own novels, *La Nouvelle Héloïse* (1761) and *Emile* (1762). The cult of sensibility was not mere entertainment; it also carried the political and philosophical message that honest emotion was a "natural" virtue and that courtly manners, by contrast, were irrational and degrading. The enormous popularity of Rousseau's novels, for example, came from the fact that their intense emotional appeal was simultaneously felt to be uplifting.

A revival of classical subjects and styles after the middle of the century evoked what were thought to be the pure and timeless values of classical heroes. This revival revealed the influence of Enlightenment thought because the artists assumed the educability of their audience by means of example. Classical revival architecture illustrated a belief in order, symmetry, and proportion. Americans are familiar with its evocations because it has been the architecture of their republic, but even churches were built in this style in eighteenth-century Europe. The classical movement in music reflected both the cult of sensibility and the classicizing styles in the visual arts. Embodied in the works of Aus-

The Moralizing Message of Neoclassical Art *The French painter Jacques-Louis David portrays the mourning of the Trojan hero Hector by his wife, Andromache. David was well known for depicting his subjects with simple gestures—such as the extended arm of Andromache here—that were intended to portray honest and sincere emotion.* (Private Collection/The Stapleton Collection/Bridgeman Art Library International)

trians Franz Josef Haydn (1732–1809) and Wolfgang Amadeus Mozart (1756–1791), this movement saw the clarification of musical structures, such as the modern sonata and symphony, and enabled melody to take center stage.

Another trend in art and literature was a fascination with nature and with the seemingly "natural" in human culture—less "developed" or more historically distant societies. One of the most popular printed works in the middle of the century was the alleged translation of the poems of Ossian, a third-century Scots Highland poet. Early English, German, Norse, and other folktales were also "discovered" (in some cases invented) and published, some in several editions during the century. Folk life, other cultures, and untamed nature itself thus began to be celebrated at the very time they were being more definitively conquered. Ossian, for example, was celebrated just as the Scottish Highlands were being punished and pacified by the English after the clans' support for a rival claimant to the English throne. Once purged of any threat, the exotic image of another culture (even the folk culture of one's own society) could be a spur to the imagination. Thus the remote became romantic, offering a sense of distance from which to measure one's own sophistication and superiority.

EUROPEAN STATES IN THE AGE OF ENLIGHTENMENT

Mindful of the lessons to be learned from the civil war in England and the achievements of Louis XIV, European rulers in the eighteenth century continued their efforts to govern with greater effectiveness. Some, like the rulers of Prussia and Russia, were encouraged in their efforts by Enlightenment ideas that stressed the need for reforms in law, economy, and government. In the main they, like Voltaire, believed that monarchs could be agents for change. In Austria significant reforms, including the abolition of serfdom, were enacted. The changes were uneven, however, and at times owed as much to traditional efforts at better government as to enlightened persuasion.

In all cases, rulers' efforts to govern more effectively meant continual readjustments in relationships with traditional elites. Whether or not elites had formal roles in the governing process by means of established institutions such as the English Parliament, royal governments everywhere depended on their participation. However limited their "enlightened" policies, monarchs were changing their views of themselves and their public images from diligent but self-aggrandizing absolutist to servant of the state. In this way, monarchs actually undermined their dynastic claims to rule by refounding their regimes on a utilitarian basis. The state was increasingly seen as separate from the ruler, with dramatic consequences for the future.

France During the Enlightenment   It is one of the seeming paradoxes of the era of the Enlightenment that critical thought about society and politics flourished in France, an autocratic state. Yet France was blessed with a well-educated elite, a tradition of scientific inquiry, and a legacy of cultured court life that, since the early days of Louis XIV, had become the model for all Europe (see pages 513–515). French was the international intellectual language, and France was the most fertile center of cultural life. Both Adam Smith and David Hume, for example, spent portions of their careers in Paris and were welcomed into Parisian salons. In fact, the French capital was an environment that encouraged debate and dissent precisely because of the juxtaposition of the new intellectual climate with the difficulties the French state was facing and the institutional rigidities of its political system. In France access to power was wholly through patronage and privilege, a system that excluded many talented and productive members of the elite.

The French state continued to embody fundamental contradictions. As under Louis XIV, the Crown sponsored scientific research, subsidized commerce and exploration, and tried to rationalize the royal administration. Royal administrators tried to chip away at the privileges, accrued since the Middle Ages, that hampered effective government—such as the exemption most nobles enjoyed from taxation. However, the Crown also continued to claim the right to govern autocratically, and the king was supported both ideologically and institutionally by the Catholic Church. A merchant in the bustling port of Bordeaux might be glad of the royal navy's protection of the colonies, and of the Crown's efforts to build better roads for the movement of goods within France. However, with his fellow Masons, he would fume when church officials publicly burned the works of Rousseau and be continually frustrated over his exclusion from any formal role in the political process.

The problems facing the French government were made worse by two circumstances: first, the strength of the privileged elites' defense of the old order, and second, mounting state debt from foreign wars that made fiscal reform increasingly urgent. Louis XIV was followed on the throne by his 5-year-old great-grandson, Louis XV (r. 1715–1774). During the regency early in his reign, the supreme law courts, the parlements, reclaimed the right of remonstrance—that is, the right to object to royal edicts and thus to exercise some control over the enactment of law. Throughout Louis XV's reign, his administration often locked horns with the parlements, particularly as royal ministers tried various expedients to cope with financial crises.

The power of the parlements came not only from their routine role in government but also from the fact that parlementaires were all legally noble and owned their offices just as a great nobleman owned his country estate. In addition, the parlements were the only institutions that could legitimately check royal power. As such, the parlements were often supported in their opposition to royal policies by the weight of public opinion. On the one hand, enlightened opinion believed in the rationality of doing away with privileges such as the ownership of offices. On the other hand, the role of consultative bodies and the separation of powers touted by Montesquieu, himself a parlementaire, were much prized. And even our Bordeaux merchant, who had little in common with privileged officeholders, might nevertheless see the parlementaires' resistance as his best protection from royal tyranny. The parlementaires, however, usually used their power for protecting the status quo.

Further hampering reform efforts was the character of the king himself. Louis XV displayed none of the kingly qualities of his great-grandfather. He was neither pleasant nor affable, and he was lazy. By the end of his reign, he was roundly despised. He did not give the "rationality" of royal government a good name. By the late 1760s the weight of government debt from foreign wars finally forced the king into action. He threw his support behind the reforming schemes of his chancellor, Nicolas de Maupeou, who dissolved the parlements early in 1771 and created new law courts whose judges would not enjoy independent power.

The Crown lost control of reform when Louis died soon after, in 1774. His 20-year-old grandson, Louis XVI, well-meaning but insecure, allowed the complete restoration of the parlements. Further reform efforts, sponsored by the king and several talented ministers, came to naught because of parlementary opposition. Not surprisingly, from about the middle of the century, there had been calls to revive the moribund Estates General, the representative assembly last convened in 1614, as well as for the establishment of new councils—local, decentralized representative assemblies. By the time an Estates General was finally called in the wake of further financial problems in 1788, the enlightened elites' habit of carrying on political analysis and criticism outside the actual corridors of power, as well as their accumulated mistrust of the Crown, had given rise to a volatile situation.

Monarchy and Constitutional Government in Great Britain After the deaths of William (d. 1702) and Mary (d. 1694), the British crown passed to Mary's sister, Anne (r. 1702–1714), and then to a collateral line descended from Elizabeth Stuart (d. 1662), sister of the beheaded Charles I. Elizabeth had married Frederick, elector of the Palatinate (and had reigned with him briefly in Bohemia at the outset of the Thirty Years' War; see page 496), and her descendants were Germans, now electors of Hanover. The new British sovereign in 1714, George I (r. 1714–1727), was both a foreigner and a man of mediocre abilities. Moreover, his claim to the throne was immediately contested by Catholic descendants of James II (see page 523), who attempted to depose him in 1715 and later his son, George II (r. 1727–1760), in 1745.

The 1745 attempt to depose the Hanoverian kings was more nearly successful. The son of the Stuart claimant to the throne, Charles (known in legend as Bonnie Prince Charlie), landed on the west coast of Scotland, with French assistance, and marched south into England. Most of the British army, and George II himself, was on the Continent, fighting in the War of the Austrian Succession (see page 593). Scotland had been formally united with England in 1707 (hence the term *Great Britain* after that time), and Charles found some support among Scots dissatisfied with the economic and political results of that union.

But the vast majority of Britons did not want the civil war that Charles's challenge inevitably meant, especially on behalf of a Catholic pretender who relied on support from Britain's great rival, France. Charles's army, made up mostly of poor Highland clansmen, was destroyed at the Battle of Culloden in April 1746 by regular army units returned from abroad. Charles fled back to France, and the British government used the failed uprising as justification for the brutal and forceful integration of the still-remote Highlands into the British state.

Traditional practices, from wearing tartans to playing bagpipes, were forbidden. Control of land was redistributed to break the social and economic bonds of clan society. Thousands of Highlanders died at the battle itself, in prisons or on deportation ships, or by deliberate extermination at the hands of British troops after the battle.

Despite this serious challenge to the new dynasty and the harsh response it occasioned, the British state, overall, enjoyed a period of relative stability as well as innovation in the eighteenth century. The events of the seventeenth century had reaffirmed both the need for a strong monarchy and the role of Parliament in defending elite interests. The power of Parliament had recently been reinforced by the Act of Settlement, by which the Protestant heir to Queen Anne had been chosen in 1701. By excluding the Catholic Stuarts from the throne and establishing the line of succession, this document reasserted that Parliament determined the legitimacy of the monarchy. In addition, the act claimed greater parliamentary authority over foreign and domestic policy in the wake of the bellicose William's rule (see page 534).

Noteworthy in the eighteenth century were the ways in which cooperation evolved between monarchy and Parliament as Parliament became a more sophisticated and secure institution. Political parties—that is, distinct groups within the elite favoring certain foreign and domestic policies—came into existence. Two groups, the Whigs and the Tories, had begun to form during the reign of Charles II (d. 1685). The Whigs (named derisively by their opponents with a Scottish term for horse thieves) had resisted Charles's pro-French policies and his efforts to tolerate Catholicism and had wholly opposed his brother and successor, James II. Initially, the Whigs favored an aggressive foreign policy against continental opponents, particularly France. The Tories (whose name was also a taunt, referring to Irish cattle rustlers) tended to be staunch Anglicans uninterested in Protestant anti-Catholic agitation. They leaned toward a conservative view of their own role, favoring isolationism in foreign affairs and deference toward monarchical authority. Whigs generally represented the interests of the great aristocrats or wealthy merchants or gentry. Tories more often represented the interests of provincial gentry and the traditional concerns of landholding and local administration.

The Whigs were the dominant influence in government through most of the century to 1770. William and Mary, as well as Queen Anne, favored Whig religious and foreign policy interests. The loyalty of many Tories was called into question by their support for a Stuart, not Hanoverian, succession at Anne's death in 1714. The long Whig dominance of government was also ensured by the talents of Robert Walpole, a member of Parliament who functioned virtually as a prime minister from 1722 to 1742.

Walpole (1676–1745) was from a minor gentry family and was brought into government in 1714 with other Whig ministers in George I's new regime. An extremely talented politician, he took advantage of the mistakes of other ministers over the years and, in 1722, became both the first lord of the treasury and chancellor of the exchequer. No post or title of "prime minister" yet existed, but the great contribution of Walpole's tenure was to create that office in fact, if not officially. He chose to maintain peace abroad when and where he could and thus presided over a period of recovery and relative prosperity that enhanced the stability of government.

Initially, Walpole was helped in his role as go-between for king and Parliament by George I's own limitations. The king rarely attended meetings of his own council of ministers and, in any case, was hampered by his limited command of English. Gradually, the Privy Council of the king became something resembling a modern cabinet dominated by a prime minister. By the end of the century the notions of "loyal opposition" to the Crown within Parliament and parliamentary responsibility for policy had taken root.

In some respects, the maturation of political life in Parliament resembled the lively political debates in the salons of Paris. In both cases, political life was being legitimized on a new basis. In England, however, that legitimation was enshrined in a legislative institution, which made it especially effective and resilient.

Parliament was not yet in any sense representative of the British population, however. Because of strict property qualifications, only about 200,000 adult men could vote. In addition, representation was very uneven, heavily favoring traditional landed wealth. Some constituencies with only a few dozen voters sent members to Parliament. Many of these "pocket boroughs" were under the control of (in the pockets of) powerful local families who could intimidate the local electorate, particularly in the absence of secret ballots.

Movements for reform of representation in Parliament began in the late 1760s as professionals, such as doctors and lawyers, with movable (as opposed to landed) property and merchants in booming but underrepresented cities began to demand the vote. As the burden of taxation grew—the result of the recently concluded Seven Years' War (discussed later in this chapter)—these groups felt increasingly deprived of representation. Indeed, many felt kinship and sympathy with the American colonists who opposed increased taxation by the British government on these same grounds and revolted in 1775.

However, the reform movement faltered over the issue of religion. In 1780 a tentative effort by Parliament to extend some civil rights to British Catholics provoked rioting in London (known as the Gordon Riots, after one of the leaders). The riots lasted for eight days and claimed three hundred lives. Pressure for parliamentary reform had been building as Britain met with reversals in its war against the American rebels, but this specter of a popular movement out of control temporarily ended the drive for reform by disenfranchised elites.

"Enlightened" Monarchy

Arbitrary monarchical power might seem antithetical to Enlightenment thought. After all, the Enlightenment stressed the reasonableness of human beings and their capacity to discern and act in accord with natural law. Yet monarchy seemed an ideal instrument of reform to Voltaire and to many of his contemporaries. The work of curtailing the influence of the church, reforming legal codes, and eliminating barriers to economic activity might be done more efficiently by a powerful monarch than by other available means. Historians have labeled a number of rulers of this era "enlightened despots" because of the arbitrary nature of their power and the enlightened or reformist uses to which they put it.

"Enlightened despotism" aptly describes certain developments in the Scandinavian kingdoms in the late eighteenth century. In Denmark the Crown had governed without significant challenge from the landholding nobility since the mid-seventeenth century. The nobility, however, like its counterparts in eastern Europe, had guaranteed its supremacy by means of ironclad domination of the peasantry. In 1784 a reform-minded group of nobles, led by the young crown prince Frederick (governing on behalf of his mentally ill father), began to apply Enlightenment remedies to the kingdom's economic problems. The reformers encouraged freer trade and sought, above all, to improve agriculture by elevating the status of the peasantry. With improved legal status and with land reform, which enabled some peasants to own the land they worked for the first time, agricultural productivity in Denmark rose dramatically. These reforms constitute some of the clearest achievements of any of the "enlightened" rulers.

In Sweden in 1772, Gustav III (r. 1771–1796) staged a coup with army support that overturned the dominance of the Swedish parliament, the Diet. In contrast to Denmark, Sweden had a relatively unbroken tradition of noble involvement in government, stemming in part from its marginal economy and the consequent interest of the nobility in participation in the Crown's aggressive foreign policy. Since Sweden's eclipse as a major power after the Great Northern War (see page 531), factions of the Diet, not unlike the rudimentary political parties in Great Britain, had fought over the reins of government. After reasserting his control, Gustav III began an ambitious program of reform of the government. Bureaucrats more loyal to parliamentary patrons than to the Crown were replaced, restrictions on trade in grain and other economic controls were liberalized, the legal system was rationalized, the death penalty was strictly limited, and legal torture was abolished.

Despite his abilities, Gustav III suffered the consequences of the contradictory position of advancing reform by autocratic means in a kingdom with a strong tradition of representative government. Gustav eventually tried to deflect the criticisms of the nobility by reviving grandiose—but completely untenable—schemes for the reconquest of Baltic territory. However, in 1796 he was mortally wounded by an assassin hired by disgruntled nobles.

Another claimant to the title "enlightened despot" was Frederick II of Prussia (r. 1740–1786), known as Frederick the Great. Much of the time, Frederick resided in his imperial electorate of Brandenburg, near its capital, Berlin. His scattered states, which he extended by seizing new lands, are referred to as Prussia rather than Brandenburg-Prussia because members of his family were now kings of Prussia thanks to their ambitions and the weakness of the Polish state, of which Prussia had once been a dependent duchy. In many ways, the Prussian state *was* its military victories, for Frederick's bold moves and the policies of his father, grandfather, and great-grandfather committed the state's resources to a military presence of dramatic proportions. Prussia was on the European stage at all only because of that driving commitment.

The institutions that constituted the state and linked the various provinces under one administration were dominated by the needs of the military. Frederick II's father, Frederick William (r. 1713–1740), had added an efficient provincial recruiting system to the state's central institutions, which he also further consolidated. But in many other respects, the Prussian state was in its infancy. There was no tradition of political participation—even by elites—and little chance of cultivating any. Nor was there any political or social room for maneuver at the lower part of the social scale. The rulers of Prussia had long ago acceded to the aristocracy's demand for tighter control over peasant labor on their own lands in return for their support of the monarchy. The rulers relied on the nobles for local administration and army commands. Thus the kinds of social, judicial, or political reforms that Frederick could hope to carry out without undermining his own power were starkly limited.

Frederick tried to modernize agricultural methods and simultaneously to improve the condition of the peasants, but he met stiff resistance from the noble landholders. He did succeed in abolishing serfdom in some regions. He tried to stimulate the economy by sponsoring state industries and trading monopolies, but too few resources and too little initiative from the tightly controlled merchant communities stymied his plans. Simplifying and codifying the inherited jumble of local laws was a goal of every ruler. A law code published in 1794, after Frederick's death, was partly the product of his efforts.

Frederick's views of the role of Enlightenment thought reflect the limitations of his situation. One doesn't have to lead a frontal assault on prejudices consecrated by time, he thought; instead, one must be tolerant of superstition because it will always have a hold on the masses. Perhaps his most distinctive "enlightened" characteristic was the seriousness with which he took his task as ruler. He was energetic and disciplined to a fault. In his book *Anti-Machiavel* (1741), he argued that a ruler has a moral obligation to work for the betterment of the state. He styled himself as the "first servant" or steward of the state. However superficial this claim may appear, Frederick compares favorably with Louis XV of France, who, having a far more wealthy and flexible society to work with, did much less.

Enlightenment and Tradition: The Case of Austria One of the most effective rulers of the eighteenth century was the Habsburg ruler Maria Theresa of Austria (r. 1740–1780). A devout Catholic, she was guided more by traditional concerns for effective rule and compassion for her subjects than by Enlightenment ideas. After surviving the near dismemberment of Austrian territories in the War of the Austrian Succession (see page 593), she embarked on an energetic program of reform to remedy the weaknesses in the state that the war had revealed. "Austria," it must be remembered, is a term of convenience; the state was a very medieval-looking hodgepodge that included present-day Austria, the kingdoms of Bohemia and Hungary, the Austrian Netherlands, and lands in northern Italy. In addition, since the sixteenth century a male member of the Habsburg family had almost always been elected emperor of the Holy Roman Empire.

Maria Theresa streamlined and centralized administration, finances, and defense, particularly in Bohemia and Austria, where she was able to exercise her authority relatively unchecked, compared with her other domains. Above all, she reformed the assessment and collection of taxes to tap the wealth of her subjects more effectively and thus better defend all her domains. She improved her subjects' access to justice and limited the exploitation of serfs by landlords. She made primary schooling universal and compulsory, in order better to train peasants for the army. Although the policy was far from fully implemented at the time of her death (only about half of Austrian children were in school, and far fewer in Hungary and elsewhere), hers was the first European state with so ambitious an education policy. Maria Theresa accomplished all of this without being particularly "enlightened" personally. For example, she had a traditional fear of freedom of the press and cherished orthodoxy in religious matters.

Maria Theresa's policies were implemented by a group of ministers, bureaucrats, and officers who shared her concern for effective government and defense, and who were well versed in "enlightened" ideas for reform. The diverse character of the Habsburg lands meant that some members of the governing elite came from the Netherlands and from Italy, where sympathy for the Enlightenment was well rooted by comparison with the relatively poorer and more rural society of the Austrian hinterland. Moreover, the language of the Habsburg court was French (Maria Theresa spoke it fluently); thus no amount of local censorship—which, in any case, Maria Theresa relaxed—could prevent the governing class from reading and absorbing Enlightenment philosophy in its original language.

Maria Theresa was followed on the throne by her two sons, Joseph II (r. 1780–1790) and Leopold II (r. 1790–1792). Each son counted himself a follower of the Enlightenment, and each, as was the family custom, served a period of "apprenticeship" governing

Habsburg territories where he could attempt to implement reform. After his mother's death, Joseph II carried out a variety of bold initiatives that she had not attempted, including freedom of the press, significant freedom of religion, and the abolition of serfdom in Habsburg lands. During his ten-year reign, the political climate in Vienna began to resemble that in Paris, London, and other capitals where political life was no longer confined to the royal court.

Like Frederick the Great, Joseph regarded himself as a servant of the state. Also like Frederick, he was limited in his reform program by the economic and social rigidities of the society he ruled. Austria had but a small middle class to insist on reform, and Joseph could not directly assault the privileges of great landholders, on whose wealth the state depended. In addition, Joseph was by temperament an inflexible autocrat, whose methods antagonized many of these powerful subjects. Joseph's policies provoked simmering opposition, even open revolt, and some of his reforms were repealed even before his death. His more able brother, Leopold, had implemented many reforms while ruling as grand duke in Tuscany (Italy) before assuming the throne in 1790. Much of his two-year reign was spent dexterously saving reforms enacted by his mother and brother in the face of mounting opposition.

Catherine the Great and the Empire of Russia
Another ruler with a claim to the title "enlightened despot" was Catherine, empress of Russia (r. 1762–1796). Catherine the Great, as she came to be called, was the true heir of Peter the Great in her abilities, policies, and ambitions. Her determination and political acumen were obvious early in her life at the Russian court, where she had been brought from her native Germany in 1745. Brutally treated by her husband, Tsar Peter III, Catherine engineered a coup in which he was killed, then ruled alone for more than thirty years.

Like any successful ruler of her age, Catherine counted territorial aggrandizement among her chief achievements. With regard to the major European powers, Russia tended to ally with Britain (with which it had important trading connections, including the provision of timber for British shipbuilding) and with Austria (against their common nemesis, Turkey), and against France, Poland, and Prussia. In 1768 Catherine initiated a war against the Turks from which Russia gained much of the Crimean coast. She also continued Peter's efforts to dominate the weakened Poland. She was aided in this goal by Frederick the Great, who proposed the deliberate partitioning of Poland to satisfy his own territorial ambitions as well as those of his competitors, Russia and Austria. In 1772 portions of Poland were gobbled up in the first of three successive "grabs" of territory. Warsaw eventually landed in Prussian hands, but Catherine gained all of Belarus, Ukraine, and modern Lithuania—which had constituted the duchy of Lithuania.

Nevertheless, Catherine counted herself a sincere follower of the Enlightenment. While young, she had received an education that bore the strong stamp of the Enlightenment. Like Frederick, she attempted to take an active role in the European intellectual community, corresponding with Voltaire over the course of many years and acting as patron to the encyclopedist Diderot. One of Catherine's boldest political moves was the secularization of church lands. Although Peter the Great had extended government control of the Russian Orthodox Church, he had not touched church lands. Catherine

Catherine the Great

Catherine was a German princess who had been brought to Russia to marry another German, Peter of Holstein-Gottorp, who was being groomed as heir to the Russian throne. Russia had crowned several monarchs of mixed Russian and German parentage since the time of Peter the Great's deliberate interest in and ties with other European states. (The Wernher Collection)

also licensed private publishing houses and permitted a burgeoning periodical press. The number of books published in Russia tripled during her reign. This enriched cultural life was one of the principal causes of the flowering of Russian literature that began in the early nineteenth century.

The stamp of the Enlightenment on Catherine's policies is also clearly visible in her attempts at legal reform. In 1767 she convened a legislative commission and provided it with a guiding document, the *Instruction,* which she had penned. The commission was remarkable because it included representatives of all classes, including peasants, and provided a place for the airing of general grievances. Catherine hoped for a general codification of law as well as reforms such as the abolition of torture and capital punishment—reforms that made the *Instruction* radical enough to be banned from publication in other countries. She did not propose changing the legal status of serfs, however, and class differences made the commission unworkable in the end. Most legal reforms were accomplished piecemeal and favored the interests of landed gentry.

Like the Austrian rulers, Catherine undertook far-reaching administrative reform to create more effective local units of government. Here again, political imperatives were fundamental, and reforms in local government strengthened the hand of the gentry. The legal subjection of peasants in serfdom was also extended as a matter of state policy to help win the allegiance of landholders in newly acquired areas—such as

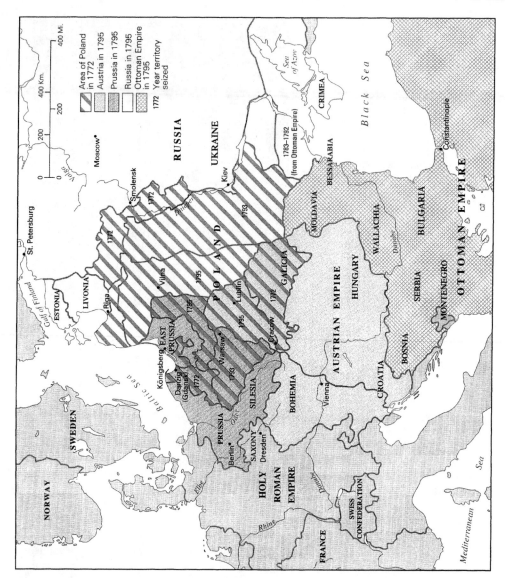

The Partition of Poland and the Expansion of Russia

Catherine the Great acquired present-day Lithuania, Belarus, and Ukraine, which had once constituted the duchy of Lithuania, part of the multi-ethnic Polish kingdom.

Ukrainian territory gained in the partition of Poland. Gentry in general and court favorites in particular, on whom the stability of her government depended, were rewarded with estates and serfs to work them.

In Russia, as in Prussia and Austria, oppression of the peasantry was perpetuated because the monarch wanted to ensure the allegiance of the elites who lived from the peasants' labor. Catherine particularly valued the cooperation of elites because the Russian state was in a formative stage in another sense as well. It was trying to incorporate new peoples, such as the Tatars in the Crimea, and to manage its relationships with border peoples such as the Cossacks. Catherine's reign was marked by one of the most massive and best-organized peasant rebellions of the century. Occurring in 1773, the rebellion expressed the grievances of the thousands of peasants who joined its ranks and called for the abolition of serfdom. The revolt took its name, however, from its Cossack leader, Emelian Pugachev (d. 1775), and reflected the dissatisfaction with the Russian government of this semi-autonomous people.

The dramatic dilemmas faced by Catherine illustrate both the promise and the costs of state formation throughout Europe. State consolidation permitted the imposition of internal peace, coordinated economic policy, and reform of justice, but it came at the price of greater—in some cases much greater—control and coercion of the population. Thus we can see from the alternative perspective of Russia the importance of the political sphere that was opening up in France and was being consolidated in England. It was in that environment, rather than in Russia, that the Enlightenment philosophy could find its most fertile ground.

THE WIDENING SCOPE OF COMMERCE AND WARFARE

In the eighteenth century a new constellation of states emerged to dominate politics in Europe. Alongside the traditional powers of England, France, and Austria were Prussia in central Europe and Russia to the east; these five states would dominate European politics until the twentieth century. Certain characteristics common to all these states account for their dominance. None is more crucial than their various abilities to field effective armies. In the eighteenth century most wars were launched to satisfy traditional territorial ambitions. Now, however, the increasing significance of overseas trade and colonization also made international expansion an important source of conflict, particularly between England and France. As warfare widened in scope, governments increasingly focused on recruiting and maintaining large navies and armies, with increasingly devastating effects on ordinary people.

A Century of Warfare: Circumstances and Rationales   The large and small states of Europe continued to make war on one another for both strategic and dynastic reasons. States fought over territory that had obvious economic and strategic value. War over the Baltic coastline, for example, absorbed Sweden and Russia early in the century. Dynastic claims, however, were still major causes of war. Indeed, the fundamental instability caused by hereditary rule accounts for many of the major wars of the eighteenth century. The century opened with the

War of the Spanish Succession, and later the succession of the Austrian Habsburgs provoked a continent-wide war. Often these conflicts were carried out in arbitrary ways that reflected a dynastic, rather than wholly strategic, view of territory. Although rational and defensible "national" borders were important, collecting isolated bits of territory was also still the norm. The wars between European powers thus became extremely complex strategically. France, for example, might choose to strike a blow against Austria by invading an Italian state in order to use the conquered Italian territory as a bargaining chip in eventual negotiations. Wars were preceded and carried out with complex systems of alliances and were followed by the adjustments of many borders and the changing control of small, scattered territories. Rulers of lesser states in Germany and Italy, particularly, remained important as allies and as potential rivals of the Great Powers. The rise of Prussia, after all, had demonstrated the benefits of zealous ambition.

The state of military technology, tactics, and organization shaped the outcomes of conflicts as well as the character of the leading states themselves. In the eighteenth century weapons and tactics became increasingly refined. More reliable muskets were introduced. A bayonet that could slip over a musket barrel without blocking the muzzle was invented. Coordinated use of bayonets required even more careful drill of troops than did volley fire alone to ensure disciplined action in the face of enemy fire and charges. Artillery and cavalry forces also were subjected to greater standardization of training and discipline in action. Increased discipline of forces meant that commanders could exercise meaningful control over a battle for the first time. But such battles were not necessarily decisive, especially when waged against a comparable force. Indeed, training now was so costly that commanders were at times ironically reluctant to hazard their fine troops in battle at all.

One sure result of the new equipment and tactics was that war became a more expensive proposition than ever before and an ever greater burden on a state's resources and administration. It became increasingly difficult for small states, such as Sweden, to compete with the forces that others could mount. Small and relatively poor states, such as Prussia, that were able to support large forces did so by means of an extraordinary bending of civil society to the economic and social needs of the army. In Prussia twice as many people were in the armed forces, proportionally, as in other states, and a staggering 80 percent of its meager state revenue went to sustain the army.

Most states introduced some form of conscription in the eighteenth century. In all regions, the very poor often volunteered for army service to improve their lives. However, conscription of peasants, throughout Europe but particularly in Prussia and Russia, imposed a significant burden on peasant communities and a sacrifice of productive members to the state. Governments everywhere supplemented volunteers and conscripts with mercenaries and even criminals, as necessary, to fill the ranks without tapping the wealthier elements of the community. Thus common soldiers were increasingly seen not as members of society but as its rejects. Said Frederick II, "useful hardworking people should [not be conscripted but rather] be guarded as the apple of one's eye," and a French war minister agreed that armies had to consist of the "scum of people and of all those for whom society has no use."[2] Brutality became an accepted tool for governments to use to manage such groups of men. From the eighteenth century on, the army increasingly became an instrument of social control used to contain and make use of individuals who otherwise might disrupt their own communities.

The costs of maintaining these forces had other outcomes as well. Wars could still be won or lost not on the battlefield but on the supply line. Incentive still existed to bleed civilian populations and exploit the countryside. Moreover, when supply lines were disrupted and soldiers not equipped or fed, the armies of a major power could be vulnerable to smaller, less disciplined armies of minor states. Finally, even supplies, training, and sophisticated tactics could not guarantee success. Not until 1746, at Culloden, could the British army decisively defeat the fierce charge and hand-to-hand fighting of Highland clansmen by holding its position and using disciplined volley fire and bayonet tactics. Warfare became increasingly professional but was still an uncertain business with unpredictable results, despite its staggering cost.

The Power of Austria and Prussia   Major wars during the mid-eighteenth century decided the balance of power in German-speaking Europe for the next hundred years. Prussia emerged as the equal of Austria in the region. The first of these wars, now known as the War of the Austrian Succession, began shortly after the death of the emperor Charles VI in 1740. Charles died without a male heir, and his daughter, Maria Theresa, succeeded him. Charles VI had worked to shore up his daughter's position as his heir (versus other female relatives who also had claims) by means of an act called the Pragmatic Sanction, which he had painstakingly persuaded allies and potential opponents to accept. When Charles VI died, rival heiresses and their husbands challenged Maria Theresa for control of her various lands. They were supported by France, the Habsburgs' perennial rival.

The Austrian lands were threatened with dismemberment. Indeed, Charles had negotiated away the wealthy Bohemian province of Silesia, promising it to Prussia in return for acceptance of his heir, and had not left his armies or his treasury well equipped to fight a war to defend it. When Frederick the Great's troops marched into Silesia in 1740, Maria Theresa's rivals saw their chance and invaded other Habsburg territories.

Maria Theresa proved a more tenacious opponent than anyone had anticipated, and she was helped by Great Britain, which saw the possibility of gains against its colonial rival, France. Fighting eventually spread throughout Habsburg territories, including the Netherlands and in Italy, as well as abroad to British and French colonies. In a preliminary peace signed in 1745, Frederick the Great was confirmed in possession of Silesia, but the throne of the Holy Roman Empire was returned to the Habsburgs—given to Maria Theresa's husband, Francis (Franz) I (r. 1745–1765). A final treaty in 1748 ended all the fighting that had continued since 1745, mostly by France and Britain overseas. The Austrian state had survived dismemberment, but Maria Theresa now embarked on the administrative and military reforms necessary to make her state less vulnerable in the future. Prussia, because of the annexation of Silesia and the psychological imprint of victory, emerged as a power of virtually equal rank to the Habsburgs.

The unprecedented threat that Austria now felt from Prussia led to a revolution in alliances across Europe. To isolate Prussia, Maria Theresa agreed to an alliance with France, the Habsburgs' long-standing enemy. Sweden and Russia, with territory to gain at Prussia's expense, joined as well.

Frederick the Great initiated what came to be known as the Seven Years' War in 1756, hoping to prevent consolidation of the new alliances. Instead, he found that he

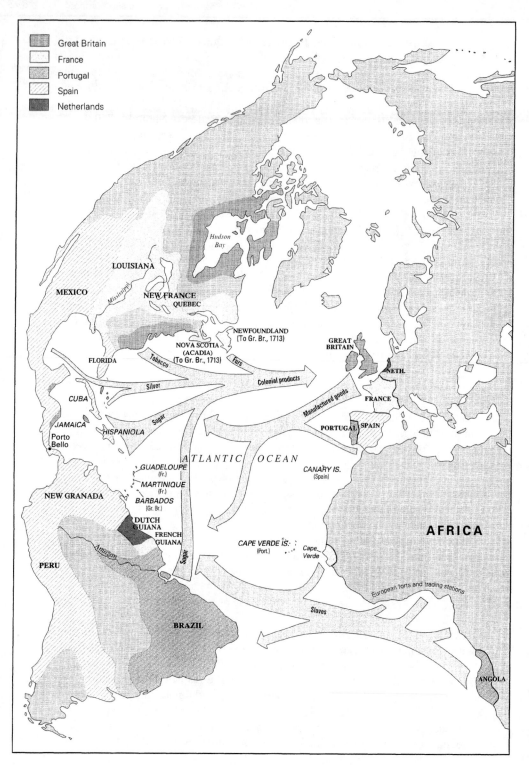

Great Britain
France
Portugal
Spain
Netherlands

Hudson Bay

LOUISIANA

MEXICO

NEW FRANCE
QUEBEC

Mississippi

NEWFOUNDLAND
(To Gr. Br., 1713)

NOVA SCOTIA
(ACADIA)
(To Gr. Br., 1713)

FLORIDA

Tobacco

Furs

GREAT
BRITAIN

NETH.

Silver

Colonial products

FRANCE

CUBA

Sugar

Manufactured goods

PORTUGAL   SPAIN

JAMAICA

Porto
Bello

HISPANIOLA

ATLANTIC   OCEAN

GUADELOUPE
(Fr.)

MARTINIQUE
(Fr.)

BARBADOS
(Gr. Br.)

NEW GRANADA

DUTCH
GUIANA
FRENCH
GUIANA

CANARY IS.
(Spain)

AFRICA

CAPE VERDE IS.:
(Port.)

Cape
Verde

PERU

Amazon

Sugar

European forts and trading stations

BRAZIL

Slaves

ANGOLA

594

had started a war against overwhelming odds. What saved him in part was limited English aid. The English, engaged with France in the overseas conflict that Americans call the French and Indian War, wanted France to be heavily committed on the Continent. Prussia managed to emerge intact—though strained economically and demographically. Prussia and Austria were confirmed as the two states of European rank in German-speaking Europe. Their rivalry would dominate German history until the late nineteenth century. Austria's and Prussia's narrow escapes from being reduced to second-class status reveal how fragile even successful states could be; Prussia's emergence as a major power was by no means assured.

The Atlantic World: Expanding Commerce and the Slave Trade   The importance of international trade and colonial possessions to the states of western Europe grew enormously in the eighteenth century. Between 1715 and 1785 Britain's trade with North America rose from 19 to 34 percent of its total trade, and its trade with Asia and Africa rose from 7 to 19 percent of the total. By the end of the century more than half of all British trade was carried on outside Europe; for France the figure was more than a third.

European commercial and colonial energies were concentrated in the Atlantic world in the eighteenth century because the profits were greatest there. The population of British North America grew from about 250,000 in 1700 to about 1.7 million by 1760. The densely settled New England colonies provided a market for manufactured goods from the mother country, although they produced little by way of raw materials or bulk goods on which traders could make a profit. The colonies of Maryland and Virginia produced tobacco, the Carolinas rice and indigo (a dyestuff). England re-exported all three throughout Europe at considerable profit.

The French in New France, only 56,000 in 1740, were vastly outnumbered by British colonists. Nevertheless, the French had successfully expanded their control of territory in Canada. Settlements sprang up between the outposts of Montreal and Quebec on the St. Lawrence River. Despite resistance, the French extended their fur trapping—the source of most of the profits New France generated—west and north along the Great Lakes, consolidating their hold by building forts at strategic points. They penetrated as far as the modern Canadian province of Manitoba, where they cut into the British trade run out of Hudson Bay. The French also contested the mouth of the St. Lawrence River and the Gulf of St. Lawrence with the British. The British held Nova Scotia and Newfoundland, the French controlled parts of Cape Breton Island, and both states fished the surrounding waters.

The commercial importance of these North American holdings, as well as those in Asia, was dwarfed by the European states' Caribbean possessions, however. The British held Jamaica, Barbados, and the Leeward Islands; the French, Guadeloupe and Martinique; the Spanish, Cuba and Santo Domingo; and the Dutch, a few small islands. Sugar produced on plantations by slave labor was the major source of profits, along

The Atlantic Economy, ca. 1750

The triangle trade linked Europe, Africa, and European colonies in the Americas. The most important component of this trade for Europe was the plantation agriculture of the Caribbean islands, which depended on enslaved Africans for labor.

The Treatment of Slaves on Carribean Plantations *These images of the brutal treatment of slaves on West Indian plantations come from a report published in England designed to convince the British public of the horrors of slavery. At left, a husband and wife are violently separated after being sold to different slaveowners. At right, a mouthpiece and neck guard are used to prevent escape. The treatment of slaves described here is also documented in other surviving accounts from the eighteenth century.* (New York Public Library/Art Resource, NY)

with other cash crops such as coffee, indigo, and cochineal (another dyestuff). The concentration of shipping to this region indicates the region's importance in the European trading system. For example, by the 1760s the British China trade occupied seven or eight ships. In the 1730s British trade with Jamaica alone drew three hundred ships.

The economic dependence of the colonies on slave labor meant that the colonies were tied to their home countries not with a two-way commercial exchange but with a three-way, or "triangle," trade. Certain European manufactures were shipped to ports in western Africa, where they were traded for slaves. Captive Africans were transported to South America, the Caribbean, or North America, where planters bought and paid for them with profits from their sugar and tobacco plantations. Sugar and tobacco were then shipped back to the mother country to be re-exported at great profit throughout Europe.

This plantation economy in the Caribbean was vulnerable to slave revolts, as well as to competition among the Europeans. Often wars over control of the islands significantly disrupted production and lessened profits for the European planters on the islands and for their trading partners back in Europe. The growing demands by Europeans for sugar and other products kept the plantation system expanding, despite these challenges, throughout the eighteenth century. The slave trade grew dramatically as a result. Approximately five times as many Africans—perhaps as many as seven million people—were forcibly transported to the Americas as slaves in the eighteenth century as in the seventeenth. The slave trade became an increasingly specialized form of oceangoing commerce (for example, slave traders throughout Europe adopted a standardized ship design) and, at the same time, one increasingly linked to the rest of European commerce by complex trade and financial ties. In England, London merchants who imported Asian goods, exported European manufactures, or distributed Caribbean sugar could provide credit for slave traders based in the northern city of Liverpool to fund their journeys to Africa and then the Americas.

Great Britain and France: Wars Overseas

The proximity and growth of French and British settlements in North America ensured conflict. The Caribbean and the coasts of Central and South America were strategic flashpoints as well. At the beginning of the eighteenth century, several substantial islands remained unclaimed by any power. The British were making incursions along the coastline claimed by Spain and were trying to break into the monopoly of trade between Spain and its vast possessions in the region. Public opinion in both Britain and France became increasingly sensitive to colonial issues. For the first time, tensions abroad fueled major conflicts between two European states.

During this century England became the dominant naval power in Europe. Its navy protected its far-flung trading networks, its merchant fleet, and the coast of England itself. England's strategic interests on the Continent lay in promoting a variety of powers there, none of which (or no combination of which) posed too great a threat to England or to its widespread trading system. A second, dynastic consideration in continental affairs was the electorate of Hanover, the large principality in western Germany that was the native territory of the Hanoverian kings of England. Early in the century especially, the interests of this German territory were a significant factor in British foreign policy. Unable to field a large army, given their maritime interests, the British sought protection for Hanover in alliances and subsidies for allies' armies on the Continent and paid for these ventures with the profits on trade.

After the death of Louis XIV in 1715, England's energies centered on colonial rivalries with France, its greatest competitor overseas. Conflict between England and France in colonial regions played out in three major phases. The first two were concurrent with the major land wars in Europe: the War of the Austrian Succession (1740–1748) and the Seven Years' War (1756–1763). The third phase coincided with the rebellion of British colonies in North America—the American Revolution—beginning in the 1770s. France was inevitably more committed to affairs on the Continent than were the British. The French were able to hold their own successfully in both arenas during the 1740s, but by 1763, though pre-eminent on the Continent, they had lost many of their colonial possessions to the English.

In the 1740s France was heavily involved in the War of the Austrian Succession, while Britain vied with Spain for certain Caribbean territories. Both France and England also tested each other's strength in scattered colonial fighting, which produced a few well-balanced gains and losses. Their conquests were traded back when peace was made in 1748.

Tension was renewed almost immediately at many of the strategic points in North America. French and British naval forces harassed each other's shipping in the Gulf of St. Lawrence. The French reinforced their encirclement of British colonies with more forts along the Great Lakes and the Ohio River. When British troops (at one point led by the colonial commander George Washington) attempted to strike at these forts beginning in 1754, open fighting between the French and the English began.

In India, meanwhile, both the French and the British attempted to strengthen their commercial footholds by making military and political alliances with local Indian

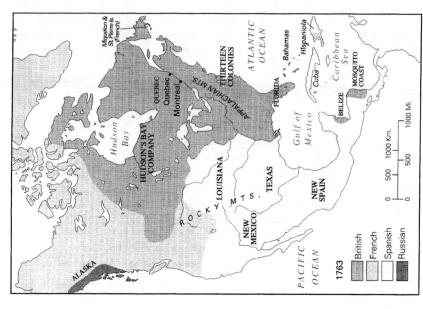

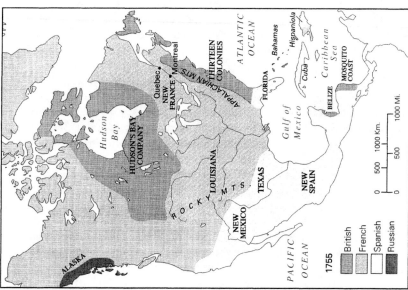

British Gains in North America The British colonies on the Atlantic coast were effective staging posts for the armies that ousted the French from North America by 1763. However, taxes imposed on the colonies to pay the costs of the Seven Years' War helped spark revolt—the American Revolution—a decade later.

rulers. The disintegration of the Mogul Empire heightened competition among regional Indian rulers and sparked a new level of ambition on the part of the European powers with interests in Asia. A British attack on a French convoy provoked a declaration of war by France in May 1756, three months before fighting in the Seven Years' War broke out in Europe. For the first time, a major war between European nations had started and would be fought in their empires, signifying a profound change in the relation of these nations to the world.

The French had already committed themselves to an alliance with Austria and were increasingly involved on the Continent after Frederick II initiated war there in August 1756. Slowly, the drain of sustaining war both on the Continent and abroad began to tell, and Britain scored major victories against French forces after an initial period of balanced successes and failures. The French lost a number of fortresses on the Mississippi and Ohio Rivers and on the Great Lakes, and then they also lost the interior of Canada with the fall of Quebec and of Montreal in 1759 and 1760, respectively.

In the Caribbean, the British seized Guadeloupe, a vital sugar-producing island. Superior resources in India enabled the British to take several French outposts there, including Pondicherry, the most important. The cost of involvement on so many fronts meant that French troops were short of money and supplies. They were particularly vulnerable to both supply and personnel shortages—especially in North America—because they were weaker than the British at sea and because New France remained sparsely settled and dependent on the mother country for food.

By the terms of the Peace of Paris in 1763, France regained Guadeloupe, the most profitable of its American colonies, although Britain gained control of several smaller, previously neutral Caribbean islands to add to its own sugar-producing colonies of Jamaica and Barbados. In India, France retained many of its trading stations but lost its political and military clout. British power in India was dramatically enhanced not only by French losses but also by victories over Indian rulers who had allied with the French. In the interior, Britain now controlled lands that had never before been under the control of any European power. British political rule in India, as opposed to merely a mercantile presence, began at this time. The British also held Canada. They emerged from the Seven Years' War as the pre-eminent world power among European states. The dramatic gains led some Britons to speak of the "British Empire" overseas.

ECONOMIC EXPANSION AND SOCIAL CHANGE

The eighteenth century was an era of dramatic change, although that change was not always apparent to those who lived through it. The intellectual and cultural ferment of the Enlightenment laid the groundwork for domestic political changes to come, just as British victories in the Seven Years' War shifted the balance of power abroad. More subtle and potentially more profound changes were occurring in the European countryside, however. Population, production, and consumption were beginning to grow beyond the bounds that all preceding generations had lived within and taken for granted.

More Food and More People　　Throughout European history, a delicate balance had existed between available food and numbers of people to feed. Population growth had accompanied increases in the amount of land under cultivation. From time to time, however, population growth surpassed the ability of the land to produce food, and people became malnourished and prey to disease. In 1348 the epidemic outbreak of the plague known as the Black Death struck just such a vulnerable population in decline.

Europeans had few options for increasing the productivity of the land. Peasants safeguarded its fertility by alternately cultivating some portions while letting others lie fallow or using them as pasture. Manure provided fertilizer, but during the winter months livestock could not be kept alive in large numbers. Limited food for livestock meant limited fertilizer, which in turn meant limited production of food for both humans and animals.

After a devastating decline in the fourteenth century, the European population experienced a prolonged recovery, and in the eighteenth century the balance that had previously been reached began to be exceeded for the first time. Infant mortality remained as high as ever. No less privileged a person than Queen Anne of England outlived every one of the seventeen children she bore, and all but one of them died in infancy. But population growth occurred because of a decline in the death rate for adults and a simultaneous increase in the birthrate in some areas owing to earlier marriages.

Adults began to live longer partly because of a decline in the incidence of plague. However, the primary reason adults were living longer, despite the presence of various epidemic diseases, was that they were better nourished and thus better able to resist disease. More and different kinds of food began to be produced. The increase in the food supply also meant that more new families could be started.

Food production increased because of the introduction of new crops and other changes in agricultural practices. The cumulative effect of these changes was so dramatic that historians have called them an "agricultural revolution." The new crops included fodder, such as clover, legumes, and turnips, which did not deplete the soil and could be fed to livestock over the winter. The greater availability of animal manure in turn boosted grain production. In addition, the potato, introduced from the Americas in the sixteenth century, is nutrient-dense and can feed more people per acre than can grain. In certain areas, farming families produced potatoes to feed themselves while they grew grain to be sold and shipped elsewhere.

More food being produced meant more food available for purchase. The opportunity to buy food freed up land and labor. A family that could purchase food might decide to convert its farm to specialized use, such as raising dairy cattle. In such a case, many families might be supported by a piece of land that had previously supported only one. Over a generation or two, a number of children might share the inheritance of what had previously been a single farm, yet each could make a living from his or her share, and population could grow as it had not done before.

Farmers had known about and experimented with many of the crops used for fodder for centuries. However, the widespread planting of these crops, as well as other changes, was long in coming and happened in scattered areas. A farmer had to have control over land in order to implement change. In the traditional open-field system, peasants had split up all the land in each community so that each family might have a piece of each field. Making effective changes was hard when an entire community had to act together. Most important, changing agriculture required capital for seed and fertilizer and for the greater number of people and animals needed to cultivate the new crops. Only prosperous farmers had spare capital. Few were inclined to take risks with the production of food and to trust the workings of the market. The bad condition of roads was reason enough not to rely on distant markets.

Yet where both decent roads and growing urban markets existed, some farmers— even entire villages working together—were willing to produce for urban populations. Capital cities, such as London and Amsterdam, and trading centers, such as Glasgow and Bordeaux, were booming. These growing cities demanded not only grain but also specialized produce such as dairy products and fruits and vegetables. Thus farmers had an incentive to make changes. Urbanization and improved transportation networks also encouraged agriculture because human waste produced by city dwellers—known as "night soil"—could be collected and distributed in the surrounding agricultural regions as fertilizer. By the late eighteenth century, pockets of intensive, diversified agriculture existed in England, northern France, the Rhineland in Germany, the Po Valley in Italy, and Catalonia in Spain.

In some areas, changes in agriculture were accompanied by a shift in power in the countryside. Wealthy landlords began to invest in change in order to reap the profits of producing for the new markets. Where the traditional authority of the village to regulate agriculture was weak, peasants were vulnerable. In England a combination of weak village structure and the attraction of urban markets created a climate that encouraged landlords to treat land speculatively. To make their holdings more profitable, they raised the rents that farmers paid. They changed cultivation patterns on the land that they controlled directly. They appropriated the village common lands, a process known as "enclosure," and used them for cash crops such as sheep (raised for their wool) or beef cattle. Among other ramifications, the clans of Scotland completely disintegrated as meaningful social units as markets for beef, wool, and other Highland commodities drew chieftains' resources and turned what remained of their traditional clan relationships into exploitative commercial ones.

Thus, although the agricultural revolution increased the food supply to sustain more people in Europe generally, it did not create general prosperity. The growth of population did not mean that most people were better off. Indeed, many rural people were driven off the land or made destitute by the loss of the resources of common lands. Peasants in eastern Europe produced grain for export to the growing urban centers in western Europe, but usually by traditional methods. In both eastern and western Europe, the power and profits of landlords were a major force in structuring the rural economy.

The Growth of Industry   Agricultural changes fostered change in other areas of economic and social life. As more food was grown with less labor, that labor was freed to take on other productive work. If enough people could be kept employed making useful commodities, the nonagricultural population could continue to grow. If population grew, more and more consumers would be born, and the demand for more goods would help continue the cycle of population growth, changes in production, and economic expansion. This is precisely what happened in the eighteenth century. A combination of forces increased the numbers of people who worked at producing a few essential materials and products.

Especially significant was the expansion in the putting-out system. Also known as cottage industry, putting out involved the production in the countryside of thread and cloth by spinners and weavers working in their own homes for an entrepreneur who bought raw materials and "put them out" to be finished by individual workers. The putting-out system expanded in the eighteenth century as the agricultural economy was transformed. All agricultural work was seasonal, demanding intensive effort and many hands at certain times but not others. The labor demands of the new crops meant that an even larger number of people might periodically need work away from the fields to make ends meet. Rural poverty, whether as a result of traditional or new agricultural methods, made manufacturing work in the home attractive to more and more people.

Overseas trade also stimulated the expansion of production by spurring the demand in Europe's colonies for cloth and other finished products and increasing the demand at home for manufactured items, such as nails to build the ships that carried the trade. The production of cloth also expanded because heightened demand led to changes in the way cloth was made. Wool was increasingly combined with other fibers to make less expensive fabrics. By the end of the century, wholly cotton fabrics were being made cheaply in Europe from cotton grown in America by slave labor.

Steady innovation in textile production allowed woven goods to be aimed at broader markets. In the Middle Ages, weavers produced luxury-quality cloth, and their profits came not from demand, which was relatively low, but from the high price that affluent consumers paid. In the eighteenth century, cloth production became a spur to a transformed industrial economy because cheaper kinds of cloth were made for mass consumption. Producing in great quantities became important, and innovations that promoted productivity were welcomed.

A crucial innovation was increased mechanization. The invention of machines to spin thread in the late eighteenth century brought a marked increase in the rate of production. Machines likewise brought profound changes to the lives of rural workers who had been juggling agricultural and textile work according to season and need. The selected areas of England, France, and the Low Countries where the new technologies were introduced stood, by the end of the century, on the verge of a massive industrial transformation that would have unprecedented social consequences.

Control and Resistance

The economic changes of the century produced both resistance and adaptation by ordinary people and, at times, direct action by state authorities. Sometimes ordinary people coped in ways that revealed their desperation. In many cities numbers of abandoned children rose greatly because urban families, particularly recent immigrants from the countryside, could not support all their offspring. The major cities of Europe put increasing resources into police forces and city lighting schemes. Charitable institutions run by cities, churches, and central governments expanded. By 1789, for example, there were more than two thousand *hôpitaux*—poorhouses for the destitute and ill—in France. The poor received food and shelter but were forced to work for the city or to live in poorhouses against their will. Men were sometimes taken out of poorhouses and forced to become soldiers.

Resistance and adaptation were particularly visible wherever the needs of common people conflicted with the states' desire for order and revenue. This scenario was evident on the high seas, for example, in the crusade to suppress piracy. Piracy had been a way of life for hundreds of Europeans and colonial settlers since the sixteenth century. From the earliest days of exploration, European rulers had authorized men known as privateers to commit acts of war against specific targets. The Crown took little risk and was spared the cost of arming the ships but shared in the plunder. True piracy—outright robbery on the high seas—was illegal, but in practice the difference between piracy and privateering was negligible. As governments and merchants grew to prefer regular trade over the irregular profits of plunder, and as national navies developed in the late seventeenth century, a concerted effort to eliminate piracy began.

Life on the seas became an increasingly vital part of western European economic life in the eighteenth century. English-speaking seamen alone numbered about thirty thousand around the middle of the century. Sea life began to resemble life on land in the amount of compulsion it entailed. Sailors in port were always vulnerable to forcible enlistment in the navy by impressment gangs, particularly during wartime. A drowsy sailor sleeping off a rowdy night in port could wake up to find himself aboard a navy ship. Press gangs operated throughout England and not just in major ports, for authorities were as interested in controlling "vagrancy" as in staffing the navy. Merchant captains occasionally filled their crews by such means, particularly when sailing unpopular routes.

Like soldiers in the growing eighteenth-century armies, sailors in the merchant marine as well as the navy could be subjected to brutal discipline and appalling conditions. Merchant seamen attempted to improve their lot by trying to regulate their relationship with ships' captains. Contracts for pay on merchant ships became more regularized, and seamen often negotiated their terms very carefully, including, for example, details about how rations were to be allotted. Sailors might even take bold collective action aboard ship. The modern term for a work stoppage, *strike,* comes from the sailing expression "to strike sail," meaning to loosen the sails so that they cannot fill with wind. Its use dates from the eighteenth century, from "strikes" of sailors protesting unfair shipboard conditions.

Seafaring men were an unusually large and somewhat self-conscious community of wage workers. Not until industrialization came into full swing a century later would a similar group of workers exist within Europe itself (see Chapter 21). But economic and political protests by ordinary people on the Continent also showed interesting parallel changes. Peasant revolts in the past had ranged from small-scale actions against local tax collectors to massive uprisings that only an army could suppress. The immediate goals of the rebels were usually practical. For example, they aimed not to eliminate taxation altogether but perhaps to protest the collection of a particularly burdensome tax. The political rationale behind such actions was not a hope that the system would disappear but rather a hope that it would operate more fairly, as it presumably had in the past. Where there was a revolutionary vision, it was usually a utopian one—a political system with no kings, landlords, taxes, or state of any kind.

Peasant revolts continued to follow those patterns in the eighteenth century. They were also driven by the localized unemployment caused by agricultural reforms or by objections to press gangs. In certain cases, however, peasants, like sailors, began to confront the state in new ways. Peasants often attacked not state power but the remnants of landlords' power, wielded over them in the shape of forced labor and compulsory use of landlords' mills. As weapons, they increasingly marshaled legal devices to maintain control over their land and to thwart landlords' efforts to enclose fields and cultivate cash crops. This change, though subtle, was important because it signaled an effort to bring permanent structural change to the system and was not simply a temporary

IMPORTANT EVENTS

1715–1774 Reign of Louis XV in France

1722–1741 Walpole first British "prime minister"

1734 Voltaire, *Philosophical Letters*

1740–1748 War of the Austrian Succession

1740–1780 Reign of Maria Theresa of Austria

1740–1786 Reign of Frederick the Great of Prussia

1746 Battle of Culloden

1748 Montesquieu, *The Spirit of the Laws*
Hume, *Essay Concerning Human Understanding*

1751–1765 Diderot, *The Encyclopedia*

1756–1763 Seven Years' War

1758 Voltaire, *Candide*

1762 Rousseau, *The Social Contract*

1762–1796 Reign of Catherine the Great of Russia

1772 First partition of Poland

1776 Smith, *The Wealth of Nations*

1780–1790 Reign of Joseph II of Austria

1792 Wollstonecraft, *A Vindication of the Rights of Woman*

redress of grievances. In part the trend toward "enlightened" revolt reflects increased access to information and the circulation of ideas about reform. A major peasant rebellion in 1775 in Austrian lands, for example, followed several years of bad harvests but specifically protested the delay in implementing changes—the subject of earnest debate among elites—in compulsory labor by peasants.

NOTES

1. Quoted in Dena Goodman, *The Republic of Letters: A Cultural History of the French Enlightenment* (Ithaca, N.Y.: Cornell University Press, 1994), p. 89.
2. Quoted in M. S. Anderson, *Europe in the Eighteenth Century, 1713–1783,* 3d ed. (London: Longman, 1987), pp. 218–219.

SUGGESTED READING

Anderson, M. S. *Europe in the Eighteenth Century, 1713–1783.* 4th ed. 2000. A general history covering political, economic, social, and cultural developments.

Black, Jeremy. *European Warfare, 1660–1815.* 1994. One of several recent books by this military historian known particularly for his studies of the seventeenth and eighteenth centuries.

Cipolla, Carlo. *Before the Industrial Revolution.* 1976. A comprehensive treatment of the development of the European economy and technology through this period.

Colley, Linda. *Britons: Forging the Nation, 1707–1837.* 1992. A history of the British that emphasizes the interrelationships of political, social, and cultural history.

Goodman, Dena. *The Republic of Letters: A Cultural History of the French Enlightenment.* 1994. Useful for understanding the social context of the Enlightenment, especially the role of women as salon leaders.

Kennedy, Paul. *The Rise and Fall of British Naval Mastery.* 1976. A comprehensive work on the rise of British sea power from the sixteenth century to modern times.

Porter, Roy. *The Enlightenment.* 1990. A brief introduction.

Roche, Daniel. *France in the Enlightenment.* 1998. A study of state and society in France by an eminent French scholar.

19

An Age of Revolution, 1789–1815

(Photos12.com-ARJ)

These militiamen marching off to defend France against the invader in September 1792 appear to be heroes already. Adoring women in the crowd hand them laurel wreaths as they pass; the men march by, resolute and triumphant. Symbols of the ongoing revolution stand out as well: the prominent tricolor flag, the tricolor cockade in each man's hat. In fact, that September France's citizen armies for the first time defeated the army of a foreign monarch poised to breach its borders and snuff out its revolution. The painting celebrates this triumph about to happen and thereby inspires confidence in the Revolution and pride in its citizen-soldiers.

Today the French Revolution is considered the initiation of modern European as well as modern French history. The most powerful monarch in Europe was forced to accept constitutional limits to his power by subjects convinced of their right to demand them. Eventually, the king was overthrown and executed, and the monarchy abolished. Events in France reverberated throughout Europe because the overthrow of one absolute monarchy threatened fellow royals elsewhere. Revolutionary fervor on the part of ordinary soldiers enabled France's armies unexpectedly to best many of their opponents. By the late 1790s the armies of France would be led in outright conquest of other European states by one of the most talented generals in European history: Napoleon Bonaparte. He brought to the continental European nations that his armies eventually conquered a mixture of imperial aggression and revolutionary change. Europe was transformed both by the shifting balance of power and by the spread of revolutionary ideas.

Understanding the French Revolution means understanding not only its origins but also its complicated course of events, and their significance. Challenges to the power of the king were not new, but the Revolution overthrew his right to rule at all. The notion that the people constituted the nation, were responsible as citizens, and had some right to representation in government became irresistible. The republican system it conjured up replaced a government by inherited privilege. Louis XVI was transformed from the divinely appointed father of his people to an enemy of the people, worthy only of execution. Central to the Revolution was the complex process by which public opinion was shaped and, in turn, shaped events. Change was driven in part by the power of symbols—flags, rallying cries, inspiring art—to challenge an old political order and legitimize a new one.

THE BEGINNINGS OF REVOLUTION, 1775–1789

"I am a citizen of the world," wrote John Paul Jones, captain in the fledgling U.S. Navy, in 1778. He was writing to a Scottish aristocrat, apologizing for raiding the lord's estate while marauding along the British coast during the American Revolution. Jones (1747–1792), himself born a Scotsman, was one of the thousands of cosmopolitan Europeans who were familiar with European cultures on both sides of the Atlantic. As a sailor, Jones literally knew his way around the Atlantic world, but he was a "citizen of the world" in another sense as well. When the Scotsman wrote back to Jones, he expressed surprise that his home had been raided because he was sympathetic to the American colonists. Like Jones, he said, he was a man of "liberal sentiments."[1] Both Jones and the Scottish lord felt they belonged to an international society of gentlemen who recognized certain Enlightenment principles regarding just and rational government.

In the Atlantic world of the late eighteenth century, both practical links of commerce and shared ideals about "liberty" were important shaping forces. The strategic interests of the great European powers were also always involved. Thus when the American colonists actively resisted British rule and then in 1776 declared their independence from Britain, the consequences were widespread and varied: British trading interests were challenged, French appetites for gains at British expense were whetted, and illusive notions about "liberty" seemed more plausible. The victory of the American colonies in 1783, followed by the creation of the U.S. Constitution in 1787, further heightened the appeal of liberal ideas elsewhere. Attempts at liberal reform were mounted in several states, including Ireland, the Netherlands, and Poland. However, the American Revolution had the most direct impact on later events in France because the French had been directly involved in the American effort.

Revolutionary Movements in Europe

While the British government was facing the revolt of the American colonies, it also confronted trouble closer to home. The war against the American colonies was not firmly supported by Britons. Like many Americans, many Britons had divided loyalties, and many who did favor armed force to subdue the rebellion were convinced that the war was being mismanaged. The prosecution of the war against the American colonies proceeded amid calls for reform of the ministerial government. In this setting, a reform movement sprang up in Ireland in 1779. The reformers demanded greater autonomy from Britain. Like the Americans, Irish elites felt like disadvantaged junior partners in the British Empire. They chafed over British policies that favored British imperial interests over those of the Irish ruling class: for example, the exclusion of Irish ports in favor of English and Scottish trading stops and the granting of political rights to Irish Catholics so that they might fight in Britain's overseas armies.

Protestant Irish landlords, threatened by such policies, expressed their opposition not only in parliamentary debates but also in military defiance. Following the example of the American rebels, middle- and upper-class Anglo-Irish set up a system of locally sponsored voluntary militia to resist British troops if necessary. The Volunteer Movement was neutralized when greater parliamentary autonomy for Ireland was granted in 1782, following the repeal of many restrictions on Irish commerce. Unlike the Americans, the Irish elites faced an internal challenge to their own authority—the Catholic population whom they had for centuries dominated. That challenge forced them to reach an accommodation with the British government.

Meanwhile, a political crisis with constitutional overtones was also brewing in the Netherlands. Tensions between the aristocratic stadholders of the House of Orange and the merchant oligarchies of the major cities deepened during the American Revolution. The Dutch were then engaged in a commercial war against the British, to whom the stadholder was supposed to be sympathetic. The conflict ceased to be wholly traditional for two reasons. First, the representatives of the various cities, calling themselves the Dutch "Patriot" Party, defended their position on the grounds of traditional balance of power within the Netherlands and invoked wider claims to American-style "liberty." Second, the challenge to traditional political arrangements widened when middling urban dwellers, long disenfranchised by these oligarchies, demanded "liberty," too—that is, political enfranchisement within the cities—and briefly took over the Patriot movement. Just as many Irish rebels accepted the concessions of 1782, many Patriot oligarchs in the Netherlands did nothing to resist an invasion in 1787 that restored the power of the stadholder, the prince of Orange, and thereby ended the challenge to their own control of urban government.

Both the Irish volunteers and the Dutch Patriots, though members of very limited movements, echoed the American rebels in practical and ideological ways. Both were influenced by the economic and political consequences of Britain's relationship with its colonies. Both were inspired by the success of the American rebels and their thoroughgoing claims for political self-determination.

Desire for political reform flared in Poland as well during this period. Reform along lines suggested by Enlightenment precepts was accepted as a necessity by Polish leaders after the first partition of Poland in 1772 had left the remnant state without some of its wealthiest territories. Beginning in 1788, however, reforming gentry in the *Sejm* (representative assembly) went further; they established a commission to write a constitution, following the American example. The resulting document, known as the May 3 (1791) Constitution, was the first codified constitution in Europe; it was read and admired by George Washington.

Poles thus established a constitutional monarchy in which representatives of major towns as well as gentry and nobility could sit as deputies. The *liberum veto*, which had allowed great magnates to obstruct royal authority at will, was abolished. However, Catherine the Great, empress of Russia, would not tolerate a constitutional government operating so close to her own autocratic regime; she ordered an invasion of Poland in 1792. The unsuccessful defense of Poland was led by, among others, a Polish veteran of the American Revolution, Tadeusz Kosciuszko (1746–1817). The second, more extensive partition of Poland followed, to be answered in turn in 1794 by a widespread insurrection against Russian rule, spearheaded by Kosciuszko. The uprising was mercilessly suppressed by an alliance of Russian and Prussian troops. Unlike the U.S. Constitution from which they drew inspiration, the Poles' constitutional experiment was doomed by the power of its neighbors.

The American Revolution and the Kingdom of France   As Britain's greatest commercial and political rival, France naturally was drawn into Britain's struggle with its North American colonies. In the Seven Years' War (1756–1763), the French had lost many of their colonial settlements and trading outposts to the English (see page 599). Stung by this outcome, certain French courtiers and ministers pressed for an aggressive colonial policy that would regain for France some of the riches in trade that Britain now threatened to monopolize. The American Revolution seemed to offer the perfect opportunity. The French extended covert aid to the Americans from the very beginning of the conflict in 1775. After the first major defeat of British troops by the Americans—at the Battle of Saratoga in 1777—France formally recognized the independent United States and established an alliance with it. The French then committed troops as well as funds for the American cause. John Paul Jones's most famous ship, the *Bonhomme Richard,* was purchased and outfitted in France at French government expense, as were many other American naval vessels during the war. French support was decisive. In 1781 the French fleet kept reinforcements from reaching the British force besieged by George Washington at Yorktown. The American victory at Yorktown effectively ended the war; the colonies' independence was formally recognized by the Treaty of Paris in 1783.

The Common People Crushed by Privilege *In this contemporary cartoon, a nobleman in military dress and a clergyman crush a commoner under the rock of burdensome taxes and forced labor (corvées). The victim's situation reflects that of the peasantry, but his stylish clothes would allow affluent townspeople to identify with him.* (Musée Carnavalet, Paris/Giraudon/Art Resource, NY)

The consequences for France of its American alliance were momentous. Aid for the Americans saddled France with a debt of about 1 billion *livres* (pounds), which represented as much as one-quarter of the total debt that the French government was trying to service. A less tangible impact of the American Revolution derived from the direct participation of about nine thousand French soldiers, sailors, and aristocrats. The best known is the Marquis de Lafayette, who became an aide to George Washington and helped command American troops. For many humble men, the war was simply employment. For others, it was a quest of sorts. For them, the promise of the Enlightenment—belief in human rationality, natural rights, and universal laws by which society should be organized—was brought to life in America.

Exposure to the American conflict occurred at the French court, too. Beginning in 1775, a permanent American mission to Versailles lobbied hard for aid and later managed the flow of that assistance. The chief emissary of the Americans was Benjamin Franklin (1706–1790), a philosophe by French standards whose writings and scientific experiments were already known to European elites. His talents—among them, a skillful exploitation of a simple, Quaker-like demeanor—succeeded in promoting the idealization of America at the French court.

The U.S. Constitution, the various state constitutions, and the debates surrounding their ratification were all published in Paris and much discussed in salons and at court, where lively debate about reform of French institutions had been going on for decades. America became the prototype of the rational republic—the embodiment of Enlightenment philosophy. It was hailed as the place where the irrationalities of inherited privilege did not prevail. A British observer, Arthur Young (1741– 1820), believed that "the American revolution has laid the foundation of another in France, if [the French] government does not take care of itself."[2]

By the mid-1780s there was no longer a question of whether the French regime would experience reform but rather what form the reform would take. The royal government was almost bankrupt. A significant minority of the politically active elite was convinced of the fundamental irrationality of France's system of government. Nevertheless, a dissatisfied elite and a financial crisis—even fanned by a successful revolt elsewhere—do not necessarily lead to revolution. Why did the French government— the *Ancien Régime*, or "Old Regime," as it became known after the Revolution—not "take care of itself"?

The Crisis of the Old Regime The Old Regime was brought to the point of crisis in the late 1780s by three factors: (1) heavy debts that dwarfed an antiquated system for collecting revenue; (2) institutional constraints on the monarchy that defended privileged interests; and (3) public opinion that envisioned thoroughgoing reform and pushed the monarchy in that direction. Another factor was the ineptitude of the king, Louis XVI (r. 1774–1793).

Louis came to the throne in 1774, a year before the American Revolution began. He was a kind, well-meaning man better suited to carry out the finite responsibilities of a petty bureaucrat than to be king. The queen, the Austrian Marie Antoinette (1755– 1793), was unpopular. She was regarded with suspicion by the many who despised the "unnatural" alliance with Austria the marriage had sealed. She, too, was politically inept, unable to negotiate the complexities of court life and widely rumored to be selfishly wasteful of royal resources despite the realm's financial crises.

The fiscal crisis of the monarchy had been a long time in the making and was an outgrowth of the system in which the greatest wealth was protected by traditional privileges. At the top of the social and political pyramid were the nobles, a legal grouping that included warriors and royal officials. In France nobility conferred exemption from much taxation. Thus the royal government could not directly tax its wealthiest subjects.

This situation existed throughout much of Europe, a legacy of the individual contractual relationships that had formed the political and economic framework of medieval Europe. Unique to France, however, was the strength of the institutions that defended this system. Of particular importance were the royal law courts, the parlements, which claimed a right of judicial review over royal edicts. All the parlementaires—well-educated lawyers and judges—were noble and loudly defended the traditional privileges of all nobles. Louis XV (d. 1774), near the end of his life, had successfully undermined the power of the parlements by a bold series of moves. Louis XVI, immediately after coming to the throne, buckled under pressure and restored the parlements to full strength.

Deficit financing had been a way of life for the monarchy for centuries. After early efforts at reform, Louis XIV (d. 1715) had reverted to common fund-raising expedients such as selling offices, which only added to the weight of privileged investment in the old order. England had established a national bank to free its government from the problem, but the comparable French effort early in the century had been undercapitalized and had failed. Late in the 1780s, under Louis XVI, one-fourth of the annual operating expenses of the government was borrowed, and half of all government expenditure went to paying interest on its debt. Short-term economic crises, such as disastrous harvests, added to the cumulative problem of government finance.

The king employed able finance ministers who tried to institute fundamental reforms, such as replacing the tangle of taxes with a simpler system in which all would pay and eliminating local tariffs, which were stifling commerce. The parlements and many courtiers and aristocrats, as well as ordinary people, resisted these policies. Peasants and townsfolk did not trust the "free market" (free from traditional trade controls) for grain; most feared that speculators would buy up the grain supply and people would starve. Trying to implement such reforms in times of grain shortage almost guaranteed their failure. Moreover, many supported the parlements simply because they were the only institution capable of standing up to the monarchy. Yet not all members of the elite joined the parlements in opposing reform. The imprint of "enlightened" public opinion was apparent in the thinking of some courtiers and thousands of educated commoners who believed that the government and the economy had to change and openly debated the nature and extent of reform needed.

In 1787 the king called an "Assembly of Notables"—an ad hoc group of elites—to support him in facing down the parlements and proceeding with some changes. He found little support even among men known to be sympathetic to reform. Some did not support particular proposals, and many were reluctant to allow the monarchy free rein. Others, reflecting the influence of the American Revolution, maintained that a "constitutional" body such as the Estates General, which had not been called since 1614, needed to make these decisions.

Ironically, nobles and clergy who were opposed to reform supported the call for the Estates General, confident they could control its deliberations. The three Estates met and voted separately by "order"—clergy (First Estate), nobles (Second Estate), and commoners (Third Estate). The combined votes of the clergy and nobles would presumably nullify whatever the Third Estate might propose.

In 1788 popular resistance to reform in the streets of Paris and mounting pressure from Louis's courtiers and bureaucrats induced the king to summon the Estates General. On Louis's orders, deputies were to be elected by local assemblies, which were chosen in turn by wide male suffrage. Louis mistakenly assumed he had widespread support in the provinces, and he wished to tap into it by means of this grass-roots voting. Louis also agreed that the Third Estate should have twice as many deputies as the other two Estates, but he did not authorize voting by head rather than by order, which would have brought about the dominance of the Third Estate. Nevertheless, the king hoped that the specter of drastic proposals put forth by the Third Estate would frighten the aristocrats and clergy into accepting some of his reforms.

Louis's situation was precarious when the Estates General convened in May 1789. As ever, he faced immediate financial crisis. He also faced a constitutional crisis. Already a groundswell of sentiment confirmed the legitimacy of the Estates General, the role of the Third Estate, and the authority of the Third Estate to enact change. Political pamphlets abounded arguing that the Third Estate deserved enhanced power because it carried the mandate of the people. The most important of these was *What Is the Third Estate?* (1789) by Joseph Emmanuel Sieyès (1748–1836), a church official from the diocese of Chartres. The sympathies of Abbé Sieyès, as he was known, were with the Third Estate: his career had suffered and stalled because he was not noble. Sieyès argued that the Third Estate represented the nation because it did not reflect special privilege.

Among the deputies of the first two Estates—clergy and nobility—were men, such as the Marquis de Lafayette (1757–1834), who were sympathetic to reform. More important, however, the elections had returned to the Third Estate a large majority of deputies who reflected the most radical political thought possible for men of their standing. Most were lawyers and other professionals who were functionaries in the government but, like Sieyès, of low social rank. They frequented provincial academies, salons, and political societies. They were convinced of the validity of their viewpoints and determined on reform, and they had little stake in the system as it was. When this group convened and met with resistance from the First and Second Estates and from Louis himself, they seized the reins of government and a revolution began.

1789: A Revolution Begins   As soon as the three Estates convened at the royal palace at Versailles, conflicts surfaced. The ineptness of the Crown was immediately clear. On the first day of the meetings in May, Louis and his ministers failed to introduce a program of reforms for the deputies to consider. This failure raised doubt about the monarchy's commitment to reform. More important, it allowed the political initiative to pass to the Third Estate. The deputies challenged the Crown's insistence that the three Estates meet and vote separately. Deputies to the Third Estate refused to be certified (that is, to have their credentials officially recognized) as members of only the Third Estate rather than as members of the Estates General as a whole.

For six weeks the Estates General was unable to meet officially, and the king did nothing to break the impasse. During this interlude, the determination of the deputies of the Third Estate strengthened. More and more deputies were won over to the notion that the three Estates must begin in the most systematic way: France must have a written constitution.

By the middle of June, more than thirty reformist members of the clergy were sitting jointly with the Third Estate, which had invited all deputies from all three Estates to meet and be certified together. On June 17 the Third Estate simply declared itself the National Assembly of France. At first the king did nothing, but when the deputies arrived to meet on the morning of June 20, they discovered they had been locked out of the hall. Undaunted, they assembled instead in a nearby indoor tennis court and produced the document that has come to be known as the "Tennis Court Oath." It was a collective pledge to meet until a written constitution had been achieved. Only one deputy refused to support it. Sure of their mandate, the deputies had assumed the reins of government.

The king continued to handle the situation with both ill-timed self-assertion and feeble attempts at compromise. As more and more deputies from the First and Second Estates joined the National Assembly, Louis "ordered" the remaining loyal deputies to

The Tennis Court Oath *It was raining on June 20, 1789, when the deputies found themselves barred from their meeting hall and sought shelter in the royal tennis court. Their defiance created one of the turning points of the Revolution; the significance was recognized several years later by the creator of this painting.* (Réunion des Musées Nationaux/Art Resource, NY)

join it, too. Simultaneously, however, he ordered troops to come to Paris. He feared disorder in the wake of the recent disturbances throughout France and believed that any challenge to the legitimacy of arbitrary monarchical authority would be disastrous.

This appeal for armed assistance stirred unrest in the capital. Paris, with a population of about 600,000 in 1789, was one of the largest cities in Europe. It was the political nerve center of the nation—the site of the publishing industry, salons, the homes of parlementaires and royal ministers. It was also a working city, with thousands of laborers of all trades plus thousands more—perhaps one-tenth of the inhabitants—jobless recent immigrants from the countryside. The city was both extremely volatile and extremely important to the stability of royal power. The king's call for troops aroused Parisians' suspicions. Some assumed a plot was afoot to starve Paris and destroy the National Assembly. Already they considered the Assembly to be a guarantor of acceptable government.

It took little—the announcement of the dismissal of a reformist finance minister—for Paris to erupt in demonstrations and looting. Crowds besieged City Hall and the royal armory, where they seized thousands of weapons. A popular militia formed as citizens armed themselves. Armed crowds assailed other sites of royal authority, including the huge fortified prison, the Bastille, on the morning of July 14. The Bastille now held only a handful of petty criminals, but it still remained a potent symbol of royal power and, it was assumed, held large supplies of arms. Like the troops at the armory, the garrison at the Bastille had received no firm orders to fire on the crowds if necessary. The garrison commander at first mounted a hesitant defense, then decided to surrender after citizens managed to secure cannon and drag them to face the prison. Most of the garrison were allowed to go free, although the commander and several officers were murdered by the crowd.

The citizens' victory was a great embarrassment to royal authority. The king immediately had to embrace the popular movement. He came to Paris and in front of crowds at City Hall donned the red and blue cockade worn by the militia and ordinary folk as a badge of resolve and defiance. This symbolic action signaled the reversal of the Old Regime—politics would now be based on new principles.

Encouraged by events in Paris, inhabitants of cities and towns around France staged similar uprisings. In many areas, the machinery of royal government completely broke down. City councils, officials, and even parlementaires were thrown out of office. Popular militias took control of the streets. A simultaneous wave of uprisings shook the countryside. Most of them were the result of food shortages, but their timing added momentum to the more strictly political protests in cities. These events forced the members of the National Assembly to work energetically on the constitution and to pass legislation to satisfy popular protests against economic and political privileges.

On August 4 the Assembly issued a set of decrees abolishing the remnants of powers that landlords had enjoyed since the Middle Ages, including the right to co-opt peasant labor and the bondage of serfdom itself. Although largely symbolic, because serfdom and forced labor had been eliminated in much of France, these changes represented a dramatic inroad into the property rights of the elite as they had been traditionally construed. The repeals were hailed as the "end of feudalism." A blow was also struck at established religion by eliminating the tithe. At the end of August, the Assembly issued the Declaration of the Rights of Man and the Citizen. It was a bold assertion of the foundations of a newly conceived government, closely modeled on portions of the U.S. Constitution. Its preamble declared "that [since] the ignorance, neglect or contempt of the rights of man are the sole cause of public calamities and the corruption of governments," the deputies were "determined to set forth in a solemn declaration the natural, inalienable and sacred rights of man."[3]

In September the deputies debated the king's role in a new constitutional government. Monarchists favored a government rather like England's, with a two-house legislature, including an upper house representing the hereditary aristocracy and a royal right to veto legislation. More radical deputies favored a single legislative chamber and no veto power for the king. After deliberation, the Assembly reached a compromise. The king was given a three-year suspensive veto—the power to suspend legislation for the sitting of two legislatures. This was still a formidable amount of power but a drastic curtailment of his formerly absolute sovereignty.

Again Louis resorted to troops. This time he called them directly to Versailles, where the Assembly sat. News of the troops' arrival provoked outrage, which heightened with the threat of another grain shortage. Early on the morning of October 5, women in the Paris street markets saw the empty grocers' stalls and took immediate collective action. "We want bread!" they shouted at the steps of City Hall. Because they were responsible for procuring their families' food, women often led protests over bread shortages. This protest, however, went far beyond the ordinary. A crowd of thousands gathered and decided to walk all the way to Versailles, accompanied by the popular militia (now called the "National Guard"), to petition the king directly for sustenance.

At Versailles they presented a delegation to the National Assembly, and a joint delegation of the women and deputies was dispatched to see the king. Some of the women fell at the feet of the king with their tales of hardship, certain that the "father of the people" would alleviate their suffering. He did order stored grain supplies distributed in Paris, and he also agreed to accept the constitutional role that the Assembly had voted for him.

That very night members of the National Guard, which had replaced the royal guard around the person of the king, saved Louis's life. A mob broke into the palace and managed to kill two members of the royal guard still in attendance outside the queen's chamber. The king agreed to return to Paris so that he could reassure the people. But the procession back to the city was a curious one. The royal family was escorted by militia and bread protesters, and the severed heads of the dead royal guardsmen were carried on pikes.

The king was now in the hands of his people. Already, dramatic change had occurred as a result of a complex dynamic among the three Estates, the Crown, and the people of Paris. The king was still assumed to be the fatherly guardian of his people's well-being, but his powers were now limited, and his authority was badly shaken. The Assembly had begun to govern in the name of the "nation" and so far had the support of the people.

The Phases of the Revolution, 1789–1799

The French Revolution was a complicated affair. It was a series of changes, in a sense a series of revolutions, driven not by one group of people but by several groups. Even among elites convinced of the need for reform, the range of opinion was wide. The people of Paris continued to be an important force for change. Country people also became active, primarily in resisting changes forced on them by the central government.

All of the wrangling within France was complicated by foreign reaction. Managing foreign war soon became a routine burden for the fragile revolutionary governments. In addition, they had to cope with the continuing problems that had precipitated the Revolution in the first place: the government's chronic indebtedness, economic difficulties, and recurrent grain shortages. Finally, the Revolution itself was an issue in that, once the traditional arrangements of royal government had been altered, momentum for further change was unleashed.

The First Phase Completed, 1789–1791 At the end of 1789 Paris was in ferment, but for a time forward progress blunted the threat of disastrous divisions between king and Assembly and between either of those and the people of Paris. The capital continued to be the center of lively political debate. Salons continued to meet; academies and private societies proliferated. Deputies to the Assembly swelled the ranks of these societies or helped to found new ones. Several would be important throughout the Revolution—particularly the

Jacobin Club, named for the monastic order whose buildings the members used as a meeting hall.

These clubs represented the gamut of revolutionary opinion. Some, in which ordinary Parisians were well represented, focused on economic policies that would directly benefit common people. Women were active in a few of the more radical groups. Monarchists dominated other clubs. At first similar to the salons and debating societies of the Enlightenment era, the clubs quickly became both sites of political action and sources of political pressure on the government. A bevy of popular newspapers also contributed to the vigorous political life in the capital.

The broad front of revolutionary consensus began to break apart as the Assembly forged ahead with decisions about the constitution and with policies necessary to remedy France's still-desperate financial situation. The largest portion of the untapped wealth of the nation lay with the Catholic Church, an obvious target of anticlerical reformers. The deputies did not propose to dismantle the church, but they did make sweeping changes: They kept church buildings intact and retained the clergy as salaried officials of the state. They abolished all monasteries and pensioned the monks and nuns to permit them to continue as nurses and teachers where possible. With the depleted treasury in mind, the Assembly seized most of the vast lands of the church and declared them national property (*biens nationaux*) to be sold for revenue.

Economic and political problems ensued. Revenue was needed faster than the property could be inventoried and sold, so government bonds (*assignats*) were issued against the eventual sale of church properties. Unfortunately, in the cash-strapped economy, the bonds were treated like money, their value became inflated, and the government never realized the hoped-for profits. A greater problem was the political divisiveness generated by the restructuring of the church. Many members of the lower clergy, living as they did near ordinary citizens, were among the most reform-minded of the deputies. These clergy were willing to go along with many changes, but the required oath of loyalty to the state made a mockery of clerical independence.

The Civil Constitution of the Clergy, as these measures were called, was passed by the Assembly in July 1790 because the clerical deputies opposing it were outvoted. More than half of the churchmen did take the oath of loyalty. Those who refused, concentrated among the higher clergy, were in theory thrown out of their offices. A year later (April 1791) the pope declared that clergy who had taken the oath were suspended from their offices. Antirevolutionary sentiment grew among thousands of French people, particularly in outlying regions, to whom the church was still vital as a source of charity and a center of community life. This religious opposition worked to undermine the legitimacy of the new government.

Meanwhile, the Assembly proceeded with administrative and judicial reform. The deputies abolished the medieval provinces as administrative districts and replaced them with uniform *départements* (departments). They declared that local officials would be elected—a revolutionary dispersal of power that had previously belonged to the king.

As work on the constitution drew to a close in the spring of 1791, the king decided that he had had enough. Royal authority, as he knew it, had been virtually dismantled. Louis himself was now a virtual prisoner in the Tuileries Palace in the very heart of Paris. Afraid for himself and his family, he and a few loyal aides worked out a plan to flee France. The king and the members of his immediate family set out in disguise on

June 20, 1791. However, the party missed a rendezvous with a troop escort and was stopped—and recognized—in the town of Varennes, near the eastern border of the kingdom.

Louis and his family were returned to Paris and held under lightly disguised house arrest. The circumstances of his flight were quickly discovered. He and the queen had sent money abroad ahead of themselves. He had left behind a document condemning the constitution. His intention was to invade France with Austrian troops if necessary. Thus in July 1791, just as the Assembly was completing its proposal for a constitutional monarchy, the constitution it had created began to seem unworkable because the monarch was not to be trusted.

Editorials and protests against the monarchy increased. In one incident known as the Massacre of the Champ (Field) de Mars, government troops led by Lafayette fired on citizens at an antimonarchy demonstration that certain Parisian clubs had organized; about fifty men and women died. This inflammatory incident both reflected and heightened tensions between moderate reformers satisfied with the constitutional monarchy, such as Lafayette, and outspoken republicans who wanted to eliminate the monarchy altogether.

On September 14 the king swore to uphold the constitution. He had no choice. The event became an occasion for celebration, but the tension between the interests of the Parisians and the provisions of the new constitution could not be glossed over. Though a liberal document for its day, the constitution reflected the views of the elite deputies who had created it. The right to vote, based on a minimal property qualification, was given to about half of all adult men. However, these men only chose electors, for whom the property qualifications were higher. The electors in turn chose deputies to national bodies as well as local officials. Although in theory any eligible voter could be an elected deputy or official, the fact that elite electors determined every officeholder meant that few ordinary citizens would become deputies or local administrators. The new Declaration of Rights that accompanied the constitution reflected a fear of the masses that had not existed when the Declaration of the Rights of Man and the Citizen was first promulgated in 1789. Freedom of the press and freedom of assembly, for example, were not fully guaranteed.

Further, no political rights were accorded to women. Educated women had joined Parisian clubs such as the *Cercle sociale* (Social Circle), where opinion favored extending rights to women. Through such clubs, these women had tried to influence the National Assembly. But the Assembly granted neither political rights nor legal equality to women, nor did it pass other laws beneficial to women, such as legalizing divorce or mandating female education. The prevailing view of women among deputies seemed to reflect those of the Enlightenment philosophe Jean-Jacques Rousseau, who imagined women's competence to be entirely circumscribed within the family. The Declaration of the Rights of Woman was drafted by a woman named Olympe de Gouges to draw attention to the treatment of women in the constitution.

Very soon after the constitution was implemented, the fragility of the new system became clear. The National Assembly declared that its members could not serve in the first assembly to be elected under the constitution. Thus the members of the newly elected Legislative Assembly, which began to meet in October 1791, lacked any of the cohesiveness that would have come from collective experience. Also, unlike the previous National Assembly, they did not represent a broad range of opinion but were mostly republicans.

In fact, the Legislative Assembly was dominated by republican members of the Jacobin Club. They were known as Girondins, after the region in southwestern France from which many of the club's leaders came. The policies of these new deputies and continued pressure from the ordinary citizens of Paris would cause the constitutional monarchy to collapse in less than a year.

The Second Phase and Foreign War, 1791–1793

An additional pressure on the new regime soon arose: a threat of foreign invasion and a war to counter the threat. Antirevolutionary aristocratic émigrés, including the king's brothers, had taken refuge in nearby German states and were planning to invade France. The emperor and other German rulers did little actively to aid the plotters. Austria and Prussia, however, in the Declaration of Pillnitz of August 1791, declared, as a concession to the émigrés, that they would intervene if necessary to support the monarchy in France.

The threat of invasion, when coupled with distrust of the royal family, seemed more real to the revolutionaries in Paris than it may actually have been. Indeed, many deputies hoped for war. They assumed that the outcome would be a French defeat, which would lead to a popular uprising that would rid them, at last, of the monarchy. In April 1792, under pressure from the Assembly, Louis XVI declared war against Austria. From this point on, foreign war would be an ongoing factor in the Revolution.

At first the war was a disaster for France. The army had not been reorganized into an effective fighting force after the loss of many aristocratic officers and the addition of newly self-aware citizens. On one occasion troops insisted on putting an officer's command to a vote. The French lost early battles in the Austrian Netherlands, but the Austrians did not press their advantage and invade France because they were preoccupied with problems in eastern Europe.

The defeats emboldened critics of the monarchy, who demanded action. Under the direction of the Girondins, the Legislative Assembly began to press for the deportation of priests who had been leading demonstrations against the government. The Assembly abolished the personal guard of the king and summoned provincial National Guardsmen to Paris. The king's resistance to these measures, as well as fears of acute grain shortages owing to a poor harvest and the needs of the armies, created further unrest. Crowds staged boisterous marches near the royal palace, physically confronted the king, and forced him to don the "liberty cap," a symbol of republicanism. The king's authority and prestige were now thoroughly undermined.

By July 1792 tensions had become acute. The grain shortage was severe, Austrian and Prussian troops committed to saving the royal family were threatening to invade, and, most important, the populace was better organized and more determined than ever before. In each of the forty-eight "sections"—administrative wards—of Paris, a miniature popular assembly thrashed out all the events and issues of the day just as deputies in the nationwide Legislative Assembly did. Derisively called *sans-culottes* ("without knee pants") because they could not afford elite fashions, the ordinary Parisians in the section assemblies included shopkeepers, artisans, and laborers. Their political organization enhanced their influence with the Assembly, the clubs, and the newspapers in the capital. By late July most sections of the city had approved a petition calling for the exile of the king, the election of new city officials, the exemption of the poor from taxation, and other radical measures.

In August the sans-culottes took matters into their own hands. On the night of August 9, after careful preparations, representatives of the section assemblies constituted themselves as a new city government with the aim of "saving the state." They then assaulted the Tuileries Palace, where the royal family was living. In the bloody confrontation, hundreds of royal guards and citizens died. After briefly taking refuge in the Legislative Assembly, the king and his family were imprisoned in one of the fortified towers in the city, under guard of the popularly controlled city government.

The storming of the Tuileries inaugurated the second major phase of the Revolution: the establishment of republican government in place of the monarchy. By their intimidating numbers, the people of Paris now controlled the Legislative Assembly. Some deputies had fled. Those who remained agreed under pressure to dissolve the Assembly and make way for another body to be elected by universal manhood suffrage. On September 20 that assembly, known as the National Convention, began to meet. The next day the Convention declared the end of the monarchy and set to work crafting a constitution for the new republic.

Coincidentally, that same September day, French forces won their first genuine victory over the allied Austrian and Prussian invasion forces. Though not a decisive battle, it was a profound psychological triumph. A citizen army had defeated the professional force of a ruling prince. The victory bolstered the republican government and encouraged it to put more energy into the wars. Indeed, maintaining armies in the field became a weighty factor in the delicate equilibrium of revolutionary government. The new republican regime let it be known that its armies were not merely for self-defense but for the liberation of all peoples in the "name of the French Nation."

The Convention faced the divisive issue of what to do with the king. Louis had not done anything truly treasonous, but some of the king's correspondence, discovered after the storming of the Tuileries, provided the pretext for charges of treason. The Convention held a trial for him, lasting from December 11, 1792, through January 15, 1793. He was found guilty of treason by an overwhelming vote (683 to 39); the republican government would not compromise with monarchy. Less lopsided was the sentence: Louis was condemned to death by a narrow majority, 387 to 334.

The consequences for the king were immediate. On January 21, 1793, Louis mounted the scaffold in a public square near the Tuileries and was beheaded. The execution split the ranks of the Convention and soon resulted in the breakdown of the institution itself.

The Faltering Republic and the Terror, 1793–1794 In February 1793 the republic was at war with virtually every state in Europe; the only exceptions were the Scandinavian kingdoms and Russia. Moreover, the regime faced massive and widespread counterrevolutionary uprisings within France. Vigilance against internal and external enemies became a top priority. The Convention established an executive body, the Committee of Public Safety. In theory, this executive council was answerable to the Convention as a whole. As the months passed, however, it acted with greater and greater autonomy not only to institute policies but also to eradicate enemies. The broadly based republican government represented by the Convention began to disintegrate.

The first major narrowing of control came in June 1793. Pushed by the Parisian sections, a group of extreme Jacobins purged the Girondin deputies from the Convention, arresting many of them. The Girondins were republicans who favored an activist government in the people's behalf, but they were less radical than their fellow Jacobins who now moved against them, less insistent on central control of the Revolution, and less willing to share power with the citizens of Paris. After the purge, the Convention still met, but most authority lay with the Committee of Public Safety.

New uprisings against the regime began. Added to counterrevolutionary revolts by peasants and aristocrats were new revolts by Girondin sympathizers. As resistance to the government mounted and the foreign threat continued, a dramatic event in Paris led the Committee of Public Safety officially to adopt a policy of political repression. A well-known figure of the Revolution, Jean Paul Marat (1743–1793), publisher of a radical republican newspaper very popular with ordinary Parisians, was murdered on July 13 by Charlotte Corday (1768–1793), a young aristocratic woman who had asked to meet with him. Shortly afterward, a longtime member of the Jacobin Club, Maximilien Robespierre (1758–1794), joined the Committee and called for "Terror"—the systematic repression of internal enemies. He was not alone in his views. Members of the section assemblies of Paris led demonstrations to pressure the government into making Terror the order of the day.

Since the previous autumn, the guillotine had been at work against identified enemies of the regime, but now a more energetic apparatus of Terror was instituted. A Law of Suspects was passed that allowed citizens to be arrested simply on vague suspicion of counterrevolutionary sympathies. Revolutionary tribunals and an oversight committee made arbitrary arrests and rendered summary judgments. In October a steady stream of executions began, beginning with the queen, imprisoned since the storming of the Tuileries the year before. The imprisoned Girondin deputies followed, and then the beheadings continued relentlessly. Paris witnessed about 2,600 executions from 1793 to 1794.

Around France the verdicts of revolutionary tribunals led to approximately 14,000 executions. Another 10,000 to 12,000 people died in prison. Ten thousand or more were killed, usually by summary execution, after the defeat of counterrevolutionary uprisings. For example, 2,000 people were summarily executed in Lyon when a Girondin revolt collapsed there in October. The aim of the Terror was not merely to stifle active resistance; it was also to silence simple dissent. The victims in Paris included not only aristocrats or former deputies but also sans-culottes. The radical Jacobins wanted to seize control of the Revolution from the Parisian citizens who had lifted them to power.

Robespierre embodied all the contradictions of the policy of Terror. He was an austere, almost prim man who lived very modestly—a model, of sorts, of the virtuous, disinterested citizen. The policies followed by the government during the year of his greatest influence, from July 1793 to July 1794, included generous, rational, and humane actions to benefit ordinary citizens as well as the atrocities of official Terror. Indeed, the Terror notwithstanding, the government of the Committee of Public Safety was effective in providing direction for the nation at a critical time. In August 1793 it instituted the first mass conscription of citizens into the army (*levée en masse*), and a consistently effective popular army came into existence. In the autumn of 1793 this army won impressive victories. In May the Convention had instituted the Law of the Maximum, which controlled the price of grain so that city people could afford their staple food—bread. In September the Committee extended the law to apply to other necessary commodities. Extensive plans were made for a system of free and universal primary education. Slavery in the French colonies was abolished in February 1794. Divorce, first legalized in 1792, was made easier for women to obtain.

In the name of "reason," traditional rituals and rhythms of life were changed. One reform of long-term significance was the introduction of the metric system of weights and measures. Although people continued to use the old, familiar measures for a very long time, the change was eventually accomplished, leading the way for standardization throughout Europe. Equally "rational" but not as successful was the elimination of the traditional calendar; weeks and months were replaced by forty-day months and *decadi* (ten-day weeks with one day of rest), and all saints' days and Christian holidays were eliminated. The years had already been changed—Year I had been declared with the founding of the republic in the autumn of 1792.

Churches were rededicated as "temples of reason." Believing that outright atheism left people with no basis for personal or national morality, Robespierre sought instead to promote a cult of the Supreme Being. The new public festivals were solemn civic ceremonies intended to ritualize and legitimize the new political order. These and other innovations of the regime were not necessarily welcomed. The French people generally resented the elimination of the traditional calendar. In the countryside massive peasant uprisings protested the loss of poor relief, community life, and familiar ritual.

Divorce law and economic regulation were a boon, especially to urban women, but women's participation in sectional assemblies and in all organized political activity—which had been energetic and widespread—was banned in October 1793. The particular target of the regime was the Society of Revolutionary Republican Women, a powerful club representing the interests of female sans-culottes. By banning women from political life, the regime helped to ground its legitimacy, since the seemingly "natural" exclusion of women might make the new system of government appear part of the "natural" order. Outlawing women's clubs and barring women from section assemblies also eliminated a source of popular power, from which the regime was now trying to distance itself.

The Committee and the Convention were divided over religious and other policies, but the main policy differences concerned economic matters: how far to go to assist the poor, the unemployed, and the landless. Several of the temperate critics of Robespierre and his allies were guillotined for disagreeing with these policies and for doubting the continuing need for the Terror itself. Their deaths helped precipitate the end of the Terror by causing Robespierre's power base to shrink so much that it had no further legitimacy.

Deputies to the Convention finally dared to move against Robespierre in July 1794. French armies had scored a major victory over Austrian troops on June 26, so there was no longer any need for the emergency status that the Terror had thrived on. In late July the Convention voted to arrest Robespierre, the head of the revolutionary tribunal in Paris, and their closest associates and allies in the city government. On July 28 and 29 Robespierre and the others—about a hundred in all—were guillotined, and the Terror ended.

The Thermidorian Reaction and the Directory, 1794–1799

After the death of Robespierre, the Convention reclaimed many of the executive powers that the Committee of Public Safety had seized. The Convention dismantled the apparatus of the Terror, repealed the Law of Suspects, and forced the revolutionary tribunals to adopt ordinary legal procedures. The Convention also passed into law some initiatives, such as expanded public education, that had been proposed in the preceding year but not enacted. This post-Terror phase of the Revolution is called the "Thermidorian Reaction" because it began in the revolutionary month of Thermidor (July 19–August 17).

Lacking the weapons of the Terror, the Convention was unable to enforce controls on the supply and price of bread. Thus economic difficulties and a hard winter produced famine by the spring of 1795. The people of Paris tried to retain influence with the new government. In May crowds marched on the Convention chanting "Bread and the Constitution of '93," referring to the republican constitution drafted by the Convention but never implemented because of the Terror. The demonstrations were met with force and were dispersed.

Members of the Convention remained fearful of a renewed, popularly supported Terror, on the one hand, or a royalist uprising, on the other. Counterrevolutionary uprisings had erupted in the fall of 1794, and landings on French territory by émigré forces occurred the following spring. The Convention drafted a new constitution that limited popular participation in government, as had the first constitution of 1791. The new plan allowed fairly widespread (but not universal) male suffrage, but only for electors, who would choose deputies for the two houses of the legislature. The property qualifications for being an elector were very high, so all but elite citizens were effectively disenfranchised. The Convention also decreed, at the last minute, that two-thirds of its members must serve in the new legislature, regardless of the outcome of elections. Although this maneuver enhanced the stability of the new regime, it undermined the credibility of the new ballot.

Governance under the provisions of the new constitution, beginning in the fall of 1795, was called the Directory, for the executive council of five men chosen by the upper house of the new legislature. To avoid the concentration of authority that had produced the Terror, the members of the Convention had tried to enshrine separation of powers in the new system. However, the governments under the Directory were never free from attempted coups or from their own extraconstitutional maneuvering.

The most spectacular external challenge, the Conspiracy of Equals, was led by extreme Jacobins who wanted to restore popular government and aggressive economic and social policy on behalf of the common people. The conspiracy ended with arrests and executions in 1797. When elections in 1797 and 1798 returned many royalist as well as Jacobin deputies, the Directory abrogated the constitution to forestall challenges to its authority. Many undesirable deputies were arrested, sent into exile, or denied seats.

The armies of the republic did enjoy some spectacular successes during these years, for the first time carrying the fighting—and the effects of the Revolution—onto foreign soil. French armies conquered the Dutch in 1795. In 1796–1797 French armies led by the young general Napoleon Bonaparte wrested control of northern Italy from the Austrians. Both regions were transformed into "sister" republics, governed by local revolutionaries but under French protection. By 1799, however, conditions had once again reached a critical juncture. The demands of the war effort, together with rising prices and the continued decline in the value of the assignats, brought the government again to the brink of bankruptcy. The government also seemed to be losing control of the French countryside; there were continued royalist uprisings, local political vendettas between moderates and Jacobins, and outright banditry.

Members of the Directory had often turned to sympathetic army commanders to suppress dissent and to carry out arrests and purges of the legislature. They now invited General Bonaparte to help them form a government that they could more strictly control. Two members of the Directory plotted with Napoleon and his brother, Louis Bonaparte, to seize power on November 9, 1799.

THE NAPOLEONIC ERA AND THE LEGACY OF REVOLUTION, 1799–1815

Talented, charming, and ruthless, Napoleon Bonaparte (1769–1821) was the kind of person who gives rise to myths. His audacity, determination, and personal magnetism enabled him to profit from the political instability and confusion in France and to ensconce himself in power. Once in power, he temporarily stabilized the political scene by fixing in law the more conservative gains of the Revolution. He also used his power and his remarkable abilities as a general to continue wars of conquest against France's neighbors, which helped deflect political tensions at home.

Napoleon's troops in effect exported the Revolution as they conquered most of Europe. In most states that came under French control, law codes were reformed, governing elites were opened to talent, and public works were upgraded. Yet French conquest also meant domination, pure and simple, and involvement in France's rivalry with Britain. The Napoleonic era left Europe an ambiguous legacy—war and its complex aftermath, yet also revolution and its goad to further change.

Napoleon: From Soldier to Emperor, 1799–1804 Napoleon was from Corsica, a Mediterranean island that had passed from Genoese to French control in the eighteenth century. The second son of a large gentry family, he was educated at military academies in France, and he married the politically well-connected widow Joséphine de Beauharnais (1763–1814), whose aristocratic husband had been a victim of the Terror.

Napoleon steered a careful course through the political turmoil of the Revolution. By 1799 his military victories had won him much praise and fame. He had demonstrated his reliability and ruthlessness in 1795 when he ordered troops guarding the Convention to fire on a Parisian crowd. He had capped his successful Italian campaign of 1796–1797 with an invasion of Egypt in an attempt to strike at British influence and trade connections in the eastern Mediterranean. The Egyptian campaign failed in its goals, but individual spectacular victories during the campaign ensured Napoleon's military reputation. In addition, Napoleon had demonstrated his widening ambitions. He had taken leading scientists and skilled administrators with him to Egypt in order to export the seeming benefits of French civilization—and to install a more lasting bureaucratic authority.

Napoleon Crossing the Great St. Bernard

This stirring portrait by the great neoclassical painter Jacques-Louis David memorializes Napoleon's 1796 crossing of the Alps before his victorious Italian campaign, as a general under the Directory. In part because it was executed in 1801–1802, the painting depicts the moment hero-ically rather than realisti-cally. (In truth, Napoleon wisely crossed the Alps on a sure-footed mule, not a stallion.) Napoleon, as First Consul, wanted images of himself that would justify his increasingly ambitious claims to power. (Réunion des Musées Nationaux/Art Resource, NY)

Napoleon's partners in the new government after the November 1799 coup soon learned of his great political ambition and skill. In theory, the new system was to be a streamlined version of the Directory: Napoleon was to be first among equals in a three-man executive—"First Consul," according to borrowed Roman terminology. But Napoleon quickly asserted his primacy among them and began not only to domi-nate executive functions but also to bypass the authority of the regime's various leg-islative bodies.

Perhaps most important to the success of his increasingly authoritarian rule was his effort to include men of many political stripes—Jacobins, reforming liberals, even former Old Regime bureaucrats—among his ministers, advisers, and bureaucrats. He welcomed many exiles back to France, including all but the most ardent royalists. He thus stabilized his regime by healing some of the rifts among ruling elites. Napoleon combined toleration with ruthlessness, however. Between 1800 and 1804 he impris-oned, executed, or exiled dozens of individuals for alleged Jacobin agitation or roy-alist sympathies. His final gesture to intimidate royalist opposition came in 1804, when he kidnapped and coldly murdered a Bourbon prince who had been living in exile in Germany.

Under Napoleon's regime, any semblance of free political life ended. Legislative bod-ies lost all initiative in the governing process, becoming rubber stamps for the consuls' policies. In any case, there were no meaningful elections. Voters chose only candidates for a kind of pool of potential legislators, from which occasional replacements were chosen by members of the Senate, an advisory body entirely appointed by Napoleon himself. Political clubs were banned; the vibrant press of the revolutionary years wilted under heavy censorship. Napoleon also further centralized the administrative system, set up by the first wave of revolutionaries in 1789, by establishing the office of prefect to govern the départements. All prefects and their subordinates were appointed by Napoleon, thus extending the range of his power and undermining autonomous local government.

Certain administrative changes that enhanced central control, such as for tax collection, were more uniformly positive in their effects. Napoleon oversaw the establishment of the Bank of France, modeled on the Bank of England. The bank provided capital for investment and helped the state stabilize the French currency. Perhaps the most important achievement early in his regime was the Concordat of 1801. The aim of this treaty with the pope was to solve the problem of church-state relations that for years had provoked counterrevolutionary rebellions. The agreement allowed for the resumption of Catholic worship and the continued support of the clergy by the state, but also accepted the more dramatic changes accomplished by the Revolution. Church lands that had been sold were guaranteed to their new owners. Although Catholicism was recognized as the "religion of the majority of Frenchmen," Protestant churches also were allowed, and their clergy were paid. Later, Napoleon granted new rights to Jews as well. Nonetheless, the Concordat removed one of the most important grounds for counterrevolutionary upheaval in the countryside and defused royalist resistance from abroad.

The law code that Napoleon established in 1804 was much like his accommodation with the church in its limited acceptance of revolutionary gains. His Civil Code (also known as the *code napoléon*, or Napoleonic Code) honored the revolutionary legacy in its guarantee of equality before the law and its requirement for the taxation of all social classes; it also enshrined modern forms of property ownership and civil contracts. Neither the code nor Napoleon's political regime fostered individual rights, especially for women. Fathers' control over their families was enhanced. Divorce was no longer permitted except in rare instances. Women lost all property rights when they married, and they generally faced legal domination by fathers and husbands.

Napoleon was careful, though, to avoid heavy-handed displays of power. He cleverly sought ratification of each stage of his assumption of power through national plebiscites (referendums in which all eligible voters could vote for or against proposals)—one plebiscite for a new constitution in 1800 and another when he claimed consulship for life in 1802. He approached his final political coup—declaring himself emperor—with similar dexterity. Long before he claimed the imperial title, Napoleon had begun to sponsor an active court life appropriate to imperial pretensions. The empire was proclaimed in May 1804 with the approval of the Senate; it was also endorsed by another plebiscite. Members of Napoleon's family were given princely status, and a number of his favorites received various titles and honors. The titles brought no legal privilege but signaled social and political distinctions of great importance. Old nobles were allowed to use their titles on this basis.

Many members of the elite, whatever their persuasions, tolerated Napoleon's claims to power because he safeguarded fundamental revolutionary gains yet reconfirmed their own status. War soon resumed against political and economic enemies—principally Britain, Austria, and Russia—and for a time Napoleon's success on the battlefield continued. Because military glory was central to the political purpose and self-esteem of elites, Napoleon's early successes as emperor further enhanced his power.

Conquering Europe, 1805–1810 Napoleon maintained relatively peaceful relations with other nations while he consolidated power at home, but the truces did not last. Tensions with the British quickly re-escalated when Britain resumed aggression against French shipping in 1803, and Napoleon countered by seizing Hanover, the ancestral German home of the English king. England was at war on the high seas with Spain and the Netherlands, which Napoleon had forced to enter the fray. Napoleon began to gather a large French force on the northern coast of France; his objective was to invade England.

The British fleet, commanded by Horatio Nelson (1758–1805), intercepted the combined French and Spanish fleets that were to have been the invasion flotilla and inflicted a devastating defeat off Cape Trafalgar in southern Spain on October 21, 1805. The victory ensured British mastery of the seas and, in the long run, contributed to Napoleon's demise. In the short run, the defeat at Trafalgar paled for the French beside Napoleon's impressive victories on land. Even as the French admirals were preparing for battle, Napoleon had abandoned the plans to invade England and in August had begun to march his army east through Germany to confront the great continental powers, Austria and Russia.

In December 1805, after some preliminary, small-scale victories, Napoleon's army routed a combined Austrian and Russian force near Austerlitz, north of Vienna. The Battle of Austerlitz was Napoleon's most spectacular victory. Austria sued for peace. In further battles in 1806, French forces defeated Prussian as well as Russian armies once again. Prussia was virtually dismembered by the subsequent Treaty of Tilsit (1807), but Napoleon tried to remake Russia into a contented ally. His hold on central Europe would not be secure with a hostile Russia, nor would the anti-British economic system that he envisioned—the Continental System (see page 630)—be workable without Russian participation.

French forces were still trying to prevail in Spain, which had been a client state since its defeat by revolutionary armies in 1795 but was resisting outright rule by a French-imposed king. In 1808, however, Napoleon turned his attention to more fully subduing Austria. Napoleon won the Battle of Wagram in July 1809, and Austria, like Russia, accepted French political and economic hegemony in a sort of alliance. By 1810 Napoleon had transformed most of Europe into allied or dependent states. The only exceptions were Britain and the parts of Spain and Portugal that continued, with British help, to resist France.

The states least affected by French hegemony were its reluctant allies: Austria, Russia, and the Scandinavian countries. Denmark had allied with France in 1807 only for help in fending off British naval supremacy in the Baltic. Sweden had reluctantly made peace in 1810 after losing control of Finland to Napoleon's ally, Russia, and only minimally participated in the Continental System. At the other extreme were territories that had been incorporated into France. These included the Austrian Netherlands, territory along the Rhineland, and sections of Italy that bordered France. These regions

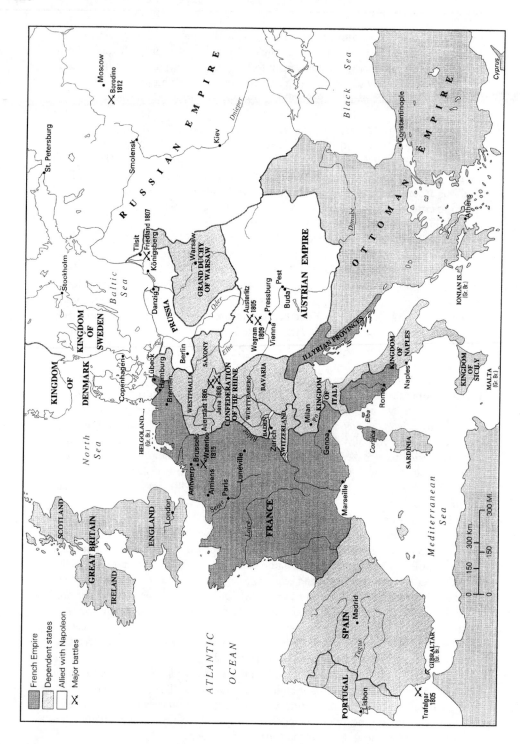

were occupied by French troops and were treated as though they were départements of France itself.

In most other areas, some form of French-controlled government was in place, usually headed by a member of Napoleon's family. In both northern Italy and the Netherlands, where "sister" republics had been established after French conquests under the Directory, Napoleon imposed monarchies. Rulers were also installed in the kingdom of Naples and in Spain. Western German states of the Holy Roman Empire that had allied with Napoleon against Austria were organized into the Confederation of the Rhine, with Napoleon as its "Protector." After a thousand years, the Holy Roman Empire ceased to exist. Two further states were created, largely out of the defeated Prussia's territory: the kingdom of Westphalia in western Germany and the Grand Duchy of Warsaw in the east.

Napoleon's domination of these various regions had complex, and at times contradictory, consequences. On the one hand, Napoleonic armies essentially exported the French Revolution, in that French domination brought with it the Napoleonic Civil Code, and with it political and economic reform akin to that of the early phases of the Revolution. Equality before the law was decreed following the French example. This meant the end of noble exemption from taxation in the many areas where it existed. In general, the complex snarl of medieval taxes and tolls was replaced with straightforward property taxes that were universally applied. As a consequence, tax revenues rose dramatically—by 50 percent in the kingdom of Italy, for example. Serfdom and forced labor also were abolished, as they had been in France in August 1789.

In most Catholic regions the church was subjected to the terms of the Concordat of 1801. The tithe was abolished, church property was seized and sold, and religious orders were dissolved. Although Catholicism remained the state-supported religion in these areas, Protestantism was tolerated, and Jews were granted rights of citizenship. Secular education, at least for males, was encouraged.

On the other hand, Napoleon would countenance in the empire only those aspects of France's revolutionary legacy that he tolerated in France itself. Just as he had suppressed any meaningful participatory government in France, so too did he suppress it in conquered regions. This came as a blow in states such as the Netherlands, which had experienced its own democratizing "Patriot" movement and which had enjoyed republican self-government after invasion by French armies during the Revolution itself. Throughout Napoleon's empire, many of the benefits of streamlined administration and taxation were offset by the drain of continual warfare. Deficits rose three- and fourfold, despite increased revenues. In addition, one of the inevitable costs of empire was political compromise to secure allies. In the Grand Duchy of Warsaw, reconstituted from lands Prussia had seized in the eighteenth century, Napoleon tampered little with either noble privileges or the power of the church. And throughout Europe he randomly allotted lands to reward his greatest generals and ministers, thereby exempting those lands from taxation and control by his own bureaucracy.

If true self-government was not allowed, a broad segment of the elite in all regions was nevertheless won over to cooperation with Napoleon by being welcomed into his

Napoleonic Europe, ca. 1810

France dominated continental Europe after Napoleon's victories.

"And It Cannot Be Changed" *This horrifying scene of an execution of rebels against French rule in Spain was one of a series of etchings by Madrid artist Francisco Goya. In the 1810 series, titled "The Disasters of War," Goya was severely critical of French actions, as well as of barbarities committed by the British-backed Spaniards.* (Foto Marburg/Art Resource, NY)

bureaucracy or into the large multinational army, called the *Grande Armée*. Their loyalty was cemented when they bought confiscated church lands.

The impact of Napoleon's Continental System was equally mixed. Under this system the Continent was in theory closed to all British shipping and goods. The effects were widespread but uneven, and smuggling to evade controls on British goods became a major enterprise. Regions heavily involved in trade with Britain or its colonies or dependent on British shipping suffered in the new system, as did overseas trade in general when Britain gained dominance of the seas after Trafalgar. However, the closing of the Continent to British trade, combined with increases in demand to supply Napoleon's armies, spurred the development of continental industries, at least in the short run. This industrial growth, enhanced by the improvement of roads, canals, and the like, formed the basis for further industrial development.

Defeat and Abdication, 1812–1815 Whatever its achievements, Napoleon's empire was ultimately precarious because of the hostility of Austria and Russia, as well as the belligerence of Britain. Russia was a particularly weak link in the chain of alliances and subject states because Russian landowners and merchants were angered when their vital trade in timber for the British navy was interrupted and when supplies of luxury goods, brought in British ships, began to dwindle.

A century of close alliances with German ruling houses made alliance with a French ruler an extremely difficult political option for Tsar Alexander I.

It was Napoleon, however, who ended the alliance by provoking a breach with Russia. He suddenly backed away from an arrangement to marry one of Alexander's sisters and accepted the Austrian princess Marie Louise instead. (He had reluctantly divorced Joséphine in 1809 because their marriage had not produced an heir.) Also, he seized lands along the German Baltic seacoast belonging to a member of Alexander's family. When Alexander threatened rupture of the alliance if the lands were not returned, Napoleon mounted an invasion. Advisers warned him about the magnitude of the task he seemed so eager to undertake—particularly about the preparations needed for winter fighting in Russia—but their alarms went unheard.

Napoleon's previous military successes had stemmed from a combination of strategic innovations and pure audacity. Napoleon divided his forces into independent corps. Each corps included infantry, cavalry, and artillery. Organized in these workable units, his armies could travel quickly by several separate routes and converge in massive force to face the enemy. Leadership on the battlefield came from a loyal and extremely talented officer corps that had grown up since army commands had been thrown open to nonaristocrats during the Revolution. The final ingredient in the success formula was the high morale of French troops. Since the first victory of the revolutionary armies in September 1792, citizen-soldiers had proved their worth. Complicated troop movements and bravery on the battlefield were possible when troops felt they were fighting for their *nation,* not merely their ruling dynasty. Napoleon's reputation as a winning general added a further measure of self-confidence.

The campaign against Russia began in June 1812. It was a spectacular failure. Napoleon had gathered a force of about 700,000 men—about half from France and half from allied states—a force twice as large as Russia's. The strategy of quickly moving independent corps and assembling massive forces could not be implemented: simply mustering so many men along the border was already the equivalent of gathering them for battle. Bold victories had often enabled Napoleon's troops to live off the countryside while they waited for supplies to catch up to the front line. But when the enemy attacked supply lines, the distances traveled were very great, the countryside was impoverished, or battles were not decisive, Napoleon's ambitious strategies proved futile. In varying degrees, these conditions prevailed in Russia.

By the time the French faced the Russians in the principal battle of the Russian campaign—at Borodino, west of Moscow—the Grande Armée had been on the march for two and a half months and stood at less than half its original strength. After the indecisive but bloody battle, the French occupied and pillaged Moscow but found scarcely enough food and supplies to sustain them. When Napoleon finally led his troops out of Moscow late in October, the fate of the French forces was all but sealed. As they retreated, French and allied soldiers who had not died in battle died of exposure or starvation or were killed by Russian peasants when they wandered away from their units. The talents of generals and the determination of troops were focused on sheer survival. Of the original 700,000 troops of the Grand Armée, fewer than 100,000 made it out of Russia.

Napoleon left his army before it was fully out of Russia. A coup attempt in Paris prompted him to return to his governing duties before the French people realized the extent of the disaster in the East. The collapse of his reign had begun, spurred by a coincidental defeat in Spain. Since 1808 Spain had been largely under French domination, with Napoleon's brother, Joseph, as king. A rebel Cortes (national representative assembly), however, continued to meet in territory that the French did not control, and British troops were never expelled from the Iberian Peninsula. In 1812, as Napoleon was advancing against Russia, the collapse of French control accelerated. By the time Napoleon reached Paris at the turn of the new year, Joseph had been expelled from Spain, and an Anglo-Spanish force led by the duke of Wellington was poised to invade France.

Napoleon lost his last chance to stave off a coalition of all major powers against him when he refused an Austrian offer of peace for the return of conquered Austrian territories. With Britain willing to subsidize the allied armies, Tsar Alexander determined to destroy Napoleon, and the Austrians now anxious to share the spoils, Napoleon's empire began to crumble. Imperial forces—many now raw recruits—were crushed in the massive "Battle of Nations" near Leipzig in October 1813, during which some troops from German satellite states deserted him on the battlefield. The allies invaded France and forced Napoleon to abdicate on April 6, 1814.

Napoleon was exiled to the island of Elba, off France's Mediterranean coast, but was still treated somewhat royally. He was installed as the island's ruler and was given an income drawn on the French treasury. Meanwhile, however, the restored French king was having his own troubles. Louis XVIII (r. 1814–1824) was the brother of the executed Louis XVI (he took the number eighteen out of respect for Louis XVI's son, who had died in prison in 1795). The new monarch had been out of the country and out of touch with its circumstances since the beginning of the Revolution. In addition to the delicate task of establishing his own legitimacy, he faced enormous practical problems, including pensioning off thousands of soldiers now unemployed and still loyal to Napoleon.

Napoleon, bored and almost penniless in his island kingdom (the promised French pension never materialized), took advantage of the circumstances and returned surreptitiously to France on February 26, 1815. His small band of attendants was joined by the soldiers sent by the king to halt his progress. Louis XVIII abandoned Paris to the returned emperor.

Napoleon's triumphant return lasted only one hundred days, however. Though many soldiers welcomed his return, many members of the elite were reluctant to throw in their lot with Napoleon again. Many ordinary French citizens had also become disenchanted with him since the defeat in Russia and with the high costs, in conscription and taxation, of raising new armies. In any case, Napoleon's reappearance galvanized the divided allies, who had been haggling over a peace settlement, into unity. Napoleon tried to strike first, but he lost against English and Prussian troops in his first major battle, at Waterloo (in modern Belgium) on June 18, 1815. When Napoleon arrived in Paris after the defeat, he discovered the government in the hands of an ad hoc committee that included the Marquis de Lafayette. Under pressure, he abdicated once again. This time he was exiled to the tiny, remote island of St. Helena in the South Atlantic, from which escape would be impossible. He died there in 1821.

The Legacy of Revolution for France and the World   The process of change in France between 1789 and 1815 was so complex that it is easy to overlook the overall impact of the Revolution. Superficially, the changes seemed to come full circle—with first Louis XVI on the throne, then Napoleon as emperor, and then Louis XVIII on the throne. Even though the monarchy was restored, however, the Revolution had discredited absolute monarchy in theory and practice. Louis XVIII had to recognize the right of "the people," however narrowly defined, to participate in government and to enjoy due process of law. Another critical legacy of the Revolution and the Napoleonic era was a centralized political system of départements rather than a patchwork of provinces. For the first time, a single code of law applied to all French people. Most officials—from département administrators to city mayors—were appointed by the central government until the late twentieth century. The conscientious attention of the government, at various stages of the Revolution, to advances for France generally reflects the positive side of this centralization. The government sponsored national scientific societies, a national library and archives, and a system of teachers' colleges and universities. Particularly under Napoleon, a spate of canal- and road-building projects drastically improved transport systems.

Napoleon's legacy, like that of the Revolution itself, was mixed. His self-serving reconciliation of aristocratic pretensions with the opening of careers to men of talent ensured the long-term success of revolutionary principles from which the elite as a whole profited. His reconciliation of the state with the Catholic Church helped to stabilize his regime and cemented some revolutionary gains. The restored monarchy could not renege on these gains. Yet whatever his achievements, Napoleon's overthrow of constitutional principles worsened the problem of political instability. His brief return to power in 1815 reflects the degree to which his power had always been rooted in military adventurism and in the loyalty of soldiers and officers. Similarly, the swiftness of his collapse suggests that although the empire under Napoleon may have seemed an enduring solution to the political instability of the late 1790s, it was no more secure than any of the other revolutionary governments.

Although Louis XVIII acknowledged the principle of constitutionalism at the end of the Revolution, the particular configuration of his regime rested on fragile footing. Indeed, the fragility of new political systems was one of the most profound lessons of the Revolution. There was division over policies, but even greater division over legitimacy—that is, the acceptance by a significant portion of the politically active citizenry of a particular government's right to rule. Before the Revolution started, notions about political legitimacy had undergone a significant shift. The deputies who declared themselves to be the National Assembly in June 1789 already believed that they had a right to do so. In their view, they represented "the nation," and their voice had legitimacy for that reason. The shift reflects not the innate power of ideas but the power of ideas in context. These deputies brought to Versailles not only their individual convictions that "reason" should be applied to the political system but also their experience in social settings where those ideas were well received. In their salons, clubs, and literary societies, they had experienced the familiarity, trust, and sense of community that are essential to effective political action.

The deputies' attempt to transplant their sense of community into national politics was not wholly successful. Factions, competing interests, and clashes of personality can be fatal to an insecure system. The National Assembly had scarcely been inaugurated when its deputies guaranteed its failure by disqualifying themselves from standing for office under the new constitution. The king also actively undermined the system because he disagreed with it in principle. The British parliamentary system, by comparison, though every bit as elitist as the narrowest of the representative systems during the

French Revolution, had a long history as a workable institution for lords, commoners, and rulers. This shared experience was an important counterweight to differences over fundamental issues, so that Parliament as an institution both survived political crises and helped resolve them. The Revolution thus left a powerful yet ambiguous legacy for France. Politics was established on new principles, yet still lacking were the practical means to achieve the promise inherent in those principles.

Throughout Europe and overseas, the Revolution left a powerful and equally complex legacy. France's continental conquests were the least enduring of the changes of the revolutionary era. Nevertheless, French domination had certain lasting effects: elites were exposed to modern bureaucratic management, and equality under the law transformed social and political relationships. Although national self-determination had an enemy in Napoleon, the breaking down of ancient political divisions provided important practical grounding for later cooperation among elites in nationalist movements. In Napoleon's kingdom of Italy, for example, a tax collector from Florence for the first time worked side by side with one from Milan. The most important legacy of the revolutionary wars, however, was the change in warfare itself made possible by the citizen armies of the French. Citizen-soldiers who identified closely with their nation, even when conscripts, proved able to maneuver and attack on the battlefield in ways that the brutishly disciplined poor conscripts in royal armies would not. In response, other states tried to build competing armies; the mass national armies that fought the world wars of the twentieth century were the result.

Naturally, the most important legacy of the French Revolution, as of the American, was the success of the Revolution itself. The most powerful absolute monarchy in Europe had succumbed to the demands of its people for dramatic social and political reforms. Throughout Europe in the nineteenth century, ruling dynasties faced revolutionary movements that demanded constitutional government, among other changes, and resorted to force to achieve it. European colonies overseas felt the impact of the Revolution and subsequent European wars in several ways. The British tried to take advantage of Napoleon's preoccupation with continental affairs by seizing French colonies and the colonies of the French-dominated Dutch. In 1806 they seized the Dutch colony of Cape Town—crucial for support of trade around Africa—as well as French bases along the African coast. In 1811 they grabbed the island of Java. In the Caribbean, the French sugar-producing islands of Martinique and Guadeloupe were particularly vulnerable to English sea power while Napoleon was executing his brilliant victories on the Continent after 1805. On the most productive of the French-controlled Caribbean islands, Saint Domingue, the Revolution inspired a successful rebellion by the enslaved plantation workers.

The National Assembly in Paris had delayed abolishing slavery in French colonies, despite the moral appeal of such a move, because of pressure from the white planters and out of fear that the financially strapped French government would lose some of its profitable sugar trade. But the example of revolutionary daring in Paris and confusion about ruling authority as the Assembly and the king wrangled did not go unnoticed in the colonies—in either plantation mansions or slave quarters. White planters on Saint Domingue simply hoped for political and economic "liberty" from the French government and its mercantilist trade policies. White planter rule was challenged, in turn, by wealthy people of mixed European and African descent who wanted equal citizenship,

Haitian Leader Toussaint-Louverture *Son of an educated slave, Toussaint-Louverture had himself been freed in 1777 but took on a leadership role when the slave revolt began on Saint Domingue in 1791. His military skill and political acumen were vital to the success of the revolt and to ruling the island's diverse population afterward.* (Stock Montage, Inc.)

hitherto denied them. A civil war broke out between these upper classes and was followed by a full-fledged slave rebellion, beginning in 1791. Britain sent aid to the rebels when it went to war against the French revolutionary government in 1793. Only when the republic was declared in Paris and the Convention abolished slavery did the rebels abandon alliances with France's enemies and attempt to govern in concert with the mother country.

Although it recovered other colonies from the British, France never regained control of Saint Domingue. Led by a former slave, François Dominique Toussaint-Louverture (1743–1803), the new government of the island tried to run its own affairs, though without formally declaring independence from France. Napoleon, early in his rule, decided to tighten control of the profitable colonies by reinstituting slavery and ousting the independent government of Saint Domingue. In 1802 French forces fought their way onto the island. They captured Toussaint-Louverture, who died shortly thereafter in prison. But in 1803 another rebellion, provoked by the threat of renewed slavery, expelled French forces for good. A former aide of Toussaint's declared the independence of the colony under the name Haiti—the island's Native American name—on January 1, 1804.

The French Revolution and Napoleonic rule, and the example of the Haitian revolution, had a notable impact on Spanish colonies in the Americas. Like other American colonies, the Spanish colonies wanted to loosen the closed economic ties the mother country tried to impose. In addition, the liberal ideas that had helped spawn the French Revolution spurred moves toward independence in Spanish America. Taking advantage of the confusion of authority in Spain, some of these colonies were already governing themselves independently in all but name. Echoes of radical republican ideology and of the Haitian experience resounded in some corners. For example, participants in two major rebellions in Mexico espoused the end of slavery and championed the interests of the poor against local and Spanish elites. The leaders of these self-declared revolutions were executed (in 1811 and 1815), and their movements were crushed by local elites in alliance with Spanish troops. The efforts of local elites to become self-governing—the attempted liberal revolutions—were little more successful. Only Argentina and Paraguay broke away from Spain at this time.

But as in Europe, a legacy remained of both limited and more radical revolutionary activity, and of its risks. Slave rebellions rocked British Caribbean islands in subsequent decades. Other colonies had learned a lesson from the Haitian revolution and were determined to avoid the horrors that had surrounded that struggle for freedom. In some regions dominated by plantations, such as some British possessions and the Spanish island of Cuba, planters were reluctant to disturb the prevailing order with any liberal political demands.

The View from Britain   Today the city of Paris is dotted with public monuments that celebrate Napoleon's victories. In London another hero and other victories are celebrated. In Trafalgar Square stands a statue of Lord Nelson, the British naval commander whose fleet destroyed a combined French and Spanish navy in 1805. Horatio Nelson was a brilliant tactician, whose innovations in maneuvering ships in the battle line resulted in stunning victories at Trafalgar and, in 1798, at the Nile Delta, which limited French ambitions in Egypt and the eastern Mediterranean. Trafalgar looms large in British history because it ensured British mastery of the seas, which then forced Napoleon into economic policies that strained French ties to France's allies and satellites. Virtually unchallenged sea power enabled the British to seize colonies formerly ruled by France and its allies.

Britain's maritime supremacy and seizure of French possessions expanded British trading networks overseas—though in some cases only temporarily—and closer to home, particularly in the Mediterranean. As long as the British had been involved in trade with India, the Mediterranean had been important for economic and strategic reasons: it marked the end of the land route for trade from the Indian Ocean. Especially after Napoleon's aggression in Egypt, the British redoubled their efforts to control strategic outposts in the Mediterranean, such as ports in southern Italy and on the island of Malta.

The British economy would expand dramatically in the nineteenth century as industrial production soared. The roots for growth were laid in this period in the countryside of Britain, where changes in agriculture and in production were occurring. These roots were also laid in Britain's overseas possessions as tighter control of foreign sources of raw materials, notably raw Indian cotton, meant rising fortunes back in Britain. In regions of India, the East India Company was increasing its political domination, and hence its economic stranglehold on Indian commodities. The export of Indian cotton rose significantly during the revolutionary period as part of an expanding trading system that included China, the source of tea.

However, economic expansion was not the sole motive for British aggression. In fact, economic expansion was often a byproduct of increased British control of particular regions or sea-lanes, and the reasons for it were as much strategic as economic. Not every conquest had direct economic payoffs, but British elites were sure that strategic domination was a desirable step, wherever it could be managed. One Scottish landholder, writing in the opening years of the nineteenth century, spoke for many when he

IMPORTANT EVENTS

1775–1783 American Revolutionary War

1779–1782 Irish Volunteer Movement

1788 U.S. Constitution ratified
Reform movement begins in Poland
"Patriot" movement ends in the Netherlands

1789 French Estates General meets at Versailles (May)
Third Estate declares itself the National Assembly (June)
Storming of the Bastille (July)

1790 Polish constitution

1791 French king Louis XVI captured attempting to flee (June)
Slave revolt begins in Saint Domingue

1792 France declares war on Austria; revolutionary wars begin (April)
Louis XVI arrested; France declared a republic (August–September)

1793 Louis XVI guillotined

1793–1794 Reign of Terror in France

1799 Napoleon seizes power in France

1801 Concordat with pope

1804 Napoleon crowned emperor
Napoleonic Civil Code
Independence of Haiti (Saint Domingue) declared

1805 Battle of Trafalgar
Battle of Austerlitz

1806 Dissolution of Holy Roman Empire

1812 French invasion of Russia

1814 Napoleon abdicates and is exiled
French monarchy restored

1815 Hundred Days (February–June)
Battle of Waterloo

said that Britain needed an empire to ensure its greatness and that an empire of the sea was an effective counterweight to Napoleon's empire on land. Much as the French were at that moment exporting features of their own political system, the British, he said, could export their constitution wherever they conquered territory.

Thus England and France were engaged in similar phases of expansion in this period. In both, the desire for power and profit drove policy. In each, myths about heroes and about the supposed benefits of domination masked the state's self-interest. For both, the effects of conquest would become a fundamental shaping force in the nineteenth century.

NOTES

1. Quoted in Samuel Eliot Morrison, *John Paul Jones: A Sailor's Biography* (Boston: Little, Brown, 1959), pp. 149–154.

2. Quoted in Owen Connelly, *The French Revolution and the Napoleonic Era* (New York: Holt, Rinehart, and Winston, 1979), p. 32.

3. James Harvey Robinson, *Readings in European History* (Boston: Ginn, 1906), p. 409.

SUGGESTED READING

Baker, Keith Michael. *Inventing the French Revolution.* 1990. A series of essays situating the Revolution amid the dramatic changes in eighteenth-century political culture.

Hunt, Lynn. *The French Revolution and Human Rights: A Brief Documentary History.* 1996. A well-presented short collection of documents, useful for a greater understanding of the impact of the Revolution on the development of human rights.

Jordan, D. P. *The King's Trial.* 1979. An engaging study of Louis XVI's trial and its importance for the Revolution.

Landes, Joan. *Women and the Public Sphere in the Age of the French Revolution.* 1988. An analysis of the uses of gender ideology to fashion the new political world of the revolutionaries.

Langley, Lester D. *The Americas in the Age of Revolution, 1750–1850.* 1996. A survey of all the American states and colonies and the impact of the Atlantic revolutions.

Popkin, Jeremy. *A Short History of the French Revolution.* 1995. A compact and readable recent synthesis of research.

Index

Cuzco, 422, 424
Cycladic islands (Aegean Sea), 53
Cynicism, 122
Cynics, 121
Cynoscephalae, battle at, 149
Cypselus (Corinth), 70
Cyril (missionary), 252–253, 287, 325
Cyrillic script, 325
Cyrus the Great (Persia), 35, 40; Sparta and, 84
Czech people: Hus and, 336, 337
Czech Republic, 493. *See also* Bohemia; Czech people

Dacia (Romania), 171–172. *See also* Romania
Da Gama, Vasco, 410(illus.), 412, 413, 415
Dalmatia, 288, 359
Damascus, 230
Damasus (Pope), 220
Danegeld, 279
Danelaw, 279, 286
Dante Alighieri, 325–326
Danube River region, 255; Magyars in, 288
Dardanelles, 58
Daric (Persian coin), 41
Darius I (Persia), 40, 41, 42; Zoroastrianism and, 44; Athens and, 84
Darius III (Persia): Alexander the Great and, 102, 103
Dark Ages: use of term, 191, 370, 372
Dating, 4n; of Jesus's birth, 181; calendar for, 545
Daughters: of nobility, 304
David (Israel), 49
David (Michelangelo), 384
Deacons: in Catholic Church, 200
Dead Sea, 7
Dead Sea Scrolls, 181
Death: Mesopotamian concept of, 17–18; Egyptians on, 21; medieval Christians on, 433–434, 433(illus.). *See also* Mortality
Deborah (Hebrew), 52
Debt: in Athens, 74
Decameron, The (Boccaccio), 371–372
Decimal system: Mesopotamian, 19
Declaration of Rights (England), 524
Decline and Fall of the Roman Empire (Gibbon), 191
Decretals, 314
Decretum (Gratian), 314
Decurians, 173; Roman taxes and, 198
Deduction: Descartes on, 554
Defenestration of Prague, 496
Defense (military): of Roman Empire, 166, 171–172, 178
Defense of the Seven Sacraments (Henry VIII), 453
De Gaulle, Charles, 275

De Humani Corporis Fabrica, see On the Fabric of the Human Body (Vesalius)
Deities, *see* Gods and goddesses
De Jure Belli ac Pacis (On the Law of War and Peace) (Grotius), 506
Delian League, 86
Deliberative branch: in Rome, 135
Delphi: oracle of, 77–78; theater at, 93(illus.)
Demesne, 256
Demeter (goddess): cult of, 124, 179
Demetrius of Phalerum, 114
Democracy: in Greece, 64; origins of term, 80; development of, 80–82; in Athens, 82–84, 109; Plato on, 90–91; Rome and, 129, 135; Cicero on, 160
Democritus (Greece), 89
Demos (people): in Greece, 60; in Athens, 73
Demosthenes (Athens), 100
De Motu Cordis, see On the Motion of the Heart (Harvey)
Denmark, 252, 286, 287, 357, 459; Vikings from, 253–254; Thirty Years' War and, 496–497; Baltic region and, 529
Deportations: by Assyrians, 37
Descartes, René, 542–543, 553–555, 556, 566; Newton and, 557
Despotism: of Alexander the Great, 103
Deuteronomy, 45
Devotio moderna (modern devotion), 437
Devotional writing: by women, 326
Dhamma (morality): in India, 112
Dhuoda, 257–258
Dialectic: Augustine on, 222
Dialogue on the Two Chief Systems of the World (Galileo), 550
Dialogues: of Plato, 91
Dias, Bartholomeu, 412
Diaspora, 51, 126–127, 185
Díaz de Vivar, Rodrigo ("El Cid"), 285, 286
Dictators and dictatorships: in Rome, 136; Sulla as, 156; Caesar as, 157–158
Dictionnaire historique et critique, see Historical and Critical Dictionary (Bayle)
Diet (assembly): in Holy Roman Empire, 451
Diet (food): in Sparta, 71; European, 354–355; Columbian Exchange and, 430
Diet of Worms: Luther and, 440, 450
Digest (Justinian), 214
Dignitas: in Rome, 141
Diocese, 193, 200
Diocletian (Rome), 178, 191; division of Roman Empire by, 191–193, 192(illus.); reforms of, 191–195; Christianity and, 195
Diogenes of Sinope, 122
Dionysus (god), 92; cult of, 179